Reading Children's Literature

Reading Children's Literature

A CRITICAL INTRODUCTION

Carrie Hintz
and Eric L. Tribunella

[SECOND EDITION]

broadview press

BROADVIEW PRESS – www.broadviewpress.com
Peterborough, Ontario, Canada

Founded in 1985, Broadview Press remains a wholly independent publishing house. Broadview's focus is on academic publishing; our titles are accessible to university and college students as well as scholars and general readers. With over 600 titles in print, Broadview has become a leading international publisher in the humanities, with world-wide distribution. Broadview is committed to environmentally responsible publishing and fair business practices.

Library and Archives Canada Cataloguing in Publication

Hintz, Carrie, 1970-, author
   Reading children's literature : a critical introduction / Carrie Hintz and Eric L. Tribunella. — Second edition.

Includes bibliographical references and index.
ISBN 978-1-55481-443-5 (softcover)

   1. Children's literature—History and criticism. I. Tribunella, Eric L., author II. Title.

PN1009.A1H56 2019   809.89282   C2018-906322-X

Broadview Press handles its own distribution in North America:
PO Box 1243, Peterborough, Ontario K9J 7H5, Canada
555 Riverwalk Parkway, Tonawanda, NY 14150, USA
Tel: (705) 743-8990; Fax: (705) 743-8353
email: customerservice@broadviewpress.com

Distribution is handled by Eurospan Group in the UK, Europe, Central Asia, Middle East, Africa, India, Southeast Asia, Central America, South America, and the Caribbean. Distribution is handled by Footprint Books in Australia and New Zealand.

Broadview Press acknowledges the financial support of the Government of Canada for our publishing activities.

Copy-edited by Juliet Sutcliffe
Book Design by George Kirkpatrick

PRINTED IN CANADA

MIX
Paper from
responsible sources
FSC
www.fsc.org   FSC® C016245

Frontispiece: Cover image by Scott McKowen, *Reading Children's Literature,* first edition.

CONTENTS

PREFACE

Reading Children's Literature: A Critical Introduction emerged out of our experiences teaching introductory children's literature courses to undergraduates. In most literature classes at the college level, students enter the course with few preconceptions about the material they are about to study. In our children's literature courses, however, we found that students were familiar with many of the titles, typically filtered through film adaptations, and often held assumptions about both children and children's books that interfered with their ability to think critically about either. These conditions required special care in designing our courses. Moreover, given the significance of audience to the study of children's literature and the fact that children's literature is almost entirely omitted from other literature courses, including both broad surveys and courses on literary analysis, we found ourselves with the added tasks of introducing students to the histories of childhood and children's literature and to the unique problems involved with analyzing works written by adults for children. *Reading Children's Literature: A Critical Introduction* seeks to lay the groundwork needed for productive discussions about literary works for children.

Readers of this book have come to a children's literature course at an exciting time, when studying this literature rigorously is especially important. Books for children and young adults are currently among the most widely read and discussed both inside and outside the academy, and many highly honored literary works for youth have been published or revisited in recent years. In addition, education, literacy, the importance of the creative arts, and the content of children's culture are among the most charged and important social issues today. While scholars have a solid foundation from which to investigate children's literature, the field remains wide open to important new discoveries and projects.

This book reflects both the history of children's literature studies and its more recent developments. Francelia Butler founded *Children's Literature*, the first scholarly journal devoted to the subject, in 1972; Anne Devereaux Jordan helped establish the Children's Literature Association (ChLA) in 1973; and the first annual ChLA convention was held the following year. Since those beginnings, the study of children's literature has responded to the changing currents of literary studies and has been influenced by both critical theory and historicist approaches to literature and culture. *Reading Children's Literature* recognizes the firm establishment of children's literature as a vibrant and serious field of scholarly inquiry, integrating theoretical, historical, and political approaches to literary study. Rather than simply describing different genres of children's literature or providing an encyclopedic catalog of children's works, *Reading Children's Literature* invites readers to participate in the critical and cultural conversations involving children's literature and demonstrates methods for reading children's literature analytically. By combining an introduction to key concepts and genres with explicit discussion about how to analyze literary texts written for children and young adults, our book reflects the sophisticated scholarly work undertaken over the past forty-five years and encourages students to participate actively in the ongoing critical dialogue. It demonstrates how to think and write about children's literature and provides the conceptual tools for doing so.

WHAT DISTINGUISHES THIS BOOK?

Several features of the book distinguish it from other children's literature textbooks. The first is our attention to history. We understand the study of children's literature as inseparable from the study of the history of childhood, and we see children's literature as both reflecting and affecting that history. Because we recognize that historicist approaches to literature are now central to literary studies, *Reading Children's Literature* pays careful attention to both historical context and literary history, providing instructors and students with the tools needed to analyze literature and history together.

The second feature that distinguishes this book from other introductions is our foregrounding of close critical analysis to make sense of literary works by actively modeling close reading and analysis. Sometimes the apparent simplicity or familiarity of children's literature makes it difficult for students to read critically, so we introduce critical and theoretical concepts and then demonstrate how to use them to read and analyze children's literature.

The third feature is our book's integration of contemporary approaches to the literary study of children's books, including unique chapters on race and ethnicity, gender and sexuality, censorship and selection, and popular culture. We address directly the critical and cultural controversies involved with these topics. Thus, *Reading Children's Literature* provides a thorough and up-to-date introduction to the field of children's literature studies.

Finally, our book includes 85 images from works of children's literature—reminding readers how vital illustrations are to works written for children.

HOW THIS BOOK IS ORGANIZED

We designed *Reading Children's Literature* to be used alongside the fiction, poetry, drama, or literary nonfiction assigned in English, education, or library science courses. The book is divided into an introduction that explores what it means to read children's literature critically and thirteen chapters on a variety of concepts and issues. Each chapter includes:

- **An introduction to key concepts and questions** foundational to the chapter topic and a review of the critical and cultural conversations or controversies surrounding it.

- **A Reading Critically section** that demonstrates how to read a literary work in light of the critical issues and debates discussed in the chapter.

- Useful **review and reflection questions** for use in class, and **suggested investigations** that students can complete outside of class.

- **An annotated list of suggested literary works** to be used in conjunction with the chapter

- **An Approaches to Teaching section** that offers a set of activities that teachers can use with primary- or secondary-school students to help connect the scholarly study of children's literature with its educational applications.

We intend the book to provide flexible support to instructors, who can assign all of the chapters or chapter sections or select those that are most relevant to his or her course. The early chapters address important foundations, such as the history of childhood and the early history of children's literature, as well as literary forms with longer histories, such as poetry and fairy tales. The middle chapters provide a survey of important forms and genres in children's literature like picturebooks, historical fiction, domestic and adventure novels, and realism and fantasy. The later chapters address contemporary critical issues such as race, gender, censorship, and popular culture. However, the book is designed so that chapters can be taught in the order of the instructor's preference and do not need to be read in the order they are presented. The chapters are as follows:

- **Introduction for Students** considers common assumptions about children's literature and explains what it means to read critically. It introduces fundamental concepts important to the study of children's literature.

- **Chapter 1: Historicizing Childhood**, investigates the history and construction of childhood and adolescence and discusses how young people have been thought about at different moments in history. It examines how this history bears upon the reading of children's literature.

- **Chapter 2: The Early History of Children's Literature**, provides an overview of the earliest literature written for children and the central problems or tensions that have dominated and shaped its history, including the opposition between didacticism and pleasure, the question of what counts as children's literature, and the role of key figures in its conception and history.

- **Chapter 3: Poetry**, looks at poetry both as a means of serious personal and political inquiry for young readers and as an extension of childhood play, especially in the form of nonsense verse. It reviews important formal qualities of poetry and of children's poetry in particular.

- **Chapter 4: Fairy Tales**, examines the importance of fairy tales to the history of children's literature and their ongoing cultural use and appeal. It also addresses some of the key questions about the fairy tale form: issues of audience, orality, and literacy, and the practice of retelling and updating tales.

- **Chapter 5: Picturebooks, Graphic Novels, and Digital Texts**, explores the conventions of the picturebook form and the importance of visual media, including graphic novels, in children's culture. It also offers techniques for interpreting picturebooks and visual media and for understanding the relationship between text and image.

- **Chapter 6: Domesticity and Adventure**, studies domesticity and adventure as key concepts in children's literature and as key genres that reflect the concerns of, and ideas about, children and childhood, for which home and venturing away from home are central concerns.

- **Chapter 7: Historical Fiction**, considers the uses and limits of the genre for educating children, and how the genre constructs history and deals with the relationship between literature and history.

- **Chapter 8: Nonfiction—History, Science, Life Writing**, discusses the narrative and aesthetic qualities of nonfiction texts, their use by children and for teaching children, and questions of perspective, simplification, and datedness in nonfiction works for children.

- **Chapter 9: Fantasy and Realism**, reviews the distinction between realistic and fantastic literature for children and analyzes how the permeable or overlapping boundaries between genres have helped shape children's literature. We also look at some of the social and political functions of both fantasy and realism.

- **Chapter 10: Race, Ethnicity, and Culture**, explores the ways children's literature has constructed racial and ethnic difference as well as how it has been imagined as a useful vehicle for multicultural education.

- **Chapter 11: Genders and Sexualities**, examines the prominence of gender and sexuality as themes in children's literature and culture and the ways in which the child audience is imagined as composed of gendered boys and girls. The chapter emphasizes more generally the socializing and constructive functions of children's literature and culture while exploring the range of genders and sexualities represented and constructed by literature for youth.

- **Chapter 12: Censorship and Selection**, addresses issues of censorship in children's literature, distinctions between censorship and selection, how and why books are challenged, ways of understanding what these controversies suggest about children's literature and the broader cultural context, and how educators and children themselves can respond to controversy.

- **Chapter 13: Children's Literature and Popular Culture**, surveys different meanings of "popular" and "popular culture" and introduces cultural studies as a theoretical approach to children's literature. The chapter also offers an overview of several genres and subgenres of popular children's literature—such as utopian/dystopian fiction, science fiction, horror, and romance—and provides a history of children's theatre, television, and film. It reviews theories of adaptation, transformation, and intertexuality and defines important terms in film studies.

WHAT'S NEW

Chapter 13: Children's Literature and Popular Culture

The second edition of *Reading Children's Literature* includes several new features. First, we have added a new chapter on children's literature and popular culture. The chapter introduction explores conflicted meanings of popularity as well as critical theories that understand popular culture in terms of political engagement and a means of exercising power or resisting control. The chapter then considers two focal points for popular culture in literary studies: 1) formula and genre fiction whose literary merit is sometimes questioned and 2) the relationship between literature and other forms of mass media like television and film. The first of these two sections, parts of which originally appeared in Chapter 9, has been expanded and placed in the context of Chapter 13's discussion of common approaches to popular culture. We then review briefly the history of children's theatre, television, and film and survey theories of adaptation, transformation, and intertextuality. The chapter provides tools for moving beyond the fidelity model of adaptation and for reading children's popular culture critically. We offer definitions of common terms used in film studies, and we explore the world of fanfiction as a form of adaptation and popular engagement with literary texts. The Reading Critically section demonstrates how to analyze a film adaptation by focusing on John Green's *The Fault in Our Stars*, an enormously popular novel, which has also been adapted into a film, that provides an excellent case study of a cultural phenomenon involving a passionate fandom and questions of genre. The annotated list of suggested works includes a selection of notable film adaptations of children's literature and examples of pedagogically useful genre fiction.

Using Models of Childhood to Read Critically

A new table in Chapter 1 (Historicizing Childhood) offers suggestions for how to use the different models of childhood to read children's literature critically. Designed to encourage students to move beyond simply identifying models of childhood in the books they read, the table suggests how to think about the implications of each model in analyzing texts.

Disability in Children's Literature

The second edition of *Reading Children's Literature* includes a new section in Chapter 1 on the body and disability in the history of childhood, titled "Child Embodiment and Disability." We have included additional references throughout the book to works that depict disabilities, including in Chapter 4 (Fairy Tales), in the section on New Realist texts in Chapter 9 (Fantasy and Realism), and elsewhere.

Race in Children's Literature

The issue of diversity in children's literature continues to be an important one among readers, civil rights activists, publishers, and scholars. Several new sections appear throughout the book, including ones on race and privilege in the history of childhood in Chapter 1, on race in fairy and folk tales in Chapter 4, and on the We Need Diverse Books movement in Chapter 10 (Race, Ethnicity, and Culture).

New Critical Reading Sections

We have added two new Reading Critically sections: one in Chapter 3 (Poetry) for Robert Louis Stevenson's poem "Escape at Bedtime" and the other in Chapter 9 (Fantasy and Realism) on Daniel José Older's urban fantasy novel *Shadowshaper* (2015).

Expanded Section on Verse Novels

In Chapter 3, we include an expanded section on verse novels, also known as the "novel-in-verse." A novel-in-verse straddles the boundary of fiction and poetry, as a book-length narrative recounted in free verse. Engaging with recent literary criticism about the verse novel, we discuss some recent examples and briefly consider the role that verse novels can play in reaching out to reluctant readers.

Expanded and Updated Section on Digital Literature

We have expanded and updated our section on digital literature in Chapter 5 (Picturebooks, Graphic Novels, and Digital Texts). Drawing on recent scholarship in the field of digital literature, we discuss recent examples of digital literature for children and young adults, including narrative tablet apps and concept books. We also contextualize current digital books within the tradition of print picturebooks and pre-digital interactive texts.

Expanded Section on Graphic Novels

Responding to readers who wanted even more discussion of graphic novels, we expanded the section on comics art and graphic fiction in Chapter 5 to consider why graphic novels have been associated with children's culture, to provide a list of key terms for reading graphic fiction, and to describe how to read graphic novels critically. We discuss additional examples of popular and critically acclaimed graphic fiction that might be read in conjunction with this chapter.

Fiction–Nonfiction Pairings

In Chapter 8 (Nonfiction—History, Science, Life Writing), we have added a chart that lists and describes ideal fiction–nonfiction pairings. We hope that literature and language arts teachers find these pairings helpful when incorporating nonfiction in the English literature classroom.

Explorations

The Explorations section of each chapter has been revised and updated to include a new set of review questions that will allow students to go over many of the central ideas of each chapter. Reflection questions are designed to inspire class discussions, and "investigate" questions suggest activities or essay topics that could be completed out of class.

Updated Reading Lists and Examples

We have updated the Suggested Readings list for each chapter to reflect important works published since the first edition of *Reading Children's Literature* that we or others have found useful in the classroom. Our references to literary and scholarly works throughout the book also reflect new publications of important works for children and young adults and new research or critical controversies in the field.

Glossary

Key terms are placed in bold in each of the chapters, and readers can now flip to the back of the book to find brief definitions of these important terms and concepts for reading children's literature critically.

INTRODUCTION FOR STUDENTS

When a blunt old sheep breaks the news to Wilbur, a pig, that he's being fattened for slaughter, the distraught Wilbur tears through the barn crying that he does not want to die. Charlotte, a kindly maternal spider, agrees to help him, and days later the farm awakens to find a magnificent web with letters spelling "Some Pig!" woven into it. This scene embodies the magic and fantasy of E.B. White's *Charlotte's Web* (1952), which depicts the extraordinary friendship between a pig and a spider while confronting child readers directly with the realities of life and death.

Children's books are full of iconic moments such as this. Think of Alice's falling down the rabbit hole into Wonderland while chasing the White Rabbit, Tom Sawyer's tricking the neighborhood boys into whitewashing Aunt Polly's fence, and Dorothy's walking down the yellow brick road to Oz. We can begin to understand what makes them memorable, and what makes such classics so important and well loved, by learning to read children's literature *critically*. While "critically" may suggest a hostile, fault-finding approach, we mean it in the sense of "critical analysis," the close reading of texts that brings our own and others' perspectives and contexts to bear on them. By reading children's literature critically, we can learn much about ourselves, our society, and indeed, our culture, past and present.

COMMON ASSUMPTIONS ABOUT CHILDREN'S LITERATURE

A number of common assumptions about children's literature can interfere with reading it critically. For example, some readers might assume that children's literature is so simple and obvious that it does not require analysis, or that all children's books are like *Charlotte's*

Web: fairly short, using simple language, and including fantastical elements. Others might think that children's literature is simply meant to be enjoyed and that treating it seriously is silly or interferes with enjoyment. Still others think they know exactly what children are like, and have not considered that what it means to be a child has changed dramatically over time, affecting how children's literature is written. Other assumptions about children's literature contribute to dismissive attitudes about it, but the following are perhaps the most common:

"Children's literature is too simple and obvious to be read critically." Elizabeth Law, a children's book editor at Viking, notes: "Many writers assume that because children are smaller, and their books are smaller, that children are less complex, easier to please— and therefore easier to write for" (17). She rejects this assumption: for an adult to write for children, which usually involves writing simultaneously for adults, requires the kind of intellectual and creative gymnastics that cannot be described as "easy." Francelia Butler, who helped establish the first scholarly journal devoted to children's literature, wrote about resistance to studying it critically: "Many arguments are advanced to justify this situation. The oft-repeated one is, 'Children's literature is so simple and obvious that any fool can understand it. It doesn't need study'" (8). If children's literature is simple, the argument goes, no special preparation or tools are needed to understand it, and a course or book on children's literature is unnecessary. For some, the very familiarity of children's stories, as represented by the iconic moments listed above, might create the impression of simplicity. However, as we explain throughout this book, children's literature can be linguistically, thematically, and formally complex even while appearing otherwise.

"Children's literature is pure, innocent, and uncontroversial." Another common assumption about children's literature is that it is devoid of elements associated with adults and adult culture, such as sexuality, racial discrimination, class distinctions, or violence and trauma. However, children's literature—in depicting the lives, pleasures, fears, and anxieties of children—often includes elements that might seem upsetting or too mature in content. The frequent controversies that surround these books, and the numerous attempts to limit children's access to them, point to the inclusion of sophisticated elements some adults find disturbing in works for young people. Children live in a world primarily created by and for adults, so no strict line divides the experiences and environments of younger and older members of a community. We should therefore expect to find elements associated with adults and adult culture in works for and about children.

"Critical analysis takes the fun out of reading children's literature." Finally, some adult readers resist thinking critically about children's literature because they worry that doing so "ruins" the work or their childhood memories of it. Such resistance reflects assumptions that children's literature is only or primarily a source of uncritical pleasure for the child and nostalgia for the adult and that critical thinking interferes with this pleasure. Some readers do not want to discover that they did not understand all the meanings or implications of a text when they were children, or they might not want to create new understandings that could compete with older ones. In this view, children's literature is simply meant to be enjoyed without requiring too much effort. However, understanding how texts work and what they mean can actually contribute to one's reading pleasure, so we encourage readers to be receptive to analyzing children's literature.

WHAT IT MEANS TO READ CRITICALLY

Reading children's literature critically enables us to challenge these assumptions. The analysis of literature—or reading critically—involves investigating what texts mean and how they work, understanding the relationships between texts and significant ideologies or social systems and experiences such as gender or race, placing texts within literary or cultural histories, and examining specific elements such as a text's themes, literary devices, production, structure, language, uses, or reception. Because no single exercise in analysis or critical reading undertakes all these tasks at once, critics must make difficult decisions about how to focus their attention and about which methodological approach is most effective for a given project. Literary critics read texts closely, learn about the history of literature and literary forms, consider the historical and cultural contexts of works, and use different theoretical concepts and approaches to understand the text, context, and reader.

Reading Closely

The practice of **close reading** involves paying careful attention to the language of the text, including the histories and meanings of words and their connotations. The critic searches for the implications of the use of particular words and explores how language is used to produce different meanings.

For instance, a close reading of Frances Hodgson Burnett's *The Secret Garden* (1911) reveals that scale (size and dimension) and Mary's perception of scale are important to understanding her feelings and actions in the novel. Reading closely, we note that the novel is mostly focalized through Mary (that is, much of the description indicates Mary's perception). When she is led to her room at Misselthwaite Manor, the narrator communicates how immense the house seems to her: "And then Mary Lennox was led up a broad staircase and down a long corridor and up a short flight of steps and through another corridor and another, until a door opened in a wall and she found herself in a room with a fire in it and a supper on a table" (15). The enormity of the house and grounds, from Mary's childhood perspective, and the novelty of the manor and landscape, offer Mary much to explore. Having spaces and mysteries to investigate makes her domestic situation, which might otherwise be dull, an extraordinary adventure. The reader is able to understand Mary and the novel better by reading Burnett's language closely.

Considering Literary History and Forms

Reading critically also involves an awareness of literary history, how literature has changed over time and what defines different movements, forms, genres, or techniques. Being able to situate a text in a particular literary movement or to recognize how it reflects, modifies, or defies the conventions of a specific genre helps direct the reader's attention and prompts discoveries that might otherwise be overlooked.

As an example, readers might note that *The Secret Garden* includes elements of gothic literature, which is characterized by a mood or tone of darkness and mystery; the depiction of large, decaying architectural structures; a focus on emotional or disturbed characters who possess psychological depth; and the intrusion of the past into the present or the experience of being literally or symbolically haunted. Given that gothic fiction is characterized by a sense in which the past lingers too long or haunts the present, we are led to question what plays that role in *The Secret Garden*. Colin, Mary's sickly cousin, and his dead mother could be said to haunt Misselthwaite Manor, creating a mystery for Mary to investigate. Reading the novel in the context of gothic literature prompts us to consider what it means that mother and son both haunt the home or even that the home is a place of fear rather than comfort. An awareness of generic conventions helps the reader make sense of these elements.

Examining Historical and Cultural Contexts

A critical reader of children's literature also examines how the historical and cultural contexts of authors affect the composition of their work and its reception by readers. Ideologies and discourses (ways of thinking and communicating) circulating at a given time and in a given place influence or construct how individuals see the world, making it possible to think in certain ways as well as impossible or difficult to imagine alternatives. Virtually all aspects of culture and society are filtered through, or constructed by, ideological and discursive frameworks that shape and create thought and perception. We are often influenced by our historical and cultural contexts without being fully aware of those influences. Even what seem like very individual choices, such as what to wear or whom to pursue romantically, are significantly encouraged, enabled, constrained, or prevented by our historical and cultural contexts.

One important way of reading critically consists of analyzing literary texts for the traces of these unacknowledged historical and cultural influences. A critical reader considers how the qualities, events, and ways of thinking and perceiving that characterize a particular historical moment are manifested in the text, constrain its production, or influence what readers notice or understand.

For instance, when Burnett was writing *The Secret Garden* in 1910, the British Empire was still at its height, and that context leaves its traces throughout the novel. M. Daphne Kutzer, considering colonialism as a context for *The Secret Garden*, develops precisely this analysis: "Mary's behavior in the garden echoes that of colonial explorers in India and elsewhere" (59). The facts of the novel also refer more explicitly to colonialism. Mary was born in India because her father held an important position as an agent of the British Empire. Mary's ill temper and disagreeable appearance are attributed to her time in India. The family's Indian servants catered to Mary's every whim, and when she arrives in England after the deaths of her parents, she expects the same treatment from the white British servants. She later refers to her tyrannical cousin as a "Rajah." Both Mary and Colin are associated with India and "Indianness," but working with the English soil and breathing the English air in the secret garden "heals" them, as though England itself heals them. Noting how these elements of the text emerge out of Burnett's historical and cultural context constitutes one of the primary strategies for reading critically.

Using Critical and Theoretical Concepts and Approaches

Since the 1960s, critical approaches to literary analysis have become increasingly diverse, offering critics and scholars a variety of concepts and methods with which to explore literature. These approaches include, among others, deconstruction, feminist and gender theory, historicist and Marxist approaches, reader response theory, psychoanalysis, postcolonial theory, biographical analysis, disability theory, ecocriticism, and queer theory. Each critical approach offers a unique focus and its own set of questions, and each is associated with a vocabulary and set of concepts with which to think and write about literature. These terms and concepts provide a critical framework that gives shape to analysis, helping to direct the critic's attention, generating useful lines of inquiry, and providing tools with which to hypothesize answers and develop explanatory claims. Reading critically benefits from a familiarity with these critical approaches, even if a specific project integrates multiple approaches or undertakes interdisciplinary work.

Critic Jerry Phillips, for example, reads *The Secret Garden* through the lens of social class. He notes, "At the center of *The Secret Garden* is an anatomy of social hierarchy, a laboratory of class relations: the great country house" (172). Phillips pays close attention to how Mary interacts with Martha, a domestic servant, and Ben Weatherstaff, the gardener. Martha, for instance, "refuses to see herself as a mere instrument of her social superiors. She resolves to do her duties, but no more," and Ben similarly refuses to bow to the authority of Mary, who was accustomed to ordering her servants around in India (175). The issues of class and shifting class relations in turn-of-the-century England provide the critical framework for this analysis of the novel, but other critics have approached *The Secret Garden* from feminist, psychoanalytic, and postcolonial perspectives. Complex works such as this novel can be read from multiple perspectives.

WHY READ CHILDREN'S LITERATURE CRITICALLY?

Dual Address and Complexity

We read children's literature critically to understand its complex meanings and operations. One source of complexity is its management of multiple audiences. Many children's books that prove durable, remaining in circulation or print for decades or even centuries, are those that appeal to both children and adults. Barbara Wall coined the term "**dual address**" to describe the way some works for children move between addressing child readers and addressing adult readers (Wall 9), while U.C. Knoepflmacher and Sandra L. Beckett use the term "crosswriting" to refer to the practice of writing for children and adults at the same time (Beckett xi). Because of the dual address or practice of crosswriting, some children's literature appeals to the sensibilities of adult readers and contains allusions or references aimed at the adult audience.

Moreover, the notion of a separate literature for children is relatively recent historically, and Wall finds that Victorian children's literature was often characterized by an "adult narrative voice" that "exhibited strong consciousness of the presence of adult readers" (9). Many literary forms, such as fairy tales and fables, were meant for both adults and children and were constructed to appeal to both. Even now, adults produce and buy almost all the literature destined for child readers. Writers must thus add elements to attract and hold the interest of adults, with the result that seemingly simple books for children contain several layers of complex meaning.

Linguistic and Narrative Complexity

A book such as Lewis Carroll's *Alice's Adventures in Wonderland* (1865) is clearly a complex work of art with a sophisticated and extensive vocabulary, yet we need to rethink the assumption that books with a limited vocabulary, including picturebooks, are not complex. Iconic children's author Dr. Seuss created *The Cat in the Hat* (1957) from a vocabulary of 250 words and *Green Eggs and Ham* (1960) from a vocabulary of 50 words. Even with a limited vocabulary, though, he managed to communicate complicated thought and expression, such as the uncertain ending of *The Cat in the Hat*, where the children consider whether to tell their mother what has been happening all day. The short book ends with a question—"What would YOU do / If your mother asked YOU?"—prompting the reader to participate actively in solving a complex ethical dilemma. Seuss's illustrations are dynamic and challenging to the viewer, despite or perhaps because of their roots in the tradition of editorial cartoons. The texts of Seuss's books are their own form of unique, dense, and exhilarating poetry. Despite their immediately recognizable rhyme schemes, they feature unexpected juxtapositions, surprising rhymes, and fantastic situations.

What are the elements that lend an apparently simple and short text a form of complexity? Allan Luke draws attention to the literary depth of Arnold Lobel's Frog and Toad series, which is intended for beginning readers: "While pitched at a primer level audience, Lobel's Frog and Toad stories nonetheless employ such literary devices as stories within stories, dream and stream of consciousness sequences to portray and invite the further construction of imaginative possible worlds" (111). Lobel's Frog and Toad books, like Seuss's works, ask a great deal of their young readers. In his essay "Children, Irony, and Philosophy," Gareth Matthews discovers philosophical dilemmas in *Frog and Toad Together* (1992), such as the nature of bravery as explored in the story "Dragons and Giants." In this story, Frog and Toad wonder whether they are brave, and Frog asserts that climbing a mountain will reveal the truth. On the mountain, they encounter various terrifying perils (a snake, an avalanche, a hawk), but exclaim that they are not afraid. Still, they run away, and when they get back to Toad's house, Frog hides in the closet and Toad cowers under the covers. This story raises a number of questions: What does it mean to be brave? What is the difference between acting brave and *being* brave? Do brave people have to be brave *all the time*?

Likewise, a number of contemporary picturebooks have displayed an impressive level of complexity. For example, in David Macaulay's *Black and White* (1990), four seemingly unrelated narratives are intertwined—each with a separate visual style and story. Readers are encouraged to speculate on the connections between the narratives through subtle clues that they are related, and all offer different perspectives on the same event. Macaulay's book challenges literary and pictorial conventions and requires an extremely sophisticated engagement with narrative. We study children's literature in order to understand these different kinds of complexity and meaning, as we would with adult literature.

Didacticism and the Lessons of Children's Literature

In addition to being complex, children's literature is a key site for transmitting values and educating children. This fact makes it especially important—it has a profound impact on socialization and society. By better understanding the texts produced and given to children, we gain a stronger understanding of the broader culture in which we live. As Mitzi Myers explains, "Because children's tales perform a variety of cultural functions, they are crammed with clues to changes in attitudes, values, and behavior. Above all, these key agents of socialization diagram what cultures want of their young and expect of those who tend them" (33). Some children's books are intentionally instructional. The term "**didactic**" is used to describe books that are specifically designed to teach a lesson, whether moral, political, religious, social, or practical. Critics such as Myers have demonstrated that even didactic works can be complex, important, and pleasurable (55). As we will discuss in Chapter 2, much of the history of children's literature has been defined by didacticism or by efforts to avoid it.

The Transmission of Cultural Values

Even texts that are not intentionally didactic can teach, influence, or shape readers. Reading children's literature critically can reveal those cultural values and teach us about ourselves. *The Story of Little Black Sambo* (1899) is a striking example of a children's book that conveys the norms and assumptions of its time. Helen Bannerman, a Scottish woman living in India, wrote and illustrated the book to amuse her two daughters. The fanciful story of an Indian boy who eludes and ultimately triumphs over a ferocious tiger, *Sambo* has long been the source of controversy because Bannerman's illustrations are similar to late nineteenth- and early twentieth-century racist caricatures of Africans and African Americans. Sambo and his parents are depicted as very dark skinned and as having wooly hair, thick lips, broad smiles, and wide eyes. As Tammy Mielke explains, numerous versions of *Sambo* were published in the United States between 1900 and 1950, and many included new pictures by American illustrators who further exaggerated the characters' racial features, drawing on minstrel traditions that mocked African Americans. Mielke notes that these American illustrations "parallel historical attitudes towards African American people, showing the power of illustration in reflecting cultural attitudes and how African American childhood is constructed through visual means" (3). Though Bannerman's purpose might not have been to inculcate racist stereotypes, her book nonetheless contributed to a wider discourse that presented people of color as ridiculous and inferior. As Mielke demonstrates, a study of the book's changing American illustrations over the course of the twentieth century can illuminate evolving representations of African Americans and broader changes in American culture.

The popularity or reception of works is also indicative of prevailing cultural mores. J.K. Rowling's Harry Potter series, published between 1997 and 2007, has attained an almost unprecedented worldwide popularity. Combining various genres of children's literature—fantasy, realism, the school story, adventure—the seven-book series follows the exploits of the boy-wizard named Harry and his friends Ron and Hermione as they confront the growing threat of Lord Voldemort, an evil wizard. Given its widespread appeal, the series and readers' response to it provide useful signposts to the state of various cultural concerns. For example, readers have debated the series' representation of girls and girlhood as embodied by Hermione. Hermione appears more knowledgeable about magic than Harry or Ron, and yet her frequent emotional displays and need for rescuing create a complex picture of modern girlhood. The series also raises questions about class-based hierarchies through the treatment of the house-elves, who serve as mostly dutiful servants to the wizards. In addition, nonwizards, or Muggles, become the object of scorn by some in the wizarding community who believe that Muggles and half-Muggles lack "pure blood." These plot elements parallel aspects of racial politics and racism in Europe and North America. The series continues to engage with issues of race and gender/sexuality. When Noma Dumezweni was cast to play the adult Hermione in the play *Harry Potter and the Cursed Child*, Rowling tweeted her support of the casting of a black actor, writing, "Canon: brown eyes, frizzy hair and very clever. White skin was never specified." In 2007, after the publication of the seventh book in the series, Rowling told an audience of fans that she considered Dumbledore to be gay, prompting many readers to revisit their interpretations of the character. Moreover, the controversy surrounding the series because of opposition from some religious communities attests to the continued conflicts between secular and religious cultures, and Rowling herself has received criticism for her appropriation of Native American culture on the Pottermore website where she has continued to expand the world of the series. The changes made to editions or translations of the books for readers in different countries point to assumptions about differences in national tastes or to the operation and effect of language, such as the change from the British "Philosopher's Stone" to the American "Sorcerer's Stone" or the problem of the name Tom Marvolo Riddle as an anagram for "I am Lord Voldemort" for non-English editions.

Children's literature transmits information and values of the culture from which it emerges, and it can influence readers in subtle ways to accept and internalize beliefs, perceptions, and expectations. Narrative and language are chief mechanisms for the transmission of information and values, so literature and our ability to understand it remain vital to society. Children's literature is as diverse in content, theme, plot, character, setting, genre, and style as adult literature; as such, it addresses a wide range of human relationships, social issues, and cultural practices. Writers are always influenced by the culture of the time and place in which they live and write, even in ways that they are unconscious of, and so the traces of that cultural context can be seen in their work, whether authors intend those elements to appear or not. Critics, too, can sometimes fail to notice such elements of a work at the time, since the ideological traces of the wider culture can become more apparent as time passes and as scholars develop a critical perspective from which to analyze texts and their contexts.

Subversive or Hegemonic?

Does children's literature reinforce dominant, or hegemonic, cultural values, or does it subvert them by offering resistant representations that undermine traditional ways of thinking? Texts rarely just do one or the other, and reading children's literature critically can involve considering how a text reinforces or resists hegemonic values. Jacqueline Rose argues that children's literature imagines and constructs the figure of the child, one that she suggests is a fantasy of and for adults. In her classic study *The Case of Peter Pan, or The Impossibility of Children's Fiction* (1984), Rose investigates "what it is that adults, through literature, want or demand of the child" (137). The child of children's literature, she argues, serves as the embodiment of innocence and purity for adults who lack these qualities, and thus in this view children's literature reinforces the hegemonic values of adult culture. Alison Lurie, in contrast, argues that many writers of classic children's literature "tended to overturn rather than uphold the conventional values of their period or background" (xii). In a world dominated by economic and commercial interests, children's literature offers a subversive critique by implying that "what matters is art, imagination, and truth" (Lurie xi). Lurie notes that many child protagonists act rebelliously and question adults and the world around them by imagining different ways of thinking and being. She suggests, in fact, that part of the appeal of children's literature is its subversive or oppositional relationship to dominant, adult cultural values. In their Introduction to *Tales for Little Rebels* (2008), Julia L. Mickenberg and Philip Nel observe that "the very idea of 'radical children's literature' may be surprising, because we do not commonly think of the connections between children's literature and politics. But children's literature has always been ideological" (1). Mickenberg and Nel confirm this claim with their extensive collection of overtly political children's works, such as an excerpt from *The Child's Socialist Reader* published in 1907. Rarely does a text simply reinforce or resist dominant culture by being either entirely subversive or entirely hegemonic in its representations. To read children's literature critically, we must seek to understand the complex relationship it has to other discourses and practices. We can do so by analyzing the child it imagines and constructs, as well as the adult who participates in this construction, benefits from it, or feels threatened by it.

Literature does not just represent the world, but also constructs the world; it depicts the world not only as it is, but also as it might be. Literature, as a form of art, can help readers see the world differently or anew and thus help them envision alternatives to current or dominant beliefs and ways of living. Because children's literature, like adult literature, ultimately both reflects and constructs the world, the study of children's literature can provide critical insight into many of the most important domains of culture and society and dimensions of identity and experience: race, class, gender, sexuality, age, nation, region, religion, kinship, education, history, and others.

Pleasure and Unpleasure

As a literary art form, children's literature *is* complex, and its complexity is one reason that it is able to give so much pleasure, that it can be read over and over again and be experienced differently each time. The history of children's literature is marked not only by didacticism and the impulse to instruct but also by literary innovation and artistry. Many of the works that remain memorable or mark significant milestones in the history of children's literature are those that demonstrate innovation by expanding the definitions or boundaries of writing for youth, by experimenting with forms and themes, by playing with conventions and expectations, and by taking creative chances in using words and images in literary and artistic ways.

As we've noted, some readers worry that analyzing cultural texts interferes with pleasure, but we might also note how unsettling it is to be confused by a text or uncertain about its meaning. Learning a new skill or achieving comprehension of ideas can be a source of great relief and satisfaction. Just as understanding the history of art and artistic movements can help a viewer make sense of a work of art in a museum, thereby deriving pleasure from understanding the work's meaning or composition or its place in a larger movement or history, understanding the history of children's literature and how children's literature works can enhance the pleasure of reading it and allow us to reread with pleasure. For instance, a complex work such as *Alice's Adventures in Wonderland* contains numerous allusions to other literary texts and historical events. While the nonsense and strangeness of the book can be enjoyed without recognizing these references, understanding them allows readers to notice jokes they might otherwise miss, allowing new and different pleasures to be discovered.

Children's literature can also be unpleasurable. It can generate anxiety or discomfort or depict frightening and disturbing elements. The disorienting quality of *Alice's Adventures*

could be upsetting to some readers, as might the terrifying scissor-man of Heinrich Hoffmann's *Struwwelpeter* (1845), who chops off the thumbs of children who refuse to stop
sucking them. The unhappy fates of the children in Roald Dahl's *Charlie and the Chocolate
Factory* (1964) or in Lemony Snicket's *A Series of Unfortunate Events: The Bad Beginning*
(1999) might be frightening, as might historical fiction for children about war and atrocity, such as Toshi Maruki's *Hiroshima No Pika* (1982), a picturebook about the bombing
of Hiroshima, or Myron Levoy's *Alan and Naomi* (1977), a children's novel about a girl
traumatized by seeing her father killed in the Holocaust. Readers seek out literature about
terrible things for many reasons, including helping them to work through challenging or
horrible experiences or feelings.

Children's literature can reveal both our greatest pleasures and our deepest fears or
concerns. Understanding what pleases or frightens us the most is absolutely key to understanding what it means to be human and how human beings relate to and treat one
another. In evoking childhood memories, children's literature provides access to our most
foundational emotions or experiences; it is thus one of the few ways adults can maintain
a connection to childhood. Following Jerry Griswold, the scholar and critic, we find the
expression in children's literature of basic pleasures and fears to be especially insistent,
suggesting that we can learn about some of our most deep-seated needs and pleasures
through studying works for children. By examining what it is about childhood that triggers adult nostalgia, we can learn about our most potent and long-term fears, anxieties,
pleasures, and desires.

HISTORICIZING CHILDHOOD

Susannah Bricks, one of the children featured in James Janeway's *A Token for Children* (1671), cries out, "Behold, I was shapen in iniquity, and in sin did my mother conceive me, and I was altogether born in sin!" (59). Fortunately, she repents of her sin before dying at the age of fourteen from the plague. Such naturally sinful children also appear throughout nineteenth-century stories about boys at boarding schools, as in Thomas Hughes's *Tom Brown's Schooldays* (1857), in which the natural wickedness of boys must be constantly policed, managed, and eventually overcome by the good example of their masters and the disciplinary policies of the school. In contrast, the child speaker of William Blake's poem "The Lamb" (1789) sees himself, the lamb, and the baby Jesus as sharing a natural innocence, which the character of Little Eva in Harriet Beecher Stowe's *Uncle Tom's Cabin* (1852) also embodies. Her father, St. Clare, the owner of a large slaveholding plantation in the American South, wonders when he sees his virtuous daughter enjoying the company of the slave Tom, "What would the poor and lowly do, without children?" (185). St. Clare sees children like Eva as embodying innocence, not sin: "Your little child is your only true democrat.... This is one of the roses of Eden that the Lord has dropped down expressly for the poor and lowly, who get few enough of any other kind" (185).

The history of children's literature cannot be understood fully without considering the history of childhood, and children's literature seems inextricably bound to issues of audience. What kinds of writing are appropriate or inappropriate for children? What is useful for the instruction or education of children? What will children find interesting

Opposite: "Boy Working in a Glass Factory" by Lewis Wickes Hine, 1911. The boy is Robert Kidd, one of the young workers in the Alexandria, Virginia, factory.

or enjoyable? What are children of different ages prepared to read or understand? How we answer these questions—which might be asked by adults who write, publish, purchase, recommend, or teach children's literature—depends on how and what we think about children. Are children born into savagery or sin, inclined to delinquency in the absence of proper guidance, and in need of strict discipline? The children in the works just cited represent different models of childhood and ideas about children. While adults read and enjoy children's literature as well, understanding the history of childhood helps us to understand the readers who are presumably the primary audience for children's literature.

As historians of childhood have discovered, the nature of that audience is anything but a simple matter. Since the groundbreaking publication of Philippe Ariès's *Centuries of Childhood* in 1960 (trans. in 1962), researchers have made it clear that how childhood has been defined—indeed, who counts as a child—has often differed at different times and in different places, sometimes radically. Complicating the study of the history of childhood is the fact that at any given moment multiple and even contradictory ideas about children and childhood coexist; what we think about children and childhood and the ways real children actually live do not always correspond. In addition, age intersects with other key dimensions of social experience, such as sex/gender, class, race, nation, region, religion, and ethnicity, so that the lives of children often vary widely even at the same historical moment. Considering all these factors produces a very complex picture of what it means to be a child. What, then, *do* we mean when we speak of children or childhood? Rather than providing a historical chronology, we answer this question in the section that follows by focusing on models of childhood most prevalent in British and US cultural history since the seventeenth century, and we approach this history in terms of models of childhood in order to distinguish clearly between ideas about "the child" and the experiences of living children.

HISTORICAL MODELS OF CHILDHOOD

In the modern age, a number of competing models or conceptualizations of children and childhood circulate that affect how children are treated and perceived and how children live and perceive themselves. The history of childhood has not unfolded in a linear way, and newer understandings have not simply replaced earlier ones. Rather, different models of childhood, more or less dominant at different moments and in different places, overlap and intermingle to produce a complex and sometimes contradictory picture of what it means to be a child. We describe some of the most commonly encountered models of childhood separately, but these models rarely operate in isolation. Even seemingly outdated models continue to overlap with others and influence how we think and write about children. Rather than simply being a framework for classifying child characters, these models provide a way to think about the assumptions underlying how children are represented in children's literature so that those representations can be analyzed critically.

The Romantic Child

One such model is that of the child as the embodiment of innocence, or the Romantic child, such as Little Eva in *Uncle Tom's Cabin*. John Locke's *An Essay Concerning Human Understanding* (1690) sets forth the *tabula rasa* theory, the notion that the mind of a child is a blank slate: "Let us then suppose the mind to be, as we say, white paper, void of all characters, without any ideas; how comes it to be furnished? Whence comes it by that vast store, which the busy and boundless fancy of man has painted on it with an almost endless variety? To this, I answer in one word, From experience [*sic*]" (59). Later Locke would write in *Some Thoughts Concerning Education* (1693) that "the difference to be found in the manners and abilities of men is owing more to their education than to anything else [and thus] we have reason to conclude that great care is to be had of the forming of children's minds" (25). Locke's theory of human nature held practical consequences for the rearing of children, especially in matters of education and discipline. Locke thought that children should be left "free and unrestrained" as much as possible in order to explore the world around them and that they possess a "natural gaiety," which could be spoiled by too much adult interference (39). Similar sentiments were expressed by Jean-Jacques Rousseau in *Emile* (1762), his treatise on education. In Book II, Rousseau exhorts parents to abandon restrictive educational and disciplinary practices that make the lives of children unbearable drudgery:

> Love childhood; promote its games, its pleasures, its amiable instinct. Who among you has not sometimes regretted that age when a laugh is always on the lips and the soul is always at peace? Why do you want to deprive these little innocents of the enjoyment of a time so short which escapes them and of a good so precious which they do not know how to abuse? Why do you want to fill with bitterness and pains these first years which go by so rapidly and can return no more for them than they can for you? (79)

The child as conceived in *Emile* has natural innocence and virtue that must simply be molded by the sensitive guidance of an adult tutor, but Rousseau warns against forcing adult reason onto the child, who is not ready for it. "To know good and bad, to sense the reason for man's duties," he writes, "is not a child's affair. Nature wants children to be children before being men. If we want to pervert this order, we shall produce precocious fruits which will be immature and insipid and will not be long in rotting" (90). In statements such as these, Rousseau works to <u>emphasize the link between childhood and nature</u>.

In Harriet Beecher Stowe's controversial novel *Uncle Tom's Cabin* (1852), Eva is constructed as possessing a racialized childhood innocence denied to African American children.

By the end of the eighteenth century and the first half of the nineteenth, Romantic poets such as Blake in *Songs of Innocence* (1789) and William Wordsworth in "Tintern Abbey" (1798) further solidified the association of childhood with innocence and purity. Influenced by thinkers such as Locke and Rousseau, they found in children and childhood a contrast to the apparent corruptions of body and soul bred by industrialization. Wordsworth's 1807 publication of "Ode: Intimations of Immortality from Recollections of Early Childhood" reflects this Romantic idealization of childhood:

> Heaven lies about us in our infancy!
> Shades of the prison-house begin to close
>   Upon the growing Boy,
> But He beholds the light, and whence it flows,
>   He sees it in his joy;
> The Youth, who daily farther from the east
>   Must travel, still is Nature's Priest,
>   And by the vision splendid
>   Is on his way attended;
> At length the Man perceives it die away,
> And fade into the light of common day. (lines 66–76)

This conception of children as somehow purer and more virtuous than adults, closer to nature and God, and beautified by their naïveté persists in contemporary times, both in literary and filmic representations of children and in public policy debates involving the "protection" of children and childhood ignorance. Consider the refrain to "stay gold" in S.E. Hinton's landmark young adult novel *The Outsiders* (1967), in which teenager Johnny encourages his friend Ponyboy to retain his "childlike" wonder, or the public hysteria surrounding Surgeon General Joycelyn Elders's suggestion in 1994 that masturbation might be an acceptable means of avoiding HIV transmission among young people, an idea that clearly conflicted with the conception of childhood innocence and led to Elders's forced resignation. What we like to think about children has practical consequences.

This Romantic conception of childhood can emphasize different qualities and sometimes appears inconsistent. To some Romantics, the minds of children are blank slates, and children must be molded by adults and imprinted with culture. Others influenced by the Romantic tradition see children as naturally happy, carefree, innocent, or pure and thus likely to be disappointed, deformed, or corrupted by experience and maturation. Some Romantic thinkers regard children as savage and uncivilized in their proximity to nature and beasts, in contrast to more cultured and disciplined adults. Others emphasize their natural insights or abilities, which adults lack or have lost. What these various understandings share is the sense of children as almost superior to adults in some ways and as aligned with nature, beauty, or spirituality.

Many classics of children's literature reflect a Romantic vision of childhood. In Frances Hodgson Burnett's *The Secret Garden* (1911), the author depicts the three child protagonists as having an affinity with nature: the sickly, upper-class Mary and Colin both find health and vigor by working in the garden, and the kindly, working-class Dickon communes with animals and maintains his hardy constitution by always being outside. The eponymous protagonist of Virginia Hamilton's *M.C. Higgins, the Great* (1974), the first novel by an African American author to win the prestigious Newbery Medal, lives on a mountain and fears the dangers posed to his home and family by the after-effects of strip-mining. The novel's depiction of M.C. as crucial to his family's salvation and as the one most conscious of the dangers of technology links him to the Romantic tradition of seeing children as embodying an earlier, purer, agrarian past amid urbanization and industrialization.

The Sinful Child

Another conceptualization competes with the notion of children as the embodiment of innocence: that of the child as sinful and in need of discipline and training. Puritan theology and social customs have left us with the image of the sinful child born corrupted by the original sin of the biblical Adam and Eve, easily swayed to do wrong, and susceptible to evil. Historian Steven Mintz has examined the diary kept by New England Puritan Samuel Sewall between 1673 and 1729. As Mintz explains,

> Sewall's diary reveals a society that believed that even newborns were innately sinful and that parents' primary task was to suppress their children's natural depravity. Seventeenth-century Puritans cared deeply for their children and invested an enormous amount of time and energy in them, but they were also intent on repressing what they perceived as manifestations of original sin through harsh physical and psychological measures. Aside from an occasional whipping, Sewall's primary technique for disciplining his children was to provoke their fear of death, sin, and the torments inflicted in hell. (2)

By the mid eighteenth century, Evangelicals in Britain and the United States had reshaped religious understandings of children. Less severe than their Puritan predecessors, they permitted play and sought to restrict child labor. While the sense of children as born sinful and damned became less pronounced in Evangelical discourse, the need to save, discipline, and educate them remained central. The Sunday School movement emerged in Britain between the 1750s and 1780s in order to address these needs, with Evangelicals such as English-born Robert Raikes establishing Sunday schools to introduce children to Christian thought and provide alternatives to mischief or criminal behavior, especially for poor and working-class children.

Jessica's First Prayer (1867), written by English Methodist Hesba Stretton (penname of Sarah Smith), indicates the Evangelical view of the child in need of both spiritual and economic care. Jess, the protagonist, is dirty, hungry, and miserable, neglected and abused by her drunken mother. When Mr. Daniel Standring, who keeps a coffee stand in London, attempts to catch Jess at stealing by deliberately dropping a penny in front of her, she resists the temptation and returns it to him. She later follows him into a church and learns about God and faith from the minister and his children. Though she needs spiritual salvation and social training, she is not exactly the evil or sinful child described by Puritan writers even if the text implies that her poverty and lack of spiritual education would eventually lead her to depravity, as her mother had been led. Evangelicals, influenced by both religious doctrines and the increasingly popular views of the Romantics, imagined the child as a composite of the sinful and Romantic child.

Today, manifestations of this notion of childhood sin might take more secular forms, couched in the pseudopsychological language of impulse control and developmental immaturity or in the pseudoanthropological language of savagery or untamed wildness, but they still arise in references to the schoolyard cruelty of children or to the need for teenage curfews as a way to reduce crime. The sinful or depraved child frequently appears onscreen or in written fiction as well, as in William March's 1954 bestseller, *The Bad Seed*, which features an adorable suburban girl in pigtails who turns into a chillingly cold-blooded murderer. *The Bad Seed* was later made into a hit Broadway play and a critically acclaimed film. George R.R. Martin's fantasy novel *A Game of Thrones* (1996) was also a bestseller that was later adapted into a successful television series, and it too features a malevolent boy, Prince Joffrey, who later becomes a tyrannical child king. Clearly, the figure of the evil child still resonates. This image is remarkable for the way it contrasts so strikingly with the image of the child as the embodiment of innocence.

While the model of the sinful or evil child still persists most obviously in works of horror, it can also be seen throughout children's literature even if the child's evil is not attributed to original sin. The character Draco Malfoy in the Harry Potter series belongs to the tradition of the evil child, even though his evil is influenced by his upbringing and his family's service to Voldemort. Another evil child, Paul, in Edward Bloor's *Tangerine* (1997) blinds his younger brother, commands a friend to murder another youth, and steals from his neighbors, and yet the novel provides little explanation for Paul's horrific actions. Though representations of the Romantic or sacred child now appear more frequently and serve as the dominant conceptions of children, the evil or sinful child continues to appear in the form of bullies, criminals, or rivals.

The Working Child

One of the key developments in the history of childhood involves the way children were transformed from economically valuable sources of expendable labor into almost sacred and sentimental objects who actually cost parents money. The model of the working child, which characterized life for most children before the early twentieth century, cast children as necessary and useful contributors to the household, as practical additions to families, and as sources of labor. The early American colonies, finding themselves in desperate need of able bodies, appealed to England to send over street children. Upon one such request from the Virginia Company in 1619, the Privy Council of England responded,

> Whereas the City of London hath, by an act of the Common Council, appointed one hundred children, out of the multitudes that swarm in that place, to be sent to Virginia, there to be bound as apprentices for certain years with very beneficial conditions for them afterwards ... the City deserveth thanks and commendations for redeeming so many poor souls from misery and ruin and putting them in a condition of use and service to the State. ("Declaration" 242)

Hardly precious objects to be coddled, these children of twelve and upward, pressed into "service to the State," were to be rounded up and sent to a faraway land to do the back-breaking work of building the colonies. Not all these children were expected to go happily or voluntarily, and the English government made provisions for such a possibility: "If any of them shall be found obstinate to resist or otherwise disobey such directions as shall be given in this behalf, we do likewise hereby authorize such as shall have the charge of this service to imprison, punish, and dispose of any of those children, upon any disorder by them or any of them committed, as cause shall require, and so to ship them out for Virginia with as much expedition as may stand with conveniency [*sic*]" ("Declaration" 243).

This way of understanding children as useful labor persisted late into the nineteenth century. In his enormously influential exposé *How the Other Half Lives* (1890), Jacob Riis writes about the "army of homeless boys" living on the streets and working in New York City in the 1880s. He cites as an example the case of two brothers: "John and Willie, aged ten and eight, picked up by the police. They 'didn't live nowhere,' never went to school, could neither read nor write. Their twelve-year-old sister kept house for the father, who turned the boys out to beg, or steal, or starve" (150). The evidence gathered by Riis and others suggests that this father was no aberration nor unusually heartless; rather, his actions represent a particular way of thinking about children that differs from the image of the sacred child that is currently dominant in Euro American culture.

Nineteenth-century children's literature often described the common experience of child labor, and more contemporary historical novels reflect this earlier model. Horatio

"Street Arabs in Sleeping Quarters," Jacob Riis, 1890.

Alger's iconic rags-to-riches story *Ragged Dick* (1868) depicts orphan bootblacks who live and work on the streets of New York City, and Walter Dean Myers's historical novel *The Glory Field* (1994) includes children and adolescents from different periods who must work to support their families or themselves, such as Lizzy, a thirteen-year-old slave who escapes to freedom during the American Civil War, and fifteen-year-old Elijah, who stands up to a white sheriff and risks being lynched in an effort to help support his family financially at the turn of the twentieth century. These texts show the working child as fully capable of earning an income, engaging in exhausting physical labor, and acting independently of adults.

The <u>Sacred</u> Child   神圣的孩子 ·

Sociologist Viviana Zelizer traces the shifting conceptualization of childhood over the course of the nineteenth and early twentieth centuries, when child labor laws sought to remove children from the factories and fields and compulsory education laws relocated them to the classroom as the model of the sacred child took hold. In this model, children are understood as precious and fragile aesthetic objects to admire rather than as practical tools. As such, they must be protected, watched, fussed over. A few dates and figures sketch a picture of how the sacred child emerged in the nineteenth century as child labor declined and education became compulsory:

- In the United States, Massachusetts was the first state to enact a compulsory education law in 1852. It compelled children between the ages of six and sixteen to attend school for some portion of the year.

- The next state to pass such a law was Vermont in 1867, indicating that other states were slow to follow the lead of Massachusetts.

- It was not until the 1870s and 1880s that the trend became decisive. By 1885, twenty-two out of thirty-eight states had compulsory education laws, and by 1900, thirty-four out of forty-five did.

- It took almost sixty years, from the 1870s to the 1930s, to prohibit many forms of child labor in the United States. During this period, a significant percentage of children worked either on family farms or outside the home, including in factories (Zelizer 57).

- Not coincidentally, the 1930s marked the beginning of a shift toward an increase in attendance of secondary schools. While in 1930 the number of teenagers graduating from high school was equal to 29 per cent of seventeen-year-olds in the United States, that figure doubled to 59 per cent by 1950 (Schaller 28).

These trends occurred for a number of reasons. Zelizer cites the rise in real incomes, the institution of the family wage with which men were expected to earn enough to maintain a household, and the growing demand for educated labor in the twentieth-century economy as factors that enabled or compelled children to attend school rather than to work (62–63). In order to free up jobs for adult men and to reduce competition for work, which was heightened by the influx of immigrants during the latter half of the nineteenth century, children were gradually removed from the workforce in significant numbers. Schools evolved to give them someplace to be and something to do.

Two other possible preconditions for this shift to thinking about children as precious objects to coddle and protect were the overall reduction in the number of children born to each family and the declining mortality rate as more children survived into adulthood. As Steven Mintz explains about colonial America, "In New England's healthiest communities, around 10 percent of children died in their first year, and three of every nine died before reaching their twenty-first birthday. In seaports like Boston or Salem, death rates were two or even three times higher" (15). By the early twentieth century, families were having fewer children, which gave parents more time and inclination to invest emotionally in each child, and better public-health education and access to medical care permitted more children to survive into adulthood. As it became easier to keep children alive, parental agency over the fate of their children increased parental responsibility and vigilance over their care.

Whatever the reasons, during this period children became primarily a source of emotional reward to prize and assiduously nurture, sacred objects to protect from every conceivable danger, rather than sources of economic income and parental security in old age. At first, childhood as a time and space of play, imagination, and formal education was the province of only the most privileged children of the middle and upper classes who could afford to keep these young people out of the workforce and provided with the toys, games, books, leisure, and lack of responsibility that now characterize childhood. Gradually, over the course of the late nineteenth and early twentieth centuries, this model of childhood came to be understood as an ideal toward which all families across the economic spectrum could and should aspire.

This marked a radical shift in both the discourse and experience of childhood. The daily routines and schedules, the self-conceptions and thoughts, the interests, the behaviors, and the capacities of the nine-year-old factory worker or farm worker in the first decade of the twentieth century would differ considerably from those of the nine-year-old student who attends a suburban school in the first decade of the twenty-first. The child laborers of the early twentieth century would have dressed exactly like the adults working next to them. They would have eaten the same foods, used the same machines, and passed time alongside fellow workers, some about the same age and some much older. They would have traveled from home to factory or across stretches of land unchaperoned and unsupervised. In contrast, twenty-first-century youth might dress quite differently from adults, attend school during the day rather than work, associate primarily with those of similar ages, eat foods packaged and marketed specifically for young people, watch television programs produced expressly for a younger demographic, and be watched constantly or forced to give an account of every movement. These two cohorts, separated by about a century, had very different lives and thought about themselves in radically different ways.

Because the model of the sacred child serves as one of the more dominant understandings of children, it appears frequently in children's literature. For instance, in Eleanor Porter's *Pollyanna* (1913), Pollyanna's value to her Aunt Polly comes not from paid labor but from how Pollyanna's good behavior reflects on her upbringing. Pollyanna also occupies the center of attention, and the curmudgeonly Mr. Pendleton wants to adopt her himself because he sees children, and Pollyanna in particular, as able to bring joy into the life of adults. Pollyanna's injury finally makes her the one who needs care, and she is treated like a fragile object to be protected from the full knowledge of her prognosis. Lafayette, the youngest protagonist of Jacqueline Woodson's *Miracle's Boys* (2000), also embodies the model of the sacred child. While his oldest brother, Ty'ree, works to support his younger siblings, and the middle child Charlie works to readjust to life after a stint in a home for delinquent boys, Lafayette focuses on school, television, and dealing with his feelings stemming from the loss of his parents. Lafayette is the child who must be protected from the pain of life, and the tension of the novel springs from the gap between this ideal and the realities of poverty and orphanhood.

The Child as Radically Other

The very different experiences of the sacred child and the working child suggest yet another structuring opposition that underlies modern conceptualizations of childhood and its distinction from adulthood. Are children fundamentally and qualitatively different from adults, or are they merely incomplete or miniature versions? Does the line between childhood and adulthood represent a rupture, marking a radical difference between the child and the adult, or do childhood and adulthood exist as periods that gradually shade into each other along a continuum, with each possessing traces of the other at its fringes? Different responses to these questions produce quite different ways of thinking about various aspects of childhood and children's culture.

One model understands the child as fundamentally different from the adult, or radically Other. For instance, the child at play might represent an experience or imaginative feat unique to childhood and lost to adults, who are much too preoccupied with the empirical or the real. Bill Watterson plays with this notion in his *Calvin and Hobbes* comic strip (1985–1995). When Calvin is alone with his stuffed tiger, Hobbes is real and alive; when one of Calvin's parents enters the frame, Hobbes reverts into an inanimate toy. His parents cannot see Hobbes the same way Calvin does. Children who playact as kings and queens, then, are perhaps performing in ways unique to children, but few would claim that a performance of Shakespeare's *Macbeth* is child's play. The child at play might be imagined as a miniature actor, the playacting of childhood existing along a continuum with the enactment of adult drama. Does the play of eight-year-old Pee Wee football players belong properly to childhood, meaning that the big business of adult football is a holdover of children's culture, or are these boys prematurely enacting an adult sport? These children might be seen as playing at an adult activity, or the adults, by playing, might be seen as performing a childhood pursuit. We do not have to decide which is the case, but we do need to recognize the slippery nature of both childhood and adulthood in order to read literature for children critically.

The Developing Child

Many models of childhood include a sense in which the child is radically Other to the adult, rather than existing along a continuum with people of different ages. One model that does seem to suggest a continuum is that of the developing child. The twentieth century saw the birth of the academic child-study movement. Though philosophers, educators, and others concerned with the care and education of the young had long considered and written about children, childhood, and child-rearing, professional psychologists first turned their attention to the concentrated study of childhood beginning with works such as G. Stanley Hall's *Adolescence: Its Psychology and Its Relations to Physiology, Anthropology, Sociology, Sex, Crime, Religion, and Education*, first published in 1904. Kenneth Kidd describes Hall as "the founding father not only of child psychology but of American psychology more generally.... Hall presided over the child study movement at Clark University, where he welcomed Sigmund Freud in 1909 and trained a whole new generation of child experts" (36). Freud, another key pioneer of psychological child study, saw the child and childhood experiences as absolutely central to the workings of the human psyche, and his work on the psychodynamics of childhood popularized understandings of the child as existing along a continuum of development with the adult. Freud likened childhood in the life of the individual to the "primaeval" period in the evolution of the human species (Freud 39).

By the mid twentieth century, the field of developmental psychology had crystallized around the empirical study of children and their increasing capacities over the course of youth. Swiss psychologist Jean Piaget, who began laying out his theory of child development in the 1920s, articulated four periods of cognitive development during which children construct knowledge in different ways: the sensorimotor period from birth to two years, the preoperational period from two to seven years, the period of concrete operations from seven to eleven years, and the period of formal operations from eleven years on. While other psychologists and cultural critics have challenged this emphasis on normative, universal stages of development in recent years, what is important for the student or scholar of childhood and children's literature is that the work of Piaget and other developmental psychologists represents children neither as miniature adults nor as fundamentally different from adults. Rather, the developmental approach understands children as immature or developing beings who are slowly moving toward adulthood in a mostly unbroken line. If this sounds matter of course to the contemporary reader, it might be because this model is currently one of the most prevalent and dominant.

Since the advent of scientific child study, children's literature often conceives of the child in psychological terms and depicts the child's gradual development or maturation. The young Christopher Robin in A.A. Milne's Pooh books possesses the imagination to envision Pooh and the other animals of the Hundred Acre Wood as living beings; yet, at the end of *The House at Pooh Corner* (1928) he must abandon Pooh to go to school and sorrowfully alludes to his own development: "'Pooh,' said Christopher Robin earnestly, 'if I—if I'm not quite—' he stopped and tried again—'Pooh, *whatever* happens, you *will* understand, won't you?'" (179). Christopher Robin intuits that his growing up will change him and his relationship with his beloved bear. In *Then Again, Maybe I Won't* (1971), Judy Blume describes the physical and psychological development of twelve-year-old Tony, who must deal with common experiences of puberty, such as nocturnal emissions and uncontrollable erections. Both works show childhood as a state of transition.

The Child as Miniature Adult

French historian Philippe Ariès argues controversially in *Centuries of Childhood* that the model of imagining children as simply miniature adults prevailed until at least the thirteenth century but persisted well into the seventeenth. He cites as evidence the depictions of children in art:

> An Ottonian miniature of the twelfth century provides us with a striking example of the deformation which an artist at that time would inflict on children's bodies. The subject is the scene in the Gospels in which Jesus asks that little children be allowed to come to Him. The Latin text is clear: *parvuli* [children]. Yet the miniaturist has grouped around Jesus what are obviously eight men, without any of the characteristics of childhood; they have simply been depicted on a smaller scale than the adults, without any other difference in expression or feature. (33)

Ariès claims that "it is hard to believe that this neglect was due to incompetence or incapacity" (33); rather, he believes that this distortion of children's bodies reflects a particular conceptualization of the child, one that would have been consistent with the experience of children whose lives, whose daily existence, were not substantively different from those of the adults around them. Ariès suggests that, to the twelfth-century artist, children were simply smaller adults, not qualitatively different from their older and larger counterparts. Even though his interpretation of the historical evidence has been contested, Ariès encourages us to think about the remarkable similarities between children and adults. If Ariès were to see an image of Pee Wee football players, he might read the boys as depicting miniature adult athletes. Children's literature—along with comics, television, and film—is replete with independent, autonomous children doing remarkable things such as building elaborate contraptions and researching complex legal loopholes, as the Baudelaire orphans do in Lemony Snicket's *A Series of Unfortunate Events: The Bad Beginning* (1999); rallying warriors and lords behind a new King in

The child as miniature adult is reflected in this *Madonna and Child* (1228–36) by Berlinghiero
Berlinghieri. Tempera on wood, gold ground.

Using Models of Childhood to Read Critically

Model	Description of Model
The Romantic Child	The Romantic model of childhood prevails when children are imagined or depicted as more innocent or insightful than adults and as closer to the natural or spiritual world, including animals or angels. Since this model emerged by using the child to embody an idyllic past in the face of unsettling trends, we should ask what anxieties or events motivate the appearance of the Romantic child.
The Sinful Child	Since the child is sometimes used to represent the best in humanity, we can understand the evil child as representing cultural fears about the limits or failures of human goodness, selflessness, or self-mastery. When we find examples of the evil or sinful child, we should consider how the text points to what we fear in or about ourselves or our cultures.
The Working Child	The concept of the working child is concerned with the utility of children, or what they are good for. We may like to think about children as ends in themselves, but for most of history children have been practically useful. Examples of the working child might appear in classic books or historical fiction, but they might also appear in contemporary realist texts. The working child in contemporary texts challenges the cherished notion that children do not—and should not—work, raising questions about whether they still can be practically or economically useful.
The Sacred Child	The sacred child appears in characterizations of fictional youth as delicate, valuable objects who confer status or provide emotional payoffs, especially to adults. This child must be carefully safeguarded. Since thinking of children as sacred comes at great financial and emotional cost to adults, readers should consider signs of adult ambivalence or resentment or indications that another model is competing with this one for dominance.

Model	Description of Model
The Child as Radically Other	Depictions of the child as significantly different from adults, rather than as miniature or developing adults, can tell us what the broader culture thinks about people across the lifespan. We should ask ourselves what the radically other child suggests about adult characters or adult culture and their limitations or failings. Is the radically other child a figure of hope in the future, condemnation of the past or present, or something else?
The Developing Child	In contrast to the child who is radically other from the adult and who possesses the potential to abruptly transform from one into the other, the developing child slowly becomes the adult over time. Recognizing the figure of the developing child prompts the reader to consider the process whereby the child is transformed and the milestones that mark those transitions. Is the process a smooth or rough one? What makes it so? What happens when a child fails or refuses to develop in expected ways?
The Child as Miniature Adult	The child as miniature adult is one who possesses the abilities, limitations, or privileges of adulthood while retaining youth. What kind of adult does the child resemble? What desires, pleasures, anxieties, or fears about youth and age does the miniature adult embody, provoke, or alleviate?

the North, as the fierce Lyanna Mormont does in the *Game of Thrones* television series (2016); or determining whether a particular statue was sculpted by Michelangelo, as eleven-year-old Claudia Kincaid does in E.L. Konigsburg's children's novel *From the Mixed-up Files of Mrs. Basil E. Frankweiler* (1967). While some children might be this precocious or talented, these examples point to a gap between lived experience and representation, which suggests that the artwork examined by Ariès might not tell the whole story about how childhood was experienced in the Middle Ages. Nonetheless, the miniaturization model continues to endure in the many ways children are either treated or expected to act like adults.

Children's literature frequently depicts children as acting independently of adults and performing roles more commonly attributed to adults, such as caring for other children or undertaking journeys. These depictions suggest that children embody miniature adults. Both Peter and Wendy in J.M. Barrie's *Peter Pan* (1904) play the role of parents, pretending to be the father and mother of the lost boys, and Peter does battle with Captain Hook, rescuing Wendy and her brothers from pirates. Though Peter is "the boy who wouldn't grow up," he actually appears to function like a smaller or younger man, just as Wendy acts like a little woman. Sometimes a child character embodies the miniature adult model only at particular moments or through specific actions, as in Sharon Creech's Newbery-winning *Walk Two Moons* (1994), in which thirteen-year-old Salamanca travels cross-country with her grandparents, tracing the path her mother took from Ohio to Idaho. At a pivotal moment in the novel, Sal takes her grandparents' car and drives it at night for a hundred miles over steep, hilly terrain to discover the secret of her mother's disappearance. Through these actions Salamanca fulfills the role of the child as miniature adult, who drives, reckons with abandonment and loss, and experiences independence from adult caregivers.

THE UNCERTAIN BOUNDARIES OF CHILDHOOD

We must take care to avoid overstating differences across time. A focus on historical change might obscure differences or variations among children or youth living at the same historical moment. For example, the experiences of two children living in the first decade of the twentieth century—one, say, the daughter of an Anglo-American factory owner in Pennsylvania and the other the son of an African American sharecropper in Mississippi—would have varied drastically, and such differences might in fact still persist between children living at the same moment. Both changes across time and differences among children of the same period point to the complex and shifting boundaries between childhood and adulthood. These uncertain boundaries of childhood complicate the writing and reading of children's literature.

Child Crime

The concept of childhood continues to change as the meanings and ideals we attach to it are constantly contested, reevaluated, and modified. Cases of children engaging in crime or violence are especially likely to challenge the boundaries of childhood, given the traditional associations between childhood and innocence—defined as both moral innocence and general ignorance. A number of controversies from the past two decades have raised questions about our definitions of childhood, including the case of Lionel Tate. After one of the most controversial trials involving a juvenile defendant in recent history, Tate became the youngest offender ever to be sentenced to life in prison in the United States. In 1999, when Tate was twelve years old, he killed six-year-old Tiffany Eunick while supposedly mimicking wrestling moves he had seen on television. At the age of fourteen, Tate was convicted of first-degree murder and sentenced to life in prison without the possibility of parole. In 2004, four days before his seventeenth birthday, Tate was released from prison after an appeals court overturned his conviction, claiming that his competency to stand trial had not been properly assessed (Goodnough 12). Is a twelve-year-old sufficiently capable of understanding right and wrong to be convicted of a crime such as murder and sentenced to life in prison? Does possessing such a capacity define adulthood? Should a twelve-year-old be protected from harsh sentences, or should the sentence fit the crime irrespective of the age of the perpetrator? If children are going to be subject to the same standards and punishments as adults, should they also have access to the rights and privileges of adulthood? Tate's case raises these types of questions about our understanding of children and childhood.

Child Sex

Cases involving juvenile sex also challenge prevailing definitions of childhood. In 1997 eighteen-year-old Anthony Croce from St. Petersburg, Florida, was convicted for having sex with his fifteen-year-old girlfriend. Although the relationship began when Croce was seventeen, the girl's mother pressed charges against Croce as soon as he turned eighteen. In recent years, some US states have passed so-called Romeo and Juliet laws to provide more leeway to teenagers who engage in consensual sexual activities with each other. In some cases these laws decriminalize sex between teenagers as long as both are over the age of fourteen and not separated by more than four years in age, while in other cases the law simply allows the convicted youth to petition to be removed from sex-offender registries. Florida passed such a law in 2007, and Anthony Croce became the first convicted sex offender to be successful in removing his name from the list. In a similar case, Genarlow Wilson was convicted in 2006 of having consensual sexual relations with a fifteen-year-old girl at a party in 2003. At the time of the incident, Wilson was seventeen. He was sentenced to ten years in prison, but his case was appealed to the Georgia Supreme Court, which ordered his release in 2007 after Wilson had spent thirty-two months in prison for a consensual sexual act with a girl only two years his junior (Ave 1B). Cases such as these are, at their core, about our cultural understanding of childhood. Should a fifteen-year-old be considered a child and therefore unable to consent to sexual activity with another teenager? Is a seventeen- or eighteen-year-old who has consensual sex with another teenager, perhaps a fellow high-school classmate or boyfriend or girlfriend, a sexual predator?

Child Soldiers

The role children have played as either witnesses to or participants in wars also complicates the picture we have of children and childhood. In P.W. Singer's 2005 study, *Children at War*, he notes that in addition to those children killed in conflicts, "Six million more children have been disabled or seriously injured in wars over the last decade, and one million children have been orphaned. Almost twenty-five million more children have been driven from their homes by conflict, roughly 50 percent of the current total number of refugees in the world. Another ten million children have been psychologically traumatized by war" (6). The children cited in these statistics are presumably civilians, but Singer also describes an increasing tendency to rely on child soldiers in conflicts around the globe:

"The use of child soldiers is far more widespread than the scant attention it typically receives. In over three-fourths of the armed conflicts around the world, there are now significant numbers of children participating as active combatants. These are not just youths who are on the cusp of adulthood, but also include minors as young as six years old" (6). Examples of child participants in war can be found in British and American history as well. Before the twentieth century, it was common for armies to employ young boys as drummers or buglers, and these boys would often find themselves on battlefields carrying messages, assisting with the wounded, or even taking up arms (Mintz 120). During the eighteenth and nineteenth centuries, Britain's Royal Navy employed youths as young as nine as cabin boys. During battles they carried gunpowder to sailors manning the cannons, thereby earning the nickname "powder monkeys." More recently, the civil war that raged in Sierra Leone from 1991 to 2001 received worldwide attention for the use of child soldiers. Singer cites estimates that up to 80 per cent of soldiers fighting for the Revolutionary

An 1861 portrait of Taylor, an African American Union Drummer Boy, 78th Regiment, US Colored Infantry, during the Civil War.

United Front were between the ages of seven and fourteen and that as many as ten thousand child soldiers participated in the conflict (14–15). Mintz's comments about child soldiers point to the implications for our thinking about children and childhood: "The experience of children during the [US] Civil War forces us to rethink popular assumptions about children's fragility. It demonstrates young people's resilience, but also the indelible impression that war leaves on children's lives" (120). As with child criminals and child laborers, child soldiers reflect both another way of thinking about what children can and should do and the extreme varieties of actual childhood experience.

Child Embodiment and Disability

One of the defining features of the child is the possession of a young body as distinct from a mature or elder one. The child's body has long been understood as a medical or social problem, while what is considered the normative body is adult, white, abled, and male. Aristotle, for instance, saw women as incomplete men, writing in *Generation of Animals* (c. 350 BCE) that "the female is as it were a deformed male" (175). He similarly saw children as inferior, "born in an imperfect state" (457), only later reaching "perfection" in maturity (459). The Greek physician and philosopher Galen (c. 130–200 CE) also upheld what Susan Mattern describes as the "adult, urban, Greek male, in the prime of life" as the standard body "from which all others deviated" (105). He speculated that health was determined by bodily humors, what were thought to be the body's four fluids, and that children's bodies were ruled by excessively hot and wet humors. The important thirteenth-century scholar Bartolomaeus Anglicus also thought that humors caused illness when out of balance and were naturally overheated in children, making them "unsteadfast and unstable." Bartolomaeus writes that because of their excessive craving for and consumption of food and drink, "they fall often and many times into diverse sicknesses and evils" (46). Bartolomaeus warned that infants should not be exposed to bright light, which might harm their sight, and he notes, "And for tenderness the limbs of the child may easily and soon bow and bend and take diverse shapes. And therefore children's members and limbs are bound with lystes [bandages] and other covenable [suitable] bonds, that they be not crooked nor evil shapen" (46). The practice of swaddling infants, or wrapping them tightly in cloth, was meant to soothe them, but also to prevent them from hurting themselves or "crawling on the floor 'like an animal'" (deMause 11). These influential figures all saw children's bodies as feeble, prone to illness, and essentially flawed.

The contemporary concept of disability complicates what it means to be a child and the distinction between child and adult. While the child has long been seen as a deformed or incomplete adult, adults with disabilities, on the other hand, have commonly been described as childlike or as needing care like children. Deborah Marks notes

that "childlike goodness" has been attributed to people with disabilities, who are sometimes thought to possess "childlike innocence" (162). She observes that the disabled
have been portrayed as "closer to nature," which echoes the Romantic model of childhood, and efforts to inspire charitable giving sometimes strategically equate children
and people with disabilities to construct an image of the disabled as "helpless, pure
and innocent" (163). As disability studies scholar Paul Longmore explains, the common
and effective practice of using children to solicit charitable donations, including for the
Arthritis Telethon, associates disability with childhood: "The charities depicted the
represented disabled person as a vulnerable child, one of 'the most weak'" (38). Paradoxically, the figure of the disabled child can subvert the concept of the innocent or
unknowing youth, since the disabled child might be keenly aware of aspects of experience like pain or bias, about which young people are thought to be ignorant. As Laura
Kavesh of the *Chicago Tribune* puts it, "It Takes a Tough Kid to Be a Poster Child" (Kavesh n.p.). The children Kavesh features manage physical difficulties related to living
in a world designed for the able-bodied. Susie, a girl with spina bifida who is a finalist
to be the Easter Seal spokesperson, tells Kavesh that the selected child "needs a lot of
spunk and determination ... [to be] a very tough child" (n.p.). Emerging scholarship
in the field of disability studies calls our attention to the ways the body is constructed
in discourse and challenges our assumptions about the ideal body and the perceived
limitations of non-normative bodies. Disability studies encourages us to consider the
possibilities of extraordinary bodies—child or adult, disabled or able-bodied—and
how they challenge the social enforcement of normativity, and it offers opportunities
for reconsidering the youthful body in children's literature.

Child Privilege and Race

Contemporary childhood as a time or experience of innocence, play, education, and protection is a privilege not enjoyed by all young people, as the experiences of working and
poor children make clear. Robin Bernstein notes, moreover, that in the nineteenth-century construction of the child as innocent, "innocence was raced white" (4). Bernstein argues that the child as white, innocent angel emerges with and depends on the racist figure
of the "pickaninny," or black youth who was actually thought to be insensitive to physical
pain: "As childhood was defined as tender innocence, as vulnerability, and as the pickaninny was defined by the inability to feel or to suffer, then the pickaninny—and the black
juvenile it purported to represent—was defined out of childhood" (20). In other words,
when childhood was defined by innocence and vulnerability, the black child was excluded from the category and privilege of childhood. Black juveniles could be found ineligible
for childhood by being imagined as too knowing, tough, or guilty. The very experience of

slavery or racial injustice could be seen as disqualifying black juveniles from innocence and hence childhood.

Geoff K. Ward has documented this bias in his study of race and the juvenile justice system. He finds that in the establishment of the US juvenile justice system, which took place during the late nineteenth and early twentieth centuries and focused on rehabilitating juvenile offenders through the use of juvenile courts and detention centers, "black youths experienced ongoing commitment to adult prisons, the convict-lease system [the use of convict labor by private employers], prolonged periods in detention, and higher rates of corporal punishment and execution" (11). Ward notes that while the age of black youths was not overlooked and that black youths were sometimes treated differently from black adults, an implicit acknowledgement of black childhood, black juveniles "were culturally and politically constructed as inferior and undeserving subjects of the white-dominated parental state, with no rights to equal protection" (38). In short, the existence of a juvenile justice system was based on the assumption that juvenile offenders were less culpable and more likely to be reformed than adult criminals, but Ward shows that these assumptions were less frequently extended to black youths, denying them the privileges of childhood.

Often, when black youths experience violence in the United States, a public debate arises about the black victim's guilt or innocence, which points to the notion of childhood as defined by the privileged possession of innocence and protection rather than to the possession of a young body. In other words, black children and youths have to have their innocence asserted if they hope to be perceived as children, rather than simply being considered children because of their youth. For instance, in 1955, 14-year-old Emmett Till traveled from Chicago, Illinois, to Money, Mississippi, to visit relatives. After interacting with a white woman in a grocery store, Till was abducted, brutally beaten, shot, and dumped in a river. Rather than focusing on Till's murder, various accounts of what led to the lynching questioned whether Till himself had prompted the horrible crime by whistling at the woman (Anderson 31). More recent cases in which unarmed black youths have been shot—such as the 2012 shooting of 17-year-old Trayvon Martin in Sanford, Florida, and the 2014 shooting of 18-year-old Michael Brown in Ferguson, Missouri— have similarly involved questions about whether the youths were guilty of threatening the shooters, thereby prompting their own deaths. A New York Times feature on Michael Brown referred to him as "no angel" for "dabbling" in drugs and alcohol and being involved in an altercation with a convenience store clerk on the day of his shooting (Elgion n.p.). Following the Times article, Kia Makarechi noted in Vanity Fair that based on a search of its digital archives, the use of the phrase "no angel" in the New York Times "seems to most commonly describe either hardened white criminals, or men of color" (n.p.), supporting Bernstein's claims about the ways in which innocence, and hence childhood, is denied black youths.

Claiming that black youth should in fact be recognized as children was used as a political tactic in the anti-slavery and civil rights movements. Bernstein traces this practice to abolitionist literature of the 1850s and cites Frederick Douglass's assertion in *My Bondage and My Freedom* (1855) that "SLAVE-children *are* children" (Douglass 33). Katharine Capshaw shows how this practice of asserting the childhood of black children continued during the twentieth century: "Within the African American civil rights movement, photographs of children held immense political power" (x). She cites as examples photographs taken of Emmett Till before and after his murder, photos of the Little Rock Nine desegregating their Arkansas high school in 1957, and pictures of black youths being attacked by police during the 1963 Children's Crusade in Birmingham (x). That civil rights activists, even today, would need to argue that black youths count as children testifies to the fact that childhood is not simply a function of age. It also operates as a privilege that must be claimed, asserted, and protected. The fact that adult slaves were sometimes understood as children in need of care by their slaveholders further confirms the unstable boundaries between childhood and adulthood and the fact that childhood could sometimes be divorced from young age.

CHILDREN'S LITERATURE AND THE HISTORY OF CHILDHOOD

For those who study children's literature, these various models of the child suggest that no assumption related to children and childhood can be taken for granted. Do children have short attention spans? Not those who read Thomas Hughes's *Tom Brown's School Days*, which exceeds five hundred pages, nor those who waited in line for each hefty new installment of Harry Potter. Are children basically good but corrupted by experience and culture, or essentially evil and in need of strict control lest they unleash all kinds of chaos? How we answer this question has profound effects not only on educational and social policy but also on the kinds of books published and purchased for children. This chapter seeks to prompt an investigation into the changing and complex conceptualizations of the child in order to consider more critically the kinds of assumptions we make about the imagined child reader of children's literature. Clarifying how we think about children and knowing about the history of childhood will help us to understand literature written for and about them.

Conversely, children's literature can provide a way of tracing the history of childhood, since the kind of child it both implies and represents will be affected by the construction of children and childhood in the era of a literary work's composition. In other words, we can learn about the history of childhood from reading children's literature. For instance, *The New England Primer*, first published between 1687 and 1690, was one of the most widely owned books in the New World for about two centuries. A collection of rhymes, proverbs, alphabets, prayers, and catechisms, it provides a snapshot of the ideology and experience of childhood in early America. One of the works included in *The New England Primer* is John Cotton's 1646 *Spiritual Milk for Boston Babes* (often called *Milk for Babes*), a short catechism that is possibly the first work printed in the American colonies specifically for children. As a catechism, it provides a series of theological questions and answers to be memorized by the child. The questions pertaining to the biblical fifth commandment are indicative of the conception of childhood in the seventeenth century:

Q. What is the fifth commandment?

A. Honor thy father and thy mother, that thy days may be long in the land which the Lord thy God giveth thee.

Q. What are meant by father and mother?

A. All our superiors whether in family, school, church and commonwealth.

Q. What is the honor due unto them?

A. Reverence, obedience, and (when I am able) recompence. [*sic*]

Here the commandment to honor one's parents is expanded to include all superiors, potentially even older children, as well as church and government authorities, and the child commits to pay his or her parents back not just spiritually but financially. First and foremost, the child is to be subject to authorities and a source of compensation. Another text included in *The New England Primer* is an excerpt from Benjamin Keach's *War with the Devil* from 1673. A dialogue in which Christ and the devil vie for the soul of a youth, it concludes with the youth telling Christ that he will put off salvation until another day in order to enjoy life first. To this, Christ replies:

Nay, hold vain youth, thy time is short,
I have thy breath, I'll end thy sport;
Thou shalt not live till thou art old,
Since thou in sin art grown so bold.
I in thy youth grim death will send,
And all thy sports shall have an end. (n.p.)

Though the youth immediately sees the error of his ways and pleads for forgiveness and mercy, Christ decides to make an example of him and takes his life, condemning him to hell. In an age when one in three children might not reach adulthood and the doctrine of original sin meant that everyone was damned from the very moment of conception, there was no time to delay in seeking salvation.

Children's literature of the nineteenth century records the shifting conceptualization of the child from profitable worker to sentimental object. Charles Kingsley's *The Water-Babies* (1863) includes an important encounter between a child who embodies the traditional model of the child laborer and one who is already living the modern version of the sacred child. *The Water-Babies* is a bizarre fantasy that condemns child labor and the treatment of the poor in England while promoting Christian ideals. Its main character, the young Tom, is a chimney sweep, one of the most publicly visible kinds of child laborers in Victorian England. As Tom crawls through the maze of chimneys in the home of a wealthy family, he loses his way and falls out into the room of a young girl named Ellie. When he sees how white and clean she is, sitting up in her white, clean bed, Tom realizes for the first time that he is dirty, and he flees the house in shame only to drown in a river and be turned into a mythical water baby. After a series of adventures, Tom is turned back into a person and given a second chance to attain middle-class respectability, having been encouraged to be a better boy by his encounter with the angelic Ellie, the child of privilege. Kingsley uses the stark contrast between Tom and Ellie to promote the modern idea that becoming a sacred child is attainable by all children, even a poor, ignorant, and dirty one like Tom.

In 1862 the American Tract Society published *Step by Step; or, Tidy's Way to Freedom*, a slave narrative written by an anonymous, presumably white, author and addressed to white children. One of the many anti-slavery works published for children, *Step by Step* tells the story of Tidy, taken from her mother when little over a year old and raised to serve Miss Matilda as a slave: "Tidy was taught to work.... Tidy was an apt learner, and at eight years of age she could do up Miss Matilda's ruffles, clean the great brass andirons and fender in the sitting-room, and set a room to rights as neatly as any person in the house" (*Step by Step* 23). By the age of ten, Tidy is charged with serving as the undernurse to four other children, the eldest a girl of her own age, along with another girl of eight, a boy of three, and an infant. Throughout the narrative, the white child reader is directly addressed by the narrator, who implores the reader to compare his or her own life of privilege with Tidy's life of enforced servitude and ignorance. Although the contemporary model of the sacred child is unavailable to Tidy, *Step by Step* nonetheless records the shift from understanding this model as the province of only wealthy children to the sense that it should be accessible to and enacted by all children. The reader is repeatedly invited to share in the national shame of having deprived Tidy of her childhood.

READING CRITICALLY: THE HISTORY OF CHILDHOOD

Anne of Green Gables

When using the history of childhood to read children's literature, we must ask: How does the ideology or experience of childhood as it exists and operates at a given moment in history inform—that is, clarify, explain, or influence—the representation of the child and childhood in the text? To answer this question, investigate the ideology and experience of childhood during the era when the novel is set, the era in which it was written, or both. Are the experiences of the child character like or unlike the ones characteristic of children from a given historical moment? In what ways does the child in the text embody the "typical" experience or depart from it? What do we learn from the fictional child that we do not learn from standard historical narratives about childhood? What does knowing that history help you to notice about the text that you might otherwise have overlooked or not understood?

L.M. Montgomery's *Anne of Green Gables* (1908) provides a particularly useful example of how understanding the history of childhood helps readers to understand children's literature, and vice versa. The premise of *Anne* is simple: aging siblings Matthew and Marilla Cuthbert, who live together and run a farm called Green Gables on Canada's Prince Edward Island, send away for an orphan boy to help on the farm. By mistake, Anne is sent instead, and she spends the rest of the novel getting into mischief, softening the edges of the no-nonsense Marilla, and ultimately enlivening the home and lives of the Cuthberts. We can better understand Anne's trajectory in the novel and her effect on other characters by recognizing the way Anne's experience parallels the history of childhood and the changing functions and uses of the child.

Matthew and Marilla initially conceive of their desired adoptee in terms of the working child. Marilla tells her neighbor Rachel, "We thought we'd get a boy. Matthew is getting up in years, you know—he's sixty—and he isn't so spry as he once was. His heart troubles him a good deal. And you know how desperate hard it's got to be to get hired help" (6). The language of the opening section objectifies Anne almost as a tool the Cuthberts have ordered. Matthew and Marilla have gotten the idea to adopt from another neighbor who is adopting a child from the same asylum. "So in the end we decided to ask Mrs. Spencer to pick us out one when she went over to get her little girl," Marilla explains (7). The Cuthberts are not especially particular about the orphan, except that he be Canadian and "a smart, likely boy of about ten or eleven … old enough to be of some use in doing chores right off" (7). When Matthew arrives at the station to pick up the orphan, the stationmaster reveals that it is a girl who is waiting for him, saying, "Maybe they were out of boys of the brand you wanted" (11). After Matthew explains the situation to Marilla, she exclaims, "Well, this is a pretty piece of business!" (24), and she concludes that "this girl will have to be sent back" (29). It is as if the wrong item has been shipped, or like a damaged product, Anne must be returned for exchange. A little girl is not what they need because, they think, a girl can be of no use. Matthew needs help with the physical work of the farm, but Marilla does not need a girl to help keep the home.

Anne disappoints their expectations by embodying the sacred child rather than the working one. The talkative girl entertains Matthew with her stories all the way from the train station in town to the siblings' country farm, and her theatrics upon arriving even cause the otherwise stoic Marilla to smile. When Matthew suggests that they keep her, Marilla responds, "What good would she be to us?" (29), but Matthew's answer betrays the shift from thinking about their adopted child as one who can benefit *them* to one they can benefit: "We might be some good to her," Matthew tells his sister (30). This view of Anne reflects the model of the sacred child whose function it is to bring parents joy, to be an object of emotional investment rather than an economic contributor, and to be nurtured and served by parents rather than the reverse. Keep her they do, and as predicted, the Cuthberts find Anne of little customary use. Marilla thinks that perhaps she will be able to use Anne in the kitchen, but some of the most comedic episodes in the novel involve Anne's disastrous efforts to cook and entertain, two traditional tasks for girls and women. Much of the humor of the novel comes from precisely this gap between the Cuthberts' expectations of the orphan they plan to adopt and the girl they end up raising, between the child laborer they need and the sacred child they enjoy. Anne does indeed make herself useful, but not in the conventional or practical sense. Matthew is a shy, quiet man, and Marilla, as we have seen, is impassive. The two live routine, uneventful lives as they gradually slip into old age. The exciting and excitable Anne becomes a source of constant amusement and energy, but also a source of parental pride and emotion. At one particularly ebullient moment, when Anne is overjoyed by the prospect of a Sunday-school picnic, she kisses Marilla in her excitement: "It was the first time in her whole life that childish lips had voluntarily touched Marilla's face. Again that sudden sensation of startling sweetness thrilled her" (91). Ultimately, Anne comes to be of emotional use, filling Matthew and Marilla's life with excitement, affection, and love.

Recognizing the distinction between the laboring child and the sacred one clarifies the trajectory of the novel and the turn of its conclusion. Over the course of the novel, Anne endears herself to the Cuthberts and forms emotional bonds with them as she comes to embody the modern conception of childhood. When Anne graduates from Queen's Academy and wins the Avery Scholarship, which will fund her college education, the Cuthberts beam with pride. "Reckon you're glad we kept her, Marilla?" Matthew asks (290). Nevertheless, near the conclusion, the novel defies this simple sense of historical progression. Matthew dies, killed by the shock of the news that the bank holding their accounts has failed. With their savings gone and Marilla's

Opposite: Anne travels through "The White Way of Delight" en route to her new home. Cover illustration by Scott Mckowen, from *Anne of Green Gables* by Lucy Maud Montgomery, Sterling Classics edition.

eyesight failing, Anne decides to forgo her scholarship and college in order to stay home, teach at a school nearby, and care for Marilla: "You surely don't think I could leave you alone in your trouble, Marilla, after all you've done for me.... Oh, I have it all planned out, Marilla. And I'll read to you and keep you cheered up. You shan't be dull or lonesome. And we'll be happy here together, you and I" (304). Anne proves to be a useful child after all, supporting Marilla in her old age and infirmity. Thus, by understanding the history of childhood, we can see that Anne represents a transitional or hybrid figure, both the working and the sacred child—a source of assistance and support, but also of pleasure and companionship. Montgomery, writing at the turn of the twentieth century, provides an index of changing conceptualizations of the child, and recognizing these changes helps us see more clearly the shape and significance of the novel.

This brief analysis points to only one possible reading of *Anne of Green Gables* in relation to the history of childhood. The models of childhood sketched in this chapter represent different frameworks for understanding children that operate simultaneously to shape how children are imagined and treated both as a group and as individuals. Because Anne never embodies only one model, it is possible to read the novel in various ways. Though we suggest that the opposition between the working and the sacred child provides a key structuring principle for *Anne of Green Gables*, others might focus on the ways Anne embodies the Romantic child: she demonstrates an affinity with nature, appears pure and uncorrupted despite her challenging experiences and circumstances, enjoys poetry and storytelling and revels in the imagination, and possesses a special vision of the world that most of the adults in the novel lack. Anne, like most complex child characters in children's literature, can be understood in multiple ways, and reading children's literature critically involves using the history of childhood to provide that understanding.

EXPLORATIONS

Review

1. This chapter argues that there is no such thing as a universal childhood. What are some of the factors that account for differences between children, both in terms of historical difference and differences between children in our own time? Discuss the statement: "Both changes across time and differences among children of the same period point to the complex and shifting boundaries between childhood and adulthood" (58).

2. Here are some quotations taken from the chapter you just read; each one applies to a particular model of childhood. Identify which model of childhood is captured by each quotation, and why it embodies such a model:

- "[this model of childhood] conceives of the child in psychological terms and depicts the child's gradual development or maturation."

- "[children are] somehow purer and more virtuous than adults, closer to nature and God, and beautified by their naïveté."

- [children are] "in need of discipline and training … easily swayed to do wrong, and susceptible to evil."

- "[children make] necessary and useful contributors to the household, as practical additions to families, and as sources of labor."

- "the child at play might represent an experience or imaginative feat unique to childhood and lost to adults, who are much too preoccupied with the empirical or real."

- "children [are seen] … acting independently of adults and performing roles more commonly attributed to adults, such as caring for other children or undertaking journeys."

- "[children are seen as] … precious and fragile aesthetic objects to admire rather than as practical tools. As such, they must be protected, watched, fussed over."

3. One of the many debates about the inherent nature of children focuses on whether children are innately good and become corrupted as they are immersed in society, or whether children are born sinful and need to be taught good behavior. Give examples from the chapter you just read of each view of childhood. Did you find examples in the chapter which don't fit into either model?

4. How do the following phenomena challenge the boundaries of adulthood?

- child crime

- child sex

- child soldiers

5. How does literature provide a glimpse into the history of childhood? Give some examples from the chapter. What are some ways that knowing about the history of

childhood helps us understand literature for and about them? What do we learn from the fictional child that we do not learn from historical narratives about childhood?

6. In the Reading Critically section we discuss *Anne of Green Gables*. What does Anne embody about the sacred child and the working child? What other models does her character sometimes embody?

Reflect

1. Think about how a children's book you have recently read makes use of different models of childhood. Does one model dominate the text? How might the text represent overlapping models of childhood?

2. When does childhood end? What rituals, ceremonies, or rites of passage mark its ending? What kind of activity or experience can you imagine that might be used to achieve or recognize the end of childhood? How have children's books you have read marked the end of childhood?

3. Imagine for yourself what would constitute an ideal childhood. What would it be like? What would the ideal child do or be able to do? What would the ideal child not do or not be able to do? Compare your version of the ideal childhood to the different ways children have lived in history as described in this chapter. Compare your imagined child to the kind of child depicted in a literary text for children.

4. What can children do that adults cannot, and what can adults do that children cannot? Provide exceptions to your expectations for these age-defined limitations. What are examples of adults doing things we think of as typical of children and vice versa? What do your answers suggest about the child as either radically Other to, or existing along a continuum with, the adult?

5. Consider a television commercial featuring children that solicits charitable donations. How does the commercial construct the child? What expectations does it have about the viewer's response? Why is a child used and not an adult? How does the commercial fit into the history of childhood as described in this chapter?

6. Examine the photograph of a child laborer taken by Lewis Hine during the first decade of the twentieth century (see figure on p. 73). Analyze the way the child is posed and the effects of the way she is posed. How do incidental or background elements

affect your reading of the photograph? What argument about childhood is Hine making in the photograph? What elements of his photography might be most effective politically?

"A Little Spinner in the Mollahan Mills, Newberry, SC" by Lewis Wickes Hine, 1908.

Investigate

1. Interview someone under the age of eighteen and someone over the age of seventy-five and have each interviewee describe his or her experience of childhood. What kinds of words or experiences are used by the interviewees to describe their childhoods? What childhood activities do they describe? Do these reflect a "typical" childhood experience? How do the two descriptions differ? How are they similar?

2. Have a group of children, either of the same age or of different ages, record their activities and the amount of time spent on each activity, both on a weekday and on a Saturday. How do they spend their time? What does the list of activities and the amount of time given to each activity suggest to you about the way childhood is experienced and

constructed now? How does the economic status of the children affect the types of
activities on their lists? How do their lists for the weekday and weekend differ?

3. Examine family photographs of your own childhood. What do the photographs say
    about your experience of childhood? What do they say about the conception of child-
    hood at the time the photographs were taken? How do the impressions created by the
    photographs differ from your own memories and impressions of childhood? What do
    the photographs not say about your experience of childhood? What experiences or
    feelings are missing from the photographs?

4. Locate a magazine or periodical published before 1940 and one published after 2000
    and examine advertisements featuring children. What kinds of products are adver-
    tised using children? What are the children doing in the advertisements? Who is the
    intended audience? What do the advertisements tell you about the construction of
    childhood in these two eras?

5. Select a film in which the main characters are children, such as Fritz Kiersch's *Children
    of the Corn* (1984) or Steven Spielberg's *E.T.: The Extra-Terrestrial* (1982), and consider
    which of the descriptions of childhood from this chapter it employs, constructs, or
    modifies. Put the film in dialogue with a literary work that employs a similar model
    and consider how the two overlap or differ or how one informs the other.

6. Select a recent controversial case from the region where you live involving the
    criminal activity of a child. What laws are relevant to the case? How is the child in the
    case represented in news accounts or court documents? How is the case described in
    public discourse? How has the community responded to the case? What does the case
    suggest about the ways childhood is defined and contested in your community? How
    might this research inform your reading of a fictional depiction of child crime?

SUGGESTED READINGS

Alger, Horatio. *Ragged Dick; or, Street Life in New York with the Boot Blacks* (1868).
One of *the* classic American boys' books and one of the works popularizing the rags-
to-riches myth in the United States, *Ragged Dick* focuses on the life of Dick, a homeless orphan who lives in New York City and supports himself as a bootblack. Dick and
the other working boys navigate nineteenth-century New York competently and fearlessly, providing perspective on the capacities of children who are forced to fend for
themselves.

Barrie, J.M. *Peter and Wendy* (1911). In J.M. Barrie's novel *Peter and Wendy*, based on his stage play *Peter Pan*, the boy who refuses to grow up whisks Wendy and her two brothers away to Neverland, where the lost boys are happy to have Wendy mother them. *Peter and Wendy* offers the opportunity to consider exactly what it is that Peter doesn't want to grow up to be, and hence to consider the notion of what it means to stay a child.

Burnett, Frances Hodgson. *The Secret Garden* (1911). Frances Hodgson Burnett's *The Secret Garden* associates childhood with nature, as Mary and Colin attain social and physical health through their work in the secret garden and their relationship with the nymph-like Dickon. Set on England's Yorkshire moors and stressing the child's connection to nature, the novel suggests a particularly Romantic notion of child-rearing and discipline.

Coolidge, Susan. *What Katy Did* (1872). When the tomboyish twelve-year-old Katy disobeys her aunt and plays on a damaged swing, she suffers a severe back injury that leaves her paralyzed. Disciplined by her injury, Katy learns to be a good girl and to manage successfully the family's domestic affairs in place of her mother, who had died years before. Written at a moment when the dominant conception of childhood was in a state of flux, *What Katy Did* ultimately punishes the playful child and honors the practical one.

Gantos, Jack. *Joey Pigza Swallowed the Key* (1998). Joey Pigza, diagnosed with Attention Deficit Hyperactivity Disorder, takes his "meds" to help calm him down. After several episodes of self-harm, Joey finds himself reassigned to the special education classroom. Jack Gantos's *Joey Pigza Swallowed the Key* not only represents an image of childhood as a social and medical problem but also implies a child reader who can relate to and learn from Joey's pathology.

Hinton, S.E. *The Outsiders* (1967). The troubled teenagers of S.E. Hinton's young adult novel *The Outsiders* find themselves struggling between a desire to remain innocent and childlike and the implicit recognition that they already know and have experienced too much to do so. As youths who earn their own income, live without parental authority, and encounter violence on a daily basis, their experiences challenge popular notions of what it means to be a child.

Janeway, James. *A Token for Children* (1671 and 1672). One of the most widely read children's books of the seventeenth century, and popular well into the eighteenth and nineteenth centuries, James Janeway's book of everyday child martyrs provides vignettes of "real" children who go to their graves fearing God and longing for salvation. The anxious appeals to God by these sick, dying children indicate the experience of Puritan children, who were believed to be inherently sinful. Published in a period of high child mortality, *A Token for Children* communicates the importance of seeking salvation early in life.

Taylor, Mildred. *The Land* (2001). Mildred Taylor's novel provides an account of how Paul-Edward, a boy of mixed race who grows up on a plantation in the years after the Civil War, experiences life differently from his white half-siblings. A Coretta Scott King Award winner, *The Land* explores the ways that conceptions of childhood and race intersect in the lives of youth.

Williams, Sherley Anne, and Carole Byard. *Working Cotton* (1992). A Caldecott Honor book written by Sherley Anne Williams and illustrated by Carole Byard, *Working Cotton* depicts a family of African American cotton pickers. Told in dialect from the perspective of young Shelan, this picturebook explores childhood in the context of child labor.

Yolen, Jane. *The Devil's Arithmetic* (1988). As a novel about the Holocaust, Jane Yolen's *The Devil's Arithmetic* suggests what happens to the concept of childhood in the context of atrocity. A winner of the National Jewish Book Award, *The Devil's Arithmetic* raises the question of whether childhood is even possible in such a context, thereby challenging the notion of childhood as a natural, transcultural, and transhistorical state.

APPROACHES TO TEACHING *ANNE OF GREEN GABLES* [SECONDARY SCHOOL]

Preparation for the Lesson

Students will have a week to read the novel. If desired, provide reading comprehension questions daily to ensure students are following the plot and characters. Once all of the students have read the novel, bring them together for the following discussions and activities. This lesson could be spread over several days if desired, especially if the students will do oral presentations.

Learning Goals

- To explore the novel's portrayal of a child's life in late nineteenth-century and early twentieth-century Canada

- To reflect on the role of imagination in Anne's character and what it means for her as a child

- To analyze Anne's development from the beginning to the end of the novel, considering how her character changes

- To practice imaginative description, essay writing, and oral presentations.

Activity One: A Child's Life in Anne of Green Gables

Using the board or a projector, the class should make a list of expectations for children's lives and behavior that the novel takes for granted. Here are some possibilities:

- Girls are expected to help with chores in the home; boys are expected to help with farm work.

- Children should say their prayers and attend church.

- Poor children will live in orphanages or in foster care.

- Children must be respectful of their elders.

- Children must work hard in school.

- Children are expected to socialize with other children, but not to the exclusion of work responsibilities.

- Children are expected not to be vain or care about their appearance.

After this list is complete, discuss whether these expectations are also true of all children today or might apply to *some* children today. If the class is team-taught with a social studies or history teacher, develop a unit about the lives of young people at the turn of the century or ask students to do independent research on this topic.

Activity Two: Anne's Imagination

One of the most striking things about Anne is her imagination. Her sense of wonder at the world around her reflects qualities often considered to be "childlike." As a class, look closely at a passage in the novel where Anne looks at an ordinary scene and imagines it to be extraordinary (the "Lake of Shining Waters" scene is one example). Then ask the students to choose a place from their lives—whether beautiful or not—and give it an imaginative name as Anne does in the novel. If they are having difficulty choosing a place, suggest a place on the school grounds (the gym, the library, or the basketball court might work). Students should write a one-page description of the newly renamed place, imagining it to be more exciting than it actually is. Students should then present their descriptions.

After students have presented, discuss whether they found it difficult or easy to produce their imaginative descriptions of a familiar place.

This would be a good opportunity to explain what is meant by a "Romantic" child (emphasis on the imagination; closeness to nature; a love of poetry and storytelling; emotional spontaneity and innocence).

Activity Three: Anne's Changes

Anne changes a great deal in the novel. As a class, discuss the difference between Anne's character at the beginning of the novel and at the end. Here are some useful starting points:

- At the beginning, she is supported by Marilla and Matthew; at the end, she helps support them.

- She is more serious about both housework and schoolwork.

- She comes to appreciate Gilbert Blythe and no longer sees him as a rival (paving the way for a romance).

- She is less prone to daydreaming and flights of fancy.

As a take-home assignment, students should write an essay about the changes Anne has undergone in the novel. They are free to judge her changes any way they like, but here are some questions that can be used to prompt them to write:

- Are you nostalgic about Anne as she was when she first arrived at Green Gables?

- Do you relate to the changes she goes through?

- Do you like Anne better at the beginning of the novel, or at the end?

- Why do you think Anne changes?

- By the end of the novel is Anne still a Romantic child?

THE EARLY HISTORY OF CHILDREN'S LITERATURE

Tracing the history of children's literature poses a number of problems, in part because what counts as children's literature is not always clear. Does children's literature comprise what children read, or what is written specifically for children? If the former, then the history of children's literature is largely coextensive or identical with the history of literature more generally, until fairly recently. If the latter—if children's literature is writing that is produced specifically for children—we run into problems as historians and critics with determining the intentions of authors, which are often unclear, as to whether a particular work was only for children, primarily for children, for both children and adults, or not intended for children at all but adopted by them or marketed to them. Does children's literature include educational works, such as primers and textbooks, or by children's literature do we mean only fiction, poetry, and drama? Scholars have different ideas about when the history of children's literature begins and about what counts and what doesn't. In the discussion that follows, we examine different ways of defining children's literature, identify important milestones in its development, and provide tools for understanding its history.

Opposite: Illustration by W. Heath Robinson from Charles Kingsley's *The Water-Babies: A Fairy Tale for a Land-Baby*, 1915. Tom converses with a dragon-fly.

QUESTIONS OF DEFINITION

Defining Literature

The problem of defining children's literature begins with the very definition of literature itself. Literature has often come to be understood as being composed of fictional works of "quality"—literary or artistic writing as opposed to popular genres such as comics or romance novels, informative texts such as newspapers or blogs, disposable products such as pamphlets or magazines, practical guides such as how-to manuals or reference books, and nonfiction works such as medical treatises or histories. However, as literary theorist Terry Eagleton explains, this has not always been the case. While "literature" might long have connoted works of privileged status, it was not always limited to fiction:

> In eighteenth-century England, the concept of literature was not confined as it sometimes is today to "creative" or "imaginative" writing. It meant the whole body of valued writing in society: philosophy, history, essays and letters as well as poems. What made a text "literary" was not whether it was fictional—the eighteenth century was in grave doubt about whether the new upstart form of the novel was literature at all—but whether it conformed to certain standards of "polite letters." (15)

So, in tracing the history of children's literature, especially before the eighteenth century, we have to consider whether to use our contemporary conception of literature or to include what readers of a given era might have termed literature.

Defining Children's Literature

Focusing specifically on children's literature, we are faced with yet another problem of definition, as we note above. Is children's literature defined by what children read or by what is written for children? Does it include practical as well as pleasurable works, or only the latter? Scholars disagree. In his landmark history *Children's Books in England*, first published in 1932, Harvey Darton writes:

> By "children's books" I mean printed works produced ostensibly to give children spontaneous pleasure, and not primarily to teach them, nor solely to make them good, nor to keep them *profitably* quiet. I shall therefore exclude from this history, as a general rule, all schoolbooks, all purely moral or didactic treatises, all reflective or adult-minded descriptions of child-life, and almost all alphabets, primers, and spelling-books. (1)

Darton's definition is the narrowest, limited to books specifically produced for children *and* designed to give them pleasure rather than to instruct. Historian Henry Steele Commager offers a different perspective in his introduction to Cornelia Meigs's *A Critical History of Children's Literature* (1953), in which he, too, questions what "children's literature" means:

> Is it that literature written especially for the young—the fairy and wonder tales, the nursery rhymes and songs, the dull books of etiquette and admonition and moral persuasion, the stories of school and playing field or of far-flung adventure? It is all of this, to be sure, but it is far more. It is the whole vast body of literature that children have adopted, commonly to share with their elders, but sometimes to monopolize. It is, quite literally, *their* literature. (xi)

Commager supports the broadest possible definition: books that are produced for children *and* books children read. Jeanie Watson concurs in her introduction to Warren W. Wooden's *Children's Literature of the English Renaissance* (1986), in which she summarizes Wooden's perspective: "A literary work becomes a 'children's book' when a child finds pleasure in it. Children themselves claim their own literature" (xix). While Wooden emphasizes the child reader's pleasure, Daniel T. Kline argues in his introduction to *Medieval Literature for Children* (2003) that instructional texts should be included because of the prominent didactic streak that runs through the history of children's literature, from the Middle Ages to the present (3). Whether textbooks or novels, children's literature is often crafted to teach a lesson, and so to exclude didactic works from the history of children's literature is to ignore a significant portion of texts produced for and read by children, Kline concludes.

Peter Hunt complicates these attempts at definition even further, questioning the criteria of "written for" and "read by." He asks:

> Just to unpack that definition: what does *written for* mean? Surely the intention of the author is not a reliable guide, not to mention the intention of the publisher— or even the format of the book? For example, Jill Murphy's highly successful series of picture-books about the domestic affairs of a family of elephants ... are jokes almost entirely from the point of view of (and largely understandable by) parents. Then again, *read by*: surely sometime, somewhere, all books have been read by one child or another? And some much-vaunted books for children are either not read by them, or much more appreciated by adults (like *Alice's Adventures in Wonderland*), or probably not children's books at all (like *Wind in the Willows*), or seem to serve adults and children in different—and perhaps opposing—ways (like *Winnie-the-Pooh*). (5)

Hunt further questions the criterion of "read by" because so often the books read by children are thrust upon them by parents or teachers who force children to read them. Jack Zipes poses a challenge to the very notion of "children's" literature by noting that "there never has been a literature conceived *by* children *for* children, a literature that belongs to children, and there never will be.... Certainly they participate in children's literature and the process of making it what it is, but children's literature *per se* does not exist" (40). According to Zipes, adults create the institution of children's literature to serve their ideas about children, what children need, or what is best for children, and thus children's literature belongs really to adults.

Teresa Michals turns traditional approaches to children literature on their head by investigating what we mean by *adult* readers. She argues that before "the emergence of the idea of books intended specifically for adult readers" in the nineteenth century, "the novel was written for a mixed-age audience" (2). When the age-specific marketing category of children's literature developed in the eighteenth century, she claims, it was contrasted with literature for a mixed-age audience, not "adult literature" (2). The more important distinction was one of status, between gentlemen (upper-class men) and everyone else (women, children, servants, etc.). Michals reminds us that "until the early eighteenth century most people in England did not know their numerical age" and society placed far less importance on people's ages than on their social statuses and roles. Following Michals, we might say that early "children's literature" was really a subset of mixed-age literature, the way picturebooks are now a subset of children's literature, and literate children would have read—and been imagined as part of the audience for—much of what was written and published before the end of the nineteenth century. What this means for contemporary scholars and students of children's literature is that we must consider what we mean when we use a phrase like "children's literature" and take care not to impose current categories or assumptions onto the past. We cannot be too quick to dismiss certain works as not being "for" young people just because they do not meet our expectations of children's literature.

It should be clear that the definition of children's literature is an unstable and contested one. Ultimately, the definition one chooses at a given moment—and we must allow for the possibility of making different choices at different moments—will be determined largely by one's purpose. The scholar of "medieval children's literature," the university archivist, the elementary-school teacher, the youth-services librarian, the parent, the gift-buying relative, the professor in an introductory college course on children's literature, and the contemporary child are all likely to approach children's literature with different goals and investments, and thus they will define children's literature in different ways, whether or not they are conscious of the assumptions underlying their choices.

Children's Literature as Genre

Perry Nodelman argues for understanding children's literature as a coherent genre, not just as a disparate set of texts grouped artificially by virtue of their intended audience of child readers: "It might, in fact, be a specific genre of fiction whose defining characteristics seem to transcend specifics of time and place, cut across other generic categories such as fantasy or realism, and even remain consistent despite variations in the ages of intended audiences" (81). A literary **genre** is a category of literature, such as **adventure fiction** or mysteries. Readers recognize or determine whether an individual text belongs to a particular genre based on its possession of common or familiar features, tropes, or patterns associated with that genre. Works for children could be textbooks or primers, cautionary tales, domestic novels, or nonsense verse—different literary genres. Nodelman insists that children's literature itself should be thought of as a genre, as possessing a consistent set of qualities, which include the implication of children as readers, the use of a simple style, the focus on action rather than description, the use of apparent simplicity to mask hidden complexities, a matter-of-fact tone despite the strangeness of the events described, focalization through a child's perspective and the use of child protagonists, a doubleness of perspective created by the differences between the perspective of child characters and the voice of a presumably adult third-person narrator, the focus on innocence and knowledge acquisition as central subjects, a pervasive sense of nostalgia and ambivalence, and the importance of home and leaving home (76–81). According to Nodelman, most children's literature shares this list of features.

Why might these features define literature for children and young adults? Nodelman believes these qualities emerge out of the condition of adult authors writing for an audience of readers younger and less knowledgeable or experienced than themselves. He explains, "Children's literature is that literature that constructs child characters in order to satisfy adult wants and needs in regard to children" (172). In this view, the partial list of qualities just noted represents a set of "wants and needs" adults have with regard to children. As long as adults maintain this sense that children need something special, in distinction to what adults need, and as long as they believe adults can provide this for them in ways children cannot for themselves, children's literature will exist as defined by these generic conventions (248).

Not all scholars of children's literature share this thinking about children's literature as a distinct genre with a set of consistent qualities, but Nodelman's hypothesis does suggest a way to read children's literature critically. The concept of genre, or the practice of categorization, is most useful for identifying similarities and the meanings of similarities amid apparent difference, and for identifying differences amid apparent similarities. Recognizing when, how, and why individual texts for children may depart from the conventions or expectations of children's literature provides a useful strategy for critical reading.

THE "BIRTH" OF CHILDREN'S LITERATURE?

John Newbery

While remaining attentive to these uncertainties, we can sketch a rough outline of the history of children's literature. Alec Ellis adopts the standard narrative about the history of children's literature and states it boldly: "There were no children's books in England before 1600 (although there were numerous schoolbooks and guides to conduct), nor were they recognized as an identifiable branch of English literature until approximately 1700" (3). The person who is most often credited with the "invention" of children's literature is John Newbery, a London bookseller and publisher who lived from 1713 to 1767, and 1744 is often cited as the year children's literature was born. That year John Newbery

Often cited as the "inventor" of children's literature, John Newbery published his *A Little Pretty Pocket-Book* in 1744 and packaged it with a toy.

published *A Little Pretty Pocket-Book*, a work recognized as igniting the children's book industry for two reasons. First, in contrast to most of the children's books that preceded it, it was advertised and designed not only for instruction but also for pleasure. Children were meant to enjoy it, not just to learn from it. Second, Newbery began to think about children and their parents as a distinct consumer group. He designed and marketed *A Little Pretty Pocket-Book* to be especially appealing to children through its elaborate and attractive cover and binding and by such features as a letter from Jack the Giant-Killer, a youthful hero of folkloric fame, addressed to the boy or girl reader, and its teaching of the alphabet through descriptions of games. As Peter Hunt observes, it was also "a commercial, mixed-media text" (42), for it was accompanied by an object that could be described as a pincushion for girls or a ball for boys. This rethinking of children as a distinct market, the strategies to incite children's interest—including the increased attention to packaging and pleasure—along with Newbery's established printing and bookselling business poised him to influence the future of the market and garner the credit for having created it.

Newbery's Contemporaries: Thomas Boreman and Mary Cooper

Although *A Little Pretty Pocket-Book* was indeed innovative, and Newbery himself was influential, this conventional history understates the work of others who came before him. Newbery was actually not the first to publish children's books that attended to the child's pleasure; he has largely overshadowed others who worked in the business during this critical period. Newbery was preceded by Thomas Boreman, another London printer and bookseller, who appears to have begun publishing exclusively for children as early as 1730. *The Gigantick Histories of the Curiosities of London*, a series of small books sized to fit in the child's hand, was Boreman's most successful; it was published in ten volumes between 1740 and 1743. After Newbery's appearance in London in 1743, Boreman disappears from the historical record, probably because of his death (Gillespie 8, 98; Demers 120; Darton 355). Another important innovator was Mary Cooper, who ran a publishing business. A year before Newbery published his first book for children, Cooper's *The Child's New Plaything* was already in its second edition. The book contained an alphabet, traditional medieval tales, and spelling lessons. Cooper's second book, *Tommy Thumb's Pretty Song Book*, published in 1744, is considered the first collection of nursery rhymes in English. Though there were others who also contributed to the invention of commercial publishing for children, Newbery, Boreman, and Cooper signal the significant emergence of a more coherent market for children's books and a revolution in thinking about the possibilities of a distinct literature for children.

Sarah Fielding and the First Children's Novel?

One other milestone in the mid-eighteenth-century birth of children's literature was Sarah Fielding's 1749 publication of *The Governess; or, The Little Female Academy*, the first work that can be described as a novel for children. Sarah was the sister of Henry Fielding, one of the writers who, along with Samuel Richardson, pioneered the English novel in the 1740s. Richardson was Sarah Fielding's friend and her publisher for *The Governess*, a book that involves a group of young schoolgirls who take turns telling their life stories, which are interspersed with fairy tales and the moral advice of their governess, Mrs. Teachum. Though little holds the disparate elements of *The Governess* together and many contemporary readers might find it a strange amalgamation, the notion of a full-length fictional work for children was unheard of, and the novel itself was still evolving when Fielding wrote. Her relationships with key innovators of the novel directly link the history of children's literature with the history of English literature more generally. The publication of *The Governess*, along with the work of Boreman, Newbery, and Cooper, marks the birth of children's literature as we have come to know it.

With the 1740s established as a flashpoint in the history of children's literature, we turn now to the works produced before the mid eighteenth century and the developments that followed. In doing so, we show why the innovations of the 1740s proved so important and how those who came after built on the work of Cooper, Newbery, and others. Children's literature before the eighteenth century can be divided roughly into two groups:

1. General-audience and crossover texts (those written for everyone, both adults and children, or those written for a mixed-age audience but now widely associated with children).

2. Educational books (textbooks, primers, and conduct manuals), including religious texts (catechisms, books of martyrs, children's Bibles, and religious instructions), and didactic poetry and stories (imaginative works whose primary purpose is to teach a specific lesson).

GENERAL-AUDIENCE AND CROSSOVER WORKS

In the traditional history of children's literature, we would talk about adult works that "crossed over" from adult literature to children's literature, but Michals compels us to rethink "adult" works before the twentieth century as actually for a mixed-age audience. By implication, "crossover" works are never really "adult" works; rather, these books were always imagined as for a general audience but became increasingly associated with children over time, sometimes to the exclusion of adults. This section describes some of the most prominent of what have traditionally been called crossover literature, a term we retain because it continues to be widely used to refer to such texts.

Aesop's Fables 伊索寓言

General-audience and crossover texts included fables and chapbooks, and their history as children's literature is really the history of literature more broadly. Such works date to antiquity, as do instructional texts for children. The fables attributed to Aesop from the sixth century BCE came to be associated with child readers, though they were not intended only for children or enjoyed only by children. Eight years after he introduced the printing press to England in 1476, William Caxton published the first English translation of *Aesop's Fables* (1484), which includes the well-known tales of the tortoise and the hare and the boy who cried "wolf." Although Caxton did not conceive of the book as specifically for children, *Aesop's Fables* began to be used in schools as a way of teaching Greek and Latin and useful life lessons, especially after its recommendation by John Locke in *Some Thoughts Concerning Education* in 1693. During the nineteenth century, many new translators and illustrators produced editions of *Aesop* for children, ensuring that fables would come to be thought of as children's literature.

Richard Heighway's drawing of "the fox and the crow" from *The Fables of Aesop* (1894), by Joseph Jacobs. Though associated with child readers, Aesop's fables were not intended only for children.

Chapbooks 小册子

In the sixteenth and seventeenth centuries, **chapbooks** became popular. These were small booklets, ranging anywhere from eight to twenty-four pages, made by folding a single large sheet of paper. Cheap and disposable, chapbooks contained ballads; folk tales; illustrated tales of adventure, romance, mystery, and crime; and other such popular forms of textual entertainment. As with fables, chapbooks were produced for the general public

with no initial distinction made between child and adult audiences. One popular chapbook tells the story of Tom Thumb, the member of King Arthur's court who, only several
inches tall, manages to be heroic and dashing despite his diminutive size. Another chapbook was *The Interesting Story of the Children in the Wood*, or *The Babes in the Wood*, which
first appeared in some form between 1593 and 1595. It tells the story of two young children
who are left in the care of an uncle when their father dies of illness and their mother
dies of grief after their father's death. The children are left an inheritance, which they can
claim at the age of twenty-one, but their uncle soon conspires to claim it for himself. He
hires two "ruffians" to take them into the woods and murder them, but one takes pity on
them, murders his fellow thug instead, and abandons the children in the woods to fend
for themselves. However, their fate hardly improves:

> Their pretty lips with blackberries
> Were all besmeared and dy'd,
> And when the shades of night arose,
> They sat them down and cry'd.
>
> These pretty babes thus wandered long,
> Without the least relief,
> The woods, the briers, and thorns among,
> Till death did end their grief. (Rusher 11)

Although *The Babes in the Wood* is about children, it is addressed to adults, as indicated by
the opening line: "Now ponder well, ye parents dear." The tale functions in part as a warning to choose the guardian of one's children carefully. At the end of the story, the uncle is
racked with guilt, confesses, and dies in prison; and the narrator concludes:

> Ye guardians, warning take hereby
> And never prove ingrate.
> To helpless infants still be kind,
>
> And give to each his right;
> For, if you do not, soon you'll find
> God will your deeds requite. (Rusher 12)

Children are frequently endangered in children's literature, and the appeal to children
of a story about the murder of helpless babes by a relative would be peculiar if not for
the appreciation some children hold for the macabre. We can suppose that part of the
attraction to such chapbook stories was the fact that most omitted any moral, at least for

children. Being designed primarily for a mixed-age audience, they represented an exciting transgression for child readers.

Folk and Fairy Tales 童話 ·

Although today folk and fairy tales are often imagined as specifically for children, they both originated in the orally transmitted tales of peasant folk and in the parlor games of the social elite. Ruth B. Bottigheimer makes a distinction between folk and fairy tales. Folk tales, passed down and modified through generations, provided a way for ordinary people who may not have been literate to entertain themselves. They featured very ordinary protagonists and often ended unhappily (Bottigheimer 4). These tales made little distinction between child and adult listeners and were not specifically for children. Some fairy tales, which often include magical elements and happier endings, may have had their origins in orally transmitted folk tales, while others were original compositions by writers such as Giovanni Francesco Straparola (1480–1557) and Giambattista Basile (1575–1632), who wrote and published some of the first fairy tales in sixteenth- and seventeenth-century Italy.

Near the end of the seventeenth century, inventing or retelling fairy tales at private gatherings of aristocratic women, called "salons," became a popular parlor game in France. The practice might have been initiated by the Countess d'Aulnoy, who settled in Paris in 1690 and is thought to have coined the term "fairy tales" (Gillespie 44). Several figures capitalized on the fad by transcribing and publishing collections of such tales, including d'Aulnoy herself, who published *Les contes des fées* (*Tales of Fairies*) in 1697, and Charles Perrault, who published *Histoires ou contes du temps passé* (*Stories or Tales of Past Times*) that same year (Zipes 20). Perrault's collection was translated into English in 1729 and included such tales as "Cinderella" and "Little Red Riding Hood." Perrault's fairy tales usually had more grisly parts than the versions in circulation today. "Little Red Riding Hood," as written by Perrault, concludes with Red Riding Hood being gobbled up by the wolf. Unlike in later versions, no woodsman comes to slice open the wolf's belly and free her. In "Bluebeard," Bluebeard's wife opens the forbidden chamber and finds the corpses of his former wives, whom he has murdered. Perrault's "Donkeyskin" is a tale much like "Cinderella," except the heroine of this story has a different suitor. The heroine's mother, the queen, commands her husband on her deathbed not to remarry unless he finds a woman more beautiful than she. The king finds the search challenging, but he eventually stumbles upon a solution:

> Every day, he studied charming portraits of suitable princesses but not one of them was half as pretty as his dead queen had been. Then he looked at his own daughter

and saw she had grown up. Now she was even lovelier than her mother had been when the king first met her and he fell head over heels in love with her and proposed. The princess was filled with horror. (Carter 62)

As Jack Zipes emphasizes, Perrault's tales "were *not* told or written for children" (23, emphasis in original). Yet over the course of the eighteenth century, fairy tales such as these were retold for children. Like fables, they enjoyed a renaissance in the nineteenth century through the publication of such works as Jakob and Wilhelm Grimm's first collection of German fairy tales in 1812, first translated into English in 1820, and Andrew Lang's *The Blue Fairy Book* (1889), which included versions of several of Perrault's tales. While older variants of the tales sometimes employed bawdy folk humor, including sexual innuendoes, scatological references, and gruesome violence, fairy tales were increasingly domesticated and sanitized for the nursery. We discuss folk and fairy tales in more detail in Chapter 4.

Mixed-Age Works as Children's Classics

The last kind of crossover texts are those like Daniel Defoe's *Robinson Crusoe* (1719), which, though written for mixed-age readers, were read and enjoyed by children and came to be associated with them. Another such crossover hit was Jonathan Swift's *Gulliver's Travels* (1726), but Defoe's work proved particularly resonant, spawning an entire genre called the "Robinsonade." Some of the more prominent Robinsonades include Johann Wyss's *The Swiss Family Robinson* (1812), which Wyss wrote to teach his children useful lessons about family and survival, and R.M. Ballantyne's *The Coral Island* (1857), an adventurous and optimistic castaway novel for children parodied by William Golding in his much darker *Lord of the Flies* (1954). Works such as these can now frequently be found in both the adult and children's sections of libraries and bookstores in both complete and abridged versions. New Robinsonades continue to be popular among both children and adults. In addition to many books in the genre, at least four twenty-first century television programs—*Survivor* (2000–present), *Lost* (2004–2010), and *Crusoe* (2008–09) for adults and *Flight 29 Down* (2005–07) for children—have been broadcast in the United States in recent years, and films such as *Cast Away* (2000) have also been popular. Crossover hits such as *Robinson Crusoe* and its imitators raise questions about crossover fiction, such as why these narratives would be either popular with children or thought to be popular with children; why some works cross over to child readers while others don't; and how to classify such works once they have crossed over. Moreover, crossover texts again raise the question of whether children's literature is defined by what is written for children or by what children read.

Almost from the beginning, children's literature and the popularity of crossover works met with resistance. Harvey Darton refers to "the general Puritan discouragement of light reading" (94), which we might take to mean anything not explicitly religious in nature. One of the best-known critics of children's literature along these lines was Sarah Trimmer (1741–1810), a mother of twelve who wrote a number of children's books in addition to being a leader of the movement to establish Sunday schools in England. Under her editorship, *The Guardian of Education* (1802–06) became one of the first periodicals to regularly review children's books and to establish a canon of its best exemplars. In *An Essay on Christian Education*, published posthumously in 1812, Trimmer writes, "Novels certainly, however excellent, should not be read by young persons, till they are in some measure acquainted with real life" (310). Trimmer warns against tales that work "too powerfully

Though written for a mixed-age audience, Daniel Defoe's *Robinson Crusoe* (1719) was considered a crossover text, especially read and enjoyed by children. Illustration by N.C. Wyeth, 1920 edition.

upon the feelings of the mind" or give "false pictures of life and manners" (310). The opposition to J.K. Rowling's Harry Potter series can be understood in terms of this long tradition of skepticism about fiction and fantasy for children. While the condemnation of secular or imaginative literature represents one strand of resistance, another comes from those who, influenced by Locke and Rousseau, thought fantasy and fairy tales would mislead children and deform their sense of reality. According to Darton, this "fear or dislike of fairy tales ... involves the belief that anything fantastic on the one hand, or anything primitive on the other, is inherently noxious, or at least so void of good as to be actively dangerous" (99). Maria Edgeworth espouses such a view in *Practical Education* (1798), co-written with her father:

> With respect to sentimental stories, and books of mere entertainment, we must remark, that they should be sparingly used, especially in the education of girls. This species of reading cultivates what is called the heart prematurely; lowers the tone of the mind, and induces indifference for those common pleasures and occupations which, however trivial in themselves, constitute the far greatest portion of our daily happiness. Stories are the novels of childhood. We know, from common experience, the effects which are produced upon the female mind by immoderate novel-reading. To those who acquire this taste, every object becomes disgusting which is not in an attitude for poetic painting; a species of moral picturesque is sought for in every scene of life, and this is not always compatible with sound sense or with simple reality. (248)

The Edgeworths single out stories of ghosts and other mystical creatures as inflaming children's fears and passions. Although they thought these and other "sentimental" stories were particularly dangerous to girls, they considered tales of adventure especially bad for boys because "the taste for adventure is absolutely incompatible with the sober perseverance necessary to success" (251). The Edgeworths even criticize castaway novels such as *Robinson Crusoe* and its imitations. In effect, pleasurable works were condemned in favor of religious and instructional ones.

INSTRUCTIONAL WORKS AND DIDACTIC LITERATURE

Textbooks

So far, we have considered general-audience texts such as fables, chapbooks, and fairy tales, or crossover works such as *Robinson Crusoe*, which were not written for children but either were enjoyed by them or came to be associated with them. Some texts written and published before 1744 *were* specifically produced for children, but almost all these were religious or instructional texts or didactic works of fiction and poetry. Some of the very oldest texts written for children were designed for instruction. One of the oldest of such works was *Ælfric's Colloquy*, produced about 1000. Ælfric was an Anglo-Saxon abbot who lived from about 955 to about 1020 and came to serve as a teacher at a monastery near Oxford. His *Colloquy*, or written dialogue, is addressed to boys between the ages of seven and thirteen and constitutes a series of questions and answers designed to teach students Latin (Harris 114):

> STUDENTS: We children bid you, Master, that you teach us to speak correctly, for we are unlearned and we speak corruptly.
> TEACHER: What would you like to talk about?
> STUDENTS: What do we care what we talk about? As long as it's correct! Let it be useful, not worthless or base.
> TEACHER: Will you be flogged in order to learn?
> STUDENTS: We would rather be flogged on behalf of wisdom than not to know it.
> (qtd. in Harris 118)

Another early instructional text produced specifically for a child was Chaucer's *Treatise on the Astrolabe*, which he wrote for his ten-year-old son Lewis around 1391. Chaucer's text describes how the astrolabe—a device used by astronomers for locating celestial bodies and determining the time—works and the kinds of experiments that can be accomplished with it. The text is noteworthy not only because it is an early example of a work written specifically for a child but also because of Chaucer's status as one of the first writers to make his name writing in vernacular English. Again, the history of children's literature intersects with the history of English literature. Works such as Chaucer's and Ælfric's, along with textbooks and primers such as *The New England Primer* discussed in the previous chapter, alphabet books, and books of conduct and manners constitute the bulk of writing for children until the eighteenth century. Though designed for practical instruction, these texts were sometimes imaginative. *Ælfric's Colloquy* includes

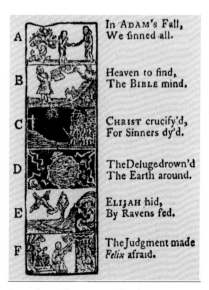

Page from the *New England Primer*, 1750.

role-playing as different kinds of laborers, such as plowmen and shepherds, for example, and *The New England Primer* uses verse to teach the alphabet. These texts can tell us what was expected of children, what children were thought to enjoy or need, and how children lived. They form an important component of the early history of children's literature.

Religious Works

In addition to secular instructional works, another major portion of writing for children before the eighteenth century was religious in nature. James Janeway's *A Token for Children*, described in the previous chapter, is one example. The Puritans, being particularly concerned with teaching children to read so that they could study the Bible, created a market of literate children that fueled the publication of many spiritual works aimed at the young, including catechisms and other texts of religious instruction or warning. Such texts included Benjamin Keach's *War with the Devil* (1673) and Nathaniel Crouch's descriptively titled *Youth's Divine Pastime, Containing Forty Remarkable Scripture Histories Turned into Common English Verse: With Forty Curious Pictures Proper to Each Story: Very Delightful for the Virtuous Imploying the Vacant Hours of Young Persons, and Preventing Vain and Vicious Divertisements: Together with Several Scripture Hymns upon Divers Occasions* (1691). Though not written for children, John Foxe's *Book of Martyrs* (1563) was, according to Warren Wooden, "regularly placed in the hands of Protestant children in England and the colonies by generations of pious parents" (73). It is a long, daunting, and sometimes gruesome catalog of persecuted Christians that pays particular attention to the persecution of Protestants by Catholics. Wooden finds evidence in the text that Foxe did consider the possibility of children as part of his audience (78). Margaret Gillespie argues that "for children, the *Book of Martyrs* was frightening and horrifying" (83), and Cornelia Meigs notes that "as reading for children it is extraordinarily unsuitable" (39). These are, of course, modern sensibilities; in contrast, Wooden calls the work "riveting" and "masterful" even for child readers (76–77). John Bunyan's *The Pilgrim's Progress* (1678) offers comparatively lighter fare. A Christian allegory, it follows the trek of a character named Christian from his home to Mt. Zion while carrying the physical burden that represents his sin. Like so many of the other works cited here, this one was not intended specifically for children.

The Sunday School and Evangelical Movements

Religious children's literature was invigorated by the Sunday School movement, which started in the mid eighteenth century, and was bolstered by the Religious Tract Society, founded in England in 1799 to produce evangelical literature. Two of the most prominent children's periodicals begun in the late nineteenth century, *The Boy's Own Paper* and *The Girl's Own Paper*, were published by this organization. The American Tract Society was founded in New York in 1825 and similarly targeted children for its evangelical mission. Peter Hunt notes the shift in emphasis in religious children's literature around this time from strictly religious or theological instruction to more social education of children, women, and the poor (45). Anna Laetitia Barbauld, a Presbyterian writer who taught at the boys' school her husband operated in Suffolk, England, explained in the preface to her *Hymns in Prose for Children* (1781):

> The peculiar design of this publication is, to impress devotional figures [feelings] as early as possible on the infant mind; fully convinced as the author is, that they cannot be impressed too soon, and that a child, to feel the full force of the idea of God, ought never to remember the time when he had no such idea—to impress them by connecting religion with a variety of sensible objects; with all that he sees, all he hears, all that affects his young mind with wonder or delight; and thus by deep, strong, and permanent associations, to lay the best foundation for practical devotion in future life. (v–vi)

Other prominent writers of religious children's literature associated with either the Sunday School movement or Evangelicalism include Sarah Trimmer, whose *Fabulous Histories* (1786), sometimes titled *The History of Robins*, uses an anthropomorphic family of robins to teach moral lessons, and Mary Martha Sherwood, whose *The History of the Fairchild Family* (1818), subtitled *A Collection of Stories Calculated to Shew the Importance and Effects of a Religious Education*, was a bestseller in Britain. Because writers such as Barbauld, Trimmer, and Sherwood worked amid the emergence of Romanticism in the late eighteenth and early nineteenth centuries, their religious children's literature reflects many of the qualities of more secular, didactic, and Romantic writing for children.

The Rational Moralists

Another group of writers—whom Patricia Demers and Gordon Moyles term "rational moralists"—includes those influenced strongly by philosophers such as Locke and Rousseau. According to Demers, these writers emphasized moral instruction rather than specifically religious instruction, and they advocated the use of rational thought to reach moral conclusions. Demers places Sarah Fielding, Maria Edgeworth, and Thomas Day in this group: "These writers were keen believers in the power of carefully designed narratives and of positive as well as negative examples to shape children's understanding" (Demers 143). Day's *The History of Sandford and Merton* (1783) translates Rousseau's educational philosophies into fiction, depicting the education of the wealthy Tommy Merton and the practical Harry Sandford, the son of a farmer, by a wise tutor. Maria Edgeworth published several collections of stories for children such as *The Parent's Assistant* (1796), which included a story called "The Purple Jar." In it, seven-year-old Rosamond begs her mother to allow her to buy a beautiful purple jar, so her mother gives her the choice between the new shoes she desperately needs and the frivolous item she wants. Despite her mother's warning, Rosamond selects the jar. When she gets home and empties her new purple vase, she is sorely disappointed: "But she experienced much surprise and disappointment on finding, when it was entirely empty, that it was no longer a purple vase. It was a plain white glass jar, which had appeared to have that beautiful colour merely from the liquor with which it had been filled" (qtd. in Demers 180). For a month Rosamond must wear her old shoes, "till at last she could neither run, dance, jump, or walk in them" (180). Rosamond learns through a combination of experience and reason what would have been the better choice. Though the literature of the rational moralists cannot be reduced to didacticism, instruction did remain its central function.

Didactic Poetry and Fiction

Works of fiction, poetry, or drama designed to communicate a practical or moral lesson are described as didactic, but not all didactic poetry and fiction can be classified as evangelical or rational moralist. As Elaine Ostry explains, authors reflected different orientations in different works, or even within the same work: "The author may be known as an Evangelical, but writes a fairy tale, a form disparaged by strict Evangelicals as a lie. Or a fanciful tale has a strong tone of moral didacticism, which is what the fantasists claimed to avoid. In fact, all children's literature conveys some kind of morality, even as it may claim to be non-didactic" (36–37). Bunyan's *A Book for Boys and Girls; or, Country Rhymes for Children* (1686) represents the last type of children's book that dominated before the eighteenth century: imaginative works of fiction or poetry whose primary function was to instruct while also crafted to delight. The emphasis on instruction is evident in this short poem from Bunyan's collection:

> The Bee goes out and Honey home doth bring;
> And some who seek that Honey find a sting.
> Now wouldst thou have the Honey and be free
> From stinging; in the first place kill the Bee. (n.p.)

In case the reader misses the point, the next stanza tells us, "This Bee an Emblem truly is of sin." Isaac Watts, a London minister and writer of church hymns, also wrote didactic poetry for children. His *Divine Songs Attempted in Easy Language for the Use of Children* (1715) was an attempt to provide a more pleasurable source of instruction for children. "What is learnt in verse is longer retained in memory, and sooner recollected," he wrote in the preface to his *Divine Songs* (qtd. in Darton 108). The collection includes such poems as "Praise to God for Learning to Read" and "Against Quarrelling and Fighting." His "Against Idleness and Mischief" is still well known:

> How doth the little busy bee
> Improve each shining hour,
> And gather honey all the day
> From every opening flower!
> How skillfully she builds her cell!
> How neat she spreads the wax!
> And labours hard to store it well
> With the sweet food she makes.
>
> In works of labour or of skill,
> I would be busy too;
> For Satan finds some mischief still
> For idle hands to do. (38)

Lewis Carroll would later parody this poem in *Alice's Adventures in Wonderland*, demonstrating how some writers resist and even lampoon the impulse to instruct child readers in children's literature. Nevertheless, instructional, religious, and didactic works for children, along with general-audience and crossover texts, prevailed until the revolution initiated by Newbery and others in the mid eighteenth century. While writing for children would remain intensely didactic through the nineteenth century, it was characterized by a trend toward increasingly imaginative and pleasurable works that would sow the seeds of the Golden Age of children's literature in the nineteenth century.

THE GOLDEN AGE

The Growth of the Children's Literature Industry

With the advent of a distinct market for children's literature during the mid eighteenth century, a struggle ensued within the enterprise of children's literature between the adult belief that children's books should be educational and the creative and commercial impulse

Mowgli and Bagheera from *The Jungle Book*, illustration by Edward Julius Detmold.

to entertain children and to craft literary works for them. Many societal changes that occurred during the nineteenth century led to a greater emphasis on innovation and imagination: children's culture expanded with the spread of industrialism and the rise of mass production, more children attended school and learned to read, more families attained middle-class status and could afford books for children, children themselves came to be seen as precious objects to spoil, and more writers looked to children as a viable audience. Although traces of didacticism would remain, children's literature would come to emphasize pleasure and creative expression in addition to instruction. Freed from the demand to craft stories or poems that taught lessons, writers were able to chart new literary paths, explore new genres and forms, and plumb more complex characters or emotions. Though we can trace the beginning of the Golden Age as far back as the 1850s, Lewis Carroll's 1865 publication of *Alice's Adventures in Wonderland,* a highly imaginative and complex work that uses nonsense and humor to lampoon didacticism and delight child readers, can stand in as one starting point for it. A significant break from the ongoing tendency to use children's literature to instruct, *Alice's Adventures* highlights the aesthetic and creative possibilities of writing for youth. While didacticism continued to be a prominent feature of children's literature after *Alice,* and remains so today, it no longer dominates writing for youth. Rather, didacticism occurs in tension with pleasure and artistry, as we discuss below.

Between roughly 1865 and 1915, the period known as the **Golden Age** of children's literature, some of the best-known classics were written and published. Even a partial list is extensive:

The Water-Babies	(1863)	Charles Kingsley
Alice's Adventures in Wonderland	(1865)	Lewis Carroll
Hans Brinker	(1865)	Mary Mapes Dodge
Elsie Dinsmore	(1867)	Martha Finley
Little Women	(1868)	Louisa May Alcott
Ragged Dick	(1868)	Horatio Alger
The Princess and the Goblin	(1872)	George MacDonald
What Katy Did	(1872)	Susan Coolidge (Sarah Woolsey)
The Adventures of Tom Sawyer	(1876)	Mark Twain (Samuel Langhorne Clemens)
Black Beauty	(1877)	Anna Sewell
Toby Tyler, or Ten Weeks with a Circus	(1881)	James Otis
Treasure Island	(1883)	Robert Louis Stevenson
A Child's Garden of Verses	(1885)	Robert Louis Stevenson
Adventures of Huckleberry Finn	(1885)	Mark Twain
Little Lord Fauntleroy	(1885)	Frances Hodgson Burnett
The Jungle Book	(1894)	Rudyard Kipling
The Story of the Treasure Seekers	(1899)	Edith Nesbit
The Wonderful Wizard of Oz	(1900)	L. Frank Baum

Kim	(1901)	Rudyard Kipling
The Tale of Peter Rabbit	(1901)	Beatrix Potter
Five Children and It	(1902)	Edith Nesbit
Rebecca of Sunnybrook Farm	(1903)	Kate Douglas Wiggin
Peter Pan (1904); *Peter and Wendy*	(1911)	J.M. Barrie
A Little Princess	(1905)	Frances Hodgson Burnett
The Railway Children	(1906)	Edith Nesbit
Anne of Green Gables	(1908)	L.M. Montgomery
The Wind in the Willows	(1908)	Kenneth Grahame
A Girl of the Limberlost	(1909)	Gene Stratton-Porter
The Secret Garden	(1911)	Frances Hodgson Burnett
Pollyanna	(1913)	Eleanor Porter
Penrod	(1914)	Booth Tarkington

When people refer to "the classics of children's literature," it is most likely the Golden Age that is being invoked.

The Crossover Appeal of Golden Age Books

Earlier we discussed works written for a mixed-age general audience that nonetheless possessed crossover appeal and became associated with children. In contrast, the classic works of the Golden Age, though ostensibly written for children or youth, held much appeal for adults. According to Jerry Griswold, "Many of the top-selling books in the United States during the [nineteenth] century were children's books. What may be equally obvious is that, since children weren't the only ones who bought and read books, these works must also have been unusually popular among adults" (viii). Beverly Lyon Clark argues in *Kiddie Lit: The Cultural Construction of Children's Literature* (2003) that during the Golden Age, children and adults were increasingly imagined as segregated and distinct audiences. Thus, while *Little Lord Fauntleroy* (1885) was read and praised by children and adults alike upon its initial publication, by the early decades of the twentieth century, books written for or marketed to children had much smaller followings among adults, testifying to the ways children's literature was coming to be imagined as only for children. There might be some notable exceptions to this trend, such as the work of J.R.R. Tolkien, and the bifurcation of child and adult audiences might have been reversed somewhat by crossover blockbusters such as the Harry Potter series. Nonetheless, as the worlds of children and adults became increasingly segregated, the distinct market of children's books emerged over the course of the eighteenth and nineteenth centuries, and the children's book as we have come to know it was born.

The Tensions that Define Children's Literature

A defining feature of the Golden Age of children's literature is that, on the whole, works published during this period emphasize pleasure and creativity, not just didacticism and education. As we have seen, the history of children's literature, both before and after the Golden Age, can be understood in terms of three sets of competing or overlapping functions:

1. Didacticism, education, and practicality: Some believed that children's literature, even fiction and poetry, should fulfill the practical function of socializing children to behave or to think properly by providing models of good behavior or by teaching children specific lessons.

2. Pleasure, popularity, and profitability: Others were primarily concerned with establishing children's literature as a commercial, money-making enterprise, and thus they were interested in producing works for children that would be pleasurable and popular.

3. Aesthetics, innovation, and literariness: Some understood children's literature as a form of creative and artistic expression and were motivated by the desire to produce aesthetic and innovative literary works for children.

The complex and layered qualities of children's literature are produced by the tensions between these different and sometimes contradictory impulses and functions. As writers and publishers attempt to negotiate between these three approaches to children's literature, individual works bear the traces of the choices or compromises made among the impulses to instruct, to please, to profit, to innovate, or to create something "serious" or "literary."

For instance, in *Alice's Adventures in Wonderland*, Carroll stresses the pleasure of the reader and the practice of literary experimentation. *Alice* is full of jokes and whimsical uses of language that work to delight readers, and Carroll experiments with children's literature by insisting on nonsense or pushing the boundaries of traditional children's fare. In these ways, the book emphasizes pleasure and craft over instruction, even if some instruction remains. Kate Greenaway's picturebook *A Apple Pie* (1886) combines prominent images of the alphabet with richly illustrated scenes and short phrases highlighting each letter. Designed to teach children the alphabet, it appears to be primarily didactic, but the illustrations, completed by Greenaway herself, are so noteworthy for their distinctiveness and merit that we cannot ignore the artistry and craft of *A Apple Pie*. Other works, such as Horatio Alger's series books, tend to follow a formula in which a poor boy, often an orphan, manages to advance in the world through a mixture of luck and pluck. These popular works often emphasized the reader's pleasure rather than literary innovation, while instruction remained a secondary motive.

All works for children represent complex negotiations between these different functions. In the chapter on censorship (Ch. 12), we will discuss how many of the controversies surrounding children's literature can be understood in terms of conflicting ideas about which set of functions should be emphasized in writing for children. During the Golden Age, pleasure and aesthetics came to the fore for the first time. Understanding this early history of children's literature and the tensions and controversies that shaped it are crucial to the study of more current works for children.

The Second Golden Age

By the twentieth century, children's and young adult literature had come into their own, and many "contemporary classics" such as C.S. Lewis's *The Lion, the Witch and the Wardrobe* (1950), E.B. White's *Charlotte's Web* (1952), Philippa Pearce's *Tom's Midnight Garden* (1958), Maurice Sendak's *Where the Wild Things Are* (1963), and S.E. Hinton's *The Outsiders* (1967) would come to be added to the distinguished list of works written during the earlier Golden Age. The mid-twentieth-century boom in the publication of beloved children's books was referred to by John Rowe Townsend in 1965 as the Second Golden Age, which spanned the years after World War II through the 1970s (151). Townsend and, more recently, Lucy Pearson both credit professional children's book editors in mid-twentieth-century Britain, such as Eleanor Graham and her successor Kaye Webb at Puffin, with promoting the publication of quality children's books during the Second Golden Age. Many of these important editors were women (Pearson 76–77). In the United States, the Second Golden Age was presided over by influential book editors such as Ursula Nordstrom, the editor in chief of the children's book division of Harper & Brothers in New York. During her tenure between 1940 and 1973, when she rose to a position as Vice President at Harper, she edited and published works by Laura Ingalls Wilder, E.B. White, Margaret Wise Brown, Maurice Sendak, and many others. According to Leonard Marcus, it was Nordstrom's "irreverent view of the field" of children's literature and her "profound contempt for its more precious tendencies" that allowed her to see the merit in what became some of the most important children's classics of the period (Marcus 160), such as Louise Fitzhugh's *Harriet the Spy* (1963), and enabled the field to escape further the constraints of strict didacticism. The 1997 publication of the first book in the Harry Potter series might be said to have ushered in the Third Golden Age of Children's Literature, which continues to be defined by the tensions between didacticism, pleasure, and aesthetics.

READING CRITICALLY: THE HISTORY OF CHILDREN'S LITERATURE

Alice's Adventures in Wonderland

Alice's Adventures in Wonderland is often taken as a starting point for the Golden Age because it seems to mark a rupture in the history of children's literature by dramatically breaking from the tradition of didacticism in works for children. *Alice's Adventures* has its origins in a story Charles Dodgson told in 1862 to ten-year-old Alice Liddell and her sisters, Edith and Lorina, the daughters of the dean of Christ Church College at Oxford University, where Dodgson taught logic and mathematics. After writing down and revising the original version, Dodgson had the tale published in 1865 under the pen name Lewis Carroll. Conceived during a series of summer afternoons and designed to amuse the Liddell sisters, *Alice's Adventures* focuses primarily on providing pleasurable entertainment while lampooning moralistic or instructional children's books. Thus, like much of children's literature, *Alice's Adventures* negotiates between the impulse to instruct child readers and the impulse to delight them. What makes the work notable is its strong emphasis on the latter. Writing children's literature without succumbing to the temptation to impart lessons required Carroll to draw upon a number of strategies, including the innovative use of nonsense, the linguistic playfulness of jokes and puns, and the explicit mockery of education and didacticism.

Part of what generations of readers have found most delightful about the work is its insistent nonsense, a literary form that plays with and defies conventional uses of language, sense, and logic. Carroll employs nonsense both as a source of amusement and as a technique for short-circuiting the coherence and sense on which instruction rests. The nonsense of *Alice's Adventures* takes a number of forms. One is Carroll's use of puns, such as when the Mouse tells Alice that his history is "a long and sad tale," and Alice replies, "It *is* a long tail, certainly ... but why do you call it sad?" (28). Carroll frequently plays with language like this to humorous effect, as in the Mock Turtle's description of what he has learned in school: "Reeling and Writhing, of course, to begin with ... and then the different branches of Arithmetic—Ambition, Distraction, Uglification, and Derision" (85). The riddle proposed by the Hatter—"Why is a raven like a writing-desk?"—is another example of nonsense; it is designed to have no answer (60). Carroll frequently includes nonsense verse throughout *Alice's Adventures*, as when the Mock Turtle sings to Alice:

> "Will you walk a little faster?" said a whiting to a snail,
> "There's a porpoise close behind us, and he's treading on my tail." (89)

The notion of a whiting, a type of fish, walking and being tread upon by a porpoise is absurd. Moreover, the very structure of the text, which shifts erratically from scene to scene, also constitutes the nonsense of Wonderland. In the first several chapters, Alice falls down a rabbit hole while playing outside, finds herself indoors somewhere but unable to get out through a tiny door, cries so much she is forced to swim in a large pool of her own tears, meets a number of animals swimming in the pool who appear out of nowhere, makes it to shore, and eventually resumes her chase of the White Rabbit, which takes her outside again, with the overly small door and its challenges having been forgotten. Characters appear and disappear, behave odd-ly, and speak incoherently. The sheer strangeness of the events, details, dialogue, and charac-ters make it extremely difficult to extract morals or lessons from the work.

Alice's Adventures in Wonderland is a funny book, and its frequent use of humor works to em-phasize pleasure over instruction. Some of that humor is grim and even mean-spirited, provid-ing opportunities to delight child readers, for whom grimness and meanness are often taboo. Many of these jokes are at Alice's expense, such as this one, which appears to allude to Alice's death: "'Well!' thought Alice to herself. 'After such a fall as this, I shall think nothing of tumbling down-stairs! How brave they'll all think me at home! Why, I wouldn't say anything about it, even if I fell off the top of the house!' (Which was very likely true.)" (10). (Alice wouldn't cry or complain after falling off the top of the house because she would be dead.) Later, when Alice finds herself growing and shrinking without any control, she begins to wonder who she is and whether she is still Alice or one of her child acquaintances. She comforts herself by thinking, "I'm sure I can't be Mabel, for I know all sorts of things, and she, oh, she knows such a very lit-tle!" (18). When Alice quotes a poem incorrectly, she thinks, "I must be Mabel after all" (19). Alice is effectively calling her friend Mabel stupid or uneducated, which is itself funny, but doubly so because seven-year-old Alice is so conscious of Mabel's and her own intellectual capacities. Alice's running monologue is precocious in its properness and diction, while simultaneously riddled with absurdities and mistakes, further adding to the humor. As Alice finds herself get-ting taller and taller, she begins to worry about her feet: " 'Oh, my poor little feet, I wonder who will put on your shoes and stockings for you now, dears? I'm sure *I* shan't be able! I shall be a great deal too far off to trouble myself about you: you must manage the best way you can— but I must be kind to them,' thought Alice, 'or perhaps they won't walk the way I want to go!'" (16). Alice appears to have internalized an adult voice; we can hear an adult encouraging a child to be independent and responsible in Alice's earnest and ridiculous comments to her own feet. *Alice's Adventures in Wonderland* is composed of joke after joke, emphasizing the pleasure of readers who are free to delight in Alice's absurdity and absurd situation.

In addition to nonsense and humor, one last key way in which Carroll's landmark work breaks from the didactic tradition of children's literature is through its outright mockery of education and didacticism. This ridicule can be seen throughout the text. Alice frequently calls upon her education at the most inopportune moments—in addition to being poorly timed, her attempts to seem educated only highlight her ignorance. For instance, as she falls down the rabbit hole at the very outset of her adventures, Alice uses the opportunity to recollect her geography lessons:

"You're nothing but a pack of cards!" John Tenniel's illustration from *Alice's Adventures in Wonderland* (1865) by Lewis Carroll depicts the moment reality destroys fantasy.

"I wonder how many miles I've fallen by this time?" she said aloud. "I must be getting somewhere near the centre of the earth. Let me see: that would be four thousand miles down, I think—" (for, you see, Alice had learnt several things of this sort in her early lessons in the school-room, and though this was not a *very* good opportunity for showing off her knowledge, as there was no one to listen to her, still it was good practice to say it over) "—yes, that's about the right distance—but then I wonder what Latitude or Longitude I've got to?" (Alice had not the slightest idea what Latitude was, or Longitude either, but she thought they were nice grand words to say.) (10–11)

This passage suggests that the knowledge of little girls is most useful for "showing off" rather than for any sort of practical application, and the narratorial aside about saying it over to herself being "good practice" alludes to the common educational technique of having children learn by rote memorization and recitations. Carroll mocks these ideas and practices by having Alice call upon her education while falling perilously down a deep hole, oblivious to the danger of her situation or the futility of her (partial) knowledge. When she finally does land safely and discovers a bottle marked "DRINK ME," Alice is again given the opportunity to draw upon her education. Here, Carroll explicitly refers to the tradition of didactic children's literature represented by works such as Elizabeth Turner's *The Daisy; or Cautionary Stories in Verse* (1807), which illustrates the dangerous consequences for children who engage in such bad behavior as playing with hot pokers or climbing up on wells. Alice attempts to use what she has learned from this kind of instruction to help her decide whether to drink what is in the bottle:

It was all very well to say "Drink me," but the wise little Alice was not going to do *that* in a hurry. "No, I'll look first," she said, "and see whether it's marked '*poison*' or not"; for she had read several nice little stories about children who had got burnt, and eaten up by wild animals, and other unpleasant things, all because they *would* not remember the simple rules their friends had taught them: such as, that a red-hot poker will burn you if you hold it too long; and that, if you cut your finger *very* deeply with a knife, it usually bleeds; and she had never forgotten that, if you drink much from a bottle marked "poison," it is almost certain to disagree with you, sooner or later. (13)

The humor here is partly in Alice's understated recollection of the lessons of these stories—a red-hot poker will burn if you hold it *at all*, and drinking poison will more than "disagree with you"—but also in her very limited application of those lessons and her failure to transfer them beyond the specific scenarios of the stories. Thus, Alice has learned that she should not drink from a bottle marked "poison," but she mistakenly concludes that if a bottle is *not* marked "poison," it must be safe to drink. On another occasion, she misremembers Sir Isaac Watts's "Against Idleness and Mischief" (1715), quoted correctly in its entirety on page 99:

How doth the little crocodile
Improve his shining tail,
And pour the waters of the Nile
On every golden scale! (19)

Carroll thus transforms a didactic verse into one of nonsense, and the fact that Alice misre-members it suggests that such works are hardly effective.

The nonsense and humor of *Alice's Adventures* make more sense, ironically, if understood both as part of the larger tradition of children's literature and as Carroll's resistance to that tradition. Of course, the fact that we are able to make partial sense of *Alice's Adventures* by reading the text in terms of the tensions between didacticism and pleasure and the fact that Carroll's allusions might occasion our learning about the original works he lampoons indicate that it is extremely difficult to avoid sense and education completely. *Alice's Adventures* and its sequel, *Through the Looking-Glass* (1871), are puzzles, and solving them requires the reader not only to draw on prior knowledge but also to seek out new information or practice new skills. In these ways, even nonsense can promote instruction. Nonetheless, Carroll's work clearly in-clines toward pleasure and away from didacticism, and his use of nonsense, linguistic humor, and literary allusion represents the kind of innovation, creativity, and complexity that ushered in the Golden Age of children's literature.

EXPLORATIONS

Review

1. What kinds of written texts were considered "literature" in the eighteenth century that not everyone would acknowledge as "literary" in our own time? What implica-tions does this shifting definition have for our study of early children's literature?

2. Perry Nodelman argues that children's literature is a distinct genre with a set of consis-tent qualities (see page 85). Make a list of these qualities. Why does Nodelman believe that all children's literature shares this list of features?

3. What kinds of strategies did John Newbery use in the eighteenth century to make his books more attractive and marketable to children? What were his goals in using these strategies?

4. This chapter includes a number of examples of early children's literature that were either enjoyed by adults and children together or that began as texts for a mixed-age audience and only became associated with children's literature specifically over time. How do these examples complicate a definition of children's literature as the literature written *for* children? What is the difference between a definition of children's literature that stresses what children *read* versus a definition that stresses what was written primarily *for* children?

5. What are some examples of morals, lessons, or skills that early children's literature was designed to teach young people?

Reflect

1. Think about the purpose of your children's literature class and your own purpose for studying children's literature. Given these purposes, discuss your ideas about what counts as children's literature. How does the syllabus for your course explicitly or implicitly define children's literature?

2. How would you define a work such as J.K. Rowling's *Harry Potter and the Sorcerer's Stone* (1997), which has been read and enjoyed by both children and adults? Are the editions of Harry Potter published with "adult" covers adult literature or children's literature? How does Harry Potter reflect or fit into the history of children's literature described in this chapter?

3. Writers such as Sarah Trimmer and Maria Edgeworth expressed concerns about the dangers of fiction or fantasy for children. What might be the uses of literature that plays with and distorts reality, as fantasy and science fiction do, as opposed to that which reflects or describes reality? Are the fears of Trimmer and Edgeworth valid? Why, or why not?

4. Identify examples of twentieth- and twenty-first-century texts for adults that have crossed over as children's literature just as *Robinson Crusoe* did in the eighteenth and nineteenth centuries. Why might these works appeal to children? Which adult books did you read as a child? How did you stumble upon or select these books?

5. Choose an alphabet or counting book such as Stephen Johnson's *Alphabet City* (1995) or *City by Numbers* (1998) and explain how it can be understood in terms of tension between pleasure and instruction. How do these books either function as or

problematize didactic children's literature? How do they emphasize pleasure or artistry? Which function of children's literature do they emphasize more?

Investigate

1. Determine the oldest children's book held in your college or university library, read it, and consider how it fits into this history of children's literature.

2. Select an adult or mixed-age text in the public domain (generally published before 1923) that might have crossover appeal, especially one available as a full text online. Abridge it for a young reader and then reflect on your editorial choices.

3. Choose a text written primarily for children and design a campaign (book cover, print or video advertisements, website, blurbs, etc.) to market the book for adult readers.

4. Select a fairy tale that has been sanitized or tamed for children, or an early version of a tale for a more general audience, and rewrite it to appeal either specifically to adults or specifically to children. Reflect on what this suggests about your assumptions regarding what adults or children might enjoy or need.

SUGGESTED READINGS

Abbott, Jacob. *Rollo at Play* (1841). An American minister and educator, Jacob Abbott wanted to teach children good morals and behavior in ways that would capture their attention and entertain them. His Rollo series, containing more than two dozen volumes, follows the development of a young boy from New England and emphasizes the use of reason in the education and rearing of children. *Rollo at Play* is an episodic novel in which Rollo explores the yard and countryside around his home with the gentle guidance of his family and his family's servant, Jonas.

Burnett, Frances Hodgson. *Little Lord Fauntleroy* (1885). A truly trans-Atlantic author, Burnett constructs a character and plot that also span the Atlantic by imagining America and the American child as the heir to Britain and British aristocracy. When his two uncles and father are all killed, Cedric Errol, the son of an American woman living in New York, becomes next in line to the Earl of Dorincourt and moves to his grandfather's estate in England, where he converts the unhappy curmudgeon into a loving philanthropist. A sentimental though enormously popular novel, *Little Lord Fauntleroy* prompts an examination of how Burnett offers a model of the ideal child while working to entertain both child and adult readers.

Fielding, Sarah. *The Governess* **(1749).** Like other early works for children, this one combines different genres to both teach and please child readers. Considered the first novel for children, *The Governess* is set at Mrs. Teachum's school for girls and follows the exploits of her young charges as they trade stories about their brief lives, exchange fairy tales, fight and make up, and derive lessons from their stories and experiences. Readers can discern Fielding's efforts to work out what a novel for children should be like.

Finley, Martha. *Elsie Dinsmore* **(1867).** Set on a Southern plantation, Finley's novel about the extraordinarily pious Elsie and her struggles with her less devout and extremely strict father was one of the most popular American children's books of the nineteenth century. The motherless Elsie is mostly cared for by her mammy in the unloving home of her grandfather and step-grandmother. When her father, whom she has never met, returns from his travels abroad, he decides to raise Elsie with an iron fist, coming into conflict with her Christian ideals. This sentimental novel raises interesting questions about the representation of race, childhood agency, the construction of girlhood, and religion in children's literature.

Hoffmann, Heinrich. *The English Struwwelpeter* **(1848).** Written for his own son in part as a parody of moralistic children's literature, Hoffmann's collection of illustrated vignettes includes characters such as Shock-headed Peter, the boy with poor personal hygiene, and Pauline, a girl who plays with matches and burns herself to ashes. A humorous book, *The English Struwwelpeter* will either delight or horrify readers with its illustrations of the worst that can happen when children fail to obey adults by not eating all their dinner or by making fun of other children.

Milne, A.A. *Winnie-the-Pooh* **(1926).** Milne's twentieth-century classic about Christopher Robin's hapless stuffed bear who comes to life and has adventures has delighted readers with its clever wordplay and satirical character sketches. A combination of fantasy and nonsense, *Winnie-the-Pooh* addresses both children and adults and can be read in the tradition of Lewis Carroll's *Alice's Adventures in Wonderland*. This first book of Milne's Pooh stories follows the adventures of Pooh, Piglet, Kanga, Eeyore, and Owl as they explore the Hundred Acre Wood.

Newbery, John. *A Little Pretty Pocket-Book* **(1744).** The work often credited with igniting the children's literature industry, *A Little Pretty Pocket-Book* is designed both to delight and to instruct. An eclectic amalgamation, it contains games, alphabets, illustrations, rules for behavior, proverbs, and poems for children. The recent reissue of an early American edition allows contemporary students to read and study Newbery's landmark text.

Ovington, Mary White. *Hazel* (1913). Ovington's *Hazel* is one of the first children's novels for and about black children with a fully realized and sympathetic African American protagonist. Though Ovington was white, she was heavily involved in the struggle for racial equality and helped found the National Association for the Advancement of Colored People (NAACP). *Hazel,* published by the NAACP through its Crisis Publishing, features a Boston girl named Hazel whose mother sends her to live with her grandmother in Alabama. Hazel encounters racial prejudice in the south, but the warm climate and welcoming community improve her physical health and outlook.

Twain, Mark (Samuel Langhorne Clemens). *The Adventures of Tom Sawyer* (1876). An American classic about a mischievous but clever boy, *Tom Sawyer* was popular with both children and adults and, like *Alice's Adventures in Wonderland,* further challenges the centrality of didacticism in children's literature. Recounting the adventures of Tom and his friends, including the discovery of treasure and their harassment of a local criminal, Twain's novel provides an opportunity to examine the construction of boyhood; in addition, since Tom's adventures are inspired by the books he has read, *Tom Sawyer* both records and contributes to the history of children's literature.

White, E.B. *Charlotte's Web* (1952). White's *Charlotte's Web* follows the efforts of an anthropomorphic spider and other farm animals as they attempt to give meaning to the life of a young pig named Wilbur and thus save him from being slaughtered. After spinning a series of webs that declare Wilbur to be "Some Pig" and "Terrific," Charlotte lays a sac of eggs and dies, prompting a discussion of how children's literature addresses such issues as the meaning of life and sacrifice and death.

APPROACHES TO TEACHING *ALICE'S ADVENTURES IN WONDERLAND* [ELEMENTARY SCHOOL]

Preparation for the Lesson

Read *Alice's Adventures in Wonderland* as a class, skipping some chapters or episodes as desired.

Learning Goals

- To practice using evidence from a text to support an argument (in the "Dream or Nightmare?" activity)

- To learn about didactic and moralizing children's literature before *Alice*

- To examine jokes and puns in *Alice.*

Activity One: Dream or Nightmare?

Ask each student: Is Alice's journey a dream or a nightmare? Why do you answer as you do? Ask the students to provide evidence from the text to support their opinions. If the students have difficulty coming up with evidence, suggest some of the following:

Dream: Alice gets to go somewhere exciting; she meets many interesting characters; the world she enters is called "Wonderland," which is a positive description; Alice has the fun of growing and shrinking; Alice is free of all the control and strictness of her regular life (including forgetting her boring lessons); the nonsense she encounters is quite enjoyable.

Nightmare: A number of the characters she meets are distant or hostile; it is frightening to grow and shrink; her life is threatened at various times; she cannot remember who she is some of the time; she doesn't remember what she has been taught; the world she encounters doesn't make sense and she doesn't know the rules; she has to go on trial.

If time permits, students can draw, paint, or use collage to depict their vision of *Alice* as either a dream or a nightmare (or both a dream and a nightmare). Each student should exchange his or her drawing, painting, or collage with another student and write a short paragraph comparing their depictions of Alice.

Activity Two: Alice's Didactic Influences and Foils

Alice's Adventures in Wonderland parodies children's literature of the past, which was often designed to teach lessons and frequently lacked humor. In this activity, an old-fashioned didactic poem will be presented in combination with the section of Alice that makes fun of it. On the board or projector, copy the passage from Alice beginning with "It was all very well to say 'Drink me,' but the wise little Alice was not going to do that in a hurry" (quoted on p. 108). Hand out the following poem, explaining that it was a typical moralistic poem from the early nineteenth century:

"Dangerous Sport," by Elizabeth Turner

Poor Peter was burnt by the poker one day,
   When he made it look pretty and red!
For the beautiful sparks made him think it fine play,
   To lift it as high as his head.

But, somehow it happen'd, his finger and thumb
   Were terribly scorch'd by the heat;
And he scream'd out aloud for his mother to come,
   And stamp'd on the floor with his feet!

Now if Peter had minded his mother's command,
   His fingers would not have been sore;
And he promised again, as she bound up his hand,
   To play with hot pokers no more. (69–70)

(For more in this vein, "Susan and Patty" is another Elizabeth Turner poem that influenced Alice. It can be found in The Cowslip; or, More Cautionary Stories in Verse [1811], available via Google Books.)

Explain that Lewis Carroll was attempting to make fun of poems such as "Dangerous Sport" in Alice and to replace them with literature that children would find more enjoyable. Talk about the cautionary tale, a genre in which children are warned about threats and dangers, especially the dangers caused by bad behavior. Ask the students which they enjoy more—Turner's poem or Carroll's book—and discuss the reasons for their answers.

An optional extension of this exercise is to have the students write a cautionary poem of their own. To begin, lead a class discussion about the dangers that children are warned against in the modern age. These might include talking to or emailing strangers, riding in a car without a seatbelt, or biking without a helmet. Ask the students to write a short poem about one of these dangers (it doesn't have to rhyme). When the students have drafted their poems, lead a discussion about what has changed between "Poor Peter's" childhood and their own. What dangers do modern children face that nineteenth-century children didn't, or vice versa? Ask the students if they have ever read a poem about the threats that modern children face, and if modern children would enjoy such cautionary poems.

Activity Three: Puns and Jokes

Define puns as "deliberate confusions of similar words or phrases for comic effect," and explain that Lewis Carroll was extremely interested in wordplay, including jokes and puns. Prepare a handout with the following puns from the chapter "The Mock-Turtle's Story":

A. "When we were little ... we went to school in the sea. The master was an old Turtle—we used to call him Tortoise—"
"Why did you call him Tortoise, if he wasn't one?" Alice asked.
"We called him Tortoise because he taught us," said the Mock Turtle angrily.

B. [The Mock Turtle describes the course he took]: "Reeling and Writhing, of course, to begin with ... and the different branches of Arithmetic—Ambition, Distraction, Uglification, and Derision."

C. "And how many hours a day did you do lessons?" asked Alice, in a hurry to change the subject.
"Ten hours the first day," said the Mock Turtle: "nine the next, and so on."
"What a curious plan!" exclaimed Alice.
"That's the reason they're called lessons," the Gryphon remarked: "because they lessen from day to day."

Discuss how these three puns work and what words are being played with. As a continuation of the lesson the next day, ask the students to bring in three or four puns they like and have them present these to the class.

POETRY

In her preface to *Hymns in Prose for Children* (1781), the English poet Anna Laetitia Barbauld questioned whether children should be exposed to poetry:

> It may well be doubted, whether poetry *ought* to be lowered to the capacities of children, or whether they should not rather be kept from reading verse, till they are able to relish good verse: for the very essence of poetry is an elevation in thought and style above the common standard; and if it wants this character, it wants all that renders it valuable. (iv)

Rather than publish hymns for children in poetry, as her predecessor Isaac Watts did, Barbauld transformed common hymns into pure prose. Parents and educators today would certainly agree with Barbauld that the "essence of poetry is an elevation in thought and style above the common standard." However, it is that "elevation in thought and style"—in its infinite diversity—that they want children to experience. Children's poetry is now regarded as a powerful means for children to explore self and world and to find joy in and appreciation for language.

In his afterword to *Laughing Tomatoes and Other Spring Poems* (1997), Francisco X. Alarcón points to the variety of poetic expression: "Poems, like tomatoes, grow in many forms and shapes" (n.p.). Some of these forms include nursery rhymes, nonsense verse, long narrative poems, lyric poems devoted to capturing a single moment or feeling, poems marking an occasion, and the skipping rhymes and playground poetry composed by children themselves. Poetry for children is created for many reasons, including

---

Opposite: "The Cat and the Fiddle" from *Hey Diddle Diddle and Baby Bunting*, illustration by Randolph Caldecott, 1880.

- To help children explore emotions and ideas

- To transmit values from adult to child, which could include religious instruction, civic education, and social education

- To encourage children to play with language, reveling in the sounds of words and vivid figurative language

- To enable political reflection on the part of the child

- To facilitate children's games and play.

This chapter looks at some of the features of poetry designed for children and explores the poetry that reflects children's own popular culture. One of the most striking characteristics of poetry is its union of form and content: what it says is entwined with how it says it. In this chapter, we will examine how the formal features of poetry—such as verse form and figurative language—contribute to the theme and message of a poem. We will also consider how the separate tradition of poetry for children fits into the dominant canonical tradition of adult poetry.

NURSERY RHYMES, VERSE, AND POETRY

Before turning to the history of children's poetry, we should distinguish between three terms: **nursery rhymes**, **verse**, and poetry. "Nursery rhymes" can be defined as traditional songs or rhymes for children, often collected under the title "Mother Goose rhymes." John Barr defines "verse" as poetry that pursues "limited objectives: to entertain us with a joke or tall tale, to give us the inherent pleasures of meter and rhyme." A large part of the pleasure of verse is its conformity to the chosen meter. Poetry differs from verse, Barr explains, in that it is "written in pursuit of an open-ended goal. It seeks to use language, in its full potential, to encompass reality, both external and internal, in the fullness of its complexity" (Barr). The difference between these forms is thus one of aesthetic depth: poetry offers a more full encounter with figurative language, and its meaning is less clearly defined than that of the more straightforward "verse," leading to a more rewarding and ongoing interpretative process. Although Barr makes a useful distinction between "poetry" and "verse," many people think of the two terms as synonyms that simply mean "the opposite of prose."

We could also make a distinction between oral and written poetry, as Morag Styles does when she contrasts "the disorderly, casual, robust world of the oral tradition" (such as nursery rhymes) with the written poetry "consciously composed with children in mind by writers who wish to communicate with young readers" (94). The first difference is obviously one of transmission: a spoken, sung, or chanted poem is experienced differently from one read on the page. The other difference is that of audience. Many works in the oral tradition were not originally composed for children; they first circulated in the popular culture as folk songs and ballads, street cries, and proverbs that were later adapted for a child audience. Written poetry is, for the most part, crafted by adults for a child readership. Scholars of children's poetry are interested in both oral and written traditions as well as in the overlap between oral and written poetic forms.

A HISTORY OF POETRY FOR CHILDREN

Bunyan and Watts

In the seventeenth and eighteenth centuries, John Bunyan and Isaac Watts wrote poetry that was meant to have particular appeal to child readers; they believed that children needed to be taught Christian ideas and that poetry could be employed for such instruction. Bunyan drew upon the natural world to describe spiritual phenomena for his child audience. For example, he compares a mole digging obsessively in the ground to a person so interested in worldly goods that he or she neglects spiritual pursuits. In contrast to Bunyan's severe allegories, Watts's poetry relied on "engaging lyric and on metrical dexterity to reach his audience. While always upholding Puritan doctrine, his poetry gently softens the Christian message of repentance and gracefully attenuates the stress on fire and brimstone" (Demers and Moyles 61). As an example of this softening, Watts's "Love Between Brothers and Sisters" begins,

> Whatever brawls disturb the street
> There should be peace at home;
> Where sisters dwell and brothers meet,
> Quarrels should never come. (lines 1–4)

Although Bunyan and Watts were didactic writers, they also sought to engage child readers with poetry featuring lively figurative language. These two figures have an important place in the history of poetry crafted both to please and to instruct child readers.

Mother Goose

The eighteenth century saw the beginning of a tradition of written Mother Goose rhymes, which captured (at least partially) a longer oral tradition. In 1697, Charles Perrault published *Histoires ou contes du temps passé, avec des moralités: Contes de ma mère l'Oye* (commonly known as *Tales of My Mother Goose*), which contains several of the major fairy tales now familiar to us, but no poetry. There is very little relation between Perrault's *mère l'Oye* and the Mother Goose of traditional rhymes, although both figures are symbols of traditional literature transmitted orally. Some American scholars argue that Mother Goose was in fact Elizabeth Foster Goose (1665–1757) of Boston, whose last name may have been Vergoose or Vertigoose (Baring-Gould and Baring-Gould 17–18). She was known for the rhymes she produced for her grandchildren, and although it was said that the verses were published by her son-in-law, there is no trace of such a book. Mother Goose is usually deemed to be fictional. Over the years, the figure of Mother Goose has become a personification of folk wisdom, and the poems regarded

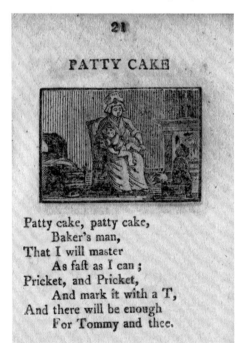

A rhyme from Mary Cooper's *Tommy Thumb's Pretty Song Book* (1744).

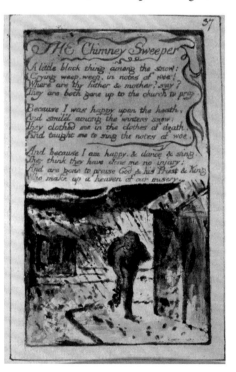

Engraving of "The Chimney Sweeper" from William Blake's *Songs of Innocence and of Experience*, 1795.

as timeless lore, even though many of them were written after the eighteenth century. In the preface to *Mother Goose's Melody*, John Newbery claimed that "the custom of singing these songs and lullabies to children is of great antiquity: It is even as old as the time of the ancient *Druids*" (v).

The earliest surviving book of nursery rhymes is Mary Cooper's 1744 *Tommy Thumb's Pretty Song Book*, published in two volumes, containing an introduction from the poetic persona "Nurse Lovechild." Later, with his typical eye for a commercial opportunity, publisher John Newbery composed *Mother Goose's Melody; or, Sonnets for the Cradle* around 1765–66 and published it in 1780. While most of these verses are familiar to today's readers, many were later modified for a younger audience. As discussed in Chapter 1, the ideology of childhood as separate from adulthood had not yet solidified when Perrault, Cooper, and Newbery were publishing; thus, it is not surprising to find adult material in earlier editions of the poems. For example, the second volume of Cooper's *Tommy Thumb's Pretty Song Book* contains the following verse:

Little Robbin red breast
Sitting on a pole
Niddle, Noddle,
Went his head,
And Poop went his Hole. (lines 1–5)

In later editions, the final line is modified to "Wiggle waggle went his tail" (Baring-Gould and Baring-Gould 26).

The adaptation of the Mother Goose rhymes into illustrated books helped establish their role in childhood culture. Some of Randolph Caldecott's best-known illustrations were based on nursery rhymes, such as his *Sing a Song of Sixpence* (1880). As Amy Weinstein notes, "Although the verses may be appreciated entirely through sound, when accompanied by brightly colored, humorous illustrations, they gain a new sensory dimension" (43). Mother Goose and other nursery rhyme books are still common gifts for children and infants. New editions are constantly produced.

The Romantic Poets and Nineteenth-Century Children's Poetry

The Romantic poets of the late eighteenth and early nineteenth centuries placed a new emphasis on children and childhood, with many writers speaking from the child's point of view. Though he did not write for children specifically, William Blake often evoked their experience. His poem "The Chimney Sweeper" is narrated in the voice of a child:

When my mother died I was very young,
And my father sold me while yet my tongue
Could scarcely cry "'weep! 'weep! 'weep! 'weep!"
So your chimneys I sweep, and in soot I sleep. (lines 1–4)

While Blake engages his readers with a tale of thwarted childhood innocence, William Wordsworth describes a divine child "trailing clouds of glory" in his "Ode: Intimations of Immortality from Recollections of Early Childhood" (1802–07). If one adheres to Wordsworth's idea of children as particularly close to the divine, not only are children capable of understanding and appreciating poetry, they are privileged readers of poetry.

One of the inheritors of the Wordsworthian tradition associating childhood and poetry was Robert Louis Stevenson. His *A Child's Garden of Verses* (1885) was written in the

Illustration for "My Bed Is a Boat" from *A Child's Garden of Verses*, illustrated by Tasha Tudor, 1984.

late Victorian period but had a Romantic emphasis on the child's point of view, evoking both life in the nursery and the yearning to explore the outside world. Poems like "My Shadow," "My Bed Is a Boat," and "The Lamplighter" are now children's classics, and *A Child's Garden of Verses* has never been out of print.

Jean Webb notes that Stevenson "attempts to recall the nature of childhood as he experienced it, and also to add to it the experience of the reflective adult, producing, therefore, innocence and experience combined" (361). Stevenson's poems, while seemingly artless, are constructed in a very sophisticated manner.

Forgotten Children's Poets of the Nineteenth Century

Much of the poetry produced for children in the nineteenth century was composed by women writers; and yet, in several cases, their authorship has been forgotten. For example, Sarah Martin, who wrote *The Comic Adventures of Old Mother Hubbard and Her Dog* (1805), is no longer well known, but her poem is still widely recited today:

> Old Mother Hubbard
>   Went to the cupboard
> To fetch her poor dog a bone;
>   But when she came there
>   The cupboard was bare
> And so the poor dog had none. (lines 1–6)

The poem becomes more and more nonsensical, with the dog dying, coming back to life, standing on his head, dancing a jig, reading the news, and ultimately greeting the dame's declaration ("your servant!") with "Bow-Wow" (Baring-Gould and Baring-Gould 111–12). Styles notes, "Sarah Martin is just one of several women poets who either composed original rhymes or brought old ones to fruition, yet whose names are not widely known" (90).

Readers might think that the poem "Twinkle, Twinkle, Little Star" is an ancient verse, passed down through history. In fact, it was written by Jane Taylor as the poem "The Star" and published for the first time in *Rhymes for the Nursery* (1806), a collection of poems by Taylor and her sister Ann. However, as early as 1864, it was credited only as a "Nursery Rhyme" in an anthology rather than being attributed to a specific author (Styles 93). Another important yet often-forgotten writer is Mary Howitt, who published "The Spider and the Fly" in 1829; it was one of the many didactic poems for children that Lewis Carroll parodied in his Alice books. "The Spider and the Fly" is a **narrative poem**, which means it tells a story. In Howitt's poem, the fly resists the blandishments of the wily spider until tempted by the chance to look at itself in a looking glass, which leads to its demise and this moral conclusion:

> And now dear little children, who may this story read,
> To idle, silly, flattering words, I pray you ne'er give heed;
> Unto an evil counsellor close heart and ear and eye,
> And take a lesson from this tale, of the Spider and the Fly. (lines 41–44)

In addition to offering a genuine cautionary tale, this poem is an early example of the cultural anxieties caused by children's contact with strangers.

Feminist scholars have recently begun to accord nineteenth-century women poets such as Martin, Taylor, and Howitt their proper place in literary history. Christina Rossetti's poetry for adults has had a place in the canon for some time now, but she also wrote poetry for children. Her *Sing Song: A Nursery Rhyme Book* (1872; expanded edition 1893) is dedicated to the "baby who suggested them." Many of the poems in the collection are lullabies or simple poems aimed at a very young child, as in this example:

> Love me, — I love you,
>   Love me, my baby;
> Sing it high, sing it low,
>   Sing it as may be.
>
> Mother's arms under you,
>   Her eyes above you;
> Sing it high, sing it low,
>   Love me, — I love you. (lines 1–8)

There are also darker aspects to *Sing Song*, such as wrenching poems about infant mortality. One such poem asks, "Why did baby die, / Making Father sigh, / Mother cry?" (lines 1–3). Lissa Paul has contextualized Rossetti's *Sing Song* within a tradition of "maternal verse" that included Ann and Jane Taylor (37). The "intimate, protected domestic space" is brought into the public sphere through maternal verse, with "hand-made, home-made verses" transformed into "mass-produced purchased ones" (38–39). Although many of them are forgotten today, the women writing poetry for children in the nineteenth century successfully translated their private experiences into a commercial literary context.

Nineteenth-Century Humorous and Nonsense Poetry

The nineteenth century saw growth in the number of humorous and nonsense poems written for children. Three writers towered over the genre during this era: Edward Lear, Lewis Carroll, and Hilaire Belloc. As we discussed in Chapter 2, though children's literature in the nineteenth century did not entirely abandon didacticism, it was increasingly oriented toward children's pleasure and entertainment. Humorous and nonsense poetry was one means to entertain children and to immerse child readers in the pleasures of playing with words. X.J. Kennedy offers a "working definition" of "nonsense in a children's book," describing it as an "account of anything that isn't likely to happen, whether or not it conceivably could" (108). Michael Heyman adds: "We may begin by classifying literary nonsense texts as those where there is a type of balance between 'sense' and 'non-sense.' Such a balance is necessary if the text is not to become either plain sense, as in a best-selling crime novel, or utter gibberish, as in a baby's babbling" (xxiv).

Nonsense poetry of the nineteenth century encouraged wordplay and experimentation with language. Edward Lear popularized the limerick form, and he is also known for comical poems such as "The Owl and the Pussycat" (1871), which begins,

> The Owl and the Pussy-cat went to sea
> In a beautiful pea-green boat,
> They took some honey, and plenty of money,
> Wrapped up in a five pound note. (lines 1–4)

The Owl and the Pussycat "sailed away for a year and a day / To the land where the Bong-tree grows," where they encounter a "Piggy-wig" with a "ring at the end of his nose" (lines 16–17; 18; 19). The absurd situation and made-up words add to the poem's construction of nonsense, yet they have their own internal logic, making sense purely on their own terms.

Lewis Carroll's poems in his Alice books were another major contribution in this era to the tradition of nonsense poetry for children. In *Through the Looking-Glass* (1872), Alice discovers a "Looking-glass book" where the writing is in reverse. Holding it up to a mirror, she is able to read the poem "Jabberwocky," with its famous opening stanza:

> 'Twas brillig, and the slithy toves
>   Did gyre and gimble in the wabe:
> All mimsy were the borogoves;
>   And the mome raths outgrabe. (lines 1–4)

Humpty Dumpty later explains the meaning of the mysterious words "brillig," "mimsy," and "outgrabe," although he is obviously not a reliable interpreter. The power of Carroll's

"The owl looked up to the stars above, / and sang to a small guitar." From Edward Lear's 1871 poem "The Owl and the Pussycat," illustrated by William Foster.

poem lies in the sounds of its words, as we see from this stanza's **alliteration** ("gyre and gimble") and the **portmanteau** word "slithy" (a word that combines "lithe" and "slimy"). Despite the nonsense words, the basic plot of the poem—the slaying of the Jabber-wock—emerges clearly. In this poem, the emphasis is on whimsy and the sheer pleasure of the invented words.

Rather than invent words as Lear and Carroll did, Hilaire Belloc wrote humorous cau-tionary tales for children, such as *The Bad Child's Book of Beasts* (1896) and *Cautionary Tales for Children* (1907). *Cautionary Tales* includes cases such as that of Matilda ("Who told lies, and was Burned to Death") and Algernon ("Who played with a Loaded Gun, and, on missing his Sister, was reprimanded by his Father"). Franklin Hyde, who "caroused in the Dirt, and was corrected by his Uncle," shares an equally mock-sobering message:

> From Franklin Hyde's adventure, learn
> To pass your Leisure Time
> In Cleanly Merriment, and turn
> From Mud and Ooze and Slime
> And every form of Nastiness— (lines 9–13)

The poem then reverses itself:

> But, on the other Hand,
> Children in ordinary Dress
> May always play with Sand. (lines 14–16)

Belloc's jovial tone inverted the well-known didacticism of previous writers of caution-ary tales. Franklin Hyde's problems and scrapes are recounted with a humor that Mary Howitt's earnest "The Spider and the Fly" lacks, as Belloc wrote in response to a vision of childhood and children's literature that stresses amusement rather than sober instruction.

Twentieth- and Twenty-First-Century Poetry

In the twentieth century, the market for children's literature grew, as did its cultural im-portance. A number of poets became primarily known as children's poets, while others considered their poetry for children to be just as important as their work for adults. A.A. Milne, author of the Winnie-the-Pooh books, also wrote poetry for children, including his collections *When We Were Very Young* (1924) and *Now We Are Six* (1927). Working largely within the tradition of Robert Louis Stevenson, his work evokes a sense of childhood in-nocence and playfulness. In "Lines and Squares" (from *When We Were Very Young*), Milne riffs on the classic children's game of trying not to step on a crack or line while walking on the street or sidewalk. Ann Thwaite remarks on the "pleasurable thrill of danger" (267) in Milne's poetry: "It is not a bland world. The menaces and uncertainties of real life are there all right, but perfectly adjusted to a small child's understanding.... The child in the poems is protected by his own egotism, is perfectly in control" (266–67).

Theodor Seuss Geisel (Dr. Seuss), known for his iconic picturebooks, made immense contributions to children's poetry. Philip Nel points to Geisel's skilled meters and rhymes and his exuberant delight in creating new words, illuminating "the pleasures of language, encouraging readers to be creative—an ideal suggestion for the child newly acquainted with the written word" (25). Like many nonsense poets, Geisel also created fantastical creatures. *Scrambled Eggs Super!* (1953) includes several dozen, among them the "Ruffle-Necked Sala-ma-goox," the "Mop–Noodled Finch," the "Stroodle," and the "Single-File Zummzian Zuks." Ultimately, Geisel "established verse at the center of the children's book genre" (Nel 35).

Another twentieth-century poet, John Ciardi, wrote several collections of children's poetry, including *The Reason for the Pelican* (1959) and *The Man Who Sang the Sillies* (1961). Ciardi's poems combine whimsy with realistic depictions of children's pleasures and frustrations. Many of his poems for children use simple vocabulary aimed at beginning readers. In his *You Read to Me, I'll Read to You* (1962), illustrated by Edward Gorey, poems meant to be read to a child alternate with poems that the child reads back to the adult, using what Ciardi calls "a basic first-grade vocabulary" (n.p.).

Eve Merriam published several collections of poetry for children, including *There Is No Rhyme for Silver* (1964) and *You Be Good & I'll Be Night: Jump-on-the-Bed Poems* (1988), illustrated by Karen Lee Schmidt. In *It Doesn't Always Have to Rhyme* (1964), Merriam draws explicit attention to poetic forms and devices in poems such as "Metaphor," "Couplet Countdown," and "Onomatopoeia" ("The rusty spigot / sputters, / utters / a splutter" [lines 1–4]). "How to Eat a Poem" includes these inviting lines:

Don't be polite.
Bite in.
Pick it up with your fingers and lick the juice that
may run down your chin. (lines 1–4)

In 1965, John Rowe Townsend coined the term "urchin poetry" for the kind of streetwise poetry written by authors such as Roald Dahl and Shel Silverstein, which was more likely to describe "disused railway lines, building sites, and junkheaps" than bucolic natural settings (cited in Styles 262). The "urchin" label does not encompass the full range of children's poetry today, since contemporary poetry for children also includes nature poetry and poems depicting rural life. Yet, at its best, "urchin poetry" makes an attempt to speak to children without idealizing them and without assuming that the world they live in is perfect.

Shel Silverstein is one of the seminal children's poets of the twentieth century; his *Where the Sidewalk Ends* (1974) is a modern children's classic. The collection includes both lyric poems that express emotion and narrative poems that tell a story. The poems combine the imagery of modern urban settings with very traditional forms. "Sarah Sylvia Cynthia Stout Would Not Take the Garbage Out" tells the humorous tale of a girl who refuses to attend to an ever-growing pile of trash until it takes on a life of its own, breaking through the roof, stretching to the sky, and extending across the state. She is eventually vanquished by the garbage, in a tongue-in-cheek update of Hilaire Belloc's humorous cautionary poems.

Roald Dahl is famous for novels such as *James and the Giant Peach* (1961) and *Charlie and the Chocolate Factory* (1964), but he also produced notable poetry collections for children, including *Revolting Rhymes* (1982) and *Dirty Beasts* (1984). *Revolting Rhymes* features verse parodies of six well-known fairy tales, all of which have surprise endings (for example, Little Red Riding Hood shoots the wolf dead). *Dirty Beasts* focuses on animals such as pigs, crocodiles, lions, and cows (and the fictional "Tummy Beast") but again features a twist, as we see in the poem "The Pig," where a brainy pig realizes he is meant for slaughter and turns on the farmer instead:

> Slowly he scratched his brainy head
> And with a little smile, he said,
> "I had a fairly powerful hunch
> "That he might have me for his lunch.
> "And so, because I feared the worst,
> "I thought I'd better eat him first." (lines 47–52)

One heir to Silverstein's and Dahl's gleeful verse is Jack Prelutsky, the first children's poet laureate of the United States. Prelutsky's *My Dog May Be a Genius* (2008), illustrated by James Stevenson, features poems devoted to animals, family, the natural world, and the pleasures of reading (even the joys of homework). The title poem refers to a dog that knows when he is getting "f-o-o-d" or his "t-r-e-a-t" because he has "learned / to s-p-e-l-l" (lines 15–16).

Other poets who wrote for children and young adults in the twentieth and twenty-first centuries include Carl Sandburg, Theodore Roethke, Maya Angelou, Dennis Lee, Nikki Giovanni, X.J. Kennedy, Eloise Greenfield, Pat Mora, JonArno Lawson, Gary Soto, J. Patrick Lewis, and Myra Cohn Livingston.

CONTEMPORARY POETRY AS A REFLECTION ON SELF AND OTHER

Contemporary poetry for children does not shy away from exploring the tensions children might feel at home or school but probes the fault lines between self and other. Jean Little's book *Hey World, Here I Am!* (1986) features poems written in the voice of her reflective protagonist, Kate. In the poem "Today," Kate grumbles:

> Today I will not live up to my potential.
> Today I will not relate well to my peer group.
> Today I will not contribute in class.
>   I will not volunteer one thing.
> Today I will not strive to do better.
> Today I will not achieve or adjust or grow enriched
>   or get involved.
> I will not put up my hand even if the teacher is wrong
>   and I can prove it.
>
> Today I might eat the eraser off my pencil.
> I'll look at clouds.
> I'll be late.
> I don't think I'll wash.
>
> I need a rest. (lines 1–14)

The poem offers a very specific form of resistance to the ideology that children must focus on achievement and cooperation. The repetition of "Today" parodies the genre of "resolution" or self-improvement, where the speaker vows to do better in his or her daily obligations. It challenges the expectations and demands teachers have of their students. This contemporary poem also provides a sharp contrast with the didacticism of the earlier poetry for children such as the poems of Isaac Watts, in which industry and hard work are praised to the exclusion of anything else.

AN EXPANDED CANON

During the twentieth century, the canon of children's poetry expanded to include more poets, alongside the publication of several multicultural and multilingual poetry collections. In 1932, Harlem Renaissance poet Langston Hughes published *The Dream Keeper and Other Poems*, a selection of previously published poems selected specifically for young readers. In his poem "Children's Rhymes," Hughes writes:

By what sends
the white kids
I ain't sent;
I know I can't
be President.
What don't bug
them white kids
sure bugs me:
We know everybody
ain't free. (lines 1–10)

In this poem written long before the election of Barack Obama, the African American child speaker reflects on the racism that has limited his destiny as an individual.

Many children's poets of the late twentieth century are motivated by a similar combination of the personal and the political. Francisco X. Alarcón's *Laughing Tomatoes and Other Spring Poems / Jitomates Risueños y otros poemas de primavera* (1997), illustrated by Maya Christina Gonzalez, is a bilingual poetry picturebook. The topics of Alarcón's poems range from the natural world ("First Rain" and "Ode to Corn") to Mexican American culture, including a poem about Cinco de Mayo (a holiday that celebrates the 1862 victory of the Mexican army over an invading French army) and one about César Chavez, the Mexican American leader who founded the United Farm Workers of America. Alarcón makes powerful use of short lines with one or two words, as we see in his short poem "Chile" or "El chile":

sometimes	a veces basta
a bite is all it takes	una mordida
for a supernova	para que explote
to explode	una supernova

Although the length of Alarcón's poems varies from a few lines to a few pages, they all invite the same focus on every carefully chosen word—and on the natural and social world. Alarcón uses **metaphor**—the literary figure of speech where two unrelated things or ideas are compared. Here the experience of eating a hot chile is likened to the power of an exploding star. The fact that his poems appear in both English and Spanish speaks to several possible audiences: Latinx students learning English, Anglophone students learning Spanish, and bilingual students who use both Spanish and English in their daily lives. Another poetry collection that combines Spanish and English words is Gary Soto's *Neighborhood Odes* (1992). An ode is a structured lyric poem in praise of an individual or thing. While the ode form is rooted in the poetic tradition of the ancient Greeks and Romans, it is also part of the poetic tradition in English, with such famous poems as John Keats's "Ode to Autumn." Soto adapts it to reflect everyday life in a Mexican American neighborhood with free verse poems like "Ode to Pablo's Tennis Shoes," "Ode to My Library," "Ode to La Piñata," among others. The use of Spanish words throughout the book reflects the life and culture of the community described in the odes. A glossary translating the Spanish terms into English reaches out to include readers who do not know Spanish.

The title poem of Guyana-born poet Grace Nichols's *Come on into My Tropical Garden: Poems for Children* (1988) begins:

> Come on into my tropical garden
>   Come on in and have a laugh in
>   Taste my sugar cake and my pine drink
>   Come on in please come on in. (lines 1–4)

Nichols's use of dialect and her employment of vivid imagery of the Caribbean expands the cultural and linguistic horizons of poetry for children. Lynn Joseph's *Coconut Kind of Day* (1990) is a picturebook poetry collection from the point of view of a young girl in Trinidad as she goes about her day: buying food from the market, going to school, and interacting with her family. It introduces many terms and words that are specific to life in Trinidad.

Janet S. Wong's *A Suitcase of Seaweed and Other Poems* (1996) reflects the reality of today's multicultural American families. The book is divided into three sections: "Korean Poems" (largely about Wong's Korean American mother), "Chinese Poems" (relating to Wong's Chinese American father), and "American Poems" (referring to her own American identity). Wong's poems are a meditation on the role of childhood memory in establishing identity and the complex ways in which identity can be experienced in a multicultural society. The "suitcase of seaweed" refers to the "seaweed / and stacks / of dried squid" that Wong's grandmother brings when she visits from Korea (lines 12–14). The final poem, "Quilt," establishes a metaphor of her family as "a quilt / of odd remnants / patched together / in a strange / pattern" but "made to keep / its warmth / even in bitter / cold" (lines 2–6; 9–12). In drawing attention to the separate norms of her Korean, Chinese, and American cultures, Wong underscores the contradictions and compromises of American identity, but also the rewards of life in her close family.

Naomi Shihab Nye's poetry is known for its focus on cross-cultural exchange; she was born in the United States but has also lived in Jerusalem. Nye is a prolific anthologist of poems by and for children, with an emphasis on international dialogue, including *This Same Sky: A Collection of Poems from Around the World* (1996). She also has an empathic understanding of the experiences of young girls, as we see in *A Maze Me: Poems for Girls* (2005). This collection includes a poem entitled "Changed," which deals with tension between peers:

> They said something mean about me
> and didn't notice it was mean
> So my heart wandered
> into the rainy night without them
> and found a canopy
> to hide under. (lines 1–6)

POETRY PICTUREBOOKS, CONCRETE POETRY, AND VERSE NOVELS

Poetry for children can be published and circulated in many ways. Many children's poets produce book-length collections of poetry, which are frequently illustrated. Sometimes poems are collected in anthologies and arranged according to theme or time period. Many children's picturebooks can themselves be read as poetry. An obvious example we have already explored is the work of Theodor Seuss Geisel ("Dr. Seuss"), whose poetry derives much of its appeal from the use of rhyme and regular meter. In *Green Eggs and Ham* (1960), the narrator rhythmically rejects the despised food of the title:

> I would not like them
> here or there.
> I would not like them
> anywhere. (16)

Margaret Wise Brown's classic picturebook *Goodnight Moon* (1947), illustrated by Clement Hurd, includes spare poetic language spread across separate illustrated pages:

> In the great green room
> there was a telephone
> And a red balloon
> And a picture of the cow jumping over the moon (n.p.)

One of the key features of poetry is economy of language: every word counts. Since picturebooks have little space, they also require an economy of language and are therefore quite suited to poetic expression—with or without rhyme.

Another distinct form within children's poetry is the concrete poem. In *A Poke in the I: A Collection of Concrete Poems* (2001), anthologist Paul B. Janeczko and illustrator Christopher Raschka note that "the arrangement of letters or words on the page, the typefaces chosen, and the way space is used, add meaning to the poems beyond that contained in the actual words" (n.p.). Concrete poems can be a single word or several words arranged into a specific shape. Janeczko and Raschka lightheartedly note that it is hard to read concrete poems out loud, since they are so dependent on visual interpretation. Concrete poems appeal to young audiences in part due to their cleverness (which can often depend on punning or the recognition of a joke). They also highlight poetry's capacity to make meaning through visual elements such as the placement of words on a page. One example of a concrete poem is John Hollander's "Kitty and Bug" (1986). The cat's unpunctuated, stream-of-consciousness musings take form as a cat shape, creating a contrast to the simple, stark three-letter word "bug."

```
              I        a
           cat    who
          coated in a
          dense shadow
          which I cast
          along myself
           absorb the
            light you
            gaze at me
          with can yet
         look at a king
        and not be seen
        to be seeing any
       more than himself
       a motionless seer
       sovereign of gray
       mirrored invisibly
      in the seeing glass
     of air whatever I am
    seeing is part of me
    As you see me now my
    vision is wrapped in
    two green hypotheses
     darkness blossoming
      in two unseen eyes
      which pretend to be
      intent on a spot of          bug
        upon
         the
         rug
        Who
        can
        see
          how
          eye
          can
          know
```

John Hollander's "Kitty and Bug" is a concrete poem.

In verse novels, a long narration is recounted in poetry rather than prose, straddling the boundaries between poetry and fiction. Another term for the verse novel is the "novel-in-poems." Some critics have reacted with skepticism to the verse novel, considering it essentially a prose form with eccentric line breaks. Others have defended the aesthetic qualities of the verse novel, including its value as poetry. Vikki Van Sickle remarked on the great potential of the verse novel as a "hybrid" form in 2006: "We need to expand our perceptions of what constitutes poetry, verse, and the novel, and look at the verse novel as an exciting form in the evolutionary literary process. Verse novels should be considered a postmodernist form of literature that is accessible, of considerable emotional impact, and here to stay" (Van Sickle). Mike Cadden agrees, noting: "we should be celebrating [the verse novel's] rich combination of generic strengths, its melding of the most engaging aspects of three genres to create a very appealing form. We have the sustained story typical of the novel, the guided pace provided by free verse's use of enjambment, and the dialogue-rich nature of drama" (27).

Recent years have seen the publication of many excellent verse novels. Kwame Alexander's *The Crossover* (2014) won both the Newbery Medal and the Coretta Scott King Honor award in 2015. *The Crossover* is divided into six sections to capture the segments of a basketball game: warm-up, four quarters, and overtime. Told from the point of view of 13-year old Josh, it describes his close-knit African American family, his rift with his twin, JB, and his father's unexpected and tragic death. Alexander draws on hip-hop and rap rhythms as well as using free verse. Words are often positioned dynamically on the page, changing in size from one line to the next or moving diagonally to evoke basketball moves like dribbling or passing. *The Crossover* includes poetic forms like list poems, advice poems, apology poems, poems built out of text messages, and even a tanka (a classical Japanese form) that Josh composes for language arts class. Like many verse novelists, Alexander wanted to reach out to readers who had no experience of poetry or who had dismissed it. In an interview, Alexander notes that he "tried to write the book to show boys—and girls—that poetry could be cool" (Barron).

Narrative verse has also been used to produce powerful memoirs. Jacqueline Woodson's *Brown Girl Dreaming* (2014) is a memoir in free verse about her family and childhood in Columbus, Ohio; Greenville, South Carolina; and New York City. Set amidst Woodson's growing awareness of the Civil Rights movement, *Brown Girl Dreaming* is above all a chronicle of the growth of her imagination and increasing awareness of herself as a writer. It won the 2014 National Book Award for Young People's Literature and the 2015 Coretta Scott King Award. Margarita Engle's *Enchanted Air: Two Cultures, Two Wings: A Memoir* (2015) describes her childhood torn between Cuba and Los Angeles during the Cuban Revolution and Cuban Missile crisis. It won the Pura Belpré Award in 2016.

Verse novels can also allow for an imaginative engagement with history, especially when told through a child or adolescent character. The poems in Karen Hesse's *Out of the Dust* (1997), set in the Oklahoma Dust Bowl in 1934–35, are narrated from the point of view of Billie Jo, a talented piano player whose hands are injured in an accident that also claims the life of her mother and her unborn brother. Thanhha Lai's autobiographical (but fictional) verse novel *Inside Out and Back Again* (2012) follows a young girl, Hà, who is forced to flee Saigon during the Vietnam War, and her difficult experiences as a refugee in Alabama in the 1970s. It won the 2011 National Book Award for Young People's Literature.

Verse novels can be particularly appealing to reluctant readers: they use a great deal of white space, are shorter than novels in prose, and explore compelling topics to which readers can relate. Dorie Raybuck, a library media specialist, notes: "Compared to a conventional novel, a novel in verse has perhaps half the number of words per page—and isn't that half the battle with reluctant readers? These readers often look at a page filled with words and think, *This is too much!* And quit before they begin" (Raybuck). The shorter length of verse novels can give a new or struggling reader a sense of accomplishment when they complete the book. Other notable verse novels include those written by Virginia Euwer Wolff (*Make Lemonade*, 1993), Helen Frost (*Keesha's House*, 2003), Ellen Hopkins (*Crank*, 2004), Sharon Creech (*Love that Dog*, 2008), David Levithan (*The Realm of Possibility*, 2006), Caroline Starr Rose (*May B.*, 2014), and Skila Brown (*Caminar*, 2014).

CHILDREN'S POPULAR CULTURE AND POETRY

In the mid-1940s, the British sociologists Peter and Iona Opie collected a number of rhymes from schoolchildren. Iona Opie reflected on their purpose for doing so:

> It was a recognition of the particular genius of rhymes that belongs to schoolchildren. They were clearly not rhymes that a grandmother might sing to a grandchild on her knee. They have more oomph and zoom; they pack a punch. Many are directly concerned with the exigencies of school life: the need for a stinging reply when verbally attacked; the need for comic complaints in the face of persecution or the grinding drudgery of schoolwork; the need to know some clever rhymes by heart, with which to win popularity. (11)

The Opies' emphasis is on children's own use of poetry, not on the great poems of the literary tradition, and they stress the oral transmission of children's rhymes. The Opies included material that would not necessarily be sanctioned by adult readers, as we can see from this rhyme, printed under "Insults":

> Tommy Johnson is no good,
> Chop him up for firewood;
> When he's dead, boil his head,
> Make it into gingerbread. (lines 1–4)

In his study of children's poetry, *Poetry's Playground: The Culture of Contemporary American Children's Poetry* (2007), Joseph Thomas Jr. argues that the frequently sexually explicit and violent poems composed by children themselves deserve to be studied alongside more canonical poetry for children, even if these verses would never find their way into a classroom. One rhyme, for example, has Abraham Lincoln jumping out a window with his "dick in his hand," saying "'Scuse me, ladies! / I'm superman!" (45). For Thomas, such playground poetry "dismantles nostalgic notions of the innocent, obedient, and controllable child and thus, in my experience, tends to disturb adults, as it implies sexualized, complicated child-agents who are able to control their world through linguistic play and sometimes violent, antiauthoritarian imagery" (42). Like the Opies, Thomas is interested in poetry as a means for children to exert control over their own social and imaginative lives.

POETRY WRITTEN BY CHILDREN

Children also create written poetry, some of which is published in anthologies or in periodicals. In 1966, Richard Lewis published *Miracles: Poems by Children of the English-Speaking World*, a project funded by UNESCO. In his introductory note, Lewis explains that the poems were "intended to be read as poetry, not as a sampling of precociousness" (7). The collection lived up to its promise to showcase excellent poetry by children and to reflect an internationalist sentiment in the middle of the Cold War. Other notable poetry anthologies of the sixties and early seventies include *The Me Nobody Knows: Children's Voices from the Ghetto* (1969), edited by Stephen M. Johnson, and *The Voice of the Children* (1970), compiled by Terri Bush and June Jordan. *The Me Nobody Knows* was adapted into a Broadway musical that was performed around the world. *The Voice of the Children* included twenty poems written by African American and Puerto Rican youths about growing up in the inner city. In 1970, Kenneth Koch reflected on teaching poetry to children in New York's public schools in his book *Wishes, Lies and Dreams*, in which he offers a number of sample assignments, such as asking children to build a poem around "the private world of their wishes": "Once they have a subject they like, but may have temporarily forgotten about, like wishing, they find a great deal to say" (13–14). Koch's work has been accused of being too formulaic, however. One of his most bracing critics, Myra Cohn Livingston, argues in *The Child as Poet: Myth or Reality* (1984) that when Koch asked students to write about "wishes," "lies," and "dreams," he foreclosed the possibility that they might write about their everyday reality.

There have also been several child poets who published their own poetry collections. Hilda Conklin's *Poems by a Little Girl* (1920), published at age ten, included a preface by well-known imagist poet Amy Lowell. Conklin created her poetry between the ages of four and ten years old by conversing with her mother, who wrote her poems down either in the moment or later by memory (she would then check with her daughter to ensure that the transcription was correct). Nathalia Crane published her first book of poetry, *The Janitor's Boy* (1924), when she was 12. *The New York Sun* published one of her poems when she was nine years old, not aware that she was a child. In 1970, eight-year old Kali Grosvenor published *Poems by Kali*, which contains poems written when she was six and seven as well as photographs by Joan Halifax and by Robert Fletcher, a photographer well known in the Civil Rights movement. In her book *Civil Rights Childhood: Picturing Liberation in African American Photobooks* (2014), Katharine Capshaw positions Grosvenor's poems within the aesthetic goals of the Black Arts Movement and the Civil Rights struggle.

THE SEPARATE TRADITION OF POETRY FOR CHILDREN

In an incisive essay called "Can Children's Poetry Matter?" (1993), Richard Flynn questions the notion "that an innocent and separate realm of children's poetry should exist at all" (40). He compares Walter de la Mare's anthology *Come Hither* (1923, 1957) with Jack Prelutsky's *The Random House Book of Poetry for Children* (1983). Of the two, he finds de la Mare's anthology infinitely stronger because it includes poetry composed solely for children as well as classics from the wider poetic tradition: "Shakespeare, Milton, Blake, Wordsworth, Coleridge, Shelley, Keats, Yeats, Hardy, and Frost alongside nursery rhymes, ballads, and doggerel" (Flynn 41). Prelutsky includes only poetry written for the child audience, which Flynn argues is an impoverishment of the range of poetry available to children (41). Several poems from the mainstream canonical tradition written in the late nineteenth century are indeed still read, such as Henry Wadsworth Longfellow's "The Ride of Paul Revere" (1866), Ernest Thayer's "Casey at the Bat" (1888), or Alfred Noyes's "The Highwayman" (1906). To steer children away from these poems is to cut children off from the wider tradition of poetry.

Just as Flynn argues that children should be exposed to the riches of the poetry canon, Livingston advocates that they be given access to a variety of poetic forms. In 1984, she lamented that most of the poetry given to children was rhyming poetry written in couplets:

> [I]t is time to rescue the child from being pulled to and fro in a struggle over ideologies and methods. It is time to respect the child's right to know, for example, not only what a couplet really is, but something about the beauty and force of a piece of free verse. Both are a piece of a poetic inheritance. (251)

Livingston's emphasis on "poetic inheritance" reminds us that young readers benefit from an exposure to all forms of poetry—free verse as much as rhyming couplets, and serious as much as comic verse.

Karen Coats notes that many scholars and critics disdain children's poetry if it exhibits "simple, rhythmic, patterned, repetitive, exaggerated speech, accompanied by movements and visual cues that also share these qualities" (136). She argues, however, that this kind of children's poetry has immense value and should not be compared to poems from the mainstream "adult" tradition:

> a children's poem is one that creates a holding environment in language to help children manage their sensory environments, map and regulate their neurological functions, and contain their existential anxieties. Rather than substituting language for sensation, a children's poem brings the body into language through strong beats

and sounds that evoke their sensory referents. It doesn't have to make sense in any conceptual way, nor does it need to challenge the adequacy of language to frame reality; rather, its particular task is to create sonorous, kinesthetic, gestural, and visual links between the heterogeneous realms of what can be said and what can only be felt (140).

Drawing on the insights of cognitive poetics, Coats notes that this kind of rhythmic or patterned children's poetry enables children to feel "at home in their own bodies as well as in their social, languaged worlds" (135).

QUESTIONS TO ASK WHEN APPROACHING A POEM FOR CHILDREN

- To what literary period does the poem belong?

The literary period of a poem often helps illuminate its themes and literary style. For example, John Bunyan's poetry reflects the religious concerns of the seventeenth century as well as his own Puritan ideology. While Robert Louis Stevenson wrote in the late Victorian period, his poetry reflects a Romantic view of an unspoiled childhood, with language designed to reflect that wonder. In contrast, Shel Silverstein's more informal poems reflect the twentieth-century focus on urban and suburban experience and the complex emotions triggered by life in a family and at school.

- How was the poem published and circulated?

Is the poem published individually, as part of a collection, or as a picturebook made up of a single poem? If the poem is printed alongside other poems in a collection, the surrounding ones affect its meaning. If it is printed in a picturebook, the illustrations influence the interpretation of the poem. If the poem stands alone, it might be published in a magazine or newspaper or on a website, which also provides the poem with a context to consider.

- Is the poem anonymous or attributed to a single author? If it is anonymous, is there some way to track the author?

As we saw with Jane Taylor's "Twinkle, Twinkle, Little Star," some poems that seem part of popular culture originally had signed authors and only later became anonymous. If a poem is signed, it is possible to learn more about an author's life and career, which can shed light on why he or she chose to write about certain topics and themes. Research into an author's biography can also help us explore how the poem reflects (or does not reflect) his or her culture and society.

- Is the poem a lyric poem (expressing an emotion) or a narrative poem (telling a story)?

A lyric poem tends to capture a moment in time, whereas narrative poems tell stories. A poem such as Sarah Martin's "Old Mother Hubbard" is a narrative poem, since it unfolds the narrative of a dog who at first seems to have died but uncannily comes back to life to sit in a chair, ride a goat, spin cloth, and engage in many other activities. Jean Little's "Today" is a lyric poem, conveying a single mood of quiet rebellion against the constraints of school.

- Is the child directly addressed?

In children's poetry, the child is sometimes addressed directly, as we see in Shel Silverstein's poem "Listen to the Mustn'ts," which contains the lines, "Anything can happen, child / Anything can be" (lines 7–8).

- What is the **diction** of the poem?

"Diction" refers to word choice. Is the language formal or casual? Does the poet use deliberately old-fashioned language? Roald Dahl's *Revolting Rhymes* uses informal—even slangy—language in order to poke fun at the fairy-tale tradition, whereas Francisco X. Alarcón uses concrete nouns and simple diction to convey a serious, solemn tone, as in his "Prayer of the Fallen Tree":

brothers
and sisters
come swiftly

make me
part of
your nests. (lines 1–6)

- What kinds of references or allusions does the poem include?

Allusions or references might be made to myths, the Bible, folklore, popular culture, visual arts, music, or other works for children. Some of these allusions might be footnoted, but others the reader must look up in order to understand their role in the poem. For example,

Marilyn Nelson's *Carver: A Life in Poems* is filled with very specific references to the life of George Washington Carver, but the reader is assisted by footnotes explaining them.

- How does the poem use figurative language?

Figurative language includes imagery and poetic tropes used in poetry that differ from the literal interpretation in order to achieve poetic effects. Figurative language is one tool that poets use to create powerful images, and to help the reader see things in a new and startling way. The critical reading of poetry involves the identification of figurative language and a consideration of how it contributes to the poem itself. See the list below detailing some common **tropes**, or figures of speech.

- Is the poem a "pattern poem" with a set and defined structure?

Some poems are written in patterns, such as the sonnet, haiku, or cinquain. Reading these poems critically includes an evaluation of how they make meaning within the very defined parameters of their structure. See the list (pp. 144–45) outlining some typical patterns used in poetry for children.

- What is the meter of the poem?

Poetry for children can rhyme or it can be written in free verse (which means it does not have a consistent pattern in either rhyme or meter). Some poems have a regular meter (such as iambic pentameter) and others do not. The form of a poem can have an impact on its mood, tone, and subject matter. See the list on pages 145–46 for some typical metrical forms for poetry in English.

COMMON FIGURES OF SPEECH

Figure of Speech	Explanation and Definition
Apostrophe	Apostrophe is a rhetorical figure in which the speaker addresses an absent or dead person, an abstraction (like "love"), or a personified object. For example, "Oh, you beautiful sun, shine brightly over us!"
Hyperbole	Hyperbole is exaggeration made for dramatic effect. An example: "There were millions of people on the bus."

Litotes Litotes is a form of irony that uses understatement. An example is saying "You are not unwelcome" to a guest whose visit you are excited about.

Metaphor A metaphor applies attributes of one thing to another thing in order to suggest the shared characteristics of the two. The metaphor "Her father is a rock" indicates that he is a reliable, steady person.

Metonymy Metonymy is a figure of speech where a thing or concept is described by one of its attributes or one of its parts. An example: "I finally got my own set of wheels."

Onomatopoeia Onomatopoeia describes words whose sounds suggest their meaning, such as "boom," "chirp," "sizzle," or "crackle."

Simile A simile is an explicit comparison between two things using "like" or "as." An example is "She is as tall as a giraffe."

TYPICAL PATTERNED POETRY FOR CHILDREN

Type of Poetry Description

Acrostic In an acrostic poem the first letters of the lines are capitalized and spell out a word or phrase.

Cinquain A cinquain is made up of a five-line stanza. The modern form, invented by Adelaide Crapsey, is arranged as follows:

First line: two syllables
Second line: four syllables
Third line: six syllables
Fourth line: eight syllables
Fifth line: two syllables

Couplet Couplets are two rhyming lines—one following the other—that share the same meter.

Haiku A haiku verse is three lines long and contains seventeen syllables, arranged as follows:

First line: five syllables
Second line: seven syllables
Third line: five syllables

Limerick Limericks are playful, humorous poems made up of five lines. The first, second, and fifth lines rhyme and have three stresses each, while the third and fourth lines rhyme with each other and have two stresses each.

Quatrain A quatrain is a stanza composed of four lines. It may be rhymed or unrhymed.

Tanka A tanka is a five-line verse with thirty-one syllables. All lines contain seven syllables except the first and third lines, which each contain five syllables.

TYPICAL METRICAL FORMS FOR POETRY IN ENGLISH

Metrical Form	Example
Anapestic trimeter has four feet within a line, with each foot containing two unstressed syllables followed by one stressed syllable.	"The Assyrian came down like the wolf on the fold, And his cohorts were gleaming in purple and gold; And the sheen of their spears was like stars on the sea, When the blue wave rolls nightly on deep Galilee." —Lord Byron, "The Destruction of Sennacherib," lines 1–4
Blank verse is unrhymed and often in iambic pentameter.	"But soft, what light through yonder window breaks? It is the east, and Juliet is the sun." —William Shakespeare, *Romeo and Juliet*, 2.2.2–3
Free verse avoids patterns such as rhyme and meter. There may be a rhyme, but not a pattern of rhyming.	"I celebrate myself, and sing myself, And what I assume you shall assume For every atom belonging to me as good belongs to you." —Walt Whitman, "Song of Myself," lines 1–3

Metrical Form	Example
Iambic pentameter is a line that has five metrical feet, each consisting of one iamb. An iamb is an unstressed syllable followed by a stressed syllable.	"Shall I compare thee to a summer's day? Thou art more lovely and more temperate; Rough winds do shake the darling buds of May, And summer's lease hath all too short a date." —William Shakespeare, Sonnet XVIII, lines 1–4
Trochaic tetrameter contains four feet within a line. Each foot is composed of a stressed syllable followed by an unstressed syllable, except for the last foot, which contains only a stressed syllable.	"Tyger! Tyger! burning bright In the forests of the night." —William Blake, "The Tyger," lines 1–2

READING CRITICALLY: POETRY

"Escape at Bedtime," from *A Child's Garden of Verses*

The lights from the parlour and kitchen shone out
   Through the blinds and the windows and bars;
And high overhead and all moving about,
   There were thousands of millions of stars.
There ne'er were such thousands of leaves on a tree,
   Nor of people in church or the Park,
As the crowds of the stars that looked down upon me,
   And that glittered and winked in the dark.

The Dog, and the Plough, and the Hunter, and all,
   And the star of the sailor, and Mars,
These shown in the sky, and the pail by the wall
   Would be half full of water and stars.
They saw me at last, and they chased me with cries,
   And they soon had me packed into bed;
But the glory kept shining and bright in my eyes,
   And the stars going round in my head.

"Escape at Bedtime," from Robert Louis Stevenson's *A Child's Garden of Verses* (1885), is animated by the tensions between a child's independent experience of the wonders of the night sky and the constraints of parental control. Many of the poems in *A Child's Garden of Verses* are structured around bed or bedtime, which is often attributed to Stevenson's own sickly childhood. The poet-narrator of *A Child's Garden of Verses* frequently contemplates the outside world from inside a domestic space, using play as vicarious adventure ("My Bed Is a Boat"). In "Escape at Bedtime," the child briefly moves into an outdoor space, achieving temporary autonomy. When the child is again "packed into bed," the poem asserts the persistence of the visionary imagination and yearning for the outside world: "the glory kept shining and bright in my eyes" (line 15).

Ann Colley notes that *A Child's Garden of Verses* "collapses the distant and the contiguous and, simultaneously, expands the immediate into the distant ..." (309). This is true of "Escape at Bedtime" in many ways. The speaker—drawing on the literary device of **hyperbole** or exaggeration—exclaims over the "thousands of millions of stars" which gives a sense of a vast scale: more stars than can be counted (line 4). Stevenson's use of **personification**—endowing non-human objects or phenomena with human traits—evokes stars that are actually sentient:

"crowds ... that looked down upon me, / And that glittered and winked in the dark" (lines 7–8). The distant, majestic stars make direct contact. More contact between the human world and the stars is found in the zeugma "the pail by the wall/ Would be half full of water and stars" (lines 11–12). A **zeugma** is a figure of speech where a word is applied to two other words, even when it actually only applies to one. Here the pail is said to be "half-full" of both "water" (which makes immediate sense) and "stars" (which cannot be literally true). These lines mean, simply, that the stars are reflected in the water, yet the use of the zeugma implies that the stars have been brought down to earth. The number of stars are also brought down to earth by being compared to "thousands of leaves on a tree" (line 5) and framed in reference to bastions of human civilization like "people in church or the Park" (line 6).

Many critics have described *A Child's Garden of Verses* as driven by nostalgia. Hugh Cunningham, for example, describes it as the "middle-class sentimentalizing of childhood" (154). Stevenson did indeed dedicate *A Child's Garden of Verses* to his nurse Alison Cunningham in very sentimental terms ("From Her Boy"). But the protected—and privileged—childhood of the collection is also one of constraint ("the blinds and windows and bars," line 2). Exulting in the night sky, the child is ultimately interrupted by adults: "They saw me at last, and they chased me with cries, / And they soon had me packed into bed" (lines 13–14). The "at last" here implies that the child's capture is inevitable. The "cries" of the adults express alarm over the way he has slipped out, or at minimum some excitement. The way in which the adults "packed" the speaker into bed render him or her an object to be controlled.

While adults clearly encroach on a child's freedom of movement, the imagination remains free, a hallmark of *A Child's Garden of Verses*. Colley explains the dynamic between children and adults in the collection as follows: "Adults are outsiders who enter momentarily to put the child to bed. As voices from another 'estate,' they intrude and call the child home to tea…. None, not even the kindly aunt ('Auntie's Skirts'), is fully part of the child's subjective and self-contained space" (Colley 179).

While the poem is clearly written from a child's point of view, Michael Rosen—himself a Children's Laureate in England—points to the ways that many of the poems in *A Child's Garden of Verses* move from the point of view of a child to that of a 'near-adult' (64–65). In "Escape at Bedtime," this burgeoning adult consciousness can be seen most clearly in the poem's mythological references (perhaps a marker of class privilege and male privilege, since access and knowledge of the classics was a sign of a gentleman's elite education in the period). The stars in the poem are named by their constellations, drawing on mythology. The "Dog" is Sirius (the Dog Star): the brightest star in the constellation *Canis Major*. The "Plough" is *Ursa Major* (the Big Dipper in the US); the Hunter is the constellation Orion. The "star of the sailor" is likely Polaris, the brightest star in the constellation *Ursa Minor*, which was used by sailors in the northern hemisphere to navigate because it seems as though it stays in the same location in the sky.

Many critics have grappled with what they call the "imperialist/colonial adventuring sensibility" in *A Child's Garden of Verses* as Jean Webb notes: "His numerous references in the collection to kings and soldiers, the foreignness and 'otherness' of places named, such as Africa or Malabar, catch both Stevenson's own desire and interest in travel, and also the spirit of exploration of the 1890s" (364). The child's wish in "Escape at Bedtime" to leave the domestic world and to embrace the vastness of night sky and bring it down to earth can be said to participate in kinds of exploratory imagination that might later be expressed in imperialist ventures but the poem does not engage this imperialist script very directly, unlike other poems in *A Child's Garden of Verses*.

Webb notes of *A Child's Garden of Verses* that it draws on a Romantic notion of childhood but combines it with "a Modernist sensibility, which intimates the nostalgic loss of childhood mingled with the knowledge of the darker sides of the imagination and the complexity of experience" (365). The regular rhymes and rhythms of "Escape at Bedtime" (two rhyming quatrains with alternating four-stress and three-stress lines, like a ballad) might tempt readers to consider the poem as old-fashioned—which it is in many ways—but there are elements here that look forward to modernist aesthetic innovations. The child speaker's description of continuing to dream even from bed ("And the stars going round in my head") prefigures Joycean epiphanies or Virginia Woolf's stream-of-consciousness in its stress on heightened internal experience. The poem points not only to a young person's encounter with nature, but also to the imaginative engagement that will make him a creator in his own right.

EXPLORATIONS

Review

1. What are some reasons that children are encouraged to read poetry? What were some of the reasons children were given poetry to read in the past?

2. How did poetry for children shift in the Romantic period and the nineteenth century? What kinds of childhood experiences did poetry of that period attempt to capture?

3. Name some major poets of the twentieth or twenty-first century who became well known specifically for their children's poetry. What aspects of their poetry appeal to children?

4. Summarize the debate about whether a separate tradition of poetry for children should exist. What are some examples of poems from the mainstream tradition (written for both adults and young people) that have attained the status of classics for children?

5. What is the difference between a children's poem with a regular rhythm and one written in free verse?

Reflect

1. What poem or poems from your childhood did you particularly like? How did you discover this poem or these poems?

2. Recall the skipping rhymes or other playground rhymes from your childhood. How were they different from the poems you were taught in school? What do you think adults would think of these playground rhymes?

3. Do poems in the twenty-first century still have morals? In what ways do contemporary poems or songs for children offer serious lessons?

4. Nonsense poetry and light verse are a major part of the tradition of poetry for children. Why do you think nonsense has played such an important role in children's poetry?

Investigate

1. Choose a poem that you are sure is inaccessible or difficult for child readers (a sonnet by William Shakespeare might be a good choice). Why do you think this poem would not resonate with child readers or listeners? Read the poem to a young child and take notes on his or her reactions, impressions, and ideas of what the poem is about. Did the results of this exercise match your preconceptions?

2. Think of a danger children face in the twenty-first century. Write a humorous cautionary tale in verse, looking at Shel Silverstein and Hilaire Belloc for inspiration. Then write a serious poem about the problem. How are these poems different?

3. Imagine that a friend of yours is a caregiver for an elementary-school-aged child who claims to dislike poetry. Your friend has asked you to come up with a bibliography of good poems to read to the child to change his or her mind. Compile a bibliography of six or seven poems that you think might be effective for this purpose and explain why you chose them. Verse novels could also be included in this bibliography.

4. Much of the poetry for children is based on the world that surrounds them: the immediate experience of a child. Review contemporary anthologies sold in bookstores and note any poems that reflect global concerns (such as the environment, global injustice, or historical atrocity). Repeat this exercise for collections aimed at older readers. What differences do you see between the poems written for children and those written for adults?

SUGGESTED READINGS

Ciardi, John. *The Man Who Sang the Sillies* (1961). Illustrated by Edward Gorey. This collection includes twenty-four rhyming nonsense poems celebrating eccentric behavior, silliness, and the absurdities of family life.

Clifton, Lucille. *Some of the Days of Everett Anderson* (1970). Illustrated by Evaline Ness. This is one of Clifton's eight books featuring Everett Anderson, an energetic young African American boy. The book follows the seven days of the week for its protagonist, and many of its poems deal with city life. With its illustrations by Evaline Ness, the book is a good example of a poetry picturebook.

Hughes, Langston. *The Dream Keeper and Other Poems* (1932). This is Hughes's only collection of poems specifically for young people; it contains fifty-nine of his poems. Poems in one section of the book use the pattern of blues folk songs. Other poems reflect on the importance of dreams and explore the complexities of the African American experience.

Lawson, JonArno. *Down in the Bottom of the Bottom of the Box* (2012). Illustrated by Alec Dempster. Lawson has won The Lion and the Unicorn Poetry Award several times due to the sophistication and power of his poetry. He has been compared to poets like Dennis Lee, Dr. Seuss, and Ogden Nash. Decorated with paper cuts by artist Alec Dempster, *Down in the Bottom of the Bottom of the Box* includes many poems reminiscent of nursery rhymes, and several that invoke fairy-tale imagery.

Milne, A.A. *Now We Are Six* (1927). Illustrated by E.H. Shepard. This is Milne's follow-up collection to *When We Were Very Young* (1924). It contains thirty-two poems, including "In the Dark," "The Emperor's Rhyme," and "The Knight Whose Armour Didn't Squeak." Pooh and Christopher Robin make an appearance in some poems, such as "The Journey's End," "Sneezles," and "Us Two" (a poem about "Pooh and Me"). The poems engage with a child's daily experience as well as with the realm of fantasy.

Nichols, Grace. *Come on into My Tropical Garden* (1988). In this collection, Guyana-born poet Grace Nichols sets her poems in the Caribbean, sometimes using dialect. In addition to poems that invoke domestic pleasures, the collection also includes poems about history, such as "They Were My People," which describes the experience of Nichols's ancestors, who were cane cutters.

Nye, Naomi Shihab. *A Maze Me* (2005). Illustrated by Terre Maher. *A Maze Me* is aimed at preteen girls and is divided into five sections: "Big Head," "Secret Hum," "Magical Geography," "Sweet Dreams Please," and "Something True." The poems capture the excitement and anxieties caused by friendships, family relationships, and crushes. They also include observations about the natural and social world in general.

Opie, Peter, and Iona Opie. *I Saw Esau: The Schoolchild's Pocket Book* (2000). Illustrated by Maurice Sendak. Folklorists Peter and Iona Opie first published more than 170 schoolyard rhymes in this book in 1947. *I Saw Esau* includes tongue twisters, insults, and skipping rhymes.

Silverstein, Shel. *Where the Sidewalk Ends* (1974). Known for its combination of words and images, *Where the Sidewalk Ends* is now iconic in our popular culture. It contains both serious and humorous poetry, including "The Edge of the World," "Ickle Me, Pickle Me, Tickle Me Too," and "Afraid of the Dark."

Volavková, Hana, editor. *I Never Saw Another Butterfly: Children's Drawings and Poems from Terezin Concentration Camp, 1942–1944* (1964; 1993). Expanded second edition with a foreword by Chaim Potok. The collection includes several poems by children written in the Terezin (Theresienstadt) concentration camp, nurtured by the artists who were also incarcerated there and who awaited deportation orders to concentration camps such as Auschwitz. The poems by children describe both the harsh realities of their incarceration and a happier world of creativity and natural beauty.

APPROACHES TO TEACHING "ESCAPE AT BEDTIME" [MIDDLE SCHOOL]

Learning Goals

- To analyze poetic form and the ways in which figurative language creates poetic meaning

- To write an argumentative essay (as students argue for their favorite musical setting of the poem)

- To bring together poetry and nonfiction to show how factual information can enhance the appreciation of poetry, and the ways in which poetry can in turn enhance our understanding of the natural world.

Activity One: Poetic Form

Part 1: "Escape at Bedtime" is a narrative poem written in past tense, a poetic choice that may well contribute to the critical view that nostalgia animates the poem. Ask the students to rewrite one of the poem's stanzas in present tense, modeling the process by doing a couple of lines together. Reassure them that their rewritten poem might lose poetic shape, including rhyme and rhythm. Reconvene the class to discuss how the poem changes if its verb tenses shift. Discuss Stevenson's choice to write the poem in past tense, and the mood it creates for the reader.

Part 2: Listen to three or four musical settings of "Escape at Bedtime" (these can be found on Spotify and YouTube as well as in music libraries). Discuss some of the artistic choices made by these composers as they set the poem to music. Students will then choose their favorite setting and write one or two pages describing why they chose it as the best setting, giving reasons for their answers.

Part 3: Discuss the following question in class. How do the allusions to various stars, planets, and constellations work in the poem? Do you need to know what they are in order to understand the poem? Can they be figured out by context? From the answers to these questions, discuss whether the poem is aimed at a child reader, an adult reader, or both and how it reaches out to multiple audiences. The students will then write a page about the intended audience(s) for the poem, and how it affects their interpretation of the poem.

Part 4: Poetic Devices and Diction

A. In "Escape at Bedtime," the literary device of personification is used for the speaker; the stars look down on the speaker and they wink. Explain the use of personification to the class, reading the relevant lines out loud as you do so. Discuss why Stevenson wanted to describe the movement of the stars in terms of human action.

B. Explain the concept of **diction** or word choice to the students—the word choice and style of speaking used in a poem. Talk about the use of the following words or phrases in the poem (or any others you wish to include):

- "shone out"

- "high overhead"

- "There ne'er were"

- "glittered"

- "glory"

Consider what mood Stevenson was trying to convey by using these particular words and phrases. As a class, write out some alternative word choices that Stevenson could have used, and discuss how the meaning and experience of the poem shifts with changes in word choice and diction.

Activity Two: Discovery of the Natural World

Read "Escape at Bedtime" alongside a book identifying the constellations, and then go out (weather and visibility permitting) and view the stars, planets, and constellations mentioned in "Escape at Bedtime" yourself. Alternatively, you can use the iPad application "Night Sky" or a star chart to observe the night sky. Ask the students to write a page responding to the following questions:

- Did you feel connected to the stars and constellations, as the speaker in the poem does? Did you find it difficult to identify the constellations?

- Were you inspired by the speaker of "Escape at Bedtime" to have your own encounter with the night sky? Did the book about constellations (or star chart, or iPad App) help you understand the poem better, and in what ways?

FAIRY TALES

Hoodwinked (2005), directed by Cory Edwards, Todd Edwards, and Tony Leech, recounts the story of "Little Red Riding Hood" in a way it has never been told before. In this animated film, a confrontation between the Wolf, the Grandmother, "Red" herself, and a Woodchopper triggers a criminal investigation. A detective frog named Flippers collects a statement from each character in turn. However, each one offers a contradictory story—a postmodern twist on the old tale, stressing multiple points of view and the difficulty of getting to the "real" story.

The film offers comic and ironic touches, many of which appeal to the sophistication of adult viewers. For example, the Grandmother is portrayed not as a fragile old lady but as a wild adventurer devoted to extreme sports. The crime in question is the theft of several coveted recipes that Grandmother uses in her bakery business; the culprit is a cute, seemingly innocent bunny. The arch humor of the film undercuts the traditional sincerity we tend to associate with fairy tales, acknowledging fairy-tale conventions while making fun of them.

Hoodwinked is one of a number of contemporary movies that lampoon fairy-tale conventions. Even the Disney Studios parodied their own fairy-tale tradition with *Enchanted* (2007), starring actress Amy Adams as a princess stranded in the very gritty "real" world of New York City. In one sequence, she sings a "Happy Working Song" (a parody of Snow White's "Whistle While You Work") to a chorus of rats, cockroaches, and pigeons. The popular movie *Shrek* (2001) features romance and adventure with the green ogre Shrek, the princess Fiona (who is more than a little ogre-like herself), and stock characters from fairy tales.

Opposite: "Snow White" by Arthur Rackham, 1909.

The fact that fairy tales are continually used and reinvented in film, television, and written literature shows that they still play an important role in both popular and childhood culture. Yet, in modern times, the social and political functions of fairy tales have been examined critically because of the messages they send about social class, gender, and sexuality. While some critics see fairy tales as containing radical or subversive potential, others see them as enforcing traditional social and political norms.

This chapter will consider the following critical questions:

- What is the relationship between the oral tales of the premodern period and the fairy tales that were written down after the sixteenth century?

- How do we define the fairy tale?

- What are some of the social functions of fairy tales?

- What are some ways of reading the happy endings of fairy tales? How do we interpret fairy tales that lack a happy ending?

- What themes and messages do fairy tales offer about class, gender, and sexual identity?

- What are the racial politics of traditional and modern fairy tales?

DEFINITION OF THE FAIRY TALE

The term "fairy tale" is a literal translation of *conte de fées*, a term coined by the seventeenth-century women writers in France who were some of the most important innovators in the written fairy-tale form. The name "fairy tales" is in fact somewhat misleading, since very few fairy tales actually include fairies. Some literary fairy tales are derived from medieval sources, some have their origins in ancient stories and myths, and others were the original compositions of nineteenth- and twentieth-century writers.

One definition of the **fairy tale**—from the *Oxford English Dictionary*—is as follows: "any of various short tales having folkloric elements and featuring fantastic or magical events or characters." Yet scholars continue to debate the meaning of the term. In his introduction to *The Oxford Companion to Fairy Tales: The Western Fairy Tale Tradition from Medieval to Modern* (2000), Jack Zipes notes that "fairy tales have been defined in so many ways that it boggles the mind to think that they can be categorized as a genre" (xv). Many scholars of the literary fairy tale define it as a genre that draws on the oral folk tale, which is collectively authored and shared. However, the literary fairy tale is distinguished from the oral folk tale by the fact that it is written down and has a definite author, such as the Grimm brothers, Charles Perrault, or Hans Christian Andersen. As Zipes explains, the oral folk tale "was (and still is) an oral narrative form cultivated by non-literate and literate people to express the manner in which they perceived and perceive nature and their social order and their wish to satisfy their needs and wants" (*Breaking* 7). In contrast, the literary fairy tale of the sixteenth, seventeenth, and eighteenth centuries "experimented with and expanded upon the stock motifs, figures and plots of the fairy tale," and "reflected a change in values and ideological conflicts in the transitional period from feudalism to early capitalism" (*Breaking* 10).

Fairy tales can be distinguished from **legends**, traditional stories featuring a notorious or legendary figure, where the story has not been verified, proven, or authenticated. They are also distinguished from **myths**, which are stories that take place outside human time, often featuring supernatural heroes and gods and goddesses. While myths (such as those featuring the gods and goddesses of Ancient Greece) are closely tied to religious and ritual practices and regarded as true by believers, folk tales and fairy tales are regarded as fictional stories. In her own attempt to describe the fairy tale, Maria Tatar calls them narratives "set in a fictional world where preternatural events and supernatural intervention are taken wholly for granted" (*Hard Facts* 33).

Fairy tales are known for their transformation and reinvention of very basic story structures, as we see in the following synopsis by Roger Sale:

> A girl is in a wood. Give her a brother and one has "Hansel and Gretel," give
> her many brothers and sisters and one has "Hop o' My Thumb," send the girl to
> dwarves and one has "Snow White," to bears and one has "Goldilocks," to grand-
> mother and one has "Little Red Riding Hood." (29)

While the differences among the tales he cites are more significant than Sale indicates here, folklore scholars have long identified common fairy-tale motifs, including—but not limited to—magic spells, animal helpers, powerful talismans, wishes, and threatening forest spaces. Fairy tales have even been classified by the use of these motifs and the patterns that emerge when these are repeated in different tales.

Fairy Tales and Revision

Fairy tales tend to exist in multiple versions. Some of those variations date from centuries ago, as storytellers and compilers drew on previous stories to create their own versions. Fairy tales are also constantly subject to the change and modification known as **revision**.

"Revision" refers to a change or amendment of a text, which is also sometimes described as "**adaptation**." In a fairy-tale revision, an author or teller introduces fresh elements to the plot, setting, or characters of a story but retains enough similarity to the original to make it recognizable as essentially the same tale. Contemporary writers often turn to older fairy tales to reinvent them for a new audience (sometimes with an ironic or humorous twist). In that case, "revision" is also "re-vision," or seeing fairy tales anew.

FAIRY TALES WORLDWIDE

There are variants of familiar fairy tales all over the world. For example, variants of "Cinderella" can be found in Zimbabwe, the Philippines, Korea, Turkey, Cambodia, Hawaii, the Caribbean, and Egypt (Hurley 229–30). One of the oldest, "Yeh-hsien," comes from China and was first recorded by Tuan Ch'eng-shih (800–863 CE) in his book *Yu-yang Tsa-tsu*. Like Cinderella, Yeh-hsien is mistreated by her stepmother. She befriends a fish, who thrives under her care, but her stepmother kills it and buries the bones. An old man descends from the sky and leads her to the bones; the bones grant her wish to go to a local festival dressed in great finery. She leaves behind a slipper, which is sold to a king. Adoring its small size, he tries to fit it on all the women of the country until he finds Yeh-hsien and weds her. These variants on the "Cinderella" tale are likely the result of continued cultural and literary exchange between countries, with common narratives adapted in response to local circumstances. Alternatively, common themes in fairy tales might have arisen because people in different cultures confront similar challenges in human life, such as sibling rivalry, scarcity, and oppression.

FAIRY TALES AND ANCIENT MYTH

Some fairy tales are derived from ancient myths. Jeanne-Marie Leprince de Beaumont published a version of "Beauty and the Beast" in 1756. Beauty's ill-fated request for a rose causes her father to be threatened by a powerful and ungainly beast; she saves her father by promising to live with the Beast in his stead. Though she expects that the Beast will devour her, Beauty is instead well treated. The Beast expresses his love and repeatedly asks her to marry him, but she refuses until the Beast becomes ill. Realizing her love for him, Beauty accepts the Beast's proposal, whereupon he is turned into a handsome prince. While this tale seems original, the ancient myth of Cupid and Psyche, first written down in Apuleius's *Golden Ass* (c. 150 CE), is a possible source. In the myth of Cupid and Psyche, a woman is forbidden to look at her divine husband—or she will face doom. Breaking the taboo, she is exiled, but in the end is united with her husband, who

The Chinese version of the "Cinderella" story, called "Yeh-hsien," retold in 2006 by Dawn Casey and illustrated by Richard Holland.

sincerely loves her. Jerry Griswold contends that "Beauty and the Beast" and this myth might have "different looks," but "if we were to x-ray both stories, we would notice that they share similar skeletal structures ... both tales tell of an inequality between marriage partners: in 'Cupid and Psyche' between gods and mortals, in Beaumont's tale between a merchant family and an aristocrat" (86). The links between myths and fairy tales are both thematic and structural, and both can be said to address common human anxieties, concerns, and hopes. However, fairy tales tend to address the experiences of mortal people rather than gods and goddesses, even though they do include supernatural elements such as magic.

A HISTORY OF THE LITERARY FAIRY TALE IN THE WESTERN WORLD

The Early Modern Roots of the Literary Fairy Tale

In the Western world, the tradition of written literary fairy tales is thought to have begun in the sixteenth century with stories that were definitely not aimed at children. Giovanni Francesco Straparola's *Le Piacevoli Notti* (*Pleasant Nights*) (1550–53) features stories— many of them fairy tales—told by a group of aristocrats living near Venice in a rented castle. Later, Giambattista Basile published the *Pentamerone* (1634–36), which also featured urbane stories recounted through conversation.

Several women wrote fairy tales in the 1690s in France, including Marie-Catherine le Jumel de Barneville (Countess d'Aulnoy), Madame de Murat, and Marie-Jeanne L'Héritier de Villandon. These women writers never claimed to capture a "folk" tradition but rather tried to evoke some of the sophistication of the literary "salons" of the day: social gatherings that featured learned discourse and wit. D'Aulnoy's "L'île de la félicité" ("The Island of Happiness"), which appears as a tale in her novel *L'histoire d'Hypolite, Comte de Duglas* (1690), is often credited as the first published fairy tale. Before the 1980s and 1990s, little attention was paid to the contributions of these writers, despite the fact that "more than two-thirds of the tales that appeared during the first wave of fairy-tale production in France (between 1690 and 1715) were written by women" (Harries 17).

In 1697, Charles Perrault published his *Histoires ou contes du temps passé, avec des moralités: Contes de ma mère l'Oye*, introducing his versions of several fairy tales of iconic significance, such as "Little Red Riding Hood," "Sleeping Beauty," and "Cinderella." Perrault's frontispiece features the "mère l'Oye" or "Mother Goose" of the title, playing on the fiction that a wise old woman had crafted the tales. However, to please an aristocratic and courtly audience, he recast the folklore and oral tales by adding details about the fashions of the day and sly asides about human

The frontispiece from Charles Perrault's *Histoires ou contes du temps passé,* modified for a later English edition.

nature. Perrault was himself a frequent attendee of the salons and gatherings hosted by the women writers of fairy tales. Jack Zipes describes the fairy tales of Perrault and his female contemporaries as "complex symbolic acts intended to reflect upon mores, norms, and habits organized for the purpose of reinforcing a hierarchically arranged civilizing process in a particular society" (*Happily* 3).

As suggested by his book's title, Perrault always ended his fairy tales with a moral, although these lessons sometimes sat unevenly with the tales themselves. Perrault's moral for "Little Red Riding Hood," for example, compares the wolf to men with bad intentions:

> Young ladies whom they talk to on the street
> They follow to their homes and through the hall,
> And upstairs to their rooms; when they're there
> They're not as friendly as they might appear:
> These are the most dangerous wolves of all. (103)

Perrault's moral is obviously not intended for children, but his desire to infuse the tales with a moral was the beginning of the tradition of associating fairy tales with moral instruction.

Fairy Tales in the Nineteenth Century

Fairy tales in the nineteenth century were collected and written by three major figures: Hans Christian Andersen; Andrew Lang; and Jakob and Wilhelm Grimm, who published their two-volume collection *Kinder und Hausmärchen* (1812–15) in order to preserve Germanic folklore for other scholars. Part of the Romantic movement, the Grimm brothers were working at a time of increased national consciousness: "They wanted to capture the 'pure' voice of the German people and to preserve in print the oracular poetry of the common people" (Tatar, *Annotated* 341). As Vicki Roberts-Gassler points out, however, the Grimms "actually gathered material from a very limited area, using written tales sent by a small circle of friends, mostly educated, unmarried young women of a middle- or upperclass background, many of whom had French Huguenot connections, rather than scouring the countryside in search of peasant informants" (252). This is not to say that the tales were not rooted in myth and folklore, but that they were changed by being written down for an educated audience. In fact, the brothers "rewrote extensively and continuously from the first edition to the seventh" (Roberts-Gassler 252).

One of the Grimms' most distinctive changes to the tales was a movement toward a child audience. As Maria Tatar notes, "What had originally been designed as documents for scholars gradually turned into bedtime reading for children" (*Annotated* 343). In *The*

Hard Facts of the Grimms' Fairy Tales (1987; rev. ed. 2003), Tatar considers the way in which the Grimm brothers altered the stories to aim them more explicitly at children. In the preface to the 1812 first edition, the Grimms wrote, "We have tried to collect these tales in as pure a form as possible" (translated by Tatar, *Hard Facts* 210). In the second edition of 1819, they had quite a different approach: "We have carefully eliminated every phrase not appropriate for children" (Tatar, *Hard Facts* 217). To make the tales more suitable for children, the Grimms purged them of sexually explicit material and emphasized the traditional roles of women. Perhaps surprisingly, they *enhanced* the violence of the tales. In 1825, the Grimms created the "Small Edition" ("Klein Ausgabe") for children, whittling down their collected 210 tales to the 50 tales they deemed best for children—their own contribution to the establishment of a fairy-tale canon. Eventually the tales made their way to the English-speaking world through Edgar Taylor's 1823 translation, *German Popular Stories*.

Hans Christian Andersen wrote literary fairy tales in Denmark in the mid nineteenth century. Tess Lewis notes that unlike Perrault and the Grimms, who "collected or embellished existing myths and oral folklore," Andersen "created original symbols that have entered our cultural consciousness as deeply as any primal myth" (679). Andersen's artistic goals were different from those of the Grimm brothers. While influenced by the oral folk and fairy tales of his youth, he was trying to write original material. Andersen's fairy tales include uplifting stories such as "The Ugly Duckling," who triumphs at the end as a resplendent swan; tragic stories such as "The Steadfast Tin Soldier," with its plot of unrequited love; and "The Little Match Girl," whose indigent heroine perishes in the cold night. Andersen's "The Emperor's New Clothes" has a hard edge as a satire of the "vanity and pretensions of Denmark's staid, conformist merchant class with just enough humor and distance to soften the satirical bite" (Lewis 679).

In England, Andrew Lang did much to popularize the fairy tale in his twelve "color books," which include *The Blue Fairy Book* (1889) and *The Green Fairy Book* (1892), containing collections of mostly European folk and fairy tales, many of which are given a very English spin. Joseph Jacobs was another influential figure in the publication of fairy tales in England. A scholar of folklore, Jacobs also produced several collections of English fairy tales for young readers, including *English Fairy Tales* (1890) and *More English Fairy Tales* (1894). *English Fairy Tales* contained versions of "Jack and the Beanstalk" and "Henny Penny."

Translations of classic fairy tales by Perrault, the Grimms, Andersen, and others also proliferated, often in lavishly illustrated editions. As readers began to expect the fairy tale to be a compact story, this succinct form became the default model for the genre. Whereas the seventeenth-century *conteuse* (storyteller) had used "elaborate framing techniques, embedded stories, transformations of old tales and motifs into new constellations" (Harries 100), the brief and compact form was now the dominant nineteenth-century mode.

As fairy tales became a literary tradition, a "classical fairy tale canon" came into existence at least as early as the nineteenth century, according to Jack Zipes. A **canon** can be defined as those texts that by social and cultural consensus have been acknowledged as the most important or central works of a period, country, or genre. The fairy-tale canon includes tales such as "Cinderella," "Little Red Riding Hood," "Sleeping Beauty," "Hansel and Gretel," "Rapunzel," "The Frog Prince," "Snow White," "Bluebeard," "Beauty and the Beast," "Jack and the Beanstalk," "The Princess and the Pea," "The Little Mermaid," "The Ugly Duckling," "Aladdin and the Magic Lamp," and "Ali Baba and the Forty Thieves" (*Why Fairy Tales Stick* 1). A fairy-tale **classic** is one that has endured over several generations and which is esteemed on both aesthetic and cultural grounds.

From the sheer familiarity of Jack Zipes's list of fairy tales, it is clear that the notions of "canon" and "classic" continue to matter. Yet there have been many challenges to the dominance of the existing fairy-tale canon, partly because folklore and fairy-tale scholars are always learning more about the genre and making neglected tales more available. The inclusion of the seventeenth-century women writers of fairy tales mentioned above is one example of the revision of the canon. Most literary scholars agree that there is no such thing as an entirely stable "canon" or "classic," since the tastes and aesthetic judgements of readers are always changing.

Oral Tales versus Literary Fairy Tales

In *Fairy Tales: A New History* (2009), Ruth B. Bottigheimer challenges prevailing notions of the "folk" origins of literary texts, arguing instead for a "book-based" history of the fairy tale. She claims that fairy-tale writers such as Perrault and the Grimms derived their tales from their literary predecessors, not from "folk" informants who recounted the tales out loud. Bottigheimer points out that there is no empirical proof that fairy tales originated from oral stories, since the oral transmission of a tale is by its nature impossible to trace. However, fairy-tale scholars continue to stress the interaction of oral and written elements in the invention and transmission of fairy tales. In her review of Bottigheimer's book, Cristina Bacchilega remarks that although contemporary scholars have been aware for a long time that the Grimms collected fairy tales not from illiterate peasants but from educated informants, "most of us are not jumping to the conclusion that tales of magic or fairy tales were not also circulating orally among the lower classes in Europe" (470). The relationship between written and oral tales continues to this day, which adds further support to Bacchilega's critique of Bottigheimer's purely text-based model of fairy tales. Written fairy tales are continually retold in oral form (sometimes using new media such as film and streaming video). In turn, oral tellers make constant changes to the themes, characters, and emphases of written tales as they recount the stories out loud.

Fairy Tales: Mass Media and Film

Zipes notes that by the early twentieth century, fairy tales were "transmitted by radio and film, through advertisements of different kinds, and a plethora of illustrated books and postcards. With the rise of film, cartoons, comic strips, and musical shows at the beginning of the twentieth century, fairy tales became a major staple of all forms of the mass media" (*Why Fairy Tales Stick* 99). The Disney Studios are known for their iconic films dramatizing fairy tales, which largely draw from Perrault or the Grimms, including *Snow White* (1937), *Sleeping Beauty* (1959), and *Beauty and the Beast* (1991). One of Walt Disney's goals was to make European culture accessible and appealing to American audiences, and he was therefore drawn to the European fairy-tale tradition. Many fairy-tale critics and readers lament the fact that Disney's versions have become so dominant in the public consciousness that many children are no longer aware of fairy tales in any other spoken, written, or cinematic form.

THE SOCIAL FUNCTION OF FAIRY TALES

Critics and creative writers disagree on the social and political impact of the fairy tale. In their oral form, fairy tales united families and communities. Many tales were a means to express the ambitions (of wealth and status), fantasies (of royalty and power), and fears (infanticide, maternal neglect, rape, etc.) of the folk. In his study *The Great Cat Massacre* (1984), historian Robert Darnton points out, for example, how the emphasis on food and satiety in many tales were the ultimate fantasy for individuals who never had quite enough to eat.

Marina Warner refers to the "optative" qualities of fairy tales: "Fairy tales are not passive or active; their mood is optative—announcing what might be" (xx). **Optative** is a grammatical term for sentences that express a wish or hope ("If only I were rich!"). Warner means, then, that fairy tales have a quality of "wishing" or "desiring." They have a utopian quality, which means in part that they help envision a better world. A tale such as "Puss in Boots," for example, imagines a disenfranchised younger brother triumphing through the wiles of his extremely clever cat. On the other hand, fairy tales might encourage indifference to real conditions in favor of a belief in wish fulfillment. This quality has led to some of the feminist critiques of fairy tales such as "Cinderella"—that they offer a sense of false hope or the unrealistic goal of being rescued by a prince.

Joyce Carol Oates notes that many fairy tales are not subversive but rather are "politically and morally conservative to a degree that seems puzzling" (262):

To interpret "Cinderella: or, The Little Glass Slipper" as a populist rags-to-riches romance is to totally misinterpret its fundamental story, which has to do with the putative injustice of denying one of aristocratic birth her rightful privilege, and with the drama of disguised worth.... In a crucial sense fairy tales work to subvert romantic wishes, for they repeatedly confirm "order" and redress dislocations of privileged birth while leaving wholly unchanged the hierarchical basis for such privileging. (263)

Yet any conclusion about the social or political impact of fairy tales depends on which tale or set of tales one focuses on. A tale such as "Puss in Boots" inverts the established order, as the wily cat elevates his low-born master to a position of power and wealth. A tale such as "The Goose Girl" affirms the established order by stressing the importance of noble birth. All readers bring their own vantage points and social positions to their readings of the tales.

FAIRY TALES AND UNHAPPY ENDINGS

Some fairy tales end with the line "And they lived happily ever after." Not all fairy tales end happily, however, and they never have. An obvious example is Perrault's version of "Little Red Riding Hood," in which the young girl is in fact eaten by the wolf and not rescued. Several of the original Grimm fairy tales were notable for their grisly, unhappy endings.

Fairy tales written by Hans Christian Andersen often strike a melancholy, tragic note. "The Little Match Girl," for example, depicts a match seller who lights her remaining matches one by one in the bitter winter, experiencing radiant visions of a Christmas tree, a holiday feast, and the reassuring voice of her dead grandmother before she dies. As Jackie Wullschlager notes, "The difficulties, indignities and sense of exclusion that made up Andersen's childhood underlay every word he wrote: his sympathy for the outsider, his identification with the child or an animal such as the duckling or the nightingale, ignored or unheeded above the crowd and babble; his vision of life as a solitary struggle often ending in tragedy" (12). Writing in part for an adult audience, Oscar Wilde used the fairy-tale form to make trenchant points about the selfishness and mob mentality of individuals and communities. "The Happy Prince," for example, tells the story of a gold-covered statue—the prince of the title—and the swallow who comes to live with him. The statue, filled with compassion for the destitute of the city, asks the swallow to distribute the jewels of his eyes and his gold leaf to the poor of the town. The swallow gives up his own desire to go to Europe and freezes to death. In the end, the townspeople discard the denuded statue, throwing it "on a dust heap where the dead Swallow was also lying." The tale ends with a poignant dialogue:

"Bring me the two most precious things in the city," said God to one of His Angels; and the Angel brought Him the leaden heart and the dead bird. "You have rightly chosen," said God, "for in my garden of Paradise this little bird shall sing for ever-more, and in my city of gold the Happy Prince shall praise me." (Wilde 22)

Here there is a striking combination of unappreciated sacrifice and spiritual redemption. The unhappy endings of some fairy tales, then, have multiple functions: to wring pathos out of a touching situation, to arouse pity for the downtrodden, or to spur readers to envision a better world by considering the cruelties of our current social organization.

INTERPRETING FAIRY TALES

Fairy tales are so enduring and persistent across cultures that they have become a magnet for theorists of all types to explore questions of human development, psychology, and social organization. Some intellectuals and thinkers focus on the insights that fairy tales offer into the human mind and human emotions. Others look to the fairy tale to illumi-nate the aspirations of non-elite people in the premodern age. Others focus on the ways in which fairy tales reflect and shape gender roles and sexuality.

Psychoanalytical Approaches

Both Sigmund Freud and Carl Jung viewed the fairy tale as shedding light on individual and collective psychology. With their rich symbolism, fairy tales have a unique capacity to speak to emotional experience. A Freudian reading of the fairy tale stresses individual development, dream imagery, and family relations. One of the most famous applications of Freudian psychoanalytical criticism to fairy tales is the work of Bruno Bettelheim, who argues in *The Uses of Enchantment: The Meaning and Importance of Fairy Tales* (1976) that children use fairy tales to come to terms with their desires and struggles on an uncon-scious level as they move through the requisite stages of development, including the oe-dipal conflict and sibling rivalry. To Bettelheim, "Hansel and Gretel" speaks to anxieties children might have that their parents will abandon them and helps to equip a child to move toward independence in adulthood. When the children nibble on the witch's gin-gerbread house and use an unreliable trail of bread crumbs to find their way home, their actions constitute an unsuccessful "oral regression" that sets them back on their progres-sion to maturity. At the time of its publication, Bettelheim's book was very influential as a response to parents and teachers who felt that children should be shielded from the darker side of fairy tales. Since that time, he has been criticized for his ahistorical vision of the fairy tale, because he did not account for historical variations in the fairy tales he used to describe universal psychological experiences.

A Jungian reading stresses how fairy tales speak to what Carl Jung called the "collective unconscious": the unconscious mind universally shared by all humanity. The collective unconscious is organized into preexisting forms called **archetypes**: symbols, plots, and patterns that organize all human psychological experience. Carl Jung's disciple Marie-Louise von Franz wrote several studies of fairy tales, including *The Interpretation of Fairy Tales* (rev. ed. 1996; originally published as *An Introduction to the Interpretation of Fairy Tales*, 1970). She viewed fairy tales as the purest expression of the recurring archetypal images and symbols explored by Jung, including the Self (which regulates identity); the Shadow (the opposite of the ego but part of the Self); the Anima (the feminine image in a man's psyche); and the Animus (the masculine image in a woman's psyche). In contrast to Bettelheim's interpretation, von Franz sees "Hansel and Gretel," with its mutual support and cooperation between brother and sister, as speaking to the need to balance both male and female elements of the unconscious.

Sociohistorical Approaches

While the psychological approach stresses the symbolic and universal power of the fairy tale, other critics see the fairy tale as reflecting specific sociohistorical realities. Robert Darnton calls French fairy tales "one of the few points of entry into the mental world of peasants under the Old Regime" (18). Ruth B. Bottigheimer cautions, however, that "it is very easy to mistake fairy tale conventions for historical evidence" ("Fairy Tales" 346). For example, a fairy tale with seven brothers does not necessarily indicate the historical prevalence of large families; rather, it might simply manifest the fairy-tale convention of significant numbers such as three and seven.

The sociohistorical work of Jack Zipes is a useful corrective to Darnton's approach, as Zipes embeds fairy tales in their literary contexts while nonetheless retaining a historical focus. In his *Breaking the Magic Spell: Radical Theories of Folk and Fairy Tales* (1979; rev. ed. 2002), Zipes argues

Kay Nielsen's 1925 illustration of "Hansel and Gretel," as told by the Grimm brothers.

that as a narrative form expressing the hopes and aspirations of the folk, fairy tales were based on a utopian idea of a better future and the empowerment of the powerless. He places "Hansel and Gretel" in the context of the famines and wars at the end of the eighteenth century, noting the very real threat of child abandonment during the period: "The struggle depicted in the tale is against poverty and against witches who have houses of food and hidden treasures" (38). In killing the witch, Hansel and Gretel "allow the common people to learn how they might survive in an unjust society and struggle with hope" (39). Zipes believes that mass media distribution of fairy tales through film, television, and popular books (which he calls the "culture industry") has drained tales such as "Hansel and Gretel" of their radical potential. Becoming aware of the original and subsequent history of the tales is to "break the magic spell." Zipes's emphasis on the need "to grasp the socio-historical forces" bearing on the tales (xi) applies to each teller of the tales, each writer, each publishing situation, and each reading situation.

Jack Zipes's most recent work expands on his previous sociohistorical approach, drawing on the cultural evolutionary theory of memes—units of information transmitted through culture—to consider the shifting nature of folktales as well as their continued existence. In this vision, fairy tales "are informed by a human disposition to action ... to transform the world and make it more adaptable to human needs, while we also try to change and make ourselves fit for the world" (*Irresistible Fairy Tale*, 2). As Zipes notes,

> At their best, fairy tales constitute the most profound articulation of the human struggle to form and maintain a civilizing process. They depict symbolically the opportunities for humans to adapt to changing environments, and they reflect the conflicts that arise when we fail to establish civilizing codes commensurate with the needs of large groups. The more we learn to relate to other groups and realize that their survival is linked to ours, the more we might construct social codes that guarantee humane relationships. In this regard, many fairy tales are utopian, but they are also uncanny because they tell us what we need, and unsettle us by showing what we lack and how we might compensate. ("Why Fairy Tales Are Immortal")

Feminist Responses to Fairy Tales

The most prolonged critique of fairy tales over the last several decades has been from feminist critics who feel that the tales reinforce gender stereotypes such as female passivity and an emphasis on stereotyped forms of female beauty. Feminist critics of the 1970s and 1980s rebelled against the traditional canon of fairy tales—those by Perrault, the Grimms, Andersen, Lang, and Disney Studios. One early debate unfolded between Alison Lurie and Marcia Lieberman. Lurie cited the presence of assertive girl and women characters in fairy tales, most notably Gretel, who instigates her brother's and her own escape from an evil witch. Marcia Lieberman argued to the contrary in a 1972 article called "'Some Day My Prince Will Come': Female Acculturation Through the Fairy Tale." In Lieberman's estimation, most fairy tales feature passive female characters who rely on beauty and meekness for success in plots that are essentially competitions between women. Most of her article is a close reading of the tales in Andrew Lang's *The Blue Fairy Book* (1889). Neither Lurie nor Lieberman used a wide sampling of texts for their investigations.

One insight of Lieberman's that has endured is the idea that fairy tales contribute to a child's socialization, or their entrance into the wider culture:

> These tales present a picture of sexual roles, behavior, and psychology, and a way of predicting outcome or fate according to sex…. A close examination of the treatment of girls and women in fairy tales reveals certain patterns which are keenly interesting not only in themselves, but also as material which has undoubtedly played a major contribution in forming the sexual role concept of children, and in suggesting to them the limitations that are imposed by sex upon a person's chance of success in various endeavors. (384)

In a study of the link between fairy tales and perceptions of the importance of physical beauty for women and girls, Lori Baker-Sperry and Liz Grauerholz argue that "[c]hildren's fairy tales, which emphasize such things as women's passivity and beauty, are indeed gendered scripts and serve to legitimatize and support the dominant gender system" (711). Their work reveals "strong associations between beauty and goodness and rewards" (724). They end, however, on a hopeful note: "The recent film *Shrek*, whose main woman character is ultimately transformed into an ogre rather than the beautiful woman she was believed to be, may begin to challenge the value and meaning of women's beauty" (725).

It should be noted that there are feminist alternatives to the social-realistic approach that Lieberman and others represent. Vanessa Joosen opens up the possibility of "interpreting [fairy tales] as fantasies" (131), arguing that the events of the tales are not meant to reflect life as it is lived—or should be lived. The kind of critical thinking that Joosen advocates can potentially include child readers, especially if parents, teachers, and friends encourage a critical perspective on the fairy tales and are willing to discuss both the "make-believe" fantasies of the stories and the kinds of values those "make-believe" stories offer.

Fairy-Tale Revision as Critical Practice

Many second- and third-wave feminists seeking to challenge the traditional fairy-tale canon embraced feminist fairy-tale revisions, which functioned as "fairy tales with a twist."
Examples include Babette Cole's *Princess Smartypants* (1986), about a princess "who enjoyed being a Ms.," and *Prince Cinders* (1987), in which the protagonist is not a girl suffering from an evil stepmother and stepsisters but an ungainly and awkward young man
whose brothers abuse him while they party at the Palace Disco. Robert Munsch's *The
Paper Bag Princess* (1980) is one of the most popular feminist revisions of fairy tales from
the period. A dragon has destroyed Elizabeth's kingdom, burning her clothes so that she
needs to wear a paper bag and kidnapping her fiancé, Prince Ronald. She challenges the
dragon to a series of tasks such as burning forests with fire and flying around the world
multiple times. Tired from these labors, the dragon falls asleep. Elizabeth rescues Ronald,
but he tells her to return when she is dressed more appropriately. Elizabeth, disgusted
with Ronald, retorts with the famous line, "You look like a real prince, but you are a bum"
(n.p.). She is last seen walking into the sunset, head held high.

In recent years some critics have seen Munsch's narrative as an inadequate response
to sexism in the traditional fairy tale. Leslee Farish Kuykendal and Brian W. Sturm claim
that "to truly re-vision a fairy tale, thereby creating a work that is artistically new and
rings true to a child, feminist authors must cease attempting to simply reverse gender
roles. Rather, they must re-vision the entire work and create something from the ground
up" (40). Their call is provocative and opens the question of what a revision needs to be
successful. Judging from its strong sales figures, Munsch's book remains popular, perhaps
demonstrating that the gender reversal in the book can still be effective for young readers
who are put off by the sexism of the traditional fairy tale and enjoy puncturing the myth
of the passive princess.

Several recent retellings have, however, offered the complex rereadings that Kuykendal and Sturm advocate, in part because they are aimed at a young adult market whose
readers are imagined to be more sophisticated. For example, Gail Carson Levine's *Ella
Enchanted* (1997), inspired by the tale of "Cinderella," tells the story of a girl given the
"gift" of obedience by the fairy Lucinda, a curse that makes her obey any order she receives. With great struggle, Ella ultimately defies an order, finally breaking the curse. Here
the focus is not on heroes and villains but on the psychology of a young girl who seeks
genuine independence and freedom from manipulation.

Vanessa Joosen argues that fairy-tale retellings create powerful opportunities for critical reading:

> Fairy-tale retellings can provide children and adolescents with a new perspective
> on a well-known narrative. By exploiting the critical potential of their intertextual

link with the traditional story, these "alternative" tales may give young readers a first impression of what literary theory can bring about: fairy-tale retellings try to make children and adolescents who make the connection with the original tale aware of issues and possible interpretations in the texts which they had not noticed before. This experience may lead to a greater alertness and understanding when they read similar stories in the future. (131)

In Joosen's model, retellings are an opportunity for critical thinking because fairy tales are part of a common culture, even if they are familiar only through Disney film versions. When she speaks of **intertextuality**, Joosen means the relationship between a prior text and a new text created when an author borrows from the prior one or references it within the new text. Retellings are capable of shedding new light on old texts, which Joosen sees as a productive critical process in its own right: revision as "re-vision."

QUEER FAIRY TALES

The love stories and marriages that are so often the focus of traditional fairy tales have been increasingly under scrutiny for their exclusive emphasis on heterosexual relationships. The mainstream fairy-tale tradition can be said to contribute to **heteronormativity**, a worldview that assumes that heterosexuality is a natural social norm, and makes the assumption that all people are or should be heterosexual. Just as feminists have sought to rewrite and revise fairy tales by elevating women to heroic roles, writers have also **queered** fairy tales to explore the lives of gay men and lesbian women and to address the heterosexist bias in a tradition that rarely depicts queer men and women and same-sex love. This is an especially urgent pursuit, given the belief that fairy tales speak to the core questions of children's development.

Linda de Haan and Stern Nijland's *King and King* (2002) is a picturebook about a young prince named Bertie "who never cared much for princesses" (n.p.). Presented with a long series of potential brides, he falls for the brother of one, Prince Leo. The two princes wed and ascend to the throne, where they live happily ever after and are known as "King and King." For the young adult audience, Malinda Lo's *Ash* (2009) is a lesbian retelling of the "Cinderella" story, in which the heroine is ultimately paired not with the prince but with the king's powerful and enigmatic huntress Kaisa. For an adult audience, Peter Cashorali's *Fairy Tales: Traditional Stories Retold for Gay Men* (1995) and Emma Donoghue's *Kissing the Witch: Old Tales in New Skins* (1997) recast fairy tales to feature same-sex unions (Cashorali's book draws on classic fairy tales and locates them in a contemporary situation). In 2014, editors and anthologists Radclyffe and Stacia Seamon published *Myth and Magic: Queer Fairy Tales*, a collection of often-erotic fairy tale retellings.

While writers have rewritten traditional tales to include same-sex love, many fairy tales in the traditional canon lend themselves to a queer reading. The Grimm brothers' tale "The Frog King, or Iron Heinrich" is one example. Faithful Heinrich is the prince's servant, and is so saddened by his master's transformation into a frog that three hoops are placed around his chest to keep his heart from bursting with grief. When he is "elated" by his master's transformation back into a prince, the hoops around his heart break.

Oscar Wilde's tales frequently feature bonds of love and friendship between male characters, such as those between the Swallow and the Happy Prince, who sleep entwined and are deeply attached. John-Charles Duffy asks whether Wilde's tales represent "an attempt to create images that embody desires he experienced as a child, but for which he could find no written representation?" (345).

The strategy, then, for thinking past the "compulsory heterosexuality" of the traditional fairy-tale corpus is to reclaim those tales that might possess a queer subtext as well as to create new fairy-tale retellings with a wider, more inclusive view of sexuality and romantic unions.

FAIRY TALES AND DISABILITY

Reading fairy tales using a disability studies approach involves critical attention to the social and political construction of physical and/or cognitive disabilities in fairy tales and retellings, as well as attention to the embodied experiences of people with disabilities in these tales. It also involves attention to narrative patterns that idealize able-bodied people or stigmatize those with disabilities. For example, in her study of disability in the Grimm's fairy tales, Ann Schmiesing discovered that physical ability often signaled virtue or goodness, while impairment signaled evildoing:

> In many fairy tales, able-bodied protagonists are thus contrasted with antagonists who exhibit or are punished with impairment. And when a disabled hero is portrayed, his heroic qualities are often brought to the fore as he triumphs despite the social stigma of his disability—a triumph typically rewarded in fairy tales with the magical erasure of his physical anomaly. (1–2)

When she noted that able-bodiedness was idealized by many of the tales, Schmiesing was describing **ableism**, an ideology that assumes "that all disabled people aspire to an able-bodied norm," and which also includes the beliefs "that disabled people are inferior to nondisabled people" and that "individuals should be defined by their disability" (5). To reject ableism is to combat the idea that able-bodied people are superior to those with disabilities, and the assumption that disabled people seek a "magical erasure of [their] physical anomaly." Schmiesing draws on a core idea of disability studies known as the social model, which contends that disability is "a social construct, requiring change in the body politic, instead of in the individual body" (5). The social model is contrasted to the medical model, which sees disability as a defect that medical intervention must cure. One historical complication of the social model is that many fairy tales with folk origins reflect the economic and cultural strictures of life as a peasant, which required much physical labor for sheer survival.

In the introduction to her book, Schmiesing argues that the term "disability" should be "an expansive and inclusive term not hemmed in by rigid categorizations." Rather than try to pin down a medical definition of disability—or even to try to ascertain the exact nature of a disability or impairment in any given Grimm tale—she examines "how the character's society constructs his or her difference as a disability" (6). For example, Schmiesing also included disease in her study, considering it within a spectrum of disability, because it too can be socially stigmatized and involve impairment. Disability also intersects with other forms of difference, as we see from Schmiesing's analysis of the gendering of disability in the Grimm tales: "females are typically given disabilities that make them more passive, whereas males often—but not always—have disabilities that mark them as Other without significantly reducing their agency" (82). Gender affects the meaning of disability in Grimm's tales and the roles that women can—or cannot—take on.

There is still a great deal of research to do in children's literature with regards to disability. Fairy tale studies are no exception, with a need to research disability in major writers like Perrault, the Grimm Brothers, and Hans Christian Andersen, but also non-canonical fairy tale writers. One striking example of a lesser-known fairy tale writer who engages with disability is Victorian writer Dinah Mulock Craik, whose *The Little Lame Prince and His Travelling Cloak* (1875) offers a complex representation of disability. In Craik's tale, Prince Dolor is dropped by a nurse as a baby. His legs stop growing so he is unable to stand. Exiled to a tower by a wicked uncle, his fairy Godmother ("Stuff-and-Nonsense") gives him some gifts: a magical flying travelling cloak to give him freedom of mobility, as well as golden spectacles and silver ears that help him see and hear from a distance. He travels around his entire kingdom and defeats his country's enemies and his own. Crowned king after his uncle's death, he is known for the wisdom he has acquired from his travels. At the end of the

Hope Dunlap illustration from the 1909 edition of *The Little Lame Prince and His Travelling Cloak*.

story, however, he abdicates in favor of his able-bodied cousin. Dolor's disability does not inhibit him from being an excellent king, but the fact that he steps aside for his cousin shows that he remains defined by his impairment.

In addition to a reexamination of the fairy tale tradition, contemporary fairy tale retellings are beginning to seek a more inclusive representation of differing abilities. The work of Jewel Kats (Michelle Meera Katyal) moves in this direction. Kats produced a series called Fairy Ability Tales, which feature characters with disabilities and other embodied differences, including works like *Cinderella's Magical Wheelchair: An Empowering Fairy Tale* (2011), illustrated by Richa Kinra, and *The Princess and the Ruby: An Autism Fairy Tale* (2012).

Kats consistently engages with ideologies of ableism in fairy tales, and many of her works also tackle society's enforcement of normative beauty standards. A project by sometimes-controversial artist aleXsandro Palombo has similar aims; he created a set of pictures of disabled Disney princesses. In his series, for example, Snow White uses a wheelchair, Pocahontas is on crutches due to a missing leg, and Sleeping Beauty is missing an arm. Palombo, who self-identifies as disabled himself, describes his motivations as follows: "I think that disabled people doesn't [sic] match Disney's standards of beauty so my message is very simple: Disabled people have rights and are part of the world" (Dicker). The Disney Princesses are ubiquitous in popular culture. Seeing them with disabilities startles the viewer into an acknowledgement that idealized representations like those produced by Disney often exclude people with disabilities.

RACE IN DISNEY'S FAIRY TALE FILMS AND TELEVISION

The Disney studio has invited criticism for its use of racial stereotypes in films such as *Aladdin* (1992) and *Pocahontas* (1995). In 2005, Dorothy L. Hurley argued, "The problem of pervasive, internalized privileging of Whiteness has been intensified by the Disney representation of fairy tales which consistently reinforces an image of White supremacy" (223). In 2009, however, Disney released *The Princess and the Frog* (2009), which not only led to the celebration of the first African American princess offered by Disney but also contributed to a long-running discussion about race in fairy tales. Journalist Ann Hornaday greeted the film with palpable relief and pleasure:

> The film's setting in New Orleans, with its African, European, Caribbean and Native American influences, allows for a gratifyingly diverse mix of ethnicities and hues among its characters, which also include a Cajun firefly named Ray and a trumpet-playing alligator named Louis. Most important, [the princess] Tiana turns out to be not just pretty but competent and self-sufficient, embodying the

principle that wishing upon a star might help you express your dreams, but hard work, character and perseverance make them come true. (n.p.)

The reception of the film was largely positive, although not without reservations. The film is set in 1920s New Orleans but does not acknowledge the history of racism there and in the United States in general; some viewers were uneasy about a film set in a city still reeling from the damage of Hurricane Katrina at the time of the film's release. Tiana's love interest, Prince Naveen, also raised ire: his skin is a very light brown. This might suggest that he is not African American but Middle Eastern in origin, implying that African American princesses are possible, but African American princes are not. Alternatively, he could be read as a light-skinned African American, which some viewers might read as a privileging of lighter skin.

In July 2016, Disney debuted a television show on the Disney channel called *Elena: Princess of Avalor*, featuring the studio's first Latina Princess. In an opinion piece for the *Guardian* newspaper, Melissa Lozada-Oliva praised Elena as a possible role model for Latina girls but also questioned the show's setting, Avalor, a "Latin-American-esque kingdom that exists in a pre-colonial, pre-Columbian world" (Lozado-Oliva). The choice to make Avalor pre-colonial might be an attempt to avoid engaging with the violent histories of the colonization of Latin America. Lozada-Oliva also described Elena as "ambiguously brown," and not located in a specific Latin-American cultural identity, which she saw as a shortcoming. By contrast, Manuel Betancourt sees Elena as a successful Latina heroine precisely because she cannot be pinned down to any country or cultural tradition:

[Producer Nancy] Kanter, creator Craig Gerber and his crew have lent Elena of Avalor the universality that fairy tales depend on precisely by borrowing and adapting influences that never tie the show to any specific country or historical period. Elena is "Latina" in the broadest sense possible (Betancourt).

Other reviewers have praised Elena as a strong role model for young Latina girls—and all girls—because at her young age she is focusing on her self-development and becoming an excellent future Queen, not on pleasing a romantic partner.

In 2016, Disney released *Moana*, featuring its first Polynesian princess. She is the daughter of a chief in a Polynesian village. The ocean chooses her to approach Maui, a demigod, to help her return a mystical relic—a *pounamu* stone—to the goddess Te Fiti. Directors John Musker and Ron Clements worked with a group of cultural experts called the Oceanic Story Trust, who advised on the film's cultural accuracy and sensitivity. The film was a box office and critical success, with a lush visual palette. The film's portrayal of Moana's strength and resilience in undertaking this journey was widely praised. However, there were still some criticisms, such as the fact that the film took cultural elements from many Pacific native groups, which seemed to elide the diversity of Polynesian cultures (Herman). The character of Maui was seen by some as insulting, given his blustering, impulsive character; he was also lacking his companion goddess Hina (Herman). The film can also be seen as exoticizing Polynesia as a travel destination, especially given Disney's partnership with Hawaiian airlines to promote the film (Liberman). Travel and tourism has traditionally had a negative effect on native communities and the natural environment. Finally, Disney marketed a "skin suit" Halloween costume for the character of Maui the demigod, which has been described as an insensitive act of cultural appropriation. It was subsequently removed from stores (Andrews).

RACE IN FAIRY TALES AND FOLK TALES

The creation of African American, Latina, and Polynesian Disney princess show how many readers and viewers—including parents—wish to see more diversity in fairy tales, including in the popular genre of stories about princesses. Wider racial and ethnic representation in fairy tales has been slow in coming. Contemporary picturebook fairy tale retellings include Joyce Carol Thomas and David Diaz's *The Gospel Cinderella* (2004) and John Kurtz's *Little Red Riding Hood*, part of Disney Hyperion's Jump at the Sun series (2005). Kelly Greenawalt and Amariah Rauscher's *Princess Truly and the Hungry Bunny Problem* (2015) is another example of a book in the princess genre featuring a young African American girl.

It is important not only to think about the relative dearth of fairy tale retellings featuring protagonists of color, but also to critically examine the ones that do exist. In an insightful chapter in *Fairy Tales with a Black Consciousness* (2013), Tyler Smith engages critically with Marilyn Joshua Shearer's early fairy tale retelling *Snow White* (1990). *Snow White*, illustrated by Daryl Joseph Moore, modifies the Grimms' tale by setting it in Africa, with Snow White as an African princess. Although her skin is dark "like the night," she gets her name from a snowflake-shaped birthmark on her cheek. Shearer's *Cinderella and the Glass Slipper* (1990), illustrated by Ron Edwards, features Cinderella as a beautiful African American woman. Smith notes: "there is more to revising a traditional European fairytale to reflect an African worldview than just altering the physical representation of the character and the setting ... By trying to impose the Europeanized tale she enters into the waters of assimilative practice" (191). Smith argues instead for an approach like Patricia McKissack's *Flossie and the Fox* (1986), illustrated by Rachel Isadora, "where the characterization of Little Red Riding Hood/Flossie is revised to reflect traditional African American storytelling tropes" (190). In McKissack's tale, Flossie's grandmother asks her to take some eggs to a family friend. Encountering a fox (reminiscent of the wolf of the traditional tale), Flossie tells him she is not frightened of him: "why should I be scared of you and I don't even-now know you a real fox for a fact?" (n.p). The fox repeatedly tries to prove his identity to Flossie, only to be outwitted at every turn. Ultimately, a hound catches up to them and chases away the fox, and Flossie reveals that she knew he was a fox all along. *Flossie and the Fox* is an obvious retelling of *Little Red Riding Hood* but resists its Eurocentrism by being set in an African American community in Tennessee.

Many teachers, parents, and librarians dissatisfied with the lack of racial diversity in the mainstream fairy-tale tradition and in fairy tale retellings turn to folk tales instead.

Dorothy L. Hurley sees the promise in this approach but cautions readers about its limits:

> One area of criticism is centered on the contamination process that could be involved depending on the person or persons who collected and possibly altered the fairy tales, perhaps to fit an internalized preconception. It is legitimate to speculate on how much may be lost or altered in translation. And since the folk tales are in fact cultural agency, the question arises regarding the extent to which this agency is diminished or tainted by an "outsider" who collected and translated the tales. (230)

Hurley's warning reminds us of the importance of critical evaluation: attention to the writer, the means of production, the motives of the producer, and the intended audience. We discuss a problematic instance of the use—and appropriation—of folk tales in Chapter 10, when we consider Joel Chandler Harris's volumes of Uncle Remus tales.

READING CRITICALLY: FAIRY TALES

Trina Schart Hyman's Retelling of "Little Red Riding Hood"

Trina Schart Hyman's picturebook of "Little Red Riding Hood" can be read both as a faithful retelling of Jakob and Wilhelm Grimm's *Rotkäppchen* (*Little Red Cap*) and as an exploration of what the tale meant to Hyman personally. Her nostalgic visual style in the book and her close adherence to the Grimms's plot make her interpretation a faithful reading rather than a revisionist change of the text. At the same time, she includes many elements that tie the text to her personal story, such as changing the setting from Europe to America.

Although anthropologists, folklorists, and historians contend that the plot of "Little Red Riding Hood" might derive from "ancient myths about the sunrise and sunset," with the red riding hood representing the sun and the Wolf personifying darkness, Jack Zipes asserts that the tale is of "fairly modern vintage" (*Trials* 18). Arguing that the story developed as an oral tale warning against wolves in France, Tyrol, and northern Italy, Zipes concludes that this was probably the tradition that inspired the most important version before Grimm: Charles Perrault's *Le Petit Chaperon Rouge* (1697) (*Trials* 18).

By using the Grimm version, Hyman draws on some of the most characteristic features of the tale, such as the famous exchange between Little Red Riding Hood and her Grandmother:

> "Grandmother! What big, hairy ears you have grown!" she said.
> "The better to hear you with, my dear."
> "Oh, Grandmother! Your eyes are so shiny!"
> "The better to see you with, my dear."
> "Your hands look so strange, Grandmother!"
> "The better to catch you and hug you with, my dear."
> "Please, Grandmother, why do you have such big, sharp teeth?"
> "Those are to eat you up with, my dear!" (Hyman n.p.)

This famous exchange, so suited to transmission through oral folklore, is just as effective in a picturebook that will be read out loud to a child.

Like the Grimms's fairy tale, Hyman's text emphasizes manners and decorum. As the young girl is sent to her Grandmother, she is ordered to use good manners and told to stay on the forest path. When the Wolf encounters her, he sees her as a "plump morsel" and tells her she should instead enjoy herself in the forest:

> Just look at those beautiful wildflowers, Red Riding Hood! They are a sight even for my tired, old eyes. For goodness' sake, why don't you relax a bit, look at the world, and see

Trina Schart Hyman's illustration for her *Little Red Riding Hood* (1982) has the appearance of a woodcut.

how lovely it is? Why, I don't believe you even hear the birds sing, or enjoy the sunshine! You are just as solemn and well behaved as if you were going to school. Everything else is so gay and happy out here in the forest. (n.p.)

It is this diversion that allows the Wolf to close in on the Grandmother and eat her whole. After her rescue by the Huntsman, Red Riding Hood pledges, "I will never wander off the forest path again, as long as I live. I should have kept my promise to my mother" (n.p.).

Unlike other illustrators who seek to modernize the tales, Hyman clothes this fairy tale in a nostalgic aura. Every page with text has an elaborate border that looks like an old-fashioned quilt or woodcut. The visual style of Hyman's *Little Red Riding Hood* is very much in keeping with the fairy-tale genre itself, as Elizabeth Wanning Harries notes:

> We should think of the tales we know as belonging to a "distressed genre," as "new antiques," to borrow Susan Stewart's terms. They are often *imitations* of what various literary cultures have posited as the traditional, the authentic, or the nonliterary. They have been "distressed" like a supposedly antique pine chest, given the patina of age, surrounded by signs that suggest simultaneously their great age and their agelessness. (4)

The combination of age and agelessness is a hallmark of Hyman's version of "Little Red Riding Hood." Hyman herself explains her choice of a past setting:

> I decided to set the story a century ago here in the hills and forests of rural New England, instead of in the mountains of Bavaria. After all, this was an autobiography of sorts; although I may have sauerbraten in my genes, I have never actually seen the Black Forest and I am a New Englander by choice. Strangely enough, not one reviewer caught it; they all said things like "set in the forests of Germany." (Hyman, "'Cut It Down'" 299)

The reviewers' mistake is, in fact, understandable. There are very few geographical markers other than the fact that the Huntsman wears a buckskin jacket that does look like American dress of the past; on the other hand, the border designs could be read as Germanic.

Hyman's choice to move the tale from the Old to the New World is a sign of her personal claim on the tale and her desire to translate it to American audiences. In her picturebook autobiography, *Self-Portrait*, Hyman describes her unusual affinity for the "Red Riding Hood" story because it was one of the first books she was capable of reading on her own: "My mother sewed me a red satin cape with a hood that I wore almost every day, and on those days, she would make me a 'basket of goodies' to take to my grandmother's house" (n.p.).

"Red Riding Hood" is sometimes read as a fairy tale about rape and violence. Hyman's pictures, while never sexual in nature, do bring out the predatory relationship between the Wolf and Red Riding Hood. He is depicted very realistically—as a wild animal. Red Riding Hood herself is clearly

Gustave Doré's 1867 illustration of "Little Red Riding Hood" as told by Charles Perrault.

a child, not a teenager, with chubby cheeks and wide eyes. The Wolf towers above her; on one page, he clutches her shoulder so she cannot move. The Wolf deceives Red Riding Hood in two ways: by tempting her to diverge from the path and by dressing as the Grandmother.

Writers who retell "Little Red Riding Hood" can choose between two traditions of how the story ends. In the Grimm version, there is a heroic rescue by the Hunter or Woodchopper; in the Perrault version, Red Riding Hood is eaten up. Hyman stays true to the Grimm tradition as the Huntsman cuts the little girl and the Grandmother out of the Wolf's stomach. In adhering so closely to the Grimm tale, Hyman replicates many of its cultural meanings. Critics have drawn attention to the ways in which the rescue of Little Red Riding Hood and her Grandmother in the Grimms's tale reinforces the patriarchal idea that women need the rescue and protection of men. Hyman's affinity for the story prevents her from significantly adapting or revising its message as many feminist fairy-tale revisions do. The changes that Hyman makes instead allow her to explore the fairy tale as a form of nostalgia for her own past and for the past she shares with other readers of the fairy tale.

EXPLORATIONS

Review

1. What are some definitions of fairy tales? Why is it hard to come to a set definition of the term "fairy tale"?

2. How might fairy tales be distinguished from legends or myths?

3. What are some explanations for why there are fairy tale variations all over the world?

4. What are some of the changes the Grimms made to make their fairy tales more suitable for children? Are there any surprising aspects to the changes they made?

5. What are some of the theoretical approaches used to interpret fairy tales and to explore questions of human development, psychology, and social organization?

6. How do some of the early feminist revisionist fairy tales, such as *The Paper Bag Princess* and *Princess Smartypants*, revise the traditional fairy tale? Are these revisions effective? Why or why not?

Reflect

1. Before fairy tales were marketed largely to children, they were traditionally read (or listened to) by adults and children alike. When was the last time you read a fairy tale? What books or movies do you read or watch that are directly influenced by fairy tales?

2. We tend to take the presence of magical elements in fairy tales for granted. But what would fairy tales be like without magical elements, such as talking animals or fairy godmothers? What role does magic play in fairy tales?

3. When you hear the term "fairy tale," what thoughts come to mind? Is the term "fairy tale" always used in a positive way, or can it have negative connotations?

4. What are some of the ways in which fairy tales might exhibit radical or subversive potential? What are some ways in which they reinforce social and political norms? Can you generalize about the social and political function of fairy tales? Why or why not?

5. Fairy tales are frequently critiqued for their "happily ever after" endings, which are viewed as simplifying the complexity of life. Yet some writers of fairy tales ended their tales with sad, bittersweet, or ambivalent endings. What changes when a fairy-tale ending is unhappy? What are some possible motivations in offering tales without happy endings?

Investigate

1. A number of recent retellings of fairy tales stress the villain's point of view. Make a short bibliography of such retellings, some of which are for an adult audience. Do you find any villains who have not been granted a tale from their point of view? Write a two-page letter from the point of view of that villain, arguing that someone should write his or her story.

2. Take four fairy tales and write an description of the settings of the tales. Then think about setting these fairy tales in another time and place. What would change for each fairy tale? Make a chart of the similarities and differences between the original fairy tales and the relocated ones. From this chart, can you draw any conclusions about the importance of setting in fairy tales?

3. Choose a fairy tale that is part of the Western canon of classic fairy tales. Research two global or international versions of the tale and compare them with their Western counterpart. How do cultural and national differences affect the significance and literary impact of the tales?

4. Read a postmodern fairy-tale text such as *The True Story of the Three Little Pigs* by Jon Scieszka. Consider how reliant the book is on a reader's understanding of the "original" fairy tale that the book parodies. Write an essay arguing either that postmodern fairy-tale parodies rely on a knowledge of traditional fairy tales, or that they can be understood and enjoyed without reference to the source text.

SUGGESTED READINGS

Andersen, Hans Christian. *The Stories of Hans Christian Andersen: A New Translation from the Danish*, edited and translated by Diana Crone Frank and Jeffrey Frank (2005). This collection includes the twenty-two translated tales considered most critical to Andersen's career as a writer of fairy tales, including classics such as "The Little

Mermaid," "The Emperor's New Clothes," "The Snow Queen," and "The Little Match Girl." A number of the tales are known for their satirical tone, while others have a tragic sensibility, with an outsider protagonist suffering and even dying at the margins of society.

De Haan, Linda, and Stern Nijland. *King and King* **(2002).** This vividly illustrated picturebook tells the story of the young prince who "never cared much for princesses" and who finds love instead with young Prince Leo. They ultimately reign as "King and King."

Grimm, Jakob, and Wilhelm Grimm. *The Complete Fairy Tales of the Brothers Grimm,* **translated by Jack Zipes (2003).** Arguably the most influential writers in the canon of classic fairy tales, the Grimm brothers collected their fairy tales not for children but for folklore scholars interested in Germanic culture. Later editions grew increasingly oriented toward young readers.

Hyman, Trina Schart. *Little Red Riding Hood* **(1982).** Hyman produces a lavishly illustrated version of the fairy tale with an old-fashioned style (it is actually set in New England one hundred years ago). Hyman follows the Grimms's version quite closely, with an emphasis on the young girl's diversion from the path to her grandmother's house and their rescue by the hunter.

McKissack, Patricia. *Flossie and the Fox.* **Illustrated by Rachel Isadora (1986).** In this picturebook retelling of Little Red Riding Hood, a young African American girl outwits a predator by pretending not to know he is a fox, and denying she is frightened of him. The book ends with the fox being chased away by a local hound. While clearly a retelling of the Grimm fairy tale, it challenges Eurocentrism by being set in Tennessee and through its use of African American vernacular speech.

Munsch, Robert. *The Paper Bag Princess* **(1980). Illustrated by Michael Martchenko.** *The Paper Bag Princess* is an example of a second-wave feminist retelling of a fairy tale and has enjoyed continuing popularity. After a fire-breathing dragon burns her kingdom, chars her clothes, and kidnaps her fiancé, Princess Elizabeth tricks the dragon while wearing only a paper bag. Prince Ronald tells her to return when she is dressed more like a princess, but she leaves, with the scathing line, "You look like a real prince, but you are a bum."

Perrault, Charles. *The Complete Fairy Tales of Charles Perrault,* **translated by Christopher Betts (2010).** Perrault originally published his tales in 1697. Known for his elegant and spare prose, Perrault combined his folk sources with a sophisticated awareness of fashion and the aristocratic court.

Wiesner, David. *The Three Little Pigs* **(2001).** In this postmodern picturebook retelling of the famous fairy tale, the pigs escape the frame of their book—and the pursuit of the big, bad wolf—and go off to visit characters in other classic fairy and nursery tales, traveling on paper airplanes. Wiesner's book reflects a trend toward postmodern retellings of traditional fairy tales in printed books, animated film, and live-action film.

Wilde, Oscar. *Complete Fairy Tales of Oscar Wilde* **(1990).** Wilde's tales are known for their irony and social critique, along with opulent imagery, sacrifice for love, and observations on friendship. They were intended for both adult and child audiences. Wilde wrote two fairy-tale collections: *The Happy Prince* (1888) and *The House of Pomegranates* (1892). This edition includes major tales such as "The Happy Prince," "The Devoted Friend," and "The Fisherman and His Soul."

APPROACHES TO TEACHING "LITTLE RED RIDING HOOD" [ELEMENTARY SCHOOL]

Learning Goals

- To compare an original fairy tale (in this case the Grimms's version of "Little Red Riding Hood") with a retelling such as Trina Schart Hyman's

- To become aware of the main roles of fairy-tale characters, introducing the terms "protagonist," "villain," and "rescuer," and to trace the actions of these characters

- To practice memorizing and performing dialogue between characters

- To learn more about the setting of a fairy-tale text.

Part One: Comparing and Contrasting Two Versions of the Same Tale

Read Hyman's book out loud, then read the original Grimm tale out loud. On the board or using a projector, make a list of the two versions' similarities and differences. How similar is Hyman's retelling to the original? What did she change? What did she keep the same?

Part Two: Characters and Their Roles

Using the board, make a list of the three major types of characters by their roles: the "protagonist," the "villain," and the "rescuer." Talk about how these character types work in fairy tales. Identify these roles in "Little Red Riding Hood" (Red Riding Hood, the Wolf, and the Huntsman). Spend a few minutes looking at the book and talking about the way that these characters are portrayed physically. Some topics to focus on might be the size of the characters and the colors with which they are drawn.

Then make a list of each character's activities, in collaboration with the class:

- Little Red Riding Hood (protagonist): being warned by her mother, walking through the forest, talking to the Wolf, going off the path to pick flowers, talking to the Wolf disguised as the Grandmother, being eaten by the Wolf, being rescued by the Huntsman, promising never to stray from the path again.

- Wolf (villain): tempting Little Red Riding Hood to go off the path, plotting and scheming, eating the Grandmother, disguising himself as the Grandmother, eating Red Riding Hood.

- Huntsman (rescuer): hearing the Wolf snore, rescuing Red Riding Hood and her Grandmother by cutting them from the Wolf's stomach, rejoicing with the rescued characters.

At the end of this exercise, review what is meant by a "role" in a fairy tale (that every character has a defined part to play) and explain the distinction between "flat" and "round" characters. Flat characters, which are less developed than round ones, are typical in a fairy tale. Discuss the male character's rescuing both the young girl and the older woman, and the ways in which this is also typical of a traditional fairy tale. If time permits, you could bring in Roald Dahl's poem "Little Red Riding Hood and the Wolf," in which Little Red Riding Hood kills the Wolf herself.

Part Three: Understanding Dialogue

Hand out a sheet of paper on which you have copied the dialogue between Red Riding Hood and the Wolf. Read it out loud with the class. Then split the class into two groups, assigning Red Riding Hood's role to one half of the class, and the Wolf's role to the other. Then reverse the roles. After this exercise, bring the class together and talk through the following questions:

- How did it feel to be Little Red Riding Hood in this dialogue?

- How did it feel to be the Wolf in this dialogue?

If time permits, or if you are seeking a linked writing exercise, you can ask the students to write a few paragraphs describing how they felt when they played Little Red Riding Hood and when they played the Wolf.

Part Four: Setting

Explain that the setting of a book is the place and time where the action unfolds. Examine the portrayal of the forest, the path, and the Grandmother's house in Hyman's book.

If time permits, students could draw Little Red Riding Hood in the threatening forest or in the Grandmother's house.

PICTUREBOOKS, GRAPHIC NOVELS, AND DIGITAL TEXTS

In *Alice's Adventures in Wonderland* (1865), the protagonist's adventure begins when she becomes bored by the book her sister is reading: "'What is the use of a book,' thought Alice, 'without pictures or conversations?'" (Carroll 7). Alice's desire for a book with pictures demonstrates a link between childhood and visual culture. The association of childhood reading with pictures grew even stronger in the twentieth century. Now picturebooks are thought of as the books we read aloud to children who don't know how to read yet and as the first books children read on their own. As such, they are sometimes dismissed as "simple" to interpret. Yet Barbara Bader draws attention to the many elements in a picturebook:

> A picturebook is text, illustrations, total design; an item of manufacture and a commercial product; a social, cultural, historical document; and, foremost, an experience for a child.... As an art form, it hinges on the interdependence of pictures and words, on the simultaneous display of two facing pages, and on the drama of the turning of the page. (1)

To read a picturebook critically is not only to consider each element in isolation but also to analyze the way in which all the elements work together. This chapter focuses on the elements that make up a picturebook, with particular attention to the relationship between word and image.

Opposite: Illustration from *Hondo and Fabian* by Peter McCarty, 2002.

We will also look at two emerging frontiers of children's literature that require visual literacy: the graphic novel and interactive digital fiction for children. Comic books have been a longstanding influence on children's books, in addition to being a staple of childhood reading, and Japanese manga have recently made an impact as well. The recent growth of the graphic novel for children and adolescents builds on and extends this tradition. Digital books (often featuring hypertext links) and other interactive fiction demand the ability to navigate a text as if it were a game. While they are emerging genres with a role to play in the future of children's literature, both graphic novels and digital media for children have several aspects in common with the traditional picturebook. They all require the interpretation of text and image together in the process of making meaning.

DEFINING THE PICTUREBOOK

A **picturebook** can be defined as a narrative or non-narrative book in which words and images form an artistic whole. In *How Picturebooks Work* (2000), Maria Nikolajeva and Carole Scott established that "picturebook" should be spelled as one word rather than as two words ("picture book") in order to signify that text and image are combined into a unified form. The picturebook is often defined in opposition to the illustrated book. Whereas the text of an illustrated book can stand alone without the pictures, a picturebook relies on the interdependence of word and image. Most illustrated books have more text than images. If the illustrations were removed, the story itself would remain intact. If the illustrations were removed from a picturebook, the continuity and lucidity of the narrative would break down. An example of an illustrated book is Louise Fitzhugh's *Harriet the Spy* (1964), which includes pictures of characters and scenes from the novel but does not rely on those pictures to advance the story. This is different from a picturebook such as Margaret Wise Brown's *Goodnight Moon*, illustrated by Clement Hurd, where a little bunny in bed for the night says goodbye to all of the objects and furniture in his or her room, with a steady darkening of the light. The pictures of all of the objects and the furniture are necessary to understand the action, and without them the book would make no sense. While *Harriet the Spy* and *Goodnight Moon* are obviously different types of books, the distinction between "illustrated book" and "picturebook" may not be as clear-cut as it seems. Though the text of *Harriet the Spy* does not need pictures to communicate the basic narrative of the book, the pictures (which Fitzhugh drew herself) do add a great deal to a reader's knowledge of characters and events, and are therefore integral to the book's meaning and artistic impact.

The picturebook, however, also relies heavily on its design and production to make meaning. Kenneth Marantz calls the picturebook "a unique expressive form that gains its strength from the totality of its making, including its paper stock, typography, binding, and design" (149). In many picturebooks, design and production elements are as important as the words and images. For example, Eric Carle's *The Very Hungry Caterpillar* (1969) incorporates literal holes in the pictures of the leaves and fruit that the ravenous caterpillar eats so that the reader can touch the caterpillar's track as well as view it and read about it.

While picturebooks have a standard length of thirty-two pages, they can be longer or shorter and have several possible physical formats. Board books are smaller books intended for babies and toddlers. Made of heavy cardboard with coated pages and rounded page edges, board books resist wear and tear while ensuring the safety of the child. Picturebooks for older children are issued in both paperback format and lavish hardcover editions.

A HISTORY OF PICTUREBOOKS

Precursors to Picturebooks

Picturebooks have their roots in instructional texts. *Orbis Sensualium Pictus,* or *The Visible World in Pictures* (1658), was a seventeenth-century precursor to the picturebook for children (it is sometimes described as the first picturebook). The book was written in Latin and German by Czech educator Johann Amos Comenius, with an English edition published in 1659. It is devoted to teaching Latin (to a German or English audience, respectively) while also explaining the physical world of objects, natural phenomena, and even ideas. Each page of *Orbis Sensualium Pictus* is divided into two parts: a numbered picture and an explanation of the picture. *Orbis Sensualium Pictus* is not that different from the concept books of today, in which a picture of an object is placed next to the words representing that object. As in many modern picturebooks, the reader moves between text and image to make meaning. Other pedagogical texts such as *The New England Primer* (c. 1683) continued this tradition of using intertwined text and image to divert and educate children.

Orbis Sensualium Pictus (1658) by Johann Amos Comenius offered explanations of objects, natural phenomena, and ideas.

The Picturebook as a Commercial Form

In the nineteenth century, the visionary English publisher Edmund Evans saw the commercial potential for illustrated books and began to publish the work of master illustrators such as Walter Crane, Randolph Caldecott, and Kate Greenaway. Walter Crane produced *The Baby's Opera* (1877), which combined music and nursery rhymes. Caldecott illustrated nursery rhymes and well-known poems in books such as John Gilpin's *This Is the House That Jack Built* (1878). His illustrations evoke a rural and traditional world. Kate Greenaway is remembered today for her pictures of idealized children, as in her alphabet book *A Apple Pie* (1886). The children's clothing she depicted in her illustrations was of her own design and influenced the fashions of the day. All three artists used bright, attractive colors and strong shapes in an effort to appeal to children or, more importantly, to the adults who were increasingly interested in acquiring books specifically for their children. Caldecott in particular did a great deal to develop the picturebook as a form that required word and image to work together. In the words of Maurice Sendak, himself a master of the picturebook, "Caldecott's work heralds the beginning of the modern picture book. He devised an ingenious juxtaposition of picture and word, a counterpoint that never happened before. Words are left out—but the picture says it. Pictures are left out—but the word says it. In short, it is the invention of the picture book" (21). Sendak uses the notions of "juxtaposition" and "counterpart" to indicate a harmony of words and pictures. The words and pictures work together, but they each have a different role to play in the narrative.

Another transitional figure was Beatrix Potter, whose watercolor illustrations and engaging stories moved the picturebook to a new level. Potter, as Linda Lear notes, created a new kind of "continuity of time and place, fantasy and reality" (154). In *The Tale of Peter Rabbit* (1902), the setting and costuming of the rabbit characters are of immense importance. On the one hand, Potter's books include anthropomorphized animals (animals that are depicted with the characteristics of human beings, such as wearing clothes). Yet there is also close observation of animals as they are in nature. Potter was also notable for producing physically small picturebooks because she thought they would be easy for young children to hold and enjoy.

An illustration from Kate Greenaway's *A Apple Pie* (1886) featuring her influential fashion designs for children.

Twentieth-Century Picturebooks

The twentieth century saw advances in printing techniques and mass production and a number of notable artist-illustrators, among them Wanda Gág, Jean de Brunhoff, N.C. Wyeth, Jessie Wilcox Smith, Virginia Lee Burton, Munro Leaf, Eric Carle, and Robert Lawson. Many twentieth-century picturebooks became an iconic part of childhood culture, most notably *The Cat in the Hat* (1957) by Theodor Seuss Geisel (Dr. Seuss) and Maurice Sendak's *Where the Wild Things Are* (1963).

Awards such as the Caldecott Medal (first given in 1938) and, in the United Kingdom, the Kate Greenaway Medal (first given in 1955) were developed to honor excellence in illustration. In the modern age, picturebooks functioned as both literary works of art and mass-marketed products. Simon & Schuster's Little Golden Books, produced in partnership with Western Printing and Lithography Company, were cheaply manufactured and sold in supermarkets to families that did not have access to more expensive books. Often met with hostility by librarians, they nonetheless had an enduring impact on younger readers, and some of the Golden Books were written by major authors and illustrators such as Ruth Krauss and Mary Blair (*I Can Fly*, 1951) and Margaret Wise Brown (*Home for a Bunny*, 1956).

The late twentieth and early twenty-first centuries have seen an efflorescence of creativity from picturebook authors like Philip C. Stead, Doreen Cronin, Laban Carrick Hill, Tomie dePaola, Matt de la Peña, Don Tate, Faith Ringgold, Chris Van Allsburg, and Jane Yolen, to name just a few writers. Postmodern picturebooks have been an especially exciting area of growth and experimentation. In the words of Ann Grieve, postmodern picturebooks are known for their "use of metafiction; the manipulation of the whole physical space of a book; parody; and intertextuality" (16). Jon Scieszka and Lane Smith's *The Stinky Cheese Man and Other Fairly Stupid Tales* (1992) fits this description perfectly. It includes nine short **fractured fairy tales**, or tales made humorous through surprising changes or unexpected modernizations, narrated by Jack (of Beanstalk fame). **Metafictionality** occurs when a fictional text reveals awareness of its own fictional status, which we see in *The Stinky Cheese Man* when the title pages and end pages are shuffled

Robert Lawson's pen-and-ink drawing from *The Story of Ferdinand* (1936) by Munro Leaf.

around, and the character Chicken Licken finds herself squashed by the table of contents that falls on her. Designer Molly Leach helped establish the postmodern qualities of Scieszka and Smith's book by manipulating the physical form of the book, especially one page where the font grows smaller and smaller until it is unreadable. The parodic and intertextual status of the text is also obvious, as Scieszka and Smith refer to traditional fairy tales in order to subvert them, including an ugly duckling who grows up to be … an ugly duck, and a princess who kisses a frog and gets only froggy slime.

A number of recent picturebooks also experiment with multiple story lines or points of view. The pages of David Macaulay's *Black and White* (1990), for example, are divided into four distinct and visually different stories that seem unconnected at first: a boy on a train, parents acting in a silly way, a prisoner's escape, and a late commuter train. As the book progresses, it grows increasingly clear that the four stories combine into a fifth story that unites them. Anthony Browne's *Voices in the Park* (1998) features four anthropomorphized chimps who each recount the same story from their own point of view: a snobbish mother, her disconsolate son, an unemployed man, and his cheerful daughter. Each version of the story is told in a different voice and with a separate color palette, emphasizing that point of view in a story makes a huge difference to the mood and meaning of a scene.

Despite the creativity of these works and their sophisticated literary techniques, contemporary picturebook publishers face many challenges. A recent report by Julie Bosman in the *New York Times* claimed that "publishers have scaled back the number of [picture-book] titles they have released in the last several years, and booksellers across the country say sales have been suffering" (Bosman, n.p.). Part of this slump can be attributed to cost cutting in the aftermath of the 2008 recession. Also, many parents who are ambitious to push their children scholastically are not willing to allow their children to enjoy picturebooks, steering them toward chapter books in the (mistaken) belief that chapter books are more challenging for young readers.

HOW WORDS AND IMAGES RELATE

To understand both classic and contemporary picturebooks, it is important to focus on the interrelation of word and image. As Perry Nodelman notes in *Words about Pictures: The Narrative Art of Children's Picture Books* (1988), "Words can make pictures into rich narrative resources—but only because they communicate so differently from pictures that they change the meaning of pictures. For the same reason, also, pictures can change the narrative thrust of words" (196).

Denise I. Matulka in *A Picture Book Primer: Understanding and Using Picture Books* (2008) articulates three types of interaction between words and pictures:

1. Symmetrical: the words and pictures have the same message, and the pictures rein-force the words. This kind of relationship between word and picture is common in concept books, which help children learn to read. One example is Dr. Seuss's *One Fish Two Fish Red Fish Blue Fish* (1960). In this book, each description of a fish is accompa-nied by an image of the fish being described.

2. Complementary: Words and images are interdependent, and words and pictures fill in each other's narrative gaps. Maurice Sendak's *Where the Wild Things Are* (1963) is a good example of a complementary picturebook. The images advance the story of Max's journey to the world of the Wild Things beyond what the text says, while the text provides information not conveyed by the pictures.

3. Contradictory: Words and pictures say opposite things. This interaction is used to create **dramatic irony**, establishing a tension between what a character knows or sees and what is presented to the reader. Pat Hutchins's *Rosie's Walk* (1971) is an example of a contradictory text. The text narrates the quiet, uneventful walk of the hen Rosie. In contrast, the pictures show a fox in hot pursuit. (118–20)

Wordless Picturebooks

Wordless or nearly wordless picturebooks, such as David Wiesner's *Tuesday* (1991) or JiHyeon Lee's *Pool* (2015), rely purely on their images to tell a story. In *Tuesday*, frogs float mysteriously over a suburban development on their lily pads. In *Pool*, two children meet in an extremely overcrowded pool and go exploring in its vivid depths, forming a friend-ship in the process. If an entire story can be constructed from pure image—or at most a phrase or two—it implies that images are the central requirement for a picturebook narrative to function. This becomes even more likely when the reader considers that there is no such thing as a picturebook *without* images. On the other hand, many definitions of the picturebook stress the interrelation of *both* text and image. Wordless books might not qualify as picturebooks under this stricter definition.

The narrative of a wordless book could emerge in any number of ways. A reader might supply the words or "translate" pictures into verbal language. When wordless books are shown to children, they are often asked to explain in words the narrative they are seeing. Yet wordless books can also be enjoyed and understood without verbalization. Looking at David Wiesner's *Tuesday* in this light, readers might supply an interpretation or "back story" for why the frogs float on lily pads into the suburban area, or they might enjoy the visual sweep of the frogs' journey and follow along without putting it into words.

The Relationship of Authors and Illustrators

Some picturebooks are written and illustrated by the same person. An example would be Tomie dePaola's *Strega Nona* (1975), with dePaola responsible for both the exuberant illustrations and the whimsical text about Big Anthony's encounter with Strega Nona's magic pasta pot. Sometimes the author and illustrator are different people, as is the case with the Newbery-award winning *Last Stop on Market Street* (2015), written by Matt de la Peña and illustrated by Christian Robinson. In *Last Stop on Market Street*, CJ and his grandmother ride the bus on a Sunday morning. CJ asks a number of questions about why they do not own a car and why he does not own an iPod like the other boys on the bus. His grandmother responds with explanations that point CJ to the beauty and warm human relationships that surround him. In response to the question about lacking a car, for example, CJ's grandmother responds: "Boy, what do we need a car for? We got a bus that breathes fire, and old Mr. Dennis, who always has a trick for you" (n.p.). An imaginative response to the world ("a bus that breathes fire") and attention to other people are revealed as far more important than material wealth. Using acrylics and collage as a medium, and a bright color palette, Christian Robinson evokes the vividness and diversity of the cityscape that CJ's grandmother emphasizes, as they head to serve others at a local soup kitchen on Market Street. De la Peña and Robinson both make important contributions to the artistic achievement of the book.

Many contemporary publishing houses will match the author of a text with an illustrator; in these cases there could be a great deal of contact between the author and illustrator, or very little. But whatever the interaction between the book's creators, words and images need to be evaluated both separately and together. The text of a picturebook can be similar to a poem in the economy and deliberation of its phrasing (and sometimes the text of a picturebook literally *is* a poem, sometimes even a rhyming one). The images in a picturebook could in theory stand alone as if they were artworks suitable for framing on a wall, but in a true picturebook the quality of the interdependence between word and image is what is important.

ARTISTIC CHOICES IN THE PRODUCTION OF PICTUREBOOKS

All books require cooperation between the author and illustrator and the various people responsible for book production. Reading picturebooks critically means being aware of the many artistic choices that are required in putting them together, down to the minute details of production. Here are some of the design choices that go into making a picturebook.

The Size of the Book

Picturebooks come in many sizes. Suzy Lee's 2008 wordless book *Wave* is remarkable for its elongated, rectangular format (12.1 × 6.9 × 0.6 inches), in which a long picture of an ocean dominates each double-page spread, with the tiny figure of a young girl playing joyfully at the water's edge. Miniature books such as Margaret Wise Brown and Garth Williams's *Little Fur Family* (1946) or Maurice Sendak's *The Nutshell Library* (1962) give an impression of intimacy. Their small size may be a result of an assumption that children are well suited to small things (as we see in the tradition of miniature models or dollhouses).

The Size of the Picture against the Page

The designer of a picturebook needs to decide to what extent a picture will fill a page and the amount of "white space"—the empty area—on the page. Some books, such as Richard Scarry's *Busy, Busy World* (1965), are known for cramming pictures into the margins, setting a mood of hectic activity. In contrast, Ian Falconer's *Olivia* (2000) has a number of pages on which the charismatic titular heroine is isolated against white space, making her the undisputed star of the action.

The Composition of Objects on the Page

In her book *Picture This: How Pictures Work* (2000), Molly Bang considers how the placement of visual objects on the page creates narrative and artistic effects. Using a hypothetical layout of a retelling of "Little Red Riding Hood" as her case study, she establishes several compositional principles, including:

- Smooth, flat horizontal shapes give us a sense of stability and calm.

- Vertical shapes are more exciting and more active.

- Diagonal shapes are dynamic because they imply motion or tension.

- The middle of the page is the most effective "center of attention" because it is the point of greatest attraction.

- The larger an object is in a picture, the stronger it feels. (Bang 42–80)

The Use, Amount, and Quality of Color

Authors and illustrators need to decide whether to use color, and if so, how to use it. Will the entire illustration include color? What is the overall mood that the color or lack of color aims for? Warm colors (such as reds, oranges, and yellows) add energy, whereas cool colors (such as blues and greens) are more tranquil. If colors are less saturated (with more grey in them), they can seem restful; highly saturated colors add intensity. Also important is whether the images are depicted with their shadows or other forms of shading; if the objects are shown to be shaded, they appear to have more depth, and shadows also add a sobering dimension. Kay Thompson and Hilary Knight's *Eloise* (1955)—the story of an insouciant little girl who lives at the Plaza Hotel in New York City—combines black-and-white drawings with bright and saturated colors, especially pink. Cynthia Rylant and Diane Goode's *When I Was Young in the Mountains* (1982) has a muted palette of greens, browns, and blues. The gentle colors add to the book's lyrical and quiet depiction of a childhood in the Appalachian Mountains of West Virginia.

The Strength of Line

Lines can be very thin or very thick, and these choices will affect the kind of image produced. A text with a number of fine lines will seem very detailed and intricate, whereas bold lines are more vigorous and may seem less realistic. Mitsumasa Anno's *Anno's Journey* (1977) is a wordless story about one traveler's journey through a nation in northern Europe, depicted from a vantage point in the air. Anno uses very fine lines to create a delicate, detailed, and intricate landscape that resembles an old-fashioned painting. In contrast, Lauren Child's *I Will Never NOT EVER Eat a Tomato* (2000) renders brother and sister protagonists Charlie and Lola in expressive bold black lines that impart a cartoonish effect.

The Medium Used

The actual material used in the creation of picturebooks, especially the visual aspects, is called a medium (the plural form is media). Each medium comes with both possibilities and limitations, and each medium creates a definite mood. For example, crayon drawings are traditionally associated with the drawings of children. Oil paintings bring to mind high art. In the Explorations section of this chapter, you will choose a picturebook and consider how it would be different if composed in a different medium.

SOME MEDIA USED IN THE PRODUCTION OF PICTUREBOOKS

Medium   Description of the Medium

Acrylic Paint Acrylics can give both the transparent brilliance of watercolor and the density of oil paint. They dry more quickly than oil paints and are less fragile (less subject to damage).

example: *Ladder to the Moon*. Maya Soetoro-Ng, author; Yuyi Morales, illustrator (Candlewick Press, 2011).

Block Printing Block printing is achieved through woodcutting, wood engraving, or a similar relief printing technique; this creates a white line on a black surface. Lines created by block printing are often bold and rugged. Subtler effects and greater tonal depth are also possible by scoring and scratching the surface or by using the wood's grain itself.

example: *Only a Witch Can Fly*. Alison McGhee, author; Taeeun Yoo, illustrator (Feiwel & Friends, 2009).

Cartoon Drawing Picturebook artists who use the cartoon form often use bold lines that are simple and energetic.

example: *Harold and the Purple Crayon*. Crockett Johnson, author and illustrator (HarperCollins, 1955).

Collage Collage is the assemblage of different forms, including—but not limited to—fabric, newspaper, cardboard, and tissue. It allows the artist to play with the artistic significance of objects, textures, and surfaces. Sometimes the artist chooses materials of personal significance, and sometimes the materials for collage are chosen because of their texture (or a combination of both).

example: *Pocketful of Posies: A Treasury of Nursery Rhymes*. Salley Mavor, author and illustrator (Houghton Mifflin Harcourt, 2010). Fabric collage.

Digital Production Through digital software tools and manipulation, artists combine digital painting with scanned images, paintings, and collages. Alternatively, the whole book can be created digitally.

example: *The Loud Book!* Deborah Underwood, author; Renata Liwska, illustrator (Houghton Mifflin Harcourt, 2011). Pencil and digital color.

Ink and Watercolor Ink drawings and "ink wash" techniques (the latter technique originated in China) "render atmospheric effects while simultaneously suggesting spatial depth" (Osborne 582). When combined with watercolors, the effect varies based on the method of watercolor painting used (*see* Watercolor).

example: *Finding Winnie: The True Story of the World's Most Famous Bear.* Lindsay Mattick; Sophie Blackall, illustrator (Little, Brown and Company, 2015).

Oil Paint Oil paint dries slowly, and it registers brush strokes in great detail. It can be quite opaque or quite transparent. Paul Zelinsky noted of his choice of oils for Rapunzel, "I wanted to evoke the sense of heightened, but also distanced, reality that I feel looking at paintings from the Renaissance in northern Europe" (qtd. in Cummins 225).

example: *Rapunzel*. Paul O. Zelinsky, author and illustrator (Dutton, 1997).

Pencil Drawing Pencils use a mineral called graphite, which is capable of a large range from black to very light gray. Graphite material also allows for variations in density and depth, depending on the softness or hardness of the pencil lines. Pencil can also create a black-and-white cinematic effect.

example: *In Coal Country*. Judith Hendershot, author; Thomas B. Allen, illustrator (Scholastic, 1987). Charcoal and pastels.

Photography Photography creates a naturalistic and realistic effect. It is used in picturebooks to create a kind of documentary accuracy particularly suited to the depiction of historical events.

example: *My People*. Langston Hughes, author; Charles R. Smith Jr., illustrator (Simon & Schuster Children's Publishing, 2009).

Watercolor Watercolor can appear transparent and luminous (filled with light). The watercolor medium is also known for its free, loose strokes. Watercolor creates different visual effects depending on the base and thinness (that is, the amount the paint is watered down). Thinner paint has a lighter tone and shows the paper more, creating a dreamlike atmosphere. Thicker watercolor paint is more realistic.

example: *The Boy in the Garden*. Allen Say, author and illustrator (Houghton Mifflin Harcourt, 2010).

Mixed Media

Many books make use of mixed media to tell a story. In contemporary children's books, we often see what Julie Danielson describes as a "blending of handcrafted and digital techniques, the latter being woven into the process, just one part of many steps" (45). One contemporary example is Dan Santat's Caldecott-award winning *Beekle: The Unimaginary Friend* (2014), where the imaginary friend of the title makes a difficult journey to find someone to play with. The copyright page explains: "The illustrations for this book were done in pencil, crayon, watercolor, ink, and Adobe Photoshop. The text was hand-lettered." The book demonstrates considerable visual range, with stark grays and blues when Beekle is on his lonely trek to find a friend, and warmer, busier pages when he connects with the young girl, Alice, who has already drawn a picture of him: "they realized / they were perfect together" (n.p).

Even before the use of digital illustration, some picturebooks were produced using mixed media. One example is Eve Bunting and David Diaz's *Smoky Night* (1994), in which the ongoing tensions between two families (one African American and the other Asian American) are defused as they help each other during the Los Angeles riots of 1992. The main illustrations are done on the right side of the page in acrylic paint and watercolor. Text on the left-facing page is photographed against a background of objects from the riots. The account of the robbery of a Korean grocery store, for example, is placed over a photograph of dried rice and cereal, signifying the damage to goods and property. A description of a man fleeing the violence while stumbling over his dry cleaning is placed above a photograph of tangled plastic and hangers. The photographic backgrounds provide a realistic backdrop, while the bright colors and bold lines of the acrylic paintings underscore the struggles of the characters at a time of strife.

Setting

Picturebook authors and illustrators must decide whether the setting or background will be highly developed or minimal, and whether it will be rendered in a fanciful or realistic way. Sometimes books include no setting whatsoever, often relying on a pure color or white background. This is often true of board books and "basic concept" books such as Sandra Boynton's *Doggies: A Counting and Barking Book* (1984). The dogs in the book are portrayed against blank backgrounds, and—along with the counting and barking activities detailed—they are the only focus of the reader's attention. Emily Hughes's *The Little Gardener* (2014) is a story about a very small boy who toils in a large garden, encouraged by the blooming of a single flower but daunted enough to make a wish for help in cultivating it, which he receives from some other local children. The garden setting in the book is wild and lush and fills the page, evoking the beautiful but sometimes challenging garden.

Text within the Pictures

Sometimes the author or illustrator will include some text within the illustrations to add an extra layer of interpretation or even irony. Maurice Sendak's *We Are All in the Dumps with Jack and Guy: Two Nursery Rhymes with Pictures* (1993) weaves together two traditional rhymes: "We Are All in the Dumps" and "Jack and Guy Went Out into the Rye." In contrast with the innocent rhymes, the illustrations show homeless children living in an urban slum. The children hold (and take shelter) under newspapers featuring woeful headlines about war and poverty and also real estate advertisements hawking property at inflated prices. These "texts within the illustrations" draw the reader's attention to the troubled world in which the book is set and to the great division between rich and poor. Many of Mo Willems's books (such as *Don't Let the Pigeon Drive the Bus* [2003]) or Dev Petty's *I Don't Want to Be a Frog!* (2015), illustrated by Mike Boldt, use speech bubbles within the text to indicate the dialogue between the characters.

CONCERNS ABOUT PICTUREBOOKS

Picturebooks are an important part of childhood culture and literary culture, but their literary and cultural status raises many critical issues which we will explore below.

Availability and Cost of Picturebooks

Availability and cost are ongoing concerns about quality picturebooks. As one example among many, Kevin Henkes's picturebook *Waiting* (2015), a Caldecott Honor Book, sells for $17.99 as of this writing. Compared to a mass-market paperback retailing at a fraction of this price, this is expensive and raises questions about the accessibility of well-produced picturebooks, especially given the chronic underfunding of public libraries. Susan B. Neuman describes the results of a 2001 study she completed with Donna Celano focusing on the "differences in resources for low- and middle-income families":

> Whereas children in the middle-income neighborhoods had multiple opportunities to observe, use, and purchase books (estimated at about 13 titles per individual child), few such occasions were available for low-income children (estimated to be about 1 book for every 300 children). Further, other avenues of access were limited or lacking. School libraries in poor communities were closed and sometimes boarded up, unlike school libraries in middle-income neighborhoods, which were thriving, with approximately 12 books available per child. Public libraries were open only for brief hours in low-income neighborhoods, compared with many open hours in middle-income neighborhoods. (Neuman 31)

Disparities in the amount of access children have to books is certainly not unique to the picturebook form, but it hard to deny the high cost of quality picturebooks.

Books as Toys

When Dorothy Kunhardt's *Pat the Bunny* appeared in 1940, the book was viewed as promoting infant development, including motor control and reading skills. The infant reader was asked to touch the fur of the bunny, look in the mirror, and complete a variety of other activities. Today's bookstores now sell a myriad of board and cloth books, including ones that are shaped like animals and inanimate objects. For example, *Little Shark: Finger Puppet Book* (2013), part of the Little Finger Puppet Board Books series, features a plush shark finger puppet attached to the book and peek-a-boo holes on every page that makes the puppet seem like it is swimming through the pages of the book. For older readers, there are toy books such as P.H. Hanson's *My Granny's Purse* (2003, mini edition 2013), and *My Mommy's Tote* (2007, mini edition 2013). Touted for their "**interactivity**," they allow children to play with the objects inside the various bags—whether house keys, glasses, a secret spider collection, or a laptop and cell phone. Books such as *My Mommy's Tote* might stimulate the minds of young readers by helping them associate reading and play so that they are more eager to engage with books in the future. On the other hand, the books might not be as imaginatively and aesthetically stimulating as other books and certain educational toys. Some adults might regard them as too gimmicky to be worthwhile as books for children.

Similar concerns circulate around books that are tie-ins to marketing and movies. What is the literary status of books that themselves create a merchandising frenzy, such as Marcus Pfister's *The Rainbow Fish* (1992), which spurred an animated series on HBO with accompanying games, purses, paint sets, themed diaries, and the like? A book such as *The Rainbow Fish*, which inspires so many toys, could eventually be regarded as merely a toy. On the other hand, as we saw in Chapter 2, marketing has long been an element of books for children. Several classic picturebooks included and continue to include accompanying toys without necessarily compromising their quality as literature.

NEW FRONTIERS FOR VISUAL TEXTS

In recent years, we are increasingly seeing texts that are mixing forms like the graphic novel, comic book, picturebook, chapter book, and digital book, challenging the boundaries of each of these forms. Kate DiCamillo's *Flora & Ulysses: The Illuminated Adventures* (2013) is an illustrated book rather than a picturebook, but it requires some of the same critical visual reading skills that are necessary to read picturebooks. Flora Belle Buckman is a 10-year-old "natural-born cynic" dealing with her parents' divorce and her often-distracted mother. Ulysses is a squirrel who receives superpowers—and the ability to compose poems on a typewriter—when he is inadvertently swept up by a vacuum. The book alternates between Flora's point of view and that of Ulysses. While the book is largely narrated using a classic chapter book format, there are several moments when the storyline is advanced using comic book panels. This is a fitting nod to the superhero genre given Ulysses's abundant powers, as well as Flora's devotion to comics like "Terrible Things Can Happen to You!" and "The Illuminated Adventures of the Amazing Incandesto!" Reading *Flora & Ulysses* involves multiple interpretive practices.

Brian Selznick's *The Invention of Hugo Cabret* (2007) is another book that sits on the boundaries between visual genres, in this case film and the illustrated novel. *Hugo Cabret* is the story of a young orphaned boy who lives in a Paris train station, winding the clocks daily, but who seeks to solve the mystery of the automaton (a self-moving machine) his father was working on before he died. Wordless pages alternate with pages of text—like a silent film. The drawings are done in pencil, allowing for a somber palette that evokes a black-and-white movie. Sometimes the words advance the plot, and sometimes the images do; sometimes the illustrations move more closely into the details of a scene, like a film close-up. The book challenges the boundaries of the picturebook form while in some ways being an ideal expression of the form, since it is so heavily reliant on the interaction of text and image. It won the Caldecott Medal in 2008.

Reinventing the Concept Book

Concept books are written to instruct children in concepts such as shapes, colors, counting, time, and the alphabet. Although concept books may seem simple, several recent authors and illustrators have produced innovative and challenging examples of the form. Stephen T. Johnson's *Alphabet City* (1996) and *City by Numbers* (2003) are good examples of this reinvention. *Alphabet City* is a take on the traditional primer and uses realistic paintings or drawings in pastel, watercolor, gouache, and charcoal; they look almost like photographs. Johnson uses illustrations in place of words such as "A is for apple." His books ask their readers to pick out numbers and letters within depictions of city scenes— without any further text. The artistry of the book lies in the naturalness of the cityscape and the pattern that emerges from it. Johnson's approach adds a new dimension to a very old picturebook form. It is in some ways a traditional alphabet book, but readers learn to decode more than just the letters; they also learn to read the urban environment. The picturebook—so apparently simple and straightforward—always involves complex forms of interpretation. It works on multiple levels to encourage both visual and verbal literacies. Digital books and apps have also contributed to the reinvention of the concept book. Roberto de Vicq de Cumptich's *Bembo's Zoo: An Animal ABC Book* (2000) is a print picturebook that uses the Bembo typographical font to shape the letters from each animal's name into a pictorial representation of the animal named.

In Vectorpark's digital app *Metamorphabet*, users tap, drag, tilt or spin each of the 26 letters of the alphabet. Each letter transforms multiple times into a word that begins with the letter. For example, "A" grows "antlers," then forms an "arch," and then begins to move around in a leisurely "amble." A narrator reads both the letter and the words they spell. An app like *Metamorphabet* evokes the traditional abecedary, or alphabet book, but adds digital sound, and the ability to trigger movement of the images onscreen.

GRAPHIC NOVELS

Charles Hatfield and Craig Svonkin argue for reading comics and graphic novels alongside other illustrated books for children, noting their shared qualities and appeal to young readers: "Both picture books and comics participate in children's culture and literacy learning. Both are popular forms of *imagetext* (to use W.J.T. Mitchell's influential term) which build narratives visually as well as, or sometimes instead of, verbally. Both allow for varied ratios and relationships between image and text, yet offer their readers compellingly if not dominantly visual (though sometimes also tactile and multisensory) experiences" (431). Hatfield and Svonkin observe, however, that while picturebooks have been authorized by adults as proper childhood reading as a means of literacy instruction, comics and graphic novels "are often seen as fugitive reading" that is more about pleasure than instruction (431). Some adults have actually considered comics dangerous to children, most famously the psychiatrist Frederic Wertham, who warned in his book *Seduction of the Innocent* (1954) that "Constructive and creative forces in children are channeled by comic books into destructive avenues" (94). Wertham's book was part of a broader hysteria over the dangers of comics that culminated in 1954 with the formation of the Comics Code Authority, which issued a strict set of guidelines about what could be shown in comics. Both the popularity of comics among child and adolescent readers and the fears this popularity inspired among some adults testify to the importance of this artistic form in children's culture.

A Brief History of the Graphic Novel

Graphic novels are not, strictly speaking, children's or young adult literature. Like folk and fairy tales or chapbooks, most are not intended specifically for young readers. The prominence of superhero comics as the popular face of graphic narratives may contribute to the impression that such works are primarily for children, since superheroes have been marketed to children, especially in the form of cartoons and toys. However, even superhero comics contain mature content and primarily target adult readers. Nevertheless, like the crossover and mixed-audience works discussed in Chapter 2, some comics and graphic novels are read by both children and adults. Moreover, as visual texts, they share qualities with children's illustrated works and picturebooks.

According to Stephen Weiner, comic books, or magazines with illustrated stories, emerged in the early 1930s, and the earliest examples were collections of comic strips reprinted from newspapers (2). When it became clear that a market existed for this new medium, original stories and art were commissioned: "Early comic book magazines consisted of genre stories told in comic book format, including mysteries, adventure, and romance" (Weiner 2). As Weiner explains, Jerry Siegel and Joe Shuster's creation of Superman in the early 1930s and his debut in the 1938 publication of *Action Comics #1* helped propel comics to popular success. Scott McCloud defines **comics** as the juxtaposition of "pictorial and other images in deliberate sequence intended to convey information and/ or to produce an aesthetic response in the viewer" (9). In other words, comics combine image and text, visual and verbal information, presented sequentially to tell a story. Starting in 1950, the Belgian artist Hergé published his Tintin comics in a series of "comic albums," or large-format collections, which were immensely popular across Europe and eventually translated into English and published in the United States by the same company that produced the Little Golden Books. Experiments with longer visual narratives continued between the 1940s and 1970s with a variety of terms suggested for these works: picture novels, picto-novels, novels in graphic form, graphic stories, and graphic novels. The latter term, which eventually prevailed, was coined in 1964 by comic-shop owner and publisher Richard Kyle and was popularized in the late 1970s by comics pioneer Will Eisner. Eisner used the term to market *A Contract with God* (1978), a book-length collection of stories in graphic form, and he sought specifically to differentiate graphic works with literary aspirations from the more popular, mass-produced comic books (Arnold n.p.). Weiner defines **graphic novels** as "book-length comic books that are meant to be read as one story" (xi). The term is now used indiscriminately to refer to literary works telling a single graphic story, collections of reprinted comic books, and manga.

Works that would now be called graphic novels preceded Eisner's, but the late 1970s and early 1980s saw increased attention to the literary possibilities of graphic literature. Art Spiegelman published the first volume of *Maus: A Survivor's Tale* in 1986, followed by a second volume in 1991. Spiegelman's *Maus* depicts his father's experience as a Polish Jew during the Holocaust and his eventual deportation to and survival of Auschwitz, with different types of characters represented by different animals: mice for Jews, and cats for German soldiers and Nazis. The two-volume work was awarded the Pulitzer Prize in 1992, making it one of the most distinguished graphic novels ever published. Other landmark graphic works include Alan Moore and Dave Gibbons's *Watchmen* (1986–87) and Frank Miller's *The Dark Knight Returns* (1986), both of which were initially published serially as monthly comics before being collected in single volumes. They reflect a much darker perspective on superheroes, combining the fantastical elements of superhero comics with the grittier realism of young adult and adult literature, and they have proved enormously influential on the direction of comics since their appearance. Originally published in French, *Persepolis* (2000) by Marjane Satrapi tells the story of her childhood in Iran after the 1979 revolution; because of its focus on childhood, it has drawn the attention of children's literature critics. Gene Luen Yang's *American Born Chinese* (2006) engages with the themes of immigration, cultural hybridity, self-acceptance, and the corrosive impact of racial stereotypes using a unique blend of fable, fantasy, and realism. *American Born Chinese* received the Printz Award as the most distinguished work for young adults in 2007. Alison Bechdel's *Fun Home* (2006), although not for young adults per se, details the childhood and young adulthood of its lesbian protagonist and her relationship with her gay or bisexual father. The graphic novel has been adapted into a Broadway musical, and some called on it to be banned based in part on fears that children would read it (Sims n.p.). The US Congressman John Lewis's graphic novel trilogy *March* (2013–16), cowritten with Andrew Aydin and illustrated by Nate Powell, details his participation in the Civil Rights

Illustration from *American Born Chinese* by Gene Luen Yang, 2006.

Movement of the 1950s and 1960s as a young man. The third volume was honored with the National Book Award for Young People's Literature, the Coretta Scott King Author Award, and the Printz Award. These are only a few of the most critically acclaimed graphic novels, many of which have become crossover hits with children and young adults, if not published specifically for them.

Graphic Narratives and the Child and YA Reader

As visual, relatively inexpensive, and popular texts that tell exciting tales of horror, adventure, or heroism, comics and graphic narratives have been commonly perceived as children's or YA literature. Moreover, the content of comics storytelling—issues of identity, transformed or mutated bodies, and stories of empowerment and adventure—resonates with the concerns and experiences of young readers. For instance, some of the most popular comics heroes, such as Superman and Batman, are orphans, and in Superman's case, his biological parents were important figures on his doomed home world, in contrast to his humble adopted family in Kansas. This origin story sounds like what Freud calls the family romance in which a young person fantasizes that he has been adopted and that his "real" parents are actually much more important than his known ones. One of the consistent themes of Superman mythology is his experience as an alien out of place on earth. He is surrounded by much weaker earthlings and must decide how he will fit in with them and what he will do with his powers. This character, who is both different from and more powerful than those around him, represents an attractive fantasy for young people who may similarly feel alienated but disempowered. In many cases, comics heroes are physically or temporally displaced from home. Buck Rogers, whose comic strip appeared in 1929, is a man who awakes from suspended animation hundreds of years in the future. Flash Gordon, the eponymous hero of a comic strip that debuted in 1934, must travel to a distant world to save the earth. The comic character who finds himself far from home becomes the outsider who must adjust to or conquer an alien environment before returning, replicating the home-away-home structure that Nodelman sees as characterizing children's literature. Many comics heroes have strange, mutant, or transforming bodies, echoing the physical experience of childhood and adolescence. *The Fantastic Four* (1961), *Spider-Man* (1962), and the *Hulk* (1962) all feature characters whose bodies are transformed by freak accidents and who must contend with their strange new bodies and powers. This changing body also appears in the Ms. Marvel series, which features Marvel comics' first Muslim heroine, Kamala Khan. The first five issues were collected in the volume *Ms. Marvel Volume 1: No Normal* (2014). Kamala is a teenaged Pakistani American from New Jersey who idolizes the previous Ms. Marvel, Carol Danvers. Kamala learns that she has shapeshifting abilities and embraces the role of Ms. Marvel, with some trepidation. For the mutants of the X-Men comics, the emergence of their powers actually coincides with adolescence, making the direct parallel between the sometimes monstrous or out-of-control bodies of superheroes and those of children and teenagers. Graphic novels build on these traditions of comics and comic strips.

Given that graphic novels occupy the boundary between children's and adult literature, one must also be attuned to how they address, imply, or construct their audiences. Yang's *American Born Chinese*, for instance, uses the graphic form to address the concerns of young adults, juxtaposing and overlapping the movement from child to young adult—the experience of adolescence—with the movement from China to the United States—the experience of immigration. Both situations involve a kind of hybridity that is explored both visually and verbally in the work. Vera Brosgol's *Anya's Ghost* also explores the immigrant experience, tapping into the gothic roots of graphic novels in horror and crime comics. Anya, a first-generation Russian immigrant, is struggling to fit in at her American high school when she falls down a well and encounters the ghost of a girl named Emily, who died nearly a century earlier. Anya's own life as a contemporary teenager is contrasted with Emily's simpler farm life, and the ghost appears to become increasingly corrupted by her exposure to teen culture. Anya must eventually contend with the increasingly threatening spirit, which represents the worst in herself. In Lila Quintero Weaver's graphic novel *Darkroom* (2012), Lila and her family emigrate from Argentina to Alabama in the early 1960s and experience life as Latinx immigrants in the Deep South during the Civil Rights movement. Weaver's work suggests a way of thinking about the child or young adult reader of graphic novels in that Lila is positioned in the text as herself a keen reader of the world around her, though she sometimes finds herself mystified by the tense race relations of her small town.

With the association between images and accessibility or simplicity, presumably stemming from the use of images to convey information to illiterate people, graphic fiction has been used to appeal to youth while teaching them about literature, politics, society, and history. Some of the first long-form comics were volumes in the Classics Ilustrated series that adapted canonical literary works such as Daniel Defoe's *Robinson Crusoe*, Herman Melville's *Moby Dick*, and James Fenimore Cooper's *Last of the Mohicans*. Published by Albert Lewis Kanter between 1941 and 1971, the Classics Illustrated series originally comprised 64-page comics published under the "Classic Comics" label. Each issue included additional educational content and omitted advertisements to appeal to educators (Jones 16). For instance, Willam B. Jones Jr., notes that the *Romeo and Juliet* issue contained "a description of Elizabethan playhouses," and most included author biographies (16). The character of Wonder Woman debuted the same year as the Classics Illustrated series. Created by psychologist William Moulton Marston, Wonder Woman was meant to teach readers about the possibilities of empowered womanhood. "Frankly, Wonder Woman is psychological propaganda for the new type of woman who should, I believe, rule the world," Marston reportedly wrote (qtd. in Lepore front matter). More recently, Roland Owen Laird, Taneshia Nash Laird, and Elihu "Adofo" Bey's *Still I Rise: A Graphic History of African Americans* (2009) presents important moments in African American history using the graphic novel form. The sophistication of graphic novels—their mature content, the complex relationship between visual image and verbal text—suggests the often-overlooked sophistication of children's picturebooks or comics for younger readers. Placing graphic novels alongside picturebooks prompts a reevaluation of each form and raises questions of how the two differ, how they address different audiences, and how their marketing affects public perception of what they are and how they work.

Reading Graphic Novels Critically

As with picturebooks and other visual media, reading graphic novels critically requires the reader to attend to both image and text. The content and style of the illustrations, their placement on the page, the content and placement of the verbal text, and the interplay between verbal and visual elements are all crucial features of graphic literature. According

Illustration from *Darkroom: A Memoir in Black and White* by Lila Quintero Weaver, 2012.

to McCloud, the less detailed and more abstract a cartoon, like a stick figure or emoticon, the more amplified and general the message. For example, a simple smiley face can convey pure happiness, and a broader range of people of different backgrounds can identify with the more simple and iconic face. For McCloud, this possibility for amplification and generality is what makes comics so appealing and effective for a broad audience. Some of the concepts we have discussed in relation to picturebooks will be useful for analyzing graphic novels, but the analysis of graphic novels does require its own techniques and terms.

TERMS FOR THE ANALYSIS OF GRAPHIC NOVELS

TERM	DEFINITION
Panel	A panel is a basic visual unit comprised of a single image, usually framed by a four-sided outline or border, though some panels are round or lack borders.
Gutter	The gutter is the space between panels. Usually action is contained to a panel, but sometimes illustrators can violate panel boundaries and extend action into the gutter to communicate something extraordinary, like a violent action.
Thought or Speech Bubble	These white spaces filled with text usually float above a character's head and indicate dialogue or thought. Bubbles that occur in a sequence of smaller white circles, with the words printed in the largest circle, usually indicate thoughts not spoken aloud.
Caption	Words that appear in boxes inside a panel or gutter constitute a caption. Usually captions represent the voice of the narrator, though if the text appears in quotation marks it might represent a character's speech or thought.
Motion Lines	Lines immediately adjacent to a figure within a panel are used to indicate movement or feeling. For instance, several lines might be drawn from a fist to create the impression of the arm moving through space during a punch, or several squiggly lines coming off a head could convey surprise or confusion.

Symbols McCloud uses the general term "symbol" to describe visual objects with culturally specific meanings. He gives the example of a small pear-shaped object drawn on a figure's forehead, which could be read as sweat and signify physical or mental exertion. Below the eyes, the same symbol could be read as tears, indicating sadness or grief.

Sound Effects Sound in comics can be represented textually, using onomatopoeias like "pow" or "thud."

Closure The term "closure" is borrowed from Gestalt psychology and refers to the process of filling in missing information to form a complete mental picture. Closure usually occurs automatically and unconsciously as the reader looks at a panel and moves between panels. McCloud provides the example of a sequence of two panels with a human figure and a top hat; in the first, the figure is wearing the hat and touching the brim of it with his hand. In the second, the figure is holding the hat above his head. The viewer likely achieves closure by imagining the action of lifting the hat off, though we only see two static images. Sequential art relies on closure for meaning.

We can use these terms to analyze a page from Weaver's *Darkroom* on which Lila's young brother, having grown up in Argentina, sees an African American man in Alabama for the first time. The man appears in a borderless panel occupying the full vertical length of the page, with Lila's brother, Johnny, seated in the background playing with his toy dump truck. Johnny is also depicted in two much smaller panels to the left of the man. In the first, his whole body is shown seated, his face looking up and alarmed. The second panel is a close-up of his face, his eyes wide as he calls out to his father. The three figures of Johnny indicate movement in time, since he does not notice the man in the first panel and then transitions from being silently alarmed to calling out. Because of Johnny's movement, the reader experiences the closure of imagining the man walking, though his singular image is static. Moreover, the man's eyes are closed. We assume he is blinking, not that he is walking with his eyes closed, but the juxtaposition of his closed eyes and Johnny's wide open ones makes clear that Johnny is the one looking and that the man is the object of Johnny's gaze. Because the reader also looks at the man who cannot or does not look back, the page creates equivalence between Johnny and the reader and privileges Johnny's perspective, and ours, over that of the African American man in a way that could jar the reader. The images and their arrangement on the page mean something, and we would miss those meanings if we did not think carefully about the form of graphic narratives.

DIGITAL MEDIA FOR CHILDREN

Digital media is ubiquitous in contemporary life. Many texts are "born digital," which means they have no print counterpart. When it comes to child readers, there has been much speculation about how their digital reading differs from their print reading and how children can develop literacies in multiple media and formats. This is made all the more complicated because children and adolescents are considered "digital natives," who have never known a world without computers. They live in an exploding media landscape that includes hundreds and hundreds of electronic apps, games, and books—including many books and apps whose aims seem to be more commercial than literary or educational. To consider digital media for children is to acknowledge that the boundaries between "game" and "book" are not always clear, since a great deal of digital media—whether picturebooks, games or apps—have elements that require the reader to interact with the text just as a game does. This is sometimes described as **interactivity**, which means that there is an interchange between a person and her device. On a tablet computer or phone, this can involve tapping, clicking on hotlinks, swiping across the screen, triggering sound or animation, tilting or rotating the device, or other actions. One well-known contemporary example is the "Alice for iPad" app sold by Atomic Antelope, in which readers touch the screen to help Alice shrink, grow, and navigate the spaces of Wonderland. Other online books ask a child to fill in a word or phrase, changing the narrative: An example is *Emily Elizabeth Goes to School* on the Scholastic website, where as early as the first page a child might choose whether Emily will learn to "leap," "read," or "weave."

As early as 2008, N. Katherine Hayles sought to establish the nature of digital texts and distinguish them from print literature, noting that "electronic literature performs the additional function of entwining human ways of knowing with machine cognitions" (135). She argued that readers coexist or even coevolve alongside computers, and the fact that the machine processes data alongside the reader is significant. She also notes that intermediation, or "re-presenting material in different mediums," changes our sensory experience of the material and therefore the "kinds of knowledge represented" (135).

Several of the unique functions we associate with digital literature—such as movement or the need to trigger a book's action—were, however, anticipated by or embodied by pre-digital print literature. For example, pop-up books have always relied on the reader's participation to make the pages "move" by pulling levers, turning pages, pulling folds, and so on. The pop-up book is an old form, ranging back to nineteenth-century authors, including the German illustrator and writer Lothar Meggendorfer. In our time, author and pop-up engineer Robert Sabuda has created several notable pop-up books, including *The Wonderful Wizard of Oz: A Commemorative Pop-Up* (2000). Pop-up books prefigure the kinds of spatial movements we might see in a digital picturebook. They demonstrate that the development of digital literature can be viewed as building on older traditions as well as breaking from them.

In a recent article, Junko Yokota considers the development of the digital picturebook from the 1990s to the present, noting that some recent developers of electronic literature for children have begun to take fuller advantage of the creative potentials of digital literature. Early digital children's books, Yokota contends, were often simple PDFs of print picturebooks. She notes that the next generation added extras like "audio narration, music, sound effects, panning in film-like close ups and wide shots as early attempts to embed movement, game features (i.e., puzzles, drawing, matching) and more" (77). Ultimately, however, "the tablet interactive book was essentially the same as the print book" (77). In the present, and looking towards the future, creators of children's tablet book apps should attempt to "avoid the pitfall of merely trying to reproduce digitally what was created in the print medium" (81). She names David Wiesner's app *Spot* (2015) as an example of what picturebooks are capable of in narrative and aesthetic terms. We have already seen Wiesner's work as a producer of imaginative wordless picturebooks, and his print picturebook *The Three Pigs* (2001) pushed the boundaries of postmodern picturebooks. In *Spot*, he has created five connected worlds—Lower Rügg, a miniature world underneath an armchair; Oceana Prime, an underwater world; Mekanikos, populated by robots; Katzaluna, a world where cats are having an exuberant parade; and an intergalactic space station. To navigate between them, the reader pinches the screen, uses two figures to swipe in opposite directions, or taps on a menu. Ultimately, the app involves the free and self-directed exploration of very different—yet connected—fantastic worlds, and it is also an exercise in perspective. Zooming in on a detail in one world (by swiping in opposite directions) allows you to enter another world-space. This begins with the opening screen, where a ladybug crawls across the screen, and you begin by touching the spot on the ladybug's back and swiping in opposite directions. *Spot* is reminiscent of the print picturebooks by Istvan Banyai, like *Zoom* (1998), where the reader's turning of the pages recreates the mechanism of a "zoom out" by a camera, showing every scene as part of a wider picture.

Another digital app for young people that demonstrates the ability for open-ended exploration and non-linear storytelling is Simon Flesser and Magnus Gardebäck's app *The Sailor's Dream* (2014), developed by Simogo. In *The Sailor's Dream*, readers scroll through a wide ocean space with several locations to explore, including "The Seven-Song Cottage," "The Secret Lighthouse," and "The Celestial Sanctuary." Each site has rooms to explore, and you can tap on objects like lanterns or hanging sculptures whose chiming tones create haunting music. Sometimes by swiping on a link in one of the rooms, a page of text comes up. From these fragments of text, the reader can piece together a kind of narrative. As reviewer J. Nicholas Geist notes, "These snippets of story each describe a young girl, or her mother, or her absent, seafaring father, but having come as close as possible to finishing the game, I still can't say with certainty whose dream we are in" (Geist).

The app requires repeated viewing, not only to piece together some of the narrative, but to experience the parts of it that are time-dependent. For example, there is an hourly radio transmission in the "Transmission Horloge" and a floating bottle that plays a folksong when you "pop" the cork of the bottle: one for each day of the week. Lucas Ramada Prieto comments that in *The Sailor's Dream* "we are offered the possibility of navigating freely through the literary spaces that make up the world of fiction" (50).

Because digital platforms also offer users the capacity to produce their own content, they allow for the production of fanfiction and children's own stories. There are a number of apps and other platforms where children and young adults are encouraged to craft their own stories. The increasingly thin boundaries between "producer" and "consumer" help challenge the assumption that adults produce children's literature which is then passively received by child consumers—because children are increasingly writing their own online stories. Digital fanfiction is another area where child readers can negotiate their relationships to authors and cultural products, crafting stories and fan art that offer their own take on pre-existing fictional universes. We discuss fan fiction further in Chapter 13.

Forking Path Storylines

We also associate digital literature with the use of "forking path" storylines, where readers are asked or forced to make choices about the way the story needs to proceed. The Choose Your Own Adventure series (1979–1998) included books such as Edward Packard's *Cave of Time* (1979) and R.A. Montgomery's *House of Danger* (1983). In these books, a reader would read up to a certain point and then be offered a choice of what action to follow. The choice determined the ultimate outcome of the book and the fate of the protagonist (who was addressed in second-person point-of-view as "you"). The Choose Your Own Adventure books enjoyed great popularity, whetting the appetite of readers for works that were not organized in a purely linear way and that allowed the reader to have some impact on the outcome of the story. A recent print graphic novel that plays with forking paths or multiple story lines is Jason Shiga's *Meanwhile* (2010), which is subtitled "Pick Any Path. 3,856 Story Possibilities." Readers move between story panels connected by thin tubes, which sometimes lead off a page and onto a tab on another page. The majority of the story lines end with disaster or doom; the reader is asked to find the one path that will lead to "happiness and success" (n.p.). Several of the original Choose Your Own Adventure Books have been modified to be digital apps by Edward Packard in collaboration with the company U-Ventures. Wiesner's *Spot* could be seen as a contemporary version of the Choose Your Own Adventure Books because readers have the choice of which of the app's five worlds to visit, and in what order.

Print and Online Combinations and Relationships

Many print books for children include a digital or online component. One example is Jon Scieszka, Shane Prigmore, and Francesco Sedita's *SPHDZ Book #1 (Spaceheadz)* (2010), in which readers are asked to recruit millions of people to become "Spaceheadz" and save the planet. After becoming an official "SPHDZ" on the website, you can surf various book-related websites to learn more about the Spaceheadz mission. The physical book can stand on its own but is enriched by digital components. Augmented reality technologies offer the illusion—at least to some extent—of "entering into" the world of a print book. For example, readers can hold up selected pages of Tony DiTerlizzi's fantasy text *The Search for WondLa* (2010) to their digital cameras and explore three-dimensional interactive settings from the book. Augmented reality such as we see in Niantic's 2016 runaway hit game *Pokémon Go* (2016) can also function within a purely digital book or app, such as the "Princess and her Pals 3-D" Augmented Reality storybook from Popar Interactive Books for Kids.

Yokota notes the contemporary trend of producing a given cultural product in multiple formats: "These days, an app might emerge first, later become a film and then, a print book, as in the case of *The Fantastic Flying Books of Mr. Morris Lessmore.* For her, this raises some provocative critical questions:

> Should the same story be played out in so many different formats? Is there a format that is better suited to the story than another? Is there a format to which the art is more suited than the other? Perhaps these are the questions we should be analysing in terms of how story plays out in different formats. In which format is a particular story *best* conveyed? In what ways are the formats different in how they show story features? (77).

One interesting case study in the interaction between print and digital forms is Hervé Tullet's *Un Livre* (2010), translated into English as *Press Here* (2011). Tullet's print picturebook mimics a digital app or book. Consisting of small circles in red, yellow, and blue placed in simple arrangements, the reader is asked to complete activities like pressing one or more of the circles multiple times or tilting the book. The reader then turns the page to see a doublespread where the impact of the reader's actions is clear. For example, given a page with three yellow dots, the reader is asked to "Rub the dot on the left … gently." When the page is turned, the dot on the left has turned red. Bettina Kümmerling-Meibauer contends that *Press Here* "obviously refers to the increasing impact of digital media on children's literature, but might also be interpreted as a book that makes fun of these new trends" (57). In this comment, we see an acknowledgement not only of the influences of picturebooks on new digital media, but the way digital media is in its turn influencing the children's books that are produced.

Digital media is a relatively new form; its narrative and artistic potential is not yet fully realized. Yet as we continue to develop a critical language to talk about digital media, we can draw on our understanding of the classic picturebook. Digital books—like classic picturebooks—require many types of literacy at once. A picturebook expects the reader to decode words, images, and design. A digital book might require attention to animation and recorded sound, the navigation of links, and the solving of games or puzzles. To read a digital text critically is to build on the kinds of reading skills exacted by picturebooks and to extend them further.

READING CRITICALLY: PICTUREBOOKS

There Is a Bird on Your Head!

Mo Willems's *There Is a Bird on Your Head!* (2007) is a text for beginning readers that relies on a complex mix of words and images to tell its story. The book derives its humor from the escalation of a situation as birds nest first on Elephant's head and then on Piggie's. The repetition of words and phrases—combined with visual slapstick—is ideal for beginning readers and is also in keeping with the absurd situation in which Elephant and Piggie find themselves.

There Is a Bird on Your Head! is sixty-four pages long, twice the conventional length of a picturebook. The title page prominently features the seal of the Theodor Seuss Geisel Award, which honors excellence in books for beginning readers. The invocation of one of the most critically acclaimed and popular picturebook authors might appeal to parents, teachers, and librarians seeking the legitimacy of Seuss's own series for beginning readers, the I Can Read books.

As of 2018, thirty Elephant and Piggie books have been produced, underscoring their status as a commercial product. Turning to the title page, we see that Hyperion Books for Children is identified as "An Imprint of Disney Book Group." While *There Is a Bird on Your Head!* might appear to be a quirky, independent book, it emerged not from a small publisher but from a multinational company. Willems's Pigeon Book series is also very successful; the Pigeon always makes a cameo appearance in the Elephant and Piggie books, hidden somewhere in the book. This book is no exception: there is an image of the Pigeon on the endpapers of the book, eating what appears to be a hamburger.

The relationship between Elephant and Piggie, and their dialogue, is the focus of *There Is a Bird on Your Head!* The two characters have distinct personalities: Elephant bears a quizzical or dismayed expression indicating a cautious or even melancholy character, while Piggie is diminutive and enthusiastic. Together, the pair create an "odd couple" comedy with the contrasting personalities of the characters adding to the humor. From the illustrations, their genders are unclear, but the blurb on the back of the book identifies Elephant as a male named Gerald and refers to Piggie using female pronouns. Elephant's circumspect and somewhat grumpy character and Piggie's exuberance can be seen as fitting gender stereotypes.

On the title page, *There Is a Bird on Your Head!* is rendered as a speech balloon emanating from Piggie. In fact, all dialogue in the text comes from speech balloons, indicating the book's indebtedness to the comic book or the graphic novel. Elephant's text balloon is gray like him, and Piggie's text balloon is a form of pink slightly lighter than Piggie herself. Like many comic books, the book proceeds with a combination of text and wordlessness, showing a unity between text and image. The lines of the illustrations are very thick as well, evoking children's coloring books. The medium is acrylic paint with some elements of pencil. The colors are a

Mo Willems's *There Is a Bird on Your Head!* (2007) features comic, simple dialogue between Elephant and Piggie.

basic and saturated pastel, with no shading visible. Characters are associated with a particular color—Elephant is rendered in gray, Piggie in pink, and the various birds in the text are green or yellow.

The book begins wordlessly with Elephant and Piggie sitting serenely. A bird lands on Elephant's head; its flight path is depicted by a curvy line of dots descending from the top right of the page and lengthening as he prepares to land. The wordless page shows Elephant expressing surprise, with the next page showing a speech balloon saying "Piggie!" (5). Informed by Piggie of the bird on his head, Elephant runs off yelling, "Aaaaaaaaaggghhh!" which temporarily scares off the birds (10–11). The exclamation, depicted in large font over two pages, adds expressive drama to a spoken reading of the book.

Subsequent pages show the conversation of Elephant and Piggie, using a great deal of repetition. While simple, this dialogue moves the action along:

Piggie: There is a bird on your head.
Elephant: There is a bird on my head? (8–9)

The verbal repetition here and the subtle modulations and variation in language throughout the book create both comedy and suspense. For example, Piggie's statement changes to Elephant's incredulous question, causing us to dwell on Elephant's surprise and creating a melodious echo effect. The simplicity in the language is deliberately crafted to encourage young children to read on their own, and *There Is a Bird on Your Head!* could well be one of the first books they read independently of adults. In his Pigeon books, Mo Willems established a formula in which very modest action takes place, and the rapport between the characters (often the Pigeon and a bus driver) is the main focus. In addition to the comic verbal repetition, Willems's approach includes a great deal of visual slapstick that relies on the movement of characters on the page and their expressions. The subtle, delicate movements of the birds in *There Is a Bird on Your Head!* form a cohesive narrative on their own. Each visual element of the text enhances the portrayal of both minor and major characters.

Willems's Pigeon books tend to include a surprise twist, and there is one here too—or, in fact, two twists. The first occurs when Elephant shoos the bird off his head, only to have *two* birds land there. They turn out to be lovebirds who build a nest, hatch three chicks, and proceed to feed a worm to the chicks. Once again repetitive structures convey Elephant's struggle.

The second twist centers on the ultimate destination of the lovebirds and their family. When Piggie asks Elephant where he wants the birds to go, he says, "SOMEWHERE ELSE!" This is again rendered in a large font with uppercase letters, indicating volume and emphasis. The whole nest on his head is knocked flying, including the worm, with movements indicated by two short curvy lines placed around the figures. Piggie is also knocked for a loop. From her prone position, she asks, "Why not ask them to go somewhere else?" (48). Elephant duly asks the birds to leave, and the adult birds respond, "No problem" (52). Once the birds are gone, a jubilant Elephant thanks Piggie for her advice. The final page shows a vexed Piggie with connected eyebrows and narrowed eyes, saying, "You are welcome…." (57). All five birds and their nest are now on *her* head.

While children are often assumed not to understand irony and sarcasm, the ending of the book demands an understanding of both. When she tells Elephant, "You are welcome," the usually gleeful Piggie is being sarcastic. Piggie's plight also introduces the young reader to irony. After Piggie advises Elephant to direct the birds "somewhere else," Piggie is upset when that "somewhere else" is her own head. The book introduces young readers to absurdity in both text and image as a silly situation spirals out into an ever sillier situation.

EXPLORATIONS

Review

1. Why do Maria Nikolajeva and Carole Scott argue that picturebooks should be spelled as one word rather than two ("picture books")?

2. What are the main characteristics of a picturebook? Would you call a longer book such as *The Invention of Hugo Cabret* a picturebook? If not, what genre best describes it?

3. What are the differences between a picturebook and an illustrated book?

4. What are some ways in which picturebooks rely on design and production elements for their artistic effects and to make meaning?

5. What is a concept book?

6. How do wordless picturebooks tell a story? What are some ways that they can be "read" and experienced?

Reflect

1. What do you think is added to a picturebook when it is read out loud? Have you recently read a picturebook to a child? Talk about your experience of reading picturebooks out loud or having them read to you.

2. Select a picturebook from your own collection or that of a friend. How would it be different if it was composed in a different medium, i.e., if a book produced using modeling clay used watercolors instead?

3. Consider books that are published in multiple formats: hardcover, softcover, and board book. How does the publishing format change the experience of reading the book?

4. While graphic novels are not necessarily children's literature, some of their themes of empowerment or identity resonate with young readers. What are some situations

or characters from comics or graphic novels that you think would be meaningful to a child reader?

Investigate

1. Choose a classic picturebook. Type out the text on a separate sheet of paper. Read the text out loud and write a brief analysis of what is lost without the pictures. Photocopy four or five pages of the same picturebook and then cut out the text. Comment on what it is like to view the illustrations without any text.

2. Interview classmates about their favorite picturebooks during childhood. What books did they name, and what details do they remember about them? Interview an older adult about his or her favorite book. What are the generational differences?

3. Take a page from a picturebook and draw an alternative picture for the page, choosing whatever medium you wish to work in or have available. How is your picture different from the existing image for the book?

4. Examine any digital text aimed at children or an electronic game for children. How does it compare to a picturebook? Would you describe the video game or electronic book as educational? Why, or why not?

SUGGESTED READINGS

Brown, Margaret Wise. *Goodnight Moon* (1947). Illustrated by Clement Hurd. The book dramatizes a small rabbit saying goodnight to the familiar objects in its room, with a simple rhyming text reminiscent of a lullaby. There are several small and subtle details in the illustrations, including shifting objects inside the room and a slow moonrise outside. The book has bright and cheerful colors, which yield to the slow darkening of the room as the night progresses.

Carle, Eric. *The Very Hungry Caterpillar* (1969). The book teaches both counting and days of the week as it follows a ravenous caterpillar munching its way through various foods, emerging at the end in a double-page image of a butterfly. Each meal the caterpillar eats has a die-cut hole to indicate where it has eaten through.

De la Peña, Matt. *Last Stop on Market Street* (2015). **Illustrated by Christian Robin-son.** Matt de la Peña and Christian Robinson follow CJ and his Grandmother as they take a bus ride across a city, with CJ asking multiple questions, such as why they do not have a car and why he doesn't have an iPod. CJ's Grandmother responds to him with affection and honesty, encouraging him to see the world less in terms of material objects and with more imaginative engagement with the environment and people around him. Christian Robinson's bold, brightly colored illustrations evoke the vibrancy and diversity of the cityscape and the people who share their bus ride with them.

Kunhardt, Dorothy. *Pat the Bunny* (1940). An early "touch and feel" book for infants, *Pat the Bunny* has many interactive elements, such as a cotton ball to simulate a rabbit's tail and sandpaper to function as "daddy's beard." The book has recently become available as a board book.

Potter, Beatrix. *The Tale of Peter Rabbit* (1902). The tale of Peter Rabbit's escape from Mr. McGregor's garden uses pages of alternating text and images. Potter mixes fantastic details with realistic ones, such as depicting rabbits wearing clothes but surrounded by a realistic and highly detailed natural setting. The book is known for its vivid watercolors with subtle colors and the accuracy of the paintings of the rabbits and other creatures.

Selznick, Brian. *The Invention of Hugo Cabret* (2007). The winner of the Caldecott Medal in 2007, *Hugo Cabret* is much longer than the average picturebook and includes elements from film and graphic novels. Illustrated in heavily shaded black and white, it alternates wordless pages with text, as in a silent film. Hugo, an orphaned boy who lives in the walls of a Parisian train station, solves the mystery of a broken automaton left to him by his father, with the help of a book-loving young girl and a brusque toy shop owner, who turns out to be the reclusive cinema legend Georges Méliès. The book ends with a celebration of Méliès's films, with several still photographic images.

Sendak, Maurice. *Where the Wild Things Are* (1963). Mischievous Max, wearing a wolf suit, is sent to his room without supper and undertakes an imaginary journey to the kingdom of the Wild Things. The book uses dark colors and an innovative cross-hatched drawing style. Sendak also includes expansive double-spreads, adding to the sense of the fantastic in the book.

Steptoe, John. *Mufaro's Beautiful Daughters* (1987). *Mufaro's Beautiful Daughters* tells the story of two sisters, the kind Nyasha and the bad-tempered, prideful Manyara. When the king of the land asks them to appear in front of him so he can choose a queen, they are confronted with people who need their help (a test of their worthiness to be queen).

Manyara pushes these people away, but Nyasha helps them, and is therefore chosen as queen. In a note at the beginning of the book, Steptoe comments that the setting of the book is based on the ruins of an ancient city in Zimbabwe and the flora and fauna of the region.

Wiesner, David. *Tuesday* (1991). This nearly wordless book has surreal images of frogs floating on their lily pads over a suburban neighborhood. Other than an indication of the time and date, there is no interpretation of what the flying frogs might mean, beyond the surprise of a few human witnesses. In addition to the innate absurdity of the frogs, the humor comes from the final image of flying pigs mobilizing in a fashion similar to the flying frogs. Wiesner used computer graphics to create the images and uses a color scheme heavy in blues and greens—evocative of both the flying amphibians and the night itself.

APPROACHES TO TEACHING *THERE IS A BIRD ON YOUR HEAD!* [ELEMENTARY SCHOOL]

Preparation for the Lesson

Read *There Is a Bird on Your Head!* out loud twice, with the second reading conducted by two students taking the roles of Elephant and Piggie. Ask the student readers to act out the expressive physical gestures of the characters in the book.

Learning Goals

- To familiarize students with vocabulary to describe the comic and absurd

- To teach vocabulary about feelings and emotions, and to consider how those are expressed both verbally and visually in Willems's book

- To explore how design elements function in a picturebook

- To examine how the punctuation on the page changes the meaning and tone of a sentence, with particular attention to the movement from a statement to a question.

The following activities emphasize the book's use of text and image to make meaning, and the contribution that the book's design makes to the book.

Activity One: Emotions and Mood in There Is a Bird on Your Head!

Part A: Characters' Emotions

On the board or projector, make a chart of the emotions experienced by each character in the book. Emotions covered could include surprise, alarm, frustration, annoyance, satisfaction, and amusement. Discuss how the book portrays these emotions in both pictures and words.

Part B: The Ending of the Book

Discuss the ending of the book. Were you expecting the book to end that way? What are some words for how Piggie feels at the end? How would you feel if you were her?

Part C: Mood and Tone

Generate words for the overall mood of the book, introducing the following words: absurd, ironic, whimsical, silly, comic.

Activity Two: Punctuation and Tone

Choose sections from *There Is a Bird on Your Head!* that involve repetition, changing your tone of voice to indicate a shift from a statement to a question to an exclamation. How does punctuation such as a question mark change the meaning of the text?

Activity Three: Analyzing the Visuals of a Book

Lead the class in a discussion about some of the striking visual and design elements of *There Is a Bird on Your Head!* such as the following:

- Consider Willems's choice to draw the flight of the birds using broken lines. Ask students to draw some birds in flight like the ones in the book. How do the broken lines capture the movement of the birds? How else could an artist draw a bird in flight?

- Discuss why the print in the book gets bigger or smaller at different points in the book.

- Examine the endpapers of the book (the leaves of paper before the title page and after the text). Explain that the endpapers are not part of the narrative of the book but help set its mood and visual style.

- Bring in a comic strip such as *Peanuts* or *Garfield* (or any other comic strip you like) and ask the students to compare the visual style of *There Is a Bird on Your Head!* to a comic strip in a newspaper.

DOMESTICITY AND ADVENTURE

In Louisa May Alcott's *Little Women* (1868), four sisters lament their family's financial hardships as they prepare for Christmas and wonder what they will give to their beloved mother. In Mary Norton's *The Borrowers* (1952), the Clock family borrows ordinary objects to supply their miniature home with the usual household comforts, and Arrietty longs to help her father support their family by joining him on his excursions. Jim Hawkins of Robert Louis Stevenson's *Treasure Island* (1883) leaves his parents' inn to join Long John Silver and the crew of the *Hispaniola* to find buried treasure, and Stanley Yelnats and Zero dig for treasure at a camp for delinquent boys before running away in Louis Sachar's *Holes* (1998). Like these beloved works, many of the most popular children's books are either domestic or adventure novels. The idea and experience of home and leaving home are tied to the very definition of what it means to be a child, so domestic and adventure fiction have emerged as two central genres of children's literature. Examining the distinction between the two provides a useful framework for reading children's literature critically.

DEFINING DOMESTICITY AND ADVENTURE

The genres of domesticity and adventure speak directly to key dimensions and experiences of childhood, including the centrality of home in the life of the child and the

---

Opposite: "The Birds Were Flown," from J.M. Barrie's *Peter and Wendy* (1911), illustrated by F.D. Bedford. Mr. and Mrs. Darling with Nana, the dog, are left at home to mourn the loss of their children, who have just embarked on a great adventure with Peter Pan.

exploration of the wider world for which the child is meant to prepare. Perry Nodelman argues that "a basic pattern of movement from home to away and then back home again" constitutes one of the defining features of children's literature (80). Hence, the pairing and opposition of the two genres provide a useful rubric for understanding children's and young adult literature. This chapter examines the conventions and implications of both domestic and adventure stories, and it explores how adventure and domesticity are linked to conceptualizations of childhood, development, and the lived experiences of children for whom home and the movement away from home are crucial.

Domestic fiction is set primarily in and around the home and focuses on social relationships within the private sphere of the household. Due to real and imagined vulnerabilities—physical, emotional, legal, economic—children are tied to the home and to the family, which is charged with protecting them from the dangers of the outside public sphere. Thus, children are prone to experience the home as the center of the world, and they are restricted to the home in ways that adults are not. Moreover, conceiving and raising children are linked closely to meanings of domesticity and domestic work, or the making and sustaining of homes and families. Since the home for many children is coextensive with the world, domestic fiction constitutes a large portion of children's literature.

However, since childhood and adolescence also involve the experience of learning about and exploring the wider world, we find too that children's literature frequently turns to adventure, which foregrounds discovery and travel. In contrast to domestic fiction, adventures are set primarily outside and typically involve motifs of exploration, escape, and survival. These motifs reflect key childhood fantasies or desires springing from the limited experience many children have had of the world. Because they are often confined to the home, limited in their freedom to roam and lacking in knowledge or experience, children are primed to take particular interest in narratives of both domesticity and adventure, the former reflecting a closer approximation of more common realities and the latter providing alternative fantasies of the extraordinary.

We summarize some of the major conventions of domestic and adventure fiction before we consider how they are employed specifically for children.

Domestic fiction
- is set primarily in and around the home with little significant movement or travel across great distances

- addresses social and personal relations within a family and community

- involves concern with poverty, wealth, property, and social class

- provides psychological insight into characters; explores psychological motivations

- depicts little physical action or activity

- imagines danger in the form of illness or disease, social intrigues or insults, or the loss of status or reputation

- represents rewards as moral, spiritual, or social

- traditionally focuses on girls or women as protagonists

- often includes romance or flirtation as a component of the plot.

Adventure fiction
- is set primarily outside, often in locales that are exotic to the protagonist or the implied reader and require travel across great distance

- involves escaping an undesirable situation, surviving dangerous obstacles, discovering or retrieving a valued object, or achieving an extraordinary goal

- focuses more on action and plot than on psychology and character development

- depicts much physical activity, violence, or struggle

- imagines danger as overt, external, and unusual

- understands rewards as material treasures or as personal experience or transformation

- traditionally focuses on boys or men as protagonists

- often includes romance or flirtation as a component of the plot

- sometimes involves relations between races or nations.

We can think about domestic fiction as operating on a smaller scale than adventure so that the action of a domestic novel might include the microscopic progression of disease or a subtle social slight, whereas the action of adventure might be a violent attack by a mountain lion or a dramatic escape from pirates. The events, plots, movements, and characters of adventure fiction are bigger, larger than life, and extraordinary; hence, the scale is larger. Scale is one of the key differences between the two.

DOMESTIC FICTION FOR CHILDREN

Many classics of the Golden Age can be classified as domestic fiction, including Alcott's *Little Women*, Susan Coolidge's *What Katy Did* (1872), Kate Douglas Wiggin's *Rebecca of Sunnybrook Farm* (1903), L.M. Montgomery's *Anne of Green Gables* (1908), and Eleanor H. Porter's *Pollyanna* (1913). All these works are set in or around the home, even if their protagonists wander into the yard, play in the garden or in nearby fields, or walk to school or the homes of friends. Each of these novels focuses on domestic and social relationships. *Little Women* is centered on the March home and on the relationships between the four sisters, between the girls and their mother, and sometimes between the girls and others in the community, such as Aunt March or the Hummel family. The action of the novel involves everyday interactions between the girls, as when the sisters stage a play in the attic, or domestic squabbles, as when youngest sister Amy burns Jo's book of writings. The girls play, make friends with the neighbor-boy Laurie, argue with one another, attend parties, care for poorer neighbors, learn to manage their vices, and talk to one another.

Much of this action occurs indoors, and much of it relates to each of the sisters as unique individuals with fully developed psychologies. The obstacles they overcome are also internal. Amy struggles with vanity, for instance; Jo with pride and anger; and Meg with envy of other people's wealth and possessions. Beth struggles with shyness and timidity and with illness and the fragility of her own body, a common feature of domestic fiction. *Little Women* also involves a concern with economic status and social class; the March family suffers from the contradictory and complex circumstances of genteel poverty. Though they have enjoyed relative wealth and security in the past and are a family of high status in their community, their father has ruined them financially and forced them to the brink of economic disaster. This situation becomes especially apparent when the girls must dress for a fashionable party or when they have to rely on their wealthy and difficult Aunt March for support. The March sisters also enjoy rewards for their triumphs, but those rewards are typically moral or spiritual, such as learning patience or the pleasures of being industrious rather

The four sisters gather around in Louisa May Alcott's *Little Women* (1868), illustrated by Jessie Willcox Smith.

than slothful. Other rewards include finding a husband, as each of the sisters does, except Beth. These qualities indicate that *Little Women* can be understood as a quintessentially domestic novel.

Realism and Everyday Life

Because of the traditionally close association between women and the domestic sphere, critical studies of women's writing have been especially likely to theorize about domestic fiction. Writing about nineteenth-century women authors of domestic novels, Nina Baym notes,

> Their fiction is mostly about social relations, generally set in homes and other social spaces that are fully described. The detailed descriptions are sometimes idealized, but more often simply "realistic." And, in accordance with the needs of plot, home life is presented, overwhelmingly, as unhappy. There are very few intact families in this literature, and those that are intact are unstable or locked into routines of misery. Domestic tasks are arduous and monotonous; family members oppress and abuse each other; social interchanges are alternately insipid or malicious. (27)

The realism of domestic fiction involves its representation of the quotidian details of everyday home life, in contrast with the extraordinary events or circumstances of romances (long tales of heroic exploits or quests dating to the medieval period) or fantasy works (narratives involving magic or supernatural elements). Those everyday details include domestic acts such as cooking and eating, which feature as sources of humor and tension in *Anne of Green Gables,* or pursuing leisure activities such as storytelling and unearthing family lore, which figure in works such as *Pollyanna.* Domestic fiction uses elements of everyday life like these to create the appearance of realism: real life can also be extraordinary and unbelievable, but realist fiction focuses on its more ordinary features. Moreover, it often involves the use of humor, wit, or satire to transform these otherwise common experiences into sources of entertainment and pleasure for readers, without which they might be dull.

The Home as a Dangerous Place

As Baym notes, because domestic fiction is mostly restricted to the home, the home itself must be the source of the tension, uncertainty, or threat driving the narrative. The idea of the home as a dangerous place mirrors data concerning actual child victims of violent crimes. According to the United States Department of Justice, for children between the ages of twelve and seventeen, 12 to 16 per cent of all violent crimes occur in the child victim's home (OJJDP *Statistical Briefing Book*). Both lived experience and children's domestic fiction therefore defy expectations of the home as a safe haven from the dangers of the outside world and can include physical or emotional threats, abuse, or strife. Often the mildest form this tension takes is the conflict between a rambunctious and imaginative child and his or her strict, cold, or cantankerous caregiver. This plot appears in almost all the turn-of-the-century orphan stories, such as *Anne of Green Gables, Rebecca of Sunnybrook Farm*, and *Pollyanna*. While the protagonists' emotional deprivations may not rise to the level of abuse, they are typically experienced as threatening or distressing to the already vulnerable and fearful orphans, who lack nurturing and protective parents. Usually, the severity of a new guardian functions as an obstacle for the orphaned child of domestic fiction to overcome, and in most of these examples the child triumphs in softening her stern elder, as Anne does with Marilla, and Pollyanna with Aunt Polly. In works such as Martha Finley's *Elsie Dinsmore* (1867), the emotional abuse Horace Dinsmore inflicts upon his daughter Elsie is more severe, as he subjects her to deeply humiliating trials that torment her—for example, making the timid girl perform in front of an audience or refusing to see or address his sensitive, motherless child until she betrays her religious convictions.

Illness and Disease

While domestic fiction represents the interior of the home as a source of threat or fear, it frequently depicts the interior of the body itself as another site of danger through illness, injury, or disease. In *Little Women*, for example, Beth contracts scarlet fever while helping the Hummels, a poor family of German immigrants. This scene also suggests how the poor or immigrants—those excluded from the domestic space of the home or nation or seen as intruding upon it—might figure as a source of danger or contagion to both the middle-class protagonist and the larger social body. Though Beth recovers, she is left physically weakened and with damage to her heart, which leads to her death near the end of the novel. Beth's case connects extreme self-sacrifice and self-effacing femininity to actual physical vulnerability and illness, suggesting the ways domestic work, including the care of others, physically endangers girls and women. Katy, the eponymous protagonist of Susan Coolidge's *What Katy Did*, suffers a severe spinal injury and spends much of the novel paralyzed, though she manages to replace her dead mother and run the household from her bed. Pollyanna is also paralyzed when she is struck by a motorcar, and her ability to play the "glad game" is severely threatened by her long convalescence. Emotional deprivation or abuse, physical injury, or disease often provides the narrative tension of domestic fiction for children.

Power Relations

Given the emphasis in domestic fiction on social relations, which are marked by interactions between participants of imbalanced levels of influence and authority, these works inevitably address the ways characters attempt to exert their will and defy the will of others. Writing about adult domestic novels of the nineteenth century, Jane Tompkins explains, "It is no exaggeration to say that domestic fiction is preoccupied, even obsessed, with the nature of power" (160). Tompkins focuses in particular on how domestic fiction by and about women in the nineteenth-century United States reflected an attempt to reconceive of the domestic sphere as a space where women, otherwise disempowered, could exercise authority and influence:

> The fact is that American women simply could not assume a stance of open rebellion against the conditions of their lives for they lacked the material means of escape or opposition. They had to stay put and submit. And so the domestic novelists made that necessity the basis on which to build a power structure of their own. Instead of rejecting the culture's value system outright, they appropriated it for their own use, subjecting the beliefs and customs that had molded them to a series of transformations that allowed them both to fulfill and transcend their appointed roles. (161)

Since childhood also is defined by a lack of power, children's domestic fiction is a similarly useful site for working out different scenarios in which children might exercise power within the household. The experience of childhood is marked by negotiations between one's desires and the restrictions placed on those desires by other people, available resources, and the conditions of the environment. It is in the home and within domestic relationships between caregivers and children where one first encounters the gulf between one's desires and the ability to satisfy those desires, between one's own will and the will of others. Thus, domestic fiction for children typically involves subtle power struggles between different members of the community, social classes, men and women, and adults and children.

This exploration of conflicting desires and differentials of power varies in form from text to text. In *Little Women*, Marmee, the girls' mother, and Mr. March, their father, are absent for much of the novel, which permits the girls to operate independently of adult authority. Even when their parents are present, the narrative seems to attribute more influence and authority to Marmee than to Mr. March, indicating the novel's complex implications for gendered authority. *Elsie Dinsmore* is almost entirely defined by the power struggle between Elsie, who maintains very strict ideas about religious observance, and her father, who wishes to dominate his daughter in every respect. In the well-known turn-of-the-century novels about girl orphans, characters such as Anne and Rebecca exert power over others through their personal charm and seductive imaginations, and they engage in battles of will with their stern caregivers, who come to rely, at least emotionally, on the girls they adopt. In many of these works, the children come to influence adult characters and the tone of the household as much as or more than the adults influence them. It becomes conventional for the protagonists of children's domestic fiction to be characterized by adept social skills that empower them both to vie successfully with adults and to exert a certain degree of control over their situations and homes.

Social Class

One of the central dimensions of domestic fiction related to the issue of power is its emphasis on class and social status. As Baym notes about women writers of domestic fiction for adults, "Their depiction of home life showed the home thoroughly penetrated at every point by the world ... and vulnerable to the various empty temptations of wealth as well as the possibility of poverty" (48). The distinct material qualities and comforts of the home and the success of its mission as a shelter from the outside world and the elements are enabled and determined by the economic stability, if not prosperity, of the family. The state of one's home is one of the key markers of social and class status, and domestic fiction set in the home almost always, whether overtly or implicitly, bears on these concerns. Moreover, because one's social relations and social interactions are frequently marked and limited by one's social background and class, domestic fiction, even for children, almost always reflects anxieties about wealth and poverty. These issues are central to Alcott's *Little Women*, which famously opens,

> "Christmas won't be Christmas without presents," grumbled Jo, lying on the rug.
> "It's so dreadful to be poor!" sighed Meg, looking down at her old dress.
> "I don't think it's fair for some girls to have plenty of pretty things, and other girls nothing at all," added little Amy, with an injured sniff.
> "We've got Father and Mother and each other," said Beth contentedly from her corner. (3)

The March family's reversal of fortune hurts Meg, the oldest sister, worst of all because she remembers what prosperous living was like. Now Meg works as a governess in order to contribute to the family income, and though she dreams of a life of luxury, she falls in love with John Brooke, a tutor of modest means. Meg's wealthy Aunt March warns her, "You ought to marry well and help your family; it's your duty to make a rich match and it ought to be impressed upon you" (213). When Meg defends her choice, Aunt March gives voice to the novel's concerns with wealth and poverty: "So you intend to marry a man without money, position, or business, and go on working harder than you do now, when you might be comfortable all your days by minding me and doing better? I thought you had more sense, Meg" (213). The class prejudice of Aunt March toward Brooke and her opposition to the match only fuel Meg's desire for him, and the first volume of *Little Women* concludes with their engagement.

In most nineteenth-century domestic novels for children, the adult characters in particular are aware of their status in the community. Consequently, part of the tension of the novel involves the adults' concern with how the behavior and character of the child protagonist reflect upon the reputation or standing of the family. This common conflict mirrored anxieties likely to be felt by the growing body of newly middle-class readers who were fueling the expansion of the children's literature market at the time. As Gail Schmunk Murray notes about nineteenth-century children's literature, "Writers of mid-century domestic fiction targeted their novels to a middle-class acutely aware that genteel behaviors and activities brought them closer to the upper-class society they emulated. Likewise, the distance between them and common and uncultured laborers and immigrants served as a reminder of their own status" (57). Domestic children's fiction was especially suited to accommodate the concerns of an upwardly mobile reading public interested in characters who were models of good conduct and who shared their struggles with achieving or maintaining social status and economic security.

Psychological Complexity

One of the hallmarks of the novel as a literary form is the development of three-dimensional characters with complex motivations and "realistic" psychologies. Domestic fiction is known for its focus on character development (Murray 52). As Nancy Armstrong argues, "The novel developed sophisticated strategies for transforming political information into any one of several recognizable psychological conditions" (36). Armstrong cites Jane Austen's *Pride and Prejudice* (1813), a domestic novel, as an example: "The novel redistributes authority between Darcy and Elizabeth in a manner that clearly demonstrates its ability to translate political conflict [between social classes] into psychological terms. Their union miraculously transforms all social differences into gender differences and gender differences into qualities of mind" (51). In other words, Austen foregrounds the psychological interiority of her two protagonists, thereby recasting their class-based conflict as one between unique personalities. Children's domestic fiction also examines individual psychology and frequently turns on the fears, desires, anxieties, and motivations of its child protagonists. Given the importance of the figure of the child to the development of psychology as a discipline and to the articulation of psychological theories, domestic literature for children plays an important cultural role in contributing to the discourses of psychology, childhood, and child development.

Alcott is particularly effective in constructing the psychological complexity of her characters, and so *Little Women* clearly demonstrates the ways domestic fiction explores the workings of the mind. The scene between Aunt March and Meg cited on page 241 not only reveals the individual psychologies of these two characters but also depicts motivations likely felt by other youths and adults:

> Now Aunt March possessed in perfection the art of rousing the spirit of opposition in the gentlest people, and enjoyed doing it. The best of us have a spice of perversity in us, especially when we are young and in love. If Aunt March had begged Meg to accept John Brooke, she would probably have declared she couldn't think of it; but as she was peremptorily ordered *not* to like him, she immediately made up her mind that she would. (Alcott 212)

Alcott's depiction of her characters' motivations is both detailed and psychologically sophisticated. *Little Women* is concerned in many other ways with the psychologies of the March sisters. Each of the girls struggles with a vice that is linked to her emotions, such as Jo's anger, which she learns to control over the course of the novel, or Amy's vanity, which she comes to temper by insistently acknowledging the limits of her talent. These are not flat, two-dimensional character types but round characters with complex and contradictory feelings and impulses that drive the narrative and provide moments of climax and insight. Thus, domestic fiction can be understood as focusing on interiors and interiority, both of the home and of the mind.

ADVENTURE FICTION FOR CHILDREN

Just as the children's domestic novel came to prominence during the Golden Age of children's literature, so did the children's adventure story. With its origins in historical epics and the popular dime novels designed for adults but read by children, the adventure story for children became wildly popular during the mid nineteenth century with the publication of works such as Frederick Marryat's *Masterman Ready* (1841), R.M. Ballantyne's *The Coral Island* (1857), Mark Twain's *The Adventures of Tom Sawyer* (1876), James Otis's *Toby Tyler; or, Ten Weeks with a Circus* (1881), and Robert Louis Stevenson's *Treasure Island* (1883) (Darton 246).

Adventure has its roots in ancient mythology, argues Joseph Campbell, who describes adventure in terms of the hero's journey or quest. From his extensive research on world mythology, Campbell concludes that the "standard path of the mythological adventure of the hero is the magnification of the formula represented in the rites of passage: *separation—initiation—return*" (23). For Campbell, this journey involves standard elements such as the initial "call to adventure," aid from a supernatural or extraordinary being, a series of trials, and the victorious return home. He notes that the scale of adventure and consequent achievement can range from a "domestic, microcosmic triumph" to a "world-historical, macrocosmic triumph" (30).

John G. Cawelti defines the basic outline of adventure fiction: "The central fantasy of the adventure story is that of the hero—individual or group—overcoming obstacles and dangers and accomplishing some important and moral mission" (40). Cawelti argues that the adventure story has been ubiquitous across history and cultures, and he articulates a number of reasons for its widespread appeal:

> At least on the surface, the appeal of the form is obvious. It presents a character, with whom the audience identifies, passing through the most frightening perils to achieve some triumph. Perhaps the basic moral fantasy implicit in this type of story is that of victory over death, though there are also all kinds of subsidiary triumphs available depending on the particular cultural materials employed: the triumph over injustice and the threat of lawlessness in the western; the saving of the nation in the spy story; the overcoming of fear and the defeat of the enemy in the combat story. (40)

We can see how these qualities might be especially appealing to children. The adventure novel typically involves leaving home and exploring the world, which most children have not yet had the opportunity to do in reality, thereby fueling an interest in literary alternatives. Children have much to discover about the world, and adventure fiction thematizes discovery as one of its defining features. Moreover, to the extent that children are restricted to home and school and limited in their ability to travel or move about without supervision, adventure fiction provides pleasure in reading about protagonists who roam about or travel to new and exciting places. Whereas children are typically disempowered, the adventure story usually attributes to its protagonist either extraordinary skills or some special status that allows him or her to triumph over challenging obstacles. Most significant, the protagonist of the adventure story becomes important, often by making a valuable discovery or rescuing an important person, if not the nation or the world itself. In these ways, adventure embodies fantasies that compensate for some of the conditions or deficiencies of children and childhood.

Ballantyne's *The Coral Island* provides a useful example because it reflects so many of these conventions of the children's adventure novel. First, it was written in the tradition of Daniel Defoe's *Robinson Crusoe* (1719), a landmark in the history of adventure fiction that spawned many imitators, or so-called Robinsonades. In *The Coral Island*, a Robinsonade for children, three boys between the ages of fourteen and eighteen leave their homes in

England as ship's boys, become stranded on a Fijian island after their ship sinks, learn to survive as Robinson Crusoe did, encounter pirates, and attempt to rescue a young woman from native cannibals. As in most adventures, *The Coral Island* is set far from the protagonists' homes in a locale that both the boys and the novel's British and American readers might find exotic. Stranded on a remote island, the boys learn to fend for themselves, free from the constraints of civilization and the presence of authority figures, which provides them with the experience of independence. They encounter numerous dangers, from the initial shipwreck to sharks and hunger, and they confront a tribe of native Fijians, who are represented as violent, lawless cannibals. The novel depicts numerous escapes—a common element in adventure stories. The boys escape the island itself, of course, and one of them, Ralph, escapes after being captured by pirates. They intervene in a domestic dispute involving the Fijian chief, and they attempt to rescue his adopted daughter, who is being forced to marry a man she does not want. Though Ralph's narration provides some insight into his mental state and psychological motivations, most of the characters remain relatively flat. The novel instead focuses on their survival of physical obstacles and dangers. The experience of three British boys interfering in the affairs of a Fijian tribe in the mid nineteenth century represents the actual colonial history of Fiji, which was ceded to Great Britain after Chief Cakobau's conversion to Christianity just three years before the publication of *The Coral Island*. (In the novel, Chief Tararo also converts to Christianity.) Thus, the novel glorifies the expansion of the British Empire by presenting the boys as achieving independence and empowerment at the expense of Fijian independence, as using faraway lands to experience new and exciting adventures, and as finding purpose by participating in global affairs.

Power Relations and Superheroics

Adventure fiction, like domestic fiction, is defined in part by an interest in power, and the protagonist of an adventure is usually empowered by special knowledge or skills. Cawelti distinguishes between two types of adventure heroes: one that is "a superhero with exceptional strength or ability" and the other type that is "'one of us,' a figure marked, at least at the beginning of the story, by flawed abilities and attitudes shared by the audience" (40). Both represent the fantasy of transcending one's limitations and either being or becoming extraordinary and powerful. Achieving the goal in works of adventure— whether making an important discovery, retrieving a valuable object, or rescuing a loved

---

Opposite: The adventure story for children exploded as a genre during the mid nineteenth century with the publication of works such as R.M. Ballantyne's *The Coral Island* (1857). This 1927 edition was illustrated by W.H.C. Groome.

or valued person—often requires the hyperbolic superheroics needed to triumph over extraordinary obstacles or situations. Adventure fiction allows the reader to imagine himself or herself as powerful in ways that are impossible in everyday life; the pleasure of this fantasy is likely to appeal to children, who are denied access to most forms of material power, including physical strength or skill, income or wealth, or reputational status or prestige. Most children simply have not had the time to master skills, acquire purchasing power, or earn respect and influence. Nevertheless, the child protagonists of adventure fiction either possess or acquire extraordinary power or skills or perform in remarkable ways. Because adventures depict superheroic powers or extraordinary feats, such fiction departs from the realism that characterizes domestic works.

The Coral Island provides a number of examples of empowerment and heroic feats in the context of adventure. That the three boys manage to survive the shipwreck is itself miraculous, especially since it is Jack's presence of mind while the ship is going down that prevents them from crowding onto the overloaded lifeboat. Once on the island, Jack's encyclopedic knowledge of vegetation permits the boys to thrive, and their eternal optimism despite the apparent hopelessness of the situation is extraordinary as well. When a group of native islanders land and threaten the life of a female prisoner, Jack rushes to her aid, pitting himself heroically against twenty-eight hostile natives. Later, Ralph is captured by pirates and taken out to sea, but he manages to escape when the pirates land on another island and he captures their unmanned vessel. He describes himself as being "alone, in the midst of the wide Pacific, having a most imperfect knowledge of navigation, and in a schooner requiring at least eight men as her proper crew!" (Ballantyne 265). Despite these limitations, the fifteen-year-old Ralph manages to sail the large vessel alone back to the Coral Island to rescue his friends who had remained stranded there. These feats require extraordinary courage and skill, and the boys' consistent success would be unbelievable outside of adventure fiction.

The quintessential adventure story is Edgar Rice Burroughs's Tarzan of the Apes (1914), often associated with or imagined as children's literature. Comparing Tarzan with Mark Twain's Adventures of Huckleberry Finn, Jerry Griswold writes, "Just as Huck wished to light out to the territories to escape the civilizin' of the Widow Douglas, the appeal of the Tarzan stories (and the Wild Child stories in general) is the wish 'to get away' from it all" (110). Raised by apes after the deaths of his human parents, who had been marooned on the coast of Africa, Tarzan nevertheless teaches himself to read the books his parents left behind—even though he never acquired human language before their deaths (studies of other so-called feral children have revealed this to be impossible). Tarzan is unaffected by the elements, seems to possess the superheroic strength necessary for hand-to-hand combat with great apes, fights with and triumphs over lions, and swings on vines through the trees. At one point, after Tarzan reenters human civilization at a French mission in Africa, a drunken man begins attacking guests at the town hotel. Men scatter, but Tarzan confronts the drunkard fearlessly and disarms him easily. On another occasion, a group of men question Tarzan's courage, and so he plunges into the jungle naked, armed only with a knife and a rope, hunts and kills a lion, and reemerges with its huge carcass, which he has carried unaided through the jungle. Such a task would, of course, be impossible for an ordinary man. Whereas *The Coral Island* portrays ordinary boys accomplishing extraordinary feats, *Tarzan* depicts a man with apparently superhuman powers.

Escaping Civilization or Home

Both *The Coral Island* and *Tarzan* demonstrate the connection between adventure and the escape from civilization or home. In the scene from *Tarzan* just described in which he accepts the challenge of slaying a lion, Tarzan exults in the freedom of the jungle after months of being trained for "civilized" life by the Frenchman Paul D'Arnot. As Tarzan plunges into the jungle in response to the dare, he sheds his clothes and thinks, "This was life! ah, how he loved it! Civilization held nothing like this in its narrow and circumscribed sphere, hemmed in by restrictions and conventionalities. Even clothes were a hindrance and a nuisance" (Burroughs 259). Part of

the novel's appeal, along with that of castaway adventures such as *The Coral Island*, is precisely this fantasy of escaping civilization, which is associated with domesticity. In addition to teaching Tarzan human language, D'Arnot insists that he learn to eat his meals with utensils—to use domestic manners. Though he longs to find and marry Jane, Tarzan nonetheless misses jungle life, which he associates with freedom: "At last he was free. He had not realized what a prisoner he had been" (259). This desire for freedom similarly motivates Robinson Crusoe to leave his home and go to sea, just as it motivates Ralph in *The Coral Island*. Thus, adventure not only provides readers with models of extraordinary heroism and superhuman powers but also feeds into a gendered desire to escape the confines of the home, which is associated with the influence of women.

Such fantasies of escape from the confines of domesticity for children, and for boys in particular, underlie childhood institutions such as the

Frontispiece from the first edition of *Tarzan* (1914) by Edgar Rice Burroughs.

Boy Scouts, which was directly inspired by Rudyard Kipling's adventure fiction *The Jungle Books* (1894/95) and *Kim* (1901). The influence of women on boys in early childhood had long aroused concerns about the "feminizing" effect of home life, which had been one motive for sending boys to live as apprentices in the homes of others or to attend boarding schools run by men. As Michael Kimmel explains, by the turn of the twentieth century, many men feared that "a new generation of young boys was being raised entirely by women, who would turn America's future men into whiny little mama's boys. Men sought to rescue their sons from the feminizing clutches of mothers and teachers and create new ways to 'manufacture manhood'" (157). Steven Mintz notes that organizations such as the Boy Scouts, which enacted adventure scenarios, emerged precisely to "revital-ize masculinity" in boys:

> Fears that boys were "overcivilized" and cut off from physical challenges prompted a yearning for a return to the primitive life in the rugged, invigorating wilderness. Deeply fearful of feminine weakness, worried that modern life was emasculating, they wanted to prepare boys for the strenuous life. Emphasis on bodily vigor, outdoor exercise, and other wholesome activities would ensure boys would not become sissies, itself a new word coined around the turn of the century. (193)

The practices associated with movements such as the Boys Scouts, designed to ensure that boys became proper men, replicate almost exactly many of the conventions of ad-venture fiction: outdoor settings, physically strenuous activities, goal-oriented tasks, and all-male companionship.

Concerns about the emasculation of boys, which became especially notable during the late nineteenth and early twentieth centuries, were compounded by the perceived effects of class status on gender performance. As Julia Grant explains, "Middle-class boys were thought to be victims of over-civilization and nervousness due to the repression of their masculine impulses, while working-class and non-Caucasian boys were believed to be in need of having their masculine impulses controlled and directed into productive activity" (832). Concerns regarding the health and vigor of poor urban children similarly motivated the American summer-camp movement for working-class children, especially boys (Paris 53–54). Leslie Paris observes that while some reformers "sought to toughen the elite," others "aspired to uplift the poor" (54). The concern with the health and virtue of working-class and immigrant boys in the United States had its own gendered impli-cations for the practice of conventional manhood. As in domestic fiction, class remains a significant component of adventure since the class status of boys presumably affected their enactment of masculinity or femininity.

Many of the classic adventure novels make the fear of "feminine" domesticity and civi-lization explicit. Most famously, Twain's *Adventures of Huckleberry Finn* (1885) begins with

Huck explaining his adoption at the conclusion of *The Adventures of Tom Sawyer*: "The Widow Douglas she took me for her son, and allowed she would sivilize [*sic*] me; but it was rough living in the house all the time, considering how dismal regular and decent the widow was in all her ways; and so when I couldn't stand it no longer I lit out. I got into my old rags and my sugar-hogshead again, and was free and satisfied" (Twain 32). Huck is subsequently kidnapped by his biological father, a drunkard who disapproves of Huck's going to school, but he eventually escapes with Jim, an escaped slave, and embarks on their adventures traveling down the Mississippi River. At the conclusion, Huck decides to head for the frontier territories rather than be adopted by yet another woman who wants to "sivilize" him. Tarzan's joy in the "freedom" of the jungle thus echoes Huck's earlier frustration with domestic life. This desire for escape and freedom from the confines of the home that lies at the center of adventure accounts for the prominence of the outdoors, travel, and exotic locations that are perceived to be outside of familiar and hence applicable social norms.

Colonialism and Imperialism

The tendency to set adventure fiction in exotic locales far from home is part of the genre's association with nation and empire. Moreover, adventure fiction shares with imperialism the practice of leaving home to travel abroad, and the fact that the term "domestic" can refer to either the household or the nation indicates the political implications of both adventure and domestic fiction. According to Martin Green, "The adventure tale has been the literary form in which war and the warrior virtues were celebrated and analyzed. It has also been the form which reflected and served the West's cult of expansion—political and economic and military expansion, material and spiritual" (viii). Green refers to adventure as "the energizing myth of empire" (4). Given their generic conventions and ideological investments, many novels of adventure are concerned with colonialism, imperialism, and international politics; the more traditional adventures of US and British origin tend to reinforce, either tacitly or explicitly, the ideologies of empire and conquest, including racialized hierarchies. Edward Said includes British children's writer George Alfred Henty, who wrote more than eighty books for or about boys, in a list of writers whose names are synonymous with "the genre of adventure-imperialism" (155). In Henty's *With Clive in India* (1884), for instance, sixteen-year-old Charlie takes a job with the East India Company and eventually participates in establishing British military control in parts of India. Whether on the frontier of the North American West, in the jungles of Africa, on the islands of the South Pacific, or in the colonies of the Indian subcontinent, adventure fiction is often set in imperial or colonial landscapes because they provide "unexplored" spaces, ready-made antagonists and dangers, possibilities for physical action and violence, and opportunities for concrete and material rewards and treasures.

Because adventure fiction is premised on travel away from home to explore unfamiliar lands, it requires a space in which to enact adventure. Historically, exploration has been linked to commercial interests: the discovery of new trade routes, markets, and resources. Tainted by greed or economic urgency, these commercial interests have engendered the exploitation, manipulation, and domination that define colonial and imperial encounters. Moreover, understanding adventure as motivated by the desire to escape from domesticity clarifies exactly what the adventuring hero is escaping from: feelings of boredom and monotony, the confinement of established law and settled order, and a lack of clear and constructive purpose, all of which are likely to be exacerbated by the conditions of modern urban and suburban life in an industrial or postindustrial economy. Colonial and imperial spaces provide antidotes to these conditions, but they often come at the expense of native and nonwhite populations. Many Euro American adventure stories constitute Western fantasies of transcending the sometimes painful conditions of modern life in societies perceived as established and unchangeable. It should be unsurprising then that the genre of adventure was particularly prominent in the nineteenth century as both the United States and Great Britain experienced an age of expansion and empire.

Though colonial or imperial themes might seem unique to adult texts, Daphne Kutzer notes of children's literature, "Empire is everywhere in classic works of the late nineteenth century, and its presence continues well into the twentieth" (xiv). The reason for this ubiquitous presence of what might appear to be mature content involves the didactic, socializing, and sometimes satirical or subversive functions of children's literature. As Kutzer explains, "The widespread appearance of empire in children's texts of the period is connected to the question of the production and use of children's fiction. Children's books are written by adults, for children, who until fairly recently had little opportunity to shop for their own books, depending on adults to supply them with reading material" (xv). That children's literature representing colonial and imperial ideals and practices would emerge out of cultural and historical contexts in which those ideals remain dominant should come as no surprise. Children and children's culture are subject to the same discourses as adults and adult culture, and they are marked by the same motives and investments, even if the details and modes of representation differ somewhat.

Images of conquest or empire appear even in children's literature intended for very young readers. Claire-Lise Malarte-Feldman and Jack Yeager cite a number of critics who have read Jean de Brunhoff's picturebook *The Story of Babar* (1931) for its colonial themes. After Babar's mother is killed in the jungle by hunters, he wanders into what Malarte-Feldman and Yeager describe as a French city in colonial Africa, where he accepts money from a wealthy woman, buys himself a suit and shoes, begins walking upright, sleeps in a bed, and learns to drive. After receiving an education, he returns to the jungle to be crowned king of the elephants. Babar's experience of being "civilized" and returning to rule his land reflects a colonial fantasy in which native African or Indian peoples are encouraged to adopt European styles, practices, and ideologies in order to "improve" their lives. As Kutzer observes, "tropes that suggest that empire and imperialism are good things" appear throughout classic children's literature (10).

HYBRIDITY: DOMESTIC ADVENTURES AND ADVENTUROUS DOMESTICITY

So far we have discussed domestic and adventure fiction as distinct and almost opposite genres in order to provide a clear introduction to many of their key qualities. However, individual texts sometimes straddle the line between the two, and even works that seem clearly to embody one genre contain traces of the other. Megan Norcia notes, "In actuality, however, no such neat divide was possible between the two realms, and elements of the domestic were often present within the adventurous" (346). For instance, we described *Little Women* as a quintessentially domestic novel, and yet it invokes adventure in a number of ways. First, Mr. March is absent from the household because he is serving as an army chaplain during the American Civil War, which affects the family's economic situation, and later both Marmee and John Brooke travel to care for him when he is wounded. War and travel appear frequently as components of adventure fiction, which means that adventure elements function as part of the backdrop to this domestic novel. Moreover, in the second volume, Jo discusses with Marmee the idea of leaving home to forestall Laurie's unwelcome courtship: "Jo liked the prospect and was eager to be gone, for the home nest was growing too narrow for her restless nature and adventurous spirit" (Alcott 305). She travels alone to New York City to work as a governess, and the city is, to her, an exotic and faraway place, like the setting of an adventure novel. She even begins writing sensational fiction for publication, some of which sounds like adventure: "Mr. Dashwood [her editor] rejected any but thrilling tales, and as thrills could not be produced except by harrowing up the souls of readers, history and romance, land and sea, science and art, police records and lunatic asylums, had to be ransacked for the purpose" (320). Jo scours the city looking for material on which to base her sensational writings, and so *Little Women* itself both incorporates adventure—in Jo's sojourn in New York— and alludes to adventure and its contrast with domesticity through her moral struggle between writing lurid tales in the city and her ultimate determination to write about her own family life.

While domestic novels often contain elements of adventure, quintessential adventure fiction such as *The Coral Island* and *Tarzan* also include important domestic elements.

As is typical for a castaway novel, *The Coral Island* depicts the boys' efforts to establish a home on their island, and they play out an almost domestic scenario, with Jack frequently providing fatherly lectures on edible vegetation or hunting and Peterkin acting as if he were the two older boys' child. They take to calling the portion of the beach where they set up camp "home" (Ballantyne 46), and Ralph explains that their situation comes to seem permanent: "But as day after day passed, and neither savages nor ships appeared, we gave up all hope of an early deliverance and set diligently to work at our homestead" (47). The domestic elements of *Tarzan* are even more striking, since the first several chapters of the novel relate how John and Alice Clayton, Tarzan's parents, are marooned by mutineers at a remote point on the African coast and must learn to survive while they wait for help. Unlike the *Coral Island* boys, the Claytons are left with many of their things, including cooking utensils, books, and other household items, and John uses his tools to construct a rather elaborate cabin. Alice's pregnancy and delivery of a son further establish this section of the novel as conventionally domestic, and even after the adult Claytons are killed and Tarzan is adopted by a female ape, the novel continues in a semidomestic mode during the chapters devoted to his childhood. That the concluding section of the novel involves Tarzan's search for Jane and wish to mate with her means that domesticity is his and the novel's ultimate goal. These examples suggest that few works reflect only the conventions of a single genre, and many are actually hybrid texts, containing elements of both adventure and domesticity.

QUESTIONS OF AUDIENCE: BOY AND GIRL READERS OF DOMESTIC FICTION AND ADVENTURE

Not only are the boundaries between genres sometimes blurry and unstable, but the audience for these works can also be equally difficult to pin down. In some cases, authors leave hints as to their intended audience, as Arthur Conan Doyle does in his dedicatory note to his adventure novel *The Lost World* (1912):

> I have wrought my simple plan
> If I give one hour of joy
> To the boy who's half a man,
> Or the man who's half a boy. (n.p.)

However, we cannot take for granted that only girls read domestic fiction, nor can we assume that only boys read adventure. In 1908 Mark Twain famously praised *Anne of Green Gables*, writing, "In 'Anne of Green Gables' you will find the dearest and most moving and delightful child since the immortal Alice [of *Alice's Adventures in Wonderland*]" (qtd.

in Gammel 235). Of course, at the time of *Anne's* publication and Twain's praise of it, he was already an adult reader near the end of his life and a literary man who read widely. Yet others have provided confirmation that men and boys did indeed read domestic fiction. Despite focusing on girls, girlhood development, and female concerns, *Little Women* was read and enjoyed by a variety of readers. According to Beverly Lyon Clark,

> In consciously writing for girls, Alcott was not necessarily excluding adults or boys, at this time when the ideals of masculinity were not yet completely dominated by those of the self-made man or the masculine primitive. What strikes the latter-day reader about many reviews of Alcott's work [at the time of its publication] is the assumption not only that both old and young will enjoy it but that both males and females will. (114)

Clark cites one review that specifically addresses both "young ladies and gentlemen," and she notes that President Theodore Roosevelt, known for his ruggedly masculine persona, recalled in his 1913 autobiography, "I worshipped *Little Men* and *Little Women* and *An Old-Fashioned Girl*" (qtd. in Clark 114). Unlike Twain, Roosevelt is recalling fondly his childhood reading of a domestic novel that we might think of as being "for girls."

While children's domestic fiction written by men was uncommon during the Golden Age (men such as Henry James and E.M. Forster did write domestic novels for adults), women sometimes wrote adventure fiction for and about both boys and girls. Norcia argues,

> Women writers in England also were imaginatively entering the spaces of adventure through their writings, though they themselves may never have left their own island. Women writers of children's books—such as Anne Bowman, Angela Brazil, Bessie Marchant, and L.T. Meade—were charting new territory by placing their girl heroes in adventurous settings. The proliferation of these tales suggests the avidity with which girl readers read them. (346)

L.T. (Elizabeth Thomasina) Meade provides a particularly compelling case, since her 1892 publication of *Four on an Island: A Story of Adventure* is a castaway novel modeled on *Robinson Crusoe* but with a girl protagonist. Norcia claims that it "merges, rather than polarizes, the domestic and adventure spheres" (347). Bessie Marchant was another prolific author of girls' adventure stories such as *The Half-Moon Girl* (1898), in which the experiences of a native girl from Borneo and the adventures of an English girl converge and result in the latter's inheriting her uncle's estate.

Just as some boys read and enjoy domestic works, many girls read and enjoy adventure, whether marketed to them or not. Clark notes that one reviewer of *The Adventures of Tom Sawyer*, usually perceived as a boys' book, referred to it as "intended for boys and girls" (82), and while Twain issued a number of contradictory statements about his intended audience for *Tom Sawyer*, he did refer to it as "for boys & girls" and as "a boy's & girl's book" (qtd. in Clark 80). Sally Mitchell observes: "It became commonplace by the turn of the century to suggest that girls liked their brothers' books better than their own," a perception that she claims inspired writers such as Meade to try writing adventure specifically for girls (15). All this suggests that the audience for domestic and adventure fiction is not as straightforward as it would appear, for both boys and girls have enjoyed works of both genres written by men and women.

CONTEMPORARY DOMESTIC AND ADVENTURE STORIES

Can contemporary literature still be classified in terms of domestic and adventure fiction? What forms do contemporary domestic and adventure stories take? Both genres coalesced in the nineteenth century, when many of the most recognizable landmark works of adventure and domesticity were published. Because both genres are tied so directly to cultural constructions of gender and nation, we would expect domestic and adventure novels to change as our definitions of what it means to be a man, woman, boy, or girl have changed, and as our sense of national identity has changed in an increasingly globalized and postcolonial world. Since the women's and national independence movements of the mid twentieth century, which offered critiques of gender and empire and compelled more critical reflection on their construction or practice, the literature of adventure and domesticity has increasingly reflected a greater degree of self-reflection, often pointing to the problems associated with gender or nation through satire and comedy. Changing social practices or social systems, such as the expansion of the middle class and the rise of the suburbs, have resulted in some cases in the displacement of traditional domestic and adventure fiction by the suburban realist or problem novel. In other cases, works of adventure or domesticity have incorporated elements of different genres, such as fantasy, in order to appear fresh. While clear examples of each genre continue to be published, most children's books with claims to these designations appear quite different from their nineteenth-century forebears. Reading these contemporary examples critically involves understanding their indebtedness to earlier forms.

"Does a Boy Get a Chance to Whitewash a Fence Every Day?" from Mark Twain's *The Adventures of Tom Sawyer* (1876), illustrated by Norman Rockwell.

Contemporary Examples

Contemporary children's literature includes a diverse range of adventuring children. Martin Green distinguishes between seven types of adventure in terms of their protagonists, who, he says, generate or characterize the type of adventure they have (21): the castaway (modeled on Robinson Crusoe), the musketeer (for Green this is the swashbuckling hero of historical adventures), the frontiersman (who is similar to the castaway but has more interaction with civilization), the avenger (whose story Green links with gothic elements), the wanderer (a picaresque hero whose adventure is defined by travel), the sagaman (who follows the model found in Icelandic sagas and myths), and the hunted man (the hero of contemporary thrillers). Many of these different kinds of protagonists can be found in children's literature of the twentieth and twenty-first centuries. The girls of Carol Ryrie Brink's *Baby Island* (1937) are child castaways, while Charlotte Doyle from Avi's *The True Confessions of Charlotte Doyle* (1990) may approximate the musketeer character. The autobiographical protagonist of Laura Ingalls Wilder's *Little House on the Prairie* (1935) is an obvious frontier girl; and while Bod from Neil Gaiman's *The Graveyard Book* (2008) does not seek vengeance per se, he does want to uncover the mystery of his family's murder, like an avenger. Bud of Christopher Paul Curtis's *Bud, Not Buddy* (1999) is a kind of wanderer, while J.R.R. Tolkien's Bilbo Baggins of *The Hobbit* (1937) shares qualities with Green's sagaman. Adam Farmer, the protagonist of Robert Cormier's *I Am the Cheese* (1977), is a contemporary hunted boy. One can see from this list that adventure overlaps considerably with other genres, especially historical fiction and fantasy.

Some clear examples of domestic fiction have been published since World War II. Madeleine L'Engle, best known for her science-fantasy novel *A Wrinkle in Time* (1962), published *Meet the Austins* in 1960. A fairly conventional domestic novel, it focuses on the Austin family, who live in an old house in a small New England town. Twelve-year-old Vicky, who narrates the novel, must cope with her three siblings and the troubled orphan girl staying with the family. Katherine Paterson's *Jacob Have I Loved* (1980), a winner of the Newbery Medal, embodies many of the traditional elements of domestic fiction as well. It traces the maturation of Sara Louise Bradshaw, who envies her beautiful, talented twin sister, Caroline. After Caroline and Call, Sara Louise's best friend, leave home and eventually marry, disappointing Sara Louise, she too leaves home to become a nurse and makes peace with her lifelong sense of isolation. Both works focus on family dynamics, are set mostly in or around country homes, have female protagonists, and explore the individual psychologies of their main characters.

Reimagining Adventure and Domestic Fiction

Many contemporary examples of adventure or domestic fiction for children revise or reimagine the conventions dominating their nineteenth-century precursors. Like *The Coral Island*, Scott O'Dell's *Island of the Blue Dolphins* (1960) is a castaway story of sorts, though its protagonist, Karana, is abandoned on her island home rather than being shipwrecked somewhere unknown to her. Like traditional castaway stories, *Island of the Blue Dolphins* focuses on the heroine's survival in a dangerous natural environment before her rescue, but it also invites a postcolonial reading: the real Native American woman on whom Karana's story is based died mere weeks after being "rescued" and brought to mainland California, probably because she lacked the necessary immunity to Western diseases (Robinson 3). Gary Paulsen's *Hatchet* (1987) similarly focuses on survival. Thirteen-year-old Brian fights to stay alive in the Canadian wilderness after his plane crashes. Like Sara Louise in *Jacob Have I Loved*, who suffers deeply from the painful disappointments of life, Brian struggles as much with the secret knowledge of his mother's infidelity as he does with the physical dangers of his situation. Both *Island of the Blue Dolphins* and *Hatchet* add a psychological complexity often missing in more traditional adventures of the nineteenth century.

Other works represent modifications of traditional adventure and domestic forms by incorporating elements of fantasy or comedy or by modifying expectations such as those for setting or character. For instance, Mary Norton's *The Borrowers* combines elements of domestic fiction with both fantasy and adventure. A boy goes to live with his great-aunt in a large country home in England to recover from illness, and while there he meets a family of very small people who live in the wall and use everyday objects they "borrow," such as postage stamps that they use as wall art or chess pieces used as sculptures. Clearly the Borrowers are fantastic creatures, and the experience of borrowing to survive while avoiding detection by full-sized humans suggests adventure. However, the focus on the social dynamics of the Clock family, thirteen-year-old Arrietty's maturation into a young woman, the practice of homemaking, and the experience of illness place *The Borrowers* in the tradition of domestic fiction, while the adventurous practice of borrowing, which involves repurposing everyday objects, suggests how the conventions of the domestic novel are being repurposed by Norton herself. E.L. Konigsburg similarly reimagines adventure for the contemporary suburban child in *From the Mixed-up Files of Mrs. Basil E. Frankweiler* (1967). Eleven-year-old Claudia decides to run away with her nine-year-old brother Jamie, but because they are used to the comforts of middle-class suburban life, the two decide not to rough it in the woods or on the road but in the Metropolitan Museum of Art in New York City. While traditional adventures take place in distant, exotic locations, the decision to set this novel in the Met, where elaborate exhibits of Egyptian tombs and ancient Greek artifacts are housed, suggests the ways in which adventure is available

to many modern children only in safe, contained spaces that preserve and institution-
alize history and adventure for casual tourists. Judy Blume's comedic approach to dealing with a new sibling in *Tales of a Fourth Grade Nothing* (1972) and the satirical take on
middle-class life in contemporary gated communities in Edward Bloor's *Tangerine* (1997)
offer new perspectives on traditional domestic fiction. The intensely psychological narrative of Adam Farmer, who may be in the witness protection program, as he presumably
journeys to reunite with his father in Robert Cormier's *I Am the Cheese* (1997), reimagines
physical and literal journeys and explorations as internal, psychological ones.

Adventure and Domesticity in Picturebooks

Because of their brevity, individual picturebooks tend not to incorporate or develop
enough conventions of adventure or domestic fiction to place them squarely in those
categories even as they might resonate with them. Cynthia Rylant and Diane Goode's
When I Was Young in the Mountains (1982) contains domestic elements because it focuses
on aspects of everyday life for a family in the rural, presumably Appalachian, mountains,
but it does not explore in detail family dynamics or individual psychology, as we might
expect from a full-length domestic work. Valerie Flournoy and Jerry Pinkney's *The Patchwork Quilt* (1985), winner of the Coretta Scott King Award for illustration, follows young
Tanya as she learns to quilt from her ill grandmother, and it contains domestic elements
by depicting family and home life and including references to illness and domestic work.
Maurice Sendak's celebrated *Where the Wild Things Are* (1963), for which he won the
Caldecott Medal, clearly contains elements of adventure: Max travels to the land of the
Wild Things, conquers them, and returns home. So does Allen Say's *Grandfather's Journey*
(1993), another Caldecott winner, which depicts a Japanese man's emigration from Japan
to the United States, his exploration of the landscapes and cities of North America, and
his return home. Even in their abbreviated forms and narrow focuses, picturebooks can
be described as adventure or domestic stories without embodying as many conventions
as their full-length fictional counterparts.

READING CRITICALLY: DOMESTICITY AND ADVENTURE

Holes

Placing a text in its generic context clarifies aspects that might otherwise remain opaque or invisible. Reading children's literature critically involves noting how a text both employs and departs from the conventions of a particular genre. Louis Sachar's *Holes* (1998), which won the Newbery Medal in 1999, can be described as a contemporary adventure story that contains three intersecting narratives involving journeys from home, deadly physical dangers, and the discovery of treasure. The two main characters, Stanley Yelnats and Zero, are sent to a camp for convicted juvenile offenders, where they are supposed to reform their delinquent behavior. Eventually they attempt to escape the camp, which the boys refer to as "home," by fleeing into the Texas desert. The novel explicitly connects elements of adventure to the experience of discipline and reformation, and by depicting the boys' escape from the camp, the novel equates home life with incarceration. In these ways, *Holes* exposes both adventure and domesticity as punishing and confining, offering comedy, coincidence, and absurdity as alternatives to the usual rewards of exploration or home.

Stanley Yelnats is sent to the juvenile correctional facility, called Camp Green Lake, after being falsely convicted of stealing a valuable pair of shoes donated to a homeless shelter by a famous baseball player. Camp Green Lake is run by a woman known only as the Warden, who makes the boys dig holes in the Texas desert. The novel cuts between Stanley's story and that of Kate Barlow, a late nineteenth-century outlaw who robs people and banks. Kate, a white woman, had been a schoolteacher who fell in love with a black man named Sam. When the town found out, Sam was killed and Kate was run out of town, leading to her transformation into a criminal. She buries her stolen fortune somewhere in the vicinity of what would become Camp Green Lake, and the Warden, a descendant of a man scorned by Kate, uses the boys to search for it. In a third narrative, Stanley's ancestor makes a deal with an "old Egyptian woman," Madame Zeroni, to help him win the heart of a girl in exchange for carrying her up a mountain. Though Madame Zeroni helps him, he ultimately discovers the girl is not worth his love and reneges on his promise to Zeroni, thereby bringing a curse upon his family. Stanley's ancestor then immigrates to the United States, where he earns a fortune that is later stolen by Kate Barlow. These three narratives converge on Stanley and Zero, who is the descendant of Madame Zeroni. When the two boys flee into the desert, Stanley ultimately carries Zero up a mountain, thereby fulfilling his ancestor's promise to Zero's ancestor. The curse is broken, and the boys find the treasure, prove Stanley's innocence, and win their release.

Each of the three narratives reflects elements of adventure and associates adventure with punishment or discipline, especially Stanley's story. Stanley leaves home, travels to a remote place, undertakes physical labors, experiences extreme dangers, rescues someone in distress, and finds a treasure—all elements that are consistent with the conventions of adventure. The setting of the novel at a boys'"camp" connects *Holes* to the history of children's camps and their development as an "artificial" opportunity for adventure, much like scouting. As Kenneth Kidd explains, "The camp was an artificial space of enclosure that … offered a temporary, healing remove from the city" (42). Kidd observes that "early advocates praised camping as an antidote to enervation, effeminacy, and sexual dysfunction" (42). Before his time at Camp Green Lake, Stanley was overweight and bullied by smaller boys, mocked even by his teachers. By the conclusion of the novel, Stanley has lost weight, made friends, and developed courage: "While Mrs. Bell, Stanley's former math teacher, might want to know the percent change in Stanley's weight, the reader probably cares more about the change in Stanley's character and self-confidence" (Sachar 228). Just as early twentieth-century advocates of camps stressed their use for building character (Kidd 43), adventure literature depicts the protagonist developing character as a result of his or her experience. That this change takes place in *Holes* at a camp that serves as a juvenile correctional facility suggests how adventure functions as a form of discipline and reformation: Stanley is supposed to be corrected by his experience there (Sachar 12). Mr. Pendanski, who is referred to as a camp counselor, explains that the purpose of Camp Green Lake is to make the boys "useful and hard-working members of society" (Sachar 19). *Holes* therefore exposes adventure as a form of discipline.

Like other adventure novels, *Holes* also includes elements of domesticity. The boys refer to the camp as "home," and they call Mr. Pendanski "Mom" (19). As we discuss in this chapter, adventure is often framed by the escape from and return to the home. Stanley's and Zero's decisions to escape from Camp Green Lake in the context of an adventure novel further positions the camp as home, and understanding the camp this way points to the novel's equation of home with incarceration. While traditional adventures might imply that the home is a place of confinement or suffocation, *Holes* exaggerates those implications by making the domestic space a literal prison. Camp Green Lake is governed by a woman, the Warden, who abuses and exploits the boys rather than care for them. Cruel and sadistic, she paints her nails with a mixture of nail polish and rattlesnake poison and then scratches her victims to cause great pain. The Warden is an absurd character whose exaggerated cruelty satirizes the depiction of homes and mothers as dangerous or smothering to the would-be adventurer.

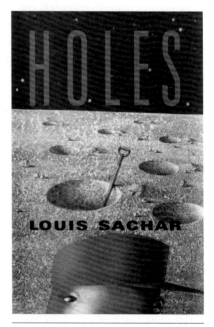

In Louis Sachar's contemporary story *Holes* (1998), the experience of discipline and reformation lead to adventure.

Holes demonstrates the self-reflexivity of contemporary adventure by exaggerating common implications of the genre: the idea that adventure benefits the protagonist and the notion that homes must be escaped. While conventional adventure stories often involve remarkable coincidences or unbelievable feats that are depicted seriously, as though they are really possible, Sachar's novel embraces and foregrounds absurdity, using many of the tropes of adventure as sources of comedy and parody. For example, Stanley is falsely accused of stealing a pair of smelly sneakers, the boys survive in the desert by eating onions, their family histories are significantly intertwined across continents and centuries, and they discover a fortune-making remedy to stinky feet. Ultimately, the novel presents two ordinary boys whose success is overtly ridiculous, lucky, and coincidental. By suggesting that traditional adventures, with their daring acts of bravery and skill by extraordinary heroes, can no longer be taken seriously, *Holes* therefore replaces adventure with comedy.

EXPLORATIONS

Review

1. How is the idea and experience of home and leaving home tied to the definition of what it means to be a child?

2. How is the domestic sphere imagined as a place of protection for children? What are some of the dangers that appear in domestic fiction and how do they compare to the dangers of adventure fiction?

3. Consider Joseph Campbell's argument that adventure has its roots in ancient practices and follows the formula "separation-initiation-return." How does this pattern function in some of the children's literature discussed in this chapter?

4. What are some texts that combine elements of both domesticity and adventure? How do these combinations work in the books?

5. Some people might assume that domestic novels are read by a female audience and adventure tales are read by a male audience. What are some examples from the history of children's literature that complicate these assumptions, and how do they do so?

Reflect

1. In the introduction to this chapter, we suggest that the differences between adventure and domesticity can be understood in terms of scale. Consider how the concepts of scale, magnitude, or size might be useful for thinking about a specific work of adventure or domesticity. In what ways are the dangers, actions, events, or feelings large or small, obvious or subtle?

2. Romance is often a component of both adventure and domesticity. Select examples examined in this chapter or listed as suggested reading and reflect on how adventure and domestic fiction represent romance or romantic relationships differently. Identify differences in perspective, protagonist, setting, rewards, etc.

3. How do adventure novels with girl protagonists (such as Carol Ryrie Brink's *Baby Island* or Scott O'Dell's *Island of the Blue Dolphins*) differ from adventure novels with boy protagonists? How are they similar?

4. Can we still classify children's literature in the contemporary period in terms of domesticity and adventure, or are these classifications specific to the nineteenth century? Give reasons for your answer.

Investigate

1. Retell a domestic novel to emphasize or introduce elements of adventure, or an adventure novel to emphasize or introduce domestic elements. How does the story change? Were these changes easy or difficult to imagine?

2. Research opportunities for urban or suburban children to experience elements of adventure in their lives or communities, such as parks and playgrounds, after-school programs, organizations, or extracurricular activities. How are elements of adventure maintained in the lives of these urban or suburban children?

3. Compile a list of domestic and adventure works for children. What patterns do you notice in the titles from these lists? What do these titles suggest about each of the genres? Can you determine the genre of a work based on its title?

4. Examine two classic picturebooks such as Maurice Sendak's *Where the Wild Things Are* and Ezra Jack Keats's *The Snowy Day* (1962) and discuss how they contain

elements of both adventure and domesticity. How are these elements depicted visually by picturebook authors and illustrators?

SUGGESTED READINGS

Alcott, Louisa May. *Little Women* (1868). Focusing on the four March sisters, who suffer from genteel poverty and the absence of their father during the Civil War, *Little Women* offers different models of girlhood and young womanhood. This New England family must navigate a variety of domestic situations and trials as the girls mature over the course of the novel. Jo, the most prominent of the four sisters, has inspired the passionate admiration of generations of readers for her outspoken brashness and tomboyish unconventionality.

Ballantyne, R.M. *The Coral Island* (1857). Ballantyne's *The Coral Island* depicts the quintessential castaway adventure for children, complete with utopian island life, ruthless pirates, damsels in distress, and cannibalistic natives. The novel not only inspired works such as Stevenson's *Treasure Island* and Barrie's *Peter and Wendy*, but it also was the basis for William Golding's satirical retelling in *Lord of the Flies* (1954). *The Coral Island* usefully provides insight into the ideology and practice of nineteenth-century British imperialism and gendered social relations.

Birdsall, Jeanne. *The Penderwicks: A Summer Tale of Four Sisters, Two Rabbits, and a Very Interesting Boy* (2005). A National Book Award winner, *The Penderwicks* features four sisters ranging in age from four to twelve who spend the summer on a large estate in the Berkshire Mountains, which includes a mansion named Arundel Hall. There, they meet a lonely, artistic boy and a handsome young gardener. Reminiscent of Alcott's *Little Women*, Birdsall's novel combines elements of domestic family stories with the kinds of summertime explorations that suggest modern versions of adventure.

Burroughs, Edgar Rice. *Tarzan of the Apes* (1914). Burroughs's first Tarzan book has inspired countless adaptations, including nearly two dozen sequels, numerous comics, film adaptations, television programs, and Tarzan memorabilia. The story is now widely known even to those who have not read the original novel, which depicts Lord Greystoke and the pregnant Lady Alice, British aristocrats stranded by mutineers at a remote spot along the African coast. Alice gives birth to a boy shortly before the couple is killed by intelligent apes, who possess a primitive language and political structure. The baby is adopted by one of the female apes and named Tarzan, and he goes on to experience a number of adventures that are typical for life in the jungle. Tarzan eventually falls in love with a marooned American woman named Jane, and he sets off to find her after she is rescued and returns to the United States.

Kipling, Rudyard. *Kim* **(1901).** In Kipling's *Kim,* an orphaned Irish boy living in India at the end of the nineteenth century is so "dark" and street savvy that he passes for an Indian child. Because he is so clever and stealthy, he is recruited to work as a spy on behalf of the British against Russian interests in Central and South Asia. The novel refers to the actual conflict between Britain and Russia during the 1880s and 1890s known as "the Great Game." Kipling's work was one of the key inspirations of Robert Baden-Powell, the British Army officer who founded the Boy Scouts and included portions of *Kim* in the first guide to scouting.

Montgomery, L.M. *Anne of Green Gables* **(1908).** Probably the best-known and most beloved classic of Canadian children's literature, *Anne of Green Gables* focuses on the humor of the talkative and indefatigable Anne acclimating to her new life as the adopted daughter of Marilla and Matthew Cuthbert, a pair of aging, unmarried siblings. Like Rebecca before her, Anne sweeps into town and manages to charm almost everyone she meets with her uninhibited extroversion and bewitching imagination, ultimately inspiring many sequels, television and film adaptations, tourism, and an entire industry of Anne paraphernalia.

Otis, James. *Toby Tyler; or, Ten Weeks with a Circus* **(1881).** Though less known now than in the late nineteenth and early twentieth centuries, *Toby Tyler* is the prototypical story about a boy who runs away from home to join the circus. Toby Tyler, an orphan who lives with a neglectful foster father, is seduced by the possibility of adventure and is forced into servitude by the abusive taskmaster Mr. Lord. Toby soon discovers that the life of a child worker with a traveling circus is not the way he imagined it would be. He eventually escapes the drudgery of manual labor for the life of a performer, but he longs to return to the imperfect home he fled.

Porter, Eleanor. *Pollyanna* **(1913).** Its title has become synonymous with a person who is obnoxiously and naively optimistic, but the novel *Pollyanna* is more compelling than one might expect based on popular caricatures of its protagonist. What distinguishes Pollyanna from other orphan girls who reform their stern caregivers is her almost unfailing optimism and her addictive "glad game," which involves finding something to be glad about in everything. Her ability to stay glad is tested when an accident leaves her paralyzed, but even from her sickbed she manages to inspire an entire community.

Stevenson, Robert Louis. *Treasure Island* (1883). Stevenson's *Treasure Island* built on Ballantyne's foundation to turn the pirate into a complex, charismatic anti-hero in the figure of Long John Silver. The novel exemplifies many of the conventions of the pirate story. Jim Hawkins, an ordinary boy whose parents own an inn and tavern, gets mixed up in the discovery of a treasure map and an expedition to Skeleton Island to recover the lost treasure. His father dies early in the novel, but Jim finds no shortage of male society aboard the *Hispaniola*, which provides him with the opportunity to leave home, experience adventure, and find his fortune.

Wiggin, Kate Douglas. *Rebecca of Sunnybrook Farm* (1903). Wiggin's publication of *Rebecca* triggered a flurry of imitative orphan-girl novels. One of the more linguistically and stylistically sophisticated of such works, *Rebecca of Sunnybrook Farm* follows its eponymous protagonist as she moves to live with her prim and proper aunts Miranda and Jane in order to receive a better education under their care and to relieve her mother of the burden of feeding another child. With her wit and imagination, Rebecca eventually charms her aunts and the town.

APPROACHES TO TEACHING *HOLES* [SECONDARY SCHOOL]

Preparation for the Lesson

Students should read the novel in advance of the activities.

Learning Goals

- To determine the ways in which the different elements of Sachar's plot work together

- To trace the emergence of a single theme (in this case the theme of destiny) as it is woven through a book

- To evaluate the impact of the novel's open ending, and to explore the idea of "ambiguity"

- To identify the domestic and adventurous spaces in *Holes*, emphasizing safety and danger

- To practice letter writing and short essay writing.

Activity One: Characters and Plot

Ask students to write a list of the major events in *Holes* as they happened chronologically in the history of Stanley, Zero, and their respective families. These events constitute the story of the novel. Next, ask them to make a list of these major events in order of their presentation in the novel. This way of ordering the story is the plot.

Lead a discussion about the effect of presenting the events in the way Sachar does rather than in chronological order. How would the reader's experience of the novel be different if the story were presented chronologically? What recurring images, actions, or characters does Sachar use to tie the different elements in the novel together? Ask the students to write a short essay on the following topic: How does Stanley's story relate to the stories of characters from the past (especially Elya Yelnats and Madame Zeroni and Kissin' Kate Barlow)?

Activity Two: Destiny and the Open Ending in Holes

Part A: Destiny

Trace the theme of destiny through the book. Here are two passages to begin with:

1. Stanley couldn't help but think that there was something special about the shoes, that they would somehow provide the key to his father's invention. It was too much of a coincidence to be a mere accident. Stanley had felt like he was holding destiny's shoes. (24)

2. As Stanley stared at the glittering night sky, he thought there was no place he would rather be. He was glad Zero put the shoes on the parked car. He was glad they fell from the overpass and hit him on the head.

    When the shoes first fell from the sky, he remembered thinking that destiny had struck him. Now, he thought so again. It was more than a coincidence. It had to be destiny. (187)

Ask the students to find other passages in *Holes* that have to do with destiny. Does the novel endorse the notion that characters have a special destiny? Are the characters in *Holes* free to live as they wish, or are their lives determined by destiny?

Part B: The Open Ending in *Holes*

At the end of the novel, it is not clear whether the improvement in Stanley's family fortunes is the result of coincidence or Stanley's carrying Zero up the mountain and ending the curse. Read the following passage out loud with the class:

> Stanley's mother insists that there never was a curse. She even doubts whether Stanley's great-great-grandfather ever stole a pig. The reader might find it interesting, however, that Stanley's father invented his cure for foot odor the day after the great-great-grandson of Elya Yelnats carried the great-great-great grandson of Madame Zeroni up the mountain. (229)

Ask the students: Why do you think rain finally fell on Camp Green Lake?

Define "ambiguity" as the "ability to have more than one interpretation." Note that this deliberately ambiguous open ending allows the reader the freedom to believe that there is a curse, or to agree with Stanley's mother that there never was a curse. Why does Sachar want to leave this question open? Why is it important that a reader can decide what he or she believes about the curse? If you wish, you can ask students to write a brief essay responding to this question: Do you think that the curse on the Yelnats family was real, or do you agree with Stanley's mother that there never was a curse?

Activity Three: Adventure and Domesticity in Holes

Part A: Danger in the Novel

On the blackboard or on the projector, list the dangers Stanley faces in the novel. Here are some of them.

- Bullying by Derrick Dunne at school; possible bullying by X-Ray and Armpit

- Walking home from school and being accused of stealing Clyde Livingston's sneakers

- The heat at Camp Green Lake and the lack of water

- Yellow-spotted lizards

- The threat of the Warden's poisonous nails.

Lead the class in a discussion of the following questions:

1. How does Stanley deal with all these threats?

2. While there is danger at Camp Green Lake, Stanley still faces difficulties such as poverty and bullying at home. How do the difficulties Stanley faces at both Camp Green Lake and home make him more able to cope with the challenges of each environment?

3. Stanley and Zero find "refuge" on God's Thumb. How do they find refuge? Why is it important that they find refuge? Is danger represented in the novel as exciting, valuable, or desirable? How does the presentation of danger compare with its presentation in other adventure stories you have read?

Part B: Stanley's and Zero's Memories of Home

Ask the students to read the following dialogue, which starts with Stanley's explaining something about his family life:

> "Well, see my dad is trying to invent a way to recycle old sneakers. So the apartment kind of smells bad, because he's always cooking these old sneakers. So anyway, in the letter my mom said she felt sorry for that little old lady who lived in a shoe, you know, because it must have smelled bad in there."
> Zero stared blankly at him.
> "You know, the nursery rhyme?"
> Zero said nothing.
> "You've heard the nursery rhyme about the little old lady who lived in a shoe?"
> "No."
> Stanley was amazed.
> "How does it go?" asked Zero.
> "Didn't you ever watch *Sesame Street*?" Stanley asked.
> Zero stared blankly.
> Stanley headed on to dinner. He would have felt pretty silly reciting nursery rhymes at Camp Green Lake. (75–76)

Lead a discussion using the following questions:

1. Is Stanley's home perfect? What is wrong with Stanley's home environment?

2. What advantages does Stanley have that Zero does not? Why hasn't Zero seen *Sesame Street*?

3. What is Zero's first memory of home? When his mother leaves him, where does he live? How does he understand his situation?

4. What kind of home life do the characters establish at the end of the story?

Part C: Serious or Funny?

Make a list of humorous and serious moments in the book. Lead a discussion about the ways in which the book combines humor and seriousness.

Activity Four: Letters from Camp

In *Holes*, Stanley doesn't tell his mother the truth about what is happening at Camp Green Lake because he does not want to worry her. Pretend that you are Stanley. Choose a scene depicting the events at Camp Green Lake and write a letter home describing the events of the scene. When you are done with your letter, write a brief (page-long) answer to the following questions:

1. Did you tell the truth about your experience at Camp Green Lake, or did you sugar-coat a bad situation as Stanley did in the novel?

2. When you were pretending to be Stanley, did you imagine that his family could help you deal with the camp? Why, or why not?

3. Is Stanley homesick in the novel? How would you feel in his place? How is your situation different from Stanley's?

HISTORICAL FICTION

Historical fiction is a thriving genre of children's and young adult literature. Its popularity can be linked to the history of didacticism in writing for youth and to the continuing sense that works for children and young adults should be educational. This chapter discusses the qualities and uses of historical fiction for children, the problems engendered by the enterprise of historical fiction, and how historical fiction functions both to entertain and to educate children and young adults.

DEFINING THE HISTORICAL NOVEL

The **historical novel**, a work that is set in a period earlier than the one in which it was written, is generally thought to have coalesced as a form in the early nineteenth century. Among its first practitioners were Scottish writer Sir Walter Scott, whose novel *Waverley* (1814) is set during the mid eighteenth century, and American author James Fenimore Cooper, whose novel *The Spy* (1821) takes place during the American Revolution. Scott's *Waverley* is sometimes viewed as the first historical novel, while Cooper's *The Spy* is the first American historical novel. Suzanne Rahn identifies Harriet Martineau's *The Settlers at Home* (1841) and Frederick Marryat's *The Children of the New Forest* (1847), both novels about the seventeenth-century English Civil War, as the first historical novels specifically for children; both were likely influenced by Scott. Scott is perhaps best known now for *Ivanhoe* (1819), which takes place during the Middle Ages, while Cooper's *The Last of the Mohicans* (1826), set in the 1750s, remains a popular classic. Notably, both works have

---

Opposite: From *Ivanhoe* by Sir Walter Scott, illustrated by Milo Winter, 1918.

been abridged and published for children repeatedly. That the works of these two ground-breaking writers of historical fiction would be recast as children's literature suggests the perception that the historical novel might be both popular with children and useful for its educational value.

Georg Lukács (pronounced GAY-org LU-cotch), a Hungarian theorist of the novel, distinguishes between works simply set in an earlier period and true historical novels. He notes that works before the nineteenth century were sometimes set in earlier periods such as ancient Greece or Rome, but he argues that these typically treated the historical settings as an "external choice of theme and costume" (Lukács 19). For Lukács, the real histori-cal novel does not just treat history as an incidental backdrop for events or interactions that could just as well take place in the present. Instead, historical fiction makes the peri-od of its setting a defining and integral feature of the work, and it attempts to convey the events, manners, customs, and psychologies of the past seriously and with care. Yet Rahn notes that "the historical novel is more controversial to define than one might expect" (1). She cites Robert Louis Stevenson's *Treasure Island* (1883) as an example of a novel from an earlier moment that might not qualify as historical: though it is set in the eighteenth century, about a hundred years before its composition, its focus is not on depicting eigh-teenth-century life or events but rather on using the time period as an occasion for its

Last of the Mohicans by James Fenimore Cooper, illustrated by N.C. Wyeth, 1919.

pirate adventure. In historical fiction, history ac-tually impinges on characters and scenes rather than simply serving as a backdrop, and the histor-ical period is rendered distinctively with concrete detail. Historical fiction sometimes, though not always, includes historical figures as characters, and it usually situates its main characters amid well-known historical events, such as the Amer-ican Civil War or the Holocaust. Typically, in order to be termed a historical novel, the work needs to take place much earlier than the period of its composition. This creates a sense that the era represented is significantly different from that in which it was written. The greater the gap be-tween the two periods and the more distinct the qualities of its place in time, the more clearly a work can be described as a historical novel. Sim-ply being set before the life of the reader does not qualify a work as a historical novel.

COMMON MOMENTS OR EVENTS IN HISTORICAL FICTION FOR CHILDREN

The Use of Historical Settings in Children's Literature

Many classic children's books have been works of historical fiction, such as Esther Forbes's *Johnny Tremain* (1943), which is set during the American Revolution, and Elizabeth George Speare's *The Witch of Blackbird Pond* (1958), set in seventeenth-century colonial America. Both of these books won the Newbery Medal, which has repeatedly been awarded to historical novels. In fact, more than twenty-five works of historical fiction have won the Newbery Medal between 1922, when it was first awarded, and 2016, making it one of the most consistently honored genres in American children's literature. Some of the most prolific American writers for children, such as Ann Rinaldi and Avi, have made careers out of writing historical fiction, as have British writers such as Geoffrey Trease and Rosemary Sutcliff. The historical novel for children remained consistently popular over the course of the twentieth century, and that popularity seems to have only intensified in recent decades, as evidenced by the enormous success of the American Girl collection of dolls and books featuring girls from different moments in American history.

As with the writing of history, works of historical fiction tend to cluster around certain events or periods. Reading historical fiction for children critically involves noting why these periods might be represented and what stories or themes they make possible. Some of the most frequent historical settings include medieval England, the American Revolution and Civil War, frontier life, World War I, the Great Depression, the Civil Rights Movement, and the Holocaust. Notable examples include

The Middle Ages
Marguerite de Angeli, *The Door in the Wall* (1949)
Karen Cushman, *The Midwife's Apprentice* (1995)
Avi, *Crispin: The Cross of Lead* (2002)

The American Revolution
Esther Forbes, *Johnny Tremain* (1943)
Christopher and James Lincoln Collier, *My Brother Sam Is Dead* (1974)
M.T. Anderson, *The Astonishing Life of Octavian Nothing, Traitor to the Nation* (2006)

The American Civil War and Reconstruction
Harold Keith, *Rifles for Watie* (1957)

Irene Hunt, *Across Five Aprils* (1964)
Mildred Taylor, *The Land* (2001)

The Frontier Experience
Laura Ingalls Wilder, *Little House on the Prairie* (1935)
Patricia MacLachlan, *Sarah, Plain and Tall* (1985)
Louise Erdrich, *The Birchbark House* (1999)

World War I
Michael Foreman, *War Game* (1994)
Linda Newbery, *The Shell House* (2002)
Theresa Breslin, *Remembrance* (2002)
Michael Morpurgo, *Private Peaceful* (2003)

The Great Depression
Mildred Taylor, *Roll of Thunder, Hear My Cry* (1976)
Karen Hesse, *Out of the Dust* (1997)
Christopher Paul Curtis, *Bud, Not Buddy* (1999)
Pam Muñoz Ryan, *Esperanza Rising* (2000)

The Holocaust
Ian Serraillier, *Escape from Warsaw* [also published as *The Silver Sword*] (1956)
Jane Yolen, *The Devil's Arithmetic* (1988)
Lois Lowry, *Number the Stars* (1989)

The Civil Rights Movement
Christopher Paul Curtis, *The Watsons Go to Birmingham—1963* (1995)
Rita Williams-Garcia, *One Crazy Summer* (2010)
Andrea Davis Pinkney, *The Diary of Dawnie Mae Johnson: With the Might of Angels* (2011)
Deborah Wiles, *Revolution* (2014)

Of course, these are periods or events that loom large in the cultural imagination, and they constitute major events or eras in Euro American history. Historical fiction often requires a basic familiarity with and an interest in the period depicted, so it makes sense for historical novels to turn to major events such as these for their settings. Moreover, the kinds of events or moments that constitute traditional history are those that involve the most conflict, drama, upheaval, or danger, and these elements are also fruitful for the writing of fictional stories. Rahn's discussion of the historical novel for children suggests as much when she notes that nineteenth-century children's writers sometimes "chose a historical setting partly because it offered greater opportunities for adventure" (4). Wars, the Middle Ages, the settling of the frontier, and economic disasters are all periods of chaos and uncertainty that demand the kind of action characterizing adventure. The past offers a temporally exotic setting that can promote reader interest or narrative gravitas. Perry Nodelman and Mavis Reimer offer yet another explanation, suggesting that the popularity of certain historical periods is linked to the school social studies curricula; they note that "it's increasingly difficult for publishers to find a market for novels set in periods of history that aren't often studied in schools" (115). School curricula also tend to reflect the traditional approach to history that constructs it from political and military conflict. These different explanations effectively amount to the same set of self-perpetuating reasons that historical fiction tends to depict the same periods or moments over and over again.

Trauma and Historical Children's Fiction

Another way to think about the popularity of historical fiction may be provided by what is known as "trauma theory," the interdisciplinary study of trauma and culture, including literary and cultural constructions or representations of trauma. Since Sigmund Freud, studies of trauma have frequently addressed the connection between repetition and trauma; Freud noted that some veterans of World War I experienced terrible nightmares that forced them to relive their traumatic experiences (10–12). He gained insight into these experiences by observing children's play and their tendency to reenact frightening or unpleasant events. Freud speculated that this practice of repetition transformed something painful into something pleasurable by restaging the trauma under more controlled circumstances, thereby enabling a sense of mastery or familiarity (15–17).

Following Freud, Kirby Farrell notes the widespread obsession in Euro American culture with news and other cultural texts about disaster and trauma: "Disaster stories model a range of human relationships to misfortune and keep our defenses exercised. They may function as a reality check even as they frame, and distance us from, horror. As a form of post-traumatic repetition, our obsessiveness about disaster headlines may represent an effort to assimilate what has frightened us since childhood, desensitizing us" (17). To the extent that history is constituted by trauma, the stories we tell ourselves, and the stories that we call "history," can be understood as attempts to repeat, work through, and master traumatic events. Children are often imagined as both extremely vulnerable—and therefore susceptible to trauma—and especially resilient and adaptable, thus making them ideal candidates to bear cultural traumas and to work through them on behalf of everyone, as Jonas does for his community in Lois Lowry's *The Giver* (1993). In its repetition of trauma, historical fiction for young readers provides an opportunity for children and young adults to engage with trauma, and this offers one explanation for why particular historical moments or events that were experienced as traumatic tend to be the ones most frequently represented.

Anastasia Ulanowicz argues that "children's literature has come to imagine itself as a medium through which the unruly ghosts of the historical past might be channeled" (3). She considers the ways in which children's literature, including historical fiction, represents and produces second-generation memory, the collective memories of the generation that follows the direct experience of a traumatic historical event. For example, Ulanowicz discusses Judy Blume's 1977 novel *Starring Sally J. Freedman as Herself*, which takes place two years after the end of World War II. Ten-year-old Sally, a Jewish girl from New Jersey, struggles with trying to understand the murder of her aunt and cousin in the Holocaust, which she does not experience directly. She devises a game with other children in which they pretend to be in a concentration camp, a puzzling and disturbing form of play. However, Ulanowicz sees Sally's game as an act that resonates with Freud's theories about repetition as a way of managing trauma (78). Children's literature becomes a site for the transmission and construction of second-generation memory, as child characters and readers learn about historical events experienced by previous generations.

Historical fiction for children provides a way to reckon with historical events or circumstances that continue to haunt the present. For instance, the United States continues to struggle with racial and ethnic prejudice, the legacies of slavery, and systemic practices of ethnic and racial inequality. Historical fiction focusing on race relations and the Civil Rights Movement represents ongoing effort to work through the complexities of race relations and the persistent traumas of racial injustice. Donna Jo Napoli's *Alligator Bayou* (2009) is based on the true story of five Sicilian immigrants who were lynched in the town of Tallulah, Louisiana, in 1899. In Napoli's novel, fourteen-year-old Calogero and the family of Sicilian grocers who care for him fail to understand and refuse to respect the Jim Crow rules of the South: Calogero befriends an African American girl named Patricia, and Francesco serves Black customers before white ones when they arrive first. Increasing racial tensions at a time when Italian immigrants were not considered white eventually lead to the family's being lynched. Ashley Hope Pérez's *Out of Darkness* (2015) similarly depicts an illicit romance, in this case between an African American boy, Wash, and a Mexican American girl, Naomi, in 1930s New London, Texas. Because of segregation, neither one can attend the town's white school, which has profited from the Texas oil boom. The novel builds towards the gas explosion at the school that kills more than 300 students and teachers, a real event considered the worst school disaster in American history (see Brown and Wereschagin). Published at a time of ongoing racial tension in the United States and a number of school disasters involving mass casualties, Pérez's representation of the New London tragedy provides a way to think through both historical and present experiences that are painful and difficult to comprehend. Rita Williams-Garcia's *One Crazy Summer* (2010) tells the story of three sisters who travel in 1968 from New York City to visit their mother in Oakland, California, where the girls find themselves at the center of Black Panther Party activities. Historical fiction for children and young adults about the history of race relations and Civil Rights Movement of the 1950s and 1960s continue to be used to teach readers about important events and to help them make connections between the past and present.

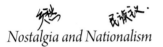

Nostalgia and Nationalism

While historical fiction might constitute a method for coming to terms with traumatic moments or events, it can also be fueled by nostalgia for certain eras or conditions. In American culture, the Western frontier persists as a source of nostalgic reflection in popular culture because it is associated with freedom from the restrictions of civilized life, opportunities for creating wealth and achieving upward mobility, hard work with clear and direct objectives and outcomes, "traditional" or "wholesome" values and standards of behavior, a sense of community or family, and the exciting enterprise of nation building. The less glamorous conditions of frontier life—including the possibility of disease, starvation, dull and physically exhausting work, geographic and social isolation, the lack of recourse in cases of domestic abuse or violence, the absence of infrastructure such as roads or sewage, and the genocidal treatment of Native Americans—are overlooked, minimized, or used as conditions of "adventure." Frontier fiction such as Laura Ingalls Wilder's Little House series (1932–43) or Carol Ryrie Brink's *Caddie Woodlawn* (1935) tap into these positive associations with frontier life by depicting the frontier as a space of familial harmony and adventurous play.

The popularity of medieval England in historical fiction for children might result from a similar motivation. Rebecca Barnhouse notes that "many of our stereotypes about the medieval period come from the Victorian era, which idealized and romanticized the Middle Ages" (x). The Middle Ages, which cover the extensive period from 500 CE to 1500 CE, are linked in the popular imagination with images of knights and squires, the social privileges of royalty and the intrigues of court, ideals of chivalry and heroism, and opportunities for adventure and discovery. Like the American frontier of the nineteenth century, the Middle Ages are frequently imagined in popular culture as a period of lawlessness and social upheaval that engendered mystery and myth. Both Marguerite de Angeli's *The Door in the Wall* and Avi's *Crispin: The Cross of Lead* involve dangerous quests, travel through dark forests, explorations of enormous castles or manors, opportunities for upward mobility, and demonstrations of bravery. Tales of King

Arthur and his knights have been popular since the sixteenth- and seventeenth-century chapbooks that inspired John Newbery, attesting to the long history of historical fiction for children.

The appeal of the American frontier or medieval England in children's literature seems likely to be related to a nostalgic sense of these periods as times of national or cultural origin, and the earliest works of historical fiction for adults were similarly rooted in nationalism and national history. Many of the most common events or periods depicted in historical fiction, such as the American Revolution, are linked to a distinctly national history that provides opportunities for laying the foundation of states or societies. The popularity of these periods, and the general connection between history and nationalism,

Marguerite de Angeli's *The Door in the Wall* (1949), with illustrations by Nina de Angeli Kuhn.

suggests the nationalist implications of historical fiction. History itself is traditionally understood as the history of the nation, and historical fiction has tended to reinforce this approach to conceptualizing and representing the past. This raises the question of whether or to what extent historical fiction promotes jingoism, ethnocentrism, or the whitewashing of past national abuses and atrocities in favor of national pride. As Kim Wilson notes, "Historical novels, holding the peculiar position of being both fiction and fact simultaneously, are effective vehicles to promote values and attitudes pertinent to the formation and perpetuation of a national identity" (130).

In articulating national identity, there is a tendency to exaggerate differences between groups and to promote a divisive sense of conflict or competition. For instance, the Little House series has been criticized for its portrayal of the Native American experience (Seale and Slapin 49). In *Little House on the Prairie*, Mrs. Scott says of the Indians, "Land knows, they'd never do anything with this country themselves. All they do is roam around over it like wild animals. Treaties or no treaties, the land belongs to folks that'll farm it. That's only common sense and justice" (Wilder 211). The narrator reports that Mrs. Scott thought, "The only good Indian was a dead Indian" (211). Mrs. Scott is arguably an unlikeable character, prompting the reader to suspect her viewpoints, but the series includes other instances of Native American characters depicted as flat, threatening, or inferior to the Ingalls family and other Anglo American settlers. Wilson cites other historical fiction published for children, including Ann Rinaldi's *The Journal of Jasper Jonathan Pierce: A Pilgrim Boy* (2000), as reinforcing the national myth of the United States "as the Promised Land of liberty, equity, and justice" and therefore as superior to others (130). Jasper Pierce is an indentured servant who arrives with the Pilgrims at Plymouth in 1620, but he asserts the right to "think or write what we believe" centuries before a notion of free speech would be codified. Historical fiction reveals current concerns, values, or biases, in addition to those of the past (52).

Popular Culture and Series Books

In recent years the children's publishing industry has produced and marketed a number of series of historical novels for children, indicating that the genre has proved profitable and popular. In the United States, Scholastic Press, one of the largest publishers of children's literature, has produced the Dear America series for girls, the My Name Is America series for boys, and the My America series for younger readers. The books in these series take the form of diaries or journals authored by fictional boys or girls who experience important events or periods in American history firsthand. All three series group individual volumes under major historical categories: the colonial period, the American Revolution, westward expansion, the Civil War and slavery, nineteenth- and twentieth-century immigration, World War I, the Depression, World War II, and the Vietnam War. However, a few volumes do defy these big categories, such as Kathryn Lasky's *A Time for Courage* (2002), about a girl suffragist who fights alongside her mother for the right of women to vote; Lois Lowry's *Like the Willow Tree* (2011), which features a girl orphaned by the Spanish Flu epidemic of 1918 who goes to live with her uncle in a Maine Shaker community; and Andrea Davis Pinkney's *With the Might of Angels* (2011), a novel about an African American girl who integrates her Virginia school following the 1954 Brown v. Board of Education decision by the Supreme Court. There has been a clear attempt to make the series ethnically and racially diverse, with characters including Wong Ming-Chung, who emigrates with his family from China during the California gold rush; Zipporah Feldman, a Russian Jewish immigrant at the turn of the century; and Jesse Smoke, a Cherokee boy forced to relocate with his family on the Trail of Tears.

While children's series fiction is usually denigrated by adults for being formulaic and mass-produced, Scholastic has engaged many prominent and critically acclaimed authors to write for the series, attesting to both the clout of the press and the creative interest of historical fiction writers. Notable contributors to the three "American" series include Walter Dean Myers, Joseph Bruchac, Laurence Yep, Marion Dane Bauer, Karen Hesse, and Lisa Rowe Fraustino. Scholastic has published similar series in the United Kingdom and Australia under the title My Story, and these too tend to address important historical eras. Another brand, the American Girl line of books and dolls, which features girls from different times throughout American history, has also proved enormously successful. Both the Scholastic series and the American Girl products have begun to be examined closely by scholars and students of children's literature and culture. In the following section, "Fiction Versus History," we offer a set of tools that might be used for approaching these and other historical works critically.

Awards for Historical Children's Literature

Since 1984, the Scott O'Dell Award has been given annually to honor a work of historical fiction for children or young adults. O'Dell, best known for his novel *Island of the Blue Dolphins*, established the award in 1982 to encourage children's writers to produce quality historical fiction. To be considered for the award, a work must have been issued by a US publisher, have been written by a US citizen, and be set in North or South America. Notable winners include Karen Hesse for *Out of the Dust* (1997), a novel in verse about the life of an Oklahoma girl during the Dust Bowl; Mildred Taylor for *The Land* (2001), part of the Logan Family series about the life of an African American family in the South from the Civil War to the late twentieth century; Louise Erdrich for *The Game of Silence* (2005), the first sequel to *The Birchbark House* about a nineteenth-century Ojibwe girl; and Laurie

Halse Anderson for *Chains* (2008), a novel about a Black slave in New York City during the American Revolution. The Geoffrey Bilson Award, established in 1988, similarly honors excellence in historical fiction for children in works written by Canadian authors. Christopher Paul Curtis won both the 2008 O'Dell and Bilson Awards for *Elijah of Buxton* (2007), a story about a boy born in Ontario's Buxton Settlement for escaped slaves before the American Civil War. Winners of these awards often depict major historical events or periods, such as the American Revolution, the Civil War, the Great Depression and Dust Bowl, and World War II, demonstrating how these moments continue to dominate the construction of history.

Mildred Taylor's *Roll of Thunder, Hear My Cry* (1976) is part of her award-winning Logan Family series. Illustration by Jerry Pinkney.

FICTION VERSUS HISTORY

Rethinking the Writing of History

Historical fiction is often used to teach the content of history, but it also might be used to examine how history is written. Fiction and history are usually thought to constitute radically different projects, but a closer examination of the writing of nonfiction history points to a number of parallels between the two. According to Perry Nodelman, the work of historians involves "shaping events into acceptable patterns of cause and effect," and thus "the stories they tell are much like the plots of fiction" (71). In his landmark work *Tropics of Discourse* (1978), historian Hayden White argues that historical writing always includes "tropes" or figurative language, such as metaphor or irony. He contends that "the techniques and strategies" used by historians and creative writers "can be shown to be substantially the same, however different they may appear on a purely surface, or dictional level" (121). Some historians feel that White's work elided important boundaries between history and fiction, therefore casting doubt on the importance of "facts." However, White is merely pointing out that even nonfiction histories involve elements of narrative and acts of interpretation. Peter Novick concurs in his history of the notion of objectivity in historiography, or the professional writing of history, and he casts doubt on whether neutral, disinterested observation of transparent, absolute truth or fact is ever really possible (6). While authors of historical fiction use historical events and details to tell a story, historians writing narrative histories use the techniques of fiction to explain what happened in the past. Well-known writers of historical narratives include Shelby Foote, whose three-volume *The Civil War: A Narrative* was published between 1958 and 1974, and the Pulitzer Prize–winning David McCullough, whose *1776* (2005) provides a narrative history of the American Revolution.

Historiography uses primary sources to tell a story about the past:

- Letters, memos, telegrams, and other forms of correspondence

- Government documents such as census records, birth and death certificates, legislative records, and court transcripts

- Diaries and journals

- Family records such as genealogies and event invitations

- Eyewitness accounts and personal interviews

- Photographs, film footage, or other documentary evidence

- Maps, architectural plans, or real estate records

- Newspaper articles that make use of sources such as these or record opinions.

Once the historian assembles these records, he or she needs to make sense of them, and that task is by no means straightforward. The use of letters, an important source for the writing of history, highlights many of the problems. In the case of handwritten letters, handwriting must be deciphered, and portions of letters might prove indecipherable. Because the uses, meanings, and connotations of words change over time, words must be understood in the context in which they are used. Sometimes these meanings can be misunderstood or be ambiguous. In a regular correspondence between two people, the historian might possess only one correspondent's letters, which means that the other half of the conversation must be reconstructed. Letters might be missing from the sequence. The letters might be undated, making their chronological order difficult to determine. Letters might have been edited or destroyed to conceal information. The correspondents might use code words or private slang, complicating the ability to make sense of the letters. A letter writer might lie or exaggerate. In some cases the validity of the letter's contents can be confirmed by another source, but in other cases the historian might be misled. Everyone's perspective is unique, and two witnesses to the same event will notice different details, perceive the event differently, and describe it in different ways. Thus, the letter being examined constitutes only one perspective.

This all means that the historian working with primary sources must interpret them, make educated guesses, evaluate and judge between conflicting sources, fill in gaps, and put the sources in context. All the disparate and unique sources are gathered, sorted, studied, and transformed into a coherent narrative that will make sense to readers without overwhelming them. Thus, the historian interprets sources and constructs a narrative, making connections between details, putting them in a particular order, and selecting some details to relate while omitting others. Put this way, the work of the historian—the writing of history—begins to resemble the writing of fiction: both are stories and reflect a set of choices. Historical fiction might be accused of constituting an interpretation of history, as reflecting or being guided by a contemporary perspective, but the same is true of history. Works of history are sometimes controversial, as is the case with Daniel Goldhagen's *Hitler's Willing Executioners: Ordinary Germans and the Holocaust* (1996). Some historians objected to the book's lack of new empirical data and others to its interpretation of that data: the idea that ordinary German citizens were aware of the scope of the Holocaust and willingly participated in it or allowed it because of pervasive anti-Semitism (Wehler 80). While using historical fiction to teach history might be problematic, the study of historical fiction can demonstrate that history, too, involves interpretation, perspective, and narrative.

The Strengths of Historical Fiction

To note that both history and fiction are stories is not to say that they are the same kind of story. History might be written as a narrative and involve interpretation, but it is a narrative and interpretation of an event, moment, or phenomenon that presumably happened. Fiction, by definition, is not limited in the same way, and it might include a story about an event that did not happen, dialogue that did not take place, or a person who did not exist, even though it is set against the backdrop of an actual event or era. Fiction is permitted greater latitude for invention, and the scale of fiction might be different from that of history. Historians assemble information to construct an overarching narrative—about the American Civil War, for instance—and its scale is usually larger than that of fiction. The historical narrative is pieced together from details about many lives over time. Fiction tends to be more specific, operating on a smaller scale, often at the level of a small slice of an individual life. As a result, readers might become attached to literary characters, identify with them, and perceive them as relatable human beings. A history of the Holocaust might present facts and details about the chronology and mechanisms of genocide, along with the abstraction of corresponding numbers, such as six million Jews killed. On the other hand, a historical novel about the Holocaust, such as Jane Yolen's *The Devil's Arithmetic*, encourages the reader to identify with the fictional Hannah, care deeply about her well-being, and examine the horrors of genocide through her unique perspective. Perceiving the historical event through the eyes of this one relatable character might help make an incomprehensible event easier to assimilate.

Much about history—events, facts, experiences—is missing from the historical record because the details were never documented or the documentation has been lost and some details are too fleeting, ephemeral, or intangible to be captured by historical narratives: emotions, the demeanor of historical figures, reactions to painful or traumatic events, humor and irony, terrible smells or beautiful sights, and many other subjective aspects of people or situations. Fiction can fill in the gaps of history with its speculative imaginings. Though perhaps not grounded in fact, these imaginative constructions and additions might provide a fuller sense of history, and though not factual in the strict sense, they offer a different kind of truth. Elizabeth Wein, who has written a number of historical novels for children, observes that "fiction is the lie that tells the truth" (164). Nineteenth-century Italian writer Alessandro Manzoni, one of the first to write critically about the historical novel, articulated the virtues of literature to the writer of historical fiction:

> The aim of your work was to put before me, in a new and special form, a richer, more varied, more complete history than that found in works which more commonly go by this name.... The history we expect from you is not a chronological account of mere political and military events or, occasionally, some other kind of extraordinary happening; but a more general representation of the human condition, in a time and place naturally more circumscribed than that in which works of history, in the more usual sense of the word, ordinarily unfold. (63)

The subjective experience of the world and events, what Manzoni calls "the human condition," is often constituted by precisely those intangible and ephemeral elements that literature is especially good at representing and communicating. As historical narratives increasingly adopt the conventions of fiction, they, too, may begin to develop these strengths.

Take, for instance, Christopher Paul Curtis's fictional treatment of the actual 1963 bombing of an African American church in Birmingham, Alabama, that killed four girls. In *The Watsons Go to Birmingham—1963* (1995), ten-year-old Kenny runs to the church after the bomb goes off, thinking his sister is still inside. Describing the mixture of fear and confusion experienced by the children poses a problem for historians. Even if a child were interviewed shortly after witnessing such an event, he or she might find it difficult or impossible to describe his or her feelings, as would an adult witness, and an adult who looks back on having experienced this event would have to reconstruct his or her childhood perception, which would be filtered through all the accumulated knowledge and thinking of the intervening years. Curtis, as a fiction writer, assumes the challenge of conveying how the scene outside the church might have looked from the perspective of a child. It requires imagination. By this point in the novel, the reader has become familiar with Kenny and his relationship with his family and sister. Kenny is a likable character, and the reader may care for him. The reader's sympathy for Kenny and the sense of intimate familiarity with him make the scene that much more painful, and Curtis's imaginative rendering of Kenny's fractured perspective communicates an ephemeral and subjective dimension that is probably missing from a traditional historical account of the event. The novel includes an epilogue in which the facts of the event are described:

> The characters and events in this novel are fictional. However, there were many unsolved bombings in Birmingham at the time of the story, including the one that took place at the Sixteenth Avenue Baptist Church on September 15, 1963. Four young-teenage girls—Addie Mae Collins, Denise McNair, Carole Robertson, and Cynthia Wesley—were killed when a bomb went off during Sunday school. (209)

These few sentences of history provide a stark contrast with the literary representation of the same facts from the perspective of a fictional boy who thinks his sister may have been inside the church. The reader's experience reading the novel is entirely different from the experience reading the historical epilogue; noting this contrast involves recognizing that fiction can achieve something distinct from, and as valuable as, history.

PROBLEMS WITH REPRESENTING THE PAST

Although historical fiction might provide invaluable contributions to our understanding of history, it has sometimes proved controversial, just as works of history have. Ann Rinaldi's contribution to the Dear America series, *My Heart Is on the Ground* (1999), has been criticized as depicting "an ahistorical conception of female voice" (Hubler 99) and as "rife with glaring factual errors" (Reese et al. n.p.). The novel is told from the perspective of Nannie Little Rose, a Sioux girl who is forced to attend the Carlisle Indian School, a Pennsylvania boarding school for Native American children where they were taught to abandon their heritage and customs and assimilate to Anglo American culture. Children were renamed, forbidden to speak their native languages, and exposed to various forms of physical and emotional abuse (Atleo et al.). Angela E. Hubler argues that "Rinaldi seems to be more influenced by such contemporary issues as the self-esteem and voice of adolescent girls" (99), and the reviewers for Oyate, a website on Native Americans in children's literature, claim the book contains numerous historical inaccuracies and implausible details of an Ojibwe girl's life (Reese et al.). For instance, they dispute the idea that Nannie Little Rose would describe herself as Sioux rather than by her band or location, and they doubt that she would have openly criticized in her diary the adults running her boarding school because they might have inspected her writing. Similarly, they argue that she would not have spoken her native language while at school, since this would have resulted in punishment. These critiques of Rinaldi's work indicate the range of possible problems created by historical fiction: problems of accuracy, authenticity and plausibility, and presentism.

Accuracy

The problem of **accuracy** involves the faithfulness of the work with regard to the historical record, which might itself be inaccurate. In some cases, inaccuracies are deliberate, as when an author creates a character who is a composite of several real people, or a place that is an amalgamation of several actual places. Other inaccuracies might constitute oversights or result from unverified assumptions. Does historical fiction have a responsibility to remain completely faithful to the historical record or historical consensus, or is it free to alter the facts for dramatic effect or literary expedience? Is it important to remain faithful to all known facts, or are some more important and demanding of fidelity? What makes certain inaccuracies acceptable and others not? Does a departure from historical consensus constitute a literary failure or just a historical one? These questions can be answered only through the negotiations of a community of readers, keeping in mind the motives for reading and the knowledge readers already bring to works. Readers who read primarily for pleasure might be unconcerned with the question of accuracy, but even these readers might expect to learn something from the work and might therefore have an investment in its faithfulness. Moreover, the reader who lacks the knowledge to combat or counterbalance misinformation might be left with false impressions of the historical moment or of the characters represented by a work. Sometimes accuracy is difficult to determine. While historical fiction might be thought useful for teaching children about history, it might also rely on historical ignorance for its success.

Readers unfamiliar with a historical figure or era are unable to object to inaccuracies—a situation that can pose real problems. In some cases, historical inaccuracy and a false sense of history can be positively dangerous. For instance, the depiction of German soldiers in works such as Lois Lowry's *Number the Stars* as flat, brutish, and wholly

villainous men might create the false sense that only simple, brutish people can participate in acts of atrocity and that one's own neighbors, or even oneself and one's family,
are incapable of them. Few see themselves as simple-minded brutes, and yet ordinary
people have participated in acts or systems of violence and oppression. Whereas the understanding of history can compel the correction of wrongs or the avoidance of disaster,
inaccurate or disputed details may lead to complacency or inaction. Depictions of Native Americans, for instance, as either mystical guides or violent warriors may undermine
efforts to educate Americans about the mistreatment of Native peoples. Nora Murphy
points to the opening page of Laura Ingalls Wilder's *Little House in the Big Woods* (1932),
which reads, "As far as a man could go to the north in a day, or a week, or a whole month,
there was nothing but woods. There were no houses. There were no roads. There were
no people" (Wilder 1). As Murphy reminds us, "There *were* people who lived in and near
Wilder's woods" (286). To imagine the American frontier as uninhabited encourages an
uncritical sense of ownership of the land and indifference to the legacy of the Euro American treatment of indigenous populations. The stakes of inaccuracy are heightened by
children's historical fiction because it is often used to introduce children to history.

Authenticity

More common, perhaps, than outright historical inaccuracies are failures of historical
authenticity. Accuracy depends upon the correspondence between recorded history
and fictional representation, whereas authenticity indicates how a literary work fills in
the gaps of the historical record and whether the imaginative components of the work are
plausible. While accuracy is a matter of how faithful the work is to what is thought to be
true, authenticity is a matter of whether the fictional additions or imaginings are within
the realm of likelihood or possibility. Anne Scott MacLeod takes a number of critically
acclaimed historical novels for children to task for failing to represent plausible scenarios.
In Patricia MacLachlan's *Sarah, Plain and Tall*, set in the mid to late nineteenth century,
Sarah travels alone from Maine to a farm in the Midwest to live with the widowed Mr.
Witting and his children in response to the newspaper advertisement he places for a wife.
She agrees to stay with the family for a month to determine whether the situation is ac-
ceptable. MacLeod finds this premise unlikely:

> The realities of nineteenth-century social mores are at odds with practically all of
> this. It was unusual (though not impossible) for a woman to travel such distances
> alone, and much more than unusual for her to stay with a man not related to her
> without another woman in the house. Had she done so, however, it is unlikely that
> she could return home afterward with her reputation intact. MacLachlan has said

Sometimes criticized for being implausible, Patricia MacLachlan's *Sarah, Plain and Tall* (1985) tells the story of a nineteenth-century mail-order bride who settles on a midwestern farm. Illustrated by P.J. Lynch.

that her story is based on a family experience a couple of generations ago, and I have no reason to question that. Even so, the story as told is highly uncharacteristic of its time and place. (28)

Because Sarah is an entirely fictional character, whether she would have traveled alone, lived with a man to whom she was neither related nor married, or worked side by side with Mr. Witting on reshingling the roof are matters of plausibility rather than accuracy. Similar questions have been raised about Karen Cushman's *Catherine, Called Birdy* (1994). For instance, critics have suggested that the independent spirit demonstrated by Birdy (MacLeod 30), a girl in thirteenth-century England who drives away various suitors selected by her father, and the extraordinary promotion of literacy represented by her diary keeping (Barnhouse 9) are implausible. The reader of historical fiction might understandably wonder whether a character living at a particular moment could be expected to perform certain actions and think or speak in certain ways. Historically informed readers may disagree in their judgements about a text's accuracy and authenticity, but reading children's historical fiction critically nonetheless involves thinking about these issues.

Presentism

Problems with the authenticity or plausibility of a work are often related to the notion of **presentism**, or the idea that the work depicts an ideology or psychology more characteristic of the present than of the past. We can never fully recover how people in the past thought, and all constructions and understandings of history are only retrospective, informed by present knowledge and present ways of thinking. Perry Nodelman observes that "history is always about the present," and he continues, "As is the case in other kinds of narrative, the stories history tells reveal as much or more about the events of current history and the values of the historian as of the historical subject" (71). This is also true of the historical novel. Sometimes authors use historical fiction deliberately to comment on the present, while in other cases presentism marks the work without the author's conscious deliberation. It is an inescapable effect of the fact that an author is situated in a particular historical moment and is shaped by that moment, including the discourses and ideologies that dominate the day, what is thinkable or knowable. That Elizabeth George Speare's *The Witch of Blackbird Pond*, first published in 1958 and set in the seventeenth century, is really about the 1950s cannot be an accident. Arthur Miller's play *The Crucible*, also about the Salem witch trials of 1692 and 1693, preceded Speare's novel by five years. First produced on Broadway in 1953, Miller's play was a commentary on McCarthyism and the hearings that the House Committee on Un-American Activities held on the role of communists in Hollywood during the late 1940s and early 1950s. The notion of a witch hunt became a paradigm for understanding the intense xenophobia and persecution of difference that came to characterize 1950s America, and Speare's novel about the trial of an outspoken, educated girl as a witch reflects this historical context, as Sara L. Schwebel observes in her study of the novel ("Historical Fiction").

Sometimes the presentism of the novel is less a form of intentional social commentary on the present than a reflection of present values. Joseph Zornado ultimately defends the work of Karen Cushman on the grounds that fact and fiction are not so easily distinguished, as we saw earlier. He summarizes her critics, who note the novel's presentism:

Skeptics charge that Cushman's work is not "real" historical fiction, but rather, simply "fiction" because her work sacrifices historical "facts" in order to tell what amounts to contemporary stories about female adolescence. Alyce, the main character in *Apprentice*, does, says, and thinks in a way young women in the fourteenth

century simply could not. In Cushman's first book set in medieval England, Catherine, the daughter of a knight—and by rights a "lady"—develops a keen sense
for the logical inconsistency that surrounds and makes up her life, and grounds
her demands for fair treatment on this way of seeing the world. Some argue, then,
that the history in these novels reflects more of Cushman's late twentieth-century
concerns about women than it does historical truths of English medieval culture
and countryside. (252)

Because presentism is almost unavoidable, to read historical children's literature critically
demands understanding that a text is a product of the historical context of its composition. In fact, historical fiction often reveals more about the present than it does about the
past. The problems of accuracy, authenticity, and presentism make historical fiction one
of the most complex genres of children's literature.

Artistic Freedom and Historical Responsibility

These possible problems with historical fiction create opportunities for conflict between authors' artistic freedom and their responsibility to history. Are authors free to
reimagine or use the past in limitless ways, or should accuracy and authenticity constrain them? Should the fact that children or teachers might use historical fiction to
learn about the past impinge on the creative process of storytelling? How might historical inaccuracies for the sake of literary or dramatic effect disrespect the experience
of—and even cause pain to—individuals or cultures? Historical fiction clearly requires
a complex negotiation between the historical record and the imagination, between creative freedom and ethical responsibility, between the pleasure of story and the didactic
uses of literature. Literature provides a variety of ways to negotiate these conflicts. Elizabeth Wein, known for her historical fiction for children—such as *The Winter Prince*
(1993), *A Coalition of Lions* (2003), and *The Empty Kingdom* (2008)—refers to the kinds
of books she writes as "sort of historical fantasy" (Wein 163). Though she ultimately
differentiates herself from the "true writer of historical fiction," her approach to writing
historical fantasy is instructive nonetheless (167). She explains that she is meticulous
about details:

> I have a tendency to get stuck on details like what kind of flowers are growing in
> the palace gardens in San'a. Are there fireflies in the Rift Valley? When was the
> crossbow invented? What is a slingshot normally made out of? This shirt so-and-so
> is wearing: is it cotton or linen? Is there oil-based paint on the walls, or lime-wash?
> I once spent two solid hours verifying the possible existence of a Chinese compass

before AD 500, just so I could put one in a room. The compass doesn't ever get used. It gets mentioned in the Mark of Solomon books twice, I think, as a piece of furniture. But such details can be as evocative as an elaborate description of landscape or pageantry. (164)

Nevertheless, she uses her imagination freely to tell stories that are missing from the historical record and to speculate about alternative possibilities. She writes, "I do my best to limit these speculations to the possible. That way, coincidence can only work in my favor. I don't bestrew my novels with anachronisms (I try not to, anyway)—only with the unlikely and unproven" (166). The enterprise of literature is capacious; it can contain a range of possibilities. We should not expect all works to represent the same answer to the questions posed above, as different authors will answer these questions differently. The student or scholar of children's literature should consider how texts embody different ways of negotiating these apparent conflicts, including how those negotiations affect readers in ways that are sometimes painful or harmful, as when minority groups are misrepresented or the abuses of history are minimized.

Controversy and Historical Fiction

Sometimes an author's or illustrator's choices—how they navigate these issues of accuracy, authenticity, and artistic freedom—can be controversial. In 2016, Scholastic published Ramin Ganeshram and Vanessa Brantley-Newton's picturebook *A Birthday Cake for George Washington*, about Washington's enslaved cook Hercules, a real historical figure. Told from the perspective of his daughter Delia, the book involves Hercules's efforts to bake a cake for the President without sugar. It concludes with his triumph and a successful birthday celebration. The book was controversial because the slaves are depicted as smiling, happy, and devoted (Stack n.p.), a representation that fits with the myth of the happy and contented slave popular as a justification for slavery both before and after the Civil War. As critics have noted, Hercules had a daughter who worked at Washington's plantation at Mt. Vernon, probably not in Philadelphia where *A Birthday Cake* is set, and Hercules eventually sought freedom by escaping, while Delia remained a slave. Ganeshram notes Hercules's escape, but this information does not appear in the narrative itself. Delia's location during Washington's presidency is a matter of accuracy, and readers and critics might debate the significance of this detail. The issue of whether Hercules and Delia were content as slaves raises questions of both accuracy *and* authenticity. While Hercules no doubt experienced moments of pleasure and gratification while enslaved, his escape implies that he was not as happy as the book's narrative and images suggest. In fact, in a period after the setting of *A Birthday Cake*,

Hercules was put to work on the plantation as a field laborer ("Hercules" n.p.), a very different situation from the privileged position of chef depicted in the book. For some, this impression lacks authenticity and minimizes the terrible pain of slavery as a historical atrocity with ongoing reverberations.

Both Scholastic and the book's author have commented on the controversy. Concerns about the book were so acute that on 17 January 2016, Scholastic took the rare step of stopping the distribution of the book, and it is now out of print. They noted on their website,

> While we have great respect for the integrity and scholarship of the author, illustrator, and editor, we believe that, without more historical background on the evils of slavery than this book for younger children can provide, the book may give a false impression of the reality of the lives of slaves and therefore should be withdrawn. Scholastic has a long history of explaining complex and controversial issues to children at all ages and grade levels. We do not believe this title meets the standards of appropriate presentation of information to younger children, despite the positive intentions and beliefs of the author, editor, and illustrator. ("New" n.p.)

Ganeshram offered a defense of the book, noting she approached it as a historian and citing her intention to tell a story about a little-known but compelling historical figure: "Hercules represents just one of the many overlooked, yet remarkable people of color who personally triumphed over their terrible circumstances to their advantage through their dignity and intellect" (n.p.). Ganeshram acknowledges that writers of historical fiction must make choices in filling in the gaps of history, writing, "I can't know exactly what [Hercules] thought or how he felt, of course. But in writing the book my aim was always to represent him as he saw himself: dignified, commanding and proud" (n.p.). She concludes, "Hercules's story is complex, but that is exactly why to my mind it deserves to be told in books for children and adults" (n.p.). *A Birthday Cake for George Washington* provides a useful case study for understanding the challenges of historical fiction for children.

THE USE OF AFTERWORDS, AUTHORS' NOTES, AND EPILOGUES

One of the problems posed by historical fiction is how best to balance a commitment to imaginatively constructing the story with a responsibility to present instructive historical information. One strategy that has been used frequently to resolve this dilemma is the author's note, afterword, or epilogue, which typically provides facts to inform the reader and complement the narrative. This paratextual material is an important component of the book that should not be overlooked, and its frequent inclusion in historical novels confirms the expectation that historical fiction will be used as an educational tool. These notes supply different kinds of information. The brief author's note to Speare's *The Witch of Blackbird Pond* is used only to confirm that the story is fictitious and to distinguish between fictional characters and real people. This is important because the real people who appear as characters in the novel—a few men important in the colonial politics of seventeenth-century Connecticut—are unlikely to be recognized by readers. The note therefore helps establish the historical authenticity of the fictitious narrative. Michael Morpurgo's note to his *Private Peaceful*, a novel about World War I, gives an overview of the war and facts such as the dates of its beginning and end. It also describes more specifically the practice of executing traumatized soldiers for deserting their posts, something that is likely to be little known about the war and is a key plot point in the novel. Morpurgo's note concludes with a statement about the value of reading the novel and learning these forgotten details.

The epilogue to Christopher Paul Curtis's *The Watsons Go to Birmingham—1963* presents a fairly thorough overview of the Black Civil Rights Movement as well as adding information about the specific church bombing depicted near the conclusion of the novel. Curtis's afterword to his Newbery-winning *Bud, Not Buddy* also acknowledges that the work is fictional but claims that "many of the situations Bud encounters are based on events that occurred in the 1930s, during a time known as the Great Depression" (237). Rather than furnish general information about the Depression, Curtis's afterword spends several pages describing the real people, mostly members of Curtis's own family, on whom some of the characters are based. He uses his description of these relatives to introduce details about the historical context, such as the fact that "the jobs of Pullman porter and redcap were among the few open to African American men at that time and carried a certain prestige in the black community" (238).

The epilogue to *The Devil's Arithmetic*, entitled "What Is True about This Book," is used to explain that the family Seder depicted in the novel is "not strictly a traditional one" but similar to the kind practiced by Jane Yolen's own family. Yolen goes on to confirm that "all the facts about the horrible routinization of evil in the camps is true" and that "only the characters are made up" (168). She also explains that the concentration camp in the novel is a composite of several real camps, and the epilogue actually offers a meditation on what fiction can and cannot do with regard to representing history. The author's note to M.T. Anderson's *The Astonishing Life of Octavian Nothing, Traitor to the Nation, Volume I: The Pox Party* (2006) similarly is a metadiscussion about historical fiction, especially the difficulties of rendering the speech of its eighteenth-century characters and treating the complex themes of the American Revolution within the confines of the novel. Afterwords stress different facets of the enterprise of historical fiction; they can be examined to understand how the author approaches the writing situation and what information is most important for the reader to learn.

TIME-TRAVEL AND TIME-SLIP NARRATIVES

Time-travel narratives occupy an uncertain place in the category of historical fiction because they usually insert characters from the present—the author's or the novel's—into
the past, thereby altering the past and adding a fantastic element to the depiction of history. Some organizations exclude time-travel narratives from the category of historical
fiction, such as the Canadian Children's Book Centre, which selects works for the Bilson
Award. Time-travel narratives are expressly ineligible for nomination. One subcategory
of time-travel fiction is the time-slip narrative, which Anne Balay describes as "a genre of
fantasy fiction in which time travel happens accidentally, without the traveler's consent
or control" (131). In some time-travel or time-slip narratives, a contemporary protagonist
travels back in time, and the work mostly focuses on this past setting, while being framed
by the present, with the character returning to his or her own time at the novel's conclusion. Yolen's *The Devil's Arithmetic* is an example, with Hannah traveling from present-day
New York to Poland during the Holocaust and then back again, having witnessed terrible
historical events firsthand. In Edward Bloor's *London Calling* (2006), a New Jersey boy is
given a magic radio that transports him to London during the Blitz of World War II.

Other time-slip narratives may not entail actual time travel but alternate between sections set in the present and in the past. For instance, Aidan Chambers's *Postcards from No
Man's Land* (1999), a Printz Award and Carnegie Medal winner, alternates between the
contemporary story of seventeen-year-old Jacob, who travels from England to the Netherlands, where his grandfather was wounded during the Second World War, and the story
of his grandfather during the war, as told by the woman who nursed him after his injury.
Linda Newbery's *The Shell House* (2002) similarly alternates between the life of a teenager
in present-day England, who begins to develop feelings for a same-sex classmate, and the
life of a World War I soldier, who has experienced romance with a fellow soldier.

Do time-travel and time-slip narratives belong properly to the category of historical
fiction? As we discuss in other chapters, works of one genre almost always contain elements of others, so that adventure stories usually refer to domestic elements, and domestic novels include scenes of adventure. Historical fiction—works that are set in and depict
the past—can be imagined as contrasting with contemporary realist fiction or problem
novels, which are set in the present and usually depict aspects of modern life. Time-travel
and time-slip narratives combine elements of both the historical novel and the contemporary realist novel, including elements of fantasy or science fiction. Some time-travel
or time-slip narratives may appear to fit more easily in the category of historical fiction,
such as *The Devil's Arithmetic*, which takes place almost entirely in the past, while others,
such as *Postcards from No Man's Land*, might be described as emphasizing the present.
Nevertheless, both are hybrid works, and we include them in this chapter because reading
time-travel and time-slip narratives critically requires understanding the conventions of

historical fiction and the problems and questions raised by the depiction of history in fiction. As with more conventional historical novels, they tend to depict certain moments in history, and they are informed as much by the historical contexts of their compositions as by the periods of their chronological settings. In most cases, works of these genres use the past to provide a new perspective on the present or to make the contemporary character appreciate the present more or gain insight on the present; other works use terrible experiences of the past to discipline the more comfortable or safer contemporary child or young adult. By depicting the past as beneficial, time-travel and time-slip narratives make explicit the ways in which historical fiction itself uses the past.

READING CRITICALLY: HISTORICAL FICTION

Johnny Tremain and *My Brother Sam Is Dead*

Esther Forbes's *Johnny Tremain* is one of the classic historical novels for children. Published in 1943, it won the Newbery Medal in 1944. The same year *Johnny Tremain* was published, Forbes won the Pulitzer Prize for her biography of Paul Revere, suggesting her special qualifications for writing historical fiction. The novel focuses on the life of a fourteen-year-old silversmith's apprentice who lives in Boston and becomes involved in the nascent American Revolution during the two years leading up to the battles of Lexington and Concord. It demonstrates all the key qualities of historical fiction: it takes place in a period much earlier than the one in which it was written, the historical setting is absolutely central to the characters and plot, and real historical figures even appear as minor characters, including Paul Revere, Dr. Joseph Warren, John and Samuel Adams, and James Otis Jr. Though set in the eighteenth century, *Johnny Tremain* is as much about the mid twentieth century; in fact, this novel about the American Revolutionary War can even be read as a novel about World War II.

Edward Jennerich notes that Forbes began writing the novel the day after the bombing of Pearl Harbor in December 1941. Though she had initially conceived of a book about the Revolution in which the main character remains neutral, Jennerich claims that the beginning of America's involvement in World War II changed those plans. In her Newbery Medal acceptance speech, Forbes states outright that her writing of *Johnny Tremain* was influenced by the events taking place in the world around her and that she wanted to link the experience of young men serving in the war with that of the young people called to serve during the Revolution ("Appendix A" 145). Other traces of the novel's historical context are subtler. Johnny eventually finds himself working as a spy on behalf of the Sons of Liberty in Boston and attends their secret meetings. At one such meeting, James Otis gives a rousing speech to the assembled men, enflaming their support for war: "We give all we have, lives, property, safety, skills ... we fight, we die, for a simple thing. Only that a man can stand up" (Forbes, *Johnny* 180, ellipsis in original). Anita Tarr acknowledges the connection between Forbes's historical context and Otis's idealistic rhetoric: "Admittedly, Forbes is adamant in her attempts to solidify an idealistic foundation for the rebellion, but this insistence is forgivable, especially since she was writing the book during the dramatic events of World War II" (179).

Paul Revere, one of the men at the meeting, responds to Otis in a way that even more clearly reflects the values of the mid twentieth century rather than those of the mid eighteenth. He says, "You know my father had to [flee] France because of the tyranny over there. He was only

Opposite: Johnny and his horse, Goblin, flee the British in Esther Forbes's *Johnny Tremain* (1943), illustrated in this 1998 edition by Michael McCurdy.

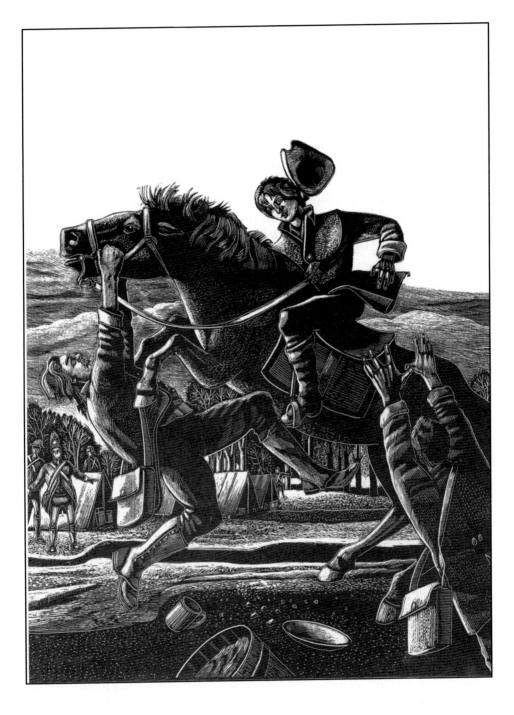

a child. But now, in a way, I'm fighting for that child ... that no frightened lost child ever is sent out a refugee from his own country because of race or religion" (Forbes, *Johnny* 181). Revere's statement articulates support of the American Revolution in terms of universal human rights and the global good, and this, along with his reference to refugees who must flee their home countries because of race and religion, likely reflects the growing awareness in the early years of World War II of the refugees fleeing wartime devastation or the genocide of Jews in German-occupied territories. Tarr notes of this passage, "That Forbes is referring to events current to World War II is evident" (182). The motives of the American Revolution would not have been articulated in the same terms during the eighteenth century, so Revere's comments in the novel reflect traces of presentism.

While critics of the novel debate the complexity of Forbes's representation of the war and whether it reflects pacifist sensibilities (Collier 138; Tarr 178), it does appear to depict the American Revolution in morally unambiguous terms, as the Otis speech indicates. James Lincoln Collier and Christopher Collier's *My Brother Sam Is Dead*, another children's novel about the American Revolution, provides a useful contrast to *Johnny Tremain* and makes clear the effect of historical context on the representation of history. First published in 1974, just as the Vietnam War was coming to a close, *My Brother Sam Is Dead* offers a far more conflicted depiction of war than *Johnny Tremain* does. The novel focuses on fourteen-year-old Tim Meeker, whose parents run a tavern in Connecticut. Tim's older brother, Sam, joins the militia to fight on the side of the colonies, while his father remains loyal to the British Crown. This forces Tim to confront different perspectives on the war. The family business suffers because the war upends the colonial economy, and the wartime abuses Tim witnesses from both sides cause him to question the validity of war itself. Ultimately, in the confusion of war, his father is arrested and dies in a British prison ship, despite having supported the British, while Sam is tried and executed by his own army after he is mistakenly convicted of stealing meat from his family. Reflecting the political divisiveness and moral ambiguity of the Vietnam era, the novel calls into question the motives for war, the righteousness of the participants, and the very idea of war as a justified solution.

The tone of *My Brother Sam* is radically different from that of *Johnny Tremain*. It is far less hopeful, and the idealism expressed by Sam is exposed as self-serving. Tim accuses him of joining the war because of his desire to be a part of something exciting and important rather than out of a commitment to the ideals and goals of the Revolution. In *Johnny Tremain*, the death of Johnny's friend Rab, who had been like an older brother to him, is treated sentimentally, as heroic. In contrast, Sam's death is depicted as utterly meaningless and absurd, reflecting Forbes's and the Colliers's radically different perspectives on the sacrifices of war. The ironic deaths of Tim's father and brother at the hands of those whose side they support invoke the feeling some had that the American government was responsible for sending its own youth to their deaths in Vietnam. Tim's mother never accepts the war or forgives the Continental Army for her older son's death, demonstrating that the Revolution was not universally supported in the colonies and that it embittered as much as it liberated. The novel concludes with Tim's looking back on the war, as does the reader: "But somehow, even fifty years later, I keep thinking that there might have been another way, beside war, to achieve the same end" (Collier and Collier 211). The different perspectives on war in *Johnny Tremain* and *My Brother Sam Is Dead* attest to how critical an understanding of historical context is to reading and comprehending literary works.

EXPLORATIONS

Review

1. If a book is set in the past, is that enough to qualify it as a work of historical fiction? If not, what makes historical fiction distinct from books merely set in the past?

2. In earlier chapters, we talked about the opposition between instruction and delight in children's literature. When it comes to the historical novels discussed in this chapter, what strategies are used to instruct and delight simultaneously? Do historical novels stress instruction over delight, or vice versa?

3. Why are certain periods—such as the Great Depression or the Holocaust—so frequently represented in children's historical fiction? Why might authors and publishers expect children to be interested in these times?

4. What do afterwords, epilogues, or authors' notes in historical fiction reveal about their authors' choices? What do they tell us about their theories of history and of historical fiction?

5. What are some ways that historical fiction works to create nostalgia? What are some ways in which that nostalgia intersects with nationalism?

Reflect

1. Discuss what a historical novel can accomplish that a conventional history about the same subject could not. What are the distinctly literary elements of the work? What kinds of details are especially powerful, evocative, or enlightening? In what ways are historical fiction and conventional history similar?

2. Reflect on a picturebook such as Billie Holiday and Arthur Herzog's *God Bless the Child* (2003), with illustrations by Jerry Pinkney, which represents the Great Migration—the movement of millions of African Americans from the South to northern cities such as Chicago and New York during and in the decades following the First World War—and identify the possibilities of the historical picturebook. How are the text and illustrations used to represent history? How do the strategies or effects of the book differ from those of a historical novel?

3. Consider the prizing of historical fiction for children. Review the list of winners of the Newbery and Coretta Scott King Awards. Which winners appear to be works of historical fiction? Given popular uses or expectations of children's literature, why might historical fiction be honored so frequently with prizes?

4. Reflect on the role of trauma in historical fiction. How does historical fiction represent trauma and its uses with regards to child characters or readers? Why might children be imagined as especially important readers of historical trauma narratives?

5. Discuss different ways in which authors might address or manage the challenge of representing the past, such as presentism and the tension between artistic freedom and historical accuracy. How might authors retain artistic freedom to (re)imagine the past without misleading readers who might assume historical fiction always matches historical records?

Investigate

1. Select a historical novel and rewrite a scene, placing the text in an entirely different historical era. What has to change for this to work? What effects does this change have on the characters, the nature of the event, or the tone? What do the results of this experiment suggest about the importance of the historical setting in the original work?

2. Examine the American Girl brand and design a historical toy for boys. Write a fictional narrative and marketing campaign to advertise your historical boys' toy.

3. Select one of the historical American Girl dolls and one of its corresponding series of books; analyze how the doll and books represent history. How does the American Girl series contain elements of presentism?

4. Visit Scholastic's website and look for the list of books in the Dear America, My Name Is America, and My America series.[1] Which historical events or eras are represented? Are any of these choices surprising? Which books defy easy categorization? Which subjects complicate traditional conceptions of history as composed of national, political, and military events? Visit Scholastic's site for its British My Story series[2] and compare the British series with the American one. Does the British My Story series reflect a different approach to history?

SUGGESTED READINGS

Anderson, M.T. *The Astonishing Life of Octavian Nothing, Traitor to the Nation, Volume I: The Pox Party* (2006). A historical novel for young adults set near the outbreak of the American Revolution, *The Astonishing Life of Octavian Nothing* depicts the life of a slave boy who is given a classical education by a philosophical society seeking to test the intellectual capacities of Africans. When the fortunes of the society change, Octavian begins to question his treatment as a slave and to wonder how the fight for independence might affect him. This novel offers a unique perspective on the American Revolution, and its depiction of Octavian's training also comments on the state of education in the early twenty-first century.

Bruchac, Joseph. *The Journal of Jesse Smoke: A Cherokee Boy, The Trail of Tears, 1838* (2001). A volume in the My Name Is America series of historical novels for boys, Bruchac's *The Journal of Jesse Smoke* depicts the life of a Cherokee boy during the forced relocation of the Cherokee Nation from the American South to the Oklahoma Territory during the winter of 1838. Thousands of Cherokee died during the march. Sixteen-year-old Jesse relates these events in his journal. The book provides an opportunity to evaluate historical series fiction and the apparatus of the My Name Is America and Dear America series.

Cushman, Karen. *Catherine, Called Birdy* (1994). A Newbery Honor book, *Catherine, Called Birdy* is set at the end of the thirteenth century in England. In the form of a diary, the novel details the life of the fourteen-year-old daughter of a knight and noblewoman, who fends off marriage suitors while fulfilling her domestic duties, including practicing household medicine, sewing, and spinning. *Catherine, Called Birdy* has received mixed reviews for the accuracy and authenticity of its depiction of medieval England.

1   www.scholastic.com/dearamerica
2   http://shop.scholastic.co.uk/series/52

Hesse, Karen. *Out of the Dust* (1997). A novel written in verse, Hesse's *Out of the Dust* won the Newbery Medal in 1998. Set in 1930s Oklahoma, it depicts the difficult life of a farming family during the Dust Bowl. When an unspeakable tragedy strikes thirteen-year-old Billie Jo, she must struggle with how to make her life livable amid the bleakness of the landscape and the apparent hopelessness of her situation. The use of poetry complicates the usual didacticism of historical fiction and makes a useful case study for the intersection of genre, function, and form.

Lowry, Lois. *Number the Stars* (1989). Lowry's Holocaust novel *Number the Stars* focuses on the efforts of non-Jewish Danes to rescue Jews during the German occupation of Denmark. The novel centers on the ten-year-old Annemarie, who plays a key role in helping her friend Ellen Rosen and her family escape by boat to Sweden. The only children's Holocaust novel to win the Newbery Medal, *Number the Stars* attempts to balance the importance of teaching children about the Holocaust with a concern about revealing too much troubling information.

Matas, Carol. *Daniel's Story* (1993). Written in conjunction with the children's exhibit at the United States Holocaust Memorial Museum in Washington, DC, Matas's *Daniel's Story* is an explicitly didactic novel that provides a far more sweeping introduction to the Holocaust than *Number the Stars*. It includes scenes of German Jewish life in the late 1930s, the experience of the Jewish ghettos, and life at the Auschwitz concentration camp. Carefully crafted with significant input from historians, the novel makes a useful case for how historical fiction for children balances the demands of history with those of literature.

Morpurgo, Michael. *Private Peaceful* (2003). Morpurgo's *Private Peaceful* is a novel about two young brothers from England, Tommy and Charlie, who enlist to fight in World War I. Flashbacks of their lives at home are interspersed with scenes of war, which allows for an exploration of both the home front and the trenches. Charlie's refusal to obey an order under extraordinary circumstances leads to a dramatic conclusion that calls into question the very notions of war, justice, and loyalty.

Myers, Walter Dean. *The Glory Field* (1994). Like Alex Haley's *Roots* (1976), Myers's young adult novel *The Glory Field* depicts several generations of one African American family, from the capture of Muhammad Bilal in Africa to the contemporary teenage lives of two cousins living in New York City. The novel provides brief snippets of the lives of different members of this family at key moments in American history, including the Civil War, the turn-of-the-century Jim Crow South, 1930s Chicago, the 1960s Civil Rights Movement, and the 1990s. Because the protagonist of each section is an adolescent member of the family, the novel depicts not only American history but also the changing experience of adolescence itself over the course of the past two centuries.

Speare, Elizabeth George. *The Witch of Blackbird Pond* **(1958).** Set in seventeenth-century colonial America, Newbery-winning *The Witch of Blackbird Pond* focuses on sixteen-year-old Kit Tyler, who leads a life of comfort and leisure in Barbados until her grandfather's death leaves her without support. She travels to the colony of Connecticut to live with her aunt, uncle, and cousins, where she must become accustomed to the dreary toil of colonial life. Because of her odd ways, Kit stands out in the Puritan village and is eventually accused of being a witch and tried for witchcraft.

Williams-Garcia, Rita. *One Crazy Summer* **(2010).** Winner of the Scott O'Dell Award for historical fiction, a Newbery Honor book, and a National Book Award Finalist, *One Crazy Summer* follows eleven-year-old Delphine and her two younger sisters as they travel from New York City to Oakland, California, to visit their estranged mother in 1968. Their mother is affiliated with the Black Panther Party, which had been founded in Oakland just two years prior, and Delphine and her sisters come to learn more about the Panthers and their approach to Civil Rights.

APPROACHES TO TEACHING *JOHNNY TREMAIN* [SECONDARY SCHOOL]

Preparation for the Lesson

Johnny Tremain could be linked with a social studies or history unit on the Revolutionary War or stand alone. While students are reading the novel, the class could cover the timeline of the war itself, biographies of important people in the Revolution, and elements of material culture (including silver manufacture and other trades depicted in the novel). The three activities emphasize understanding how historical fiction combines the true and the fictive and how the novel represents the past.

Learning Goals

- To analyze a historical novel in terms of its combination of fictional elements and historical fact

- To practice close reading of literary passages

- To practice summarizing information found in good reference tools like encyclopedias.

Activity One: Johnny Tremain's Engagement with History

Part A: Historical Figures

Provide students with the following list of historical figures in the novel:

1. Samuel Adams
2. John Hancock
3. Paul Revere
4. James Otis Jr.
5. Governor Thomas Hutchinson
6. George III

Ask students to provide the following information for each historical figure:

1. Name of historical figure
2. Birth and death dates
3. A list of scenes where he appears in the novel, including page numbers (it is fine if the appearance is very short) and a summary of each scene
4. A biography of the real historical figure summarized from at least two reference sources (this should be about one page in length)
5. Questions:
   a. Did you learn anything from your biographical research that you didn't learn from the novel?
   b. What is the novel's attitude toward the historical figure? Does it match the attitude of the reference sources you used?

Part B: Women in Colonial America

Have students conduct research on the lives of women of different classes in colonial America. One good source for them to use is Carol Berkin's *First Generations: Women in Colonial America* (1996). Ask students to recall how Forbes's depiction of women confirms, contradicts, or overlooks the experiences of women as described in nonfiction histories. Which historical women could Forbes have included in *Johnny Tremain*?

Part C: Child Workers and Child Slaves in Colonial America

Ask students to describe the historical lives of either child indentured servants and domestic workers or child slaves in colonial America. One good source for them to use is Steven Mintz's *Huck's Raft: A History of American Childhood* (2006), especially chapters 2, 3, 5, and 7. Ask students to explain how Forbes's depiction of child workers and slaves confirms, contradicts, or overlooks the experiences of such children as described in nonfiction histories.

Activity Two: Invented Characters

After students have completed the worksheets devoted to historical characters, lead the class in discussing the three main invented characters: Johnny Tremain, Rab Silsbee, and Priscilla Lapham.

The discussion should focus on the ways in which *Johnny Tremain* combines historical figures with purely invented characters. Some points for discussion:

1. Using the blackboard or a projector, note terms that could be used to describe each character. How would you describe the relationships between the characters?

2. How old are Johnny, Rab, and Priscilla? What kind of impact does their relatively young age have on the novel?

3. Using the blackboard or a projector, write out the terms "sympathy" and "empathy" and define them for the class. Make a list of the ways in which Johnny, Rab, and Priscilla suffer in the novel and what causes their suffering. How do we sympathize or empathize with the characters? What do we learn about the colonial period and the Revolutionary War from these struggles?

4. Why did Esther Forbes invent new characters to tell her story of the American Revolution? How would the novel have differed if only historical figures had been used?

Activity Three: Scene Study

Each student should choose two scenes from the novel: one scene in which the historical setting and events do not seem particularly significant and one scene in which the historical setting is emphasized. If students experience difficulty choosing, a list of possible scenes in each category can be made available.

The students should compose answers to the following questions in complete sentences and paragraphs.

1. Summarize the scenes you chose from the novel (each summary should be one or two paragraphs each). Why did you choose these two scenes?

2. One of the scenes you chose emphasizes the historical events of the Revolutionary War; one of the scenes does not feature historical events. Compare and contrast these two scenes. In the scene you chose depicting history, how does the novel represent the historical setting? In the scene that does not feature historical events, how is history still important?

3. Consider the hopeful ending of the novel. Why does it end on such a positive note? What does the ending tell us about the novel's view of war?

4. How might the historical context in which Esther Forbes wrote—the beginning of World War II—help explain the events depicted in these two scenes?

NONFICTION—HISTORY, SCIENCE, LIFE WRITING

In *Cathedral: The Story of Its Construction* (1973), David Macaulay uses words and images to describe the construction of a French Gothic cathedral. Macaulay, a former architect, created pen-and-ink drawings that resemble architectural sketches. The book covers all elements of the construction process, from foundations to flying buttresses to the placement of the windows. Yet despite the meticulous factual detail of the book, *Cathedral* also raises questions about the role of fictional narrative elements in nonfiction for children. First of all, Macaulay sets his book in the fictional village of Chutreaux. Second, he acknowledges that the process of constructing a French Gothic cathedral was more prolonged and uncertain than the story would suggest: "Owing to either financial or structural problems or both, the completion of many such undertakings was delayed for as long as two hundred years" (Macaulay n.p.). *Cathedral* presents an eighty-six-year process of uninterrupted construction, which Macaulay notes is a "somewhat ideal situation" (n.p.). Finally, Macaulay is as interested in "motivating forces" as in technical details (Stott 15), imagining that the people of Chutreaux "did not wish to be outdone, on earth or especially in heaven" (n.p.). Despite these additional narrative elements—and the very fact that neither Chutreaux nor its cathedral really exists—the book offers a scrupulously accurate portrayal of the construction of a French Gothic cathedral in the thirteenth century.

When we think about nonfiction for young people, we often conceive of it as a purely didactic—or teaching—genre. History, science, and life writing can seem purely fact

---

Opposite: David Macaulay's *Cathedral* (1973) tells the detailed story of the construction of a thirteenth-century Gothic cathedral in France, including the construction of the vaulted ceiling.

based, and it is undeniably true that such books aim to communicate factual information. Yet nonfiction for young people often includes stories designed to enliven the reading experience and spark an imaginative response. Reading such texts critically involves
discerning whether the fictive elements diminish the capacity of the nonfictional text
to communicate ideas and information, but it also involves an understanding of how a
fictional element might add to a nonfictional text. Nonfiction works without fictive elements can also be read critically, with attention to the way they structure information,
whether through a comparison/contrast structure, the exposition of a process or cycle, a
question-and-answer format, or some other arrangement.

Nonfiction trade books frequently overlap with the kind of reading that children complete in school classrooms, where they often use textbooks. However, nonfiction trade
books are a thriving literary genre in their own right. The American Library Association
(ALA) acknowledged the literary and cultural value of nonfiction in 2001, when it began
awarding the Ronald F. Sibert Informational Book Medal for the best informational book
published in English in the United States. Likewise, the National Council of Teachers
of English (NCTE) offers the Orbis Pictus Award for Outstanding Nonfiction for Children, named after Johann Amos Comenius's *Orbis Sensualium Pictus* (*The Visible World
in Pictures*, 1658), considered the first work of nonfiction for children as well as the first
picturebook. Nonfiction and informational books produced for children can be:

- advice and conduct books, including books about health and the human body

- biography, autobiography, memoirs, and published diaries

- life writing in picturebook and graphic form

- books about historical events or phenomena

- books about nature

- books about the physical and geological sciences.

As varied as these types of nonfiction are, they raise common questions:

- Fictional stories in nonfiction: What is the boundary between fiction and fact in nonfiction books? Can the presentation of facts be enhanced by the presence of a fictive
  element?

- Simplification and complexity: When presenting scientific processes, historical events, or life stories to younger readers, how much simplification is acceptable without losing accuracy?

- Accuracy and new research: Is there any such thing as a classic work of nonfiction, or do works of nonfiction inevitably become dated in the light of new research and discovery?

NONFICTION AND INFORMATIONAL BOOKS: SOME DISTINCTIONS

The terms "nonfiction" and "informational" tend to be used as synonyms. However, we might benefit from making some distinctions between them. **Nonfiction** refers to any text understood to be factual. **Informational books** are a subset of nonfiction, defined by Nell K. Duke and V. Susan Bennett-Armistead as books that convey "information about the natural or social world," addressing entire classes of things in a timeless way that has a generalizing quality (16). A book such as Macaulay's *Cathedral* would not fit this precise definition of an "informational book," since it does not discuss a phenomenon in a timeless or generalized way: it describes the building of a single cathedral. Duke and Bennett-Armistead also exclude books that "tell about an individual life, an event or series of events, or how to do something" from their definition of informational texts (17).

Informational books usually include graphical devices such as diagrams, charts, and tables, all of which help readers quickly grasp the material presented. For example, Gail Gibbons's *From Seed to Plant* (1991) uses text and diagrams with labels to explain how the production and dissemination of seeds results in plants, including natural cycles such as germination that are necessary for plants to grow. Despite these distinctions, for the purposes of this chapter, we will treat "nonfiction" and "informational" as interchangeable terms, except when it is important to make distinctions between them. This is consistent with the broader definition used by the ALA for the Sibert Award, when it notes, "Information books are defined as those written and illustrated to present, organize, and interpret documentable, factual material for children" ("Welcome").

This chapter will discuss a variety of nonfiction and informational books for children, beginning with conduct literature: one of the first genres to be geared toward children and one that continues—albeit in a modified form—into the present. We will continue with life writing, considering the main features of autobiography, biography, memoirs, and diaries aimed at a child audience. Shifting from personal histories to collective ones, we will review what historical nonfiction teaches children about the past and suggest strategies for reading those representations critically. Finally, we will look at science writing for children, through which readers learn facts about the physical world and are introduced to scientific practice and experimentation itself.

CONDUCT LITERATURE

Conduct books advise their readers on social norms and offer a guide for behavior. Historically, they were written for adults as well as for children. One of the most famous conduct books for adult audiences was Baldassare Castiglione's *The Book of the Courtier* (1528), which enumerated the ideal attributes of a courtier (or man in attendance at the court of a king), including knowledge of the classics, fluency in the fine arts, and elegant manners. Several conduct books through the centuries were aimed specifically at women, encouraging chastity, modesty, and good household management. Other conduct books were written for a child audience. As Lynne Vallone remarks: "Advice-givers of today and ages past have felt with some conviction that the conduct of young men and young women was a subject worthy of notice, and thus the conduct manual that codified behavior— domestic and social—was a genre published consistently from the Middle Ages to the nineteenth century" (27–28).

We noted in Chapter 2 that conduct books constituted much of the writing for children until the eighteenth century. Sometimes parents offered direct advice to their children in the form of published letters, as we see from conduct books such as John Gregory's *A Father's Legacy to His Daughters* (1774) and Lady Sarah Pennington's *An Unfortunate Mother's Advice to Her Absent Daughters* (1781). In this variety of conduct literature, a parent advises a child or children when he or she cannot nurture them in person, whether due to impending death or absence.

The long tradition of conduct literature for children—and its continuance in a modified form today in health and sexual education books—may indicate a desire on the part of adults to control and shape the behavior of young people. At the same time, conduct literature can empower children and adolescents, offering them guidance in how to achieve maturity and navigate the challenges of life.

Nineteenth-Century Conduct Books

The Victorian and Edwardian periods were years of vigorous production of conduct books in both England and the United States. Benet Davetian states that "good conduct (obedience, pleasantness, industriousness, and lack of egotism) was ... enlisted in favour of a functional familial and communal harmony" (234). To that end, a conduct book such as *Mentor; or, Dialogues between a Parent and Children; on Some of the Duties, Amusements,*

Pursuits, and Relations of Life (1828), published anonymously, "covered a range of practical topics such as play, vanity, work, truth, lying, effective use of time, cursing, and deference" (Davetian 234).

Elaine Ostry has observed that conduct books of that period "may simply offer advice, or include information on natural history and other subjects" (28). One example of this kind of mixed-genre conduct book is William Clarke's *The Boy's Own Book: A Complete Encyclopedia of All the Diversions, Athletic, Scientific, and Recreative, of Boyhood and Youth* (1828), which includes "minor sports," "athletic sports," "aquatic recreations," "scientific recreations," "games of skill," and so on. The scientific recreations include a myriad of ingenious skills, such as producing luminous writing in the dark ("fix a small piece of solid phosphorus in a quill," Clarke 192) or boiling water over the surface of ice (195).

Instructions in "Calisthenics" from Lydia Maria Child's conduct guide, *The Girl's Own Book* (1833).

The Girl's Own Book (1833) by Lydia Maria Child is likewise a compendium of games, "active exercises," crafts, and needlework (including the making of baskets and ornaments) alongside instructive dialogues. Child situates her book within a specifically American discourse of democratic uplift and self-improvement, as the following passage suggests:

> In this land of precarious fortunes, every girl should know how to be *useful*; amid the universal dissemination of knowledge, *every mind should seek to improve itself to the utmost*; and in this land of equality, as much time should be devoted to *elegant accomplishments, refined taste*, and *gracefulness of manner*, as can possibly be spared from holier and more important duties. (iii–iv)

When it comes to active exercise, Child writes, "Little girls should not be afraid of being well tired: that will do them good; but *excessive* fatigue should be avoided, especially where it is quite unnecessary" (107). She also gives a great deal of advice about appearing graceful:

> A tendency to stoop should be early corrected. It is very destructive to health. This habit, together with the very ungraceful one of running the chin out, may be cured

by the practice of walking the room frequently with a heavy folio volume balanced on the head, without the aid of the hands. (Child 282)

Exercise involves disciplined—even painful—practice, in the service of encouraging health and promoting a full development of mind and body.

In conduct books written for both boys and girls, behavior, decorum, and comportment are important—but they encompass all aspects of a child's life by including material about play and recreation as well.

Reinventing the Boy's Own Book *and* Girl's Own Book *Tradition*

In 2006, Conn and Hal Iggulden's *The Dangerous Book for Boys* attracted media attention when it was promoted as bringing needed adventure to the overprotected childhood of contemporary boys. However, *The Dangerous Book* itself was mainly a compendium of activities and crafts (such as skin tanning, tying knots, and folding paper napkins) and informational segments about topics such as famous battles and secret codes. A counterpart for girls appeared in 2007: Andrea J. Buchanan and Miriam Peskowitz's *The Daring Book for Girls*. In their introduction, Buchanan and Peskowitz note that they present "stories and projects galore, drawn from the vastness of history, the wealth of girl knowledge, the breadth of sport, and the great outdoors" (viii), with sections on "Great Queens of History," "Reading Tide Charts," and "How to Negotiate a Salary." Both *The Dangerous Book for Boys* and *The Daring Book for Girls* are self-conscious throwbacks to the *Boy's Own Book* and *Girl's Own Book* tradition, with covers that mimic those of nineteenth-century children's books and contents that evoke a pre-internet world where collections of facts could be browsed for amusement. While the success of these books may be due to the publicity they attracted for their ostensibly "dangerous" and "daring" content, they show how literary traditions can be updated successfully for the contemporary age.

Contemporary Health and Sexual Education Books

The tradition of didactic conduct literature diminished as the twentieth century went on, but it was reinvented in self-help literature as well as in health and sexual education books produced for child and adolescent readers. One example is Kelli Dunham and illustrator Steven Bjorkman's *The Boy's Body Book: Everything You Need to Know for Growing Up YOU* (2007), which covers male puberty, bodily changes, and peer pressure. An equivalent for girls is Mavis Jukes and Lilian Wai-Yin Cheung's *Be Healthy! It's a Girl Thing: Food, Fitness, and Feeling Great!* (2003), illustrated by Debra Ziss, which puts a great deal of emphasis on nutritious food and a healthy body image.

Contemporary health and sexual education books are less didactic than nineteenth-century conduct books, but they nevertheless socialize children and adolescents into cultural norms and expectations, establishing what is "normal" in terms of health and sexuality, and seeking to integrate children into their peer groups. At the same time, contemporary conduct books, especially sexual education books, address the concerns and worries that children themselves express—sometimes bypassing parental guidance and sometimes acting as a supplement to such guidance.

Robie H. Harris and illustrator Michael Emberley's *It's Perfectly Normal: Changing Bodies, Growing Up, Sex, and Sexual Health* (rev. ed., 2009) addresses the child reader as "you" and seeks to anticipate his or her questions, as we see in Part I, "What Is Sex?":

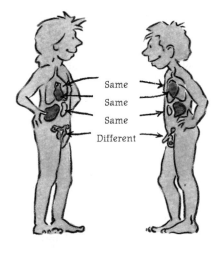

Robie H. Harris's *It's Perfectly Normal* (2009), illustrated by Michael Emberley, provides up-to-date information on sexual health for tweens and teens.

> What is sex? What is it … exactly? What is it all about?
>
> These are questions lots of kids wonder about. You needn't feel embarrassed or stupid if you don't know the answers, because sex is not a simple matter.
>
> Sex is many things, and people have many different feelings and opinions about it. That's why there is more than one answer to the question, What is sex? (Harris 10)

To explore the many possible answers to the question, the book explains various meanings of the word "sex," including the "sex of a baby" (male or female), sexual reproduction, sexual desire, and sexual intercourse. Emberley's drawings are anatomically detailed and present a range of human bodies, often in the nude. The function of sexual organs in both development and reproduction is described in both text and image. Educators and medical professionals have lauded *It's Perfectly Normal* for its accuracy and for making the facts about sexual maturation and sexuality comprehensible to very young readers. However, it has also sparked censorship attempts, due in large part to the detailed drawings of nude human bodies and sexual organs, which some call pornographic. The censorship controversy around *It's Perfectly Normal* shows that some adults continue to want control over what their children learn about human life and human sexuality, in keeping with the older traditions of the conduct book. Yet it also shows how most conduct literature has changed by affirming that children have a right to have any of their *own* questions answered fully and without the use of euphemisms.

LIFE WRITING: BIOGRAPHY, AUTOBIOGRAPHY, MEMOIR, DIARIES

Life Writing for Children

Biographies for children, like conduct books, are another nonfiction genre with a long history. As we noted in Chapter 2, James Janeway's *A Token for Children* (1671) gave child readers "real-life" stories of repentant children to inspire them to embrace the Puritan faith (and in some ways it functioned as a kind of conduct book in its own right). Although biography became more secularized by the nineteenth century, the conventions of the early religious biographies continued to hold sway, as Donna Norton points out:

> Nineteenth century biographies in full-length versions and in textbooks were affected by the didactic themes of the earlier Puritan era, by the Victorian emphasis on duty to God and parents, by the values associated with the American frontier, and by the belief that children should be educated in a highly structured environment in which the teacher molds the student, the student follows the rules, and the adult authority provides punishment for any disobedience. In addition, nineteenth century biographers believed that children's biographies should be teaching tools for religious, political, or social education. Consequently, emulation of biographical heroes was considered desirable. (79)

Biographies that upheld the religious, social, and political status quo were produced well into the twentieth century, but there were also biographies that sought to catalyze progressive social change. Julia Mickenberg describes the biographies of African American civil rights leaders written in the 1940s and 1950s by leftist authors:

> These biographies showed children a model of civic duty that hinged upon the need for brave, non-conforming individuals to struggle against injustice and to rally members of the community to join in that struggle. Within these historical tales was an implicit or explicit commentary on the power of history and stories,

and on education in general. This embedded commentary encouraged children to connect what they were reading to the world in which they currently lived; that is, to a social and political landscape dominated by Cold War repression and conformity on the one hand, and an increasingly militant struggle for African American civil rights on the other. (71)

Biographies such as Shirley Graham's *There Was Once a Slave: The Heroic Story of Frederick Douglass* (1947) and Dorothy Sterling's *Freedom Train: The Story of Harriet Tubman* (1954) taught child readers to resist authority when it was morally wrong. At the same time, these books present an idealistic vision of the United States as encouraging and nurturing ideals of protest for the purpose of enacting political change.

All biographies, whether written for adults or children, need to grapple with questions about what parts of a person's life should be revealed or emphasized. Such questions are often intensified when it comes to child readers, who are imagined as needing protection from the seamy or violent side of life. But while the twentieth century saw an ongoing "tradition of biography as inspirational literature" (Segal 12), biographies for children were also expected to be more frank about the lives of their subjects than they had been in the past. In a 1980 article, Elizabeth Segal criticized Dorothy Aldis's *Nothing Is Impossible: The Story of Beatrix Potter* (1969) for glossing over some of the frustrations of Potter's life, including the way the scientific career she desired in mycology (the study of mushrooms and other fungi) was thwarted by a lack of support from her parents and the scientific community. Segal argues:

> Many students and writers of biography and historical fiction for children in recent years have recognized that it is more encouraging to a child to know that others shared the doubts and fears he or she feels and yet were able to work out a productive and fulfilled life than to be told that as children the great remained cheerful and confident in the face of all difficulties. Precisely because Beatrix Potter's childhood was so unhappy, Aldis' hewing to the old conventions here is especially damaging. (8)

Segal argues that major parts of a subject's life should not be omitted to achieve a purely uplifting story.

Russell Freedman's *Lincoln: A Photobiography* (1987) has been praised for its nuanced portrayal of the political and personal dimensions of President Abraham Lincoln's life and career, including the shifting reasons for the Civil War ("At first the issue had seemed the salvation of the Union, but in the end, slavery had become the issue" [112–13]). The deaths of two sons are dealt with frankly, as are his wife Mary's "depression and imaginary fears" (Freedman 121) and Lincoln's own concerns for his safety. Freedman treats with respect Lincoln's rise to prominence from humble beginnings, but at the same time he makes plain the costs of Lincoln's political career and his abiding melancholy. One set of photographs taken from 1861 to 1864 shows how the "pressures and anxieties of the war became etched in his face" (116). A lengthy recitation of the events of Lincoln's assassination gives way to a stirring account of the mundane contents of his pocket on the day of his death. Overall, the biography portrays Lincoln as an iconic national figure but does not shy away from the darker sides of his character and the troubled world that surrounded him.

Autobiographies, Memoirs, and Diaries

Autobiographies are stories about the life of a person written by that same person. Rocío G. Davis observes that autobiography for children tends to center on childhood itself, which "allows for a greater sense of identification and, subsequently, a more effective story" (186). Jerry Spinelli's *Knots in My Yo-Yo String: The Autobiography of a Kid* (1998) is a good example of an autobiography written for a child audience, focusing as it does on his hardscrabble youth in Pennsylvania. In this passage, Spinelli talks about his many childhood enthusiasms:

> Grownups have gone ahead and answered the question: "*What* shall I be?" They have tossed out all the whats that don't fit and have become just one. Teacher. Truckdriver. Businessperson. But a kid is still becoming. And I, as a kid alone, was free to be just about anything.
>
> So many careers came and went through me: salamander finder, crawfish annoyer, flat-stone creek skipper, cedar chest smeller, railroad car counter, tin can stomper, milkweed blower, mulberry picker, snowball smoother, paper bag popper, steel rail walker, box turtle toucher, dark-sky watcher, best-part saver. They didn't last long, these careers of mine, but flashed into and out of existence like mayflies. But while they employed me, I gave them an honest minute's work and was paid in the satisfactions of curiosity met and a job well done. (85–86)

Though Spinelli is an adult writing about childhood, he effectively captures the amusements and pastimes of a child.

Memoirs are similar to autobiographies, although they cover "a segment of a life, not its entirety" (Smith and Watson 274). One intriguing memoir aimed at the young adult audience is Jack Gantos's *Hole in My Life* (2002), in which he writes about his time in prison for a drug-smuggling operation from Puerto Rico to the mainland. Although he spent the majority of his incarceration as a medical technician, Gantos pulls no punches

From Anne Frank's diary.

in describing the violence and hopelessness of prison life. In one way, the book fulfills a didactic purpose, underscoring the importance of staying on the right side of the law—but it also displays a powerful lack of sentimentality about the author's life both before and during prison. Yet the memoir is also a narrative of vocation, since Gantos becomes the successful writer he always longed to be once he is released.

Diaries also immerse readers in the voice of an individual speaker, although they are for the most part written with the intention to be private and are only published later. Anne Frank's diary, written when she was thirteen to fifteen years old, has been read by millions of children as well as adults. First published in Dutch as *Het Achterhuis* in 1947, it was translated into English as *Anne Frank: The Diary of a Young Girl* in 1952. Anne Frank was a Jewish girl living in Amsterdam during the Nazi occupation of the Netherlands. After hiding for two years in the annex of her father's office building with her family and four other people, the family was ultimately apprehended by the Nazis, and Anne died of typhus in the Bergen-Belsen concentration camp right before the end of the war in 1945. A skillful writer with great literary ambition, Anne wrote about living in a confined space, the people confined with her, her aspirations for her life after the war, and her shifting romantic feelings for Peter Van Daan (the real-life Peter van Pels, a fellow teenager who lived in the annex with her). While Anne is a powerful symbol of the unspeakable losses of the Holocaust, her voice is also that of a teenaged girl who yearns for freedom and its pleasures.

Blogs are similar to diaries in that they chronicle daily life. Unlike diaries, however, they are published online and read by the public. *IraqiGirl: Diary of a Teenage Girl in Iraq* (2009), developed by John Ross and edited by Elizabeth Wrigley-Field, is a printed collection of four years of blog posts by Hadiya (not her real name) writing from the city of Mosul during the American occupation of Iraq, beginning in 2004. Hadiya writes a great deal about her school and family but also about the loss of life caused by the war and its disruption of every aspect of her life. The end of the book contains a series of spirited discussions on politics and identity between Hadiya and some American teenagers. Hadiya wrote her blog in English partly in order to reach readers outside of Iraq and to express her anger about the American presence in her country and the shadow of violence the war cast over her childhood. Hadiya's blog is an example of an online blog that became a book. The dominance of electronic social media like blogs, Facebook, Instagram, Twitter and other platforms might mean that the printed tradition of diaries and journals will come to an end, in favor of online forms.

Picturebook and Graphic Autobiographies, Biographies, and Memoirs

Biographies and autobiographies are also written in the form of picturebooks largely aimed at younger readers. All life writers must be selective about what to reveal about their subject's life, but such choices are more pronounced in a picturebook biography because there is less space for detail. While a picturebook biography contains limited text, the visual elements communicate the physical appearance of the subject—through illustrations or photographs—and the physical world where the subject lives. Jennifer Berne's *Manfish: A Story of Jacques Cousteau* (2008), illustrated by Éric Puybaret, describes Cousteau's childhood love of water, passion for movies, and enthusiasm for science, which led him to his ultimate vocation as an oceanographic researcher, scientist, and filmmaker. Many of the book's pages are a light greenish-blue, depicting the sea creatures and ocean scenes that always fascinated Cousteau; the book also includes an illustration of *Calypso*, the warship that Cousteau converted into an explorer's vessel. The ending of the book appeals directly to child readers: "Jacques dreamed that someday it would be you, exploring worlds never seen, never imagined. Whole new worlds, silent and shimmering. Worlds that are now yours. To discover. To care for. And to love" (Berne n.p.). Carol Boston Weatherford's *Voice of Freedom: Fannie Lou Hamer, Spirit of the Civil Rights Movement* (2015) recounts the life of Civil Rights activist Fannie Lou Hamer in first-person verse, illustrated by Ekua Holmes. Growing up, Hamer experienced poverty and grueling labor as a sharecropper in Mississippi in the 1920s and 1930s. A white doctor gave her a hysterectomy without her consent, a racist policy designed to reduce the poor African American population in the state. Hamer did not realize that African Americans could vote—and that voting was her right as a citizen—until a grassroots activist came to her town when she was in her 40s. She became active in voter registration, a national spokesperson for the Student Nonviolent Coordinating Committee, and a major force in passing the 1965 Voting Rights Act. She was known both for her powerful speeches and her singing, which boosted morale. An inspiring figure to many, she suffered violent opposition throughout her activist career. In 1963 she was jailed and brutally beaten after demanding to be served in a whites-only café. Weatherford's book includes a timeline of Hamer's life and major Civil Rights landmarks. Some of the artwork is derived from or inspired by photographs from her life. Illustrator Holmes used boldly colored mixed-media collage to evoke Hamer's energy, bravery, and determination.

Graphic autobiographies, memoirs, and biographies (sometimes misleadingly termed graphic "novels") are another emerging form in which both text and image communicate a life story. Siena Cherson Siegel's *To Dance: A Ballerina's Graphic Novel* (2006), with artwork by Mark Siegel, is a memoir about a young dancer's ballet training at the School of American Ballet and her performances in ballets at Lincoln Center in New York. Although Siena gives up professional ballet at eighteen after an injury, she continues to dance, noting simply: "Dancing fills a space in me" (Siegel n.p.). The pictures evoke the joyful movement and rigorous training of dancing bodies in a way that words alone cannot capture; throughout the book, illustrator Mark Siegel uses ribbonlike lines to convey the vitality of ballet practice and performance.

Life writing engages child readers in many ways. Autobiographies, memoirs, and diaries encourage child readers to put themselves in the place of the writer and imagine other ways of living. Biographies can provide role models, while giving readers a glimpse into the choices and contingencies that make up a life. They also introduce children to the major figures of both history and our contemporary age.

HISTORY WRITING

Exploring the Past in Nonfiction

In historical nonfiction, children are presented with a factual narrative about the past. In theory, historical nonfiction differs from biography in its focus on an entire culture, nation, or group. We will see, however, that much historical nonfiction focuses on important individuals in history or is told from the point of view of an individual.

To explore the evolution of historical nonfiction for children, it is useful to compare two books about the same historical event: Maurice Boutet de Monvel's 1896 *The Story of Joan of Arc* (English translation, 1912) and Diane Stanley's 1998 *Joan of Arc*. Boutet de

Monvel tells the story of Joan of Arc as an encouragement to French national pride, which at the time of the book's composition was still smarting over defeat in the Franco–Prussian War of 1870–71. He doesn't gloss over the suffering of war, and the book's illustrations portray bitter conflict, but he also reads Joan of Arc as a figure worthy of emulation: "Her history will teach you that in order to conquer you must believe that you will conquer. Remember this in the day when your country shall have need of all your courage" (Boutet de Monvel vi). Stanley's more contemporary book emphasizes Joan's personal feelings and impressions rather than the national story.

Contemporary theories of historiography stress the process of sifting evidence and the ways in which historical sources can contradict one another. In keeping with this modern approach, Stanley's book ends by foregrounding doubts about the visions Joan of Arc saw:

> But now that we have the story, what are we to make of it? How, in reading a historical account that is based on hard facts and documentary evidence, are we supposed to make sense of miraculous visions and voices? Depending on our point of view, we can account for them in one of three ways. First, they were exactly what Joan said they were: divine revelations. Second, they were hallucinations produced by some illness of mind or body. And third, seeing the terrible state of her country and having heard the prophecy about the young girl who would save France, she began to wish, and then actually to believe, that she was the chosen one. To this day, however, no historian has been able to do more than spin the occasional theory. Sometimes, in studying history, we have to accept what we know and let the rest remain a mystery. (n.p.)

Stanley's book, unlike Boutet de Monvel's, is more honest about what we cannot know, inviting the child reader to participate in the ongoing debates about historical fact and allowing for the presence of doubt.

In Chapter 7, we saw how an author's choice of historical period is associated with cultural values of various kinds. As one example, fiction set on the frontier enables a story stressing adventure and self-reliance. Historical nonfiction also advances cultural and social narratives. Elizabeth Mann's *Empire State Building: When New York Reached for the Skies* (2003), for example, interprets the construction of the Empire State Building as a symbol of hope for New Yorkers during the darkest days of the Great Depression: "When it was completed, it continued to lift their spirits. It had not been defeated by the Depression, and neither would the city" (40). Mann assigns a particular value to American technology, extolling the flexibility and ingenuity of construction engineers. Individual expertise in the service of collective activity is also lauded, as in this description of the workforce in August of 1930: "There were 3,500 workers on the site every day doing 60 different kinds of jobs" (Mann 26). At the end of the book, the author points out that the Empire State Building remained the tallest building in the world until 1972.

While nonfiction does reflect the social and political values at the time of its publication, it can also present conflicting values within the historical event it is covering, and differing ideas about history. Steve Sheinkin's *Bomb: The Race to Build—and Steal—The World's Most Dangerous Weapon* (2012) is a gripping account of the discovery of nuclear fission; the development of the atomic bomb (the "Manhattan Project") under theoretical physicist Robert Oppenheimer; and the often-successful attempts of Soviet spies (allies in World War II) to attain scientific information about the bomb, ultimately setting the stage for the alarming nuclear proliferation of the Cold War period. Many reviewers compared Sheinkin's book to an exciting spy thriller; the use of chapter openers with file folders and pictures of the main historical figures creates the impression of looking into "secret files." The American development of the atomic bomb was a suspenseful race because Nazi scientists were believed to be close to developing their own atomic bomb. Sheinkin fully acknowledges the ingenuity of the scientists who worked on the Manhattan Project in Los Alamos, New Mexico, but the book does not shy away from the bitter and tragic implications of the scientists' work. It presents the moral dilemma involved in President Truman's choice to use the bomb on Hiroshima and Nagasaki, acknowledges the catastrophic sufferings of the people in those cities, and ends with a description of the continued threats of nuclear war in our time, linking us directly to the historical events presented in the book: "The making of the atomic bomb is one of history's most amazing examples of teamwork and genius and poise under pressure. But it's also the story of how humans created a weapon capable of wiping our species off the planet. It's a story with no end in sight.... And, like it or not, you're in it" (236). Jonathan Fetter-Vorm's *Trinity* (2012) is a graphic novel that similarly treats the development of the atomic bomb and the Manhattan project. It shows the sufferings of the people in Hiroshima and Nagasaki, with full-page spreads of people reeling from the effects of the bombs, many of them dying a terrible death.

Innovative Approaches to Historical Nonfiction

Historical nonfiction often tells the story of a past event or phenomenon using narrative, but several contemporary history series for children present the past using other formats. Scholastic's If You Lived ... series uses a question-and-answer structure to explore everyday life in the past. Ann McGovern and illustrator Anna DiVito's *If You Lived 100 Years Ago* (1999) explores life in historical New York by answering questions such as "Where did people take baths?" and "What did things cost in the 1890s?" Anna Kamma and illustrator Linda Gardner's *If You Lived with the Hopi* (1999) imagines membership in the Hopi tribe of the high desert in Arizona approximately five hundred years ago, with questions such as "What clothes would you wear?" and "Where would you find water?" The questions and answers break up the factual information into readable segments and speak to a child's curiosity about the actual experiences of living in the past. This format also represents a shift from a "big events" approach to history to one that explores the needs and concerns of quotidian life.

Some recent historical nonfiction makes good use of humor. Terry Deary's Horrible Histories series offers an irreverent look at the past in books with such alliterative titles as *The Savage Stone Age* (1999), *The Vicious Vikings* (1998), and *The Terrible Tudors* (2003). With their jaunty texts and inset cartoons, the books have the feel of "unofficial histories" although they are detailed and factual.

The You Wouldn't Want to Be series uses a boldly cartoonish style to explore the unenviable lot of various individuals and groups in history, in books such as Fiona MacDonald and David Antram's *You Wouldn't Want to Be a Medieval Knight: Armor You'd Rather Not Wear* (2013) and Andrew Langley's and Antram's *You Wouldn't Want to Be a Viking Explorer: Voyages You'd Rather Not Make* (2013). The series describes the lives of individuals from a wide variety of historical groups—from Pyramid Builders to Civil Rights Soldiers to Victorian millworkers—with Handy Hints on how to navigate danger, challenges, and unpleasant situations. The books tend to end with an upbeat conclusion about the contributions that the individuals or groups that "you wouldn't want to be" actually made to history. For example, the conclusion of Peter Cook and illustrator Kevin Whelan's *You Wouldn't Want to Sail on the Mayflower! A Trip That Took Entirely Too Long* (2005) reads: "You may have risked everything during that dangerous voyage to a new land, but your descendants now enjoy the freedom that the Pilgrims were seeking when they first set sail: beginning a voyage that, in the end, you are glad you made" (28).

The You Wouldn't Want to Be series is notable for representing the points of view of laboring non-elites and enslaved people. At the same time, it remains selective of the historical events included in the series. For example, there is an examination of the terrible lives of slaves in Ancient Greece and Sumer in MacDonald and Antram's *You Wouldn't Want to Be a Slave in Ancient Greece! A Life You'd Rather Not Have* (2000) and Jacqueline Morley and Antram's *You Wouldn't Want to Be a Sumerian Slave: A Life of Hard Labor You'd Rather Avoid* (2007), but the series does not cover the more politically sensitive topic of slavery in the United States. Despite these shortcomings, the books' playful visual style and engaging narratives may encourage young people to read historical nonfiction as a source of entertainment and pleasure as well as edification.

SCIENCE AND DISCOVERY

Early Science Books: A Sense of Wonder

The scientific revolution of the late seventeenth and eighteenth centuries established the scientific method of using empirical observation and experimentation, a process that fostered many scientific discoveries. Yet the desire to communicate scientific discoveries to the general public found much of its momentum in the Romantic movement's fascination with the beauty and power of the natural world, as Richard Holmes argues: "It was the age when science began to be taught to children, and the 'experimental method' became the new, secular philosophy of life, in which the infinite wonders of Creation (whether divine or not) were increasingly valued for their own sake" (xix). Many science books for children of the later nineteenth century stressed the thrill of scientific understanding, as we see in this passage from Arabella Burton Buckley's *The Fairy-Land of Science* (1885), where she compares the unseen forces of nature to the supernatural beings of fairy tales:

> Exactly all this which is true of the fairies of our childhood is true too of the fairies of science. There are *forces* around us, and among us, which I shall ask you to allow me to call *fairies*, and these are ten thousand times more wonderful, more magical, and more beautiful in their work, than those of the old fairy tales. (6)

In Buckley's approach, both imagination and observation are needed to understand scientific principles such as gravitation and condensation.

In the early decades of the twentieth century, the scientific and technological education of children was intensified with the hope that they would grow up to play a role in expanding technological industries. In the United States, further acceleration occurred after World War II due to the "space race" and the "race to the moon." The increasing emphasis on an information economy—one that stresses the manipulation of ideas rather than tools—in the late twentieth and early twenty-first centuries has also stimulated the production of science and discovery books. Books on science and discovery are also meant to help instill an appreciation for science and scientific literacy in the general population.

Contemporary Science Books

Contemporary science books continue the earlier tradition of science writing and include many works we might term "informational," using the definition offered by Duke and Bennett-Armistead at the beginning of this chapter. Patricia Lauber argues that the difference between science writers of the past and those working today is an emphasis on interdependence and process:

> Within memory, natural scientists have moved from finding and classifying plants, animals, and protists, to anatomy and physiology, and to understanding the relationships that exist among living things and their environment. Today it does not suffice to produce, even for very young readers, a book that simply shows, names, and describes turtles. Every young reader is capable of grasping a bigger picture— how turtles make a living, how some can survive in cold water, who and what their enemies are, and what role turtles play in the natural world. Young children are perfectly capable of understanding how a big cactus survives in a desert and how, in surviving, it provides food and shelter for desert animals. The total picture is more complex and more interesting. It is significant and important because it permits children to grow up knowing about the interdependence of living things. ("What Makes" 6)

Such a focus on process reflects recent environmental concerns, which emphasize that all natural and inorganic elements form a holistic system. One example of a nonfiction text that presents a holistic view of the natural world—with attention to its interrelated processes—is Caroline Arnold's *A Warmer World: From Polar Bears to Butterflies, How Climate Change Affects Wildlife* (2012), illustrated by Jamie Hogan. *A Warmer World* is unflinching in its portrayal of how rising world temperatures have affected the habitats of many animal species, showing how both plants and animals have responded to the change in temperature. For example, Arnold notes that the warming temperatures have made it harder for polar bears, who need solid ice on which to hunt: "Now that the sea ice in the Arctic is freezing later each fall and melting earlier in spring, polar bears have less time to hunt and build up fat in the summer. They are now thinner and less healthy than they were twenty years ago, and females are giving birth to fewer cubs" (14). Not only does Arnold's book introduce young people to a pressing human and scientific problem; it stresses the interrelation of organic and inorganic forces and assesses the impact of human activity on the natural world.

Another book about science lauded for its depiction of interrelated factors—including politics and economics—that affect the natural world is Susan L. Roth and Cindy Trumbore's *Parrots over Puerto Rico* (2013), a colorful, large-format picturebook that describes the efforts of the Puerto Rican Parrot Recovery Project to prevent the extinction of Puerto Rico's parrot population, which faced extinction in the 1960s. It covers the history of the island and the threats exploration, colonialization, and overdevelopment pose to the parrot's habitat. It is a poignant experience to read the book now, given the lasting impact of Hurricane Maria (2017) on the people and natural environment of Puerto Rico. Efforts to restore the Puerto Rican Parrot were significantly set back, although some wild and captured parrots have survived (Giaimo).

The National Science Teachers Association (NSTA) has compiled lists of the best science trade books since 1973. Here are NSTA's criteria as articulated on its website:

- The book has substantial science content.

- Information is clear, accurate, and up-to-date.

- Theories and facts are clearly distinguished.

- Facts are not oversimplified to the point that the information is misleading.

- Generalizations are supported by facts, and significant facts are not omitted.

- Books are free of gender, ethnic, and socioeconomic bias. (National Science Teachers Association)

The NSTA criteria stress scientific content, skillful presentation, accuracy, and precision in communicating scientific ideas. While these criteria do not specifically address the use of fictional narrative in science writing, they neither exclude fictional frames for scientific writing nor advocate for them. They do, however, stress the writer's need to be alert to the changing understanding of scientific fact in the wider world and to make sure that scientific principles and processes are fully explained.

Experimentation in Science Writing for Children

Many science and discovery books for children encourage them to carry out scientific investigations of their own. For example, Donald Silver's book *One Small Square: Pond* (1994) invites young readers to scrutinize one small section of a pond in their area. As in all the One Small Square series, the reader is urged to measure a small square twenty-four inches long and wide with a yardstick: "Visit your square often: in the morning, at midday, and before sunset" (Silver 9). Child readers are told to keep a notebook to record the activity within the square they've chosen. The child observer in *Pond* takes on the authority of a scientist but also the risks of scientific endeavor; while the pond offers many possibilities, no one can predict what will appear in the square at any given moment and how the creatures they witness will relate to one another. The child is asked to look and to interpret, piecing together a narrative of the pond's natural cycles based on what he or she observes.

Some science books for children also explain how professional scientists work as they seek to make discoveries or solve problems. Sy Montgomery's *The Octopus Scientists: Exploring the Mind of a Mollusk* (2015), with photographs by Keith Ellenbogen, follows a team of researchers—among them a professor of psychology, a behavioral ecologist, and a marine ecologist—as they visit the Tahitian Island of Moorea to study the Pacific day octopus (*Octopus cyanea*). They seek to investigate "how these intelligent invertebrates make decisions" (4), so they go to Moorea to gather information about how the *Octopus cyanea* decide what to eat while avoiding predators themselves. Fieldwork proves unpredictable, and the octopuses are frequently elusive, but the researchers do manage to see some of the mollusks and to gather data. Ultimately, the scientists are not able to fully answer their initial questions about the eating habits of the *Octopus cyanea* in Moorea, since they behave so differently from *Octopus cyanea* previously studied in Hawaii—opening the possibility that maybe this research team had encountered an entirely new species of octopus. Montgomery, who participated in the research while writing his book, remarks: "our field expedition generated more questions than answers" (66). Lead scientist Jennifer Mather places the team's results within the context of ongoing scientific exploration: "Science doesn't usually give you clear answers of the type you wanted, especially fieldwork. But we got information—that's what it's all about" (66). *The Octopus Scientists* makes it clear that fieldwork can be valuable, but that scientific work is often not conclusive or final.

Many contemporary science books point to ongoing questions in science and opportunities for research. In *Next Time You See a Spiderweb* (2015), Emily Morgan not only explains types of spiderwebs and their functions but also points to the ways in which they can inspire human technological or scientific innovation: "Engineers and architects are intrigued by the durability of spiderwebs. They have noticed when a spiderweb is damaged, only part of it breaks, while the rest of it remains stable. Studying the construction of spiderwebs might help engineers and architects design structures that can withstand disasters such as earthquakes" (27). Once again, we see the interaction of human concerns and the natural world, with the natural world a potential inspiration for human technology.

CRITICAL ISSUES IN NONFICTION

Fictional Stories in Nonfiction

In opening this chapter with David Macaulay's *Cathedral*, we raised the issue of fictive elements within nonfiction. "Made up" elements do not necessarily diminish the value of a text as nonfiction, and might even enhance it. Yet reading critically involves an evaluation of how much fictionalization is acceptable for a work to retain its nonfiction status, and an awareness of how those standards can shift with time. In an interview with Roger Sutton, for example, Lincoln biographer Russell Freedman notes that it is increasingly unacceptable to include imagined scenes and dialogue in biography for children:

> Fictionalizing is no longer a controversial subject: you simply don't do it. That's been a total change since I first started writing. My first book, *Teenagers Who Made History*, which was published in 1961, is full of invented dialogue. That was the standard of the time, and, in fact it was fun to write, but I'm glad the standard has changed. I think that today's books, in which every quote, every conversation, is taken from a memoir, an autobiography, an interview, or what-have-you, are much more convincing. (697)

In a publishing environment with standards that have shifted so much, a biography containing some pure fabrication might ring false for child and young adult readers. The text may veer so close to being fiction that it no longer seems factual; the invented scenes cannot be tested or verified.

One science series that combines fiction and fact is Joanna Cole and illustrator Bruce Degen's Magic School Bus series in which a class of students goes on a magical journey (through the solar system, inside a beehive, into the human body) to learn about scientific phenomena. In *Lost in the Solar System* (1990; rev. ed. 2010), a bus trip to the planetarium veers into an interplanetary journey through the solar system beginning with the inner planets (Mercury, Venus, Mars), traveling through the asteroid belt, and moving to the outer planets (Jupiter, Saturn, Neptune, and Uranus; Pluto's change in status from a planet to a Kuiper Belt object is noted in the revised edition). In the process, the teacher, Ms. Frizzle, is lost in the asteroid belt between Mars and the outer planets. The students must carry on without her until they can double back to the asteroid belt and pick her up again.

Many pages of the Magic School Bus series include lined paper with "reports" ostensibly written by the students, representing the fruits of their research. For example, *Lost in the Solar System* offers a report by Phoebe, entitled "What Makes Night and Day?": "The spinning of the Earth makes night and day. When one side of the Earth faces the Sun it is daytime on that side. When that side turns away from the Sun, it is night" (Cole 7). Readers derive much of the factual information about the solar system from these mock-handwritten notes. As the students progress through the solar system, a small map outlines "Our path so far," with planets identified one by one. Another feature is called "Your weight and fate on [fill in the planet]." The scale for Venus notes that someone who weighs 85 pounds on Earth would weigh 77 pounds. The "fate" reads, "Your future looks cloudy," and the students exclaim, "So does Venus!" (Cole 17).

Joanna Cole and Bruce Degen's *The Magic School Bus: Lost in the Solar System* (1990; rev. ed. 2010) combines narrative, dialogue, and factual reports to create an adventure story within a science lesson.

Some science teachers appreciate the Magic School Bus series because it appeals to child readers and conveys a great deal of information. Yet the series has such an elaborate fictional narrative that it might be better described as science fiction (as it is in Scholastic's official guide to the series). On the other hand, the opposition between "real science" and "fantastic narrative" in a book such as *Lost in the Solar System* might not matter to young readers who will generally be able to distinguish between the truthful (facts about the atmosphere, solar system, and gravity of the planets) and the fanciful (a school bus that suddenly flies into orbit).

Even if it is best categorized as science fiction, the Magic School Bus series can be seen as valuable for the factual information it does include and for encouraging children to speculate about science. Educator and naturalist Chet Raymo thinks that an emphasis on "sheer factuality" in science writing has detracted from children's enjoyment of science. In an essay originally published in the journal *The Horn Book*, he argues that Dr. Seuss books and other fantastic texts are the most important for young readers: "Pick any Seussian invention, and nature will equal it" (Raymo 169). Raymo concludes:

> Let's not be too overly concerned about providing science facts to children. A child absorbs quite enough science facts from school and television, from computers and the other rich technologies at the child's disposal. If we want to raise the children who will grow up to understand science, who will be citizens who are curious, skeptical, undogmatic, imaginative, optimistic, and forward-looking, then let's turn [the Victorian rule against fantasy] on its head and put into the hands of children books that feed imagination and fantasy. (175)

To Raymo, fantastic literature instills scientific habits of mind more than science nonfiction, and it is clear that works of fiction—science fiction in particular—have always inspired scientists. At the same time, nonfiction science books without any fictive elements can also encourage creativity and imagination by depicting the astounding and often-mysterious natural world.

When approaching questions of fictionality within nonfictional texts, it is important to acknowledge how children's literature more often than not straddles the line between instructional books and narrative fiction. This combination of the fictional and the nonfictional is due in part to children's literature's didactic roots and the persistence of the "teaching function" in children's literature. A 2016 Children's Literature Association conference panel composed of scholars Amy Pattee, Cathryn Mercier, and Lauren Rizzuto discussed this issue in reference to Chris Raschka's postmodern picturebook *Arlene Sardine* (1998). *Arlene Sardine*, written in second person ("you"), recounts the tale of a young brisling (fish) who wishes to become a sardine. The vivid and beautifully illustrated book tells the story of how Arlene is caught, dies, and is put in a can. The book is puzzling to most. Mercier countered reviewers who dismissed the book for its defiance of traditional genre conventions, and Rizzuto considered the politics of its anthropocentrism. Pattee's paper in particular focused on the ways in which the book could also be read as a detailed and informative nonfiction explanation of how fish become sardines. We might, for example, consider the following passage: "Arlene swam around in the net for three days and three nights and did not eat anything, so her stomach would be empty. There is a word for this. The word is thronging" (n.p.). This is a solid explanation of a necessary stage in the industrial production of sardines. Many—if not most—fictional texts impart some form of information to their young readers, which is another reason that the fiction/nonfiction divide is an artificial one.

When we think of nonfiction, we think of texts that impart information or increase the understanding of the reader, whether of historical events, scientific processes, life narratives or the contours of the geographies that surround us. We have also seen non-fiction and informational books contributing to an ethic of mastery of the physical and human world, as in the expansion of science education during the Cold War period. But nonfiction can sometimes open up as many questions as it answers and promote a sense of the world as strange and alienating. Sheinkin's *Bomb*, for example, immerses its reader into a morass of unresolvable moral dilemmas about the intersection of warfare, politics, and science, despite its elegant structure and narrative pacing. In nonfiction, the world often appears beyond human control. One recent example is Don Brown's *Drowned City: Hurricane Katrina and New Orleans* (2015), a work of graphic nonfiction, illustrated with watercolor images in a subdued—often eerie—color palette dominated by blues, grays, and sober browns. *Drowned City* presents the events and aftermath of Hurricane Katrina, including harrowing evacuations, people stranded on roofs or trying not to drown in attics, and the harrowing conditions at the Superdome where many took refuge. The book makes a full accounting of the many who lost their lives. Governmental failures at the local and federal level are depicted, as are grassroots attempts to assist. Brown's narrative not only shows a lack of human control over natural forces, but also a strange and unfathomable world, where many people can no longer call New Orleans their home.

Simplification and Complexity

Biographies, science writing, historical writing, and conduct/advice literature all grapple with the problem of presenting a complex reality to young readers. Reading these forms critically involves evaluating how successfully they inform a young person about complex facts and realities. This task becomes more difficult when writers work within the shorter form of the picturebook. Speaking of biography for children, Russell Freedman conceded: "A picture-book biography can't deal with the same complexities and nuances as a 150-page biography for older kids. You can't use the picture-book format if you want to get into all those complications, and yet, you still want to capture a sense of a life being lived" (qtd. in Sutton 699–700). This difficulty is also found in science writing. Seymour Simon argues that he writes for children only through the upper elementary grades, since "any junior-high-school-age child who is interested in science tends to read adult books on science, rather than children's books" (qtd. in DeLuca and Natov 23). Yet many science picturebooks are successful in communicating to very young readers that the natural world involves complex processes and systems; they also get child readers to practice what it is like to study those systems through observation and experiment.

   In an article entitled "Writing Science Books for Children," Frances R. Balkwill talks about the importance of the "distillation" of ideas, by which she means breaking down the content to its most crucial elements. The notion of distillation appears often when science writers talk about their writing; we also see it in life writing and historical nonfiction. Distillation is a complex endeavor, as Balkwill explains:

> The difficulty is deciding what *not* to include, and in maintaining accuracy without complicating the story. Young readers gain confidence by grasping one or two simple concepts that they can return to with maturity. Science fact is stranger and often more exciting than science fiction. As with simple fiction picture books, children respond to a narrative style, but it is important to convey information sparingly. (Balkwill)

One way of thinking about simplification in literature for children and young adults is that complex ideas need to be made clear for any audience, no matter what their age. Educational psychologist Jerome Bruner famously noted that "any subject can be taught effectively in some intellectually honest form to any child at any stage of development" (33). Scientists often need to explain their complex work so that nonscientists will understand it; this is not a fundamentally different process from what an author of a science book for children must do: boil down complex ideas without oversimplifying them.

Accuracy and New Research

Nonfiction works present factual information about the world. As scientific, technological, historical, or biographical knowledge evolves, nonfiction books need to keep up. Patricia Lauber says of science writing,

> Gone are the days when "facts" stayed reliably the same for years on end. Gone, too, are the days when research could be done in the comfortable convenience of a good home library. To be up-to-date, writers must go to primary sources: scientific papers and journals and the scientists who know in what direction research is moving. ("What Makes" 7)

One potential reward of a science writer's need to stay alert to our changing understanding of scientific principles is the possibility of conveying the vitality and dynamism of scientific change.

> The reader should realize that because science is a human activity, it contains errors. The point is important partly because the reader should realize that science is, sooner or later, self-correcting, that questioning minds are always probing, questioning, doubting. It is also important because the writer must take cognizance

of the errors that are incorporated into textbooks and encyclopedias, which even adults tend to view as gospel, but which by their very nature are years in the making, always partly out-of-date, and constantly being revised. It is confusing for a child to find "facts" that are categorically stated in a textbook being flatly contradicted in another book. The considerate writer will indicate what is a new discovery, or even go so far as to tell what it was that other scientists "used to think." ("What Makes" 8)

This approach invites children to become aware of science as a human creation, beset by error and change. At times, young readers are asked to put themselves in the place of a scientist making discoveries.

Nonfiction can also become dated when social or cultural norms shift. For example, both life writing and biography present a wider range of human stories than they have in the past, with more emphasis on racial diversity, women's contributions to history, and the experiences of working-class people. Old-fashioned language and a stiff prose style can also render a work of nonfiction obsolete. One example is Henrik Van Loon's *The Story of Mankind* (1921), which won the first Newbery Medal in 1922. Van Loon recounts key events in human history from the first Mesopotamian civilization to World War I. Kathleen T. Horning draws attention to the book's "quaint and dated" prose style, citing the following sentences: "The history of man is the record of a hungry creature in search of food. Wherever food was plentiful, thither man has travelled to make his home" (12). Horning's sense of the datedness of Van Loon's book is all the more striking in light of the fact that the book has often been updated to reflect new historical events, most recently by Robert Sullivan in 2013. Sullivan brings the history up-to-date by adding topics like global warming, terrorism, and the election of Barack Obama. Writing about the previous 1999 update by John Merriman, Horning wearily comments:

It appears that *The Story of Mankind* will be updated ad infinitum, as long as human history continues and the book stays in print. One might question whether a book that is so clearly dated in other respects should be kept alive artificially, simply because it won an award almost a century ago. If it had been left with its original ending, just after World War I, with an illustrated chronology showing the highlights of the last century as "League of Nations ... World War ... rivalry in armament ... large scale production ... combustion engine perfected," would today's young readers see the book for what it truly is: a product of its time? (12)

Horning makes a good point here. If nonfiction books reflect the time period in which they were written, they can be a helpful window into societies and cultures of the past even if they are no longer compelling as texts that inform readers about their contemporary realities.

While some works of nonfiction are perceived as dated and stale, others attain classic status and can still be read by contemporary readers even if they were published in an earlier time. For example, Cornelia Meigs's *Invincible Louisa: The Story of the Author of* Little Women was published in 1933, but readers can still appreciate its unflinching account of Louisa May Alcott's struggle with poverty and her determination to provide for her family through her writing. Alcott's Civil War context is vividly evoked; she worked as a nurse in an army hospital in Washington, DC. The political debates around slavery and abolition are fully outlined, as is Alcott's personal and intellectual rapport with philosophers and intellectuals such as Henry David Thoreau and Ralph Waldo Emerson. However, even if some nonfiction books do attain classic status, most nonfiction books are superseded by newer, more accurate works, or must be updated to reflect new research and information.

READING CRITICALLY: NONFICTION

We Are the Ship: The Story of Negro League Baseball

Kadir Nelson's *We Are the Ship* (2008) is a picturebook history of the Negro National Baseball League from its beginnings in 1920 to 1947, when Jackie Robinson joined the major leagues. *We Are the Ship* presents three different kinds of history. First of all, it explores a little-known time in the history of baseball, detailing how African Americans were systematically excluded from major league baseball, forming their own league so that they could keep playing profession-ally. It reveals how major events such as the Great Depression and World War II shaped life in the United States in general and the lives of Negro League baseball players specifically. Finally, it contributes to our understanding of African American history before the Civil Rights Move-ment, showing the hardships and discrimination Negro League players faced as they worked and traveled.

When baseball began as a professional sport in the nineteenth century, it included African American players. But in the first two decades of the twentieth century, African Americans "began to disappear from professional baseball teams and were soon gone from them alto-gether" (Nelson 2). In response to this racist exclusion, African American players created their own league, catalyzed by the strenuous efforts of Andrew "Rube" Foster, a baseball manager.

> Rube aimed high. He wanted to create a league that would exhibit a professional
> level of play equal to or better than the majors, so that when it came time to integrate
> professional baseball, Negroes would be ready. See, Rube didn't want to put just one
> or two Negroes in the major leagues, he wanted to put a whole *league* into the major
> leagues. There would be the American League, the National League, and the Negro
> League. Rube knew that if Negroes were to play in a professional league, we'd have to
> organize it ourselves. "We are the ship," he proudly declared; "all else the sea." (Nelson 9)

Nelson takes his title *We Are the Ship* from Rube Foster's metaphor, evoking the self-reliance of the Negro Leagues in the absence of other forms of support.

Historical nonfiction is a genre related to biography; it often focuses on individuals who were important in a given historical period. Nelson's book is notable for its focus on the players and managers who were participants in the history of the Negro Leagues. We read about some of the very best players, including Leroy "Satchel" Paige, Josh Gibson, and Cool Papa Bell, but also discover lesser-known players such as George "Mule" Suttles, Norman "Turkey" Stearnes, Oscar Charleston, and William Julius "Judy" Johnson. Nelson notes, "The Negro Leagues were full of guys who were stars in their own right. Many of our guys could have rewritten the record books if they had been given the chance to play in the majors" (41).

We Are the Ship: The Story of Negro League Baseball (2008), written and illustrated by Kadir Nelson, tells the story of the unsung heroes of Negro League Baseball in the first half of the twentieth century.

As a picturebook, *We Are the Ship* relies on images as well as text. Nelson includes portraits of players and managers that he first produced as large oil paintings, many of which have been exhibited in museums such as the National Baseball Hall of Fame and the Eric Carle Museum of Picture Book Art. With their clear outlines and warmly saturated colors, Nelson's paintings are reminiscent of not only those by American painter and illustrator Norman

Rockwell but also those by Renaissance painter Sandro Botticelli. Even when reduced from their full size on a museum wall to pages in a book, Nelson's portraits give off an impression of heroic achievement.

Nelson pays homage to many talented and charismatic individuals and yet narrates the book in "a collective voice, the voice of every player, the voice of we" (80). While the information presented in the text is factual, there is some fictionalization, as Nelson wove together a single narrative from the many interviews and books he consulted during his research. The text gives the impression of a shared historical experience transcending any single narrator.

We Are the Ship contributes a great deal to baseball history. Divided into nine innings (with some "Extra Innings" at the back of the book), it traces the formation and organization of the league but also captures the flavor of the game itself: "Negro baseball was fast! Flashy! Daring! Sometimes it was even funny. But always very exciting to watch" (Nelson 17). Besides emphasizing the exhilaration of the games, Nelson acknowledges some of their harsher elements, including occasional altercations between the players or violent pitching. The constrained finances of the Negro Leagues also posed challenges for baseball players, including playing on bad fields and the fact that they could not afford to have umpires travel with the teams. Though the games themselves were sometimes rough, the players exhibited great professionalism and dedication to the game. Nelson draws the reader's attention to the innovations Negro League teams offered to the sport of baseball, such as the Kansas City Monarchs' being the first baseball team to play a night game using a portable lighting system. The book ends with Jackie Robinson's entrance into the major leagues, which signaled the beginning of the end for the Negro Leagues. Ultimately, 58 out of 200 Negro League players ended up in the major leagues (77).

The book also depicts the significance of global political events, acknowledging their influence on the nation as a whole but emphasizing their impact on the Negro Leagues specifically. Nelson observes of the October 1929 stock market crash: "Businesses collapsed and banks closed, taking people's life savings with them. People were losing their jobs left and right, and soon it seemed everybody was out of work. What little money people had left could only be spent on food and heat" (31). The resulting Depression "hit white baseball hard and Negro baseball even harder. The Eastern Colored League and the great Negro National League that Rube Foster had built fell apart after twelve seasons. Most teams disappeared. The teams that remained drifted around barnstorming wherever they could, passing the hat" (31). World War II also reshaped the Negro League, as many of the Negro League teams lost players to the draft, and many played in exhibition games to entertain the troops. Large-scale historical events are treated in the book not as abstractions but as forces that disrupted and changed the lives of both individuals and groups.

We Are the Ship contributes to African American history by discussing the exclusion of African Americans from the major leagues and by showcasing the achievements of African American baseball players. It is particularly eloquent in describing the hardships faced by Negro League players because of their race, especially when traveling in the South. They were not allowed to use public restrooms and often could not find a restaurant that would serve them: "We would have to travel several hundred miles without stopping because we couldn't find a place where we could eat along the way. It's a hurtful thing when you're starving and have a pocket full of money but can't find a place to eat because they 'don't serve Negroes'" (Nelson 24). The North was also segregated and sometimes northerners also refused to serve the players in a restaurant or offer them rooms in a hotel: "Many times, we would get to a town after riding all day, only to spend a few more hours searching for a place to stay. The minute we arrived, inexplicably, every hotel would be full. If we couldn't find anyplace to stay, we would have to sleep on the bus" (24). Hotels were often too expensive: "Some teams slept at the YMCA, the local jail, even in funeral homes" (Nelson 24).

At the end of the book, the narrator asks whether the players were understandably bitter because they had been barred from the major leagues, but he asserts that most players were, surprisingly, not: "Most Negroes back then had to work in factories, wash windows, or work on some man's plantation, and they didn't get paid much for it. We were fortunate men. We got to play baseball for a living, something we would have done even if we hadn't gotten paid for it…. When you can do what you love to do and get paid for it, it's a wonderful thing" (Nelson 77–78). Modern-day players such as Bob Gibson and Ken Griffey Jr. "stand on our shoulders. We cleared the way for them and changed the course of history. And knowing that satisfies the soul. How can you be bitter about something like that?" (Nelson 77–78). This upbeat ending can be difficult to reconcile with the book's overall narrative of exclusion from the major leagues, as well as the racial discrimination and hardships faced by players in the Negro Leagues. A critical reading of the book might examine this positive resolution of the book as bound up with its status as a work for younger readers, requiring a note of hope and pride rather than one of bitterness or anger at manifest injustice: a hold-over from the tradition of children's inspirational biography. But a different critical reading might equally note the well-deserved pride of the collective narrator, underscoring the historical and cultural importance of the Negro League and its players.

EXPLORATIONS

Review

1. In this chapter, we note that conduct books constituted the bulk of writing for children until the eighteenth century, and that the tradition of conduct literature persists today in modified form. Why are adults so motivated to give conduct books to children and adolescents?

2. How are autobiographies, biographies, memoirs, and diaries different from each other? What do they have in common? How do they engage child readers?

3. What are some ways in which contemporary science books for children facilitate children's own scientific discoveries or connect them to real scientific work in the field?

4. How has the tradition of biography as inspirational literature about idealized people changed with more recent examples? What are some ways in which the tradition of inspirational biography continues in biographies for children?

5. How do contemporary health and sexual education books address the concerns and worries that children themselves sometimes express? How does the frank content in these books sometimes spark censorship attempts? Why do some adults maintain that frank and honest health and sexuality books are so important?

Reflect

1. When you consider children's books about science, mathematics, and nature, do you associate them with excitement or with drudgery? Choose two science, math, or nature books for children and compare them to two textbooks written for high school or college-level science classes. How are they different?

2. When you were a child, did any of the biographies you read inspire you to embrace their subject as role models? If so, was it a biography written for a child audience? When you grew up, did you learn anything new about the figure you idolized or discover any information that contradicted the portrayal you saw in the children's biography you read?

3. How are nonfiction books such as biographies, science writing, or historical nonfiction different from works of fiction? Do you see any common elements?

4. How important do you think illustrations are in works of science and discovery? Recall some of the best science books you know. Would these books be as effective without their visual components?

5. How does a biography written for an adult audience compare to a biography of the same figure written for a child reader? After listing the differences you see, reflect on how the intended audience for the text affects the kind of works produced.

Investigate

1. Visit a local art gallery, museum, or science center and examine the nonfiction books available for younger readers in the gift shop. If possible, speak to the manager of the bookstore about what he or she chooses to stock. Is the display an appealing one? Are the books expensive? If you were a young child, would you want to read or buy any of the books that are on offer there? Why, or why not?

2. Speak to one of the following people, if you can:

    a. A professional scientist, engineer, mathematician, or museum curator
    b. A doctor, nurse, or medical lab technician
    c. A science or math teacher (either K–12 or at a university)
    d. Someone with a strong amateur interest in science.

Ask the person what his or her favorite nonfiction books were as a young child. If possible, look up these books yourself and make some notes about them. How influential were the books when these people were imagining careers in science or technology?

3. Photocopy five to six pages of a science or technology book for a child, choosing one that includes several technical or scientific terms. Circle those technical or scientific terms. How do the authors deal with this specialized vocabulary? If there is a glossary, how effective is it in explaining specialized terms? If there is no glossary, what terms would benefit from being included in a glossary, and why?

4. Go to the children's nonfiction section of the local library and collect about a dozen books at random. How many are serious in tone? How many are lighthearted in tone? Do you have a preference for the serious books or the ones that use humor?

SUGGESTED READINGS

Floca, Brian. *Locomotive* (2013). *Locomotive* is set in the summer of 1869, and describes what it was like to ride America's first transcontinental railroad, from the point of view of a mother and her two children. It is written in free verse, and uses a great deal of onomatopoeia (words that sound like what they describe). In addition to evoking the experience of the journey itself, *Locomotive* offers many technical details about nineteenth-century railroad travel. The work also describes how the railroad crosses the land of the Cheyenne, Pawnee, and Arapaho nations of the West, and it notes that bison once roamed there; however, the book has been criticized for eliding the colonial history of the railroad and for the implication that these Indian nations simply vanished.

Freedman, Russell. *Lincoln: A Photobiography* (1987). This biography is notable for its use of photographs from Lincoln's time and its nuanced vision of Lincoln's political career and personal life. Extensive suggestions for additional reading are included.

Gantos, Jack. *Hole in My Life* (2002). Gantos, well known for his "New Realist" novels for young people (most notably the Joey Pigza series), writes about his arrest and incarceration for drug smuggling in 1971. At times graphic and candid in its description of violence, the book ends with Gantos leaving prison and finding a career as a writer.

Macaulay, David. *Cathedral: The Story of Its Construction* (1973). The book covers the building of a French Gothic cathedral in painstaking detail with black pen-and-ink drawings of each stage. Noted for the accuracy of its description of the construction process, it is set in the fictional village of Chutreaux.

Mann, Elizabeth. *Empire State Building: When New York Reached for the Skies* (2003). Illustrated by Alan Witschonke. Mann's picturebook is a history of the construction of the Empire State Building, using text, photographs, illustrations, and maps to explain how it was designed and built. The Empire State Building is portrayed as a triumph of American engineering and a symbol of hope in the midst of the Great Depression.

Meigs, Cornelia. *Invincible Louisa: The Story of the Author of* **Little Women** (1933). This biography places Alcott within her family context, with an emphasis on the influence of her father, Bronson Alcott. Although *Invincible Louisa* was published in 1933, it has stood the test of time due to its vivid and frank depiction of the challenges Alcott faced and her determination to write in order to alleviate her family's financial struggles.

Murphy, Jim. *An American Plague: The True and Terrifying Story of the Yellow Fever Epidemic of 1793* (2003). *An American Plague* is a nonfiction history of the yellow fever epidemic that killed thousands of people in Philadelphia in the eighteenth century. The book combines a narrative account of the epidemic with images of newspaper accounts, engravings of the city at the time of the fever, and portraits of various individuals who responded to the epidemic, including doctors, politicians, and the free Black Philadelphians who played an important role in helping the plague victims. The book also describes the clashing views of the medical professionals of the day about the cause of the epidemic and includes a final chapter on insect-borne diseases in the contemporary world.

Roth, Susan L. and Cindy Trumbore, *Parrots over Puerto Rico* (2013). *Parrots over Puerto Rico*—a vivid, colorful large-format picturebook—depicts the efforts of scientists to save parrots in Puerto Rico as part of the Puerto Rican Parrot Recovery Program. It also includes a great deal of Puerto Rican history and explains the reasons why the parrots almost went extinct in the 1960s: foreign occupation and overdevelopment that encroached on the parrot's natural habitat.

Sheinkin, Steve. *Bomb: The Race to Build—and Steal—The World's Most Dangerous Weapon* (2013). *Bomb* is the story of the development of the atomic bomb by Robert Oppenheimer and his team at Los Alamos, New Mexico ("the Manhattan Project") and their efforts to beat Nazi scientists to that technology. Much of the book is devoted to the efforts of Soviet spies to obtain scientific knowledge for the USSR. Paced and structured like a spy thriller, *Bomb* also offers insights into the moral dilemmas raised by atomic technology, with an examination of President Truman's decision to use the bomb, and a conclusion dealing with the ongoing global consequences of nuclear proliferation.

Silver, Donald. *One Small Square: Pond* (1994). Illustrated by Patricia J. Wynne. Silver asks his young readers to measure out a small section on a pond (while obeying safety rules) and observe it in all weathers and times of day. Through words and illustrations, Silver and Wynne present the different forms of pond life and their interrelation, and provide a visual glossary of all species at the end of the book.

APPROACHES TO TEACHING *WE ARE THE SHIP* [SECONDARY SCHOOL]

Preparation for the Lesson

Students should read *We Are the Ship* in advance of the class discussion.

Learning Goals

- To analyze Kadir Nelson's research and compositional process for *We Are the Ship*

- To consider Nelson's invention of a first-person-plural speaker who represents the collective experiences of the players in the Negro Leagues

- To evaluate Nelson's portraits as works of art and depictions of historical individuals

- To see how Nelson's primary documents and artifacts evoke a historical past

- To position *We Are the Ship* within the civil rights movement, within twentieth-century history, and within the history of baseball.

Activity One: Nelson's Compositional Process and the Collective Voice of the Narrator

Go over the following quotation from Nelson's Author's Note with the students.

> I chose to present the voice of the narrator as a collective voice, the voice of every player, the voice of we. Under the leadership of Rube Foster, who declared the leagues' independence from major league baseball by saying, "We are the ship; all else the sea," the owners and players formed and sustained a successful league, demonstrating the power of the collective. And after reading interviews and listening to former players speak about their lives in baseball it became clear that hearing the story of Negro League baseball directly from those who experienced it firsthand made it more real, more accessible. I hope that the way I have chosen to present the story has the same effect. (Nelson 80)

Explain that the voice of the narrator is a composite voice and includes information gleaned from the many first-person accounts of players in the Negro Leagues. Discuss whether this narrator can be called a fictional or nonfictional one, and what the narrative gains from having a narrator who represents the totality of the experiences of players in the Negro Leagues.

Choose a page where Nelson has footnoted several of the sentences and copy the page and the notes for the students; demonstrate how the footnoted sentences are based on interviews from actual players in the Negro Leagues.

Lead a discussion of Rube Foster's words, "We are the ship; all else the sea." Why did Nelson choose this quotation for the title of his book?

Activity Two: Portraits and Documents

Part One: Portraits

Show the class images of some of Kadir Nelson's artistic influences, including the illustrations of Norman Rockwell and Renaissance paintings by artists such as Sandro Botticelli. Explain that the portraits in *We Are the Ship* were originally large oil paintings that are impressive and heroic in scale. As a class, discuss the artistic impact of the paintings and how they function as works of art.

Ask each student to choose one of Nelson's portraits and write half a page summarizing the accomplishments of the person depicted in the portrait. They should write three adjectives to describe the person in the portrait and add a sentence for each adjective explaining why they chose it.

Finally, they should compose a paragraph about why they were drawn to that particular portrait.

Part Two: Documents

As a class, look at some of the paintings of primary documents included in the book, such as the reproduction of a ticket from a baseball game and the sign reading "Bronzeville Inn Cabins for Colored." Discuss why Nelson included these images and how they evoke a historical era. How do these images affect the reader?

Activity Three: We Are the Ship *as History*

Part One: *We Are the Ship* and African American History

Lead a discussion on why the Negro Leagues were formed. How were African American players shut out of the major leagues? Ask the students to write a list of the hardships athletes in the Negro Leagues faced. These might include not being able to use segregated bathrooms or eat at segregated restaurants, having to sleep in the bus when touring, or constantly struggling to make ends meet. After they complete this list, have the students choose one of these hardships and find quotations from the book that discuss this hardship. What is the speaker's attitude toward those hardships, and how did the players cope with these problems?

Part Two: Global Historical Events

We Are the Ship engages not only with the history of the Negro Leagues but also with major international crises and events such as the Great Depression and World War II. Ask the students to write a list of the major international crises and conflicts that occur in the book. Discuss the impact that these events had on the daily lives of the players in the Negro Leagues.

Part Three: *We Are the Ship* as Baseball History

Ask the students to identify an avid baseball fan, preferably someone who is interested in the history of baseball. This could be a parent or caregiver, a teacher at the school, a friend, or an acquaintance. The students should each write an email to this baseball fan to explain what he or she has learned from Nelson's book, asking if the recipient knew anything about the Negro Leagues. Once the student gets an answer, he or she should complete one of the following exercises.

a. If the baseball fan does know about the Negro Leagues and their importance to the history of baseball, the student should ask how the fan found out about this time in baseball history. The student should write a page summarizing what the baseball fan says about the Negro Leagues and compare it to Nelson's account.

b. If the baseball fan does not know about the Negro Leagues, the student should email the fan a summary of what Nelson's book tells us about the Negro Leagues, arguing for their importance in baseball history.

SOME FICTION–NONFICTION PAIRS AND GROUPS

Fiction–nonfiction pairings, or groupings, can animate classroom discussions and promote inquiry for young students outside of the classroom. Fiction can be effectively compared and contrasted to informational books, historical nonfiction, and biography/autobiography. Here are a few pairings and groupings to begin with.

HISTORICAL FICTION AND NONFICTION

Nonfiction	Fiction	Description
Jim Murphy, *An American Plague: The True and Terrifying Story of the Yellow Fever Epidemic of 1793*. Clarion Books, 2003.	Laurie Halse Anderson, *Fever 1793*. Simon & Schuster Books for Young Readers, 2000.	Jim Murphy's comprehensive and detailed nonfictional history of the 1793 yellow fever epidemic in Philadelphia pairs well with Laurie Halse Anderson's historical novel about the same epidemic, which focuses on protagonist Mattie Cook and her struggle to survive both the yellow fever and its catastrophic social and economic consequences.
Jerry Stanley, *Children of the Dust Bowl: The True Story of the School at Weedpatch Camp*. Crown Publishers, 1992.	Karen Hesse, *Out of the Dust*. Scholastic, 1997. Matt Phelan, *The Storm in the Barn*. Candlewick Press, 2009.	Karen Hesse's historical verse novel about the Oklahoma Dust Bowl between January 1934 and December 1935 depicts the struggles of protagonist Billie Jo as she grapples with economic and ecological devastation and an accident that kills her mother and infant brother. It pairs well with Jerry Stanley's *Children of the Dust Bowl: The True Story of the School at Weedpatch Camp*, which describes the western migration of Oklahomans who sought to move west, often encountering fresh struggles when work and social acceptance eluded them in California as well. Weedpatch School in Bakersfield, California, was a place for both practical and academic education, and was built by teachers, parents and students. In her verse novel, Hesse depicts struggles like the topsoil blowing away and ailments like dust pneumonia, which Stanley's nonfiction history also explores. Matt Phelan's *The Storm in the Barn* is a graphic novel combining fantasy and realism. Eleven-year old protagonist Jack Clark, suffering with his family through the threats and deprivations of the Dust Bowl, discovers a phantom in the barn with a face that resembles rain, prompting rumors that he suffers from dust dementia. Jack struggles to release this phantom storm from the barn, precipitating the return of rain and renewal of the crops.

WORLD WAR II BOOKS

When fiction and nonfiction are paired, students might consider the ways in which fictional characters help bring alive the historical experience of the war, but also the way in which nonfiction is capable of revealing nuances of character and of action.

Nonfiction	Fiction	Description
Kenji Kawano, photographer. *Warriors: Navajo Code Talkers*. Northland Publishing Company, 1990	Joseph Bruchac, *Code Talker: A Novel About the Navajo Marines of World War Two*. Penguin, 2005.	These four books—fiction and nonfiction—engage with the Navajo (Diné) Code talkers who made such significant contributions to the American war effort in World War II. Brynn Baker's *Navajo Code Talkers* is an overview of the Navajo Code Talker program for younger readers. *Warriors: Navajo Code Talkers* is a series of photographs of Navajo code talkers, now veterans. The photographer is Kenji Kawano, a Japanese photographer who notes, "these soldiers had been my father's enemies at one time" (xiv).
Brynn Baker, *Navajo Code Talkers: Secret American Indian Heroes of World War II*. Capstone Press, 2016.	Sara Hoagland Hunter, *The Unbreakable Code*, illustrated by Julia Miner. Rising Moon Books, 1996.	In Joseph Bruchac's novel *Code Talker*, protagonist Ned Begay enlists in the Marines as a Navajo Code talker and goes to war in the Pacific. In Sara Hoagland Hunter's picturebook *The Unbreakable Code* a Navajo Grandfather speaks to his grandson about his experiences at a government boarding school (which he was forced to attend) and his later service as a Navajo code talker for the Marines.
Pearl Witherington Cornioley, *Code Name Pauline: Memoirs of a World War II Special Agent*, edited by Kathryn J. Atwood. Chicago Review Press, 2013.	Elizabeth Wein, *Code Name Verity*. Hyperion, 2012.	Kathryn Atwood shaped material from interviews with Pearl Witherington Cornioley into a first-person memoir of her time in the Special Operations Executive (SOE), where she worked with the French resistance as a clandestine courier and then helped coordinate a resistance network of 3,500 men. Elizabeth Wein's intricately plotted historical novel *Code Name Verity* depicts the deep friendship between two women contributing to the British war effort. Maddie Brodatt (code name "Kittyhawk") is a commoner and talented pilot flying with the ATA (Air Transport Auxiliary) and Julie Beaufort-Stuart (code name "Verity") is a Scottish aristocrat working for the SOE (Special Operations Executive). The book is notable for its dual narration (first "Verity," then "Kittyhawk"), for its portrayal of women's aviation work in the war, and for its surprising plot twists and revelations.

Nonfiction	Fiction	Description
Tanya Lee Stone, *Courage Has No Color: the True Story of the Triple Black Nickels: America's First Black Paratroopers*. Candlewick, 2013.	Shelley Pearsall, *Jump into the Sky*. Alfred A. Knopf, 2012.	Stone's long-form nonfiction history of the 555th Parachute Infantry Battalion (the "Triple Nickels") pairs very well with Pearsall's historical novel set in 1945 and featuring thirteen-year-old Levi Battle who travels from Chicago to North Carolina (through the Jim Crow South) and ultimately to Pendleton, Oregon, to reunite with his father: a paratrooper and officer in the 555th Parachute Infantry Battalion. Although the Triple Nickels never saw combat overseas due to racism and unwillingness on the part of the army to integrate white and black paratroopers, they were assiduously well trained. In Oregon, they were deployed on "Operation Firefly"—a response to the threat of forest fires caused by Japanese balloon bombs. The Triple Nickels did indeed spend most of their time on the west coast fighting forest fires, although none caused by balloon bombs. Pearsall's novel explores the emotions and perceptions of her fictional characters; Stone draws on historical photographs of real paratroopers and military figures, and interviews with these figures.

SCIENCE, THE NATURAL WORLD, AND TECHNOLOGY BOOKS

These pairings can be discussed in terms of the contrast between the often-fanciful fictional elements and the fact-based nonfiction. Students might also discuss the ways in which the fictional texts can often reflect some of the scientific/physical realities of their subject even if they include clearly fictional elements.

Nonfiction	Fiction	Description
Sally M. Walker and Tim Flannery, *We Are the Weather Makers: The History of Climate Change*. Candlewick Press, 2010.	China Miéville, *Un Lun Dun*. Del Rey, 2008.	Sally M. Walker and Tim Flannery's *We Are the Weather Makers* is a comprehensive look at the causes, trajectories, and potential effects of global warming, as well as key moments in earth's climatological history. It also includes sections that give advice about reducing one's carbon footprint and conserving energy. China Miéville's fantasy *Un Lun Dun*—the title is a transformation of "UnLondon"—imagines an alternative London populated by trash and discarded items from the London we know in the real world. Un Lun Dun is menaced by the Smog: an evil, sentient cloud of pollution. Both *Un Lun Dun* and *We Are the Weather Makers* imagine a world where extreme weather has a negative impact on human life, and (in their very different ways) explore ways to save the environment.
Robin Page, *A Chicken Followed Me Home!: Questions and Answers About a Familiar Fowl*. Beach Lane Books, 2015.	David Ezra Stein, *Interrupting Chicken*. Candlewick Press, 2010.	Robin Page's beautifully illustrated informational book is structured as a series of questions about chickens (diet, varieties of chickens, keeping chickens safe etc.). It pairs well with David Ezra Stein's *Interrupting Chicken*, which features an irrepressible young chicken who interrupts every classic bedtime story his father tries to tell him.
Linda Glaser, *Wonderful Worms*, pictures by Loretta Krupinski. The Millbrook Press, 1992.	Doreen Cronin, *Diary of a Worm*, pictures by Harry Bliss. HarperCollins Children's Books, 2003.	Cronin's witty picturebook imagines a fictionalized, anthropomorphized worm who keeps a diary about family, school, career aspirations (he wants to be a Secret Service agent) and the various pleasures of living in the earth and eating garbage. Linda Glaser's informational book explains the digging habits of earthworms, with particular attention to their enrichment of the soil.

Nonfiction	Fiction	Description
April Pulley Sayre, *Vulture View*, illustrated by Steve Jenkins. Henry Holt and Company, 2007.	Jane Yolen, *Owl Moon*, illustrated by John Schoenherr. Philomel Books, 1987.	*Owl Moon* is a narrative picturebook centering on a young girl's "owling" expedition with her father; *Vulture View* is an informational nonfiction picturebook which describes the scavenging habits of turkey vultures in the present tense: "Vultures like a mess / They land and dine. / Rotten is fine" (n.p.). *Owl Moon* represents a human presence in the woods, whereas *Vulture View* entirely excludes people, revealing the vulture's consumption of carrion as entirely a natural process. Jenkins's illustrations depict the wilderness from the "bird's eye view" as the vulture spies its prey, but Schoenherr has a tendency to depict the owling journey from the human point of view, except for a couple of page spreads that show the scene from the owl's level.
Patricia Lauber, *Be a Friend to Trees*, illustrated by Holly Keller. HarperCollins, 1994.	Alan Zweibel's *Our Tree Named Steve*, illustrated by David Catrow. Puffin Books, 2005.	In Alan Zweibel's *Our Tree Named Steve*, a father writes his now-adult children a letter reminiscing about how a large tree near their house, now destroyed in a storm, was an important part of their family life while they were growing up. Patricia Lauber's nonfiction picturebook *Be a Friend to Trees* presents scientific facts about trees, exploring their place in the natural ecosystem and the ways in which humans use trees. It ends with some advice about saving paper, recycling, and planting trees.
Melissa Stewart, *Robots*. National Geographic Society, 2014.	Gordon Korman, *Ungifted*. Balzer + Bray/ HarperCollins, 2012.	In Gordon Korman's *Ungifted*, Donovan Curtis is accidentally sent to the Academy of Scholastic Distinction (ASD), a program for gifted and talented students instead of being punished for a prank he pulled. The novel emphasizes that he is ill prepared for the academics at ASD, but his creativity and warm personality make him a valuable friend for his classmates. Much of the novel centers on the class's participation in a state robotics meet that "combined creativity, design, engineering, mechanics, electronics, pneumatics, and computer science, all in an atmosphere of healthy competition" (241). Melissa Stewart's nonfiction photobook *Robots* presents the history of robotics (and mechanical "humans"), a definition of the term "robot," and an explanation of a robot's components and how robots are used in a variety of commercial, military, scientific, and leisure activities.

Additional Resources

The sources below provide lists and suggestions for these pairings; they have many more suggestions for teachers and researchers to work with:

Ansberry, Karen and Emily Morgan. *More Picture-Perfect Science Lessons: Using Children's Books to Guide Inquiry, K–4*. NSTA Press [National Science Teacher's Association], 2007.

Baer, Allison L. "Pairing Books for Learning: The Union of Informational and Fiction." *The History Teacher* 45.2, February 2012, pp. 283–96.

Eastern Connecticut Roundtable. "Fiction/Nonfiction Book Pairs." *ECYA Blog*, 2014, ecya. wordpress.com/fictionnonfiction-book-pairings.

Jordan, Helen Labun. "Using the Craft of Fiction to Tell Nonfiction Stories." *Bear Pond Books: Matching Readers with Books*, 21 September 2013, montpelierbearpond.blogspot. com/2013_09_01_archive.html.

"Non-Fiction Books of the Month (2016 Nonfiction Book)." *Idaho Commission for Libraries*, libraries.idaho.gov/page/non-fiction-books-month.

"Pair Nonfiction with Fiction to Enhance Literacy." *University of Texas Arlington Online*, 11 January 2016, academicpartnerships.uta.edu/articles/education/pair-nonfiction -with-fiction-to-enhance-literacy.aspx.

"Resources: Native Words, Native Warriors." *National Museum of the American Indian* (NMAI), 2007, http://www.nmai.si.edu/education/codetalkers/html/resources.html, 2007.

An illustration for the song "I Saw Three Ships" from Walter Crane's *The Baby's Opera* (1877), which includes music and nursery rhymes accompanied by pictures.

Jean de Brunhoff's *The Story of Babar* (1931) features appealing and brightly colored illustrations. Here, Babar is reunited with his cousins Arthur and Celeste over pastries.

Written by Margaret Wise Brown and illustrated by Clement Hurd, *Goodnight Moon* (1947) invites readers to say "goodnight" to various objects rendered in vibrant colors.

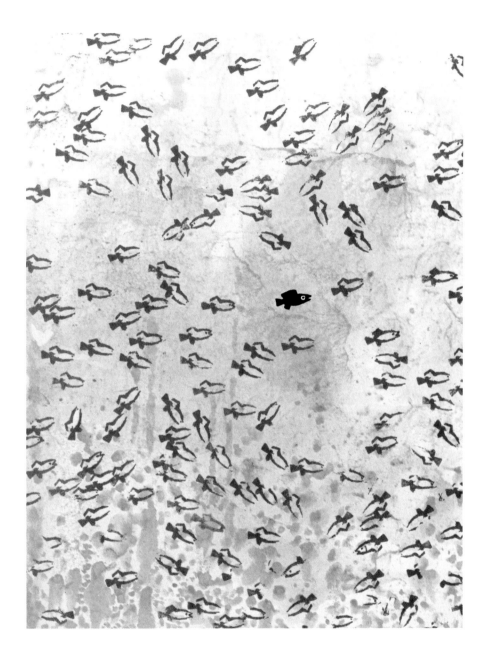

Leo Lionni's story of *Swimmy* (1963) features colorful block prints.

In Virginia Lee Burton's story of *Mike Mulligan and his Steam Shovel* (1939), Mike and Mary Anne offer to dig the cellar for the new town hall of Popperville.

David Wiesner's *Tuesday* (1991) relies solely on images to tell a story of frogs floating through a suburban community on lily pads.

Cassie and her brother, Be Be, fly over New York City in Faith Ringgold's *Tar Beach* (1991).

and eggs.

The strikingly landscaped hedges in Lane Smith's *Grandpa Green* (2011) depict different moments in the life of a boy's great grandfather.

Beatrix Potter's evocative illustrations for *The Tale of Peter Rabbit* (1902) are rendered in subtle but detailed watercolors.

Paul O. Zelinsky's rich oil paintings bring new life to the story of *Rapunzel* (1997).

A French Creole version of Cinderella by Robert D. San Souci, *Cendrillon* (1998) is illustrated by Brian Pinkney using a combination of scratchboard and oil paint.

FANTASY AND REALISM

In C.S. Lewis's *The Lion, the Witch and the Wardrobe* (1950), Lucy Pevensie enters a wardrobe in a sprawling old house and discovers a new world, the kingdom of Narnia. Her siblings—Peter, Susan, and Edmund—soon follow her there and discover that Narnia is a magical place inhabited by talking animals and pagan figures including fauns, giants, and centaurs—all living under the oppressive rule of a cruel White Witch. Lured by her offers of Turkish delight, Edmund falls under the thrall of the enchanting White Witch and must be redeemed by Aslan, the lion, in a Christ-like sacrifice. The children themselves do battle against the White Witch's forces and are ultimately crowned kings and queens.

Nothing could be more different from the Narnia series in both tone and plot than Jack Gantos's Joey Pigza series (1998–2015). Joey is a young boy dealing with an illness that is likely attention deficit disorder or attention deficit hyperactivity disorder. He struggles with school and life at home. His parents have a dysfunctional relationship, frequently reconciling only to split up again. In the second book, Joey's father, Carter Pigza, appears and urges his son to go off his "meds," causing Joey to become increasingly "wired." A good-natured kid, Joey struggles to stay on an even keel with the help of his chihuahua, Pablo. Joey's problems continue to trouble him all through the series. In the fourth book, *I Am Not Joey Pigza* (2007), Joey is pulled out of school and forced to stand at the side of a highway in a bee suit to advertise the family's new bee-themed diner. In the fifth and final book, *The Key That Swallowed Joey Pigza* (2015), Joey's parents leave him alone with his infant brother Carter Junior, his mother checking into a hospital with post-partum depression and his dad absent after botched plastic surgery. At the end of the novel, the

Opposite: *Edmund and the White Witch* (1997), adapted by Frederic Thomas from C.S. Lewis's *The Lion, the Witch, and the Wardrobe*. Illustration by Deborah Maze.

family reunites, with the implication that, as unlikely as it may seem, they might actually become a functioning family unit.

With their enchantments and powerful opposition between good and evil, the Narnia books fall within the genre of fantasy. The Joey Pigza books, with their family turmoil and struggling protagonist, fall squarely within the tradition of realism. While this chapter will explore fantasy and realism as separate phenomena—and define them in opposition to each other—it will also explore the ways in which fantasy and realism are permeable genres with multiple points of contact. For example, the Narnia and Joey Pigza books share thematic and structural elements despite their differences. Both feature children who must navigate an unfamiliar world with an absence of reliable parental guidance, and both wrestle with the nature of good behavior and responsibility to others. Fantasy and realism, then, can function in similar ways despite obvious differences. We will also turn to books that combine fantasy and realism, such as magical realism.

Lucie Armitt offers a good functional definition of the fantastic when she notes that "fantasy sets up worlds that genuinely exist *beyond* the horizon, as opposed to those parts of our own world that are located beyond that line of sight but to which we might travel, given sufficient means" (8).

Attributes of **fantasy** include:

- Elements of the magical or supernatural

- An imaginary world unlike the world we know (either completely different or with strikingly different elements)

- A distant setting, both in place and time

- Events and experiences that could not take place in the known world, with a reality that does not map onto the observable world as we know it, defying known laws of physics and science.

Attributes of **realism** include:

- A world we already know, at least to some extent; in the case of certain types of realism, it is a quite faithful rendition of environments familiar to children and young adults

- An emphasis on verisimilitude, which means that events in the novel *could* happen

- Avoidance of the magical and supernatural in favor of things that are scientifically and physically possible.

Fantasy and realism are different generic modes. Responding to this difference, educators, parents, and librarians have developed theories about the importance of fantasy or realism in children's reading, sometimes championing one to the exclusion of the other. Yet both fantasy and realism have important roles to play in childhood reading.

Throughout the chapter, we will look at what we gain from reading children's literature with a critical awareness of genre.

GENRE

Genre as a Guide for Readers

To examine the impact of genre on children's literature, it is important to ask an even more fundamental question: What is a genre? In what ways does a work's genre determine the nature of a work or the reader's experience of it? **Genre**, as we noted in Chapter 2, is often defined as a class of works. Literary works that share certain features are classed together. Genre, however, is more than a taxonomy or classification system; it is also a guide to readers that conditions their responses to a work. Jonathan Culler defines genre as a "conventional function of language, a particular relation to the world which serves as norm or expectation to guide the reader in his encounter with the text" (159). A genre is thus less a classification than a series of signals to guide a reader.

Sheldon Sacks argues that children can respond appropriately to works based on their genre from a very young age:

Imagine a child watching respectively an animated cartoon in which a favorite, mischievous animal character is squashed into a pretty pancake-shaped object and the same child viewing a television episode of *Lassie* in which the noble collie is temporarily separated from her unhappy master. The first elicits laughter. The second tears, or, more moderately, anxiety, though surely in some everyday sense the mischievous cartoon figure is more seriously threatened than the noble dog. It is clear that in each case the child has made a correct intuitive judgment based on the manner in which the plight of a character is represented. In other words, he has had to intuit an artistic end to which such characters are represented from the manner in which they are represented. (qtd. in Cawelti 47–48)

A work's genre includes the clues and norms that help a reader or viewer interpret it, which include what Sacks describes as "the manner in which it is represented." The cartoon is marked by its bright colors, strong lines, goofy music, and absurd tone, which send the message that the violent action is not to be taken literally: no one really dies. In contrast, the live-action episode of *Lassie* is filmed with a real dog and human actors, indicating that Lassie's difficulties should be taken seriously. Generic conventions might be seen, then, as a contract between reader and audience where an awareness of genre comes through wide exposure to different texts and genres and through watching other readers respond to them as well.

In addition to guiding readers in their reaction, genre can help establish the boundaries of what is possible for a work's plot. In her article "Pig in the Middle" (2000), Sophie Mills explores the ways in which fantasy and realism establish the destinies of pig characters in children's and young adult literature.

> Human beings have always imagined a fantastic world in which change and death are no longer necessary: Peter Pan never grows up; Hercules conquers death and acquires immortal life. Within this framework, the pigs can go down one of two paths. In stories in which realism predominates, they must die according to the laws of "the real world," which also insist that children must grow up, that they must take responsibility, be initiated into sexuality, and so on. However, in narratives that incorporate some fantasy, the pigs experience a miracle which enables them to find a world devoid of change and insecurity. (108–09)

For example, Wilbur in E.B. White's fantasy *Charlotte's Web* (1952) lives and flourishes, while the pig in Robert Newton Peck's realistic *A Day No Pigs Would Die* (1972) perishes. Mills draws a bold contrast between these two porcine destinies: "Either we are given a fantastic vision of a world in which we may escape change and pain, or we are shown that the change and the pain are necessary and beneficial for our development" (123). Genre conditions both the characters and the moral lessons we might draw from the characters' experiences.

FANTASY

Early Roots of Fantasy

Fantasy fiction has its roots in the earliest oral literature, such as Homer's *Odyssey*, which features gods, heroes, monsters, and a quest to return home. Fairy stories are another root of fantasy writing. In English literature, many works from the medieval period center on magical and supernatural beings—from Beowulf's fight with the monster Grendel to the enigmatic wizard Merlin in stories about King Arthur. Although these works influenced later fantasy writers such as C.S. Lewis and J.R.R. Tolkien, readers at the time may not have seen supernatural or magical figures as "fantastic" in the same way that later readers did. Because early listeners or readers drew less of a distinction between faith and reason, it is possible that they understood magical incidents as just one of many possible realities. In contrast, the Enlightenment of the seventeenth and eighteenth centuries emphasized scientific principles, rational thought, and phenomena that could be proven, drawing a sharper line between the true and the fictional. The Romantic movement of the late eighteenth and nineteenth centuries was rooted partly in the desire to explore the aesthetic and moral dimensions of supernatural and spiritual realms shunted to the side by Enlightenment rationalists. In the realm of children's literature, the Romantic emphasis on the world that could not be seen—the world of fantasy—was explored to great effect beginning in the late nineteenth century.

Nineteenth- and Early Twentieth-Century Fantasy

Lewis Carroll's *Alice's Adventures in Wonderland* (1865) is a watershed moment in fantasy literature for children. Much of the fantasy of the Alice books is based on the experience of nonsense, in the form of nonsense poetry such as "Jabberwocky" and the absurd behavior of its characters. For example, at the Mad Hatter's tea party, all the attendees shift places rather than cleaning the dishes, creating perpetual confusion and resentment. Another important writer in the history of fantasy was George MacDonald. His *At the Back of the North Wind* (1871) presents the night flights of a boy named Diamond with Mistress North Wind. In MacDonald's *The Princess and the Goblin* (1872), the Princess Irene is saved from goblins by the miner's son Curdie (she then saves him in return). *The Princess and Curdie* (1883) follows their further adventures. J.M. Barrie ensured his place in the history of fantasy literature by creating Peter Pan, a boy who never grows up and who flies with the enraptured Darling children to Neverland. Peter Pan made his first appearance in a novel Barrie wrote for adults, *The Little White Bird* (1902), and subsequently in his 1904 stage play, *Peter Pan; or, the Boy Who Wouldn't Grow Up*. The play was adapted and expanded as the novel *Peter and Wendy* (1911). E. [Edith] Nesbit was another innovative fantasy author of the period. In *Five Children and It* (1902) and *The Phoenix and the Carpet* (1904), she developed a form of fantasy in which magic appears in the modern world. In *Five Children and It*, a magical creature named the Psammead grants the children three wishes. Comic disaster ensues as the wishes create unpleasant effects (one of the children wishes to be taller, for example, and ends up awkwardly towering over everyone at eleven

feet). In the United States, L. Frank Baum created many books set in the magical country of Oz. In *The Wonderful Wizard of Oz* (1900), Dorothy's adventures with Toto, the Scarecrow, the Lion, and the Tin Woodman brought the world of fantasy a very American heroine from Kansas but also harked back to the episodic framework of Lewis Carroll's books about Alice.

Fantasy gained an avid audience in the nineteenth century and early twentieth century for many reasons. Eric Rabkin points to one cause when he muses on Barrie's 1911 novel about Peter Pan:

> When the fantastic Peter Pan rejects maturity in favor of childhood, we know that a failure to shoulder responsibilities is an iconoclastic assault on the Victorian perspective toward personal achievement; when we find that Barrie's book is ostensibly directed to children, we know something more about both the Victorian conception of childhood and the means by which iconoclasm—escape—may be made acceptable; and when we realize that all those best-selling copies of the books were bought by adults and read to children by adults, we know something further about the yearnings of normal Victorian adults. In their children's fantasies are revealed their own perspectives. (75)

Fantasy offers direct commentary (in Rabkin's words, "an iconoclastic assault") on a culture that valued adult professional achievement and a high level of dignified decorum and control. For the Victorians, fantasy was also a means of creating a protected childhood marked by whimsy and the imagination.

Postwar Twentieth-Century Fantasy

Twentieth-century postwar fantasy for children and young adults was in many ways dominated by two figures: C.S. Lewis and J.R.R. Tolkien. Colleagues at Oxford University, they were also members of the informal literary discussion group known as the Inklings. Lewis's best-known fantasy novels for children constitute his Chronicles of Narnia series: seven fantasy novels published between 1950 and 1954. Tolkien's *The Hobbit* (1937) begins when the wizard Gandalf enlists the home-loving hobbit Bilbo on a quest to rescue treasure from the formidable dragon Smaug. On the way, Bilbo encounters the creature Gollum, who is enthralled by a magical ring that is the "One Ring" forged by the Dark Lord Sauron. In *The Lord of the Rings* (1954–55), Frodo Baggins undertakes a grueling

Opposite: Illustrated by W.W. Denslow, Dorothy, Toto, and the Tin Woodman are whisked away to the Wicked Witch of the West in L. Frank Baum's *The Wonderful Wizard of Oz* (1900).

but successful quest to destroy the ring in the fires of Mordor, accompanied by his friend Samwise ("Sam") Gamgee and fellow hobbits Merry and Pippin.

Fantasy for children and young adults grew significantly in popularity after Tolkien and Lewis, with hundreds of texts being produced for devotees of the genre. T.H. White, Susan Cooper, and Ursula K. Le Guin are some major postwar figures. White's *The Once and Future King* (1958)—an Arthurian fantasy that collects works written earlier between 1938 and 1941—traces Arthur's ascent to the throne and his aspiration to rule. Cooper's The Dark Is Rising series (1973–79) draws on Arthurian and Celtic imagery to tell the coming-of-age story of Will Staunton. Le Guin's Earthsea fantasy series, beginning with *A Wizard of Earthsea* (1968), follows a wizard named Ged who battles a rival, Jasper, and in the process summons a shadow-monster. Over the course of the novel, Ged develops mastery both over his magic and himself. Diana Wynne Jones wrote several fantasy books and series, among them *Howl's Moving Castle* (1986), the Dalemark quartet (1975–93), and the Chrestomanci series (1977–2006). Other notable writers of fantasy from the period include Anne McCaffrey, Natalie Babbitt, Madeleine L'Engle, and Terry Pratchett.

Recent Children's and YA Fantasy

At the turn of the millenium, J.K. Rowling's Harry Potter series was a major landmark in fantasy literature that seems destined to achieve classic status, as a generation that grew up with the series passes down their love of the books to new children. Philip Pullman's His Dark Materials trilogy (1995–2000) is a sweeping high fantasy where protagonists Lyra and Will, and various allies, travel through multiple universes. In Rick Riordan's Percy Jackson & the Olympians series, beginning with *The Lightning Thief* (2005), a young boy discovers that he is the son of Poseidon and travels across the United States to recover Zeus's lightning-bolt. In Neil Gaiman's *The Graveyard Book* (2010), Gaiman's homage to Kipling's *The Jungle Book*, protagonist Bod survives a murder and spends his childhood among the congenial ghosts in the Graveyard, where he feels entirely at ease. Nnedi Okorafor writes science fiction, speculative fiction, and fantasy. Her *Zahrah the Windseeker* (2005) incorporates West African folklore to tell the story of Zahrah Tsami, who is born with "dadalocks" (dreadlocks with vines growing through them), showing that she has special powers. In Zahrah's world, the Ooni Kingdom, computers are grown from plant seeds, and buildings are also grown. Zahrah's quest begins when she must venture into the Forbidden Greeny Jungle to procure an unfertilized egg from an elgort to save her friend Dari, who has fallen into a coma. Other contemporary fantasy authors include Jane Yolen, Robin McKinley, Zetta Elliot, Ransom Riggs, and Daniel José Older.

TYPES OF THE FANTASTIC

John Rowe Townsend divides the fantastic into three categories: "anthropomorphic fantasy, in which animals or inanimate objects are endowed with human qualities; fantasies that create imaginary worlds or countries; and fantasies that inhabit the world we know but require some disturbance of the natural order of things" (211). In the section that follows, we will explore these three categories of fantasy.

Anthropomorphic Fantasy

E.B. White's *Charlotte's Web* (1952) is a good example of an anthropomorphic fantasy. It is set in a homely barnyard in a farm belonging to the Zuckerman family, who are dependent on the slaughter of animals for their livelihood. However, the animals in the barnyard have a fully developed society of their own—from the devious rat Templeton to the naive pig Wilbur. Facing slaughter, Wilbur is aided by the nurturing and savvy spider Charlotte, who spins a web praising Wilbur's virtues ("SOME PIG"), making him famous and saving his life. The fantasy of the book lies in the fact that it asks the reader to imagine talking animals banding together against the human world. Other notable anthropomorphic fantasies include Anna Sewell's *Black Beauty* (1877), featuring a horse who eloquently testifies to animal cruelty; Brian Jacques's Redwall series (1986–2010), with its mice living at the great

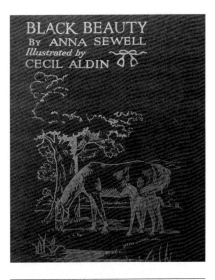

Black Beauty by Anna Sewell (1916 edition).

Redwall Abbey; William Steig's *Abel's Island* (1976), about a shipwrecked mouse; and Kate DiCamillo, *Tale of Despereaux* (2003), which centers on a mouse who lives in a castle and is devoted to music and reading. It includes other animal characters.

Secondary Worlds and High Fantasy

Some of the most important works of fantasy create "secondary" worlds, running parallel to our world. In Philip Pullman's His Dark Materials trilogy, for example, there are literally billions of interconnected worlds, although the protagonists move between only a few of them. The trilogy begins in a somewhat realistic setting in Oxford, England, and yet his protagonists Lyra Belacqua and Will Parry, along with other characters, have visible *daemons* (or souls) in the form of animal companions. The characters move between worlds by means of the Northern Lights (Aurora Borealis) or with the help of a subtle knife forged three hundred years earlier, which belongs to Lyra's friend (and ultimately lover) Will. At the end of the series, however, the doors between worlds are shut forever.

High fantasy is the subset of fantasy most associated with elevated quests and lofty struggles between good and evil. Lois Kuznets outlines the characteristics of high fantasy as follows:

- it "puts a premium on the presence of the 'marvelous'" (19)

- it is dependent on the writer's "subcreation" of a world sustained enough "to serve as a fitting background for a story in which the forces of good and evil clash and in which evil is, at least temporarily, defeated" (19)

- it features a protagonist who is "ordinary in ways with which most modern readers can identify" but who "must perform heroic acts in the course of the story, which usually has a romance-quest structure" (20)

- it "must never convey within its text any sense that the fantasy world is unreal or that the hero's experience is untrue" (20), which excludes any fantasy that takes place in a character's mind or a dream.

Tolkien's Lord of the Rings series and Lewis's Narnia books are examples of high fantasy because of their moral seriousness and the struggle they depict between good and evil. In contrast, Carroll's *Alice's Adventures in Wonderland* does not qualify as high fantasy since it takes place in a dream and does not involve an explicit moral struggle between good and evil. Many secondary-world fantasies and books of high fantasy are produced in series form, which has the effect of making the magical setting itself the focus of the books.

Fantasy that Inhabits Our World

Edward Eager's *Half Magic* (1954) is a good example of Townsend's category of "fantasies that inhabit the world we know" (211), since it depicts magic without creating a fully elaborated secondary world. In this comic novel, four children discover a coin that grants wishes, only to find that the coin only fulfills *half* the wish, which the children cope with

by doubling their wishes. Eager paid explicit homage to E. Nesbit, who also featured ordinary children encountering magical beings. A more contemporary example is David
Almond's *Skellig* (1998). The protagonist, Michael, discovers a strange man, Skellig, in his
garage. With his friend Mina, he discovers that Skellig has wizened angel wings growing
from his body. When Michael's infant sister faces a life-threatening operation, his mother
dreams about Skellig, and the baby survives. The book is never clear on Skellig's nature—
whether man, angel, or some combination—but it shows the miraculous touching upon
ordinary life.

EXPERIENCING THE FANTASTIC

Fantasy as a Reversal of Expectations

Eric Rabkin uses the two Alice books to talk about the reader's experience of the fantastic,
defining it as "a quality of astonishment that we feel when the ground rules of a narrative
world are suddenly made to turn about 180 degrees. We recognize the reversal in the reactions of characters, the statements of narrators, and the implications of structure, all
playing on and against our whole experience as people and readers" (41). Alice moves
from the real world of the Victorian nursery into Wonderland, where she cannot even be
sure of her own size, and the lessons she has been taught come out inexplicably mangled.
Wonderland is a place where flamingos are used as croquet mallets, where playing cards
are soldiers, and where a white rabbit is a servant of the Queen. To read *Alice's Adventures
in Wonderland* is to discover ground rules that are very different from the ones we live
with. This disorientation can be one of the great pleasures and challenges of fantasy.

Fantasy Literature and Responsibility

Rabkin's reversal of expectations—and his idea that fantasies like *Peter Pan* provide opportunities to vicariously escape from responsibility—offers one model of the experience
of the fantastic. However, fantasy characters just as often have to take on leadership roles
in fighting "real world" struggles and/or problems within their fantasy worlds. For example, in Ransom Riggs's books about "Peculiar" children, starting with *Miss Peregrine's
Home for Peculiar Children* (2011), the protagonist Jacob must, first of all, come to terms
with his grandfather's grisly murder. Traveling to the remote island where his grandfather
grew up in an orphanage, he learns more about his grandfather's history, which involved
a traumatic escape from Nazi Germany but also lifelong efforts to preserve a world of

"peculiar" children who live in a time-warp protected by "ymbrynes." Peculiar children are distinguished by their striking talents and qualities, such as being able to levitate or control fire. An ymbryne is a type of female peculiar who can turn into a bird and preserve a time loop, ensuring her young charges never die. When Jake learns that he, too, is Peculiar, he takes up his grandfather's mantle and works to save his new Peculiar friends and their protector, the ymbryne Miss Peregrine. Some recent fantasy literature has grappled with questions of racism and violence. For example, in Daniel José Older's *Shadowshaper*, a villainous white academic, Jonathan Wick, seeks to appropriate the spiritual knowledge and power of the shadowshapers, whose magic is centered in a diverse Brooklyn community. Protagonist Sierra Santiago must confront Wick while emerging into her own magic destiny and exploring her powers as a shadowshaper. Fantasy, therefore, is not always a removal from real world concerns, but a means to dramatize deeper commitments to the struggles of the world we know, or to struggles that unfold simultaneously in the fantastic and natural worlds.

The Fantastic and the Natural World

In *Rhetorics of Fantasy* (2008), Farah Mendlesohn writes, "I believe that the fantastic is an area of literature that is heavily dependent on the dialectic between author and reader for the construction of a sense of wonder, that it is a fiction of consensual construction of belief" (xiii). She sets up a working model of fantasy based on the relationship of our world to the fantasy world and creates four loose categories based on the "means by which the fantastic enters the narrated world" (xiv). Mendlesohn's categories are as follows:

1. The "portal-quest," in which "we are invited through [a point of entry] into the fantastic" (xiv). An example of a portal-quest would be Baum's *The Wonderful Wizard of Oz* (1900), in which the cyclone is the portal from the realistic world of Kansas to the fantasy world of Oz.

2. The "immersive fantasy," which "presents the fantastic without comment as the norm both for the protagonist and for the reader: we sit on the protagonist's shoulder and while we have access to his eyes and ears, we are not provided with an explanatory narrative" (xx). An example is Diana Wynne Jones's *Howl's Moving Castle* (1986), which plunges the reader into the magical kingdom of Ingary, where fairy-tale tropes are literally true.

3. The "intrusion fantasy," in which "the fantastic enters the fictional world" (xiv) and "is the bringer of chaos. It is the beast in the bottom of the garden, or the elf seeking

assistance" (xxi). An example is Neil Gaiman's *The Wolves in the Walls* (2003), illustrated by Dave McKean. In this book, a young girl hears noises in the walls, which turn out to be wolves encroaching on her family's peace and quiet.

4. The "liminal fantasy," where "the magic hovers in the corner of our eye" (xiv). Mendlesohn views Louis Sachar's *Holes* (1998) (see Chapter 6) as a rare example of a "liminal quest fantasy" because Stanley is unaware that in rescuing Hector (Zero) Meroni, he is breaking a longstanding family curse; Stanley and the reader are not conscious of whatever fantasy or magic elements hover in the background of the action.

Mendlesohn notes that these categories are not absolute and that several fantasy books combine elements of the four categories. For example, she refers to the Harry Potter series as "one of the few crossovers" (2). J.K. Rowling's *Harry Potter and the Sorcerer's Stone* (1997) begins as an intrusion fantasy (with the unexpected appearance of a Hogwarts owl at Privet Drive) but transmutes into a portal fantasy when Hogwarts students enter the magic world on the Hogwarts Express and discover a fully realized magic environment there. Mendlesohn's taxonomies represent a shift from Townsend's earlier categories of "anthropomorphic fantasy," "secondary-world fantasy," and "fantasy in the world we know" (Townsend 211). She is more interested in how the *reader* is positioned toward the magic of the books, and how he or she comes to understand and accept the fantasy world of the books.

There is much variation within the fantasy genre. Yet a common feature of fantasy texts is their engagement with settings, events, and experiences outside the known possibilities of our world. In our next section, we will see realism as a contrasting genre, focusing as it does on events that could actually happen within the parameters of our known reality and on situations from everyday life.

REALISM

Defining Realism and the "New Realism"

In a 1981 article, Linda Western defined "realism" in two ways. In the first instance, **realism** "characterized those stories which could actually happen—those containing no element of magic." This definition of realism is quite a broad one and could include any number of books for children. Literary realism itself has a long history and is notoriously difficult to pin down. It is grounded in the concept of **mimesis**, a Greek term that refers to imitation or representation of the physical world. In his *Rise of the Novel* (1957), Ian Watt argued that the development of the early novel in England was characterized by "formal realism" associated with an increased focus on the individual and the rejection of traditional forms such as allegory and romance. Literary realism as a movement is associated with nineteenth-century French writers such as Honoré de Balzac, who were committed to portraying "life as it actually was," focusing in on mundane daily events. Later, the literary movement known as **naturalism** extended literary realism by depicting characters as products of their environments.

Western's second definition of "realism" is more specific and referred to the "New Realism" of certain children's and young adult books written after the 1960s and into the present. **New Realism** encompasses books that deal with "taboo topics," including (but not limited to) "pregnancy, sexual abuse, adolescent physical change, birth, drugs, the elderly, and physical and mental disability" (Western 9). These books often feature common conventions or tropes such as urban settings, a focus on the working class, and the use of vernacular (or slang). The New Realism in children's and young adult fiction arose partly as a response to the social upheaval and change of the 1960s and 1970s, as adolescent readers in particular sought fiction that spoke to their immediate experiences—a concern for "relevance" and a rebellion against idealized and sanitized images of childhood and teenage life.

Early New Realism and the Problem Novel

Sheila Egoff traces the impact of Louise Fitzhugh's *Harriet the Spy* (1964) as a watershed book in the New Realism for children: "Its harshness and candor gave a new definition to realism. It was satirical and astringent in its portrayal of adult society and, even more shocking, it questioned what had heretofore been an inviolable tenet in a child's life: do not tell a lie" (33). In *Harriet the Spy*, a privileged young girl who is being raised by her nanny, Ole Golly, keeps a blunt diary based on her daily "spy route" and her unflattering observations of her peers at school. When her diary falls into the hands of her classmates, she must face their anger and apologize. The end of the novel shows her growing into her vocation as a writer by taking on a partial editorship of the school newspaper, and subtly growing in empathy toward her friends and classmates.

A number of New Realist works were developed for the young adult market. Robert Lipsyte's *The Contender* (1967) tells the story of Alfred, a high-school dropout living in a chaotic and violent Harlem neighborhood. Training as a boxer in Donatelli's gym, he is inspired not to become a professional fighter but to complete high school and seek out a meaningful vocation. S.E. Hinton's *The Outsiders* (1967) dramatizes the violent tension between two rival gangs: the impoverished Greasers and the affluent Socs. Michael Cart writes of Hinton: "She wasn't writing about tree-shaded streets in small-town America.

Instead, she was writing about mean urban streets where teenagers didn't have time to agonize over first love and dates for the prom; they were too busy agonizing over whether they would survive the next battle in their ongoing war with a rival gang" (43–44). Hinton wrote *The Outsiders* while in her teens, which deepened the impression that the book reflected genuine adolescent culture, as recounted by an insider: the quintessence of realism. Paul Zindel's *The Pigman* (1968) is the story of a group of adolescents who befriend an older, vulnerable man whom they later betray. With Robert Cormier's *The Chocolate War* (1974), there was further development of the form, as Cormier took an unstinting look at the role of conformity and social pressure by depicting an adolescent boy's refusal to sell chocolates in defiance of his teachers and the Vigils, a secret society in his school. Not only was the book critical of bullying, it explored corruption among teachers and school administrators.

Judy Blume was one of the most important figures in the development of New Realism for children and young adults, especially for female readers. Joseph Michael Sommers argues that Blume's writing "spoke to [young women] about difficult issues when no one else would" (262). Evidence of this power to connect with readers can be found in a collection of essays edited by Jennifer O'Connell: *Everything I Needed to Know about Being a Girl I Learned from Judy Blume* (2007), in which women writers link Blume's stories to their lives, usually in terms of sexual maturation and coming of age but just as often in terms of family conflicts such as divorce or a dominant younger brother.

New Realist works are often conflated— not always fairly—with a genre known as the **problem novel**. In problem novels, plot, characters, and even language are defined—and constrained—by a focus on a single problem or set

Aspiring Spy Harriet M. Welsch, illustrated by author Louise Fitzhugh in *Harriet the Spy* (1964).

of problems, such as drug use, divorce, or teen pregnancy. The term "problem novel" is often read as indicating that a work is not well crafted or aesthetically significant. Sheila Egoff argues that in problem novels "the conflict stems from the writer's social conscience; it is specific rather than universal, and narrow in its significance rather than far-reaching" (67). She complains that problem novels, with their "clear-cut topical subjects, their lack of background and depth, and the prevalence of dialogue, require little adjustment from the inveterate TV watcher" (77). Michael Cart traces the fall in the literary status of the problem novel, noting, "Though technically the problem novel and the realistic novel are synonymous," the difference between them grew at the end of the 1970s, as the realistic novel was "gradually evolving into a richer and more rewarding kind of fiction" (71). New Realist novels, unlike problem novels, cannot be reduced to a single problem or resolvable situation; they address a wider sphere of child and adolescent experience.

Contemporary New Realism

Writers working in the realist tradition today include Louis Sachar, Susan Patron, Jack Gantos, Jeff Kinney, Sharon M. Draper, Linda Sue Park, Jacqueline Woodson, John Green, and Jerry Spinelli. This already long list leaves out several dozen authors working to produce realist books for children and young adults, testifying to the variety of realist works on the market. Below we discuss some of the themes explored by contemporary New Realism.

Diversity in New Realist Fiction

Emerging from a desire to provide fiction relevant to readers' lives, contemporary realist works sometimes address questions of gender, sexuality, race, ethnicity, social class, and disability directly. In terms of appealing to female readers, Sarah Dessen's recent YA novels are reminiscent of Judy Blume's work in their focus on the problems and opportunities faced by young girls. In *Saint Anything* (2015), when the brother of protagonist Sydney severely injures a young boy when driving while intoxicated, she is disturbed by her family's denial of his guilt. The friends Sydney makes at her new school, and her new boyfriend Mac, are a source of solace and help her come to terms with her family's dysfunction and her own shame over her brother's crime. Dessen has a thriving fan community which reaches out in particular to female readers.

We discuss several realist works that engages with race in Chapter 10, sometimes intersecting with concerns of social class. One example among many works of realist fiction that engage with both race and class is Eric Gansworth's *If I Ever Get Out of Here* (2014), which tells the story of Lewis "Shoe" Blake, who lives on the Tuscarora Indian reservation (New York) in the 1970s. He makes friends with a white boy, George Haddonfield, who shares his enthusiasm for music (particularly the Beatles); their friendship ultimately remains strong, but the novel frankly explores the complexities of navigating race and class differences. Gansworth's novel is also notable for its exploration of racially motivated bullying at school, including the failure of school authorities to respond to it effectively. In Chapter 11, we discuss several realist works that engage with sexuality and gender roles.

For example, emily m. danforth's *The Miseducation of Cameron Post: A Novel* (2012), which is set in Miles City, Montana, depicts the recently orphaned Cameron Post's discovery of her lesbian sexuality and resistance to it from her conservative Christian Aunt Ruth, and a broader evangelical Christian community.

Several recent texts in the realist vein have explored the issue of disability, especially in reference to social acceptance and schooling. In Sharon M. Draper's *Out of My Mind* (2012), Melody is a brilliant young girl with cerebral palsy, who is unable to communicate with the people around her until she gets a MediTalker and begins to express herself in language, emerging into a sometimes stressful but ultimately rewarding world of social relationships. In R.J. Palacio's *Wonder* (2012) August (Auggie) Pullman is a fifth grader with a facial abnormality which has required him to have many surgeries. He has been homeschooled all of his educational career, but the novel begins as his parents send him to Beecher Prep for fifth grade, where he endures bullying and social friction, but also makes friends. The novel is told from multiple points of view, including those of his schoolmates, his sister, and his sister's boyfriend, ultimately charting not just Auggie's development but also the gradual emergence of a supportive community outside his family. Many readers find the book stirring and inspiring, although the novel's stress on interpersonal amity and Auggie's heroic endurance of the challenges that face him might also be read as sentimentalizing disability. The affluence of Auggie's family—and the lack of attention to the financial costs of his medical treatments and assistive technology—is another way in which the book can be said to gloss over some of the challenges of disability. In Francisco X. Stork's *Marcelo in the Real World* (2011), the titular character has an unspecified cognitive impairment, described in the text as "Asperger's-like," where he hears music no one else can hear and has a singular devotion to religion. Marcelo's father, a driven lawyer, forces him to take a summer job in the mailroom of his firm, to force him to acquire experience of the neurotypical "real world." Sorting through case files, Marcelo finds a picture of an injured girl: one of their clients is trying to evade responsibility for defective windshields. Under pressure to defend his father's interests and overlook the evidence, he follows the ethical imperative to hold the manufacturer responsible. The "real world" of the title is implicitly critiqued by Marcelo's burgeoning awareness of treachery, although disability scholars also note that Marcelo's work in the "real world" could be read as implying that people on the autism spectrum must be integrated into neurotypical and mainstream society to be successful.

New Realism and Series Books

In the fantasy genre, series books are well suited to facilitating **worldbuilding**, or the construction of a consistent, coherent, and developed fantasy environment. Realist texts are also frequently published in series form, which allows for a similar development of the characters and their environment. The eight books of Beverly Cleary's Ramona series, for example, are for younger readers and center on a young girl's interactions with school, friends, and family. Annie Barrows's Ivy and Bean series, illustrated by Sophie Blackall, centers on the friendship of two apparently different young girls, who find that they in fact have a great deal in common and who cement their friendship through a series of adventures and pranks. Phyllis Reynolds Naylor's Alice series (1985–2013) comprises 25 books in the main series and three prequels. Because the Alice books were published over a period of 28 years, Naylor was able to explore Alice throughout her growth and development (and the last book takes her all the way to age 60). Naylor deliberately set out to write a series about an ordinary girl, as opposed to one with extraordinary talents, and this is perhaps one reason that readers have embraced it so fully. Alice McKinley grows up in Silver Springs, Maryland, with her father and her brother, Lester, her mother having died when she was five. The series includes the exploits of her three best friends, her first boyfriend, Patrick, and second boyfriend, Sam, and the remarriage of her father to her language arts teacher Sylvia Summers. The series deals frankly with issues of maturation and sexuality and has been the target of censorship attempts, like Blume's work. The Alice series is particularly notable for moving from middle-grade books to young adult books, as Alice herself grows up.

New Realism and Trauma

Several works of realism, particularly those written for the young adult audience, depict extreme trauma that the reader may have experienced or may only be empathizing with at a distance. Laurie Halse Anderson's *Speak* (1999) features Melinda, a protagonist who isolates herself and stops speaking altogether, until her work on an art project leads her to confront the fact she was raped by a classmate at an end-of-the-year party. Stephen Chbosky's *The Perks of Being a Wallflower* (1999) is an epistolary novel in which Charlie, an introverted teenager, writes a series of letters to an anonymous stranger. Charlie's best friend Michael has committed suicide, and his favorite Aunt Helen dies earlier in his childhood. Later in the novel, it is revealed that his Aunt Helen sexually abused him as a young child, and he has repressed the memory.

Reading realistic books critically involves attention to the literary techniques used to create believable plots, characterizations, and settings. Even if the young reader has not directly experienced the events depicted in the novel, the author must evoke them in such a way that the reader feels they could happen. The prominence of trauma narratives for children and young adults suggest a need on the part of young readers to master difficult experiences. Stories are used to learn about or heal from psychological wounds.

FANTASY AND REALISM IN PICTUREBOOKS

Picturebooks are produced in both fantastic and realistic modes. As in longer chapter books, a picturebook's plot and characters help determine whether it is fantastic or realistic. Fantasy texts include magic; realistic texts include only things that could happen in the real world. In the case of picturebooks, however, a book's visual style also helps position it as fantastic or realistic. *Alexander and the Terrible, Horrible, No Good, Very Bad Day* (1972) by Judith Viorst, with illustrations by Ray Cruz, is one example of a realistic picturebook. Its depiction of the frustrations of a young boy—who wakes up with gum in his hair, trips on a skateboard, and learns he has a cavity at the dentist—speaks to children who have had similar experiences (or have themselves experienced a "terrible, horrible, no good, very bad day"). Ray Cruz's pen-and-ink drawings are also quite lifelike, with detailed depictions of Alexander's facial expressions. William Steig's *Sylvester and*

Alexander starts his day on the "wrong side of the bed" in *Alexander and the Terrible, Horrible, No Good, Very Bad Day* (1972) by Judith Viorst, illustrated by Ray Cruz.

the Magic Pebble (1970) is an example of a fantasy picturebook. Sylvester is a donkey who collects unusual pebbles; he finds a bright red pebble that grants wishes when he holds it. Encountering a lion, he rashly wishes he was a rock and then is unable to reach the pebble that would allow him to transform from a rock back into a donkey. When his grieving parents go for a picnic, they use the Sylvester-rock as a picnic table, notice the pebble, and place it on top of the table, which allows him to wish himself back into donkey form. One of the most intriguing aspects of the book is its imagination of both animal and mineral sentience, especially during Sylvester's time as an immobile rock who wishes he could become a donkey again.

AUTHORS WORKING IN BOTH FANTASY AND REALISM

Whereas some authors excel at one genre only, others produce work within both fantasy and realism. Madeleine L'Engle was a prolific writer who moved freely between fantasy and realism, producing science fantasy, realistic coming-of-age stories, and political thrillers. L'Engle's fantastic works (which straddle the boundaries between fantasy and science fiction) include time travel, magic talismans, and travel to different planets and galaxies. In her realistic works, characters struggle with the difficulties of family life, school, relationships, and other travails of growing up. It is clear that genre has an important role in shaping her novels, not only setting the tone of the books but determining the kind of events possible in the plot. In her fantasy *A Wrinkle in Time* (1962), a young girl must travel to a distant planet to fight the intractable will of the evil giant brain "IT." In her realistic text *A Ring of Endless Light* (1980), the action focuses on a young girl's coming to terms with the impending death of her grandfather, her own vocation, and the competing (and inconsistent) attentions of three young male suitors. *A Wrinkle in Time* might well be described as **science fantasy**, a mixed genre that combines elements of both fantasy and science fiction. *A Ring of Endless Light* combines the conventions of romance with the young adult coming-of-age novel, or **bildungsroman**. Despite these differences, both novels explore the notion of the contribution that single individuals can make to the world around them. In newer editions of some of L'Engle's works, she includes a "family tree" of the major characters from her corpus of books and how they are related. Most of her books revolve around two families: the Murry-O'Keefes, who represent "kairos" ("real-time, pure numbers with no measurement" [L'Engle n.p.]) and the Austins, who represent "chronos" ("ordinary, wrist-watch, clock time" [L'Engle n.p.]). This division seems quite clear, but it is complicated by the fact that all the novels—whether kairos or chronos—are interrelated. Some of the characters from L'Engle's realistic books also appear in her fantastic books, indicating that there is less of a gap between the fantastic and the realistic than there might seem. The overlap between kairos and chronos implies that the everyday matter of life—the material usually treated by realistic fiction—is connected to the magical and supernatural conditions we would ordinarily describe as part of the fantastic.

Virginia Hamilton is another author who made major contributions in both genres. Her Newbery Medal–winning *M.C. Higgins, the Great* (1974) is a realistic coming-of-age story set in eastern Kentucky, where the protagonist confronts the environmental degradation caused by strip mining that threatens his family's home. In Hamilton's fantasy novel *Dustland* (1980) (the second book in the Justice Cycle), Dorian, Thomas, Levi, and Justice possess extrasensory perception and travel to a decimated future world in order to share much-needed information with the mutated humans there. Lois Lowry has written speculative fiction, especially *The Giver* (1993), which posits a world of "sameness," devoid of color, emotion, and historical consciousness. She is equally well known for her realistic fiction, such as *A Summer to Die* (1977), which explores a young girl's reaction to her sister's death, and the Anastasia Krupnik books, a series about a young girl aimed at readers in the middle grades.

Rainbow Rowell directly explores the relationship between fantasy and realism in her companion books *Fangirl* (2013) and *Carry On* (2015). In *Fangirl*, she describes protagonist Cath's devotion to a fictional wizard named Simon Snow who appears in books written by Gemma T. Leslie. Cath is the author of a popular online fan fiction named *Carry On*, which romantically pairs Simon and his nemesis Baz. *Fangirl* is a realist text that explores the transformative aspects of being a fan of fantasy literature and the intricacies of family and romantic relationships. *Carry On: The Rise and Fall of Simon Snow* is a fantasy text that began when Rowell asked herself "what I'd do with [Simon] if he were in *my* story, instead of Cath's or Gemma's" (Author Note). While the Simon Snow of *Carry On* has some similiarities with the character in *Fangirl*, including his romantic relationship with his roommate Baz, it mostly stands alone, as it depicts Simon at Watford Academy of Magic battling the Insidious Humdrum, who seeks to drain the world of magic.

LITERARY GENRES AS A RESPONSE TO CHILDREN'S NEEDS

Debates about the role of fantasy and realism are often fueled by beliefs about what genres children need the most. We might return to an earlier moment in the twentieth century to get a sense of this conflict. The Superintendent of the Department of Work with Children at the NYPL from 1906 to 1941, Anne Carroll Moore, believed that children thrived on stories of the fantastic, in particular fairy tales. Stimulation of the imaginative faculties was of key importance to children's development as readers. In contrast, the educational researchers based at New York's Bank Street School, led by Lucy Sprague Mitchell, held that stories should be based on the objects, people, and things familiar to children from their immediate experiences. The anthology of readings they produced, the *Here and Now Story Book* (1921), represented, in the words of Leonard S. Marcus, "a direct challenge to the widely held view of librarians and publishers that fairy tales, myths, legends, and traditional nursery nonsense—the literature of 'once upon a time'—comprised the best introduction to literature for the young" (53).

Though individual readers may prefer either fantasy or realism to the exclusion of the other genre, most contemporary educators, librarians, and parents regard both modes as equally important for child and young adult readers, and so they try to make a wide range of fantasy and realistic texts available to young people. Fantasy is valued for its capacity to stretch children's imaginations and to help them learn to adapt to an unfamiliar world. Realism provides insight into existing human realities, helping children to reflect on the world they know well, but to see it from a new angle.

FANTASY ELEMENTS IN REALISTIC TEXTS, REALISTIC ELEMENTS IN FANTASY TEXTS

Realistic and fantastic modes are often seen as not mixing well. As one example, we might look at the early development of the TV show *Sesame Street* in the 1960s. Experts consulted in preproduction were concerned that children would not be able to distinguish between human actors and the fantastical puppets. Jim Henson explained to Caroll Spinney, the actor who portrayed both Big Bird and Oscar, that "the bird puppet and the trash grouch were created to add a fantasy element to the street scenes, which had tested so flat following the test shows." The production team had "overridden the objections of researchers who had advised against mixing the Muppets with humans on the street. The scientists preferred there be a line between fantasy and reality" (Davis 185). Yet both in *Sesame Street* and in the world of books, fantasy and realism mix all the time, and they mix quite well.

Predominantly realistic texts often contain fantastic elements. As Lewis Roberts observes,

> Realism does not necessarily preclude an author from utilizing other narrative techniques and borrowing from other literary genres, such as nonsense literature, symbolism and metaphor, and even fantasy. A number of realistic stories for children and adolescents employ magical realism by introducing a single element of the impossible into otherwise realistic settings in order to highlight or comment upon the reality that the story describes and the characters inhabit. (124–25)

In their turn, fantastic texts often include realistic concerns and conventions. Roni Natov remarks about the Harry Potter series,

> During a recent radio interview, a child called in to ask if [author J.K.] Rowling could please bring back Harry's parents. Respectfully and sorrowfully, she said she regretted that she couldn't do that. "You can't bring dead people back," she said. She had to set limits on what magic could and couldn't do, since it was important to keep these characters real. Even the magical ones are defined by their human as well as magical traits. The real world, then, becomes somewhat illuminated by these characters who can span both worlds. For example, teachers at Hogwarts can be imaginative and compassionate; they are also flighty, vindictive, dim-witted, indulgent, lazy, frightened, and frightening. Students are clever, kind, weak, cruel, snobbish. Lessons are inspiring and tedious—as in the best and worst of real schools. (253)

Readers can be engaged not only by Rowling's fantasy environment but also by the realistic interpersonal dynamics of Harry and his friends, including the teenage romances that play an increasing role in the later books.

Both fantasy and realism have the capacity to engage children on political and social issues. For example, the Harry Potter series tackles race and class discrimination when a Pureblood Wizard faction targets "Mudbloods" (Muggleborn wizards and witches). Although such struggles are set in a fantastic world, they have obvious relevance to struggles in our own political and social spheres.

Magical Realism

Magical realism, which has traditionally been associated with Latin American writers such as Gabriel García Márquez, combines realism and fantasy. In Don Latham's words, **magical realism** presents "a matter-of-fact world in which the extraordinary exists side by side with the mundane realities of everyday life" (59). Magical realism does not involve the creation of a separate fantasy environment such as Narnia or Middle Earth. It does, however, include the presence of magic in our own world, and in this way is similar to Townsend's notion of fantasy that inhabits our world and Mendlesohn's concept of the intrusion fantasy. In Latham's view, magical realism for young adults helps portray "an alternative—and perhaps subversive—view of society" (62). He offers three examples: Francesca Lia Block's *Baby Be-Bop* (the fifth of the Weetzie Bat series, 1995), David Almond's *Kit's Wilderness* (1999), and Isabel Allende's *City of the Beasts* (2002). In *Baby Be-Bop*, Dirk is beaten to a semiconscious state by a group of neo-Nazis but is visited by the ghosts of his father and great-grandmother. He sees a vision of his future boyfriend, Duck, with the help of a genie. In *Kit's Wilderness*, the title character encounters the spectral presence of all the children who were victims of mining disasters in his mining town in northern England and develops a magical, mystical connection with his friend John Askew. In *City of the Beasts*, Alex is initiated into the community of the People of the Mist in the Amazon and is transformed into his totemic animal: a black jaguar. As Latham notes:

> Each of these novels depicts a world that is realistic yet contains a kind of magic that is visible to those who know how to see, and each of the protagonists has, or develops, this ability to see. As a result, each learns things about himself, including the fact that he possesses a capacity for discerning the magic that permeates the physical world. While the realism provides a credible context, the magic drives the plot and plays a major role in shaping the identities of the protagonists. Moreover it is the incongruity between the realism and the magic that calls into question other aspects of the rational world and causes the protagonists to question the values and assumptions of the dominant society. (63–64)

As a genre, magical realism is marked by hybridity (or mixture), indicating that the line between the fantastic and the realistic is not absolute.

There are several fantasy–realism hybrids that do not fall into the magical realist category. One well-known example is Jack Gantos's *Dead End in Norvelt* (2011), which balances the realistic and the far-fetched in its depiction of a young boy's eventful summer in 1962 Norvelt, Pennsylvania. It won the Scott O'Dell Award for historical fiction, and it includes a series of photographs and background about the book's settings and references. The autobiographical nature of the book is further underscored by the fact that the main character is named Jack Gantos. Grounded for the summer after he is caught playing with his father's World War II rifle, Jack is only allowed to run errands and help out their neighbor, Miss Volker, who writes lively obituaries for the local paper and who has lost the use of her hands. Norvelt is a New Deal town built for poor families and is named after Eleanor Roosevelt, and Miss Volker's obituary project is a means for her to remain true to her pledge to Roosevelt to memorialize all of the town's original inhabitants. What shifts the book from straightforward memoir or realistic fiction are a number of elements that are—if not fantastical strictly speaking—highly implausible. In addition to the exaggerations of various quirky characters—especially the larger-than-life character of Jack Gantos's father—there is also an elaborate murder-mystery plot which stretches credulity. *Dead End in Norvelt* is, perhaps, best described as drawing from the tradition of the **tall tale**, where a story has unbelievable elements or exaggerates real events.

READING CRITICALLY: FANTASY AND REALISM

Shadowshaper

Daniel José Older's *Shadowshaper* (2014) combines fantasy and realism to tell the story of protagonist Sierra Santiago, a Puerto-Rican girl living in Bed-Stuy, Brooklyn. In Older's novel, Sierra
discovers that she is a shadowshaper, with the power to "transform spirit into form" (225). Sierra's development as an artist and shadowshaper is entangled with her defense of her community's culture against the interloper Dr. Jonathan Wick, a professor at Columbia University
who seeks to appropriate the magic powers held by Sierra's community for himself, and to kill
all of the original shadowshapers. Ultimately, Sierra discovers that she has inherited the role of
Lucera—the leader of the shadowshapers—from her grandmother Maria Carmen. Reviewers
have characterized Older's book as an "urban fantasy"—which simply indicates that it is a fantasy text that takes place in a city—and pointed out its debt to magical realism, which throws
the distinction between the real and the magical into doubt. Understanding *Shadowshaper*,
then, involves attention to both its realist and fantastic elements, as Sierra faces both quotidian challenges and enemies in the spiritual realm.

   In *Shadowshaper*, Older sought, first of all, to create a novel that represents the experiences
of people of color and one that reflects Brooklyn's ethnic and racial diversity. In an interview
with Ashley C. Ford, he noted that fantasy texts should represent our society's cultural and
racial diversity: "Even if it's infused with magical powers, or zombies, or whatever you'll have,
we should still be trying to tell the truth. Then, it becomes a question of what truth, how are
we telling it, and whose truth do we take the time to repeat?" (Ford). Sierra's Bed-Stuy neighborhood has a buzzing street life, where friends, family, and acquaintances banter affectionately. That community is also dealing with racialized police violence and gentrification. Her
best friend's brother Vincent "had been killed by the cops in the adjacent corner, just a few
steps from his own front door" (81), reflecting concerns about police violence in minority communities. As affluent white people move into the neighborhood, Sierra begins to feel like "the
out-of-place one" in a neighborhood she has lived in all her life:

> The place Sierra and Bennie used to get their hair done had turned into a fancy bakery of
> some kind, and yes, the coffee was good, but you couldn't get a cup for less than three
> dollars. Plus, every time Sierra went in, the hip, young white kid behind the counter gave
> her either the "don't-cause-no-trouble look or the I-want-to-adopt-you look." (81)

The novel opens when Sierra's friend Manny asks her to paint a mural on the "Tower," an unfinished high-rise: "the developers built the outer structure and then left it, abandoned and

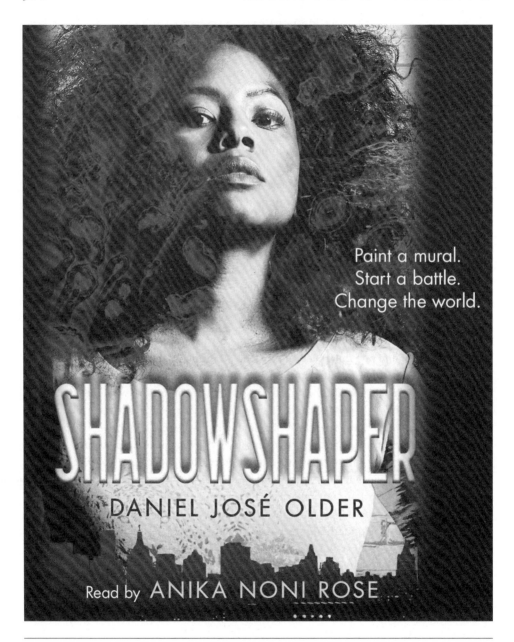

Paint a mural.
Start a battle.
Change the world.

SHADOWSHAPER

DANIEL JOSÉ OLDER

Read by ANIKA NONI ROSE

Cover image for *Shadowshaper* by Daniel José Older (2015).

unfinished, its unpaned windows staring emptily out into the Brooklyn skies" (2). Sierra's mural—an explicitly public form of art, free to all—is an act of defiance against the economic and political forces that exclude her because it is not sanctioned by the owners of the Tower and therefore carries some risk.

As we often see in realist novels, Sierra also faces opposition and friction within her own family. Her Tía Rosa disparages her romantic interest in Robbie because of his Haitian ancestry and his darker skin, an example of colorism within the Latino community, which occurs when lighter skin is privileged. Sierra's Abuelo (grandfather) Lázaro has suffered a stroke, moaning "lo siento" ("I am sorry") over and over again, drifting "further and further away as time went on" (69). Although he had told Sierra's brother about the shadows when he was ten years old, he withheld the knowledge from her out of the conviction that women should not be shadowshapers. Sexism, racism, and violence are portrayed realistically in the book and form the backdrop for the magic that Sierra discovers in her world and within herself.

In addition to the problems Sierra faces in the everyday, she is plunged into a spiritual or magical crisis. Early in the novel, Sierra is startled when the mural of her old family friend Papa Acevedo starts crying, and other murals in the neighborhood follow suit. Her grandfather urges her to contact Robbie, whom she barely knows, to ask him for help in completing her own mural. Robbie reveals his identity as a shadowshaper and explains to Sierra:

> The shadows come to me. When they're just in shadow form, they can't do much in the living world, just whisper and run around mostly. Some can do other stuff, but it takes a lot of their energy. But when I put their spirits into the painting—a form—they take on way more powers. (93)

Some of the shadows are "ancestors of us shadowshapers, some are just other folks that passed on and became spirits. But they're like our protectors, our friends even" (62–63). But Lucera, the leader of the shadowshapers, has gone missing. With her gone, the murals' connection to the spirits will be obliterated and they will fade. Robbie and Sierra—who are slowly falling in love—must try to find the true Lucera so that she can restore the magic of the shadowshapers again. Meanwhile, Jonathan Wick has been attempting to take on the role of Lucera—or Lucero—himself. Sierra gets access to Wick's journals, where he writes: "thanks to my extensive knowledge of other cultures and cosmological systems, I could benefit in far greater ways than anyone could foresee from [Lucera's] magic" (71). *Shadowshaper*, then, offers an interrogation of knowledge and power and the ways in which figures like Jonathan Wick, expert in "urban spirituality systems," attempt to control knowledge for themselves. As one of the other characters in the book, the archivist Nydia Ochoa, comments: "Who gets to study and who gets studied, and why? Who makes the decisions, you know?" (51).

Sierra and Robbie track Lucera to Coney Island, but are pursued by corpuscules, dead bodies with other spirits shoved into them. A terrified Sierra throws herself into the water, but to her surprise she hovers several feet over the water instead of drowning. Lucera comes to her and lifts her higher. Lucera is Maria Carmen, her own grandmother, dead in the physical world but living as a spirit. Hovering high over Brooklyn, Sierra learns that she is destined to take on the role of Lucera herself, although at the great cost of having to say goodbye to her grandmother, whose spirit will move on.

The final scenes in the novel are a direct showdown between Sierra and Wick, who has kidnapped Robbie and brought him to the abandoned Tower to co-opt his shadowshaping powers for evil purposes. It is no coincidence that the abandoned tower—a symbol and manifestation of gentrification—is the venue for this pivotal scene. As Amal El-Mohtar astutely notes in an NPR review: "the creeping gentrification of Sierra's neighbourhood and the person actually eliminating shadowshapers share the same narrative root: A well-meaning savior complex that, under the auspices of rescuing people, actually exploits, possesses and harms them" (El-Mohtar). Jonathan Wick is tied both to the gentrification that is stressed in the realist part of the novel and to the eradication of Shadowshapers that is part of the fantastic plot of the novel.

The book is clearly indebted to magical realism, where magic appears as part of the world we know. One example is a scene when Robbie takes Sierra to Club Kalfour, where he has painted several murals in his "distinctive graffiti-like style" (91). As Sierra and Robbie dance, she notices that they are infused with the spirits, and "bursting to life" (93). This rootedness in the world of spirit—the world that is hard to perceive unless very attentive to it—roots the book in fantastic traditions, but the book has an equal claim to realism, especially if you have a perspective that allows for the presence of the magical in the everyday. In a similar vein, Debbie Reese describes the magic in *Shadowshaper* as "that fabric of life that is the norm for Sierra's family and community" (Reese). Echoing one of the book's central themes, Robbie notes that to perceive magic people they need to look closely at the world around them: "It's just that people don't usually see it. Their minds won't let them, so it looks like a regular painting, not movin' or nothin'" (63). *Shadowshaper* is, ultimately, a novel about the permeability of the natural and spiritual realms, and the need to pay attention to both the world of the everyday and the world of magic.

EXPLORATIONS

Review

1. How would you define "genre"? How does the genre of a work condition or shape a reader's experience?

2. What are some of the attributes of fantasy? What are some of the attributes of realism? What are some similiarities between fantasy and realism?

3. Consider John Rowe Townsend's division of the fantastic into three categories: anthropomorphic fantasy, fantasies that create imaginary worlds or countries, and fantasies that inhabit the world we know but require some disturbance of the natural order of things. What are some examples of each kind discussed in the chapter? How are these modes of fantasy distinct?

4. Farah Mendelsohn has developed four categories of fantasy, largely based on how a reader is positioned vis à vis the magic or fantasy world. Name these four categories and explain how they work.

5. Why did new realism emerge as a genre in the 1960s and 1970s? What are some of its earliest examples, and how do they represent a shift from previous works for children and young adults?

6. Can realistic and fantastic modes be mixed in a single work? Are realism and fantasy always distinct genres? Why or why not?

Reflect

1. When you read a book, how aware are you of its genre? Based on your answer to this question, how important do you think genre is to the work produced?

2. Realistic books for children and young adults (such as Robert Cormier's *The Chocolate War*) are often described as "frank" and "disturbing." Yet fantasy texts also contain disturbing tropes of violence, conformity, and evil. Are realistic texts more prone to critique than fantasy texts? Why is this so? Draw on two or three books from any genre for your answer.

3. Consider a text that combines fantasy and realism, such as one of the texts listed in the magical realism section (pp. 377–78). How does magic work within the predominantly realistic setting?

4. Choose a fantasy text such as one of the Harry Potter books. If this fantasy text were to be turned into a realistic text, what elements would you need to remove? How much of the book would be lost? What sort of realistic elements would you need to add?

5. Sometimes in fantastical fictions, magical or fantastic actions are completed through very ordinary, nonmagical objects. At other times fantasy works rely on magical talismans. Consider two fantasy books and reflect on their use of objects (magical, nonmagical, or both). What is the significance of magical or nonmagical objects in fantasy literature?

Investigate

1. Read a fantasy series and evaluate the final work. Are you satisfied with the ending? If not, write a proposal for a new final installment. What made the original ending unsatisfying to you? What does your continuation tell you about the series?

2. Compare the illustrations of two realistic and fantastic texts. Do you see a difference in the way that realistic and fantasy books are illustrated?

3. Ask friends to list their favorite characters in children's literature, dividing these into fantastic and realistic characters. Do you see any patterns, or are the differences between these characters largely arbitrary?

4. The theme of coming of age is treated in both fantastic and realistic texts. Choose an aspect of the coming-of-age story and look at how it is treated in both fantastic and realistic texts. How does the genre of a work affect the treatment of this theme in the story?

SUGGESTED READINGS

Fantasy

Le Guin, Ursula. *A Wizard of Earthsea* **(1968).** In Le Guin's Earthsea fantasy series, a wizard named Ged battles a rival, Jasper, which brings forth a shadow-monster. The series follows Ged as he gains control over his own temperament and grows in magical ability.

Lewis, C.S. *The Lion, the Witch and the Wardrobe* **(1950).** Part of a seven-book series devoted to the fantasy land of Narnia, this book follows four children who enter this world through a wardrobe, then battle the evil White Witch. The book is notable for its overt Christian allegory as well as pagan elements such as fauns and talking animals.

Miéville, China. *Un Lun Dun* **(2007).** Heavily influenced by Lewis Carroll's Alice books, *Un Lun Dun* is set in an alternative London inhabited by trash discarded by the inhabitants of the actual city. Twelve-year-old Zanna is destined to save the city of Un Lun Dun from the evil, sentient cloud of pollution known as the Smog, but her friend Deeba (the "UnChosen") completes the task instead. The book presents both a fully elaborated secondary world and a series of magical objects who act independently, such as Unbrellas (broken umbrellas) and the pet milk carton Curdle.

Tolkien, J.R.R. *The Hobbit; or, There and Back Again* **(1937).** Bilbo Baggins goes on an epic quest to win treasure from the dragon Smaug. This book is the precursor to the vast epic *The Lord of the Rings*. As a high fantasy text, *The Hobbit* also includes elements of the fairy tale and initiated a tradition of quest fantasy writing.

Realism

Blume, Judy. *Deenie* **(1973).** Told from a first-person point of view, *Deenie* is about an attractive girl who is diagnosed with scoliosis and who must then wear a back brace and navigate parental pressure. The book has been repeatedly subject to censorship attempts due to a brief scene in which Deenie masturbates.

Fitzhugh, Louise. *Harriet the Spy* **(1964).** Precocious Harriet keeps a diary where she records blisteringly frank thoughts about her family, friends, and classmates. When her classmates find her notebook, she is ostracized and must learn to balance her budding vocation as a writer (and spy) with increased empathy toward others.

Spinelli, Jerry. *Wringer* (1997). Palmer lives in a town where a pigeon shoot is held every year at Family Fest, an event to raise money for a community park. Once the pigeons have fallen, ten-year-old boys are expected to wring the pigeons' necks and kill them. Palmer rebels against this tradition due to his rapport with a pigeon called Nipper. The book is a clear example of realism, but it has an almost surreal quality due to the bizarre rituals of the town and its violent child culture.

Combinations of Fantasy and Realism

Almond, David. *Skellig* (1998). Almond's realistic novel begins as Michael encounters a strange, wizened man called Skellig in the garage of his new family home. With his friend Mina, he discovers Skellig has wings, leading them to speculate that he is an angel. When Michael's infant sister goes for a heart operation, his mother dreams of Skellig, and the surgery is successful. Though unclear about Skellig's true nature, Almond implies that the family has been helped by supernatural intervention.

Funke, Cornelia. *The Thief Lord* (2000). After their mother's death, brothers Prosper and Bo run away to Venice, where they become members of a gang led by Scipio, the Thief Lord of the title, and live in the "Stella," an abandoned movie theater. The realistic criminal underbelly of Venice is combined with a carousel's startling magic, which transforms adults into children and ages children into adults.

Stead, Rebecca. *When You Reach Me* (2009). Set in 1970s New York, the book follows the protagonist, Miranda, a huge fan of *A Wrinkle in Time*, as she attempts to understand the mysterious notes she is receiving. Despite the realistic setting, the book is both a science fiction text, since it includes time travel, and a mystery novel, since Miranda must figure out who left the notes and what they mean.

APPROACHES TO TEACHING *SHADOWSHAPER* [SECONDARY SCHOOL]

Preparation for the Lesson

Students will read the novel in advance of the class.

Learning Goals

- To consider the ways in which Daniel José Older's *Shadowshaper* draws on both fantasy and realism

- To reflect on the heroines of YA fantasy, and the ways Older sought to reflect Brooklyn's racial diversity in fantasy fiction as he crafted *Shadowshaper*

- To practice writing a compare and contrast essay with two different literary texts.

Activity One: Fantasy and Realism

Part 1: Enemies: Realistic and Fantastic

Sierra and her friends and family face many antagonists, both supernatural and realistic. As well, she faces opposition within her family (particularly her Tía Rosa and grandfather). In class, make a list of the antagonists and combative characters Sierra encounters in the book. What are the differences between the antagonists she encounters in everyday life and those she confronts as she deals with the crisis in shadowshaping? Students will then write a brief essay comparing the enemies of the realist plot of the book with those of the fantastic plot of the book, with some attention to how these antagonisms overlap.

Part 2: Art Making in *Shadowshaper*

Much of the art making in *Shadowshaper* centers on murals and public art. In class, take a look at the passages in the novel that describe Sierra and Robbie's art making, and consider why Older chooses to foreground this kind of artistic activity in the book. If there is public art near your school, bring in photographs of it, or ask the students to visit it, and discuss the ways it functions in the urban landscape. For more information about public art, and/or for images to use in class, you might consult Rafael Schacter and John Fekner's *The World Atlas of Street Art and Graffiti* (2013) and Nicholas Ganz's *Graffiti World: Street Art from Five Continents* (updated edition, 2009). Students would then write a brief essay about the role of public art in their community (if applicable) as compared to Sierra's. If students do not have any public art near them, they can focus their essay on the uses and importance of public art in *Shadowshaper*.

Activity 2: Conventions of Fantasy

Part 1: Magical Destiny

In many fantasy novels, the character becomes aware of their singular destiny or role when they are informed of it directly. For example, Hagrid famously tells Harry: "You're a wizard, Harry!" In class, discuss the ways in which Sierra becomes aware of her identity as a shadowshaper and as Lucera in Older's novel. Write a brief essay comparing Sierra's emergence into her magic destiny with that of Harry, or another magical figure. How does Sierra's discovery of her magic powers and destiny as Lucera affect her development as a person?

Part 2: Diversity in Children's and YA Fantasy Fiction

In a guest post on the blog *The Brown Bookshelf*, Daniel José Older described his motivations for writing *Shadowshaper*: "I had grown up like many sci-fi/fantasy dorks, wondering where I fit into all those wild worlds of monsters and space battles. I was working with black and brown kids in Bushwick and Bed-Stuy and they were wondering the same thing" (Older, *The Brown Bookshelf*). With this quotation in mind, read one or two examples of recent children's or YA fantasy fiction recommended by the We Need Diverse Books Tumblr or blog. If you need some place to start, try one or more of these books:

> Octavia Butler, *Fledgling* (2005)
> Nnedi Okorafor, *Zahrah the Windseeker* (2008) and *Akata Witch* (2011)
> Sabaa Tahir, *An Ember in the Ashes* (2016)

After reading one of the recommended fantasy texts from the We Need Diverse Books Tumblr, compare the heroine or hero in that book to Sierra in *Shadowshaper*.

To build on this exercise you might compare Sierra to some other fantasy female protagonists you might know from your previous reading, such as Katniss Everdeen, Hermione Granger, Tris Prior, or Meg Murry. What does she have in common with these heroines, and how is she different?

RACE, ETHNICITY, AND CULTURE

Children, childhood, and children's culture have served as key sites for constructing and representing racial and ethnic communities and identities. In some cases, children's literature has worked to reproduce and reinforce racial and ethnic hierarchies, while in others it serves as an important vehicle for antiracist thought. The representation of different races, ethnicities, or cultures in children's literature involves a complex set of issues that demand we read critically and think carefully. This chapter is divided into two major parts. In the first, we briefly survey the history of racial, ethnic, and cultural representation in children's literature, including depictions of peoples of African and Asian descent, Jewish and Latinx cultures, Native Americans and First Nations, and colonized subjects of the British Empire. Rather than providing a comprehensive catalog, we note a few landmark moments, texts, or authors that stand out as either especially groundbreaking or particularly problematic, and we include an overview of various awards and prizes being used to recognize and promote the publication of ethnically or culturally diverse children's literature. In the second part, we encounter some of the more controversial aspects of this history and provide a set of tools and concepts to help the reader think critically about these controversies.

Opposite: Shaun Tan's wordless graphic novel *The Arrival* (2007) tells the story of immigrants of all creeds and colors attempting to forge new lives for themselves in a city that is both strange and awe-inspiring.

THE HISTORY OF RACE, ETHNICITY, AND CULTURE IN CHILDREN'S LITERATURE

The Early History of Racial Representation in Children's Literature

The history of ethnic children's literature is much briefer than the history of children's literature more generally. In nineteenth-century American children's literature, characters of color appeared mostly as secondary to white protagonists and as stereotyped caricatures. Gail Schmunk Murray explains,

> When black characters appear in children's fiction in the latter half of the nineteenth century, they are rarely distinguished from the slaves of the old South.... [Children's writers] portrayed African-Americans only in subservient roles, in which their docility, simple-mindedness, and penchant for having a good time bolstered their creator's confidence in the racial hierarchies they embraced. (125)

Martha Finley's *Elsie Dinsmore* (1867), one of the top-selling children's books of the latter half of the nineteenth century, is set on a Southern plantation before the Civil War and depicts the slaves as flat characters who speak in dialect and appear only when serving or being spoken to by white characters. According to Donnarae MacCann, "With the exception of a few abolitionist narratives, [nineteenth-century] children's books have generally treated Black characters stereotypically, or they have excluded them entirely" (xvi). When African Americans were depicted as central characters, as in Jacob Abbott's *Congo* (1857), they were presented in ways that reinforced racial hierarchies and racist thought. Congo's white employer is told by his grandfather, "It is one of the characteristics of the colored people to like to be employed by other people, rather than take responsibility and care upon themselves" (qtd. in MacCann 13). Usually produced by white writers with little investment or experience with thinking beyond traditional racial hierarchies, these depictions of racial difference in children's literature socialized child readers into the racist ideologies of the broader culture.

The abolition movement during the middle decades of the nineteenth century did produce a number of slave narratives for children that had African American protagonists, but many of these works were written by anonymous white authors to promote abolitionism among white children. Though designed as anti-slavery propaganda, these abolitionist stories often promoted racial stereotypes and the inferiority of African Americans. MacCann notes that even publications such as *The Child's Anti-Slavery Book: Containing a Few Words about American Slave Children and Stories of Slave-Life* (1859) contained "mixed signals with regard to the humanity and equality of Blacks" (10). Though white abolitionists opposed the institution of slavery, they did not always embrace the full humanity of African Americans or take care to transcend the racial stereotypes that defined the dominant ideologies of their historical and cultural contexts.

Even works that served to critique slavery or racism, such as Harriet Beecher Stowe's *Uncle Tom's Cabin* (1852) or Mark Twain's *Adventures of Huckleberry Finn* (1884), also tended to fall back on easily recognizable stereotypes or expectations of people of color. In the latter, for instance, Jim repeatedly endangers himself in rescuing Huck, and he ultimately sacrifices his freedom to care for the wounded Tom Sawyer. Jim also allows Huck and Tom to torture him while the boys plan Jim's escape as a game. Moreover, while Tom's and Huck's family situations are explored and developed, the novel provides little insight into Jim's relationship with his wife and children. The emphasis of the novel is clearly on the lives and psychologies of the two white boys even as Twain uses the depiction of the slave Jim to critique the experience of African Americans during Reconstruction.

British children's literature of the nineteenth century was similarly mired in racist representations and racial hierarchies that privileged white Britons over colonial subjects of color. R.M. Ballantyne's *The Coral Island* (1857), discussed at length in Chapter 6, depicts the native Fijian islanders as lawless and violent savages who are tamed by European conquest and Christian values. Such sentiments were typical of British children's literature in the nineteenth century. M. Daphne Kutzer contends that "some of the most revered of British children's texts support the culture of imperialism" (xv); she defines "imperialism" as including as a central component "the promotion of the racial superiority of white Europeans, and especially Englishmen, over darker-skinned non-Europeans" (xvii). Mavis Reimer discusses one classic text, Frances Hodgson Burnett's serialized novella "Sara Crewe" (1887), which was later expanded into the novel *A Little Princess* (1905), in precisely these terms. Reimer argues that the story "is as much about an imperial child coming to power as it is about a powerless child beset by powerful adults," which, she says, is "evident in Burnett's representation of the racialized other. In the 1887 text, the unnamed servant is a curious composite of British stereotypes of Indian men" (116).

This kind of problematic representation of racialized "Others" continued in British children's literature well into the twentieth century, from Hugh Lofting's *The Story of Dr. Dolittle* (1920) and *The Voyages of Dr. Dolittle* (1922) to Roald Dahl's *Charlie and the Chocolate Factory* (1964), each of which has been criticized for its depiction of race. *Dr. Dolittle* includes the character Bumpo, an African prince who lives in a palace made of mud and longs to be turned white because Sleeping Beauty, whom he loves, does not like Black men. Contemporary editions of the novel eliminate this plot point entirely. In the original version of *Charlie and the Chocolate Factory*, the Oompa-Loompas are African pygmies Willy Wonka has saved from extinction and brought to England to work in his factory. Newer editions of the work describe them as fantastic creatures from Loompaland, seeking to eliminate the overt racial references.

African American Children's Literature

The late nineteenth and early twentieth centuries saw an increase in ethnic children's literature, and writers of color began to make their own contributions that combated the mostly racist and stereotyped depictions that prevailed. In their collection on African American children's literature before 1900, Katharine Capshaw and Anna Mae Duane identify Amelia E. Johnson's *Clarence and Corinne; or, God's Way* (1890) as the first children's novel by an African American author (xix), though they note its ambiguous status because of the "absence of clear racial descriptors for the characters" (xxii). Violet J. Harris cites Paul Laurence Dunbar's book of dialect poems titled *Little Brown Baby* (1895) as one possible starting point for a distinctly African American children's literature (544). Capshaw Smith has written about the importance of children's literature during the New Negro Movement, or Harlem Renaissance, beginning in the 1920s. "At the dawn of the Harlem Renaissance, intellectual giant W.E.B. Du Bois reinvented conceptions of black childhood and instituted the genre of black children's literature," Smith writes (*Children's Literature* 1). Du Bois and the National Association for the Advancement of Colored People (NAACP) began publishing a children's issue of the literary journal *Crisis* in 1912, and they started a magazine specifically for children called *The Brownies' Book* in 1920. The Crisis Publishing Company released Mary White Ovington's *Hazel* (1913), about an African American girl who travels from Boston to Alabama to live with her grandmother and recover her health. *Hazel* offers a fully developed and sympathetic black protagonist, and Ovington, who was white, describes her book as written for African American children who might like to see characters like themselves in fiction.

Compiled by Julius Lester and illustrated with paintings by Tom Feelings, *To Be a Slave* (1968) tells the story of slavery in the United States through the words of slaves and ex-slaves.

Harlem Renaissance writers such as Langston Hughes and Arna Bontemps also began writing for children in the 1930s. According to Capshaw Smith, Du Bois wanted to "include children in the fight for civil rights" and "politicize young people" (*Children's Literature* 28). This racially affirmative children's literature of the first few decades of the twentieth century, which raised the social and political consciousness of a generation of children, helped pave the way for the Civil Rights Movement of the 1950s and 1960s. Murray notes that the period after World War II marked a turning point in American children's literature: "After the civil rights activity of the 1950s and early sixties, more literature featuring African American and Native American protagonists appeared at all levels, from picture books to young adult novels" (201). By the 1960s, the age of multicultural children's literature was in full swing.

The 1970s were a landmark decade in African American children's literature. Virginia Hamilton became the first African American writer to win the Newbery Medal in 1975 for *M.C. Higgins, the Great* (1974), and two years later Mildred D. Taylor would win for *Roll of Thunder, Hear My Cry* (1976). Lucille Clifton published her first books for children in 1970, *The Black BCs* and *Some of the Days of Everett Anderson*. Julius Lester's career was well under way by the 1970s after his *To Be a Slave* (1968) received Newbery Honor status in 1969. Walter Dean Myers also began his career in the 1970s, and he too would receive the Newbery Honor award in 1989 for *Scorpions* and again in 1993 for *Somewhere in the Darkness*. His book *Monster* (1999) was the first winner ever of the Printz Award for young adult literature. These writers paved the way for others such as Angela Johnson and Jacqueline Woodson, who started publishing children's and young adult literature with African American protagonists in the late 1980s and early 1990s.

The importance of African American representation to the Civil Rights Movement's anti-racist struggles foregrounds the social and political implications of African American children's literature. For instance, in Renée Watson's Coretta Scott King Award winner *Piecing Me Together* (2017), Jade repeatedly encounters bias because of her race, such as being asked to leave her bag behind the counter at a store while white shoppers are permitted to keep theirs. The novel shows racism as a fact of everyday life for an African American teenager. Other recent works contribute to the ongoing struggle for social and political equality by addressing issues like police violence against young people of color. Jason Reynolds and Brendan Kiely's *All American Boys* (2015) depicts the police beating of an African

First published by W.E.B. du Bois and the NAACP in 1920, *The Brownies' Book* promoted the publication of black children's literature.

American youth wrongly accused of shoplifting. Reynolds and Kiely use alternating narrators to provide different perspectives: Rashad, the boy who is beaten, and his white classmate Quinn, who witnesses the incident. Angie Thomas's *The Hate U Give* (2017), inspired by the Black Lives Matter movement, focuses on an African American girl named Starr who witnesses her unarmed friend Khalil get shot and killed by a police officer. Thomas's bestselling novel depicts the community protests following Khalil's death and the teenage Starr's important role in response to the tragedy. These works suggest the ongoing need for literature to represent the lives of African American youth and their contributions to social change.

Jewish Children's Literature

Landmarks of ethnic children's literature came in swift succession in the latter half of the twentieth century, and a number of Jewish American writers made significant contributions to writing for children. H.A. and Margret Rey, German-born Jews who fled Paris to escape the German invasion, published their first Curious George book in 1941. In 1951, Sydney Taylor published the first of her All-of-a-Kind Family series, which June Cummins describes as bringing "Jewish children's literature into the mainstream of American society" (395). Judy Blume, a Jewish American author, published her first children's book in 1969; her third, *Are You There God? It's Me, Margaret* (1970), was published only a year later and deals explicitly with Margaret's Jewish heritage. Johanna Reiss's *The Upstairs Room* (1972), a novel about the Holocaust, was designated a Newbery Honor book in 1973. A number of other Jewish writers were among the most important and successful children's writers during this period, including Ezra Jack Keats, whose *The Snowy Day* (1962) was the first Caldecott-winning book with an African American protagonist, and Maurice Sendak, whose *Where the Wild Things Are* (1963) won the Caldecott Medal in 1964, the year after Keats. In 1967, Jewish writer Robert Lipsyte published his own young adult novel, *The Contender*, a book Michael Cart argues is a greater literary success than S.E. Hinton's *The Outsiders*, also published that year. Along with *The Outsiders*, *The Contender* marks the emergence of the contemporary young adult novel. It has an African American protagonist, but one of its central characters is Jewish. More recently, David Wisniewski won the Caldecott Medal for *Golem* (1996), a picturebook retelling of the Jewish legend in which a sixteenth-century rabbi creates a golem, a supernatural being, to protect the Jewish people of Prague from racist violence.

Latinx Children's Literature

Latinx children's literature has been attaining greater prominence and literary recognition, with Latinxs of various national origins collectively constituting one of the fastest-growing demographics in the United States. A number of authors of Latin-American descent have been recognized for their work, including Pam Muñoz Ryan, whose novel *Esperanza Rising* (2000) is based on her grandmother's experience emigrating from Mexico to the United States, and Victor Martinez, whose young adult novel *Parrot in the Oven: Mi Vida* (1996), about a Mexican American boy growing up in California, won a National Book Award. Other notable writers who have contributed to the growing body of Latinx children's literature include Gary Soto, who began his career publishing poetry for adults before turning to children's literature; Pat Mora, who has written both poetry for young adults and picturebooks for younger children; and Juan Felipe Herrera, who is also a poet and picturebook writer; and recent YA writers such as Meg Medina and Isabel Quintero.

Asian American Children's Literature

The history of Asian American children's literature extends back to the nineteenth century, though only in recent decades have works by or about Asian Americans received more critical attention. According to Dolores de Manuel and Rocío G. Davis, who edited a special issue of *The Lion and the Unicorn: A Critical Journal of Children's Literature* on Asian American books for children, "These overlooked or forgotten writers continually show us how the story of Asian American writers has been marked by various forms of marginalization and erasure, and reshaped by their attempts to make themselves visible" (v). They note that Dhan Gopal Mukerji, who immigrated to the United States from India, was the first Asian American to receive the Newbery Medal in 1928 for *Gay-Neck: The Story of a Pigeon*, at the time only the seventh book to receive this prestigious prize. A number of other early Newbery Medal and Honor books, such as Arthur Bowie Chrisman's *Shen of the Sea* (1925) and Elizabeth Foreman Lewis's *Young Fu of the Upper Yangtze* (1932), depicted Asian characters or cultures, but these were written by European American writers and, according to de Manuel and Davis, possess "a decidedly Orientalist flavor" (v) that exoticizes Asian people and cultures. The early history of Asian American children's literature, like that of early books featuring African American children, is marked by racial stereotypes. One of the better-known examples is Claire Huchet Bishop and Kurt Wiese's *The Five Chinese Brothers* (1938), a picturebook that depicts the five brothers and all the townspeople as yellow colored and nearly identical, resonating with a common racist stereotype of Asians as visually indistinguishable.

The 1970s marked a critical turning point for Asian American children's literature. Chinese American author Laurence Yep published his first novel in 1973, and his book *Dragonwings* (1975) was chosen as a Newbery Honor book in 1976. De Manuel and Davis call *Dragonwings* "the first work to present a significant portrayal of the Asian American presence, dealing with Asians and their lives in America" (vi). In recent years, other Asian American writers for children have also received significant critical acclaim for works depicting Asian and Asian American characters and cultures, such as Linda Sue Park for *A Single Shard* (2001) and Cynthia Kadohata for *Kira-Kira* (2004), both winners of the Newbery Medal. In 2007, Gene Luen Yang won the Printz Award for his young adult graphic novel *American Born Chinese* (2006), which directly addresses the immigrant experience and stereotypes of Chinese Americans.

Native Americans and First Nations in Children's Literature

Perhaps because of the troubling association of Native Americans and First Nations with savagery—as well as the notion of children as savages (see Chapter 1)—and the prominence of North American frontier motifs in children's culture and games, some of the most canonical children's books in both Britain and the United States have included American Indian characters. The villain of Mark Twain's *The Adventures of Tom Sawyer* (1876) is Injun Joe, a half-white and half–Native American thief and murderer. Robert Louis Stevenson, best known for *Treasure Island* (1883), included frequent reference to Indians in his *A Child's Garden of Verses* (1885), a collection of poems for children discussed in Chapter 3. Representations of Native Americans famously appear in J.M. Barrie's classic *Peter and Wendy* (1911), in which they are referred to as "redskins." Laura Ingalls Wilder's well-known Little House series, first published in the 1930s and 1940s and detailing Wilder's life as a child pioneer, remains extremely controversial for the kind of comments about Native Americans described in Chapter 7. In Lynne Reid Banks's *The Indian in the Cupboard* (1980), a boy's plastic toy Indian comes to life and embodies many stereotypes of Native Americans, including the use of broken English: "Little Bear fight like mountain lion! Take many scalps" (37). Sharon Creech's Newbery Medal–winning novel, *Walk Two Moons* (1994), features a protagonist, Salamanca, whose great-great-grandmother was part Native American. Salamanca likes her "Indian-ness" because it makes her "appreciate the gifts of nature" and means she is "closer to the land" (57). Yet she lacks any substantive connection to the Seneca Nation, to which her great-great-grandmother presumably belonged. These works attest to the prominence of Native Americans in children's literature and the often problematic nature of these representations.

Numerous books like these by European American and British writers have engendered many of the critical controversies addressed later in this chapter, but Native

American and First Nations writers have made their own successful contributions to children's literature that speak back to and complicate these troubling and stereotypical representations. Louise Erdrich's *The Birchbark House* (1999) and its sequels provide a Native American perspective on life in the mid nineteenth century for an Ojibwe girl; they offer an alternative to the depiction of the frontier found in Wilder's Little House books. Sherman Alexie's *The Absolutely True Diary of a Part-Time Indian* (2007), a National Book Award winner, depicts the life of a fourteen-year-old Spokane Indian living in present-day Washington State. Another prominent Native American writer is Joseph Bruchac, who has published numerous folk-tale collections, novels, and picturebooks about the Native American experience. Canadian Métis writer Cherie Dimaline received the prestigous Canadian Governor General's Award for English-language children's literature for *The Marrow Thieves* (2017), a dystopian YA novel in which indigenous North Americans are hunted for a special property of their bone marrow.

When these authors write from the perspective of Native American children and young adults and with a thorough understanding of the history of indigenous peoples in North America, they are able to convey the full humanity and diversity of complex American Indian characters. Omakayas in *The Birchbark House* experiences the pain of losing loved ones and the hardships of life in the mid nineteenth century, as well as the security of being loved and wanted by her adopted family. Junior of *Absolutely True Diary* experiences common teenage challenges but also the particular feelings of a contemporary Indian youth caught between the culture of his "rez" and the opportunities of the public school in town. Jake in Bruchac's *The Warriors* (2003) plays high school lacrosse and courageously confronts stereotypes about Native Americans held by his teachers and classmates. Frenchie forms deep bonds with the other youths he lives with while on the run from the Recruiters in *The Marrow Thieves*. These characters are neither romanticized nor caricatured and offer a fuller picture of Native American and First Nations experiences that correct myths and misrepresentations and prompt deeper understandings than the statistics or summaries of textbooks or news broadcasts.

A WORD ABOUT ETHNICITY AND CULTURE

Werner Sollors points out that the term "ethnicity" dates only to the 1940s, and thus the notion that people *have* something we call "ethnicity" is a relatively recent invention (59). Whereas "race" implies some natural or essential differences between groups, the concept of ethnicity foregrounds the ways these differences are cultural, historical, and constructed. As Stuart Hall explains, "The term ethnicity acknowledges the place of history, language, and culture in the construction of subjectivity and identity" (446). In other words, one's ethnicity or ethnic identity is linked to cultural practices and markers, including language use, symbols, traditions, cuisine, and interpersonal styles, all of which change over time.

Sollors argues that the use of the term "ethnicity" has always masked a contradiction: ethnicity is both something possessed by everyone (for example, Italian Americans, Anglo Americans, German Americans, etc.) and something that marks groups as distinct from the mainstream (such as Latinxs in the United States). It is important to remember that the term "ethnicity" is applicable not only to minority communities of color. Hall advocates recognizing that "we all speak from a particular place, out of a particular history, out of a particular experience, a particular culture, without being contained by that position" (447). As Sonia Nieto observes, "White people, as the majority in US society, seldom think of themselves as *ethnic*—a term they tend to reserve for other, more easily identifiable groups. Nevertheless, the fact is that we are all ethnic, whether we choose to identify ourselves that way or not" (26).

We use the term "culture" in this chapter to refer to languages, practices, traditions, rituals, and artifacts that are associated with different ethnic groups or nations, that constitute ethnic or national identities, and that are used to signify racial, ethnic, or national differences. As Debra Dudek explains, the term "multicultural" applies to literature that depicts and respects cultural differences rather than assumes or elevates a falsely homogenous or monocultural norm (155). Multiculturalism rejects a singular norm that is used to encourage or enforce assimilation, and Dudek shows that children's literature has been seen as central to the multicultural project (159). In her 2014 keynote address to the Children's Literature Association, Katharine Capshaw notes that in the field of children's literature, the term "multiculturalism" has "an impassioned political edge"; however, she also observes that for scholars working in the field of critical race theory, multiculturalism represents "a shift away from antiracism and power and toward versions of diversity that are largely celebratory (at best) and incorporative (at worst)" (244, 245). In this latter view, the concept of multicultural undermines the potential for radical change.

Although discussions of ethnic and multicultural literatures might typically be understood as defined by attention to minority ethnic groups and their cultures and identities, this approach reinforces the sense that some cultures are normal and normative while defining others as deviant or deviations, as though the concept of ethnicity does not apply in the same way to everyone. People of European descent can also be understood as possessing a distinct ethnic and cultural identity. In the North American context, this means recognizing that Irish Americans, German Americans, Anglo Americans, French Canadians and so on also constitute ethnic groups, and that each of these groups is marked by the tensions between articulating unique identities and cultures and assimilating to undifferentiated national American or Canadian identities, regional identities within nations, or racial identities across region and nation. Works about certain ethnic groups of Western European decent are often taken to represent a universal human experience, while texts about ethnic characters of Asian, Latinx, African, or other heritages are imagined as unable to represent universal experiences. Why can't works of literature embedded in very specific ethnic, racial, or cultural contexts be read as representing "the human experience"? Thinking critically about the concept of ethnicity enables us to pose this question.

The concept of ethnicity also highlights the tensions between a celebration of cultural pluralism or ethnic pride and the pressure for ethnic groups to assimilate to a larger collective culture and identity, usually that of the nation. In the context of children's literature, this tension manifests itself as one between the impulse to emphasize the universality of humanity and similarities across ethnicities and cultures on the one hand, and the recognition of or instruction about ethnic or racial difference on the other. In other words, some works for children, in depicting ethnic or racial minorities, suggest that the "ethnic" child or family is really just like the unmarked "mainstream" family underneath superficial cultural differences, while other works emphasize the uniqueness of identity and experience. Moreover, Sollors suggests that the concept of ethnicity tends to obscure other group categories, such as the working or middle class, and similarities across groups. For the student or scholar of children's literature, this discussion of ethnicity might prompt questions about what counts as "ethnic" children's literature, how a concern with ethnicity is signaled by a work, how the ethnicity of a character is constructed and asserted, what that identity is defined against, under what conditions ethnicity and ethnic identity become especially pronounced, and to what extent the work advocates a sense of universality and similarity or uniqueness and difference.

THE NEED FOR DIVERSE BOOKS

In 1965, the founder of the International Reading Association, Nancy Larrick, published "The All-White World of Children's Books," in which she decried the children's publishing world for its lack of diversity. A children's book editor at Random House and a strong advocate for children's reading, Larrick lamented the fact that "nonwhite children are learning to read and to understand the American way of life in books which either omit them entirely or scarcely mention them. There is no need to elaborate upon the damage—much of it irreparable—to the Negro child's personality" (63). Larrick went on to note that the effect of this lack of diversity on white children "is probably even worse" in that it promotes racial bias and a sense of white supremacy. She found that only 0.008% of books published over a three-year period from 1962 to 1964 "tell a story about American Negroes today" (64). The Cooperative Children's Book Center (CCBC) at the University of Wisconsin-Madison surveys children's literature annually to assess the diversity of children's publishing. Of the 3,700 books received by the CCBC in 2017, only nine per cent were about Africans or African Americans, eight per cent about Asians or Asian

Pacific Americans, six per cent about Latinxs, and two per cent about American Indians. Larrick's concerns from over fifty years ago remain relevant.

In the spring of 2014, the We Need Diverse Books (WNDB) campaign emerged on Twitter in response to the lack of diversity in the announced children's author panel for BookCon, an event being held for the first time in New York. Since then, the We Need Diverse Books organization, whose mission is "putting more books featuring diverse characters into the hands of all children," has worked to advocate for "changes in the publishing industry to produce and promote literature that reflects and honors the lives of all young people" ("Mission Statement" n.p.). WNDB defines "diversity" as "including (but not limited to) LGBTQIA, people of color, gender diversity, people with disabilities, and ethnic, cultural, and religious minorities." Rudine Sims Bishop, a professor emerita of education and long-time advocate of diversity in children's literature, explains her sense of why the lack of diversity in children's literature is a problem: "for those children who historically had been ignored—or worse, ridiculed—in children's books, seeing themselves portrayed visually and textually as realistically human was essential to letting them know that they are valued in the social context in which they are growing up" (9). Children need mirrors, she explains, to see themselves in the books they read. Like Larrick, Bishop also sees negative effects on white children, for whom children's books about diverse characters can be windows into the lives of others. These windows sometimes need to be "sliding glass doors" that allow children into each other's lives, she says (9). Grassroots organizations like We Need Diverse Books and scholars like Bishop continue to advocate for increasing diversity among children's book publishers, authors, librarians, and critics as a way to impact the world of children's literature and the lives of children. These kinds of more diverse representation would add voices to the critical conversation and provide new ways of reading critically.

AWARDS

As a way to promote the publication and recognition of ethnic children's literature, a number of awards have been created to honor works that are by and about people of different races and ethnicities. While the Newbery Medal was first awarded in 1922, the Caldecott in 1938, the Carnegie in 1936, and the Greenaway in 1956, it was not until 1969 that the Coretta Scott King Award was established to honor African American children's literature and authors. The award was founded by two librarians, Mabel McKissick and Glyndon Greer, who noted that African American writers had not been recognized by the major awards in children's literature (H. Smith ix). Kenneth Kidd observes that for much of the history of the Newbery Medal, "African-American subjects were excluded from the scene, in keeping with social practices of segregation" (178). Only three African American authors have won the medal since 1922, Kidd adds (several others have authored New-bery Honor books), with a gap of twenty-three years separating Mildred Taylor's win for *Roll of Thunder, Hear My Cry* in 1977 and Christopher Paul Curtis's for *Bud, Not Buddy* in 2000. The King Award was given for the first time in 1970 to Lillie Patterson for *Martin Luther King, Jr.: Man of Peace* (1969), but it was not until 1982 that the award became officially associated with the American Library Association (ALA), as the Newbery and Caldecott were. For the first few years, the King Award was presented only to authors, but in 1974 the honor was granted to both authors and illustrators. According to the Constitution of the Coretta Scott King Task Force,

> The Coretta Scott King Award is given to encourage the artistic expression of the black experience via literature and the graphic arts including: biographical, social, historical, and social history treatments. The books are selected because they promote an understanding and appreciation of the black culture and experience. The Award is further designed to commemorate the life and works of Dr. Martin Luther King Jr. and to honor Mrs. Coretta Scott King for her courage and determination to continue his work for peace and world brotherhood. ("Coretta" n.p.)

Thus, the King Award is specifically designed to promote the publication of quality works depicting the Black experience, and since the early 1970s it has no doubt been instrumental in doing so. As Kidd states, "Literary prizing has been a remarkably effective mechanism" (165) for the publicity and sales of children's literature.

Awards for ethnic American children's literature continue to be established. In 1996, the Pura Belpré Award was established to honor Latinx writers and illustrators of children's literature. From 1996 to 2008, the award was given only once every two years, but since 2009 it has been given annually, indicating the growing body of children's literature authored by Latinx writers. Illustrator Yuyi Morales has won the award a number of times, including for *Just a Minute: A Trickster Tale and Counting Book* (2003) and *Just in Case* (2008), while Julia Alvarez has won twice in the narrative category for *Before We Were Free* (2002) and *Return to Sender* (2009). In 2001, the Asian/Pacific American Librarians Association (APALA) began honoring books "related to Asian/Pacific American experience" and "by an Asian/Pacific Islander American," including in the categories of children's literature and children's book illustrations ("Literature Award Guidelines" n.p.). Janet S. Wong and Bo Jia's *The Trip Back Home* (2000) received the first award for a children's illustrated book, and An Na's *A Step from Heaven* (2001), which also won the Printz Award for young adult fiction, received the first APALA children's book award. In 2006, the American Indian Library Association began presenting the American Indian Youth Literature Award every two years to works "by and about American Indians" that "present American Indians in the fullness of their humanity in the present and past contexts"

("American Indian Youth Literature Award" n.p.). Winners include Eric Gansworth's *If I Ever Get Out of Here* (2013), Tim Tingle's *House of Purple Cedar* (2013), and Richard Van Camp and Julie Flett's *Little You* (2013).

The proliferation of prizes has highlighted problems with the prominent Newbery and fostered further discussion about the merits and effects of literary prizes. In his analysis of children's literature prizes, Kidd raises the possibility that the existence of the King Award might actually undermine the likelihood of the Newbery going to African American writers, which might happen if committee members assume, even unconsciously, that they can leave African American children's literature to be recognized by the King prize. Marc Aronson, a children's writer, goes so far as to argue that the King and Belpré Awards are misguided. Writing for *The Horn Book Magazine*, a publication devoted to children's literature, Aronson explains,

> I'm sure that nearly every reader of this magazine is in favor of supporting a more diverse children's literature that is in tune with the increasingly multi-ethnic environment in which we and our children live. I am equally convinced, though, that ALA's sponsorship of three awards in which a book's eligibility is determined by the race or ethnicity of its creators is a mistake. For the Coretta Scott King, the Pura Belpré, and the (announced but as yet unnamed) Asian American awards, the creator's biography—ethnic credentials, if you will—predetermines the book's validity. I am convinced that this is wrong. It is the wrong way to bring more kinds of books to more kinds of readers; it is wrong in that it does not evaluate literature in its own terms but by extraneous standards; it is wrong because it is a very slippery slope down which we are already tumbling; and finally it is wrong because even as ALA sponsors more and more such awards, we have not openly discussed and debated their merits. (271)

Aronson ultimately argues that books should be evaluated on their literary merits irrespective of the backgrounds of their authors, and he claims that the King Award effectively "balkanizes literature" by encouraging only members of particular racial or ethnic groups to pay any attention to works by members of those groups (273). Yet the list of Newbery and Caldecott winners suggests that children's literature was already balkanized prior to the establishment of these additional prizes, and the new awards provide a mechanism for calling wider attention to works that might otherwise have been overlooked. Andrea Davis Pinkney asserts in response to Aronson, "A key aspect of awards that hold ethnicity as a criterion for winning is the exposure they afford to black and Latino talent" (536). She observes that awards are by nature exclusionary, and the work that the Coretta Scott King and Pura Belpré Awards have done to draw attention to children's literature by writers and illustrators of color represents an invaluable benefit. Because the world of children's literature is predominantly composed of white authors, illustrators, editors, and scholars, Pinkney warns, both these awards are needed to attract more diverse representation. This discussion surrounding the use of awards to promote ethnic children's literature points to many of the controversies and critical questions that have helped define the field.

KEY TERMS AND CONTROVERSIES

In the sections that follow we discuss the most important concepts and controversies associated with race, ethnicity, and culture in children's literature.

- **Authorship** and **ownership**: One controversy surrounding ethnic children's literature involves the question of who has the right to represent people of different races or cultures and whether an author can ever adequately represent people of a different race or culture.

- **Audience**: Representations of races or cultures imply audiences with different backgrounds or knowledge sets. Authors construct these representations for various kinds of audiences who are themselves of different racial or ethnic backgrounds; and the reader's familiarity with a cultural, racial, or ethnic group can affect how a work is received or interpreted.

- **Perspective**: The narrative of a work is told from a particular perspective, and that perspective can be limited or can create negative impressions. Even when a work appears to be sympathetic to a group, its narrative perspective can undermine its sympathy and result in problematic consequences.

- **Reclamation**: Many readers continue to enjoy troubling texts, while some writers, readers, and educators seek to reclaim, repurpose, or rewrite them. Can classic works with problematic or overtly racist elements be reclaimed and repurposed effectively, or should these texts be abandoned and supplanted by other ones? What ongoing use might such texts have? How might we think about the pleasure and enjoyment that can still be derived from some of these works?

- **Authenticity** and **accuracy**: One approach to ethnic representation in children's literature has involved the extent to which depictions of different races and cultures are accurate and authentic. However, authenticity can be difficult to define and determine. What counts as authentic representation? To what extent is authenticity possible? Who determines whether a text or textual element is authentic or not? How do authenticity and accuracy affect the meaning or composition of texts?

- **Artistic freedom** and **ethical responsibility**: Some authors assert the importance of maintaining their artistic freedom to represent people of different races and cultures in particular ways, however historically accurate or not, or to omit them entirely, while scholars of minority literatures have detailed the pain and offense caused by inaccurate or biased representations. What responsibility do authors have to represent other races accurately?

Our aim is not to provide definitive answers to these questions; thoughtful discussants often arrive at very different conclusions. Instead, we hope to provide the tools for participating in these discussions effectively.

Authorship and Ownership

One of the more sensitive and complex issues related to the depiction of races, ethnicities, and cultures concerns the background, experience, and identity of the author and whether an author of one ethnic, racial, or cultural group has the right or ability to write about another. Michael Cart puts the question this way: "Can a writer's imagination be powerful enough to create a viable work of fiction about a culture the writer has observed only from the outside?" (114). Respondents might be tempted to assert that authorial freedom and creativity give writers the absolute right to tell any story, or anyone's story, but the perspectives and histories of minority groups create a less certain sense of this absolute freedom. This dynamic—writing about a culture other than one's own—is especially problematic in cases where the author is a member of the culturally and politically dominant and privileged group and is writing about a subordinate or oppressed minority. This situation can be especially troubling in the context of systemic racism, where the member of the dominant group is more likely to have better access to education; more economic stability or flexibility, which makes writing possible; and a stronger chance of making the personal or professional connections to agents, publishers, and editors necessary to see a work reach print. Moreover, minority groups often already experience exploitation by the dominant majority, and to have aspects of one's culture appropriated for the profit or reputation of another—especially an outsider who already benefits from racial or ethnic privilege—can be frustrating and painful.

A stark example of such a troubling dynamic is the composition and publication of Joel Chandler Harris's *Uncle Remus: His Songs and His Sayings* (1880), a collection of folk tales that immortalized characters such as Brer Rabbit and Brer Wolf and inspired the

Disney film *Song of the South* (1946) and the Splash Mountain ride at Disney's Magic Kingdom. Born in the American South in 1848, Harris, a white man, became an apprentice printer on a working plantation in Georgia during the American Civil War. He later became a journalist and editor before retiring to devote himself fully to writing. During his time working on the plantation, he encountered slaves and listened to their folk tales, which he would later retell in his story collections about Uncle Remus, a fictitious slave who narrates tales about animal characters to a white boy at the plantation (Moore and MacCann 96). Harris described Uncle Remus as a composite of several African American men he knew, and his tales are based on old folk tales that circulated among African Americans. The Uncle Remus stories made Harris wealthy and famous, though they provided little or no benefit to the anonymous slaves whose stories he appropriated and published. Who owns these folk tales? Did Harris have the right to publish and profit from them? If the stories "belong" collectively to a particular racial group, does one member of that group have the right to give Harris permission to take the stories? Writing about the controversy surrounding Harris's Uncle Remus books, Opal Moore and Donnarae MacCann contend,

> It is a perpetual tug-of-war to decide who will "own" and interpret the art and artifacts of the Black American—determine the use to which historical and cultural materials will be put. This subtle war of wills ensues as a natural result of scholarly Black resistance to further intellectual colonization. The resisters confront the reluctance of white America to relinquish its illegitimate and unnatural proprietorship of valuable and persuasive materials. (96)

This example is especially vexing because it involves a white male Southerner, a member of the dominant race that profited from the legal enslavement of another, appropriating the stories of former slaves after the Civil War, many of whom were likely illiterate and possessed little access to education, publishing networks, or legal recourse.

Though other cases of cultural appropriation and exploitation might be less dramatic, this basic dynamic typically defines situations in which the member of a dominant group either retells stories already circulating within another culture or invents stories about that culture or its members. In *A Broken Flute: The Native Experience in Books for Children*, Doris Seale writes, "Taking something that has not been offered to you does not make it yours. That makes it stolen. Stories are never free.... Because you have conquered a People does not give you a right to their spirit" (5). A culture's stories or stories about a culture are integral to that culture and to the identity of its members. To have one's stories taken or to have stories told about one group by an outsider from a politically and culturally dominant group is to exploit the vulnerability of the minority and to do further damage. Harris's depiction of Uncle Remus, told from the perspective of a white

Southerner for a predominantly white audience, reinforced stereotypes of the happy slave who was devoted to his white master at the expense of his own best interests. This stereotype, which has done incalculable damage to generations of African Americans, was promoted through this case of literary appropriation by a man who did not himself experience slavery or racial oppression and therefore lacked the ability and commitment to understand fully why his representations were hurtful and harmful. This is not to say that it is impossible for a member of one cultural group to write about another, or that each case is as potentially troubling as Harris's Uncle Remus stories. Several landmark works with African American protagonists we have mentioned, such as Ezra Jack Keats's *The Snowy Day* and Robert Lipsyte's *The Contender*, were not written by African Americans, and yet because of the problem of authorship and ownership, even an apparently benign book such as *The Snowy Day* has proved controversial for some.

Audience

The case of Keats's *The Snowy Day* also indicates the importance of audience. When we think about the audience of a book, we need to think about the experiences that can lead to different reader responses. Readers concerned about a history of racial stereotypes such as the mammy figure might be attuned to the possibility that Peter's mother could be viewed through this tradition and therefore might find *The Snowy Day* troubling. Reading racial or ethnic representations in children's literature critically means considering how the qualities or experiences of the audience might affect interpretation and how texts imply or imagine particular audiences.

One picturebook that has provoked far more controversy than *The Snowy Day* is Carolivia Herron's *Nappy Hair* (1997). Herron, herself an African American, has explained that she based *Nappy Hair* on her own experience and intended the book to be a celebration of African American hair, a literary effort to reclaim a feature that has often been denigrated and mocked. The term "nappy" has a derogatory connotation in the United States and has been used as a disparaging descriptor for African American hair. Herron's use of the term attempts to recuperate it as a source of pride. In 1998, a controversy erupted when Ruth Sherman, a white schoolteacher in a predominantly Latinx and African American community in Brooklyn, read the book to her third-grade class. After photocopies of pages from *Nappy Hair* circulated in the community, the school received complaints, Sherman's safety was threatened, and she was forced to relocate to a school in a distant neighborhood. The controversy made news in major newspapers across the United States (Holloway n.p.).

While Sherman read the book to her class in order to promote acceptance of racial difference and to introduce children to literary representations of minorities, the long history of racial caricature, to which some thought Joe Cepeda's illustrations in *Nappy Hair* bore a resemblance, led many African American parents to respond negatively to the book. Speculating on audience helps provide some perspective on this controversy. *Nappy Hair* tells the story of an African American girl named Brenda resisting her family's efforts to tame her naturally curly hair. If the reader is meant to identify with Brenda, who takes pride in her hair, then we might infer that the implied audience of the work is African American children whose hair might be similar to Brenda's. Sherman's classroom, however, was ethnically and racially heterogeneous, and the suspicious response to the use of the book in the classroom sprang in part from the fact that Sherman herself is white. Clearly, the assumption was that a white reader trafficking in the phrase "nappy hair" must be using it to poke fun and that the white teacher did not fully realize the pain associated with the term "nappy." Indeed, though the book might have been intended to promote acceptance, in the hands of a more hostile audience, both the language and illustrations could be read as racist caricature. Other readers simply might not understand the notion of reclamation—the idea of reclaiming an abusive term and repurposing or redefining it as a self-applied term of pride—while still others might understand Herron's intentions and judge the work as a failure, ultimately working against its own purpose and reinscribing nappy hair as a source of pain and shame. The point is that different readers bring different experiences, backgrounds, purposes, desires, and knowledge to a work, and those differences will affect how a text is interpreted and understood, whatever the author's intentions.

Different books imply different kinds of readers. *Nappy Hair*, for instance, implies a familiarity with African American culture and concerns, and it does not depict responses to Brenda's hair from outside of her community. The reader of *Nappy Hair* is presented only with Brenda and members of her family as characters with whom to identify. No children of other ethnicities or races are presented in the text, so none are shown having a problem with Brenda or her hair or learning to accept Brenda's hair. We can therefore infer that the text is not designed to teach non–African American children to appreciate this kind of hair, and thus it implies an African American audience. This is not to say that the text would not be useful or meaningful to a variety of readers; rather, they may not be directly implied or addressed by the text and might have responses not anticipated by the author or managed by the text. *Nappy Hair* contains many other complex elements, such as the call-and-response cues, a practice associated with African American culture in which a speaker makes a comment and an audience voices a response. These and other elements will continue to promote a variety of responses, but understanding the kind of audience the text implies is crucial to making sense of both it and the controversy that has surrounded it. As Michelle Martin, who specializes in children's literature and African American children's literature at the university level, explains, "I have found, however, that even if students are willing to [learn] and interested in learning African-American history and culture through the texts that I choose for them to read, many of them benefit from learning some background information necessary for understanding the problems that African Americans have faced historically in this country" (184). Children's literature scholar Katharine Capshaw Smith suggests that this expectation of multiple audiences is especially in play for ethnic children's literature because of the didactic function to which it is put:

> Ethnic children's literature is often targeted both to insider and outsider groups. If part of its agenda is didactic in advancing revivified versions of history and identity, texts often consciously address both the ethnic child reader and those in other populations. For children of the ethnicity represented textually, authors encourage resistance to pejorative categorizations by asking the reader to reimagine herself, to identify herself with the texts' cultural models. For a reader from another ethnic group, texts often encourage cross-cultural amity and understanding as a means to dispel prejudice. ("Introduction" 4)

To read children's literature critically, the student and scholar must analyze the kind of audience implied by the text, what the reader is expected to know, who is being addressed or instructed by the text, and how different readers might respond.

Perspective

Part of the complexity of any text includes the perspective from which the narrative is told. In works that foreground race, ethnicity, or race relations, narrative perspective is especially important for the literary critic of children's literature. Perry Nodelman and Mavis Reimer provide an excellent example of how recognizing narrative perspective is crucial to understanding fully a text's representation of these concerns. Citing Paula Fox's explanation that she intended her Newbery-winning novel *The Slave Dancer* (1973) to expose the horrors of slavery, they point out that the novel is narrated from the perspective of a thirteen-year-old white boy named Jessie, who is kidnapped from New Orleans and taken aboard a slave ship to play the fife:

> The white author tells the story of the suffering of captured black slaves through the eyes and in the voice of a white adolescent who has himself been shanghaied onto the ship. There seems to be a "quiescent" or passive assumption that young readers of the book would probably identify with such a point of view—not with the Africans who are being so cruelly mistreated but, instead, with a white outsider who learns to feel sympathy for their plight. (Nodelman and Reimer 169)

Nodelman and Reimer suggest that "Fox's choice of point of view in *The Slave Dancer* makes the white protagonist's personal distress at having to observe suffering seem more important than the physical and spiritual pain he observes [in the captured slaves]" (169). The narrative perspective makes the novel more Jessie's story than the slaves', and the focus is on him and his response to the horrors of slavery rather than on that of the slaves themselves. In fact, the captured slaves barely speak in the novel, so they effectively become a backdrop for the adventures of a white boy who is able to feel some kinship with them because he, too, has been captured. The novel almost seems to equate Jessie's kidnapping and forced fife-playing with the situation of the captured Africans, though his experience obviously cannot compare to the far more dire, painful, and hopeless circumstances of a Black slave. Recognizing the implications of the novel's narrative perspective is crucial to understanding the novel's portrayal of race and the African American experience.

Other popular works along these lines must also be read in terms of narrative perspective. Harper Lee's perennial classic *To Kill a Mockingbird*, which won the Pulitzer Prize for fiction in 1961, is widely assigned in schools, included on summer reading lists, and made the subject of community-wide literacy programs. Part of its appeal derives from how the novel seems to expose racial injustice in the American South; but told from the perspective of a six-year-old white girl nicknamed Scout, the novel focuses on the difficulties faced by Scout's family because of her father's decision to legally defend Tom Robinson, a Black man, in a segregated Alabama town in the 1930s. It is Scout's father, an extraordinarily honest and principled lawyer, who is the hero of the novel, and since Gregory Peck's Academy Award–winning performance as Atticus in the 1962 film, the character has attained almost iconic status as a champion of justice and racial equality. However, while the feelings of the Finch family are thoroughly explored, and while Scout and her brother and father are developed fully as characters, Tom Robinson and *his* family are barely glimpsed, and they might even be understood as props for the heroic efforts of Atticus and his children on Tom's behalf. A six-year-old might be expected to have difficulty imagining or narrating the life and psychology of a man outside of her immediate family, but Scout, as the novel's narrator, is unbelievably precocious and insightful about everything else, and the very choice to narrate a story about racism and injustice from the point of view of a white child privileges a white perspective. That the novel depicts a white man attempting to rescue a Black man from racism and injustice participates in a liberal white fantasy of rescue as a way of mitigating the guilt of racist exploitation and racial privilege. To note these implications of the text is not to argue that its status as a classic of American literature is undeserved, but it is to think critically about the novel's depiction of race. These issues became even more complicated with the publication of *Go Set a Watchman* in 2015, which showed Atticus participating in his town's Citizens' Council, racist community organizations common across the South during the mid twentieth century that sought to block civil rights and maintain Jim Crow segregation.

Both *The Slave Dancer* and *To Kill a Mockingbird* examine race and racism in US history from the perspective of white characters. Works told from the perspective of African American characters make essential contributions to this body of children's literature, and the narrative perspective of these works can sometimes communicate aspects of that history that would be difficult to convey otherwise. Mildred Taylor's *Roll of Thunder, Hear My Cry* (1976), like *The Slave Dancer*, is a Newbery Medal winner, and like *To Kill a Mockingbird*, it is set during the 1930s. However, Taylor's novel is narrated by an African American girl from Mississippi named Cassie Logan, and this narrative perspective allows Taylor, herself an African American author, to convey in the first person the pain of racial injustice. The Logan family members are not flat background characters like the Robinsons in *Mockingbird*. Cassie, a fourth-grader, describes the anger at receiving an eleven-year-old textbook marked on the inside cover as being in "poor" condition and thus reserved for a "nigra" student (Taylor 25). She relates her daily efforts to avoid being run down by a school bus carrying white children who shout racist taunts through the windows as she and her siblings walk to school. Moreover, Taylor's novel does something that is usually avoided in works depicting African Americans as secondary characters or stereotypes from the viewpoint of white authors or characters: it represents a Black family from the inside, in vivid detail, and as composed of three-dimensional members with complex emotions and histories. The difference in narrative perspective among these three works produces enormous differences in characterization, plot, and other important details, and thus demonstrates the importance of examining a work's point of view.

Reclamation

One question related to the history of ethnic representation in children's literature is whether a problematic text can ever be reclaimed or enjoyed despite its potentially troubling or offensive content. Earlier we discussed Joel Chandler Harris's Uncle Remus stories, which depict a slave called Uncle Remus telling African American folk tales about characters such as Brer Rabbit and the Tar Baby to a white child. Though the stereotype of the happy and devoted slave Uncle Remus embodies is now widely recognized as deeply offensive, Harris's story collections constitute one of the largest and most significant repositories of African American folklore. Although the character of Uncle Remus is Harris's invention, as is the frame narrative of Remus's telling the tales to a white child, the tales themselves are actually derived from the oral tradition of African Americans in the nineteenth century. Harris reportedly took care to include only those stories of African American origin, and had he not collected and published them, the tales might have been lost to subsequent generations. Nevertheless, the figure of Uncle Remus, explains Julius Lester, was used as a "retrospective justification" for slavery (*Tales* xiv), and Lester argues that the character "affirmed white superiority and confirmed an image of black inferiority many whites needed" (*Tales* xv). Given the troubling use to which the character of Uncle Remus was put and the fact that Harris profited from the appropriation of African American culture and the exploitation of the slaves from whom he collected the tales, can the Uncle Remus stories ever be redeemed and reclaimed as valuable and pleasurable works of children's literature?

Famed African American children's librarian Augusta Baker describes her difficulty with both reading the tales and sharing them with children over her long career, though she states that "I still loved the stories and appreciated Brer Rabbit as a cultural hero" (qtd. in Lester, *Tales* ix). According to Lester, himself a noted African American author, "Their place and importance in Afro-American culture is singular and undisputed" (*Tales* xiii). At Baker's suggestion, Lester rewrote the stories, explaining, "The purpose in my retelling of the Uncle Remus tales is simple: to make the tales accessible again, to be told in the living rooms of condominiums as well as on front porches in the

South" (*Tales* xvi). Lester makes a strong case for the value of preserving the tales despite their problematic history and framing and Baker, who writes the introduction to Lester's collection of retellings, lauds the project. Nevertheless, Lester admits that reclaiming the tales involved sorting out many difficult questions, including how to manage the racist implications of Uncle Remus. Ultimately, Lester largely omitted the character of Uncle Remus except from the title of the collection and as what he describes as "a voice ... the voice of a people, the black people of Kansas City, Kansas; Pine Bluff, Arkansas; Nashville, Tennessee; and the state of Mississippi" (*Tales* xvii). Lester undertakes a similar project of reclamation in his retelling of Helen Bannerman's now infamous picturebook *Little Black Sambo* (1899), which Lester rewrote as *Sam and the Tigers* (1996) in order to "right the wrongs of the original and several subsequent versions" (Lester, *Sam* 4). Clearly, Lester endorses the notion of reclamation while acknowledging the

Julius Lester "reclaims" Joel Chandler Harris's stories in a 1987 retelling of *The Tales of Uncle Remus*, illustrated by Jerry Pinkney.

difficulty of such an act and the ambivalence associated with both the originals and the revisions.

Not all works that have raised concerns about their racial implications have been reclaimed as fully or as successfully as the Uncle Remus and Sambo stories. Mark Twain's *Adventures of Huckleberry Finn* (1884) has long been controversial for both its frequent use of the word "nigger" and for its representation of the slave Jim, who is depicted ambiguously as sometimes foolish and superstitious and as unbelievably accepting of unnecessary torment at the hands of Huck Finn and Tom Sawyer. Lester is far more hesitant to reclaim *Huckleberry Finn*, calling it "dangerously, fatally seductive" ("Morality" 200), and he writes, damningly,

> I am grateful that among the many indignities inflicted on me in childhood, I escaped *Huckleberry Finn*. As a black parent, however, I sympathize with those who want the book banned, or at least removed from required reading lists in schools. While I am opposed to book banning, I know that my children's education will be enhanced by not reading *Huckleberry Finn*. ("Morality" 200)

These comments suggest that Lester sees Twain's novel as qualitatively different from Harris's folk-tale collections and Bannerman's *Sambo*. He goes so far as to call it "immoral in its major premises, one of which demeans blacks and insults history" ("Morality" 201). It is the fact that the novel seems to equate Huck's captivity by his abusive father with Jim's status as a slave that Lester finds most offensive and that presumably damns it as irredeemable and unsalvageable. In contrast, Lester defends Bannerman, claiming, "It would be unfair to say Bannerman had a racist intent in creating *Little Black Sambo*," but he offers no similar defense of Twain, who he perhaps assumes should have known better (Lester, *Sam* n.p.). However, what determines whether a text can be reclaimed is not simply the intent of the original author, since Harris deliberately offers the often ridiculous sayings of Uncle Remus as something for his white readers to laugh at. On the other hand, as Gail Murray contends about *Huckleberry Finn*, "While Clemens's [Twain's] position on race relations and the abilities of African Americans seems ambivalent at best, his novel is so shot through with irony that the reader cannot always discern his narrative intent" (129). Moreover, Lester's own reclamations have not failed to meet with skeptics. Opal Moore writes of Lester, "When I encountered his *Tales of Uncle Remus* and *More Tales of Uncle Remus* as I browsed a bookstore shelf one day, I was somewhat surprised that Lester, who I considered to be of a radical black consciousness, would want to preserve not only the African American lore of Br'er Rabbit and his nemesis, but Joel Chandler Harris's 'darkie' uncle as well" ("Othello" 374). That Lester accepts a retelling of Harris and Bannerman and rejects Twain, while Moore rejects Lester, suggests that whether a text can be recuperated will rarely if ever be a matter of consensus. Readers will reach different conclusions based on evidence from the text, its historical context, the life of the author, and their own investments.

Authenticity and Accuracy

The extent to which literary texts represent racial or ethnic minorities and cultures accurately is one of the more controversial issues related to this body of work. The notion of authenticity refers to the idea that a text not only is accurate in its specific details but also captures the intangible qualities that cultural insiders deem integral or faithful to their culture. Nina Mikkelsen distinguishes between "deep" and "surface" structures as a way of determining "multicultural" authenticity, pointing out that in the case of problematic texts, "writers will attend to surface features (observable details, facts, and idioms) but miss the bigger picture—the values, beliefs, and world view of the insider that can so easily be subsumed, usurped, or crowded out entirely by an outsider's pervasive thinking" (38). Authenticity can be difficult, if not impossible, to determine, in part because members of a group might have a range of ideas about what qualities or practices are critical to a culture or identity. Consensus might not be reachable even among members of a particular racial or ethnic group, because groups are always fractured along a number of lines, including region, class, religion, sex/gender, generation, and sexual orientation. Members of privileged communities are more likely to see their work published. Therefore, if writers write only about their immediate and personal experience, literature as an enterprise might be severely limited, and fictional worlds would be even more homogeneous than they are. Nevertheless, writing ethnic children's literature requires thoughtfulness and care, and reading it critically entails being conscious of how readers might contest the accuracy or authenticity of a work and how contested details bear on the meanings of the work.

For instance, Gerald McDermott's picturebook *Arrow to the Sun* (1974), subtitled *A Pueblo Indian Tale*, won the Caldecott Medal for its illustrations in 1975, but the accuracy of its representations of Pueblo Indian traditions has been highly contested. The book describes a boy conceived by a Pueblo woman and the sun who decides one day to search for his father. Eventually, the boy is transformed into an arrow and shot to the sun where he confronts his father, who demands the boy prove himself by experiencing a set of trials held in Pueblo kivas, or ceremonial chambers. After completing the trials, the boy returns to earth, "filled with the power of the sun," and the Pueblo people "celebrate his return in the Dance of Life" (McDermott 18).

Writing in *A Broken Flute* (2005), Debbie Reese, an American Indian studies and children's literature scholar, identifies a number of troubling inaccuracies in the book. A member of the Nambé Pueblo tribe, Reese contends that the depiction of the boy as being mocked by other boys for not knowing his father is not likely. "The concept of 'illegitimate' doesn't fit with our ways of caring for children," Reese writes (342). More-over, she explains that a kiva is "a place of gathering, a place to learn, a place to worship," whereas in McDermott's book kivas are places where the boy undergoes a series of tri-als involving lions, serpents, bees, and lightning (342). Reese acknowledges that the il-lustrations "are striking, and it's easy to see why the Caldecott committee selected this book for the award" (342). What a book accomplishes aesthetically—as a work of literary art—and to what extent it is culturally accurate might thus constitute different criteria of evaluation.

However, the literary scholar is less concerned with evaluating a text and more with analyzing what it means or how it works, and recognizing both dimensions—aesthetics and authenticity—is useful for this purpose. Indeed, Jon Stott argues that the successful resonance of *Arrow to the Sun* is an effect of McDermott's integration of Pueblo iconogra-phy and cultural references with the ideas of European American scholar Joseph Camp-bell about world mythology. Campbell argued for a universal hero's journey, which Stott sees unfolding in McDermott's text using culturally specific imagery. Thus, *Arrow to the Sun* can be understood not as an example of an authentic Pueblo folk tale but as a liter-ary work of textual and cultural hybridity. Recognizing both the cultural "inaccuracies" and the sources of McDermott's ideas about heroes and myths helps explain how the book was put together and the choices leading to its specific composition. Understood this way, *Arrow to the Sun* is less a Pueblo tale and more a contemporary American tale that reflects an investment in universal motifs that transcend cultural specificity. In other words, the text reflects a 1970s multicultural ethos of integration that contrasts with our contemporary attunement to difference and cultural specificity. Reaching this conclusion requires pondering the question of authenticity and investigating whether the book is accurate and how its accuracies or inaccuracies bear on its meaning or composition.

Artistic Freedom and Ethical Responsibility

As with the historical fiction discussed in Chapter 7, the complexities of ethnic represen-tation in children's literature have raised the question of whether authors have unlimited artistic freedom to tell any story or use any character type, construct plots or perspectives, address specific audiences, or omit certain details—however problematic or troubling some may find those choices. Given the significance and impact of racial and ethnic rep-resentations on both individual lives and society as a whole, the stakes are especially high in this discussion. Some authors argue strenuously for the freedom to base their creative choices on artistic demands and to borrow the stories of other communities and cultures at will. Jane Yolen, a prolific and critically acclaimed author of award-winning children's books such as *The Emperor and the Kite* (1968) and *Owl Moon* (1988), has written publicly in defense of artistic freedom in *The Horn Book Magazine*. "To arbitrarily set borders for our writers, boxing them in with rules, is to do literature the gravest disservice. And in the end it does a worse disservice to the children," she writes (705). Marc Aronson concurs, arguing, "We should do everything in our power to encourage the growth of a more diverse literature, but not by predefining who will create it. We should do our best to encourage all readers to be receptive to every brand of literature. Which also means that we must be open to great art, no matter who creates it" (274). Yolen points to the impossibility of authenticity, noting the fallibility of memory and the inevitability of different recollections and interpretations of the same event or story: "We all view the world through individual lenses. Even those things which actually happened can be reported upon in a number of ways" (703). Yolen relates that one of her picturebooks, *All Those Secrets of the World* (1991), is based on a true story from her childhood, but her cousin has a different memory of the event. If two members of the same family can have different perspectives on the same event, then who is to decide which version has more authority? Which constitutes a more faithful, accurate, or authentic rendering of the event? If representing true and minor events can be this difficult, if their accuracy and authenticity can be contested, then how much more difficult is it to determine the authenticity of fictional stories, especially ones that depict racial or ethnic groups? And what individual can speak for an entire ethnic or racial group, especially when members of the group may disagree about accurate or authentic renderings of certain traditions, characters, or events? Yolen concludes her defense of artistic freedom by noting that some stories would never be told if no one outside of a racial or ethnic group were ever permitted to tell those stories.

Yolen makes a strong case for the value of artistic freedom, and certainly literature would be impoverished by the imposition of overly restrictive constraints on writers and stories. Yolen claims the title "empress of thieves," implying that writers steal or "borrow" stories in order to produce works of literature:

> When I speak of borrowing, I am always aware of the absolute necessity for research—cultural, physical, historical. All translations are off-center somewhere. The Italians say, "Translations, traitors,"[1] meaning that to some extent any translation misrepresents. And anytime one borrows from another culture, another time, another gender, it is translation. But our very lives are borrowed—from our own pasts, from the pasts of others. It cannot be otherwise. (703)

However, Doris Seale, co-editor of *A Broken Flute*, provides another perspective on this notion of stealing stories. Addressing the Native American experience, Seale indicates

---

1 The phrase in Italian is "traduttore, traditore," meaning "translators, traitors," which expresses the sense that translations fail to capture and thus betray the beauty of the original work.

that the practice of "borrowing" the stories of Native peoples lacks the kind of reciprocity that might ameliorate the offense. Indeed, to steal or borrow the stories of Native Americans—victims of deliberately genocidal practices, whose lands were taken and whose cultures were destroyed, whose children were "forcibly removed from their parents" to live in boarding schools where they were "forbidden to speak their own languages"—is to add terrible insult to injury (Seale 4). Seale explains why this practice is so painful:

> Since the 1980s, non-Native authors and illustrators of books for children have turned increasingly to Indian literatures, lives, and histories as sources of material for their efforts. Publication of the results has become big business. Whether retellings, adaptations, or edited versions of stories, historical accounts, photographic essays, or biographies, these works have been carefully produced, lavishly illustrated, and brought out with artfully orchestrated publicity. Several have become best sellers; some have won awards. They are nearly invariably well received, praised for their beauty and sensitivity, and frequently for their ecological messages, by reviewers who do not know enough to know that the works in question are inaccurate, inauthentic, patronizing, full of lies, and altogether a huge insult to the people out of whose lives so much money is being made. (4)

To have writers earn reputations and make careers out of telling stories that belong to another culture, often getting details wrong, either accidentally or for artistic expediency, is experienced by the people of that culture as cultural theft. *A Broken Flute* includes dozens of anecdotal accounts of the pain caused to Native American children and parents when inaccurate or racist representations of Native peoples are read in schools, turned into school plays, or made the subject of animated films. One contributor named Liz describes her third-grade class reading the 1936 Newbery-winning novel *Caddie Woodlawn*, which, she recalls, describes Native Americans as "sneaking around like dogs, and they picked up Caddie Woodlawn by her hair, and they were acting like dogs sniffing a bone.... They made the pioneers seem like angels and the Native Americans seem like inhuman monsters. I felt hurt inside, my eyes were watering and I felt like I wanted to cry" (Reese, "Liz's Story" 14). Clearly, the kind of thieving defended by Yolen can be extremely painful. Artistic and curricular freedom must be balanced with the ethical responsibility to weigh the potential of literary representations to harm others, to perpetuate racist stereotypes and racial strife, and to add to the physical, cultural, and economic violence inflicted on racial and ethnic minorities.

READING CRITICALLY: RACE IN CHILDREN'S LITERATURE

The Snowy Day

Ezra Jack Keats's *The Snowy Day*, published in 1962, has been both critically acclaimed and con-troversial. As we mentioned earlier, it is the first Caldecott-winning book to feature an Afri-can American protagonist. That depiction, which appears to be sympathetic, resulted from Keats's interest in promoting diversity in children's literature. Nevertheless, some critics have taken issue with the book and suggested that Keats, a Jewish American, might inadvertently have included racial stereotypes. Because of this mixed response and because of the apparent simplicity of the picturebook form with its limited verbal text, *The Snowy Day* makes a useful case for investigating how children's literature addresses race and ethnicity and how an under-standing of some of the critical controversies reviewed in this chapter is useful for explicating texts.

The Snowy Day is a short picturebook for young readers that depicts a young African Amer-ican boy playing in the snow. The large buildings in the background indicate that the setting is urban, and the fact that Keats was a lifelong New Yorker might suggest the city is New York. Keats's innovative artistic style combines collage with painting to produce a layered effect, as Keats explains:

> Day by day I cut out rectangles of red, yellow, orange, and purple paper and pasted
> them down. They became buildings. With a roller I spread white and pastel paints,
> blues, greens, and yellows, on a large sheet of paper. It turned into snow. From this I cut
> out shapes of hills; they became snow piled up in the city. I cut out a red snowsuit and
> pasted a brown oval on it for a head. It became Peter, my character, walking, crunch,
> crunch, crunch through the snow! ("From *Collage*" 71)

The plot is simple. Peter wakes up, goes outside to play in the snow, returns home to be un-dressed by his mother, goes to bed, and wakes up the next day to repeat his adventures. The book might not appear to provide much material for the literary critic to explore, but its appar-ent simplicity is deceptive.

The controversy surrounding the book was ignited by Nancy Larrick's 1965 article in the *Saturday Review* called "The All-White World of Children's Books," which noted the rarity of African American characters in children's literature. Larrick also singled out *The Snowy Day*, raising questions about how Keats's background complicates the book's depiction of race. Pat Cummings summarizes Larrick's claims about the book: "Larrick had found the depiction of the characters in *The Snowy Day* to be racist stereotypes and insisted that Keats had no right to do a story about blacks" (49). More specifically, Larrick expressed concern that the depiction of

Peter plays in the snow in Ezra Jack Keats's *The Snowy Day* (1962).

Peter's mother, who appears once on a single page, reflects a common way of representing the mammy figure, a stereotype of markedly subservient African American women who care for white people happily and sacrificially (Scarlet O'Hara's "Mammy" in *Gone with the Wind* is one infamous example). These figures are often depicted as heavyset, as Peter's mother is. While Larrick took issue with *The Snowy Day*, Michelle Martin's experience with the book indicates the range of possible reader responses:

> I read *The Snowy Day* many times as a child and many more times as an adult, having no idea that Ezra Jack Keats was white…. All I knew was that someone somewhere had thought that I, a young black reader, deserved an image of a child in my bedtime stories who looked more like me than the blond-haired, blue-eyed Sallies and Billies who stared out at me from between the covers of the basal readers I read every day at school. And although Keats's *The Snowy Day* has been lambasted for tokenism, this

The original strip of photos that appeared in a 1940 issue of *Life* magazine and inspired Ezra Jack Keats.

author was attempting to do what few others in the early 1960s were: giving black children the chance to see themselves and their experiences reflected positively in the literature they read. (xviii)

At the level of both reader response and authorial intention, Martin seems to exonerate *The Snowy Day*'s depiction of race.

Indeed, Keats claimed to have laudable goals that informed his literary and artistic choices. Keats was inspired to represent Peter as an African American boy by a photo of a boy from rural Georgia that had appeared in a 1940 issue of *Life* magazine and that Keats had taped above his desk. As Keats explained,

None of the manuscripts I'd been illustrating featured any black kids—except for token blacks in the background. My book would have him there simply because he should have been there all along. Years before I had cut from a magazine a strip of photos of a little black boy. I often put them on my studio walls before I'd begun to illustrate children's books. I just loved looking at him. This was the child who would be the hero of my book. ("From *Collage*" 71)

As the son of Jewish immigrants and growing up in New York during the 1920s, Keats felt an affinity with people of color because of his experience of anti-Semitism. As an adult writer he was even encouraged to change his given name—Jacob Ezra Katz—so that it would appear less Jewish. According to Keats's childhood friend Martin Pope, "His suffering in early life from economic privation and anti-Semitism, coupled with his firmly held egalitarian philosophy and love for children, made the minority child a natural subject for his creativity" (Alderson 73). However, as we saw with the controversy surrounding Carolivia Herron's *Nappy Hair*, neither the author's racial background nor the author's intentions determine or limit readers' responses to a book, and just because Keats's goals were benevolent does not mean his work is not a product of its historical context and therefore marked by race and racial bias. Works of art exceed the intentions of their authors, who are driven by unrecognized and unconscious beliefs, desires, fears, and associations. In fact, Keats admitted that he could not fully explain the origins of his story: "I approached the project with total innocence, unaware that my pre-conceptions about the rules of illustrating had disappeared.... I was in a world with no rules. As in a dream, everything fell into place" ("From *Collage*" 71). He acknowledged then that he was driven in part by unconscious drives, like those that shape our dreams, which are beyond our control and often beyond our ability to explain.

While the authorship of *The Snowy Day* raises these concerns, a close reading of the book is important to understanding it more fully. How does *The Snowy Day* construct and signal race? Peter is an African American boy, but how do we know this? The text does not verbally indicate Peter's racial background at all, nor does the interior of his home include any artifacts that might provide clues. The only markers of Peter's race are the color of his skin and perhaps the rendering of his hair. Race is therefore constructed in the book as merely a visual, surface-level trait. What difference does this make? And what does it suggest about the book's approach to race? Barbara Bader refers to *The Snowy Day* as "color-blind" in the sense that it emphasizes similarities between races rather than difference: "In *The Snowy Day* (1962), Ezra Jack Keats's joyous celebration of boyhood in winter, the race of lively, brown-skinned Peter *doesn't* matter, is immaterial" (660). In other words, *The Snowy Day* emphasizes the universality of experience across race rather than racial and cultural specificity. It absorbs the African American experience into a universal notion of the human race. As Bob Dixon explains, "[The characters] are black enough, but it's only skin deep. Nothing would be affected in Keats' stories if the characters were white. The whole social, political and cultural significance of being black is left out" (123). Peter wakes up, plays in the snow, is undressed by his mother, takes a bath, and goes to bed. His racial background has virtually no effect on his activities or on the book, which therefore represents race as inconsequential and unimportant. Even though this might look like progress, it is also a denial of reality. Race remains both consequential and important in the United States, even for children, but *The Snowy Day* does not acknowledge that. Published in the midst of the Civil Rights Movement and two years before the Civil Rights Act of 1964, which made discrimination based on race illegal, *The Snowy Day* might be read as envisioning a utopian future in which race does not matter, but it overlooks the very real and often negative and painful effects of racial status on the lives of African Americans. To acknowledge this is not to find fault with Keats or to deny the historical significance or quality of *The Snowy Day*, but it is to understand *how* the book represents race in a very particular way that is only one way among many.

The physical depiction of Peter is not the only way *The Snowy Day* addresses the issue of race. Though this aspect of the book might have been entirely unintentional on Keats's part, it is remarkable that one of the first sympathetic treatments of an African American boy in a children's picturebook has the protagonist encounter a world of almost complete whiteness. In fact, the first page of the book across from the front cover depicts Peter from behind walking toward the top of the otherwise entirely blank page. Peter, wearing his red snowsuit, appears as a red-hooded figure against a completely white space. Given both the title and the four sets of footprints that trail behind Peter, the reader is immediately meant to recognize that he is walking in the snow, but visually Peter is floating in a sea of white. This image is used again later in the book, except Peter is further up on the page with more prints behind him. The concluding illustration, a double spread, shows Peter, now accompanied by a friend, poised motionless in the cavern created by two unrealistically enormous mountains of snow that appear threatening in their ability to collapse and bury the boys. That the book ends with this ominous image of Peter, appearing smaller than he does on any other page, is telling. The world is a white one, and though Peter may frolic and have fun, this white world is still a dangerous and threatening place.

Peter, in his red snowsuit and with his head entirely covered, resembles the figure of Little Red Riding Hood, who in the earliest versions of the tale is actually devoured by the Wolf. While "Little Red Riding Hood" is a tale about a vulnerable child who encounters danger, the only conceivable danger in *The Snowy Day* is the snow itself, which we argue invokes whiteness. Little Red Riding Hood is usually represented as innocently oblivious to her predicament or the danger posed by the Wolf, and Peter is similarly unaware. He saves a bit of snow in the pocket of his suit when he returns home, and when he discovers that it melted, "He felt very sad" (Keats, *Snowy* n.p.). Peter, as a young child, does not understand that the snow will melt; similarly, the young reader of *The Snowy Day* might not make the connection between snow and whiteness and its implications for a reading of race in the book. But then neither might the adult reader who is not reading in this way. Reading the book in the context of the history of race and ethnicity in children's literature and paying attention to how children's books represent race and ethnicity make recognizing these elements more likely.

EXPLORATIONS

Review

1. How did nineteenth-century American children's literature—even that produced by abolitionists or critical of slavery—often reinforce racial hierarchies and racist thought? How was British literature of the nineteenth century similarly mired in racist representation and racial hierarchies that privileged white Britons over colonial subjects of color?

2. Consider the portrayal of Native Americans and First Nations in canonical children's literature, and especially the troubling association of Native Americans with savagery.

How have Native American and First Nations authors produced their own children's literature that speaks back to and complicates these troubling and stereotypical narratives?

3. What are some ways in which classic works of children's literature with problematic or overtly racist elements have been reclaimed and repurposed? What are some of the problems in doing so? You might consider this in reference to Julius Lester's retellings of Joel Chandler Harris' Uncle Remus stories.

4. What is meant by the term "ethnicity"? How does it compare to the concept of race? In this chapter, we note that the tension between ethnic pride and the pressure for ethnic groups to assimilate to a larger collective culture "manifests itself as one between the impulse to emphasize the universality of humanity and similiarities across ethnicities and culture on the one hand, and the recognition of or instruction about ethnic or racial difference on the other" (p. 401). Explain what we mean by this and its implications for children's literature.

5. Questions of audience are important for racially and culturally diverse literature. How can a reader's familiarity—or lack of familiarity—with a cultural, racial, or ethnic group affect how a work is received or interpreted? When it comes to books about race, culture, and ethnicity, how do other different experiences, backgrounds, purposes, desires, and knowledges affect how a text is interpreted and understood?

Reflect

1. Discuss the question of whether authors have an ethical responsibility to consider the racial implications of their fictional works or characters. If so, why? If not, why not? Are there ever any limits to creative freedom? How might authors balance a commitment to creative freedom and ethical responsibility to people of color?

2. Why might reading books by and about people of color be important or necessary for different kinds of readers? Given the different purposes of reading diverse books, why is it important to read these books critically in terms of accuracy and authenticity?

3. Review Marc Aronson's essay on awards for ethnic children's literature and respond to his call to discuss the use and value of these awards. How would you defend the existence of these awards? For what purpose or audience might they be useful or effective? Do they imply that authors cannot write about cultures, ethnicities, or races

different from their own? Could these awards actually undermine the promotion of ethnic children's literature?

4. Discuss the question of ownership. Are the stories of a particular race, ethnicity, or culture "owned" by members of that community? Is it "theft" to write about or appropriate another culture's stories?

5. Consider a work depicting people of color such as Herron's *Nappy Hair* or Luis Alberto Urrea and José Galvez's *Vatos* (2000): What kind of audience does the text imply? Does the text assume a white audience, an audience composed of children or young adults of color, or a mixed audience? What kind of knowledge does the text assume the audience possesses? What does it assume the audience does not know? What is the evidence from the text for your claims?

Investigate

1. Select a scene from a children's book known for its controversial depiction of a person of color or Native American, such as Laura Ingalls Wilder's *Little House on the Prairie* or Martha Finley's *Elsie Dinsmore*, and rewrite a scene from the perspective of the character of color or indigenous person. How does imagining this alternative perspective help you understand the text differently or better? How does your understanding of the character of color or indigenous person change or develop through this activity?

2. Examine the illustrations for several different editions of a novel or picturebook featuring people of color, such as Mark Twain's *Adventures of Huckleberry Finn* or Helen Bannerman's *Little Black Sambo*. How are these characters depicted visually? To what extent do the illustrations rely on or depart from racial or ethnic stereotypes?

3. Select a work that has been retold—such as one of the Uncle Remus tales retold by Julius Lester, or Margaret Mahy's 1990 *The Seven Chinese Brothers*, illustrated by Jean and Mou-sien Tseng (a retelling of Claire Huchet Bishop and Kurt Wiese's *The Five Chinese Brothers*, 1938)—and determine how the retelling changes the original. Is the retelling less problematic or troubling in its depiction of race or ethnicity? How does the story, language, or perspective change?

4. Select a work with a white protagonist that might not appear to address race or ethnicity—such as Louisa May Alcott's *Little Women* (1868) or *Little Men* (1871),

L.M. Montgomery's *Anne of Green Gables* (1908), or Lois Lenski's *Strawberry Girl* (1945)—and consider how race or ethnicity might actually play a role in the novel. Do the white characters seem to possess a distinct race or ethnicity? How does race or ethnicity affect the narrative in subtle ways?

SUGGESTED READINGS

Erdrich, Louise. *The Birchbark House* (1999). Telling the story of a seven-year-old Ojibwe girl named Omakayas, Louise Erdrich's *The Birchbark House* could be called a response to the controversial Little House series by Laura Ingalls Wilder because its depiction of Native American life in the nineteenth century functions as a corrective to Wilder's. Omakayas's daily life with her family on an island in Lake Superior is described, as the Ojibwe Indians must contemplate moving west ahead of encroaching Euro American settlers and contend with the dangers of smallpox.

Gansworth, Eric. *If I Ever Get Out of Here* (2013). Set in 1975, *If I Ever Get Out of Here* is narrated by Lewis Blake, who lives on the Tuscarora reservation in Niagara County, New York. The only Native American in his seventh-grade "brainiacs" class, he is initially isolated but slowly forges a friendship with George Haddonfield, a white kid whose military family has served in many countries. Their friendship is built on a mutual love of music and a shared sense of humor, but they must also navigate class division and cultural differences. Racially motivated bullying is another theme of the novel, when Lewis is bullied and school authority figures ignore it. Initially ashamed of his poverty and unwilling to invite George to visit his home, Lewis comes to a renewed appreciation of his supportive family and his life on the reservation.

Kadohata, Cynthia. *Kira-Kira* (2004). Set in Georgia between the mid 1950s and the early 1960s, Cynthia Kadohata's Newbery-winning novel *Kira-Kira* depicts the life of a Japanese American family who contend with both racial prejudice and the terminal illness of one of its members. Twelve years old when the novel ends, Katie, the narrator, struggles to understand the cruel working conditions her immigrant parents experience at a poultry factory and to work through the grief of losing her beloved older sister to cancer.

Levoy, Myron. *Alan and Naomi* (1977). Taking place in New York City while World War II continues in Europe, Myron Levoy's *Alan and Naomi* is about the friendship between Alan, a twelve-year-old Jewish American, and Naomi, a Jewish girl who has emigrated from France after her father was murdered by the Gestapo. Though set in the United

States, *Alan and Naomi* is ultimately a novel about the Holocaust. Naomi suffers from trauma, and the people surrounding her believe her friendship with Alan may help her avoid a total breakdown.

Reynolds, Jason and Brendan Kiely. *All American Boys* (2015). Co-authored by Reynolds and Kiely, *All American Boys* tells the story of Rashad, a black teen who experiences a violent encounter with a police officer, and the white teen, Quinn, who witnesses the brutality. The novel, which alternates between the two boys' stories, echoes real news-making events that have given rise to the Black Lives Matter movement. The book depicts the possibilities of youth activism around issues of race.

Ryan, Pam Muñoz. *Esperanza Rising* (2000). A historical novel set in California during the 1930s, Pam Muñoz Ryan's *Esperanza Rising* is based roughly on the experience of Ryan's grandmother, who emigrated from Mexico to the United States during the Great Depression. Esperanza, almost thirteen, leaves behind a life of relative privilege and travels to California with her mother after the death of her father. She must become accustomed to the difficult life at a camp for Mexican American migrant laborers, and after her mother becomes ill, Esperanza must assume the burden of her family's survival.

Taylor, Mildred D. *Roll of Thunder, Hear My Cry* (1976). Only the second African American author to win the Newbery Medal, Mildred D. Taylor set *Roll of Thunder, Hear My Cry* in Mississippi during the 1930s, as Cassie Logan and her family must contend with the explicit racism and hostility faced by African Americans in the United States.

Cover of *Esperanza Rising* (2000) by Pam Muñoz Ryan.

Cassie, a fourth-grade student in a segregated school where her mother teaches, provides a child's perspective as her family struggles to hold on to its land and dignity in the face of violence and threat.

Taylor, Sydney. *All-of-a-Kind Family* (**1951**). Sydney Taylor's classic children's novel *All-of-a-Kind Family* is the first in a series of books about five Jewish sisters growing up in the immigrant neighborhood of the Lower East Side in New York City during the early decades of the twentieth century. Sometimes compared to Alcott's *Little Women*, the mostly episodic novel describes the girls' various adventures, from visiting a branch of the New York Public Library to facing illnesses and celebrating holidays.

Urrea, Luis Alberto, and José Galvez. *Vatos* (**2000**). Marketed as a picturebook for young adults, *Vatos* combines a poem by Luis Alberto Urrea about vatos, a Chicano slang term for "dude, guy, pal, brother," with José Galvez's compelling black-and-white photographs of Chicano and Latino men engaging in various everyday activities. *Vatos* represents Chicano men as emotionally complex individuals, in contrast with the two-dimensional stereotypes that currently dominate American public discourse about Latino immigrants, and it uses the aesthetics of poetry to celebrate these usually unsung men.

Yang, Gene Luen. *American Born Chinese* (**2006**). Gene Yang's young adult graphic novel *American Born Chinese* won the Printz Award in 2007. It interweaves three related stories, which eventually converge: one about a Chinese folk character called the Monkey King, one about a Chinese American middle-schooler and child of Chinese immigrants named Jin Wang, and one about a European American sitcom character named Danny who is embarrassed by the stereotypical behaviors of his Chinese cousin Chin-Kee. In juxtaposing the Monkey King's story with Jin's and Chin-Kee's, *American Born Chinese* combines traditional folk tales with the conventions of contemporary realist fiction about the immigrant experience. Yang uses the graphic novel form to address racial stereotyping visually.

APPROACHES TO TEACHING *THE SNOWY DAY* [ELEMENTARY SCHOOL]

Preparation for the Lesson

The class should read the 50th Anniversary Edition of *The Snowy Day* (2011) out loud. The bonus material in the book will support some of the following activities. The teacher should also assemble various materials for a collage activity.

Learning Goals

- To learn about Keats's process in composing *The Snowy Day*

- To analyze the book's use of an urban setting

- To reflect on the book's appeal to international audiences

- To learn more about Keats's use of collage and practice collage techniques.

Activity One: The Composition Process

Read students the following description of Keats's compositional process, showing them the *Life* magazine photo stills of the African American child who inspired him (see p. 421):

> Before this book came out, in the early 1960s, very few picture books had ever featured African American characters. Years earlier, when Keats was beginning his career as an illustrator, he saw a set of photos of a little black boy in *Life* magazine and stuck them up on the wall of his studio…. The photos remained on his wall for twenty-two years before Keats finally decided he would write the book himself, and Peter and *The Snowy Day* were born. (n.p.)

Lead a discussion about the emotions the young boy expresses in the clipping and why Keats may have found the photos so inspiring. Ask students to identify moments in *The Snowy Day* when Peter demonstrates similar emotions.

Activity Two: Universality and Specificity

Part A: The Specific Setting of the Book

Lead the class in a discussion of the setting of the book. How do we know it is an urban setting? Do you live in a city, like Peter does, or in the country or a small town? How would *The Snowy Day* be different if Peter lived in the country?

Part B: The Global Appeal of *The Snowy Day*

Read Keats's remarks (in the 50th Anniversary Edition of *The Snowy Day*) about his use of materials from many countries: "The creative efforts of people from many lands contributed to the materials in this book. Some of the papers used for the collage came from Japan, some from Italy, some from Sweden, many from our own country" (n.p.). Explain to the students that *The Snowy Day* was translated into at least ten languages and show them the global editions in the 50th Anniversary Edition (if you happen to own editions of the text in translation, bring those in as well). Building on the discussion about the specific setting, explain that the book is set in a very specific time and place but that it speaks to people who live far away from the protagonist. Ask students to select a country where *The Snowy Day* has appeared in translation. Help students locate images of a city in that country and research the climate; then instruct them to describe or illustrate the typical winter day of a child in that city. Discuss with the class how their depictions differ from Keats's depiction of Peter's snowy day.

Activity Three: Collage and Illustration

Part A: Newspaper and Magazine Clippings: A Creative Response

Lead a discussion about Keats's use of collage in his book. After the discussion, present a variety of newspaper and magazine clippings featuring child protagonists of many races and ethnic backgrounds. Remind the students that Keats found inspiration in the story of a young African American boy in a magazine, and ask them to choose a clipping to serve as their own inspiration. Ask the students to create a single collage page depicting the child in the clipping they chose and to write a short narrative about the child. After the activity, ask them about the experience of working with collage and what they learned about *The Snowy Day* from making their own collages.

Part B: Joining Peter on a Snowy Day

In this exercise students will imagine that they are playing with Peter on a snowy day. As a class, make a list of the winter activities that the book depicts where Peter is playing alone. Tell the class to imagine that they are joining Peter in his play. The students will produce either an illustration or a collage of themselves playing with Peter. When their artwork is complete, each student should share his or her picture. Briefly comment on the artistic choices or the choice of a particular scene. Lead a discussion about why Peter enjoys playing by himself, but why it is also fun to be outside with someone else.

GENDERS AND SEXUALITIES

According to the Office for Intellectual Freedom of the American Library Association (ALA), seven of the top ten most frequently challenged books of 2017, whether for children or adults, were targeted for removal from schools and libraries wholly or in part because of objections to LGBT characters, sex and sex education, sexual violence, or "sexually explicit" material ("Top Ten" n.p.). Out of 10,676 challenges on record with the ALA between 1990 and 2010, sexual explicitness was cited as the reason for 3,169 cases, making it the most frequent basis for challenges, while other objections related to sexuality or gender (homosexuality, nudity, sex education, unsuited to age group) constitute an additional 4,052 cases (more than one reason can be listed for each challenge, and the person reporting the challenge must indicate to which of these categories it belongs). While a challenge could be initiated for multiple reasons, these figures indicate that between one-third and one-half were related to issues of sexuality or gender. A total of 6,103 challenges were initiated by parents on behalf of their children, and the most frequently targeted institutions were schools (4,048), school libraries (3,659), and public libraries (2,679). This data clearly indicates that sexual material is some of the most controversial content in literature when it comes to child readers, and childhood and children's culture are key battlegrounds for attitudes about gender and sexuality ("Number of Challenges" n.p.). This makes sense, given that childhood is the period when we learn or practice what it means to be a boy, girl, man, or woman, or to construct and enact alternatives to these traditional categories.

Opposite: Vivian Burnett (1886), son of Frances Hodgson Burnett, dressed in a "Little Lord Fauntleroy" costume.

THE SIGNIFICANCE OF GENDER AND SEXUALITY IN CHILDREN'S CULTURE

Gender and Sexuality in Childhood

Part of the reason sex and sexuality are so controversial as subjects for children's literature and culture is the persistent investment in what is perceived to be the innocence of children. This innocence is defined in part by children's enforced ignorance of sexual matters. Indeed, access to sex and sexuality is one of the privileges that constitutes the line between childhood and adulthood, and while adolescents are begrudgingly permitted limited opportunities for sexual exploration, sex and sexuality remain highly controversial even for young adults. Nonetheless, many of the rituals of adolescence that mark developmental milestones, such as the senior prom, are associated with courtship and the possibility of sexual activity. Dressing up, riding in limousines, dancing, and retiring to a hotel room are practices associated with both proms and weddings. This association presents a bit of a paradox, since, according to James Kincaid, youth and innocence are two of the most eroticized constructions of the past two centuries: "Innocence was that which we have been trained to adore and covet, to preserve and despoil, to speak of in hushed tones and in bawdy songs" (10). Children and adolescents are expected to be sexless, even as our culture valorizes, idealizes, and even eroticizes youth.

Moreover, children are actively socialized to behave in ways associated with one gender or another; they are encouraged and rewarded for behaving in normative and sanctioned ways for their gender while being discouraged or punished for showing nontraditional interests. They are similarly compelled to experience certain sanctioned and normative desires while others are made to seem prohibited or perverted. Because childhood is a critical time for development, children's culture is replete with artifacts or rituals that provide opportunities to practice gender and sexuality. Much of children's culture, from toys and games to television programs and novels, contributes to the gendering and sexualization of children, and many of our notions and values regarding gender and sexuality get worked out through and around children and their bodies.

Toys, Clothes, and Bathrooms

A visit to any toy store makes clear the importance of gender and sexuality to childhood. Many children's toys are specifically coded as either for boys or for girls. Baby dolls allow children, usually girls, to practice caring for infants by feeding them, cuddling them, and dressing them—actions that promote reproduction and conception itself. Barbie dolls teach child consumers about fashion and the standards of female beauty—for future heterosexual girls, how to make oneself attractive to boys or men. Products marketed to boys include G.I. Joe, a doll originally modeled on army soldiers; and Transformers, robots that transform into cars or aircraft and promote an interest in or comfort with combat and technology, which are masculine domains. Toy cooking sets or lawnmowers allow children to practice adult activities and roles that remain clearly gendered. These gendered distinctions now extend into newer technologies such as video games.

Children's clothes and room decorations also tend to come coded as specifically for boys or girls. Though blues and earth tones now dominate boys' fashions while pinks and other pastels mark similar products for girls, these pairings used to be reversed. One publication advised parents in 1918, "The generally accepted rule is pink for the boys, and blue for the girls. The reason is that pink, being a more decided and stronger color, is more suitable for the boy, while blue, which is more delicate and dainty, is prettier for the girl" (qtd. in Maglaty 1). Even small infants, whose lives might not otherwise require clear gender distinctions, are dressed in outfits to mark their sex, with female infants sometimes even having hair bands with bows or other accessories affixed to their bald heads. Clothes and toys are clearly used to teach children about gender and to reinforce conventional distinctions.

A 2015 decision by Target stores to eliminate gender labeling on signs for items like toys, costumes, and bedding caused some controversy, indicating the deep investment in childhood gender traditions (Padilla n.p.). In response to some US states' efforts to pass laws requiring people, including school children, to use the bathroom of the sex assigned to them at birth, as opposed to the one with which they identify, the US Departments of Education and Justice issued a joint statement indicating that such laws may violate federal protections from discrimination (Davis and Apuzzo n.p.); however, the Department of Education rescinded that guidance in 2017 (Balingit n.p.). Opponents of these bathroom laws note that forcing transgender students to use the bathroom of a gender with which they don't identify is embarrassing, painful, and potentially dangerous to them. Cases of both product labeling and bathroom use make clear that children and children's culture remain battlegrounds for changing cultural norms around gender and sexuality.

Disney

Even the stories read to the youngest children, such as traditional fairy tales, and Disney films based on them, often center on narratives of desire, romance, and marriage. Many of the most celebrated Disney films end in romantic pairings or even marriage: *Snow White* (1937), *Cinderella* (1950), *Sleeping Beauty* (1959), and *The Princess and the Frog* (2009). June Cummins, writing in 1995, observes that "virtually all recent Disney animated fairy tales, including *The Little Mermaid, Beauty and the Beast,* and *Aladdin,* privilege the romance plot structure" (22). Cummins contends, "While one may argue that Disney is not responsible for this tendency because fairy tales have always relied on the romance plot, it is possible to see that in fact Disney magnifies the romantic element of its versions of the tales" (23). These films, which constitute part of the common culture of generations of audiences, also depict powerfully influential images of what it means to be a man or woman and how men and women should view each other.

GENDER AND SEXUALITY IN CHILDREN'S LITERATURE

Children's literature has a long history of viewing boys and girls as distinct audiences and contributing to their gendered socialization. When John Newbery published his landmark *A Little Pretty Pocket-Book* in 1744, it was packaged with an object described as a ball for boys and a pincushion for girls. The text of the book contains two letters written by the fictional character Jack the Giant Killer, one to Master Tommy and one to Miss Polly, as a way of engaging boy and girl readers. In 1798, British educator and author

A 1787 edition of John Newbery's *A Little Pretty Pocket-Book* with the included pincushion or ball.

Maria Edgeworth and her father Richard Lovell Edgeworth cowrote a parenting guide that made distinct recommendations about appropriate reading material for boys and for girls. However, historians of childhood and scholars of children's literature have found that distinctions between boyhood and girlhood and between boy and girl readers became even more pronounced in the nineteenth century, when genres and periodicals were developed specifically for boys or girls. Newbery's significance lies in his breakthrough in thinking about children as a consumer market. As children's culture became much more elaborate and varied, and as more goods and services were produced specifically for children, more attention came to be paid to boys and girls as distinct consumers, which led to the production of even more varied goods. According to the historian John Gillis, boyhood took on new meaning in the mid nineteenth century when it came to be more clearly distinguished from an undifferentiated early childhood and from the increasingly defined period known as adolescence. He notes that it was not until the 1850s that magazines for children were published specifically for boys (Gillis 104). Sally Mitchell sees a similar phenomenon with girls beginning in the 1880s, when "the concept of girlhood as a separate stage of existence with its own values and interests was only beginning to take shape" (1). Despite the increased bifurcation of boys and girls into distinct audiences, it remained acceptable and unremarkable for boys to read fiction for and about girls, such as Louisa May Alcott's *Little Women* (1868), and for girls to read fiction for and about boys, such as Mark Twain's *The Adventures of Tom Sawyer* (1876), during the nineteenth century. While this kind of cross reading might have become more taboo in the twentieth century, some children do brave the risks of defying gender norms with reading material.

Children's literature is now thoroughly marked by and invested in distinctions between boys and girls, men and women, and gay and straight sexualities. In Chapter 6 we considered how the genres of adventure and domesticity are often used to address or represent boys and girls separately, but this tendency also extends to other genres. The assumption of a bifurcated audience of boys and girls might seem especially pronounced in nineteenth-century classics, but it remains true of more contemporary realist works of the twentieth and twenty-first centuries. This chapter explores the role of children's literature and culture in the development, emergence, or construction of gender and sexual identities and desires. We begin by unpacking the complex matrix of gender and sexuality by examining and defining key components of each, and then we go into more detail about the literature of boyhood and girlhood as well as depictions of love, romance, and relationships, both normative and queer.

DEFINING SEX/GENDER

Sex and Gender

Feminist cultural critic Gayle Rubin coined the term "sex/gender system" to refer to the "set of arrangements by which a society transforms biological sexuality into products of human activity" (28). Critics like Rubin often make the distinction between sex and gender, on which the idea of the sex/gender system rests. The term "**sex**" is used to refer to a system of biological designations such as male, female, or intersexed (individuals born with both male and female anatomical components) based on genetic and anatomical features; the term "**gender**" refers to the system of culturally and historically specific characteristics and behavior sets such as masculinity, femininity, manhood, and womanhood. Starting with a distinction between sex and gender is important to recognizing that the two do not always line up in expected ways. Male individuals can be described as feminine or can enact femininity, and female individuals can be described as masculine or can enact masculinity. Though there might be a relationship between the two, sex does not determine gender. Rubin's discussion of the sex/gender system recognizes that society creates the illusion that maleness automatically involves masculinity, and femaleness femininity. If that equation of sex and gender were true, children would not need to be taught and trained to perform gender in ways that are judged to be socially acceptable or normative. A boy would not need to be told to "be a man," nor would a girl need to be told how to "act like a lady." That gender needs to be taught and reinforced indicates that it does not emerge naturally on its own in the kinds of distinct, exaggerated ways we might expect.

Gender as Performance

Feminist and gender critics also make distinctions between **gender performance** and **gender identity**, or behaviors and ways of thinking about onself. Gender involves both. First, to be described as masculine or feminine, one has to *do* something. Even to *look* masculine involves dressing in a particular way—perhaps by wearing pants, or a specific uniform or costume, such as that of a soldier, mechanic, or business executive—while appearing feminine might require wearing one's hair longer or using cosmetics. How one carries one's body, one's posture or manner of walking, is often understood as signaling masculinity and femininity. Masculinity might be associated with physical aggressiveness or bravado, while femininity might be signaled by meekness or seductiveness. Because many of the qualities that might lead a person to be labeled masculine or feminine require action, we could say that they must be performed, and thus gender can be understood as a socialized, habitual performance of a certain set of qualities. Gender theorist Judith Butler has argued that the "reality" of gender "is created through sustained social performances" and that rather than expressing an essential difference, this sustained performance, however subtle or unconscious, creates that sense of difference (192). Moreover, the kinds of actions or qualities described as masculine or feminine can change depending on cultural location or historical moment. For instance, it became fashionable for upper-class men in seventeenth-century France and England to wear long, shoulder-length wigs, and in the eighteenth century for the wigs to be powdered. A man sporting a similar style now might be perceived as feminine. Similarly, in the 1930s famed anthropologist Margaret Mead found that the women of the Mundugumor people of New Guinea were "as assertive and vigorous as the men; they detest bearing and rearing children, and provide most of the food, leaving the men free to plot and fight" (50). Thus, gender can be understood in terms of culturally and historically specific performances.

Gender as Identity

Gender also involves identity. One not only enacts a particular set of behaviors perceived as masculine or feminine but also thinks of oneself as having a gendered identity such as man, woman, non-binary, or transgender. Such identities are partially self-determined and partially imposed or policed by others. One can perceive oneself as a man and have that identity undercut or threatened by others who might refuse to accept one's chosen status. Such refusal can be expressed as complaints that someone is not "acting like a man" or is not a "real man." This can be especially true for transgender persons whose biological sex at birth may not correspond to their present state or to their identity. Nevertheless, someone might have been designated female at birth but identify as a man and perform masculinity, while someone else might have been designated male at birth, identify as a woman, and perform femininity. The combinations of sex, gender performance, and gender identity are multiple and varied.

Gender and Class

Available gender identities and performances, and what might be normative or usual expressions of gender, depend on historical context and cultural location, but they also depend on class status. What is considered masculine or feminine, manly or womanly, or boyish or girlish is different at different times and in different places; but even at the same time and place, differences of socioeconomic or class status, race, and ethnicity can affect and intersect with gender. As Leonore Davidoff and Catherine Hall explain, for middle-class English children during the nineteenth century, "education and early work experience followed gender divisions," but "the greatest distinction came in later adolescence when the boys began to be seriously groomed for work in the outside world" (344). On the other hand, for working-class boys forced to leave home or take on more substantial work at earlier ages, gender distinctions may have been accelerated. In other cases, class status could blur gender divisions, with working-class or poor girls needing to do more physical labor, thereby affecting their gender performance and how others perceive it. Davidoff and Hall note that cleanliness and tidiness were essential to the performance of femininity for middle-class girls, but working-class or poor girls might not have had the same opportunity to remain so fastidious and dainty, altering how others would view their girlishness or femininity.

CHILDHOOD GENDER

Boys and Girls

If we look at the intersection of gender and age, we find that childhood has its own forms of gender identity and performance that differ somewhat from their adult counterparts: boys, girls, tomboys, sissies, boyhood, and girlhood. Many stereotypical expectations about gender are linked to traditional family roles and how men and women in heterosexual relationships are expected or thought to relate to one another, to divide household labor, and even to relate to children. Despite progress in thinking critically about gender stereotypes, the expectation persists, for instance, that men are or should be "providers" while women are or should be "nurturers." By virtue of their youth, children have roles expected of them that differ from those of adults of the same sex. For example, while manhood might be associated with being responsible and providing for others, boyhood is frequently associated with pranks and irresponsibility, as suggested by the phrase "Boys will be boys" as an excuse for troublesome behavior. Men are expected to wield authority, but this can be difficult or impossible for boys who are subject to the authority of adults, including women. Boys who appear to claim power or authority might be branded as having behavior problems and punished, indicating that boys are not regarded simply as miniature men. Similarly, girlhood differs from womanhood. One expectation of women is that they be sexually or romantically available to men, but the cultural hysteria surrounding child molestation makes the sexualization of girls highly problematic, as evidenced by the case of JonBenét Ramsey, the six-year-old beauty queen who was found murdered in her home in 1996. Her murder brought attention to the world of girls' beauty pageants, and the overt sexualization of JonBenét led to the cloud of suspicion that haunted her parents for twelve years following the unsolved murder. While women pageant queens might be thought by some to represent the ideal of female beauty, the phenomenon of beauty pageants for girls is still widely met with suspicion, if not outright disapproval, suggesting again that girls are not simply supposed to be little women.

Tomboys and Sissies

The figure of the tomboy is especially associated with childhood and is defined by the girlhood performance of masculinity. Michelle Abate notes that the concept dates to the late sixteenth century, though the figure of the tomboy was not prevalent in American culture until the nineteenth century, when it became popular in literature such as Louisa May Alcott's *Little Women* and Susan Coolidge's 1872 work, *What Katy Did* (xiii). In the latter novel, Coolidge describes Katy as a girl who "tore her dress every day, hated sewing, and didn't care a button about being called 'good'" (3). When Meg tells Jo in *Little Women* that she must "leave off boyish tricks," Jo responds despondently, "It's bad enough to be a girl, anyway, when I like boys' games and work and manners! I can't get over my disappointment in not being a boy" (Alcott 5). As Abate explains, "The traits most Americans are likely to name as constitutive of this code of [tomboy] conduct include a proclivity for outdoor play (especially athletics), a feisty independent spirit, and a tendency to don masculine clothing and adopt a boyish nickname" (xvi).

Abate also states that often in literature "a tomboy's closest friend is a 'sissy' boy rather than another girl" (xx). The friendship between Jo and Laurie in *Little Women* is a classic example. The sissy boy, as the boyhood corollary to the tomboy, is the boy who performs some version of femininity; this figure is often expected to avoid rough-and-tumble play in favor of milder or more artistic pursuits, to express an appreciation for finery or pretty things, and to display less bravado or machismo than other boys. When Jo first meets him, Laurie spends much of his time indoors, is considered sickly and fragile, and enjoys practicing music. He is described as having "pretty manners" (Alcott 53), in contrast to the "rough and wild" Jo (10). Over the course of the novel, Laurie becomes more conventionally boyish and then manly, while Jo vows to become more ladylike.

While gender variance in adulthood is typically associated with sexual deviance, particularly romantic and sexual desire for others of the same sex, this expectation is less true of tomboys and sissies. In fact, one important quality that differentiates tomboys and sissies from gender-variant adults is the expectation that the former will outgrow their gender variance, and one of the common plotlines involving gender-variant children is precisely their maturation into gender-conforming adults or older youths. Both Jo in *Little Women* and Katy in *What Katy Did* are eventually disciplined or tamed into becoming more traditional girls and women.

BOYS AND BOYHOOD IN CHILDREN'S LITERATURE

Thinking critically about boys and boyhood in children's literature involves examining books about boys and books for boys, or what is known as the boy book. What does it mean to be a boy in children's literature? What varieties of boys are represented? How do boys enact a range of gender performances? How are boys imagined as a market? In contrast to earlier boy books that were primarily didactic, such as Thomas Day's *The History of Sandford and Merton* (1783) and Jacob Abbott's Rollo series (starting in 1834), a number of genres crystallized in the nineteenth century for the amusement of boy readers.

The Boys' School Story

The boys' school story was one of the first genres developed specifically to entertain boy readers. Usually set in all-boys boarding schools, works such as Thomas Hughes's *Tom Brown's Schooldays* (1857) set the pattern for later school stories, including contemporary examples such as J.K. Rowling's Harry Potter series. The boys' school story typically features a fairly ordinary boy and his small circle of friends who must navigate the social, educational, and physical dangers of school life, from contending with bullies and abusive schoolmasters to temptations to cheat on exams or snitch on other boys. The school itself—with its Gothic architecture, labyrinth of rooms, and extensive grounds—provides opportunities for adventure, mischief, exploration, and physical altercations, and sports are usually a major component of school stories. This collection of experiences allows boys to enact traditional forms of boyhood while practicing many of the hallmarks of adult men's culture: political and social alliances and hierarchies, subjection to authority and the mentorship or exploitation of inferiors, and the ability to plan and carry out schemes. In *Tom Brown*, Hughes makes explicit the conventions and experiences of boyhood. Tom is described as "robust and combative" and as possessing "an excess of boyishness" in his athleticism, honesty, and pluck (Hughes 22).

Boys' Adventure Fiction

The adventure fiction described in Chapter 6 was another nineteenth-century genre that usually featured boys. It typically depicted boyhood as defined by the escape from home and accumulation of worldly experience, usually in the company of other men or boys. The boy books of Rudyard Kipling, such as *The Jungle Book* (1894) and *Kim* (1899), are key examples. Set in nineteenth-century India, *Kim* focuses on the orphaned son of an Irish soldier, who manages to pass as Indian and gets swept up in "the Great Game," the political conflict between Britain and Russia in the 1890s that played out in South Asia and the Middle East. Kim becomes involved in espionage, stealing vital maps from Russian agents. That a boy plays a crucial role in a dangerous and consequential international conflict is a fantasy that turns Kim's boyhood into an asset and transforms child's play into something real within the world of the novel. Kim is able to achieve a position of power and importance despite or because of his age, thereby transcending the limitations of boyhood.

We discussed in Chapter 6 how themes of empire and imperialism, seen clearly in *Kim*, are often central to adventure fiction, but not all boys' adventure stories so explicitly invoke empire. Robert Louis Stevenson's *Treasure Island*, inspired in part by R.M. Ballantyne's *The Coral Island* (1857), featured many elements thought to be appealing to boys. Stevenson himself explained, "It was to be a story for boys; no need of psychology or fine writing; and I had a boy at hand to be a touchstone. Women were excluded" (187). The novel, which emerged out of Stevenson's efforts to amuse his stepson, tells the story of young Jim Hawkins, who leaves behind his home and his mother and the dull work at his parents' inn to accompany an expedition of men to find a treasure. Faced with pirates, mutiny, and gun battles, Jim is able to demonstrate his courage, independence, and heart. By sharing in the discovered treasure, Jim profits from his adventure and proves himself to be upwardly mobile. With both experience and capital, Jim is prepared to take his place as a young man, indicating one common trajectory of the boy book. Gary Paulsen's *Hatchet* (1987), about a thirteen-year-old boy who survives a plane crash in the Canadian wilderness, is a more contemporary version of the boys' adventure story that, following in the tradition of *The Coral Island*, focuses on survival.

The Bad-Boy Book

While the boy book about imperial adventure was more prevalent in British children's literature, American boy books pioneered the story of the bad boy, whose adventures are more local and common. Thomas Bailey Aldrich's *The Story of a Bad Boy* (1869) and Mark Twain's *The Adventures of Tom Sawyer* (1876) are both about boys named Tom who cannot stay out of trouble. Though they cause mischief and get into scrapes, they are also depicted as especially enterprising, clever, and charismatic. Bad boys such as Tom Sawyer have been held up as icons of both boyhood and American culture itself. Like Jim Hawkins in *Treasure Island*, Tom acts as the underdog boy who nonetheless triumphs over a villainous adult, Injun Joe; also like Jim, Tom discovers a treasure that signals his upward mobility. Like the boys in these other classic boy books, he demonstrates courage and initiative, qualities that boys are clearly supposed to possess, but he also evidences a mischievousness that boys are supposed to outgrow as they become men. As with a character such as Peter Pan, it becomes difficult to imagine an adult Tom Sawyer who still possesses the qualities that define his childhood self, which indicates that Twain captures a conception of boyhood that is distinct from manhood and is even honored as such. Contemporary versions of the bad boy might include the character of Christopher from Mark Haddon's *The Curious Incident of the Dog in the Night-Time* (2003). In Haddon's book, though the mostly humorous mischief of Tom Sawyer, dismissed with the common excuse that boys will be boys, is now medicalized. Christopher lives with his father in the town of Swindon in England, and though never stated explicitly, evidence points to Christopher's having Asperger's syndrome. Over the course of the novel, he attempts to solve the mystery of his neighbor's dead dog, for which he is blamed.

The Feral Tale

Whereas the bad boy remained tied to the home, with many of the sources of drama and tension caused by the boy protagonist's chafing against his domestic anchor, survival stories and stories Kenneth Kidd describes as "feral tales," about children raised in the wild, depict boys who are unencumbered by home or civilization. Rudyard Kipling's *The Jungle Book* (1894) and *The Second Jungle Book* (1895) feature Mowgli, a boy raised by animals in the jungles of India, and Edgar Rice Burroughs's *Tarzan of the Apes* (1914) depicts a boy adopted by apes after his parents, who are stranded on the African coast, are murdered. These boys possess either extraordinary abilities themselves or intelligent animal companions who are ferocious protectors. Tarzan is immune to cold and can kill and carry a full-grown lion with relative ease. Mowgli enjoys the protection of Bagheera and Baloo, a panther and a bear, but he is also a capable hunter himself, despite being a young boy. Contemporary examples of the feral tale or animal-companion story include Maurice Sendak's *Where the Wild Things Are* (1963), in which Max travels to the land of wild monsters and briefly communes with them, and Fred Gipson's *Old Yeller* (1956), about a boy who helps care for the family farm in Texas with the help of a stray dog during his father's absence. Though both boy protagonists in these later books struggle with self-doubt, they are represented as hearty and resourceful survivalists who ultimately triumph over nature and their circumstances.

The Unconventional Boy in Children's Literature

Not all boys in children's literature fit these conventional models of the physically robust athlete, hearty survivalist, or mischievous bad boy. Children's literature also includes boys such as Laurie in *Little Women*, who are described as sensitive, saintly, sickly, or effeminate. Cedric Errol of Frances Hodgson Burnett's *Little Lord Fauntleroy* (1886) is an extremely compassionate boy who worries about the plight of the poor and who softens his curmudgeonly grandfather through his feminine sweetness. He is described as having "pretty manners" and "bright, curly hair which waved over his forehead and fell in charming lovelocks on his shoulders" (Burnett, *Little* 10). In *The Secret Garden* (1911), Burnett presents a sickly and petulant boy in the character Colin, who suffers from fits of crying, a dose of vanity, and hysteria, a mental illness historically associated with girls and women. The sickly, sensitive boy even appears in the context of the quintessential boys' school story, *Tom Brown's Schooldays*. Arthur is a shy and saintly boy who helps reform the more boisterous Tom through his gentle prodding and his fine example. Even Arthur, though, is able to demonstrate courage by bravely enduring the taunts of his peers when he insists on getting down on his knees to pray each night, and both Arthur and Colin are ultimately transformed into more conventional boys over the course of the works in which they appear. More contemporary sissy boys include Jesse from Katherine Paterson's *Bridge to Terabithia* (1977). In Paterson's Newbery Medal winner, Jesse is a timid boy who likes art and strikes up a friendship with a tomboyish new neighbor named Leslie, whose death represents a significant moment in Jesse's childhood. Jesse's father disapproves of his son's artistic inclinations and worries about his female teachers: "Bunch of old ladies turning my only son into some kind of a—" (Paterson 14). Paterson leaves out the word, but it clearly refers to Jesse's gender or sexuality. These unconventional boys evidence the fact that not all boys are depicted as performing masculinity.

Boys and Popular Literature

In her study of boys' literature, Annette Wannamaker observes that research on the reading habits of boys indicates that their preferences are often at odds with the recommendations of teachers and librarians, and she argues for classifying popular forms such as video games, manga, magazines, and comic books as boys' literature. Following Perry Nodelman, Wannamaker suggests that more popular forms of fiction tend to represent and reinforce conventional or dominant constructions of gender and race, while those works described as "literary" are more likely to complicate or critique them. Wannamaker's study implies that some readers prefer to read more normative gender representations, and that members of the literary establishment prefer oppositional or non-normative ones. Wannamaker cites Dav Pilkey's *The Adventures of Captain Underpants* (1997) and its sequels, a series about two troublemaking fourth-graders who invent silly superheroes, as examples of popular boys' literature. Another example of popular children's literature for or about boys include Jeff Kinney's Diary of a Wimpy Kid series, first published in 2007, which combines text with cartoons in what is supposed to be the diary of a middle-school boy named Greg. Works such as J.K. Rowling's Harry Potter series complicate the distinction between literary and popular texts, but understanding the kinds of works popular with boys offers insight into contemporary constructions and expectations of masculinity and boyhood.

GIRLS AND GIRLHOOD IN CHILDREN'S LITERATURE

The Girls' School Story

The girl book can be found in as many varieties as the boy book. Girl books were both adapted from models for boys and innovated independently of boy books. For instance, while *Tom Brown's Schooldays* is sometimes viewed as the prototype of the school story, Sarah Fielding's *The Governess; or, The Little Female Academy* (1749) preceded it by over a century. The first full-length narrative or novel for children, *The Governess* is set in a dame school, a small private school usually operated by a woman, and the girls in the novel achieve mutual understanding and personal insight by sharing their brief life stories. While *The Governess* anticipates the later formation of the school story and the narrative of moral reformation it often employs, Evelyn Sharp's *The Making of a Schoolgirl* (1897) parodies the boys' school story, as Becky, the novel's protagonist, mocks her brother's faulty assumptions about girls and girls' schools. Sue Sims credits Susan Coolidge's *What Katy Did at School* (1873) with helping establish the pattern for subsequent girls' school stories in the United States and Britain (6). In this second volume of the Katy series, sixteen-year-old Katy is sent to a boarding school on the East Coast with her sister Clover because their deceased mother's cousin, Mrs. Page, thinks the girls act too grown up. At school, they meet a variety of girls, from their cousin Lilly Page—who is vain, petty, and theatrically emotional—to a girl called Rose Red, who is brash and worldly. Katy and Clover are themselves depicted as saintly and virtuous, and their presence helps to reform the behavior of the other girls and steer them away from a precocious interest in boys.

Domestic and Family Stories

Books with girl protagonists can often be classified as domestic or family stories, such as Alcott's *Little Women* and other books discussed in Chapter 6. Sydney Taylor's *All-of-a-Kind Family* (1951) is a mid-twentieth-century example of the girls' family story that is often compared with Alcott's earlier classic. Set in New York City at the turn of the twentieth century, the novel depicts the life of a Jewish family that includes five sisters between the ages of four and twelve. It is mostly episodic: the girls visit the public library, learn to be diligent about doing their assigned chores, celebrate their father's birthday, and battle scarlet fever. Though the girls venture outside to visit the market or the library, much of the novel takes place inside the family's apartment and is concerned with the everyday activities of the household and immigrant life in their Lower East Side neighborhood. These girls can be said to have adventures, but as in *Little Women*, those adventures are circumscribed by the home or neighborhood.

Girls' Adventure Fiction

The domestic novel was the most common type of girl book in the nineteenth century, but some adventure fiction featuring girl protagonists also began to appear then. Lewis Carroll's *Alice's Adventures in Wonderland* (1865) combines elements of adventure with fantasy and nonsense. Alice leaves home, travels through Wonderland, encounters various dangers, overcomes obstacles, and returns to the safety of her sister's side. More conventional girls' adventure fiction was adapted from the models provided by boy books. The British author L.T. Meade published both girls' school stories and girls' adventures,

including *Four on an Island* (1892), a castaway novel featuring girls. Carol Ryrie Brink's *Baby Island* (1937) is another girls' adventure in which two sisters, Mary and Jean, survive the apparent sinking of an ocean liner and are cast away on a desert island with four babies, combining elements of domestic work with the survival aspects of adventure. Mary is the more conventionally gendered of the two, described as "a motherly girl who was never so happy as when she had borrowed a baby to cuddle or care for" (Brink 11). Jean, on the other hand, is a tomboy, so the sisters offer two different models of girlhood.

Another subgenre that combines both domesticity and adventure is the girls' frontier story. Some of the best-loved classics of girls' fiction, such as Brink's Newbery-winning *Caddie Woodlawn* (1935) and Laura Ingalls Wilder's Little House books (1932–43), are frontier stories that depict tomboyish girls who experience both conventional domestic situations and the

Frontispiece to a girls' adventure novel, *Half-Moon Girl, Or the Rajah's Daughter* by Bessie Marchant, 1898.

excitement of outdoor adventures. Even animal companions in children's literature are gendered. While boys in adventure or frontier fiction might be paired with dogs, girls are often associated with horses, as in Enid Bagnold's *National Velvet* (1935). Family life proves more prominent in these books than in counterparts for boys, but adventure and frontier fiction nonetheless provide opportunities for girls to explore the world outside of the home and family.

Orphans and Good Girls

The first decades of the twentieth century saw the publication of a number of classic orphan or foster girl books. Kate Douglas Wiggin's *Rebecca of Sunnybrook Farm* (1903), Frances Hodgson Burnett's *A Little Princess* (1905) and *The Secret Garden* (1911), Lucy Maud Montgomery's *Anne of Green Gables* (1908), and Eleanor Porter's *Pollyanna* (1913) all feature young girls missing one or both parents who are taken in by relatives or adopted by strangers. Of these girls, only Rebecca of Sunnybrook Farm has a living parent, though she spends almost the entire novel in the care of her spinster aunts. Rebecca, Mary of *The Secret Garden*, Anne of Green Gables, and Pollyanna all manage to greater or lesser degrees to convert spinster or widower relatives from cold curmudgeons into lovable caretakers. Only Sara Crewe in *A Little Princess* fails to reform the mean-spirited Miss Minchin, though Miss Minchin's sister, Miss Amelia, does stand up to her sister a bit by the conclusion of the novel.

While some of these girls lack conventional domestic skills, such as Anne, who frequently botches attempts to cook or bake, most of them possess the charm needed to play good hosts, to appease others, and to elicit care and protection. The good girl appears to be one corollary of the bad boy. For instance, the name "Pollyanna" is now synonymous with unfounded optimism, inspired by Pollyanna's habit of playing "the glad game," which involves finding something to be happy about, however dire the situation. When Miss Polly's maid, Nancy, learns that Pollyanna will be moving in, she is delighted to think of what a little girl will do for the house: "'A little girl—coming here, Miss Harrington? Oh, won't that be nice!' cried Nancy, thinking of the sunshine her own little sisters made in the home" (Porter 3). As Nancy predicts, Pollyanna does "brighten" the home with her enthusiasm and compassion. Beth of Alcott's *Little Women* is also a good girl, and her innocence and purity are linked with her physical fragility. Katy from the What Katy Did series starts off as a bad girl, but after a severe injury leaves her temporarily paralyzed, she transforms into a virtuous good girl who cares for her family and manages the household from her sickbed. These good, saintly girls echo one model of female adulthood: the angel in the house. A phrase coined by Coventry Patmore in his 1854 poem of that name, "the angel in the house" refers to a woman who demonstrates selfless devotion to the domestic care of others, especially her husband and family. As with the angel in the house, the definition of a good girl in these works indicates cultural ideals involving girls and women. The fact that the good girl typically experiences a personal catastrophe raises questions about what it means that good girls in literature are so often written as tragic figures.

Most of these girl protagonists are exceedingly good-tempered, innocent, imaginative, and extroverted. Mary is the main exception, yet one of the central plots of *The Secret Garden* is her transformation from a spoiled brat into a nurturing proto-mother to her cousin Colin. Whereas Mary's development is defined by her increasing selflessness and care for others, maturation for Rebecca and Anne involves taming some of their boisterousness and channeling it into productive work and the care of aging or less capable relatives. Sara and Pollyanna start out as models of ideal girlishness and change little. Like Jo in *Little Women*, some of these girls are depicted as needing to outgrow their tomboyishness or to temper their imaginations in order to settle into the calmness of adult womanhood.

Realist Fiction and Problem Novels for and about Girls

Literature for and about older girls and young women includes the romance, or novel of first love. Published just as the contemporary teenager was emerging as a coherent consumer market and age-based identity, Maureen Daly's *Seventeenth Summer* (1942) is about the first love of seventeen-year-old Angie for the handsome athlete Jack the summer after their senior year of high school. Their love, however, is doomed by circumstance, since at the end of the summer Angie will leave for college. *Seventeenth Summer* anticipated the emergence of the specifically young adult novel two decades later and the kind of realist fiction for girls by writers such as Judy Blume, whose novel *Forever* (1975), about the first sexual experience of a teenage girl, contains echoes of Daly's earlier novel while embracing the sexual revolution that had taken place in the interim. Blume's name is now virtually synonymous with the contemporary girl book. Her oeuvre contains numerous works, including *Are You There God? It's Me, Margaret* (1970), which walks girl readers through their first menses and first bra purchase; *Blubber* (1974), which addresses bullying among girls; and *Deenie* (1973), which depicts a girl whose vanity suffers when she is diagnosed with scoliosis. Blume's characters such as Margaret Simon, Jill Brenner, and Deenie Fenner embody the concerns and lives of contemporary girls who must contend with the social realities of modern girlhood and young womanhood.

Girls' Contemporary Series Fiction

Publishers frequently market series fiction for children specifically to either boys or girls, such as the Hardy Boys or Nancy Drew series, both published by the Stratemeyer Syndicate. While some series, like the popular Goosebumps books by R.L. Stine, seem to target readers of both sexes, some of the most successful series have been specifically marketed to and popular with girls, including the Sweet Valley High series, launched in 1983 by Francine Pascal to capitalize on the popularity of television soap operas (Carpan 120). Pascal later coached a host of ghostwriters on how to produce volumes about the everyday lives of a pair of teenage twins from California, leading to the publication of over seven hundred titles in the various Sweet Valley series (Carpan 133). According to Carolyn Carpan, the Sweet Valley High series owes its popularity to its inclusion of sexuality and romance and to its savvy marketing to both teen and younger girls with spin-offs for readers of different ages (122). The enormous success of Sweet Valley High paved the way for later girls' series books, such as Cecily von Ziegesar's Gossip Girl series, which launched in 2002; Lisi Harrison's The Clique series for middle-school age girls, which first published in 2004; and Stephenie Meyer's Twilight series, which first appeared in 2005. As Amy Pattee notes, these girls' series books have frequently been associated with the production of a variety of related commodities, such as clothing and television programs or movies, that encourage girls to associate their reading with consumerism (155).

The Diverse Girlhoods of Children's Literature

Girl books present a range of different types of girls, from tomboys such as Katy in Coolidge's What Katy Did series to the long-suffering Pollyanna, who enlivens her home through her sweetness, patience, and optimism. They include bratty girls such as Mary in The Secret Garden, who is a perversely sympathetic character in her initial refusal to conform to conventional expectations that girls be sweet and self-sacrificing, and modern girls such as Katherine in Blume's Forever, who ventures into New York City alone to visit a Planned Parenthood clinic and obtain birth control. In many of these novels, girls who are overly vain, such as Katy's cousin Lilly Page, or spitefully jealous, such as Sara Crewe's rival, Lavinia, are portrayed as villains, suggesting that proper or sympathetic girlhood must reflect certain qualities, such as a concern with fine appearance, only in moderation. To be a good girl is to suffer endless trials gracefully and without complaint, as almost all these protagonists do, and becoming a young woman typically involves taming some of the effusiveness and imagination of girlhood in order to serve others with a more moderate temperament.

SEXUALITY IN CHILDREN'S LITERATURE

Defining Sexuality

When we speak colloquially of a person's "**sexuality**," we often mean this as short-hand for which sex/gender a person most desires, but this common use of the term obscures many of its complexities. This concept of sexuality was conceived and developed over the course of the latter half of the nineteenth century, beginning in the 1860s, and the term "sexuality" to mean what we sometimes now call "sexual orientation" was not even used this way until the very end of the nineteenth century (the first recorded use, according to the *Oxford English Dictionary*, is from Havelock Ellis's 1897 study of sexual psychology). In recent decades, historians of sexuality such as Michel Foucault, David Halperin, Jonathan Ned Katz, and others have sought to explain that this concept of sexuality is a fairly recent historical development and that the practice of distinguishing between exclusive types of people based on their sexual or romantic desires has not always been employed. Sexuality is now often thought about in terms of two or three types of identities—homosexual, heterosexual, and sometimes bisexual—and as differentiating all people into one of these two or three categories. In Western culture before the mid nineteenth century, "sexuality" was more often, though not exclusively, understood in terms of sexual acts as opposed to sexual identities and in terms of morality rather than psychology. Under this system, anyone might be tempted to engage in sexual acts with someone of the same sex, for instance, and while this made one guilty of sodomy, it did not necessarily mean that one was a homosexual or that one's entire being or sense of self was linked to these acts.

While traces of this way of thinking about sexuality still persist, it is now often thought that sexual desires themselves can be used to categorize everyone, and that the sex/gender of the desired object is the most significant factor. Eve Kosofsky Sedgwick asserts,

> It is a rather amazing fact that, of the very many dimensions along which the genital activity of one person can be differentiated from that of another (dimensions that include preference for certain acts, certain zones or sensations, certain physical types, a certain frequency, certain symbolic investments, certain relations of age or power, a certain species, a certain number of participants, etc. etc. etc.), precisely one, the gender of object choice, emerged from the turn of the century, and has remained, as *the* dimension denoted by the now ubiquitous category of "sexual orientation." (*Epistemology* 8)

"Sexuality" is thus a way of bringing together under one term 1) certain "sexual" practices or acts which may or may not be genital, 2) the biology and physiology of sex/gender and

arousal/pleasure, 3) ways of perceiving or conceiving of desire and pleasure (as a matter for art and poetry, or science and medicine; as fixed and inherent or malleable and changing), and 4) ways of naming oneself and others in terms of particular and available identities.

The Sexuality of Children

It is important for students and scholars of children's literature to consider the sexuality of children because sexuality permeates both childhood and children's culture. While children's sexualities might sometimes resemble adult sexualities, they might also be different in important ways that sometimes render them invisible, or nearly so, to adults. Sexuality involves a range of possible desires, pleasures, acts, and identities. What kinds of physical or bodily acts give children pleasure? What kinds of objects, companions, or partners in pleasure or affection do they desire? To what extent are sexual identities important to children, or not? Sedgwick points out in the quoted passage that there are many other qualities besides sex/gender that could have emerged as the basis of sexual classification; this idea becomes especially apparent when thinking about children.

Sigmund Freud pioneered the study of children's sexuality. For some, Freud's claim that children are sexual beings remains contentious one hundred years after he first presented his theory of infantile sexuality. Freud published his *Three Essays on the Theory of Sexuality*, which deals heavily with children, in 1905. In it, he argues that contrary to the popular belief that sexual desire emerges only at puberty, manifestations of sexual desire and pleasure appear as early as infancy. In order for Freud to reach this breakthrough and for readers to understand this potentially surprising claim, the notion of sexual desire or pleasure must be divorced from overt genital contact and from the assumption that the genitals must be involved in order for a particular act to count as sexual. While Freud notes instances of childhood masturbation that do involve the genitals, his understanding of sexual pleasure is broader, encompassing such acts as the holding back and releasing of stool, which can be pleasurable, or the act of thumb sucking, which stimulates the lips and mimics the bodily pleasure of breastfeeding (45, 52). What these acts have in common is the stimulation of the body and what Freud calls its erotogenic zones in ways that evoke pleasure.

These insights are especially important for children's sexuality because children are not yet fully trained to limit their perception of what counts as proper or pleasurable, and thus their sexual pursuits might appear quite different from the conventional sexual

---

Opposite: "Tom's Visit to Arthur after the Fever," from *Tom Brown's Schooldays* (1857) by Thomas Hughes, illustrated by Arthur Hughes.

practices of adults. For instance, Peter Hunt refers to food in children's literature as "a substitute, quite possibly, for sex" (81), and Carolyn Daniel concurs, commenting about eating in children's literature, "But, while it can be a relentlessly mundane activity, merely a way of supplying the body with energy, it can also be one of the most sublime of all bodily experiences" (1). Thus, we see children eating throughout children's literature, from Hansel and Gretel's consumption of the gingerbread house to Alice's tea party or the various meals consumed by Harry and friends at Hogwarts. When children clutch dolls or stuffed toys close to their bodies, delight in snuggling with them, cry when separated from them, and share their most intimate fantasies with them, they are treating their toys as lovers, and they are deriving pleasure from their contact and companionship. They engage in similar relationships sometimes with other inanimate objects such as blankets and sometimes with animal companions, and the pleasures of these relationships might explain why boy-and-his-dog and girl-and-her-horse stories, or works in which toys come alive, are so prevalent in children's literature.

Children also seek such contact from other children: they hold hands, engage in rough-and-tumble play, have sleepovers, get jealous, and so on. Adults, intuiting the sexuality of childhood, sometimes find it cute when children pretend to have boyfriends or girlfriends, or they tease young children about what look like pretend romances. Children are, in part, mimicking what they see of the sexual and romantic culture that surrounds them, but they are also expressing a fundamental desire for pleasure and companionship, which are central to the notion of sexuality. Moreover, while adults have developed a system of sexual types that predefines the kinds of objects that are appropriate and gives names to particular identities based on the sex/gender of one's preference, children are still learning this system and can be less inhibited by it and less prone to use its language and terminology. Thus, the sexuality of children can often go undetected, but learning to read children's literature critically means being attentive to the desires and pleasures of children and childhood.

Queering the Classics of Children's Literature

Just as children themselves have been shown to be sexual beings, children's literature contains the traces of sexuality. At minimum, adult characters, such as parents, might be depicted as romantically paired and as sometimes bringing additional children into the world, while the adult characters of tales such as "Cinderella" engage in romance and marriage as central plotlines. Sometimes child characters themselves engage in romantic relationships, as in the case of the flirtatious courtship of Tom Sawyer and Becky Thatcher, which even includes a brief "engagement" before Becky gets wise to Tom and breaks it off.

Sometimes the sexuality is less normative, whether covert or explicit. In his introduction to a special issue of the *Children's Literature Association Quarterly* on lesbian and gay literature for children and young adults, Kenneth Kidd playfully speculates about the "decidedly queer" friendship of Mole and Rat in Kenneth Grahame's *The Wind in the Willows* (1908), in which Mole, a bachelor, leaves his home and moves in with Rat, another bachelor, and the two set up a cozy domestic partnership. In one especially poignant scene, Mole is drawn by his acute sense of smell back to his old home, and his animal instincts grip and paralyze him:

> Poor Mole stood alone in the road, his heart torn asunder, and a big sob gathering, gathering, somewhere low down inside him, to leap up to the surface presently, he knew, in passionate escape. But even under such a test as this his loyalty to his friend stood firm. Never for a moment did he dream of abandoning him. Meanwhile, the wafts from his old home pleaded, whispered, conjured, and finally claimed him imperiously. He dared not tarry longer within their magic circle. With a wrench that tore his very heartstrings he set his face down the road and followed submissively in the track of the Rat, while faint, thin little smells, still dogging his retreating nose, reproached him for his new friendship and his callous forgetfulness. (Grahame 54)

Somehow Mole manages to overcome his natural attachment to his old home to follow Rat, who turns out to be a thoughtful companion and insists the two visit Mole's old home together. Kidd clarifies that while *The Wind in the Willows* is "not a gay text per se, it is certainly about (among many other things) gendered male-male interaction" (115). The language of longing, companionship, and intimacy used to describe the relationship between Rat and Mole does suggest the near proximity of sexual, affectional, or what Freud would call "libidinal" investments and energies. Eve Sedgwick discusses these kinds of ostensibly platonic relationships between men as "homosocial," a term she uses to encompass a range of same-sex bonds including "male friendship, mentorship, entitlement, [and] rivalry" (*Between Men* 1). Though Sedgwick wrote about men, her ideas can be applied, with modification, to boys and girls. If we are attentive to these kinds of charged same-sex relationships, they become visible in all sorts of works, from the relationships between boys in Ballantyne's *The Coral Island* and Hughes's *Tom Brown's Schooldays* to those between girls in Coolidge's *What Katy Did at School* (1873) and Montgomery's *Anne of Green Gables*.

Some Golden Age authors of children's fiction consciously featured same-sex loving characters. The first known American or British author to refer to his or her own work for children as "homosexual" was Edward Irenæus Prime-Stevenson, who published two novels for boys—*White Cockades* (1889) and *Left to Themselves* (1891)—in the late nineteenth century and later referred to them as "homosexual in essence," calling the latter

book even more distinguishably homosexual than the earlier one (Stevenson 182). Writing in 1908, Stevenson surveyed a selection of books from the late nineteenth and early twentieth centuries that he described as "homosexual children's literature," making him the first to write explicitly on the subject. In *Left to Themselves*, an American adventure novel, two boys strike up a loving relationship as they travel across the northeast United States into Canada while being pursued by a mysterious antagonist. Stevenson describes the boys as remaining lifelong companions after their adventures. His first boys' book, a work of historical fiction about the Scottish Jacobite rebellion of 1745, features a romantic friendship between Bonny Prince Charlie and a Scots youth.

LGBT Representation in Picturebooks and Fiction for Younger Readers

As the system of heterosexual/homosexual identity became more prominent in the twentieth century, and as the lesbian, gay, bisexual, and transgender (LGBT) civil rights movement expanded the public visibility of LGBT people, children's literature began to depict queer sexualities more explicitly. The queerness of early childhood literature has most often taken the form of either gender-variant children—tomboys and sissy boys—or gay and lesbian parents. Lesléa Newman's *Heather Has Two Mommies* (1989) helped pioneer the inclusion of lesbian and gay parents in children's literature, and Michael Willhoite's *Daddy's Roommate* (1990) followed not long after. Since these early efforts, children's publishers have markedly increased their output of picturebooks that present a variety of family arrangements, such as Johnny Valentine's *One Dad, Two Dads, Brown Dad, Blue Dads* (1994), about a boy with two blue dads; Nancy Garden's *Molly's Family* (2004), about a girl with two moms; and Justin Richardson and Peter Parnell's *And Tango Makes Three* (2005), based on the true story of two male penguins at the Central Park Zoo who became companions and adopted a chick. By using animals to depict same-sex parenting, *Tango* associates queer sexuality with nature and strategically portrays "gay" parents as cute and lovable. Though the selection of children's novels with gay characters is still rather small, more have started to appear, such as James Howe's *The Misfits* (2001), about a group of misfit middle-schoolers, including gay twelve-year-old Joe, and its sequel, *Totally Joe* (2005).

In addition to depicting children with lesbian or gay parents, books for young readers have begun to embrace representations of gender-variant children who do not perform masculinity or femininity in conventional or normative ways. Tomie dePaola's *Oliver*

Opposite: Bachelor friends Rat and Mole establish a loyal domestic partnership in Kenneth Grahame's *The Wind in the Willows* (1908), illustrated for the 2005 Sterling Classics edition by Scott McKowen.

Button Is a Sissy (1979) was pioneering in its positive rendering of a boy who prefers to dance and play with dolls, and Sharon Dennis Wyeth's *Tomboy Trouble* (1998) offers a similar message of acceptance regarding a young girl who likes games usually played by boys. In Lesléa Newman's *The Boy Who Cried Fabulous* (2004), Roger's unconventional gender is signaled by his linguistic exuberance. If stoicism is a masculine quality, Roger's enthusiasm and talkativeness indicate his nonnormative gender presentation. More recent examples of books for younger readers featuring LGBT and queer or questioning characters include the picturebook *I Am Jazz* (2014) by Jessica Herthel and Jazz Jennings, with illustrations by Shelagh McNicholas, about Jazz's experience growing up as a transgender youth. Jazz was nearly 14 when the book was published and had previously been the subject of a television documentary and subsequently a reality show. Gayle E. Pitman and Kristyna Litten's celebratory picturebook *This Day in June* (2014) introduces readers to a gay pride parade and the different members of the LGBT community who participate. In Alex Gino's chapter book *George* (2015), a fourth-grade transgender girl, whose given name is George, slowly comes out to those around her as she seeks the titular role in the school production of *Charlotte's Web*. The twelfth volume of the Captain Underpants series by Dav Pilkey, *Captain Underpants and the Sensational Saga of Sir Stinks-A-Lot* (2015), shows a possible future in which one of the main characters, Harold, is gay and married to a man. Richard Peck treats same-sex marriage as fairly unremarkable in *The Best Man* (2016), in which a sixth-grade boy encourages the romance of his two role models: his uncle and his student teacher, who ultimately marry. As children increasingly self-identify as gay, lesbian, and transgender at younger ages, and as resistance grows to homophobic and heterosexist thinking, we are seeing an increase in representation of LGBT characters in works for younger readers.

LGBT Representation in Young Adult Literature

The literature of early childhood has so far provided relatively few depictions of LGBT children, but young adult (YA) literature has seen far more such diversity in recent decades. As Kenneth Kidd observes, "The young adult genre has been extraordinarily receptive to lesbian/gay themes, largely because coming out is often described in the idiom of adolescence as an intense period of sexual attraction, social rebellion, and personal growth" (114). John Donovan's *I'll Get There. It Better Be Worth the Trip* (1969) pioneered the gay YA novel, even as it suggested that homosexuality is a transgression to be punished. It was not until the 1980s that many additional landmark works about gay and lesbian adolescents were published for young adult readers. The intervening years were filled with highly troubled gay and lesbian youths, tortured either by their sexuality or by the culture's response to it. The character of Artie in Judy Blume's *Forever*, intimated to be gay, tries to kill himself and is eventually institutionalized. In Sandra Scoppettone's *Happy Endings Are All Alike* (1978), Peggy attempts to deny her love for Jaret, another girl, by trying to date boys, and Jaret is eventually raped by a stalker. Aidan Chambers's *Dance on My Grave* (1982), which depicts sixteen-year-old Hal's love for the reckless Barry, ends with one of the boys dying in a motorcycle accident. These early representations of lesbian or gay youth in YA literature reflected the hostile and homophobic culture of the mid-to-late twentieth century, but landmark novels such as Nancy Garden's *Annie on My Mind* (1982), Francesca Lia Block's *Weetzie Bat* (1989), and David Levithan's *Boy Meets Boy* (2003) offer gay and lesbian characters who are far less troubled, reflecting the changing cultural atmosphere and increasing possibilities for lesbian and gay young people.

The body of YA fiction for and about lesbian, gay, and queer characters continues to expand at a noticeable rate. Whereas Michael Cart and Christine Jenkins identified fewer than 40 YA books with gay, lesbian, or queer content over the course of the entire 1980s (Cart and Jenkins 74–80), Malinda Lo found that "mainstream publishers" published 47 YA books with LGBT content in 2014 alone ("2014 LGBT YA" n.p.). Many recent works have been critically acclaimed, offering complex characters, worlds, and plotlines that move beyond the tragic teens and unhappy endings of earlier decades. A debut novel by emily m. danforth, *The Miseducation of Cameron Post* (2012) features a lesbian teen growing up in rural Montana in the 1990s. In Benjamin Alire Sáenz's celebrated novel *Aristotle and Dante Discover the Secrets of the Universe* (2012), two Mexican American youths face the challenges they experience at the intersection of ethnicity and sexuality. As their friendship grows, they reexamine their feelings for each other and their different understandings of their Mexican heritage. Levithan's *Two Boys Kissing* (2013), narrated by the collective voice of gay men who died from AIDS, features a number of LGBT and queer characters and suggests the possibilities of teen activism around queer issues. Its two teen protagonists, Harry and Craig, seek to break the world record for kissing and thereby inspire other queer youth in town who are encountering the familiar joys of budding romance, the pain of being rejected by their families or being gay bashed by bullies, and the quotidian frustrations of everyday life.

Transgender characters have appeared even less frequently in young adult literature, though the list of such works continues to grow. Michael Cart and Christine Jenkins identify Francesca Lia Block's 1996 short story "Dragons in Manhattan" as the first appearance of a transsexual character in YA literature (118), and Levithan's *Boy Meets Boy* includes a secondary character named Infinite Darlene who is transgender. Julie Anne Peters's *Luna* (2004) appears to be the first YA novel to feature a transgender protagonist. In *Luna*, a seventeen-year-old decides to transition into Luna, and her sister Regan struggles with accepting the change. Ellen Wittlinger's *Parrotfish* (2007) depicts a protagonist who identifies as a boy and adopts the name Grady after he transitions, while Brian Kratcher's *Almost Perfect* (2010) features an adolescent boy who falls for the new girl in school and later learns that she is transgender. Cris Beams's *I Am J* (2012) represents its protagonist's transition to J to match his identity as a boy. As in the early history of gay YA literature, the transgender experience is most frequently a struggle for both the transgender character and his or her loved ones and community, mirroring the current cultural landscape. However, as the understanding and acceptance of the transgender experience grows, this will perhaps change as well.

Awards for LGBT Children's and Young Adult Literature

Each year, the Lambda Literary Foundation, an organization devoted to supporting LGBT literature, presents the Lambda Literary Awards in a variety of categories, including children's and young adult literature. The first children's book to receive the Lambda was MaryKate Jordan's *Losing Uncle Tim* (1989), a picturebook about a boy whose uncle is dying from AIDS. Other past winners include Jacqueline Woodson for *The House You Pass on the Way* (1997), Alex Sanchez for *So Hard to Say* (2004), and Shyam Selvadurai for *Swimming in the Monsoon Sea* (2005). In 2009, the Lambda Literary Foundation specified that winners of the award must identify as lesbian, gay, bisexual, or transgender, a move Thomas Crisp defends as necessary to help support LGBT writers (Crisp 97). In 2010, the American Library Association added a children's and young adult literature category to its Stonewall Award, which honors LGBT literature. The first recipient for a children's or young adult book was Nick Burd for *The Vast Fields of Ordinary* (2009). Crisp argues that these awards serve important functions in promoting the inclusion of LGBT characters and the quality of LGBT writing for children and young adults.

READING CRITICALLY: GENDER AND SEXUALITY IN CHILDREN'S LITERATURE

A Little Princess

Reading constructions of gender and sexuality in children's literature critically means being attentive to how conceptions and practices of boyhood, girlhood, manhood, womanhood, masculinity, femininity, desires, pleasures, and romantic or affectional relations impinge upon, direct, or shape the narrative. In Frances Hodgson Burnett's *A Little Princess*, constructions of gender and sexuality are crucial to the novel in both explicit and subtle ways. Foregrounding their operation helps us to see and understand the novel better or anew. First published as a serialized novella in 1888 called "Sara Crewe," Burnett's story about a wealthy boarding-school girl reduced to servitude by the death of her father premiered in London as a stage play in 1902 and then in New York in 1903. The play's success led Burnett to revise and expand the original novella, and the new version was published in 1905 as a full-length novel titled *A Little Princess*. The gendered figure of the princess is one of the most iconic images of womanhood and femininity (which are not the same thing), and since Burnett's novel traffics heavily in the concept of princesses, the role of gender is crucial to understanding what makes Sara Crewe a sympathetic character and how her decline in circumstances is caused indirectly by the homosocial relations of the late nineteenth and early twentieth centuries.

A Little Princess belongs to the category of the school story, which crystallized as a coherent genre with consistent and recognizable characteristics in the mid nineteenth century. Typically, school stories are set at either all-boy or all-girl boarding schools; thus, learning to be a boy or girl is usually a significant component of the educational experience. Sara is praised not only for her fine work on her lessons but also "for her good manners, for her amiability to her fellow pupils, for her generosity" (Burnett, *Little Princess* 40). Though these might sound like traits that would be universally encouraged in children, they are rarely mentioned explicitly as eliciting praise in school stories about boys. Moreover, the school permits Sara to practice being a mother. When the school's two proprietors, Miss Amelia and Miss Minchin, cannot control the temper tantrum of a small girl named Lottie, Sara intervenes and manages to calm the youngster by promising to be her mother. Later, when Sara's father dies after an illness and Sara is left in poverty, she is kept at the school as a servant and must learn to perform all sorts of domestic work. Having arrived at the school as the daughter of a wealthy man and provided with every material comfort—including a French maid—Sara transforms from princess to servant, thereby occupying a variety of traditional female roles and practicing a range of traditional womanly duties, from nurturing younger children to cleaning the home.

Nevertheless, Sara is an unconventional girl, and she is repeatedly described as either lacking traditional feminine qualities or as actually possessing masculine ones. For example, when

Captain Crewe first brings his daughter to Miss Minchin's school, Sara likens herself to a soldier going into battle (6). In contrast to traditional associations between femininity and beauty, Sara is very much resigned to being ugly. She thinks, "I am not beautiful at all. Colonel Grange's little girl, Isobel, is beautiful. She has dimples and rose-colored cheeks, and long hair the color of gold. I have short black hair and green eyes; besides which, I am a thin child and not fair in the least" (8). Sara is described as gobbling up books and reading histories, biographies, and books of poetry in both English and French. In fact, Captain Crewe is concerned that she does not play enough and asks Miss Minchin to make Sara ride a pony or play with dolls. Clearly, Sara is not perceived as girlish enough. She might be perceived as too grown up, and there- fore needing to act more childlike, but the prescribed remedies are gendered as specifically girlish: ponies and dolls. Sara eventually attempts to shield several of the other girls from the abuses of Miss Minchin, a trait her father had recognized before his departure: "If Sara had been a boy and lived a few centuries ago … she would have gone about the country with her sword drawn, rescuing and defending everyone in distress. She always wants to fight when she sees people in trouble" (29). As Rashna B. Singh notes, "To her credit, Burnett permits both the princess and the soldier to be important facets of the female" (131). We would add that Sara's combination of masculine and feminine qualities is what makes her such a sympathetic char- acter. Those girls who possess assortments of more traditionally feminine qualities without the addition of more masculine ones—Lavinia is described as jealous and vain (Burnett, *Little Prin- cess* 41), while Ermengarde is passive and dependent—are represented as far less sympathetic, if not downright unlikable. Thus, the model of ideal girlhood the novel constructs is one that combines elements of both masculinity and femininity.

Since school stories are usually set at single-sex institutions, they frequently deal explicitly with a range of same-sex relations that Eve Sedgwick calls "homosocial." Sedgwick uses that term to describe the range of same-sex relations between men, from formal business relation- ships and friendships to romantic or sexual ones (*Between Men* 4). Homosocial relations set off the conflict in *A Little Princess* because many of the events central to its plot are effects of a boyhood friendship of Sara's father from his days at a boys' boarding school. Sedgwick singles out these schools as one of the key sites in which male homosocial relations were formed: "School itself was, of course, a crucial link in ruling-class male homosocial formation" (*Between Men* 176). Many other historians and critics of British boarding schools or school stories have commented on the importance of intimate same-sex friendships at these schools (Reed 63, Quigley 126–27). Though these relationships were ostensibly platonic, boarding schools were reputed to occasion sexual and romantic relationships between boys (Ellis 45–46, Mack 126, Bamford 72). Even relationships that might have remained platonic could become passionate. Sedgwick quotes Benjamin Dis- raeli, British prime minister in the late nineteenth century, who describes boyhood friendships

Opposite: "The Sparrows Twittered and Hopped about Quite without Fear," from Frances Hodgson Burnett's *A Little Princess* (1905), illustrated for this 1917 version by Ethel Franklin Betts.

as extremely intense: "At school, friendship is a passion. It entrances the being; it tears the soul. All loves of after life can never bring its rapture, or its wretchedness; no bliss so absorbing, no pangs of jealousy or despair so crushing and so keen!" (qtd. in *Between Men* 176). Whether or not boyhood friendships turned sexual, they would form the foundation of the web of relationships between adult, ruling-class men, who relied on the connections they made while at school, or on the shared experience of having attended an elite boarding school, in the colonial, military, political, and commercial ventures they would undertake as adults.

Just such a relationship is critical to the Cinderella-like story at the core of *A Little Princess*. Sara Crewe is plunged into poverty when her father, Captain Crewe, dies after losing his fortune in an apparently bad business venture which he'd been drawn into by an intimate friend from his days at an all-boys boarding school. Captain Crewe is persuaded to invest his fortune in a colonial diamond mine by Tom Carrisford, with whom he played cricket at Eton, a prestigious and exclusive institution. Thus, his lost fortune and eventually his death are linked to his trust in and love for his boyhood friend from his school days. Carrisford is described as "an intimate friend" of Captain Crewe (Burnett, *Little Princess* 302), and as he explains in his own words, "Poor Crewe had put into the scheme every penny that he owned. He trusted me—he *loved* me" (193, emphasis in original). Of course, Sara's mysterious "Indian gentleman," who funds the magical transformation of her rat-infested, unfurnished attic room into a wonderland of comforts and delights, is none other than Mr. Carrisford, who is searching for Sara so that he can adopt the daughter of his former school chum. Eventually, Sara and Mr. Carrisford are revealed to each other. He then rescues her from the abuse and drudgery of Miss Minchin's school and returns her to a place of wealth and comfort. In these ways, both gender and sexuality are two of the novel's central concerns. Sara's hybrid gender performance offers a nontraditional model of what it means to be a princess, and Captain Crewe's boyhood friendship, though referenced only a few times, triggers many of the most crucial plot points.

EXPLORATIONS

Review

1. What are some reasons that sex and sexuality are so controversial as subjects for children's literature and culture, and what are some ways in which these controversies are manifested?

2. Name some ways in which children's culture contributes to the gendering and sexualization of children, focusing on:

- Toys and games

- Disney films and marketing

- Children's clothing

- Children's literature itself.

3. What is meant by the term "sex" and what is meant by the term "gender"? According to feminist and gender theorists, what are some typical ways that gender is taught and reinforced?

4. What does it mean to have a gender identity? What role does social class play in making available certain gender identities and performances?

5. In what ways can readers pay attention to intense or erotically charged same-sex relationships in classic texts? How does this constitute a queer reading?

6. What are some early examples of the public visibility of LGBTQ people in children's literature? What are more contemporary examples of picturebooks and diction for young readers that portray either gender variant children—tomboys and sissy boys— or gay and lesbian parents?

Reflect

1. Consider how traditional fairy tales such as "Cinderella," "Snow White," and "The Little Mermaid" represent gender (both manhood and womanhood) and sexuality (desire and courtship). How do versions by Charles Perrault or Jakob and Wilhelm Grimm compare to Disney film versions?

2. The literary critic James Kincaid argues in *Child-Loving: The Erotic Child and Victorian Culture* (1992) that while children are imagined to be sexless and taboo as objects of desire, they are nonetheless eroticized as embodying innocence, virtue, and purity. What is the evidence that children are eroticized in contemporary culture? In what instances are the bodies of children or young adults put on display for the enjoyment of the public?

3. How do works that foreground gender and sexuality, such as Brent Hartinger's *Geography Club* (2003) or Linda de Haan and Stern Nijland's *King and King* (2003), negotiate between didacticism and artistry? Do they lean more toward instruction or delight, or do they achieve a balance between the two?

4. Consider a literary work for children that depicts bodily change or pleasure, such as Alice's changing body and consumption of various substances in Lewis Carroll's *Alice's Adventures in Wonderland* or Edward or Bella's desire for and pleasure in the other's body in Stephenie Meyer's *Twilight*. How does your chosen text depict desire and its satisfaction? How can this be understood in terms of sex and sexuality?

5. How do contemporary YA representations of lesbian or gay youth such as Levithan's *Boy Meets Boy* or *Two Boys Kissing* reflect the changing cultural atmosphere and increasing possibilities for lesbian and gay people? How do they compare to the early representation of lesbian and gay youth in YA literature?

Investigate

1. Using the resources of the American Library Association (ALA) and other sources, research the list of most frequently banned or challenged books for a particular year, region, or school district. How many of these challenges were based on matters related to gender or sexuality? What were the specific concerns in these cases?

2. Research a court case related to the sexual activity of children or young adults, such as a case of a student involved sexually with a teacher or one like the case of Genarlow Wilson described in Chapter 1 (see p. 59). What does it suggest about the cultural debate over childhood or adolescent sexuality?

3. Visit a local toy store and examine how children's toys and games, including video games, are designed and marketed along sex/gender lines. What kinds of toys and games are marketed to girls? What kinds of toys or games are marketed to boys?

4. Visit a local bookstore and examine book covers for children's and young adult works. How do book covers signal concerns with sex/gender or sexuality? How are book covers used to market books to boy and girl readers differently? Are any covers sex/gender neutral?

SUGGESTED READINGS

Coolidge, Susan. *What Katy Did at School* (1873). A sequel to Coolidge's *What Katy Did*, this novel can still stand alone as the story of two teenage sisters, Katy and Clover, who are sent to an all-girls' boarding school on the East Coast of the United States because of concerns that Katy is not girlish enough. While there, the virtuous sisters have a strong effect on their classmates, who represent a range of different kinds of girls. As in many school stories, intimate same-sex friendships are central to school life.

Garden, Nancy. *Annie on My Mind* (1982). Garden's groundbreaking novel about the romance between two high school girls in New York City helped pave the way for the explosion of LGBT literature for young adults. Despite the fact that Liza attends an expensive private school in Brooklyn and Annie a public school in Manhattan, the two girls meet at an art museum and hit it off. With the help of two lesbian teachers at Liza's school, the two girls confront homophobia and the difficulties faced by lesbian adolescents.

Gino, Alex. *George* (2015). Although given the name George at birth, the fourth-grade protagonist of Gino's novel identifies as a girl and begins to come out to her family and friends as transgender. She pursues the titular role in the school production of *Charlotte's Web* and is referred to by the author using the pronouns "she, her, and hers," helping the reader experience the disconnect between how her community sees her and how she sees herself.

Hughes, Thomas. *Tom Brown's Schooldays* (1857). Thomas Hughes's classic nineteenth-century boys' school story helped establish the conventions of the genre. Set at Rugby School in the 1830s, *Tom Brown's Schooldays* depicts a variety of boys, from the ordinary and eponymous Tom and the saintly and fragile George Arthur to the sadistic bully Flashman and the eccentric scientist Martin. Rugby is an institution where boys are made men, so these boys are disciplined and transformed, in part by the intimate, same-sex friendships they form with others.

Levithan, David. *Boy Meets Boy* (2003). Levithan's fantastical novel is set in a kind of utopian alternative reality in which different sexualities are not merely tolerated but celebrated. Paul, who has been out as gay since kindergarten, falls in love with the new boy in school, Noah. Their group of friends includes Paul's bisexual ex-boyfriend, who interferes with Paul's new romance, and Infinite Darlene, a transgender youth who is both the quarterback of the football team and the year's homecoming queen.

Newman, Lesléa. *The Boy Who Cried Fabulous* (2004). Illustrated by Peter Ferguson. Newman and Ferguson's picturebook depicts a boy named Roger, who has a special love for the word "fabulous." When his parents become worried about their sissy boy, they forbid him to use the word, but the creative Roger finds other equally delightful words he can use to express himself and his love for pretty things.

Rossetti, Christina. "Goblin Market" (1862). A poem that occupies the territory between adult and children's literature, "Goblin Market" describes two sisters, Laura and Lizzie, and their encounters with a group of goblins who sell a seductive fruit. After Laura succumbs to temptation and tastes the fruit, her health declines and she appears to be dying. In an attempt to ease Laura's suffering, Lizzie visits the goblins to acquire the fruit, is assaulted and covered with the fruits' juices, and escapes home to soothe her sister with juice that covers her body. The poem addresses temptation, girlhood sexuality, and sisterly love.

Stevenson, Edward Prime. *Left to Themselves: Being the Ordeal of Philip and Gerald* **(1891).** One of the first works to be described by its author as a homosexual children's book, this American boys' novel features the romantic friendship of two youths who flee from a mysterious predator as they travel from New York to meet the younger boy's father in Nova Scotia. Philip and Gerald experience a variety of adventures, including a shipwreck, and remain lifelong companions.

Tamaki, Mariko and Jillian Tamaki. *This One Summer* **(2014).** A Caldecott and Printz Honor book, this graphic novel centers on the friendship between preteen girls Rose and Windy, who are spending the summer with their families at a fictional beach based on the Muskokas, Canada. The two friends experience crushes, witness the complex romantic relationships of older teens and adults, and come to recognize the different treatment girls and boys experience in matters of sex.

Woodson, Jacqueline. *From the Notebooks of Melanin Sun* **(1995).** Woodson's young adult novel focuses on thirteen-year-old Melanin Sun, who records all his feelings and experiences in his notebooks. An African American boy growing up in Brooklyn, Melanin must come to terms with the fact that his mother is a lesbian and dating a white woman. Thus, the novel addresses the intersections of gender, sexuality, and race, as Melanin and his family confront both racism and homophobia.

APPROACHES TO TEACHING *A LITTLE PRINCESS* [SECONDARY SCHOOL]

Preparation for the Lesson

Students will read the novel on their own. Tell the class that the first class activity will center on the ways in which the female characters fit into or challenge conventional gender roles. First, explain some of the most clearly articulated conventional and stereotypical gender roles for women at the time of the novel (e.g., maternal, self-sacrificing, tending toward dependence, concerned with physical appearance, emotional). Next, ask the students to replicate and complete the following worksheet while they are reading and collect it after the first activity.

Character	Conventional or unconventional	Passages that support claim
Ermengarde		
Lavinia		
Lottie		
Miss Minchin		
Sara		

Learning Goals

- To give students some practice in taking notes while reading (and rereading) a book and choosing relevant quotations to build an argument

- To reflect on gender, especially the novel's response to conventional femininity

- To examine the novel's representation of same-sex bonds.

Activity One: Feminine Roles

In class, review the worksheet about conventional feminine roles, asking students to read out loud the passages they chose in order to illustrate their assessments. Sara will be the last one you discuss, with emphasis on the complex ways her character draws on both unconventional and conventional femininity, as follows.

- Elements of Sara's character that fit in with conventional femininity: maternal, self-sacrificing, charitable, dutiful, good manners, amiable, owns dolls, owns fancy clothes.

- Elements of Sara's character that challenge conventional femininity: independent, tough-minded, inspired by "manly" literature (like tales of imprisonment in the Bastille), attractive but not conventionally pretty, prefers to read and needs to be encouraged to play with dolls, not concerned with clothes and appearance.

Talk about how these elements of Sara's character work together in the novel.

Activity Two: Princesses

Students will complete an independent research project comparing Burnett's vision of the "princess" with the presentation of princesses in other books, films, and TV shows. To begin, students should review the novel, noting passages that illustrate Burnett's vision of a princess. Then each student should pick out another depiction of a princess. Some possibilities include (but are not limited to)

- The Grimms' version of "Cinderella" or "Snow White"

- Meg Cabot's Princess Diaries series (or the films)

- Any of the Disney princesses.

Students will then write a brief essay comparing Sara with another depiction of a princess. What qualities does she share with that princess? How is she different? How has the princess figure changed over time?

　　Lead the class in discussion by asking the students if they or their friends were ever involved in "princess culture." What is it about princess culture that might be appealing to children? How does *A Little Princess* complicate or inform our understanding of modern princess culture? For upper grades, refer students to Peggy Orenstein's *Cinderella Ate My Daughter: Dispatches from the Front Lines of the New Girlie-Girl Culture* (2011).

Activity Three: Same-Sex Friendships and Love in the Novel

Lead the class in a discussion of the same-sex friendships in the novel, especially the friendship between Sara and Ermengarde or Becky and the friendship between Captain Crewe and Mr. Carrisford. Focus on the following questions:

1. How are these friendships a source of both physical and emotional support?

2. How do these friends describe their love and affection for each other?

3. Why is Mr. Carrisford so eager to help Sara? How does the friendship and love of Captain Crewe and Mr. Carrisford help resolve the plot? How is their friendship like or unlike that between Sara and one of her friends?

CENSORSHIP AND SELECTION

In 2011, Alan Gribben published the NewSouth edition of *The Adventures of Tom Sawyer* and *Huckleberry Finn*, bringing together Mark Twain's two "boy books" in the belief that they should be read together. Among other editorial decisions, Gribben chose "to eliminate two racial slurs that have increasingly formed a barrier to these works for teachers, students, and general readers" (9). These included the substitution of "slave" for the reviled racial slur "nigger," which occurs 218 times in *Huckleberry Finn* (plus once in the table of contents), and the replacement of the phrase "Injun Joe" in Tom Sawyer with "Indian Joe." Gribben describes the 2009 lecture tour in Alabama that inspired his new edition:

> In several towns I was taken aside after my talk by earnest middle and high school teachers who lamented the fact that they no longer felt justified in assigning either of Twain's boy books because of that hurtful n-word. Here was further proof that this single debasing label is overwhelming every other consideration about *Tom Sawyer* and *Huckleberry Finn*, whereas what these novels have to offer readers hardly depends upon that one indefensible slur. (12)

Gribben came to believe that "a significant number of school teachers, college instructors, and general readers will welcome the option of an edition of Twain's fused novels that spares the reader from a racial slur that never seems to lose its vitriol" (13). Gribben emphatically notes that the edition is not intended for academics and "textual purists," adding that "literally dozens of other editions are available for those readers who prefer Twain's original phrasing. Those standard editions will always exist" (15).

Opposite: Huck and Jim from *Adventures of Huckleberry Finn* by Mark Twain, illustrated by Scott McKowen.

Most journalists, academics, and intellectuals were squarely opposed to Gribben's edition. Elon James White, the editor in chief of "This Week in Blackness" on *Salon.com*, argues: "The book, which deals directly with racism, is not better served by erasing the racial slur. The only purpose is to erase the tension that is felt by parents and teachers of students who would read it. To pretend this is for some higher good is to insult the intelligence of the American public" (White n.p.). Other objections to the removal of the offensive word center on the notion that by removing it, the editor pretends that it was never there, glossing over or ignoring historical truth. Leonard Pitts Jr. asserts:

> The past is what it is, immutable and non-negotiable. Even a cursory glance at the historical record will show that Twain's use of the reprehensible word was an accurate representation of that era.
>
> So it would be more useful to have any new edition offer students context and challenge them to ask hard questions: Why did Twain choose that word? What kind of country must this have been that it was so ubiquitous? (Pitts n.p.)

Others argue that focusing on the offensiveness of the "n-word" ignores the arguably anti-racist message of the text and Twain's own desire to criticize racist attitudes. Some are unconvinced that "slave" is a less offensive term, as Francine Prose notes when she says, "Racial epithets are inarguably disgusting, but not nearly so disgusting as an institution that treats human beings as property to be beaten, bought and sold" (Prose n.p.).

In contrast, Boyce Watkins praises the NewSouth edition for opening the door for the book "to be enjoyed in schools that are not interested in traumatizing students in order to educate them":

> Long before I became a scholar, I was a black teenage boy. At that time, I would never have enjoyed hearing my English teacher repeat the n-word 219 times out loud in front of a class full of white students. I also would have wondered why African-Americans are the only ethnic group forced to read "classic" literature that uses such derogatory language toward us in a disturbingly repetitive way.
>
> I would have found such a presentation to be only a hurtful and highly inefficient way for me to understand slavery, and I probably would have been teased. (Watkins n.p.)

Yet Bill Maxwell, a journalist, disagrees, based on his own encounter with the text as an adolescent:

> When I first encountered the N-word, on Page 4, I took it in stride. It was a word I was accustomed to hearing uttered every day by blacks and whites. As an avid

reader, I was accustomed to seeing the word in stories by white writers and black writers such as Zora Neale Hurston, Ralph Ellison and Richard Wright. I couldn't count the number of times I'd been called the N-word by fellow blacks, sometimes to diminish me, other times as a form of endearment. The word was part of the fabric of my life.

My 10th Grade English teacher, Gloria Bonaparte, assigned *Huck Finn* to us, and we read it without a second thought. Mrs. Bonaparte said it was one of the great American novels we should read, and she explained that Twain used the N-word because it was the most natural word for Huck to refer to blacks, given his time and place. We understood. (Maxwell n.p.)

Watkins and Maxwell represent two poles of a debate on censorship: one stressing the capacity of words and ideas to affect and even traumatize young people, and the other representing the power of pedagogical framing and critical thinking to guide young people in their encounters with ideas and concepts that might be unfamiliar and even painful.

The controversy around the NewSouth edition of *Huckleberry Finn* features contrasting values: the desire to spare students of color the repeated exposure to a racial slur in a high school classroom versus the desire to respect the integrity of a classic text without alteration. Novelist Lorrie Moore attempts to find a third approach when she opposes the removal of the "n-word" but argues that "the remedy is to refuse to teach this novel in high school and to wait until college—or even graduate school—where it can be put in proper context" (Moore n.p.). Moore is technically advocating for selection (a choice to teach a text or not to teach it in any given classroom) as an alternative to censorship, standing against any modification of Twain's words. Yet she also argues that it shouldn't be shared with young people in a middle school or high school setting—thus also limiting their access to the material.

This chapter explores the role of both censorship and selection in children's and young adult literature. Studying the phenomenon of censorship as it interacts with children's literature returns us to some of the critical questions raised by the first chapters of this book. In Chapter 1, we discussed the emergence of a notion of childhood as a space apart from the demands and pressures of adulthood. Censorship in its various forms is often catalyzed by the conception of childhood as a time of innocence: a childhood that needs to be protected from the pressures of the adult world. Chapter 2 described the rise of a separate children's literature increasingly attuned to children's pleasures, desires, and concerns. With the shift from didactic works that transmit values from adults to children, to literature centering more on children's own tastes and preferences, some adults feel a loss of control over the messages and themes of children's literature. Contemporary literature for children often does not shy away from "mature" content, including depictions of sexuality, drug use, violence, social upheaval, and political controversy. The often-permeable boundaries between "adult" and "children's" literature can raise red flags for some adults. Censorship can also reveal to us what adults themselves don't want to think about, not just what they don't want children to think about.

Can children be affected adversely by their reading, or even damaged by the ideas or images they encounter in a text? To believe that works of literature are not capable of negatively affecting a child is to deny literature's power to speak to children's emotions and influence their ideas. Those who oppose censorship, however, stress children's resilience: their ability to bounce back from difficult circumstances and traumatic events (and therefore to take the disturbing material encountered in books in stride). Many anti-censorship activists take a middle position by arguing that children might well be sensitive to disturbing content of various kinds but can manage it by talking through that content with parents, teachers, and caregivers, gradually developing their own critical reading skills.

Tony Kushner, writing about the controversy sparked by some of Maurice Sendak's books, notes:

> Universal suitability and universal appeal are odd standards against which to measure a work of art. No art intended for adults would be expected to meet such standards, and one should be immediately suspicious of any work for adults, or for children, apparently qualifying as such. I found *The Cat in the Hat* rough sledding when I was a kid. The cat made appalling messes—he freaked me out. Nothing good is really universal, *Goodnight Moon* being probably the lone honorable exception. (22)

If, as Kushner suggests, children's literature is unfairly subject to a standard of "universal suitability," a book would have to meet *everyone's* standard for acceptability and ruffle no one's feathers. This seems difficult or even impossible in a world where there is much diversity in social and political opinion. Even his "universally appealing" example—*Goodnight Moon*—has its critics. In a recent blog post, Andy Hinds wrote half-seriously of *Goodnight Moon*: "The juxtaposition of a chromatically jarring setting, childish ramblings, and incongruous visual details creates a vertiginous psychological landscape with sinister undertones" (Hinds n.p.). While Hinds is (presumably) being facetious, his ability to produce such a negative reading of such an ostensibly innocuous text shows that *any* text can be the recipient of criticism or dismissal. At the same time, most parents, teachers, writers, and critics have some kind of pragmatic working standard for material they find absolutely unsuitable or beyond the pale for children's reading or viewing. Censorship is therefore a complicated phenomenon. Censorship is also significant as a set of forces and pressures that reveals the power—and lack of power—children have individually and collectively to assert their freedom to read.

German soldiers and citizens give the Nazi salute as thousands of books are burned in May 1933.

CENSORSHIP: DEFINITIONS AND KEY TERMS

In this section, we will look at the forms that censorship can take and examine some definitions and key terms.

Censorship

Censorship is most specifically defined as government restriction or legislation of materials, including the banning of books. One particularly egregious form of censorship is the destruction of books. As we will see in the Harry Potter case study later in this chapter, books are sometimes burned, an action linked to an ancient history of state and individual suppression of ideas. For example, in China in 213 BCE, Confucian books were burned by the government in power. In late nineteenth-century America, the New York Society for the Suppression of Vice, led by Anthony Comstock, destroyed literally tons of books. The most infamous instance of book burning in the twentieth century is the Nazis' burning of thousands of works because they were written by Jewish authors or otherwise termed "degenerate" by Nazi ideology. The atrocities of the Nazi regime are therefore forever associated with acts of book burning.

The Intellectual Freedom Committee of the American Library Association (ALA) defines censorship quite broadly as "a change in the access status of material, based on the content of the work and made by a governing authority or its representatives," noting that censorship encompasses "exclusion, restriction, removal, or age/grade level changes" (ALA 106). This vision of censorship extends far beyond the physical destruction or legal banning of books; it encompasses a wide number of obstacles that obstruct an individual's or group's ability to get material and a variety of roadblocks to access that are put up by a governing authority (which could include a government body, but could also be a school board, a religious group, or a parent organization).

Challenges

A **challenge** is a written, oral, or public request directed to a librarian or teacher that a book be removed from a library or classroom. In 1986, the Intellectual Freedom Committee of the ALA developed categories specifying the different forms that challenges take:

Expression of Concern. An inquiry that has judgmental overtones.

Oral Complaint. An oral challenge to the presence and/or appropriateness of the material in question.

Written Complaint. A formal, written complaint filed with the institution (library, school, etc.), challenging the presence and/or appropriateness of specific material.

Public Attack. A publicly disseminated statement challenging the value of the material, presented to the media and/or others outside the institutional organization in order to gain public support for further action. (ALA 105)

Sometimes these challenges are successful and a book is indeed removed. Another possible outcome is that books are placed on a "restricted" shelf in a library, where the student or child must obtain written permission from a parent or caregiver in order to look at them. Other times, books that are challenged simply remain in the collections of libraries (Kidd 213).

Selection

Selection is defined as the process of choosing to include or omit certain books from classrooms, curricula, and libraries. In 1953, Lester Asheim published an essay entitled "Not Censorship But Selection" that proposed selection as an alternative to censorship. Selection begins from the premise that any given library does not have the physical space or funding to possess every single book, so some books will inevitably be rejected. Asheim grounds the distinction between selection and censorship in a difference of attitude:

> The selector's approach is positive, while that of the censor is negative…. The positive selector asks what the reaction of a rational intelligent adult would be to the content of the work; the censor fears for the results on the weak, the warped, and the irrational. The selector says, if there is anything good in this book let us try to keep it; the censor says, if there is anything bad in this book, let us reject it. And since there is seldom a flawless work in any form, the censor's approach can destroy much that is worth saving. (66)

Asheim's advocacy of selection over censorship has become a cornerstone of librarianship and teacher training, and most teachers and librarians receive instruction in establishing a collection of library and classroom books that represent wide and diverse reading. Asheim argues that selection establishes a protocol for the proliferation of texts rather than the repression of texts. We also see an emphasis on selection in the words and actions of many anti-censorship activists. For example, when asked by Mark I. West about the "censorship of racist books," author John Steptoe responded that "the best way of dealing with racist garbage in children's books is to provide kids with books that aren't racist" (West, *Trust Your Children* 135). There are clearly many virtues to an anti-censorship approach that stresses selection.

PRIZING AND CENSORSHIP

In 2009, Kenneth Kidd published "'Not Censorship but Selection': Censorship and/ as Prizing," an article that challenged the existing critical consensus about censorship and selection. In a surprising juxtaposition, Kidd compares the similarities between **prizing** (the giving of awards such as the Newbery Medal) and censorship. Like prizing, lists of challenged books such as those put out on a regular basis by the ALA "point toward a canon of banned books, individual titles of which gain importance through challenge. Censorship thus achieves something like canonization" (Kidd 209). One of the ironies Kidd draws out is that despite "differences in aim and attitude," prizing and censorship achieve the same end result: "greater publicity and symbolic capital" (199). This irony is particularly pronounced because so many challenged and banned books are literary classics: "We are expected to value books because they have been controversial" (210). Kidd also challenges the long-held distinction between selection and censorship by arguing that "selection is arguably a form of censorship. With selection and prizing, many books must be judged unworthy so that a few might be celebrated" (204). While Kidd remains opposed to censorship in its many forms, his article has a nuanced attitude to the phenomenon of censorship. Anti-censorship activities, by highlighting some texts as particularly worthy of attention or critical defense, have something in common with the system of literary prizes: the valuation of certain texts and the devaluation of others.

THE FIRST AMENDMENT AND FREEDOM OF SPEECH

In the United States, the **First Amendment** protects freedom of speech from government persecution or suppression. In a landmark 1982 Supreme Court decision, *Board of Education v. Pico*, the court ruled that school boards could not restrict the availability of books in their libraries because of their content. This means that a young person's right to read anything in a school library is protected by the First Amendment. There are, however, gray areas in the amendment, and some categories of speech are not protected:

> The United States Supreme Court has ruled that there are certain narrow categories of speech that are not protected by the First Amendment: obscenity, child pornography, defamation, and "fighting words," or speech that incites immediate and imminent lawless action. The government is also allowed to enforce secrecy of some information when it is considered essential to national security, like troop movements in time of war, classified information about defense, etc. (ALA, "Intellectual Freedom")

The First Amendment therefore has its limitations, organized roughly around the idea of providing protection from physical endangerment, as evidenced by the fact that "fighting words" are not protected speech because they might incite immediate violence. Limits on speech inevitably produce interpretative debates such as whether we can always tell the difference between an angry, opinionated statement and one that incites action. It is also famously difficult to draw a line between obscenity and art.

Marjorie Heins draws a sharp distinction between exposure to ideas and physical harm in the case of child pornography, arguing that it is by no means protected speech:

Child pornography involves actual physical abuse, not exposure to words, images, or ideas. Indeed, the tendency to conflate the two separate issues is worrisome precisely because it threatens the foundation of the First Amendment: the distinction between free speech and thought on the one hand and punishable acts on the other. Allowing youngsters access to information and ideas about sex is decidedly not the same as engaging them in exploitative sexual conduct. (13)

Here Heins argues that a book or idea cannot harm a child, but she asks us to be vigilant for instances where a child is vulnerable to *actual* physical harm or exploitation.

Questions of free speech are approached differently outside of the United States. In Canada, the Charter of Rights and Freedoms (section 2 [b]) allows for "freedom of thought, belief, opinion and expression, including freedom of the press and other media of communication" ("Canadian Charter"). Canada does, however, limit free speech through a federal law that "prohibits any statement that is likely to expose a person or group of persons to hatred or contempt based on ethnicity, place of origin, religion, sex, or sexual orientation" (Cortese 17). The United Kingdom also has a long tradition of respect for freedom of speech, although "freedom of expression is only implicit and not invoked as a right in court" (Kearns 147).

Since even the First Amendment in the United States places limits on freedom of speech, it is clear that such freedom is not boundless. The question remains: Should it be? And if not, what are the proper limits of freedom of speech, and who is entitled to make these decisions?

CHILDREN'S VULNERABILITY VERSUS CHILDREN'S RESILIENCE

In *The Disappearance of Childhood* (1982), Neil Postman argues that the rightful state of childhood is one of "mystery and awe," where children are shielded from adult knowledge (86). In Postman's model, the rise of a mass media culture, with television confusing the separate spheres of childhood and adulthood, is ruining an ideal of childhood worth preserving. However, such a model of childhood presumes a childhood materially privileged and protected enough to be able to develop as "a space apart" from "adult" concerns. Robert Cormier, himself the author of a number of controversial and frequently challenged young adult books, stresses that most children are already immersed in the conflicts and difficulties of the adult world. Children, Cormier notes, are "part of the world. They watch television, ride buses, see newspaper headlines, and go to movies. Most kids have heard of corruption or terrorism or sexuality, and I see no reason not to deal with these subjects in children's books" (qtd. in West, *Trust Your Children* 73).

Another distinct strand of censorship is specifically motivated by the desire to shield children from the blandishments and imperatives of an overheated consumer culture. In 2006, the British newspaper the *Daily Telegraph* published an open letter from 101 sociologists, children's book writers, and teachers arguing that children should be protected from the decadence of contemporary culture caused by the dictates of the consumer market: "[Children] are pushed by market forces to act and dress like mini-adults and exposed via the electronic media to material which would have been considered unsuitable for children even in the very recent past" ("Modern Life"). While this argument seems similar to that of Postman, it focuses more explicitly on mass-market commodification of the spheres of childhood and adulthood alike. In this view, the steady drumbeat of mass media (including the internet) has made it impossible for children to develop as individuals away from consumerism and the dictates of the mass market.

Mark I. West argues that children have a different purpose in engaging with children's literature than adults do. Parents and teachers are drawn to the "nostalgic appeal" of children's literature, but children

> are anxious to grow up and thus seek books that help explain the mysterious worlds of adolescence and adulthood. Consequently, while children appreciate [Judy] Blume's and [Norma] Klein's willingness to write openly about menstruation, masturbation, and other taboo subjects, adults who want to read about childhood innocence may feel repulsed or even betrayed by the writers' frankness. (West, "Teaching Banned Books" 55)

The split between adult and child readers does not have to be absolute, of course. Many adult readers are capable of encountering children's texts in a spirit of discovery, while child readers might look to children's texts in the expectation that they offer a familiar, unthreatening world. But West's remarks offer a good explanation for censorship rooted in conflicting expectations not only of childhood but also of children's literature.

KEY MOMENTS IN THE CENSORSHIP OF CHILDREN'S LITERATURE

Children's literature before the twentieth century was effectively censored long before it reached publication. Many of the "crossover" books initially meant for adults or mixed audiences and then produced in versions for children were expurgated or bowdlerized. **Bowdlerization** describes the editing of texts with anything offensive taken out; the process is named after Thomas Bowdler, who edited an edition of Shakespeare in 1818 with offensive material removed to make it more suitable for women and children. For example, the children's versions of *Gulliver's Travels* edited out much of the satirical content of the work and some of the incidents deemed unsuitable for children. To begin with, the version for children tends to include only Gulliver's first two voyages (to Lilliput and Brobdingnag) and not even all that material. There is also bowdlerization of the earthy bodily activity that is such an important part of Swift's satire. Among other examples, a scene in which the giant Gulliver urinates on a tiny Lilliputian building in order to extinguish a fire was deleted in several editions intended for younger readers. As we saw in our discussion of fairy tales, there were modified and expurgated versions that omitted sexual content, violence, and social critique, draining the tales of much literary and cultural impact.

West argues that prior to the 1970s "most censorship activity took place in an author's study or an editor's office" because authors "became their own censors" when they "accepted as a given that they could not use swear words, make reference to sexuality, or address controversial social problems" (*Trust Your Children* 5). Though this is undoubtedly true, the censorship landscape then, as now, was probably more complex than we usually think. While Christine Jenkins found that some youth services librarians during the McCarthy era of the 1950s noted that books with "an intergroup and international focus became politically suspect" (116), Julia L. Mickenberg paints a different picture. In *Learning from the Left: Children's Literature, the Cold War, and Radical Politics in the United States* (2006), Mickenberg argues that many leftist authors during the McCarthy era (especially those associated with the Communist Party) turned to writing children's literature, since the established channels of mainstream literature for adults were closed to them as writers and teachers lost their jobs through graylisting or blacklisting: "The fact that children's books were viewed as outside the literary establishment—beneath it, actually—did much to explain how the field could inconspicuously 'harbor' significant left-wingers throughout the McCarthy era, despite concurrent concerns about the 'seduction' of 'innocent' youth by violent comic books, rock and roll, television, and 'un-American' schoolteachers" (15). Here we have a model of children's literature as less vulnerable to censorship because it is less scrutinized than other cultural forms. Often, however, children's literature is censored because it is *more* vulnerable to scrutiny than literature written for adults.

The rise of realistic young adult (YA) books in the 1970s ushered in a new era of frankness about social and political issues, creating a wave of censorship in reaction to this frankness. However, this wave of censorship may have been caused at least in part by the depressed economic conditions of the period, as Judith F. Krug argues: "If you trace the history of censorship, you'll find that when the economy goes down, censorship attempts go up" (qtd. in West, *Trust Your Children* 180). This tendency could be due to an upsurge in social anxiety generally, leading adults to be less tolerant of outside influences on their children; it might be an attempt by would-be censors to distract themselves from hard economic times through focusing on matters of culture that they think of as under their control; or it could perhaps be some combination of the two.

Since 1990, when the ALA began publishing lists of the most challenged books, the majority of challenged ones were written for children and young adults. This pattern continues into the twenty-first century. From 2001 to 2010, American libraries faced 4,660 challenges due (variously) to "sexually explicit" material, "offensive language," "violence," "homosexuality," "anti-family" stances, "religious viewpoints," or material deemed unsuitable to the target age group. In 2017, 354 book challenges were recorded in the USA (up from 323 in 2016). The top ten most challenged books were:

1. *Thirteen Reasons Why*, written by Jay Asher

2. *The Absolutely True Diary of a Part-Time Indian*, written by Sherman Alexie

3. *Drama*, written and illustrated by Raina Telgemeier

4. *The Kite Runner*, written by Khaled Hosseini

5. *George*, written by Alex Gino

6. *Sex Is a Funny Word*, written by Cory Silverberg and illustrated by Fiona Smyth

7. *To Kill a Mockingbird*, written by Harper Lee

8. *The Hate U Give*, written by Angie Thomas

9. *And Tango Makes Three*, written by Peter Parnell and Justin Richardson and illustrated by Henry Cole

10. *I Am Jazz*, written by Jessica Herthel and Jazz Jennings and illustrated by Shelagh McNicholas.

The majority of the books on this list were written for children or young adults. Many of these books have been on the most challenged book lists off and on for several years. Harper Lee's *To Kill a Mockingbird* (1960) is an American classic that sparked censorship attempts in 2017 due to its use of the "n-word" and its depiction of violence. Others, such as Angie Thomas's award-winning *The Hate U Give*, are new to the list (Thomas's book was challenged for its supposed "vulgarity," and for drug use and profanity). Asher's *Thirteen Reasons Why* was controversial because of its depiction of suicide. Originally published in 2007, it attracted renewed attention due to a controversial Netflix series of the same name.

Two challenged works: *Nasreen's Secret School* and *I Am Jazz*.

As we noted in Chapter 11, a number of censorship attempts occur because of objection to sexual content in books for young people, and that is abundantly true of the 2017 list. Sherman Alexie's *The Absolutely True Diary of a Part-Time Indian* attracted challenges due to some sexually explicit content, and profanity. Telgemeier's *Drama* is a graphic novel about the production of a school musical, with a gentle depiction of middle-school crushes, both gay and straight. Two of the books on this list deal with transgender identity for an elementary school audience: *I Am Jazz*, a nonfiction picturebook and *George*, a novel. *And Tango Makes Three*, also for young readers, features a same-sex relationship. The presence of Silverberg and Smyth's *Sex Is a Funny Word* attests to the continued challenges faced by books about sexuality for younger readers, especially those which engage with young people's questions with candor, and those which represent many different gender identities and sexual orientations.

SPECIFIC REASONS FOR CENSORSHIP

Sometimes groups of citizens take action against a book; at other times a censorship attempt is initiated by an individual. Amy McClure traces three major motivations for censorship: moral, psychological, and sociological. The moral argument "denotes personal behavior and connotes righteousness as defined by the teachings of religion" but can encompass a wide range of economic, social, and cultural factors bearing on morals. Psychological motives stress "the mental and emotional well-being of the child" and are "overwrought with concern for local and contemporary problems and enthusiasms." For example, one culture stresses "independence" and another culture "cooperation." Sociological motives for censorship derive from "the urge to advance or protect the concerns of one segment of society over the concerns or prejudices of other segments." This could include—variously—sexism, racism, and communism, or "books depicting violent or other socially proscribed behavior" (McClure 22). McClure's taxonomy is particularly insightful because it pinpoints and historicizes the aspirations of those who might object to books.

Douglas L. Howard writes of his reaction to the ALA list of banned and challenged books as he designed a college-level course on intellectual freedom:

> At times, the list seemed like a conservative attempt to protect teens and children from explicit sex and violence. At other times, it appeared to be a righteous response to social injustice, to drug use, to bigotry, to racism, and to emotional and sexual abuse. Still, at other times, the list made no sense at all and generally offended my sensibilities as both a reader and a professor of English. (n.p.)

Diane Ravitch finds a similar diversity in the motivations of censors. Censorship, she notes, can come from both the left wing of the political spectrum ("liberals") and the right wing ("conservatives"), with the left seeking to curtail representations that they perceive as sexist, racist, or homophobic, and with the right seeking to censor works that do not conform to the "family values" of the heterosexual and patriarchal nuclear family (Ravitch 6).

Some people attempt to censor literary works on religious grounds. Parents are often surprised to find that the books and ideas their children encounter in school (even public school) are not "value neutral"; they also must cope with the fact that their children

In William Steig's *The Amazing Bone* (1976), Pearl's walk home from school takes her past some "old gaffers" smoking, playing horseshoes, and spitting tobacco juice. The book was challenged because of the depiction of tobacco use.

encounter religious or nonreligious ideas that might be different from the ideas they learn at home. Hamida Bosmajian notes that the motivation of religious censors "rests on what James Moffett has called 'fear of knowing'" (316); besides not wanting their children to be exposed to other religious ideas, they themselves do not seek to explore other religious points of view.

Sometimes censorship is triggered by the presence of a detail in the text that is not germane to the narrative of the book or its themes but which nonetheless stirs controversy. In 1986, William Steig's *The Amazing Bone* (1976) was challenged by a parent in Lambertville, New Jersey, because one of the animal characters uses tobacco. Rather than looking at the overall message of the book, the would-be censors focused on a single (and random) detail about a character.

The electronic search techniques of the internet age have ushered in new ways for such selective and reductive reading, as we see, for example, in a 2013 request to remove David Levithan's *Two Boys Kissing* (2013) from Virginia Fauquier County Public Schools, a request unanimously denied by the school district's board committee. The "Request for Reconsideration of Learning Resources" was filed when a parent of a student in the district, Jessica Wilson, typed the keywords "kiss" and "sex" into Amazon.com and found 117 references (while the Amazon search function displays only a limited number of pages, it does search the entire text). While the book undeniably takes its title and central action from Harry and Craig's marathon kiss on the high school lawn—as they attempt to break the Guinness World record for kissing—the narrative makes it clear that the kiss is many things: an act of defiance against homophobia and exclusion; an act of friendship between the two ex-lovers; a galvanizing event for those who support them. The book is narrated by a collective group of men who died during the AIDS epidemic, who regard Harry, Craig, and other queer youth from above with mingled tenderness and admiration, adding to the book's gravitas and literary complexity. Wilson—who completed the online text search but did not read the book—wrote on her request form that such references "equate[d] to 60 percent of the book's contents being related to kissing or sexual content" (Chung). *Two Boys Kissing* appears on the ALA's 2016 list of Most Challenged Books. These cases can be regarded as based on misunderstandings of the texts or a kind of "nitpicking" of a minor detail. However, Kenneth Kidd reminds us that a "holistic" orientation to a text is an acquired skill and that many readers might not share the assumptions of literary critics who seek a holistic understanding of any given text (206).

Betty Miles opines that there is a seldom-discussed class conflict in many censorship cases:

> Many of the people who want to ban books feel intimidated by everything that books seem to stand for: education, culture, a rich life. They may feel uneasy around people who seem to know so much about books. They feel—often with

justification—put down and belittled. Misguidedly or not, many would-be censors are trying to do what they think is right for their kids, and when they find themselves dismissed as a bunch of fools, it's naturally painful to them. There's very little that's more painful than being laughed at. I've been at meetings where supposedly open-minded people snickered at their opponents' mispronunciation of words. If that's how book-reading "intellectuals" behave, I'm not surprised at anti-intellectual rage. (qtd. in West, *Trust Your Children* 85–86)

Kidd echoes Miles's concerns: "Without capitulating to the demands of censors, we can try to establish dialogue rather than dismiss their concerns as uncultivated or uninformed" (208). We might also be sensitive to parents' desires to inculcate their own values and culture in their children—desires that can sometimes be at odds with the culture children encounter at school, in libraries, or from society at large. As Miles observes, "Parents want their kids to be educated, but not so educated that they grow away. Such parents may come to view books and learning as a threat" (qtd. in West, *Trust Your Children* 86). One way of dealing with this type of anxiety is to talk with parents about how to accept that their children might hold opinions different from their own, and to consider ways in which a close relationship across these differences might be maintained.

SELF-CENSORSHIP/SUBTLE CENSORSHIP

Even in the wake of an increased frankness in writing for children and young adults, subtle curtailment of free expression continues. Judy Blume, who has written many novels subject to censorship and who is an anti-censorship activist herself, describes a moment when on the advice of her editor she backed away from a potentially controversial scene in which the adolescent character masturbates:

The scene was psychologically sound, he assured me, and delicately handled. But it also spelled trouble. I got the message. If you leave in those lines, the censors will come after this book. Librarians and teachers won't buy it. Book clubs won't take it. Everyone is too scared. The political climate has changed.

I tried to make a case for why that brief moment in Davey's life was important. He asked me how important? Important enough to keep the book from reaching its audience? I willed myself not to give in to the tears of frustration and disappointment I felt coming. I thought about the ways a writer brings a character to life on the page, the same way an artist brings a face to life on canvas—through a series of brush strokes, each detail adding to the others, until we see the essence of the person. I floundered, uncertain. Ultimately, not strong enough or brave enough to defy the editor I trusted and respected, I caved in and took out those lines. I still remember how alone I felt at that moment. (*Places* 6–7)

Blume describes her failure as a lack of strength and bravery but also as a tough choice: her editor said she would have to decide whether she wanted the book to be widely distributed or whether she wanted to hold on to the integrity of the scene. This choice raises questions about the line between market pressures (which are genuine, since most published authors wish to sell their books) and censorship. Are the modifications demanded by editors and publishing houses in order to please prospective readers censorship? Daniel Keyes, the author of the frequently challenged book *Flowers for Algernon* (1966), thinks they are. Asked by Mark West how prepublication censorship affects the writing process, Keyes replies that such pressure "has a chilling effect. You are sitting at your writing desk, and you are about to use a certain word when suddenly your fingers start to tremble. And you ask yourself, 'Do I really need to use that word?'" (qtd. in West, *Trust Your Children* 120).

Sue Curry Jansen goes even further, as she argues that market censorship touches all books commercially produced under a capitalist publishing system:

> These *market censors* decide what ideas will gain entry into "the marketplace of ideas" and what ideas will not. They inspect books, journals, dramatic pieces, etc., before publication, to ensure that they contain nothing that seriously challenges the basis of the existence of the corporate state. That is, *they decide what cultural products are likely to ensure a healthy profit margin.* (16)

In Jansen's view, freedom of expression is not possible in a corporate culture committed to profits and its own capitalist ideologies.

We might also examine censorship in the classroom. Many educators, especially in higher education, see "trigger warnings" in the classroom as a form of subtle censorship. As the name suggests, trigger warnings are short descriptors on a syllabus before a literary work is taught warning students that a book or article contains

Deenie (1973) is one of many works by Judy Blume that have been challenged or banned—in this case, due to its frank treatment of masturbation.

sensitive, explicit, or controversial content, and may "trigger" an adverse reaction. Many college and university teachers feel that the free discussion of ideas and exposure to the full spectrum of literary and artistic expression is hampered by trigger warnings, offering a challenge to the very mission of higher education: to make students think deeply and critically even about material that disturbs them. Long-term anti-censorship activist Judy Blume bluntly notes: "Why do college students need to be warned that what they are about to read might make them feel bad? These are 20-year-olds, but they need a professor to warn them? What kind of education is that?" (quoted in Baker 65–66).

Those who advocate trigger warnings note that they can help students prepare for disturbing content before they encounter it, noting that many students have experienced trauma, violence, prejudice, or abuse, and might experience pain or even physical distress when exposed to graphic content. Onni Gust explains that trigger warnings could encompass "sexual assault, racist violence, transphobic or homophobic slurs." Trigger warnings, Gust argues, are conducive to intellectual exploration and good pedagogical practice because "they help create a community of learners who acknowledge difference. Overall, trigger warnings remind everybody, regardless of their personal history, to keep breathing, and to think carefully and compassionately about what they are learning" (Gust n.p.).

One of the strongest arguments against trigger warnings is that rich and complex works of literature are boiled down to brief descriptors like "racist violence" or "explicit sexual situations," which are reminiscent of the objections filed when people submit requests to remove material from libraries and schools. Trigger warnings veer most strongly near to the territory of censorship if they are interpreted as an assurance that a student need not engage with classroom material because it contains disturbing content—although few college professors who embrace trigger warnings intend them in quite that manner. The debate around trigger warnings seems to center on a notion of a college student's vulnerability or susceptibility to disturbing content, which is reminiscent of the debate around the vulnerability children might experience as readers. The way anti-censorship activists handle this issue around children's literature is that they argue that it is not a book's *content* that poses a problem, but a lack of skillful and informed conversation about the books. Something similar may be at work when people advocate trigger warnings instead of focusing on the pedagogy that allows college students to engage with all course material openly, fully, and in a respectful atmosphere.

Individuals versus Groups

How should readers who fervently object to a book cope with or express their distaste for a particular text? Tim Hirsch describes the balancing act between being offended by a book and yet upholding the rights of others to read it:

I have to tell you in this first sentence: I consider much of *The Adventures of Tom Sawyer* offensive. I am offended that someone like Tom could be the hero of the book. I don't like the ways he bullies other kids and how he tortures animals. I don't like the way he lies to and cons both other children and adults. I don't like the way he treats women and girls. I object vehemently to the blatant anti–American Indian racism in the book, and to the more sly but equally offensive anti–African American racism. I also am troubled by the violence in the book, and by its idealization of child neglect and rebellion against "civilization." So I have no trouble at all understanding why some folks would like to ban the book. But I do not advocate censoring the book in any way. Absolutely not! (4)

The problems Hirsch has with *Tom Sawyer* are very profound ones, not to be dismissed lightly. Yet he does not think that his own passionate feelings about *Tom Sawyer* mean that the book should be made unavailable for a wider public or expurgated. He has made a distinction between his own beliefs and the rights of others.

Selection and a Parent's Rights

When navigating tensions between individual and group rights, it is worthwhile to return to questions of selection. Most anti-censorship activists would defend the right of parents and educators to be selective, to give individual children the books that reflect their values or support their own goals in the classroom. Many anti-censorship activists urge parents to monitor their child's reading or viewing—avoiding what they find offensive or distasteful—in order to dissuade parents from seeking to censor a book for everyone.

This seems like a commonsense solution to the problem of censorship. It does, however, raise the question of where selection ends and censorship begins. While it might be simple to make a distinction between censorship and the rights of a caregiver or parent to forbid a book, we might turn again to Kenneth Kidd's questioning of the tidy distinction between censorship and selection. Unlike the censor, who is "clearly Other," the parent possesses "the right to censor for their own kids, or the kids they own." Kidd asks an incisive question: "Who decides on the ownership of a child, and how might that inform the 'war' on censorship?" (212). While it may seem natural for a parent to restrict the material their children read, such control could be seen as a form of censorship in its own right, since children are not exerting their freedom to read what they wish.

Judy Blume argues that parents "have to ask themselves, 'So what if my kid browses through the books at the library and picks up a book for older kids or even adults. What can happen?' The kid might ask a question, and if he does, I say answer him" (qtd. in West, *Trust Your Children* 54). Along with children's frank questions comes the difficulty of having to navigate awkward subjects or questions to which a parent might not know the answer. Blume points to her own discovery that a number of parents lack the basic knowledge about human sexuality, anatomy, and reproduction that they would need to address their children's most elementary questions about sexuality. Given that parents and other caregivers might face gaps in their own knowledge and experience, there may need to be an adjustment of the traditional notion that adults "know all" and have as their main role the transmission of knowledge to their children. Such an adjustment necessitates giving children more responsibility to learn about the world and establishes a relationship of codiscovery between parent and child. Daniel Keyes sees this process positively, asserting that young people who grow up in "more open homes, where they are permitted to read and where full discussion is encouraged" are "generally better equipped to deal with the real world" (qtd. in West, *Trust Your Children* 121).

CRITICAL READING AS ANTI-CENSORSHIP ACTIVITY

In *Should We Burn* Babar? *Essays on Children's Literature and the Power of Stories* (1995), Herbert R. Kohl articulates his concerns about Jean de Brunhoff's Babar books, which he sees as reinforcing colonial notions, especially through Babar's socialization into European values by the Rich Lady who clothes him and makes him something of a pet. Kohl also sees sexism in the text's treatment of the female elephant Celeste and the sense that marriage is her only possible destiny. Despite these misgivings, Kohl offers useful ideas about how to have a discussion with children about a troubling book:

> Critical reading consists of questioning a text, challenging it, and speculating on ways in which the world it creates can illuminate the one we live in. A book is a wonderful tutor for the imagination which thrives on being challenging as much as it does on being challenged. Part of the experience of reading *Babar* for a child is raising questions, like Did Babar forget his mother when he met the Rich Lady? Did he ever talk to her about his mother? What happened between Celeste and Arthur in that car ride back to the jungle that led to their getting married? Why is wearing clothes so important in this story? And what would I do if I met the Rich Lady?
>
> For a more experienced and older reader, the challenges can go beyond the text itself to inquiries about the author's politics, social class, and family background, and to speculation about the emotional impact of books in general that show children losing their parents. In all of these cases, reading becomes dialogue. The text can be reimagined and invested with multiple meanings. For the active reader, there is no need for one authoritative interpretation, and even absurd fights over the meaning of the text are part of the whole experience of reading. (22–23)

This approach emphasizes the child reader's growing power to form his or her impression of the text and a teacher's capacity to guide students productively. In this model, children are not vulnerable to the messages of a text, whatever they may be, but have a say in its meaning and how much of an impact it makes on their lives—therefore avoiding the need to censor a text. Kohl remains concerned that some children do not have the necessary guidance from parents or teachers to navigate a text critically, but he does point the way forward to supporting children as they encounter a text that might either disturb them or offer values that parents and teachers cannot themselves endorse.

READING CRITICALLY: CENSORSHIP AND SELECTION

The Harry Potter Series

Along with the popularity of the seven Harry Potter books published from 1997 to 2007 came several challenges to the publication and distribution of the books. These have included attempts—both successful and unsuccessful—to remove the series from libraries, and even the extreme measure of book burning. What creates this kind of response to the Harry Potter books, seen by so many as charming and harmless? The majority of the accusations center on the notion that the Harry Potter books promote the occult—belief in the supernatural outside the parameters of conventional religious beliefs, including alchemy, magic, fortune telling, or witchcraft. Inherent in fear of the occult is the conviction that children are not only fascinated by such material but easily tempted to enter an occult subculture. This fear is particularly held by the fundamentalist Christian community, where some individuals and groups view the Harry Potter books as a genuine threat to the faith of their young people. Although the most obvious objections to the series center on occultism and magic, most censors and would-be censors are probably equally motivated by the way the books challenge authority, portraying nightmarish bureaucracies and corrupt authority figures and repeatedly siding with Harry and his friends as they flout even benign authority.

Not all Christian believers dislike the Harry Potter series; some see positive Christian models of community and personal virtue in the books, including loyalty to friends, self-sacrifice, and a willingness to combat evil (as embodied by Lord Voldemort). There are also Christian believers (including fundamentalist Christians) who express their objections to the books on websites and blogs, or in books or videos, but do not actively seek to censor the series. Yet the most high-profile incidents of Harry Potter censorship—the ones that have made headlines around the world—have been book burnings conducted in the American Christian fundamentalist community. For example, CNN reported on 31 December 2001 that the pastor and members of the Christ Community Church in Alamogordo, New Mexico, burned books in the Harry Potter series. Pastor Jack Brock claimed, "These books teach children how they can get into witchcraft and become a witch, wizard or warlock." At the same time, protestors against the burning denounced it as inappropriate in a free society. Harry Potter books were also burned in 2001 at the Harvest Assembly of God Church near Pittsburgh, by two Michigan pastors outside their Jesus Non-Denominational Church in 2003, and in several other locations. The Harry Potter series has also been the subject of a number of book challenges, which are formal requests (either oral or written) to remove books from school libraries, classrooms, or curricula. It is number one on the list of the American Library Association's Top 100 Banned/Challenged Books of 2007 and number seven on the list of the 100 Most Frequently Challenged Books of 1990–99. It is also number one on the list of the Most Challenged Books of the Twenty-First Century.

On December 30, 2001, the Christ Community Church in Alamogordo, New Mexico, held a book burning at which parishioners were urged to burn *Harry Potter* and other books and games, including Ouija boards, that were deemed dangerous and offensive.

In a newspaper column entitled "Is Harry Potter Evil?" (originally printed on the *New York Times* op-ed page on 22 October 1999), Judy Blume made an astute (and somewhat ironic) distinction between her own much-censored works and those of J.K. Rowling. Much of Blume's writing was published in the 1970s and 1980s and deals realistically with sexual maturation and tensions with family and at school. Blume observes, "In my books, it's reality that's seen as corrupting. With Harry Potter, the perceived danger is fantasy" ("Is Harry"). Yet Amanda Cockrell believes the perceived threat is exacerbated by the series' location in the "real world," since the wizarding world of the books is entwined with ours: "Rowling has abandoned the realm of high fantasy and laid her story in contemporary England, rather than in the imaginary and medievally flavored otherworld of Tolkien's Middle Earth, or in a place like Baum's Oz, which can only be reached by tornado" (25).

Cockrell explains that there may be cultural reasons for the hostility directed at the books in some sectors of the fundamentalist community, citing Deborah J. Taub and Heather L. Servaty's study of the linkage between notions of "fantasy" and "deceit" in fundamentalist culture (25). Anxieties about fantastic or imaginary literature seem rooted in a belief that such texts are not merely diversionary but actively dangerous. It is true that magic in the Harry Potter books includes not just mild spells (to find household objects, for example) but also fearsome curses and dark arts. However, Cockrell contends that fundamentalist censors are mistaken about the nature of magic in the series: "Rowling insists that magic in Harry's world is a skill to be mastered, that it has no connection with religion or theology, or with supernatural spirits good or bad. It is the wizard, the practitioner of the magic, who makes it good or evil, in the way that any science may be turned to bad ends" (27). In this model, young people would never dabble in the occult because of Harry Potter, since the magic in the series is merely "a skill" like any other and must be learned through painstaking study with qualified teachers.

Quite apart from the accusations of occultism in the books is the way in which Harry and his friends challenge adult authority. Judith Krug of the ALA writes:

> I believe, in fact, that what some parents and adults find most threatening about the Potter series is what engages young minds and fires the imagination of young people— Rowling's willingness to deal with the truth that adults in children's lives can sometimes be unthinking, authoritarian, and even evil. The best books always have raised questions about the status quo—and are the most threatening to censors who want to control what young persons read and think about. Like the tyrannical Defense Against Dark Arts Professor Dolores Umbridge, who insisted on providing a "risk-free" education to the young wizards at Hogwarts, they would limit education and information to facts so incontestable that they arouse no controversy at any level, thereby leaving young people unequipped to think about and address larger questions about the nature of our society. (Krug)

The question of an "innocent" literature is addressed directly in Rowling's *The Tales of Beedle the Bard* (2008), which includes notes to the tales from the fictitious headmaster Dumbledore. Dumbledore cites Beatrix Bloxam, who felt that Beedle's tales were "damaging to children" because of what she called "the unhealthy preoccupation with the most horrid subjects, such as death, disease, bloodshed, wicked magic, unwholesome characters and bodily effusions and eruptions of the most disgusting kind" (Rowling 17). She rewrote various stories with the aim of "filling the pure minds of our little angels with healthy, happy thoughts, keeping their sweet slumber free of wicked dreams and protecting the precious flower of their innocence." Here is Mrs. Bloxam's "pure and precious" reworking of Beedle's "The Wizard and the Hopping Pot":

> Then the little golden pot danced with delight—hoppitty hoppitty hop!—on its tiny rosy toes! Wee Willykins had cured all the dollies of their poorly tum-tums, and the little pot was so happy that it filled up with sweeties for Wee Willykins and the dollies!
> "But don't forget to brush your teethy-pegs!" cried the pot.
> And Wee Willykins kissed and huggled the hoppitty pot and promised to help the dollies and never to be an old grumpy-wumpkins again. (Rowling 18–19)

The overwrought performance of both innocence and cuteness is meant—somewhat hyper-bolically—to represent what censors propose to offer children instead of "dangerous" books, implying that censorship is an act of artistic impoverishment as well as condescension. If we remember Tony Kushner's lament that children's literature is often forced to adhere to a stan-dard of "universal suitability," we can see the insipid writing of Mrs. Bloxam as a fictitious (and ultimately undesirable) model of what "universal suitability" might look like.

One aspect of the Harry Potter series that triggers would-be censors is the way that Harry and his friends organize independently when they lack proper support from their school sys-tem. They form a secret student organization, Dumbledore's Army, in *Harry Potter and the Order of the Phoenix* (2003) when their teacher Dolores Umbridge fails to teach them defense against the dark arts properly. She allows them to read only theoretical texts on the subject and for-bids the practice of important applied skills. Would-be censors find this disturbing because of its suggestion, first of all, that school authorities can fail to meet the needs of their students. It also implies that students are capable of striking out on their own without any adult supervi-sion when necessary.

One way to respond to objections about the students' flouting of authority is to contextual-ize it within the books' narrative arc of the fight against Voldemort. Perry L. Glanzer contends:

> What these traditionalists fail to realize about Harry's moral world is that school
> rules may actually get in the way of furthering good or preventing evil. In that case,
> observing conventions becomes secondary. Staying out past curfew and breaking into
> a restricted section of the library are hardly major transgressions, although they do
> cause problems for school bureaucrats. When issues of ultimate good and evil are at
> stake, one can excuse Harry and his friends for staying out past midnight. (526)

The books become increasingly sophisticated as the series goes on, and the characters become even more daring and independent. Kate Behr points to the notorious darkening of mood later in the series: "Harry and the reader move together from wonder, innocence, and comedy, to fear, experience, and tragedy throughout the series…. Innocence cannot be maintained unless a character has no concept of time or of cause and effect, and a reader, caught by the 'passion for reading,' is actively trying to lose his/her innocence" (114).

While the books clearly engage with a struggle between good and evil, the moral universe of the series is complicated. It is not always possible to put trust in authority or even to know if a character is truly good. In this sense, the Harry Potter series is often criticized by would-be cen-sors for its moral ambiguity, in contrast to the more stable and hierarchical social organization of C.S. Lewis's books—where it is easy to tell an evil character (the White Witch) from a good character (Aslan). Harry—and by extension the reader—does not always know who is trust-worthy. The apparently evil teacher Snape turns out to be a genuine hero; the unimpeachable headmaster Albus Dumbledore turns out to have flirted with the forces of evil in his troubled youth. The moral ambiguity of the books adds to their complexity and richness as works of literature but can trigger censorship attempts from people who want literature to portray a less nuanced vision of good and evil. The Harry Potter series is popular partly due to its charm and inventiveness but also because it is a genuine coming-of-age story, in which childhood innocence gives way to increased participation in a complicated political and social world.

EXPLORATIONS

Review

1. How does the censorship of works for children reflect on our notion of childhood as a space apart from the demands and pleasures of adulthood? Why are children thought to need protection from adult concerns?

2. Summarize some of the responses from journalists, academics, and intellectuals to Alan Gribben's NewSouth edition of *The Adventures of Tom Sawyer* and *Huckleberry Finn*. What do these responses tell us about censorship and freedom to read?

3. In what ways is selection an alternative to censorship? Can selection function as censorship in its own right?

4. How do the demands of the market affect the freedom of an author to write and a publisher to publish what they want?

5. What are some strategies explored in the chapter to critically read or express distaste for a given text without resorting to censorship?

Reflect

1. Do you remember a book that you wished to read but were denied access to as a younger reader? Did you read it anyway? If so, what effect did it have on you?

2. If you were the parent of young children, what sort of books, movies, magazines, or video material would be totally off limits to them? Can you come to any conclusions about your own view on censorship and selection? Compare your list to those of your classmates. Can you see any patterns in the class?

3. In "Harry Potter and the Public School Library," Todd A. DeMitchell and John J. Carney argue that the Harry Potter novels are censored for two reasons: the characters' frequent defiance of authority and the supposed occultism in the books. Analyze the presence of these two elements in one of the Harry Potter books. Is either of these arguments a valid objection to the books?

4. Here are three types of censorship or attempted censorship: the burning of books, the attempt to remove a book from a library or classroom, and an editor who removes obscene language or sexual content from a book before its publication. Think about all these modes of restriction of the freedom to read. How should we judge an act of censorship: by its effects or by the form it takes?

Investigate

1. Choose one of the books on our Suggested Readings list. Make a list of issues, themes, or topics in the book that a young reader might find it hard to talk about. Make a list of questions a young reader might have about the book and come up with some possible answers to address them. Was it difficult to come up with something helpful to say to the young person?

2. Choose one of the books from our Suggested Readings list or the list of censored or challenged books on the American Library Association website. Imagine that you're a teacher or librarian who has to respond to a challenge to one of the books. How will you defend the book? Will you defend the book on the grounds of its aesthetic or literary qualities, or according to more general principles of freedom to read?

3. Interview the parents or caregivers of both a young child and a teen and ask them what books or movies they would deem out of bounds for their child. From these interviews, what can you conclude about the patterns of censorship based on age?

4. Choose a book with explicit or profane language (either sexual or "curse words"). Take a page and rewrite it with the language edited out (or expurgated). Write a brief essay analyzing what changed in the second version. What effect did this kind of censorship have on the meaning and literary impact of the text?

SUGGESTED READINGS

Blume, Judy. *Forever* **(1975).** The novel is known for its frank description (for its time period) of the sexual relationship between high school students Katherine and Michael. It also stirs controversy because the protagonist seeks birth-control counseling from Planned Parenthood and goes on the pill. It is number seven on the ALA list of the 100 Most Frequently Challenged Books of 1990–99.

Cormier, Robert. *The Chocolate War: A Novel* **(1974).** Jerry Renault's unwillingness to sell chocolates during his school's fundraising drive is a defiance of both the school authorities and the school "gang," led by the ruthless Archie. The violent denouement, in which Jerry is subject to a ritualized fight, leaves the reader in doubt about his very survival. This is the second most challenged book of 2007 due to "sexual explicitness, offensive language, and violence."

Levithan, David. *Two Boys Kissing* **(2013).** In *Two Boys Kissing*, Harry and Craig are two 17-year-olds who take part in a 32-hour marathon to break the Guinness World Record for kissing. Narrated by a Greek chorus of gay men who died in the AIDS epidemic, the boys' marathon kiss becomes an act of defiance against homophobia and a moment of unity for their supporters. Entangled with their story are the lives of other teenaged boys coping with romance, gender identity, and coming out. *Two Boys Kissing* was on the 2016 ALA Most Challenged Books list, with challenges arising from its representation of homosexuality and for "condon[ing] public displays of affection."

Lowry, Lois. *The Giver* **(1993).** Lowry's novel posits a world where "sameness" has been achieved. The people in Jonas's village see no color, have no genuine emotion, have no ties to a real family, and possess no memory of the past. The sole burden to remember their collective history lies with the "receiver of memory." When he turns thirteen, Jonas discovers that he is about to become the new "receiver." In this role, he learns that the secure world he knew was built upon the lies that individuals told, the suppression of emotion and sexuality, and the cruel murder of the elderly, weak, and sick. The book has been censored for its depiction of euthanasia, sexuality, and intergenerational tension. It is twenty-third on the ALA list of Most Challenged Books in 2000–09.

Pilkey, Dav. *The Adventures of Captain Underpants: The First Epic Novel* **(1997).** In this book, two kids hypnotize their principal to believe that he is Captain Underpants, the hero of a comic book they write. The book has been censored for its use of "potty" humor and its ostensible encouragement of bad behavior. It is number thirteen on the ALA list of the Top 100 Banned/Challanged Books for 2000–09.

Rowling, J.K. The Harry Potter series (1997–2007). The seven-book series about Harry Potter's adventures at Hogwarts has been frequently challenged in libraries and even burned. Fundamentalist Christians in particular accuse the books of encouraging young people's participation in the occult.

Sendak, Maurice. *In the Night Kitchen* (1970). Sendak's picturebook shows the visits of a young boy to a bakery in the middle of the night. The book is twenty-first on the ALA list of 100 Most Frequently Challenged Books of 1990–99. The book continues to attract censorship because the young boy is drawn in the nude.

Twain, Mark (Samuel Langhorne Clemens). *Adventures of Huckleberry Finn* (1884). The book was criticized for its "rough language" when it was first published and was banned from the public library of Concord, Massachusetts. In contemporary times, it is frequently challenged for its use of the racial slur "nigger" and its stereotypical portrayal of African Americans. It has been removed from classrooms and libraries, and the ALA lists it as one of its Most Frequently Challenged Books of the 1990s.

Williams, Garth. *The Rabbits' Wedding* (1958). In 1959 the book was removed to the reserve shelf of the Montgomery, Alabama, public library due to objections to its depiction of "interracial" marriage between a black and a white rabbit.

Winter, Jeanette. *Nasreen's Secret School: A True Story from Afghanistan* (2009). *Nasreen's Secret School* is a picturebook set in Taliban-controlled Afghanistan, which has outlawed formal education for girls. Nasreen's parents disappear; her father is taken away by soldiers and her mother breaks the law and goes out alone to search for him, never to return. After these wrenching events, Nasreen refuses to speak with anyone, so her grandmother enrolls her in an illegal school for girls to raise her spirits and ensure that she receives an education. Nasreen's education opens her intellectual horizons, and she makes friends, once again speaking and interacting with people. *Nasreen's Secret School* was on the 2015 ALA List of Most Challenged Books for "religious viewpoint," "violence," and the argument that it was "unsuited to age group" despite being carefully crafted for a younger audience.

APPROACHES TO TEACHING *HARRY POTTER AND THE SORCERER'S STONE* [ELEMENTARY SCHOOL]

Preparation for the Lesson

The class will read *Harry Potter and the Sorcerer's Stone* together.

Learning Goals

- To look at the ways in which the fantastic and the real intersect in *Harry Potter and the Sorcerer's Stone*, with an emphasis on the "make-believe" nature of the world J.K. Rowling has created

- To gain practice in evaluating the strengths and weaknesses of characters as literary creations, rather than as role models or peers

- To gain practice in talking about the potentially disturbing elements of a book, contextualizing them within the book's plot, and considering them as part of the book's artifice.

Activity One: Real and Imaginary

As a class, list the ways in which J.K. Rowling's wizarding world is located alongside the "Muggle" (or human) world in the novel. This might include Dumbledore's various ways of contacting Harry at Privet Drive and the location of Diagon Alley in a disguised part of London. Lead a discussion about whether the wizarding world's proximity to the Muggle world makes it feel more or less real. If the consensus is that Hogwarts and the wizarding world feels real, ask if something feels real, does that mean it *is* real? Discuss the ways in which Rowling's book functions as make-believe, and the way that Rowling uses the wizarding world's proximity to our world for comic effect.

Activity Two: Evaluating Characters

Make a list of the strengths and weaknesses of Harry, Ron, and Hermione. For each character, ask the students to list scenes from the novel where they admire or dislike that character. Discuss the ways in which a character's flaws make someone believable and also advance the plot. Discuss why Harry, Ron, and Hermione are admirable characters but not perfect role models.

Activity Three: Frightening Scenes

On the board, make a list of two or three frightening moments in the novel. If time permits, ask each student to anonymously write out one or two things that they find frightening in the novel. Collect these and go over them with the class, taking care not to reveal the identity of the student writers. If several students choose the same scene, point out the ways in which they share a reaction to the text. Lead a discussion about how to deal with frightening moments in the novel. Ask them whether there is a pleasure to being frightened if you know the events of the novel are not real; whether they remember a time in their lives when the events of the novel would be too frightening; or whether they know a younger child who would find the novel too scary. Discuss why Rowling includes the frightening or suspenseful scenes and what they add to the novel. Lead a discussion about whether the book should ever be censored, and if so, under what circumstances.

CHILDREN'S LITERATURE AND POPULAR CULTURE

Like the phenomenally popular Harry Potter series before it, Suzanne Collins's best-selling Hunger Games trilogy, published between 2008 and 2010, sold millions of copies, inspired a series of film adaptations, and spawned a merchandising empire that includes toys and dolls, clothing and jewelry, posters and room decor, school supplies and stationery, and countless other products. Collins claims to have found inspiration in both Roman gladiatorial games and contemporary reality television shows, two forms of popular entertainment from ancient and modern times. Within the series, the Hunger Games require 24 youths from 12 of Panem's 13 districts to engage in combat to the death, commemorating the nation's first rebellion and providing the people of Panem with an annual opportunity to witness violent conflict, live vicariously through their district tributes, and cheer for victories with little real effect on the wider world or the lives of citizens. Collins derives the name "Panem" from the Latin phrase "panem et circenses," which means "bread and circuses." Coined by Roman satirist Juvenal in 120 CE, panem et circenses refers to a strategy sometimes used by political authorities to prevent rebellion and appease the masses by providing minimal sustenance (bread) and distracting entertainment (circuses). For some cultural studies critics, popular culture represents the modern manifestation of panem et circenses, and children's literature has often been seen as a form of popular culture throughout its history. Other critics of children's literature see in this popularity a means for child and adolescent readers to assert their own tastes, pleasures, and cultural priorities and to enter literary culture as resistant readers and commenters.

Opposite: Fan art by Noelle Stevenson for The Hunger Games trilogy by Suzanne Collins.

This chapter draws from the academic field of cultural studies to examine the role of children's literature in popular culture, from genres of popular fiction such as mysteries and romance novels to adaptations of children's books as popular entertainment for stage and screen.

This chapter is informed by two hallmarks of cultural studies: 1) the focus on how texts are caught up in class-based systems of power and in everyday practices of resistance and 2) the rejection of strict boundaries between "high" and "low" culture. In his introduction to *The Cultural Studies Reader* (1993), Simon During attempts to define cultural studies in terms of its methodology and field of investigation, and he notes that one "distinguishing characteristic of early cultural studies was that it was an engaged form of analysis," which meant that cultural studies considered the political and social implications of the texts and phenomena it investigated (1). He explains, "Early cultural studies did not flinch from the fact that societies are structured unequally, that individuals are not all born with the same access to education, money, health-care, etc., and [early cultural studies] worked in the interests of those who have fewest resources" (2). In keeping with this defining feature of cultural studies as political, this chapter pays particular attention to the ways popular culture functions to shape and constrain people as consumers and how it creates or occasions opportunities for resistance. During also notes that for founders of cultural studies like pioneering Welsh scholar Raymond Williams, "'culture' was not an abbreviation of a 'high culture' assumed to have constant value across time and space" (2). In other words, practitioners of cultural studies sought to understand a broad range of cultural forms, including those that had been traditionally dismissed as inferior, using the same analytical practices and tools. Cultural studies could address a nearly endless array of cultural practices and texts, from youth subcultures like hipsters to contemporary genres like manga and anime, though given the fact that readers are likely to encounter this chapter in the course of studying children's literature, we limit our focus here to popular genres of fiction and to adaptations of children's books for other media, which are likely to be most relevant to the reader's immediate purpose.

POPULAR CULTURE

Defining Popular Culture

Julie A.S. Cassidy notes that "[a]ccording to the *Oxford English Dictionary* (*OED*), in the early sixteenth century the term 'popular' defined the 'common people' or people of 'lowly birth' as opposed to people of the aristocracy" (174). To be popular is also to be widely known and beloved. While "popular" came to mean that a work was esteemed by many, it also took on negative connotations because of its associations with non-elite people: "By the late sixteenth century (the *OED* cites 1599), the intention behind the word shifted slightly to invite negative similes such as low, vulgar, and plebeian" (Cassidy 174). Williams, who helped develop cultural studies as an academic enterprise, notes that by the late seventeenth century the concept of "popularity" was defined as "courting the favour of the people by undue [manipulative] practices" (111). In this latter sense, the popular also potentially elicits suspicion as possibly deceptive or manipulative.

"Culture," on the other hand, has come to mean "the distinctive ideas, customs, social behavior, products, or way of life of a particular nation, society, people, or period" (*OED*, "Culture" 7a). Used in this sense since the nineteenth century, the term "culture" refers to the collective social practices and products of a people, often understood as opposed to nature and the natural world and what exists outside of or without assistance from human civilization. An even earlier sense of "culture" defined it specifically as "Refinement of mind, taste, and manners; artistic and intellectual development. Hence: the arts and other manifestations of human intellectual achievement regarded collectively" (*OED*, "Culture" 6). This latter definition of "culture" associates it with the upper classes and their elite practices or privileges, including education, much like what we might now describe as "high culture." The concept of "popular culture" has emerged as a counterpoint to "high culture."

Williams explains that the concept of "**popular culture**," like the concept of "popular," bears both positive and negative connotations: "inferior kinds of work," but also "work deliberately setting out to win favour" as well as "the more modern sense of [work] well-liked by many people" (111). While many scholars of popular culture celebrate it for its complexity rather than denigrating it as inferior, we must nonetheless recognize the historically negative connotations of "popular" and "popular culture" that Williams documents. Scholars and students of children's literature, who frequently contest claims about the "inferiority" of works for youth, may be particularly attuned to the nuances and complexity of popular culture and the need to read it critically.

The phrases "popular culture" and "mass culture" are sometimes used interchangeably to refer to cultural practices, texts, and products that are produced for and enjoyed by a broad, nonspecialized audience. Football games, television sitcoms, spy novels, video games, horror movies, fan conventions, beauty pageants, comic books, hip hop concerts, and celebrity news magazines are all examples of pop culture. The phrase "mass culture" has a slightly more negative connotation than "pop culture" and calls more explicit attention to the mass production and dissemination of goods, which allows them to be relatively inexpensive and formulaic and therefore more widely accessible to an ordinary or even unsophisticated consumer. For example, Stephenie Meyer's Twilight series (2005–08), which details the romance between a teen girl and a vampire who is over 100 years old, was a pop culture phenomenon that included four popular novels, a series of movie adaptations, and a wide variety of mass-produced products like toys, film soundtracks, posters, magazine issues, and t-shirts. Products related to the series are examples of both popular and mass culture.

The sense of popular entertainment as primarily for the mass public and produced to be inexpensive and easily sold has reinforced an association between popularity and simplicity, accessibility, and recognizability. If pop culture is for "everyone," that means it should be readily accessible, or easily obtained and understood with little resources or preparation, to a variety of audiences young and old, literate and illiterate, wealthy and poor. These qualities, which came to be associated with popular writing, dovetailed easily with expectations of children's literature and culture: that it be simple, thrilling, plot-driven, and familiar. Sometimes the impulse to promote popularity leads to the exaggeration of these qualities, since the more familiar a text seems, the easier it is to read, view, and understand. The quest for popularity can therefore result in formulaic texts designed either to be immediately recognizable and familiar or to employ qualities or tropes that have proved successfully popular in the past. Such may be among the "undue practices" to which Williams refers. Series books, which often repeat a successful formula in each volume, are especially prone to demonstrate this market-driven impulse. Cassidy explains that "the term 'popular' was held in direct opposition to the term 'literature,'" so works that are deemed popular or achieve popularity can paradoxically result in their devaluation as literary. The term "popular fiction" has been used to describe genres with mass appeal that are thought to be formulaic or lacking literary merit: mysteries, romance novels, detective fiction, science fiction, westerns, etc. In the contemporary moment, YA dystopias like the Hunger Games and Divergent series have attracted this kind of criticism, sparked by their popularity and the perception (by some) that they lack aesthetic merit. Given the inverse relationship between popularity and cultural value, the status of children's literature often proves vexed—influential and beloved, but also dismissed and marginalized—and children's literature itself can be considered a form of popular culture.

Popular Culture, Ideology, and the Culture Industry

Clearly the terms "popular" and "popular culture" are not neutral ones, and their associations with manipulation and social class give them political dimensions. German critical theorists Max Horkheimer and Theodor Adorno, members of a group of intellectuals known as the Frankfurt School, warned about the dangers of popular culture in their essay "The Culture Industry: Enlightenment as Mass Deception," a chapter in their influential book *Dialectic of Enlightenment* (published 1944, revised 1947). Horkheimer and Adorno argue that the culture industry—the mechanical production of popular culture under capitalism—turns people into passive consumers of mass-produced products such as music and movies. They claim that "[e]ntertainment is the prolongation of work under late capitalism" in that both work and leisure are characterized by sameness, routine, mindlessness, and lack of imagination or agency (109). The consumer, they write, needs "no thought of his own: the product prescribes the reaction" (109). We are so familiar with mass media and how we are supposed to respond to it that our reactions are as scripted as the songs, television shows, and movies we consume. For Horkheimer and Adorno, one of the most troublesome effects of the culture industry is that consumers are lulled into a routine of work and leisure that distracts and drugs us and thus preempts any possibility for resistance or revolutionary change. "Culture has always contributed to the subduing of revolutionary as well as barbaric instincts," they write (123). We seek leisure as an escape from the dullness of work, but our leisure pursuits keep us going until we return to work, thereby maintaining the status quo.

A number of children's and YA works actually discuss the power and effects of popular culture on youth as well as the possibility of resisting its allure in order to see the world differently. For instance, the adolescent characters in M.T. Anderson's *Feed* (2002), a sci-fi dystopian novel, embody the relationship between consumer and mass media Horkheimer and Adorno warn about: they are too distracted by their addiction to a constant stream of television and commercials plugged directly into their brains to notice the dissolution of their world into a toxic wasteland, the destruction of their bodies by disease, and the loss of real intimacy or connection to others. Protagonists Violet and Titus eventually try to resist the feed and to cultivate critical thinking about it. Jonah in Lois Lowry's *The Giver* (1993), another popular dystopian novel, struggles to see past the colorless sameness of his homogenous community in order to imagine and create a better world.

Other theorists associated with the Frankfurt School, such as Walter Benjamin, saw the potential for subversion in popular culture, especially film. Benjamin writes, "We do not deny that in some cases today's films can also promote revolutionary criticism of social conditions" (231). The widespread access to film and to being filmed makes everyone a possible expert, according to Benjamin. More recently, pop culture theorist John Fiske has written optimistically about how cultural products can be repurposed by audiences in ways that resist oppressive political or economic authorities. He critiques a conception of mass culture that sees it simply as "imposed upon a powerless and passive people by a culture industry whose interests were in direct opposition to theirs" (17). Fiske suggests that consumers of mass culture are not as passive or helpless as some theorists of the culture industry assume them to be. He describes, for instance, "Young urban Aborigines in Australia watching old Westerns on Saturday-morning television ally[ing] themselves with Indians" (20), suggesting that consumers are capable of reading resistantly in ways that support oppositional identities or politics. Fiske concludes, "A text that is to be made into popular culture must, then, contain both the forces of domination and the opportunities to speak against them, the opportunities to evade them from subordinated, but not totally disempowered, positions" (21). When reading popular culture and children's literature critically, we must look for the ways they not only work to subject people to forms of authority but also provide people with opportunities for resistance.

Bertolt Brecht, in his early-twentieth-century writings on theater, similarly sees revolutionary potential in popular culture. Brecht, a German playwright, suggested that popular entertainment could provoke critical thinking through the "alienation effect," in which the familiar is made strange, thereby allowing audiences to see the world differently. Brecht offers as an example when an actor in a play pauses the action to address the audience directly, calling attention to the playgoer's role as spectator and the fiction of what is being viewed (91–92). Jon Scieszka uses a device like this in *The Stinky Cheese Man and Other Fairly Stupid Tales* (1992), in which the narrator, an elf-like creature named Jack, appears throughout the book as a character calling attention to the fact that a story is being told. Scieszka's book exposes the absurdity of fairy tales (if you can have a Gingerbread Man, why not a Stinky Cheese Man?), which can undermine the didactic lesson appended to stories in more traditional collections. Other forms of pop culture, such as graffiti art and blogging, have been put to revolutionary political purposes, suggesting that popular forms of expression and entertainment do not always or necessarily have the dulling effect some theorists have posited. Alison Lurie makes this point about children's literature in *Don't Tell the Grown-Ups: The Subversive Power of Children's Literature* (1990). According to Lurie, "The great subversive works of children's literature suggest that there are other views of human life besides those of the shopping mall and the corporation" (xi). In contrast to thinkers like Jacqueline Rose, who see children's literature as primarily constructing the adult's view of the child and therefore inculcating young people into adults' ideas of what children are or should be, Lurie points to works like Beatrix Potter's *Peter Rabbit* (1902), in which the reader's sympathy is really with the reckless Peter rather than his obedient siblings. Lurie presents the possibility that even popular children's literature might create opportunities for readers, child and adult, to question the world around them and to resist the stupefying effects of popular culture.

POPULAR GENRES AND GENRE FICTION

We defined "genre" in Chapter 9 as a class of works that are believed to share certain features. The term "genre fiction" is used more specifically to refer to categories of popular fiction such as mystery, crime story, detective novel, romance, and so on. Child and adult readers alike often choose a book based on its similarities to books in the same genre they have read before. Literary and cultural critics have dismissed some of these popular cultural genres, as we discussed in the beginning of this chapter. Yet it is clear that this kind of genre fiction often reflects larger currents in popular culture and addresses social and political affairs. We discuss some important popular genres below with attention to their social and political functions and the ways in which they respond to the needs and demands of their readers.

Science Fiction

Science fiction could be seen as a subcategory of fantasy. Science fiction author Arthur C. Clarke once said, "Any sufficiently advanced technology is indistinguishable from magic" (qtd. in McClintock 27). Yet Michael McClintock draws attention to the fact that in many ways the two are distinct: "Something there is in technology that does not love magic, and magic is at least as hostile to technology." Science fiction and fantasy, he argues, have different "principles of control": "In fantasies, magic works; in science fiction, technology does" (33). In fantasy, the magic is assumed, with no explanation necessary. Science fiction offers more scientific explanation of the events described, even if the story is set in another time or place.

William Sleator, a science fiction author, offers another view: "My own definition is that science fiction is literature about something that hasn't happened yet, but might be possible some day" (207). He goes on to say,

> In fantasy we are asked to believe in elves, ghosts and magic spells, which we all know do not exist. In science fiction we are asked to believe in aliens—and no one can tell me that aliens do not exist. I know I will not run into an elf tomorrow, but I can't say for sure I won't run into an alien. I tend to doubt that I will get to another world by walking into a wardrobe, but I don't doubt at all that I could get there in a space ship. (210)

Definitions of **science fiction** like Sleator's tend to imply that the genre's use of scientific explanation leads to a kind of verisimilitude—or believability—that fantasy does not seek. When Sleator says he believes in the possibility of aliens but doubts that of elves, he indicates a faith in science rather than magic, since scientists have argued that extraterrestrial life is indeed possible. At the same time, the science remains speculative, since (as far as we know) no one has actually seen an alien. The genre of science fiction at its most effective enables dreaming about the future and what it might bring, including technological and social innovations of all kinds. Like utopian and dystopian fiction, described below, science fiction includes an articulation of new and previously unimagined political formations—even extending to worlds where humans are not at the center of the action, or where humans have to collaborate with alien species on an equal basis. Though often set in the future, science fiction typically comments on the concerns of the present, much as the historical fiction discussed in Chapter 7 does.

Utopian and Dystopian Fiction

Lyman Tower Sargent defines "utopia" as a "non-existent society described in considerable detail," further dividing it into "eutopia" and "dystopia." "Eutopia" refers to "those societies that the author intended a contemporaneous reader to view as considerably better than the society in which the reader lived" and "dystopia" refers to societies that are "considerably worse" (xii). **Utopian fiction** fits within the fantasy tradition because it features imaginary worlds. These books are distinguished, however, by their focus on the political and social organization of the imaginary worlds they posit. For example, James Gurney's Dinotopia books (1992–2007) feature a world where dinosaurs and humans have built a sophisticated and just society with the two species living in harmony. Young adult **dystopian fiction** has recently experienced a great boom, including M.T. Anderson's *Feed* (2002), Cory Doctorow's *Little Brother* (2008), and Veronica Roth's *Divergent* (2011) and its sequels. Young adult dystopian fiction often extrapolates current trends, asking young people to speculate about a future world where violence, injustice, and environmental degradation have rendered the world uninhabitable. Dystopian fiction appeals to the developing political awareness of many adolescents, since the adolescent protagonists often change the world for the better. Utopian and dystopian novels reveal social and political values and encourage critical thinking about what society should be aiming to change in the future.

Detective and Mystery Fiction

Detective and mystery novels for young people can be differentiated from their adult counterparts because they feature children and young adults as the mystery-solving protagonists. Two series (and assorted offshoots) produced by the Stratemeyer Syndicate are particularly well known: the hundreds of books produced for the Hardy Boys series (written under the name Franklin W. Dixon from 1927 to 2005) and the Nancy Drew Mystery Stories (written under the name of Carolyn Keene from 1930 to 2003). Both series feature regular adolescents who are daring amateur sleuths. In Donald J. Sobol's Encyclopedia Brown series, which began in 1963, a boy solves ten mysteries in each book, drawing on his keen powers of observation and the ability to pick up on clues; a section at the back of each book reveals how Encyclopedia figured out the crime. Continuing the tradition of brainy youth who piece together complex puzzles is Michael D. Beil's Red

Blazer Girls series (2009–13), centering on four Upper East Side schoolgirls who solve crimes requiring cultural erudition and peerless math skills.

Electronic media has made a definite mark on the mystery and detective genre. Scholastic's 39 Clues series (2008–11) by Rick Riordan, Gordon Korman, Jude Watson, Peter Lerangis, and Linda Sue Park features the worldwide adventures of siblings Dan and Amy Cahill as they search for the 39 Clues, the elements of an alchemical formula developed by their ancestor Gideon Cahill. Each book comes with a packet of cards with codes that readers can use to go online and unlock clues from the book. In Patrick Carman's Skeleton Creek series (2009–11), Ryan McCray and Sarah Fincher explore a creepy abandoned dredge in a small town, discovering hidden treasure and a mysterious secret society known as the Crossbones. Ryan pours out his thoughts about the case in a handwritten diary, while Sarah records her investigations on password-protected streaming video (readers are given the log-in codes in the book itself). The reader must use both Ryan's text and Sarah's video to move ahead with the story.

The continued vitality of the mystery and detective genre for young adults is reflected in two Edgar Allan Poe Awards presented every year by the Mystery Writers of America: the best juvenile mystery (preschool to grade 7) and the best young adult mystery (grades 8 to 12). The appeal of these genres for younger readers may lie in their emphasis on children's toughness and insight. In Sobol's Encyclopedia Brown series, for example, the chief of police brings his tough cases home to his fifth-grade son to solve: "Who would believe that the guiding hand behind Idaville's crime cleanup wore a junior-sized baseball mitt?" (8).

Mystery and detective novels also allow young readers to exercise their critical thinking skills by picking up clues and solving puzzles. To the extent that dominant models of ideal childhood require children to be protected from difficult experiences or knowledge, the world must remain mysterious to them. Curious children are therefore primed to act as detectives and to find pleasure in stories about other children making discoveries, often about adult misconduct or crime. It is interesting to note that three of the four current and former female Supreme Court justices—Sandra Day O'Connor, Ruth Bader Ginsburg, and Sonia Sotomayor—cite the girl

Nancy Drew series cover.

sleuth Nancy Drew as an influence, drawn to her gumption, her powers of logic, and her authority in confronting crime, making it an example of a popular text that offered empowerment to its readers.

Horror Fiction

Horror fiction is named for the emotions it evokes in its readers, ranging from vague unease to terror. Horror includes "ghost stories," "tales of witches, devils, bogeymen, zombies, and vampires," and "tales of monstrous creatures and of other dangers" (Schwartz 1). As we discussed in Chapter 1, children are often featured as characters in horror films, but many adults are less comfortable with children as readers of horror. First of all, horror is often dismissed as "junk" literature that lacks literary quality. A key example is R.L. Stine's Goosebumps series (1992–97) for middle-grade readers and his Fear Street Saga series (1989–2005) for junior-high readers, which some educators dismiss as lacking sufficient quality and others defend as encouraging reluctant readers to pick up books. Yet teacher Peggy Timmons had success with her first-grade students when she developed a set of lessons around "scary stories":

> After hearing a number of scary stories, the students were asked to consider and identify characteristics of scary stories.... Predictably, many children identified scary characters, like monsters, mummies, bugs, ghosts, and dead things. That led to a discussion of the importance of characters in stories, and how authors create characters that make readers respond to those characters in particular ways. Some students identified scary elements related to the setting of the story, such as cobwebs, haunted houses, castles, and basements. The importance of time and place in the story became a focus lesson. Some students identified elements of plot, such as scary adventures

Stephen Gammell's illustrations for *Scary Stories to Tell in the Dark* (1981) by Alvin Schwartz were so horrific that the book became one of the most frequently challenged books.

or problems, tricks, mysterious occurrences, and no ending, as contributing factors to a story's scare quotient. (Richards et al. 834–35)

These "scary stories," dismissed by many critics, not only encouraged students to read but helped them read *critically* and with a deeper knowledge of literary structure.

Many adults are also anxious about the level of violence horror fiction entails (mirroring perennial concerns about fairy tales and other traditional stories that include their share of gore). Robert Hood, who coauthored the Creepers series with Bill Condon, defends children's capacity to cope with horror: "Children can realize, at least implicitly, that looking at the scary side of life—loss, bereavement, fear, the monster under the bed—is possible. They can examine these emotions, even play with them, and by so doing gain some power over them" (Hood n.p.). Alvin Schwartz echoes this sentiment in his collection *Scary Stories to Tell in the Dark* (1981): "Most of us *like* being scared in that way. Since there isn't any danger, we think it is fun" (1). Schwartz's own collection, originally illustrated by Stephen Gammell and later illustrated by Brett Helquist, features a number of stories taken from folklore and lists the sources prominently at the back of the book, in addition to further reading for students who might be interested in similar tales. Pleasure in horror can come from voluntarily experiencing small doses of fear in a relatively safe and controlled space. Reading horror critically involves considering what horror texts tell us about what we find scary or what we find exciting or thrilling in the grotesque or macabre, either at a particular moment in history or at a particular age. Often, depictions of monsters or the setting of horror stories point to larger cultural concerns, such as environmental devestation or the emotional and social isolation of the suburbs. For instance, in the Goosebumps volume *You Can't Scare Me!* (1994), the frightening mud people are supposedly created when a flash flood triggers a mudslide that buries a village in the distant past. The villagers, now monsters made of mud, return to terrorize a group of schoolchildren. Many other volumes in the series point to routine elements of modern suburban life as sources of fear, from household plumbing to unfeeling camp counselors.

Romance Fiction

The blockbuster success of Stephenie Meyer's Twilight series (2005–08) testifies to a wide readership for teen **romance fiction**, a literary genre defined by the focus on romantic feelings and often the development of romantic relationships between two or more characters. Bella Swan's fascination with the mysterious vampire Edward Cullen and her emotionally charged friendship with the werewolf Jacob Black have riveted millions of readers, in the process creating a boom in teen paranormal romance. As Bella's romance with Edward progresses toward marriage and consummation of their love, she makes the ultimate commitment to become a vampire. This stress on eternal commitment is a shift from earlier teen romance series such as Scholastic's Wildfire or Bantam's Sweet Dreams. Writing in 1986, M. Daphne Kutzer made a distinction between teen and adult romances: "Teen romances are also concerned with developing love, but nearly all of them imply that the one, true love is some years in the future and … not necessarily passionate. Teen romances are concerned with the beginnings of the romantic search, not with the final triumph" (91). In contrast, Bella's romance commits her to nothing short of eternity with Edward and to life as a vampire. Given Meyer's Mormon religious beliefs, the series has been read as commenting on controversial political issues like abortion and teen sexual abstinence.

Another shift in the genre in the last two decades is the increasing diversity of the romantic partnerships explored within the genre, including both interracial and same-sex pairings. Jacqueline Woodson's *If You Come Softly* (1998) deals with the romance between Ellie, a white Jewish girl, and Jeremiah, an African American boy, who meet at an exclusive New York City preparatory school. Nina Revoyr's *The Necessary Hunger* (1997) deals with the rivalry and love between two female basketball players, Japanese American Nancy Takahiro and African American Raina Webber. Nick Burd's *The Vast Fields of Ordinary* (2009) explores Dade Hamilton's conflicted feelings for Mexican American Pablo Soto and his growing love for Alex Kincaid. As cultural values surrounding sex, sexuality, and romance change, children's and YA romance fiction both records and promotes those changing values. That books for children featuring diverse expressions of romance are often targeted for censorship attests to their status as political works as well as popular entertainment.

Romance novels are often critiqued as formulaic fiction lacking in quality. This is not necessarily or always the case; several romance novels for younger readers have a strong plot, convincing characters, and good writing. Furthermore, formulaic books might have a worthwhile place in childhood and adolescence. In her now classic study of romance novels, *Reading the Romance: Women, Patriarchy, and Popular Literature* (1984), Janice Radway examined series such as the Harlequin Romances not just for their content but also for the way readers used the books actively, forming book clubs and honing their critical skills. One could readily imagine young readers using romance novels of varying quality to reflect on relationships, sexuality, and sexual identity when they are contemplating their first relationships or actually experiencing them.

FORMULA FICTION

Some fiction is treasured by readers not because it breaks the mold but because the work closely follows a set of generic expectations. This is the case with **formula fiction**, which tends to conform to a reader's expectation of plot, theme, and tone. The formula is set in part through generic expectations; many mysteries, detective stories, and romances fall into this category. John G. Cawelti offers the following definition of "formula":

> A formula is a conventional system for structuring cultural products. It can be distinguished from invented structures which are new ways of organizing works of art. Like the distinction between convention and invention, the distinction between formula and structure can be best envisaged as a continuum between two poles; one pole is that of a completely conventional structure of conventions ... the other end of the continuum is a completely original structure which orders inventions. (56)

Formula fiction is distinguished by its repetition of the same expected themes and characters, which are frequently described as "tropes."

Many works that can be classified as formula fiction are structured as books in a series, which we see, for example, in the Sweet Valley High series that included 181 books written from 1983 to 2003, plus many more in multiple spinoff series. Although the series was created by Francine Pascal, many ghostwriters chronicled the lives and adventures of Jessica and Elizabeth Wakefield: affluent, popular teenagers living in Sweet Valley, California. One of the most striking aspects of series books is how they follow predictable patterns in response to reader demand: readers want a repetition of familiar characters and settings rather than innovation. Cawelti argues that the predictable patterns of formula fiction have their uses: "The game dimension of formula is a culture's way of simultaneously entertaining itself and of creating an acceptable pattern of temporary escape from the serious restrictions and limitations of human life" (59). While by his admission formula fiction does not "break the bounds" of readerly expectations or of genre, it can provide a useful diversion and an escape from mundane obligations. This is precisely the escape that Horkheimer and Adorno, and critics following in their wake, criticized so forcefully for creating political passivity in readers. However, one of the aspects of popular literature that makes it so powerful is its ability to provide a range of readerly experiences, temporary escape among them. Formula fiction also serves, like many other popular forms, as a source of insight into cultural aspirations and fears. For example, the Baby-Sitter's Club might reveal the nature of social popularity and affluence in American society and the ways in which readers are taught to desire material possessions and social status.

ADAPTATIONS OF CHILDREN'S LITERATURE AS POPULAR CULTURE

Children's Literature as Inspiration

In Chapter 2, we discussed the popular story of "The Babes in the Wood," in which an uncle adopts his niece and nephew and plans their murder so he can steal their inheritance. Originally a narrative poem meant to be sung, "The Babes in the Wood" was registered as early as 1595 by Thomas Millington in Norwich, England, though it may have circulated in oral and print forms even earlier (McLane 147). Ending in the deaths of the two children, "The Babes in the Wood" is perhaps surprising material for children's entertainment as both crime and horror story, though it has been reproduced countless times since the sixteenth century in chapbooks, poetry and nursery rhymes, children's picture books, and children's plays. "The Babes in the Wood" was an especially popular children's **pantomime**, a musical comedy for the stage usually performed around Christmastime and often involving adaptations of traditional folk or fairy tales. According to William Davenport Adams's 1904 *Dictionary of the Drama*, "Babes in the Wood" was produced at least eighteen times on the London stage between 1856 and 1894, and Adams calls these eighteen the most "notable" productions, suggesting that there were in fact many more. Attesting to the popularity of the story in the nineteenth century is the fact that it was adapted as a children's picturebook, most famously in 1879 by Randolph Caldecott, after whom the Caldecott Medal was named. The popularity of the story was not lost on the Walt Disney Company, which produced an animated film in 1932 titled *Babes in the Wood* based partly on the traditional story and partly on the Grimm Brothers' fairy tale "Jorinda and Jorindel," in which two youths wander into the woods and meet a malevolent fairy who turns children into caged animals. The story of "The Babes in the Wood" has long been a part of children's literature and popular culture.

The practice of adapting or retelling stories is central to the history of popular children's literature and culture, as the numerous versions of "The Babes in the Wood" attest. Benjamin Lefebvre notes that for children's literature, "textual transformations have for a long time been the norm rather than the exception, and the industries that support adaptations, abridgements, and censored editions of children's texts are driven at once by financial, artistic, and ideological considerations" (2). Modifying or shortening works for different media or venues has long been a common practice in the production of children's culture to promote popularity. In 1698, Benjamin Harris published *The Holy*

Opposite: The story of the "Babes in the Wood" first appeared in some form between 1593 and 1595. Randolph Caldecott illustrated this 1879 version, showing the two orphans lost in the woods.

Bible in Verse, a rhyming edition of the Bible for children. John Newbery republished fairy tales and appropriated folk characters to build his business. Early chapbook publishers retold stories of Robin Hood and King Arthur. In 1807, siblings Charles and Mary Lamb published *Tales from Shakespeare*, 20 prose retellings of Shakespeare plays written in language "to make these tales easy reading for very young children" (6). Children's fantasy writer Edith Nesbit undertook the same task in her 1895 book *The Children's Shakespeare*, which even included illustrations of Shakespearean characters as children. Just one year after Harriet Beecher Stowe published the bestselling anti-slavery novel *Uncle Tom's Cabin* (1852), publishers like John P. Jewett & Co. produced versions for children, such as *Pictures and Stories from Uncle Tom's Cabin*, which was "designed to adapt Mrs. Stowe's touching narrative to the understandings of young readers and to foster in their hearts a generous sympathy for the wronged negro race of America" (reprinted in Haviland and Coughlan 194).

Many adaptations, like children's literature more generally, are designed to appeal to a mixed-age audience of children and adults, since it is usually adults who write, produce, direct, star in, purchase tickets for, and take children to these productions. Even in the unabridged version of Stowe's novel the narrator sometimes addresses children, while the children's adaptation includes a publishing note that it was "well suited for being read aloud in the family circle" and that "our younger friends will claim the assistance of their older brothers and sisters or appeal to the ready aid of their mamma" (n.p.). Jacqueline Rose notes that when J.M. Barrie's play *Peter Pan* debuted in 1904, "[t]he audience was made up of London's theatre-going élite, and there was hardly a child among them" (32). Andrew Adamson and Vicky Jenson's popular animated film *Shrek* (2001), an adaptation of William Steig's picturebook from 1990, includes a number of jokes directed at adults. For example, the Magic Mirror presents several women to Lord Farquaad, whose name sounds like a very adult insult, in a manner reminiscent of a dating reality show. When the Mirror introduces Snow White, it describes her as living with seven men but not being "easy." Children's adaptations that fail to address adults are less likely to be as successful as those that do, which is why many children's plays and films include situations or humor designed to amuse adults.

In short, the film industry, including the phenomenally successful Disney Company, did not invent the practice of retelling traditional stories for children; rather, the history of children's literature is a history of the appropriation, adaptation, and transformation of earlier works for different media. To read popular culture and adaptation critically, we must set aside the modern worship of authorship and originality that causes some readers to think about adaptations as simply inferior copies.

Stage Adaptations

Children's literature provided readily available material for children's theatrical productions. Fairy and folk tales and children's fiction were popular materials for dramatic adaptations. The emergence of stage productions of fairy tales coincided with the rise of the literary fairy tale in the eighteenth century, and this tradition continues through the present with hit Broadway shows like Disney's *Beauty and the Beast* (Jarvis 139). As Roger L. Bedard explains, few writers at the turn of the twentieth century were specifically writing stage productions for children, "so producers looked to writers in other mediums to fill the void" (103). The work of Frances Hodgson Burnett was especially popular. In fact, Burnett's successful 1888 lawsuit over the pirated stage adaptation of *Little Lord Fauntleroy* (1886) secured protection from unauthorized adaptations for all British authors (Gerzina 121). Burnett biographer Gretchen Gerzina calls *Fauntleroy* "the *Harry Potter* of its day," and Burnett's own dramatic adaptation of *Fauntleroy*, which premiered the same year as her lawsuit, was a sensational hit (110). Her later works were similarly adapted for the stage to great success, including *A Little Princess*. The same year *Fauntleroy* debuted on the stage, a Mrs. Freiligrath-Kroeker adapted Lewis Carroll's Alice books and published the script in *Alice and Other Fairy Plays for Children* (Varty 104). Barrie's *Peter Pan* (1904) is probably the best-known dramatic work for children, and it was adapted from a section of an adult novel that was later excerpted and republished for children as *Peter Pan in Kensington Gardens* (1906). The success of the play itself inspired Barrie to write the full novelization of the Peter Pan story in 1911. Marah Gubar notes that the play versions of *Fauntleroy* and *Peter Pan*, two adapted works, were credited in the early twentieth century "with helping establish the category of the children's play as a distinct dramatic subgenre" (175). Gubar sees children's theater as participating in the late nineteenth and early twentieth century cult of the child, which she describes as a "'mass culture' phenomenon" (179).

Children's theatre continued to draw inspiration from literature over the course of the twentieth and early twenty-first centuries. A.A. Milne, author of the Pooh books, adapted Kenneth Grahame's *The Wind in the Willows* for the stage in 1929 in the play *Toad of Toad Hall*. It has been adapted a number of times since, notably by British playwright Alan Bennett in 1991. One of the most popular Broadway musicals of the past 40 years was *Annie* (1977), which won the Tony Award for Best Musical the year it opened. *Annie* was adapted from cartoonist Harold Gray's *Little Orphan Annie* comic strip, which first appeared in 1924 and ran for 86 years. Michael Morpurgo's *War Horse* (1982) was adapted by the National Theatre in London and debuted on stage in 2007. According to the publication *American Theatre*, the sixth most produced play of the 2016/17 season was *Peter and the Starcatcher* (2009), an adaptation of Dave Barry and Ridley Pearson's 2006 prequel to *Peter Pan* (Tran). As with the children's books that inspired them, most of these stage productions had significant crossover appeal with adult audiences, and many of these same texts were adapted as films either prior to their stage debut, as in the case of *Little Orphan Annie*, or after, as with *War Horse*.

Film Adaptations

Children's literature has also inspired popular film adaptations. Film historians date the earliest children's films to the first decade of the twentieth century, and Ian Wojcik-Andrews cites Cecil Hepworth's silent film *Alice in Wonderland* as one of the earliest examples of children's cinema (54). Hepworth's Alice adaptation was followed by other silent film classics such as Cesare Antamaro's *Pinocchio* (1911) and the movies of well-known silent film star Mary Pickford, who played in *Cinderella* (1914), *A Little Princess* (1917), and *Rebecca of Sunnybrook Farm* (1917), all based on popular children's books. The Disney Company based its film empire on adaptations, both animated features such as *Peter Pan* (1953) and *The Sword in the Stone* (1963) and live-action films such as *Treasure Island* (1950) and *Old Yeller* (1957). Adaptations of children's literature continue to be big business. One of the most successful films of 2016 was the live-action remake of Disney's 1967 animated adaption of Kipling's *The Jungle Book*, a trend that continued with a live remake of *Beauty and the Beast* in 2017 and *A Wrinkle in Time* in 2018.

While not all popular children's films are adaptations, many of them are. For Wojcik-Andrews, this is no coincidence: "the aesthetic and political function novels fulfilled for nineteenth-century readers was fulfilled for early twentieth-century viewers by children's films, at least those that were adapted from canonical works of children's literature" (56). Children's films, and adaptations in particular, provide a comforting form of popular entertainment. While potentially political or subversive, children's film adaptations tend to offer relatively mild critique or commentary, giving them a titillating edge without being overly provocative. For instance, the 1939 version of *The Wizard of Oz* offers subtle references to class politics. The early sepia-toned scenes set in Kansas suggest the dreariness of home life before Dorothy is transported to the more magical and empowering land of Oz. In one of these scenes, Aunt Em tells Elmira Gulch, "Just because you own half the county doesn't mean that you have the power to run the rest of us." Gulch is played by the same actor who plays the Wicked Witch, suggesting a critique of wealthy landowners that would have resonated with Depression-era viewers. Ultimately, the film suggests that Dorothy can find the power within herself to get home, but while she might be changed by her adventures, her home remains the same dull place it was when she left.

Race in Children's Adaptations

This tradition of using adaptations to offer social commentary continued over the course of the twentieth and early twenty-first centuries, and the increasing commitment to racial and ethnic inclusiveness in children's literature and popular culture led to efforts, some more successful than others, to depict characters or cast actors of more diverse racial and ethnic backgrounds. Indeed, stage and film adaptations of children's books have been one useful way to present racial and ethnic diversity in children's culture, using texts with which audiences are already familiar to engage viewers while reimaging the traditional canon. Decades before Disney's *The Princess and the Frog* (2009), which we discussed in Chapter 4, Aduke Aremu's *Liberation of Mother Goose* was first performed by the Harlem Children's Theatre in 1974 and offered "a Black look at the traditional nursery rhymes" (Bailey 59). That same year, Charlie Smalls and William F. Brown's *The Wiz*, a retelling of Baum's *The Wonderful Wizard of Oz* set in an urban landscape with an all-black cast, debuted on stage. The play was made into a popular film in 1978 starring Michael Jackson, Diana Ross, Lena Horne, and Richard Pryor. More recently, Will Gluck directed another film adaptation of *Annie* (2014) starring African American child actor and Oscar nominee Quvenzhané Wallis as the eponymous character and Jamie Foxx in the Daddy Warbucks role. Producers of children's adaptations continue to sometimes practice color-blind casting, when roles are filled without considering the race or ethnicity of the actor or character. In 2016, Jack Thorne's stage adaptation of J.K. Rowling's *Harry Potter and the Cursed Child* cast Noma Dumezweni, an English actor of black African birth, as an adult Hermione (Ratcliffe). Her casting and the controversy that followed prompt us to ask why some readers and viewers are so troubled by reimagining the race of characters or by making texts more racially inclusive. As we have discussed throughout this book, retelling, revision, adaptation, and transformation have been central to the history of children's literature. Offering more diverse representations by reimagining the race or ethnicity of a character is consistent with the larger tradition of children's literature as reflective of social change and committed to social and ethical instruction.

Children's Television Adaptations

Children's literature has also inspired television programming for young people. The British Broadcasting Corporation (BBC) began broadcasting in London in 1936, and the 1939 World's Fair in New York City introduced television to the wider American public after many years of technological development and smaller exhibitions (Edgerton 10). World War II briefly interrupted the progress of television history. By 1946, only 0.02% of US households owned televisions. The percentage jumped to 71.6% a decade later (Sterling

864), while 36.5% of homes in the UK owned television sets by 1956 (Brittain and Clark 11). In the early years of television, programming was not differentiated by age, while the new industry worked to promote TV ownership and develop shows for broadcast. As Gary Edgerton explains, "proponents of television (broadcasters, station owners, and manufacturers of television sets) hoped TV would help cement together members of the new postwar, suburban middle-class nuclear family with a sense of renewed domestic values. Members of this new ideal family would stay at home together during their leisure time rather than run their separate ways" (92). In this way, the history of general audience and crossover television mirrors the early history of children's literature. During the Golden Age of television in the 1950s, some of the most popular family or children's programming was inspired by children's literature. For instance, *Lassie*, which debuted in 1954, was based on the novel *Lassie Come Home* (1940) by English author Eric Knight, who expanded an earlier short story he published in 1938. The original novel was set in England and Scotland, though the TV series moved the setting to the United States. Other popular programs were based on comics superheroes such as Superman and the Fantastic Four. This practice of looking to children's literature for inspiration continues into the present, with TV shows based on Enid Blyton's Famous Five series, H.A. and Margret Rey's Curious George, R.L. Stine's Goosebumps, and many different superhero comics. Television adaptations in particular are able to replicate the serial and episodic nature of children's series fiction.

Like other forms of popular culture, television inspired both fear and hope about its effects on viewers, especially children. The strong appeal of television to young people spurred concerns that children were becoming addicted to it and that TV violence would encourage bad behavior or even juvenile delinquency (Edgerton 94–95). Advertising directed at children encouraged them to ask their parents for money to buy toys, games, and food, promoting concerns that TV was indoctrinating children as voracious consumers, which conflicted with the sense of childhood as insulated from worldly concerns like commerce: "The general intensity of emotion invested in the debates about television … can be understood in the long-term desires to protect children, to preserve a sanctuary from commercial culture" (Morrow 4). Others saw television as a useful educational or progressive tool. Robert W. Morrow links the development of *Sesame Street*, an educational program for American children premiering in 1969, with the Civil Rights Movement of the 1960s and the desire to create a society "free of racism, free of poverty" (4). In the United States, the Children's Television Act of 1990 mandated that TV stations offer educational programming for children, though children's television remains very much concerned with enjoyment and profit, just as children's literature is. In the PBS animated series Curious George, which premiered in 2006, episodes typically incorporate some kind of lesson into the plot. For example, in an episode titled "Candy Counter," George takes over at the counter of a candy shop and considers different ways to arrange the candy by shape or color and even learns how to make a rhombus. Cultural studies critics might also note that George and the viewer also learn both how to sell goods and how to consume them.

THEORIZING ADAPTATION AND TRANSFORMATION

Defining Adaptation

Adaptation refers both to the process of modifying a text for a different medium or genre and to the product of that process. The traditional view of adaptation might understand it as simplifying a text to produce a revised version in a different medium, and adaptations do often involve a condensed timeframe (i.e., the length of the film in contrast to the time it would take to read the novel), fewer characters and plotlines, and visual presentation rather than prose description (Hutcheon 1). However, adaptations can also add new plots or characters and frequently do make changes or additions, such as a musical score in a film or the proliferation of stories needed for a television series, that can create new meanings and sources of complexity.

As Linda Hutcheon explains, adaptations are popular because readers or viewers derive pleasure from "repetition with variation, from the comfort of ritual combined with the piquancy of surprise" (4). One of the dominant frameworks for assessing adaptations is the "fidelity" model, which seeks to determine how faithfully or closely adapters adhere to the source material (Hutcheon 6–7). Viewers operating under the fidelity model might consider how much of the original source material is omitted, modified, or supplemented and the degree to which the adaptation conveys the tone or spirit of the original, an elusive and subjective quality of the text. This viewpoint assumes that "adapters aim simply to reproduce the adapted text" (Hutcheon 7).

Understanding adaptations strictly in terms of fidelity limits our ability to analyze them fully. The language of fidelity, which connotes "conjugal faithfulness" or sworn allegiance, can lead to a moral judgement of the adaptation ("Fidelity" n.p.). If an adaptation lacks fidelity, it might be thought of as unfaithful or as breaking a solemn vow, but moral judgement interferes with analysis. Reading adaptations critically involves thinking beyond fidelity to consider the process of adaptation, the elements that are altered, and the changes in meaning between versions. It requires asking what difference the differences make. The changes involved with adapting children's literature for the stage or screen can be demanded by the differences between media, such as the need to eliminate plotlines or characters to meet time constraints, while other changes reflect evolving tastes or values. Adaptations need to be considered in terms of both formal demands (the differences between book, stage, and screen) and historical context (how different historical events or ways of thinking at the time of production shape each version).

As we have noted, the process of adaptation involves many different kinds of changes. Characters can be omitted in order to make more time for the development of others. Multiple characters can be combined so that a single composite character performs the actions or roles of more than one character. Sometimes adaptations extend or supplement a text by adding characters or developing them, giving them more complex personalities or motivations. In some cases, a character is changed to appeal to a different audience or to introduce a new element into the story. Similarly, the plot—how the story is told—might be condensed by cutting subplots or eliminating plot points to reach the climax and conclusion sooner. Some plot points or scenes, like characters, might be combined so that a single scene does the work of several from a prior version, and plots can be changed based on expectations of what different audiences prefer. A character's traits or a plot could be amplified or altered by the musical score or actor's performance, changing its meaning or significance. The narration itself will likely differ; as John Daniel Stahl explains, "The narrative perspective is externalized in film. Except through the use of voice-over narration (and—to a limited extent—dialogue), film cannot convey thoughts going on in the minds of characters" (7). Even settings of time and place can change, with adaptations set in different countries or historical periods. Themes or values, along with depictions of social issues like race and gender, can also change as discourses, values, and ways of thinking change over time.

Recent film adaptations exemplify these different kinds of changes. For instance, Alfonso Cuarón's 1995 film adaptation of *A Little Princess* moves the setting from London to New York and from the Victorian period to World War I. The changes in setting and period result in significant changes in meaning, since the class dynamics and imperial implications of the two settings differ. In the 1905 novel version, Sara's father, Captain Crewe, is believed to be killed by a fever while operating a diamond mine in colonial India; in the film, he is a World War I soldier, eliminating the diamond mine plot and thus the fact that he profits from the English colonization of India. Disney's 2002 film *Treasure Planet* adapts Stevenson's *Treasure Island*, changing the setting from eighteenth-century earth to a distant future of interplanetary travel. Sometimes the changes can be subtle but make important differences. In C.S. Lewis's *The Lion, the Witch and the Wardrobe* (1950), Father Christmas gives Susan a bow and arrows, but she is never described using them; in Andrew Adamson's 2005 film version, she uses them repeatedly in battle, perhaps indicative of early twenty-first-century thinking about girl power. Some adaptations change the narrator or perspective in significant ways, such as Steven Spielberg's 2011 film version of *War Horse*, which differs from the novel's use of Joey, the horse himself, as the narrator. Finally, adaptations can fundamentally alter the themes of a prior version. Gil Junger's adaptation of Shakespeare's *The Taming of the Shrew* as contemporary teen film *10 Things I*

Hate About You (1999) concludes not with the subjugation of Kate, as in the play, but with Kat's empowering claim to authorship in rewriting a Shakespearean sonnet. In all of these cases, the viewer must ask how the change affects what the text means.

Transformation and Intertextuality

The process of adaptation involves not only making changes to earlier versions, but also interpreting them for a different medium, time, place, or audience. Interpreting a text requires thinking about how it works, what it means, and what effects it might have, which are necessary to reimagining the text for a different context. Sometimes, the changes are so numerous and significant that the adaption represents a significant departure from earlier versions. Some scholars prefer to use terms like "revision" or "transformation" instead of "adaptation" in order to call attention to how works that retell stories constitute independent artistic productions and may even surpass earlier versions in artistic or commercial ways. Junger sets a Shakespeare play in a contemporary high school, for example, altering the traditional version in profound ways while retaining the outline of

Film still from *Maleficent* (2014).

Shakespeare's. Phyllis Frus and Christy Williams use the term "**transformation**" to describe texts that "move beyond mere adaptation and transform the source text into something new that works independently of its source" (3). While adaptations announce their relationship to earlier versions (Hutcheon 6), the relationship between a transformed text and an earlier version may be obscured. Many viewers may not realize that *10 Things I Hate About You* retells *The Taming of the Shrew* even if they are familiar with the earlier text. Frus and Williams cite Amy Heckerling's *Clueless* (1995), a retelling of Jane Austen's *Emma* (1815), as another example of a transformation. Heckerling's movie reimagines the early nineteenth-century events of Austen's novel as taking place among wealthy teens in a 1990s California high school. Disney's 2014 film *Maleficent* transforms the 1959 animated film *Sleeping Beauty*, itself an adaptation of the Briar Rose fairy tale, by extending and developing the origins of the villain in the earlier version, ultimately offering a story of female collaboration rather than antagonism. Thinking about adaptation in terms of transformation can permit writers and directors to exercise freedom and imagination in interpreting earlier versions, and it can encourage viewers to move beyond the fidelity model to take adaptations seriously on their own terms.

Adapted and transformed texts point to the concept of intertextuality. Coined by French feminist theorist Julia Kristeva, **intertextuality** refers to the ways in which texts inevitably refer to other texts by virtue of being part of a larger system of language with shared references, codes, images, meanings, and ways of speaking, writing, and perceiving. Adaptations and transformations are usually deliberate retellings of earlier stories, but all texts are part of an interconnected textual system or web and thus are intertexts. The concept of intertextuality emphasizes the ways texts endlessly refer to other texts, either accidentally or deliberately, and reciprocally influence each other's meaning. In contrast to **allusion**, which refers to a brief and specific reference to another work, the concept of intertextuality points to the more significant ways texts are shaped, influenced by, and respond to other texts. Recognizing intertextual relationships between works offers a way to analyze them by considering how a text is composed of other texts. Isolating a part of the web to identify relationships between intertextual elements allows critics to understand possible meanings and how they are made. As Frus and Williams explain, with the concept of intertextuality, "the emphasis is not on either text, the new one or its predecessor(s), but on the relations between them" (11). We can consider the intertextual relationships between Stevenson's *Treasure Island* and Richard Donner's 1985 film *The Goonies*, in which a group of contemporary young people seek out a treasure in their own town, by asking how the latter uses, modifies, or omits elements of the earlier, prototypical story of treasure-seeking. Another example of intertextuality would be the relationship between Robert C. O'Brien's Newbery-winning novel *Mrs. Frisby and the Rats of NIMH* (1971), adapted into an animated film in 1982, and real research on mice and rats that inspired O'Brien in which John B. Calhoun at the National Institute of Mental

Health studied the disastrous effects of "utopian" conditions on rat communities. Recognizing the book's intertextual relationships with actual scientific studies can help us understand what the text suggests about science, scientific methods, and American cultural values in the late twentieth century.

A text does not need to be an adaptation to be understood in terms of intertextuality. For instance, Walter Dean Myers's YA novel *Monster* (1999), about an African American youth on trial for murder, might be read as an intertext alongside Richard Wright's adult novel *Native Son* (1940). *Monster* is not an adaptation of *Native Son*; rather, we can read the two novels as intertexts that both explore the intersections of race with concepts of guilt and innocence. Our understanding of one may trigger interpretations of the other. Similarly, Neil Gaiman's *The Graveyard Book*, a Newbery-winning novel about a boy raised by ghosts, responds to Kipling's *Jungle Book*, in which a boy is raised by animals, from a century earlier. Cece Bell's 2014 graphic novel *El Deafo*, about a deaf girl who imagines herself as a superhero, can be read as an intertext with Batman and Robin comics. Cece wears a Phonic Ear device at school, which transmits her teacher's voice from a microphone directly to her hearing aids, and she discovers that she can eavesdrop on her teacher wherever she goes in school. Cece thinks about her hearing devices in terms of Batman's various crime-fighting gadgets. Moreover, Cece and the other characters in the graphic novel are depicted as rabbits, prompting consideration of animals as sources of inspiration for superhero characters or powers: Batman, Catwoman, Spiderman, Squirrel Girl, etc. Bell's use of rabbits might also prompt consideration of other visual works with anthropomorphic rabbits, like Beatrix Potter's *Tale of Peter Rabbit*, as intertexts.

Fanfiction: The Pleasures and Possibilities of Adaptation and Subversive Repetition

Viewers enjoy adaptations because they offer both familiarity and novelty. Beloved texts can be reimagined, retold, or reinterpreted with the kinds of variations we have discussed in this chapter, offering both continued experience with aspects of earlier versions and the excitement of new possibilities. Adaptations and transformations can also provide the pleasure of mystery and discovery as viewers search for and recognize references to earlier versions. The practice of adaptation can also provide what Hutcheon describes as an "ongoing dialogue with the past" (116). This phrase suggests work that is unfinished or ambivalence on the part of writers and readers with respect to texts they may love but also find frustrating. The author Jacqueline Wilson, who rewrites Coolidge's *What Katy Did* in her novel *Katy* (2015), calls the earlier version "one of my all time favourite books," but she also expresses discomfort with it: "I thought of all the real children in wheelchairs reading these books, wondering why religion and fresh air weren't working miracles for them too…. I wanted to show what life is really like for children with serious spinal injuries" (n.p.). Adaptation allows for this kind of corrective engagement with the past, which recalls Judith Butler's discussion of "subversive repetition." She argues that "repetition is the way in which power works" to create the appearance of naturalness or normativity ("Imitation" 315). However, the reliance on repetition to create cultural norms can also provide the possibility of change through "subversive repetition," or repetition with a difference ("Imitation" 317). The possibility of introducing change through subversive repetition bolsters the claim that popular culture and adaptation can be sites of political resistance and not just hegemonic domination.

Hutcheon emphasizes the pleasures of adaptation, pointing to the fact that "[a]nother name for adaptation audiences here is obviously 'fans'" (116). Not all members of an audience are fans, though. The term "fan," a shortened form of the word "fanatic," refers to an especially passionate or extreme devotee. Henry Jenkins argues that fans are particularly active viewers who not only interpret or use cultural products but create them: "One becomes a fan not by being a regular viewer of a particular program but by translating that viewing into some type of cultural activity, by sharing feelings and thoughts about the program content with friends, by joining a community of other fans who share common interests. For fans, consumption sparks production" (88). Fans might produce fan letters, YouTube videos, film reviews, or homemade costumes. Fans can be inspired to honor, revise, reimagine, or expand the cultural products that excite them, as children and young adults have long done through play and other acts of (re)creation.

Fanfiction, or fanfic, is a particular form of fan production: fan-authored stories about characters and situations from popular literature, film, or television. One of the earliest fan communities in contemporary popular culture was the Star Trek fandom, about which Jenkins was writing, and in the years before the internet and online publishing, networks of fans wrote and published underground zines—inexpensive, self-published magazines and newsletters—devoted to fanfiction. Many of these stories contained sexually explicit content involving characters who were never romantically or sexually involved in the source material, like Kirk and Spock from Star Trek, and authors of fanfiction frequently identified as heterosexual women. As Constance Penley explains, many participants in the Star Trek fanfiction community were women who derived pleasure and pride from "having created both a unique, hybridized genre that ingeniously blends romance, pornography, and utopian science fiction and a comfortable yet stimulating social space in which women can manipulate the products of mass-produced culture to stage a popular debate around issues of technology, fantasy, and everyday life" (137). With the emergence of the internet and the world wide web, fandom migrated online and proliferated, with active fan communities for popular TV and book series such as Buffy the Vampire Slayer, Doctor Who, Lord of the Rings, the Hunger Games, and Harry Potter. Catherine Tosenberger notes that many of these communities are "mixed-age fandoms centered on youth-oriented texts," and because fandom involves fewer gatekeepers like editors and publishers, or at least less powerful or authoritative ones, it provides an opportunity for young people to reimagine and revise the popular texts that inspire them (9–10). In addition to the canon, or authorized set of official texts, the fan community has its own "fanon," which includes "the history of fannish theorizing, interpretation, and previous fanfiction (or the lack of the same) that has become widely accepted, or at least recognized as such, within the fandom" (Tosenberger 10). One popular subgenre of fanction is slash fiction, which involves stories of romantic or sexual pairings between two characters of the same sex, such as Harry and Draco from the Harry Potter series. The "slash" refers to the slash used between the characters' names in the story's label (e.g., Harry/Draco). Slash fiction may be especially prominent in fandom because it allows authors to explore and reimagine different romantic and sexual possibilities and gendered embodiments. Tosenberger notes that "[s]ince the vast majority of English-language Western literature and entertainment assumes a default straight, white, cisgender male audience, it's not surprising that transformational fandom is often populated by those considered marginal audiences, who are more likely to feel the need to rework a beloved story to suit their own desires" (8). While theorists such as Benjamin and Brecht may not have imagined fanfiction about Hermione from Harry Potter as a girl of color or about an alternate Hunger Games that romantically pairs Peeta and Gale, fanfiction provides an exciting way for fans to exert agency on popular culture and rewrite it for their own desires and pleasures.

ANALYZING CHILDREN'S FILM

The Gaze

Reading films critically requires knowing common terms in the language of film and film theory. One important concept is that of the **gaze**, which denotes the act of looking or the ability to look at another person. However, for film theorists, the gaze is not just a neutral behavior or ability; rather, it implies a power dynamic between the one who sees and the one who is seen. In traditional understandings of the gaze, the watcher holds power over the person who is seen. To look is to be active, while to be looked at is to be the passive object of the gaze. The one who gazes on the other learns information about the object that can be used to exert power, leaving the object of the gaze potentially vulnerable and exposed, while the one who looks can remain unknown. The gaze is related to scopophilia, or the pleasure in looking. As the feminist film theorist Laura Mulvey explains, "Freud isolated scopophilia as one of the component instincts of sexuality.... [H]e associated scopophilia with taking other people as objects, subjecting them to a controlling and curious gaze. His particular examples centre around the voyeuristic activities of children, their desire to see and make sure of the private and forbidden" (835). To gaze on the other is to make the other an object for the pleasure of the onlooker. For Mulvey, cinema relies on the voyeuristic pleasure of the audience, and the gaze is gendered as male: "In a world ordered by sexual imbalance, pleasure in looking has been split between active/ male and passive/female" (837). The practice of sexualizing visual representations of girls and women, especially in film, points to the cultural dominance of the heterosexual male gaze. However, the gaze can be manipulated to alter the power dynamics involved. The gaze can be turned on the one who looks in order to expose onlookers and their vulner-abilities. In other cases, the object of the gaze can derive pleasure from being watched or perform in ways that deceive or confound the watcher. For Mulvey, it was important to understand the role of the gaze in the operation of narrative pleasure so that audiences could engage critically with film, understanding their place in the relationship between watcher and watched.

The Semiotics of Film

Semiotics is the science of signs, a field devoted to understanding how signs work, from linguistic signs (words) to non-linguistic ones like icons or pictograms, which physically resemble the thing they stand for, or symbols, for which there is an arbitrary but culturally learned association. The structuralist critic and semiotician Roland Barthes analyzed the semiotics of film to understand how visual signs could symbolically code information for viewers. For example, in his analysis of Romans in films, he notes that movies frequently depict ancient Romans with their hair cut in fringes to convey their Roman-ness, even though actual ancient Romans might have worn a variety of styles or been bald (26). No matter the ethnicity or features of the actors, their Roman-ness is conveyed through the shorthand of dark-haired fringe. Similarly, Barthes notes that in Joseph Mankiewicz's 1953 film *Julius Caesar*, an adaptation of Shakespeare's play, characters are frequently shown sweating (Vaseline is used to create the appearance of sweat). According to Barthes, sweat is used to convey "moral feeling," or the sense that the character is "debating something within himself" (27). Sweat, associated with physical exertion, becomes a sign of men-tal anguish or emotional work. Reading film critically requires that viewers be sensitive to visual signs like these. For instance, Fregley's oversized glasses and braces convey his extreme nerdiness in Thor Freudenthal's 2010 film adaption of Jeff Kinney's *Diary of a Wimpy Kid* (2007). The darker shading of Scar's fur in Disney's *The Lion King* (1994) signals to the reader that he is the villain, which also could be interpreted as invoking a racial hierarchy.

COMMON TERMS FOR FILM ANALYSIS

Term	Definition
Auteur theory	Dating to the 1940s, the traditional practice in writing about film is to refer to a film's director as equivalent to a book's author, rather than the screenwriter, since the director is responsible for the overall creative vision of the film. Contemporary critics now often recognize the collaborative nature of film production and debate the authorial role of the film director.
Shot	A shot is a part of the scene captured by the camera. A shot could be a close-up of an object or of an actor's face, a medium-range look at objects or actors in their environment, or a long-distance view of the landscape or objects far in the distance. The distance of the shot—whether close or far—can communicate narrative perspective or degrees of intimacy. The closer to an object or actor, the more the shot conveys a subjective perspective, in contrast to a sense of objectivity or broader perspective constructed by a long-distance shot. A shot can communicate the perspective of an outside observer, or, in the case of a point-of-view shot, it can establish the perspective of a character by showing the audience what a character sees or might see. A tracking shot follows an object or character as it moves.
Cut and pan	A cut is the abrupt shift from one shot to another, while to pan the camera involves pointing it at different objects in one sweeping motion and recording without cutting away. James Monaco argues, "Psychologically, the cut is the truer approximation of our natural perception. First one subject has our attention, then another; we are seldom interested in the intervening space, yet the cinematic pan draws our attention to just that" (144).
Scene	Monaco defines a scene as a "complete unit of film narration. A series of shots (or a single shot) that take place in a single location and that deal with a single action" (451).
Framing	Like framing a picture, a film scene is framed. Framing a scene involves deciding how actors will be placed in a set, how they will be positioned in relation to each other and objects in their environment, and how far away or close up the camera will be.

COMMON TERMS FOR FILM ANALYSIS (continued)

Term	Definition
Storyboard	A film's storyboard is a series of visual plans for the film, usually rough sketches that lay out shots, cuts and camera movements, and scenes.
Diegesis and non-diegesis	A film's diegesis is the totality of its fictional world, and its diegetic elements are those that exist or occur in the world of the characters, including objects they see, sounds they hear, and so on. Non-diegetic elements are those aspects of the film that the audience, but not the characters, recognizes as part of the film, such as the score, voice-over narration, subtitles, or scrolling text.
Mise-en-scène and montage	The elements that are physically present in the scene, such as actors, costumes, sets, props, and even the arrangement of lighting compose the mise-en-scène. Monaco writes, "In film criticism, generally, the modification of space is referred to as mise-en-scène. The French phrase literally means 'putting in the scene.' The modification of time is called montage (from the French for 'putting together.')" (142). In a montage, multiple scenes are spliced together in rapid succession.

READING CRITICALLY: CHILDREN'S LITERATURE AND POPULAR CULTURE

The Fault in Our Stars

John Green's novel *The Fault in Our Stars* (2012) reached number one on the *New York Times* bestseller list six months before publication, after its title was released, spurred in large part by the popularity of Green's previous novels. In 2014 alone, the book sold about 1.4 million copies in paperback. The movie version was released by Fox 2000 Pictures in 2014 and was directed by indie-film director Josh Boone, with a screenplay adapted from Green's book by Scott Neustadter and Michael H. Weber. It starred the popular young actors Shailene Wood-ley and Ansel Elgort and grossed over $300 million at the box office. It also sparked a vibrant fan culture, both online and offline, much of it fueled by John Green's active digital pres-ence. As we noted at the beginning of this chapter, many theorists of popular culture—like Horkheimer and Adorno—look down on popular cultural products because they are pro-duced by large corporations within a "culture industry" and because they offer escape from the political and social arena. Others see popular culture as potentially empowering to its readers and viewers or as registering cultural anxieties and priorities in a way that helps us attain wider political and social understanding. Despite their popular status—or perhaps because of it—the *Fault in Our Stars* novel and movie facilitate an exploration of mortality, "a fully lived life," as well as exploring psychological questions of family bonds, sexual passion, and the grieving process. *The Fault in Our Stars* also builds on and responds to other popular genres and literary traditions. A central part of the phenomenon of *The Fault in Our Stars* is the fan community that has been built around it, in which Green plays an active role, and which allows fans to take a certain ownership of the book and to analyze it critically in their own right. Reading *The Fault in Our Stars* critically involves examining it as a cultural phenom-enon that includes the novel, the film, merchandising, the online fan community, and Green's interaction with that community.

Critically Reading the Novel

Green's novel tells the love story of two witty and attractive teenagers: Hazel Grace Lancaster and Augustus "Gus" Waters. But this is a love story with a difference: Hazel and Gus meet in a support group for young people with cancer, a group Hazel is initially loath to attend. Hazel suffers from thyroid cancer that has spread to her lungs. An experimental drug has prolonged her life but she is still sick and has trouble breathing. Gus has recovered from osteosarcoma, a bone cancer that causes the amputation of one of his legs; at the beginning of the book it appears that he is now cancer-free. Hazel and Gus know their time together is short, and

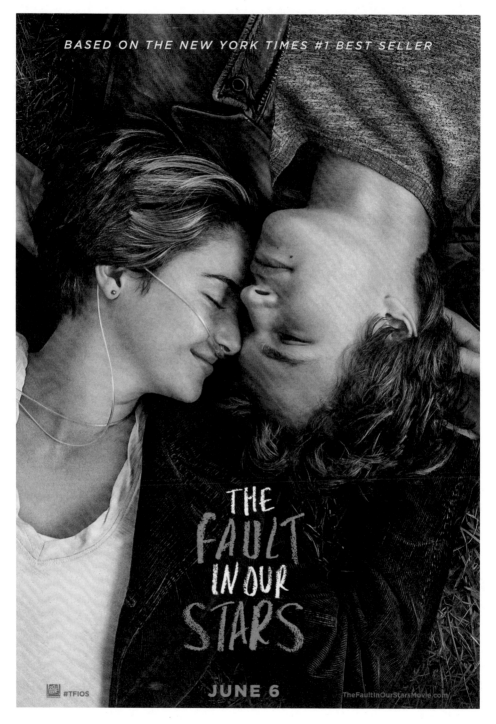

this sparks much of the philosophical and existential content of the book: meditations on the meaning of a life well lived, and the urgency of human connection even in the face of mortality. Green wanted to write a completely unsentimental cancer book that was more than a "cancer book." In keeping with this, *The Fault in Our Stars* includes a number of comic situations and scenes, and Hazel's first-person narration is often funny and irreverent. It also includes a literary adventure, as Hazel and Gus travel to Amsterdam to ask a Dutch author, Peter Van Houten, about his (cancer-themed) novel *An Imperial Affliction*, and the destinies of its surviving characters after it ends. Van Houten turns out to be cruel and capricious (Willem Dafoe plays him with impressive surliness in the movie version), but Hazel and Gus have a wonderful time in spite of him. Touring the Anne Frank House, they passionately kiss and later consummate their love at their hotel. Just before their return to the US, Gus confesses to Hazel that his cancer has returned and readers witness his wrenching decline. Before he dies he writes a eulogy for Hazel and sends it to Van Houten (with whom he has been in spirited correspondence), asking for his help in polishing it. Van Houten mails it to Hazel unamended. "I love her," Gus writes, "I am so lucky to love her, Van Houten. You don't get to choose if you get hurt in this world, old man, but you do have some say in who hurts you. I like my choices. I hope she likes hers" (313).

One of the ways the book clearly resonates with readers is its emphasis on the pleasures of reading and an assertion that popular culture plays a meaningful role in people's lives. Hazel notes:

> Sometimes, you read a book and it fills you with this weird evangelical zeal, and you become convinced that the shattered world will never be put back together unless and until all living humans read the book. And then there are books like *An Imperial Affliction*, which you can't tell people about, books so special and rare and yours that advertising your affection feels like a betrayal. (33)

Instead of keeping Van Houten's book to herself, however, Hazel shares it with Gus. Their shared fandom of the book provides the motivation to travel to Amsterdam (Gus uses his cancer "wish" to fund the trip, appealing to the philanthropic Genies for help). They also bond over films and even video games: a shared appreciation of popular culture that brings them closer together. Hazel's relationship to *An Imperial Affliction* is "fannish" in that it presumes a continued life for the characters after the book's ending. But while fans of literary works might produce fanfiction from their desire to see the fiction continued or amended, Van Houten denies Hazel the pleasure of an unofficial sequel, scornfully noting:

> This childish idea that the author of a novel has some special insight into the characters in the novel ... it's ridiculous. That novel was composed of scratches on a page, dear.

Opposite: Promotional poster for *The Fault in Our Stars* (2014).

The characters inhabiting it have no life outside of those scratches. What happened to them? They all ceased to exist the moment the novel ended." (191–92)

Hazel's desire to imagine what happens after the end of *An Imperial Affliction* is important to her as she tries to visualize a life for her parents after her own death. She gets over Van Houten's cruel dismissal by ceasing to care what he thinks, but also by coming to the understanding that her parents will endure her inevitable death and go on to live a full life. Her mother, for example, reveals that after Hazel's death she intends to go into social work in order to help families with sick and dying children.

The book was embraced by many readers not just because of its central romance, but because Hazel and Gus's discussion about what makes a life matter made those "ultimate" questions more accessible to its audiences, and it affirmed the primacy of desire and pleasure in the face of mortality. It also affirmed readerly pleasures and priorities, as the characters engaged with books and took them to heart. Part of the objection to popular culture among critics influenced by the Frankfurt School is that it impedes critical thinking, but Green's novel seems to prompt readers to ask important questions about how a better life could be imagined or created, even under circumstances that would seem to block any adventure, desire, or growth.

Critically Viewing the Movie

In this chapter, we noted that film adaptations allow a book to reach a different time, place, and audience. It is striking, however, how much the film adaptation of *The Fault in Our Stars* reaches out to existing fans of the novel. Much of the dialogue from the book—including catchphrases and signature lines—appears verbatim in the film. Even the film's credits are rendered in the same font used on the book cover. No doubt the filmmakers and the studio wanted to please the book's substantial fan base. The director and screenwriter also expressed genuine appreciation for their source material. John Green joined them almost every day on the set, which he described as seeing the book come to life. There are, however, some differences between the movie and the book. For example, Gus dies more quickly in the movie than in the book. Hazel's former best friend Kaitlyn and Gus's late ex-girlfriend Caroline are entirely omitted—perhaps to stress Hazel and Gus's isolation before they come together as a romantic pair. In the book, Hazel mounts an extensive search for the final letter Gus sent to Van Houten; in the movie Van Houten gets into her car at Gus's funeral and gives it to her directly (she crumples it up and refuses to read it until she learns it is not from Van Houten but from Gus). Most of these changes are designed to streamline the movie and to move the plot along, especially after Gus tells Hazel that his cancer has reoccurred.

A unique aspect of the movie—one that distinguishes it from the book—is the use of cinematic techniques that create a romantic but elegiac mood. We see the characters rather than imagining them, and the audience's gaze rests equally on the two characters through much of the film. The camera sometimes gets very close to Hazel and Gus, creating a sense of intimacy. We noted in this chapter that the closer the camera zooms in on an object or actor, the more a shot conveys a subjective perspective, in contrast to a sense of objectivity or broader perspective constructed by a long-distance shot. As the camera cuts from Hazel to Gus and back again—even when they are in separate locations—their connection is emphasized. Communication between people is in fact a major theme in the book and movie, reflected in the movie's projection of text messages and emails onto the screen, a technique also seen in the popular television series *Sherlock* (2010–). The use of text message and email makes the movie seem fresh and contemporary, but might be one way in which the movie will seem dated as technology evolves in the future. While the movie is striking for its close-ups, sometimes the film opens out to outdoor locations with a wider shot, most notably the scenes on the canal in Amsterdam. These scenes are meant to show moments where the characters' world is opening up and becoming more adventurous.

The film uses music to great effect, for romantic moments (such as when the camera pans out to follow Hazel and Augustus's trip down the Amsterdam canal) and also sad ones (when Hazel drives home alone from Gus's funeral). Some of the most wrenching scenes are entirely silent, such as a scene in which Hazel is taken to the hospital when she is not getting enough oxygen to her brain. Despite the fact that some scenes in the movie are raucous or celebratory, there are also quieter and more contemplative moments, designed to make the movie a meditation on human connection as well as a shared adventure.

At the beginning of the film there is an idealized cinematic montage meant to evoke a traditional Hollywood romance with a voice-over from Hazel talking about how real life is not as glamorous as in the movies—and vowing to tell a more truthful story. In the early scenes featuring the pediatric cancer support group, young people who actually have cancer are shown speaking: another attempt at realism. For a mainstream movie, the costumes of the characters are remarkably understated. They are dressed in everyday, unglamorous outfits, the one exception being when they dress up to go to an elegant restaurant in Amsterdam. Hazel herself seems to wear little or no makeup; she wears a nasal cannula and carries around a tank to provide oxygen. She often appears winded or pained by stairs and other physical challenges. Sometimes the camera is focalized from Hazel's point of view, as when she contemplates an abandoned swing set or is in the Anne Frank house, where the camera pans up to a steep and daunting set of stairs she must climb. We see her physical and mental exhaustion. The movie does not contain many special effects (such as those we would see in an action movie, for example), but they are sometimes used for maximum emotional effect, as when VFX (visual effects) supervisor Jake Braver creates a shot showing Gus's artificial leg (his osteosarcoma having forced the amputation of his real leg). Even in a movie that eschews traditional Hollywood glamour, however, the choice to cast physically attractive actors like Woodley and Elgort as the romantic pair (and for that matter, Laura Dern and Sam Trammell as Hazel's parents) adds to the glamour of the film. Elgort, for example, is described in the DVD audio commentary as "having the body of a Greek god."

The book derives much of its power from Hazel's narrative voice and the reader's immersion in her perceptions and feelings; the film derives much of its power from our ability to visualize the connection between Hazel and Gus, as we view them standing together or connected through screen shots that cut between them. The film is also striking for its visual and auditory evocation of moods ranging from joy to wistfulness to desolation. It could, in fact, be argued that the cinematic effects of the film envelop the viewer in its shifting moods, as a kind of seduction, in the process losing some of the book's critical edge. Yet the movie also tackles the existential questions raised by the book and retains Hazel's perspective through both voiceovers and her ongoing dialogue with Gus.

Intertextuality in the Novel and the Movie

Both the book and the movie challenge and cleave to some of the conventions of other popular genres. One of these genres is that of popular romance. The untimely deaths of young lovers have appeared in literary texts for centuries, as we know from our enduring cultural fascination with *Romeo and Juliet*. In keeping with the romance tradition, Hazel and Gus experience powerful physical attraction. Like typical romance characters, they verbally spar, increasing the sexual tension between them. The novel's rootedness in Hazel's point of view and emotions is also a hallmark of the frequently feminocentric romance genre: "I fell in love the way you fall asleep: slowly, and then all at once" (125). At the same time, Green plays with the gender roles of the two main characters, at first making Gus the dominant and confident pursuer (another friend describes him, affectionately, as "cocky") and then revealing his physical and emotional vulnerabilities as he weakens and dies.

The Fault in Our Stars also revises the illness (specifically cancer) narrative, as seen in such books (and movies) as Erich Segal's *Love Story* (1970), Larry McMurtry's *Terms of Endearment* (1975, film version 1983), and Iris Rainer Dart's *Beaches* (1985, film version 1988). Green's narrative, as we have noted, is explicitly unsentimental and unflinching, while remaining emotionally resonant. He also creates a unique generic mix, as Rachel Syme notes: "he tells his story with such gumption and tenderness that he almost adds a new genre to cancer-lit: romantic teen angst jumbled with big existential questions" (Syme). One of the sources of the book's popularity, perhaps, is its use of genres that are familiar and legible to many readers while offering a fresh variation on these genres. The "big existential questions" Syme notes are one of the book's signature elements, as we noted above: Gus and Hazel spar over the nature of a life well lived, with Gus arguing that only heroic deeds matter, and Hazel stressing the importance of being remembered by friends and family.

One important moment of intertextuality is Hazel and Gus's visit to the Anne Frank House, a climactic scene in both the book and the movie that ties *The Fault in Our Stars* back to a major landmark of children's literature and culture. As we noted in our nonfiction chapter, the printed diary of Anne Frank was an extremely popular book, and it was adapted into a play in 1955. In his review of the film, Matt Wolf offered a scathing objection to the scene in the Anne Frank House: "The thought that hiding out from the Nazis and dealing with cancer might be two entirely different things seems not to have crossed anyone's mind" (Wolf n.p.). Other critics have also objected to Gus and Hazel's kiss in the Anne Frank House. Hazel herself is initially uneasy, but in the book she offers this conclusion: "Anne Frank kissed someone in the Anne Frank House, and … she would probably like nothing more than for her home to have become a place where the young and irreparably broken sink into love" (202). It is well worth examining this scene critically to examine whether it adds to the major themes of *The Fault in Our Stars* (that of life going on in the face of suffering, and the fact that even those who face death also feel desire and love) or whether, as Wolf contends, it makes a false equivalency between two very different forms of suffering.

Reading critically involves knowing when Green's novel and Fox 2000's film draw on the conventions of popular genres and literary works that have come before, and when they resist them. *The Fault in Our Stars*, for example, has a mix of sentiment and irony, both indulging the emotions connected to genres like romance and the illness narrative, and signaling that the characters themselves are skeptical of the conventions and norms of genres like romance and the idealized illness narrative.

Reading the Fan Community and Merchandising Critically

In her *New Yorker* profile of Green, Margaret Talbot notes that reading has changed immensely in the contemporary age. It is no longer "an act of private communion with an author whom [readers] imagine vaguely, if at all." Instead, it is "a prelude to a social experience—following the author on Twitter, meeting other readers, collaborating with them on projects, writing fan fiction" (Talbot n.p.). In a number of ways, the presence of the online fan forums—and even the merchandising—allow readers to claim *The Fault in Our Stars* for themselves, and to analyze it critically—but also to offer critiques and objections. There are multiple fan sites and forums dedicated to the book and the movie, including wikis, Tumblrs, Reddit threads, blogs, Facebook pages, Goodreads discussions and many more. In terms of fan questions, John Green has an FAQ organized into sixteen sections on his website, with very extensive answers for most of them. Green has a robust presence on the internet generally (on YouTube, Twitter, Instagram, and Tumblr, among others). He also speaks to young cancer patients on a regular basis, many of them requesting the conversation through the Make-A-Wish Foundation. In her profile, Talbot described Green's facing a struggle "to embrace simultaneously the voluble aesthetic of the Internet and the contemplative sensibility of the novelist" (Talbot n.p.). Green has two YouTube series (Vlogbrothers, with his brother Hank, and CrashCourse, with various writers) where he discusses history, books, culture, and more. He positions himself as a student of culture and literature, and a fan himself, as Samantha Dunn argues: "rather than emphasize his authorial position, he apeals [sic] to fans by emphasizing his role as a fanatic of readers and learning communities" (35).

There is an element of canny marketing connected both to Green's books and his You-Tube presence. John Green's brother Hank started a store with Alan Lastufka, called D.F.T.B.A. ("Don't forget to be awesome"), with a section of merchandise related to John Green's books, and hundreds of other products like T-shirts, posters, mugs, notebooks, and buttons on sites like Redbubble. Just as *Love Story* became an iconic book (and then film) in the 1970s, John Green's *The Fault in Our Stars* has a good chance of becoming an iconic book for young people now. What remains to be seen is whether the popularity of *The Fault in Our Stars* will endure past our current moment to become a touchstone for another generation, or whether it will become a period piece most meaningful to the young readers who encountered it in the 2010s.

EXPLORATIONS

Review

1. In what ways has popularity been understood as both a positive and negative characteristic? Why has children's literature sometimes been understood as popular literature?

2. Why have some critical theorists expressed concerns about popular culture? What did theorists such as Max Horkheimer and Theodor Adorno warn about the effects of popular culture on the public?

3. What distinguishes a transformed text from an adapted one? What kinds of changes characterize adaptations and what kinds of changes characterize transformations?

4. Why, according to Tosenberger, does so much fanfiction reimagine representations of gender, sexuality, or race?

5. In what ways do formula fiction and genre fiction overlap? How are they different from each other? Provide examples of different kinds of genre fiction.

Reflect

1. Scholars of popular culture disagree about whether popular culture can be a site and method of political and social change. What are the arguments for and against popular culture as repressive or subversive? Provide examples for each.

2. Viewers who adhere to the fidelity model of adaptation sometimes dismiss a film or stage adaptation as an inferior copy, but some of the film scholars we cite in this chapter encourage us to resist the fidelity model. Select a film adaptation that you or others might be inclined to dismiss as unfaithful and consider how it succeeds on its own terms. How does it supplement or reimagine prior versions in inventive ways?

3. We defined "intertextuality" as referring to the ways texts are composed of references to or elements of other texts. Select a work like a version of *Peter Pan* or *Twilight* and consider all of the characters, plots, settings, themes, or other details that seem to refer to similar elements in other texts. In what ways is the story a patchwork of other texts? What does understanding it in this way help you see that you did not see before?

4. We discussed in this chapter how genre fiction like romance novels can be used by young people as models or as fantasies for how romantic or erotic relationships work. What impressions of romantic and sexual relationships might young people gather from romance fiction, TV shows, or films for young people? How do children's and YA texts represent childhood or adolescent sexuality? Is there a common formula used?

5. Dystopian fiction for young people has exploded in popularity since the 1990s. Reflect on why stories set in worlds that have experienced catastrophes, that represent a society in chaos, or that are dominated by an oppressive regime might be especially appealing at this moment in history. How do the lives of child or teen protagonists in dystopian fiction differ from the routines of child or teen readers?

Investigate

1. Select one of your favorite children's or YA texts and write a fanfiction story, either one featuring the main characters or one set in the same world. Then, compose a short reflection piece in which you explain why you added to or reimagined the story or characters in the way you did.

2. Watch a block of children's television programming and note either how children's literature might have influenced the TV shows or how some of the key terms for understanding children's literature, like the dual address (where a text is aimed at both children and adults), help you understand the shows you watch.

3. Create a storyboard and script for a scene in a film adaptation or transformation of a children's book. How would you frame the scene? How would you cast and costume the actors? What props would you need? What shots would you use?

4. Formula fiction is defined by its use of recognizable elements in similar patterns. Select an example of a formula work, such as a volume of the Babysitter's Club series, and reimagine it with one of the elements of the formula dramatically altered. Make of a list of how the one change would affect other elements of the novel. How might readers respond differently to it?

SUGGESTED READINGS AND VIEWINGS

Anderson, M.T. *Feed* **(2002). Novel.** In M.T. Anderson's prescient sci-fi dystopia, economically privileged people have the internet beamed directly into their brains through their feeds, which allow them to text, watch shows, and shop without any external devices. Growing up with the feed has impeded language development and critical thinking for most users, and they fail to notice that the world around them has descended into political turmoil and environmental devastation. After Titus meets Violet on the moon and her inferior feed begins to malfunction, she helps Titus begin to see how the feed controls them. The teens belatedly try to resist the corporations that control the feed, to mixed results.

Barrie, J.M. *Peter Pan* **(1904). Play.** Barrie's play *Peter Pan* was based on a character who first appeared in *The Little White Bird* (1902), a novel for adults. After the success of the play on the London stage, where it was enjoyed by children and adults alike, Barrie wrote the novelization, which was published in 1911. In the classic story of the boy who wouldn't grow up, Peter Pan takes Wendy Darling and her brothers to the magical Neverland, where they experience big adventures with fairies, mermaids, and pirates before defeating the menacing Captain Hook and returning home with the Lost Boys. Only Peter remains in Neverland, visiting Wendy and then her daughter over the course of a lifetime.

Burton, Tim. *Charlie and the Chocolate Factory* **(2005). Film.** Roald Dahl's novel has been adapted more than once, most recently by Tim Burton in a film starring Johnny

Depp as Willy Wonka. Some viewers found Depp's performance reminiscent of pop star Michael Jackson, who was accused and then acquitted of sexually abusing children on his Neverland Ranch. In Burton's film, Freddie Highmore plays Charlie Bucket, the poor boy who finds the Golden Ticket and wins a tour of Willy Wonka's chocolate factory, a surprisingly dangerous place for children. Burton's treatment of the Oompa Loompas, a controversial element from Dahl's novel, should be noted.

Clements, Ron and John Musker. *The Little Mermaid* **(1989). Film.** This adaptation of the Hans Christian Andersen fairy tale reignited the craze for Disney animated blockbusters in the late 1980s. A cartoon musical, *The Little Mermaid* features the story of Ariel, the titular mermaid, who longs to explore dry land. After rescuing a handsome prince from a shipwreck, she trades her voice for legs in order to be with him, and with the assistance of an assortment of animal helpers and a magical patriarch, Ariel foils the plot of a jealous witch and finds a much happier ending than her counterpart in Andersen's version.

Coppola, Francis Ford. *The Outsiders* **(1983). Film.** Acclaimed filmmaker Francis Ford Coppola adapted S.E. Hinton's groundbreaking YA novel with some of the biggest young actors of the early 1980s as the warring Greasers and Socs: Tom Cruise, C. Thomas Howell, Ralph Macchio, Patrick Swayze, Rob Lowe, Matt Dillon, Emilio Estevez, Diane Lane, and Leif Garrett. When teens Ponyboy and Johnny accidentally kill a boy from the other side of town, they go on the run from the law and become accidental heroes. In 2005, Coppola released an extended version of the film called "The Complete Novel," which adds deleted footage and period 1960s music.

Fleming, Victor. *The Wizard of Oz* **(1939). Film.** The MGM film adaptation of L. Frank Baum's *The Wonderful Wizard of Oz*, starring the famous child actor Judy Garland as Dorothy, remains a beloved classic. Known for its creative use of color and memorable musical numbers such as "Somewhere Over the Rainbow" and "If I Only Had a Brain," the film omits some of the quirkier elements of Baum's novel and represents Oz as a dream rather than a real place. However, it retains the central plot involving Dorothy, Toto, and their companions traveling down the yellow brick road to meet the wizard.

Meyer, Stephenie. *Twilight* **(2005). Novel.** Meyer's Twilight saga, featuring a teen girl and vampire more than a century old who meet in high school and fall in love, blends elements of horror and romance. A bestseller, *Twilight* spawned a blockbuster film franchise and a thriving fandom. The beautiful vampire Edward, whose body remains that of a 17-year-old, falls irresistibly and inexplicably in love with ordinary teen Bella, who must choose between Edward and the werewolf Jacob, a teen member of the Quileute nation.

Miyazaki, Hayao. *Howl's Moving Castle* (2004). **Film.** Hayao Miyazaki, a Japanese filmmaker and manga artist, is internationally renowned for his animated films. His film *Howl's Moving Castle* adapts the fantasy novel of the same name by British writer Diana Wynne Jones, winner of the Phoenix Award, in which the teenage Sophie is transformed into an old crone by a witch and must seek out the wizard Howl and demon Calcifer for help returning to her youthful self. Produced through a combination of traditional and digital animation, *Howl's Moving Castle* was a commercial and critical success around the world.

Rowell, Rainbow. *Fangirl* (2013). **Novel.** Rowell's novel explores the fandom of the fictional Simon Snow, an analogue of Harry Potter. First-year college student Cath writes Simon Snow fanfiction, and she is working to complete the conclusion of her story "Carry On, Simon," a fantastical romance between the Simon character and a vampire named Baz, who will remind Harry Potter readers of Draco Malfoy. Cath's own life reads like a YA problem novel as she struggles with social anxiety, unrequited love, and her father's bipolar disorder.

Selick, Henry. *Coraline* (2009). **Film.** An adaptation of Neil Gaiman's horror/fantasy novel, Selick's film uses stop-motion animation, a technique involving the use of physical models and objects that are put in different positions for each frame. When the speed of the frames increases, the objects appear to move. Coraline, voiced by Dakota Fanning, discovers an Other World inside her new home occupied by an Other Mother and Father with buttons for eyes. At first, the Other World seems better than her own, but it quickly becomes a nightmare from which Coraline must escape.

APPROACHES TO TEACHING *THE FAULT IN OUR STARS* [SECONDARY SCHOOL]

Preparation for the Lessons

Students will read the novel *The Fault in Our Stars* and view the film adaptation of the book in advance of the class lessons. They should also be asked to look up John Green's videos, posts, and pictures on social media (in particular YouTube, Tumblr, Twitter, and Instagram) and consider how he interacts with his fans. For more context on Green's relationship with his fans, give them Margaret Talbot's profile of Green in *The New Yorker*: "The Teen Whisperer."

Learning Goals

- To practice gathering evidence from literary texts to make arguments

- To practice close reading of a literary text

- To learn how to write a compare and contrast essay

- To analyze the differences between a novelistic source text and a movie, and what those differences mean

- To analyze cinematic techniques and how they make meaning.

Activity One: The Fault in Our Stars *as Literary Text*

Part A: Compare and Contrast/Textual Evidence: Hazel and Gus have a spirited debate about what constitutes a meaningful life, with Gus arguing that only bravery and extraordinary deeds matter, and Hazel stressing the intimate bonds of love and friendship. Working with the text, collect quotations that exemplify their differing points of view and go over these quotations in class. Talk through some strategies for structuring a compare/contrast essay. Students will then write a brief essay comparing Gus's point of view to that of Hazel. How does Gus change his mind at the end of the book? In what ways can Gus and Hazel be said to have lived extraordinary lives?

Part B: Close Reading: *The Fault in Our Stars* is known for its memorable sayings and quotations, many of which ended up in the film. In class, students should gather some of the most striking lines from the film, and then produce a short essay devoted to a close reading of the line or lines from the film.

Here are some prompts to get them started. Why did you choose this quotation? How does it function in the novel? How does it function as a standalone phrase or saying? If you are having difficulty choosing a quotation, here are three to choose from:

"Apparently the world is not a wish-granting factory." (197–98)

"That's the thing about pain … it demands to be felt." (63)

"Some infinities are bigger than other infinities." (260)

Activity Two: Fandom

Part A: Fanfiction

It is very important to Hazel to find out what happened to the surviving characters after the end of *An Imperial Affliction*. However, her conversation with the author Peter Van Houten is not successful; he turns out to be capricious and cruel. He does, however, make a powerful argument that literary characters have no existence beyond the limits of a book. In class, discuss the following questions: Do you agree with Van Houten? Why or why not? If you read and write fanfiction, or know anyone who does, how does that experience challenge Van Houten's assertions?

Part B: Online Fandom

Students will have looked up John Green and investigated his relationship with his fans. In class, discuss the following questions: Are authors obligated to answer their reader's questions? Why or why not? What do you think of Green's engagement with his fans? In the DVD audio commentary on the film version, Green talks about the inevitable gulf between an artist and his fans—even when he is open to feedback from them—and his awareness that authors sometimes disappoint their fans. What have been some of the criticisms of John Green's relationship with his fans? Write a brief essay considering some of the advantages and disadvantages of the author–fan relationship.

Activity Three: Cinema and Film

Part A: Adaptation and Change

Consider the following questions in class discussion:

1. What are some differences between the movie and the book?

2. If you read *The Fault in Our Stars* before watching the movie, were you hoping that the movie would stay faithful not only to the overall feel but also the events of the book? If you did not read it, how sympathetic are you to readers who wanted to see the book rendered faithfully on screen?

After answering these questions, students should write a short essay comparing the book version of *The Fault in Our Stars* to the movie version, considering the relationship between the book and the movie.

Part B: Cinematic Techniques and Film Interpretation

For each of the following cinematic techniques, write one or two pages explaining how they work in the film, and what they contribute to the film.

1. Close ups, especially of Hazel and Gus.

2. Scenes shot from behind Hazel (that seem to be shot from her point of view), like the scene where she is contemplating the pathetic swing set.

3. A scene where a song from the soundtrack is featured heavily.

4. A scene featuring a special effect (such as when we see Gus's artificial leg in support group).

5. The projection of texts and emails on the screen.

6. A montage scene (such as the Hollywood romance montage or the flashback to their romance at the end).

7. Scenes that cut from Hazel to Gus, and vice versa.

8. Panning shots, which track a scene in one continuous movement.

GLOSSARY

Ableism An ideology that assumes that people should be defined by their disability, and that able-bodied people are superior to disabled people. It also presumes that disabled people all aspire to an able-bodied norm. Many disability scholars are critical of ableist ideas.

Accuracy When used in reference to historical fiction, "accuracy" refers to a work's faithfulness to the historical record.

Adaptation Refers both to the process of modifying a text for a different medium or genre and to the product of that process.

Adventure fiction Works usually set in locales exotic to the protagonist in which characters face physical dangers in order to achieve an explicit goal.

Alliteration A poetic device where a series of words begins with the same consonant sound.

Allusion A brief and specific reference to another work.

Archetypes In Jungian psychology, the symbols, plots, and patterns that organize all human psychological experience.

Auteur theory   The understanding of a film director as equivalent to the author of a literary work in which the film is seen as the product of the director's vision, as opposed to that of the screenwriter, producer, or editor.

Authenticity   When used in reference to historical fiction, "authenticity" refers to the plausible representation of details in a literary text that are missing or vague in the historical record.

Bildungsroman   A coming-of-age story, often covering a protagonist's emotional, psychological or professional development, and sometimes involving a transition from innocence to experience.

Bowdlerization   The editing of texts with anything offensive taken out, named after Thomas Bowdler, who produced expurgated editions of books for children.

Canon   Books considered to be the most significant and culturally essential in any given time and place, forming a core of important cultural knowledge.

Censorship   Government restriction or legislation of materials, including the banning of books. It can also encompass a wide number of obstacles that obstruct an individual or group's ability to get material and a variety of roadblocks to access that are put up by a governing authority.

Challenge   A written, oral, or public request to a librarian or teacher that a book be removed from a library or classroom.

Chapbooks   Small, inexpensive booklets, ranging from eight to twenty-four pages, in which tales of adventure, romance, mystery, or crime were printed.

Classic   A work whose value has been recognized over time, and which is considered to be of the highest quality or of thematic or historical importance.

Close reading   The practice of paying careful attention to the language of a text, including the histories and meanings of words and their connotations, as well as the implications of the use of particular words and phrases.

Comics   Narratives told in sequential images, usually including text as well.

Crossover   A work traditionally imagined as for adults or a mixed-age audience that has come to be considered children's literature.

Cut   The abrupt shift from one shot to another in a film.

Detective and mystery novels   A category of literary works in which solving a crime or mystery through logical reasoning and investigation is a central concern of the plot.

Diction   The style of writing or speaking, determined by word choice, vocabulary, and use of figurative language.

Didactic   While readers can derive lessons from any verbal or visual text, the term "didactic" describes a text or passage that explicitly teaches a lesson, whether moral, political, religious, social, or practical.

Diegesis   A film's diegesis is the totality of its fictional world, and its diegetic elements are those that exist or occur in the world of the characters, including objects they see, sounds they hear, and so on. Non-diegetic elements are those aspects of the film that the audience, but not the characters, recognizes as part of the film, such as the score, voice-over narration, subtitles, or scrolling text.

Domestic fiction   Works usually set in or around the home and focusing on the personal relationships among members of a family or household.

Dramatic irony   The state of tension between what a character knows or sees and what is presented to the reader.

Dual address   The phenomenon in children's literature in which a text moves between speaking to imagined child readers and imagined adult readers, or when child and adult readers might understand the same passage differently based on different age-based knowledge or experience.

Dystopian fiction   A category of literary works featuring a society that is far worse than current ones and that comments on the aspects of contemporary society by imagining the nightmarish implications of current practices or values.

Fairy Tale   A short narrative including magical or fantastical events, objects, or characters.

Fanfiction Fan-authored stories about characters and situations from popular literature, film, or television.

Fantasy A genre including magical or supernatural elements, events, and experiences that could not take place in the known world.

Figurative language Figurative language includes imagery and poetic tropes used in poetry that differ from the literal interpretation in order to achieve poetic effects.

First Amendment The US constitutional amendment that protects freedom of speech from government persecution or suppression.

Formula fiction A category of literary works that replicate a familiar pattern in terms of plot and focus. Some works of fantasy, horror, mystery romance, science fiction, and utopian/dystopian fiction might be considered formula fiction if they remain close to recognizable patterns.

Fractured fairy tales Fairy tales made humorous through surprising changes or unexpected modernizations.

Framing How actors will be placed in a set, how they will be positioned in relation to each other and objects in their environment, and how far away or close up the camera will be.

Gaze A term in cultural and film theory that denotes the act of looking or the ability to look at another person from a particular perspective and in a way that creates power over the viewed object.

Gender The system of culturally specific characteristics and behaviors that characterize masculinity, femininity, boyhood, girlhood, manhood, womanhood, transgender, or other genders.

Gender identity The sense of oneself as a gendered person. Common gender identities include boy, girl, man, woman, transgender (transman or transwoman), non-binary, etc.

Gender performance How gender is enacted in the world, whether consciously or unconsciously, through a set of a repeated, ongoing, or habitual behaviors.

Genre   A class of works that share features, and often including the clues and norms that help a reader or viewer interpret texts.

Golden Age   The period from the mid nineteenth century to around World War I when many of the classics of children's literature were written and published and when children's literature became increasingly less concerned with didacticism and more with literariness or pleasure.

Graphic novels   Book-length narrative works that combine verbal text and images to tell a story.

Heteronormativity   A worldview that assumed that heterosexuality is a natural social norm, and makes the assumption that all people are or should be heterosexual.

High fantasy   The subset of fantasy most associated with elevated quests and lofty struggles between good and evil.

Historical novel   To qualify as a historical novel, a work must be set in a historical period significantly earlier than the one in which it was written and the historical setting must be significant rather than incidental to the plot and characters.

Horror fiction   A literary genre designed to elicit unease, fear, or terror or to represent experiences, characters, or situations likely to cause such emotions.

Hyperbole   A literary device where a phenomenon or object is described in an exaggerated or heightened way.

Informational books   Books that convey information about the natural, social, or biological world, in a non-narrative format (often present-tense) that seeks to offer an explanation of phenomena or processes.

Interactivity   The interchange between a person and an electronic device.

Intertextuality   The relationship between a prior text and a new text created when an author borrows from the prior one or references it within the new text. It describes how texts inevitably refer to other texts by virtue of being part of a larger system of language with shared references, codes, images, meanings, and ways of speaking, writing, and perceiving.

Legends   Traditional stories featuring a notorious or legendary figure, where the story has not been verified, proven, or authenticated.

Magical realism   Books where magical elements are depicted as coexisting along with mundane events.

Metafictionality   When a fictional text reveals awareness of its own fictional status.

Metaphor   The literary figure of speech where two unrelated things or ideas are compared.

Mimesis   A Greek term that refers to imitation or representation of the physical world.

Mise-en-scène   The elements that are physically present in the scene, such as actors, costumes, sets, props, and even the arrangement of lighting comprise the mise-en-scène.

Montage   Modifying the presentation of time in a film to splice together multiple scenes in rapid succession.

Myths   A traditional story that includes supernatural beings or events, and that is meant to explain a social or natural phenomenon.

Narrative poem   A poem that tells a story.

Naturalism   A literary movement which stresses the impersonal forces of nature that elude human control, and where the fate of characters are determined by these forces. Naturalist writers stress the importance of detached observation in the fictional portrayal of reality.

New Realism   Books that deal with controversial or taboo topics like teen pregnancy and drug use, among others, often featuring urban settings.

Nonfiction   Writing that is not fiction, and is concerned with real events and facts.

Nursery rhymes   Traditional songs or poems for children, often collected under the title "Mother Goose rhymes."

Optative   A grammatical term for sentences that express a wish or a hope; Marina Warner has used it to describe the wish-fulfillment aspect of fairy tales.

Pan   Involves moving the film camera between different objects and recording in one sweeping motion without cutting away.

Pantomime   A musical comedy for stage usually performed around Christmastime and often involving adaptations of traditional folk or fairy tales.

Personification   A literary device where non-human objects or phenomena are endowed with human traits.

Picturebook   A narrative or non-narrative book in which words and images form an artistic whole.

Popular culture   Cultural practices, texts, and products that are produced for and enjoyed by a broad, non-specialized audience.

Portmanteau   A word that combines the meanings and sounds of two other words.

Presentism   The idea that a work depicts or is influenced by a way of thinking more characteristic of the time in which it was written than the time it describes.

Prizing   The giving of awards such as the Newbery Medal.

Problem novel   Books where plot, characters, and even language are defined—and constrained—by the focus on a single problem or set of problems, such as drug use, divorce, or teen pregnancy.

Queer   Used as an adjective, the term "queer" can describe identities, acts, or people that defy norms of gender, sexuality, or other cultural systems or practices. Used as a verb, "queer" can describe ways of writing or analyzing texts to emphasize how they resist normative expectations of gender, sexuality, or other cultural systems or practices.

Realism   A mode which includes stories that could actually happen: those containing no element of magic.

Revision   A change or amendment of a text, which is also sometimes known as "adaptation."

Romance fiction   A literary genre defined by the focus on romantic relations and often the development of romantic feelings between two or more characters.

Scene   A basic unit of film comprising the shot or shots taking place in one location and involving a coherent event.

Science fantasy   A literary text falling on the boundaries between science fiction and fantasy, which draws on elements of both science fiction and fantasy.

Science fiction   A literary genre defined by works in which science and technology, usually more advanced than what is currently possible, is central to the story.

Selection   The process of choosing to include or omit certain books from classrooms, curricula, and libraries.

Semiotics   The science of signs and how they work.

Sex   Biological designations such as male, female, or intersex based on genetic and anatomical features.

Sexuality   The large category that can refer to certain "sexual" practices that may or may not involve the genitals, the biology and physiology of sex/gender and arousal/pleasure, ways of perceiving or conceiving of desire and pleasure, and ways of naming oneself or others in terms of particular and available identities and orientations.

Shot   A part of the scene captured by the camera.

Storyboard   A film's storyboard is a series of visual plans for the film, usually rough sketches that lay out shots, cuts and camera movements, and scenes.

Tall tale   A story that has unbelievable elements, or which exaggerates real events.

Transformation   The process whereby a text is modified to such a significant degree that a new text is created that echoes the previous one but that is substantially different from it.

Trope   The use of figurative language or metaphors in a literary work.

Utopian fiction A category of literary works featuring societies that are either utopian (idealized societies that are better than current ones) or dystopian (societies that are far worse than current ones) and that are used to comment on aspects of contemporary society or imagine better ones.

Verse Poetry that conforms to strict meters and rhymes and that is meant primarily to entertain, especially when referred to as "light verse." It can also refer to all forms of poetry.

Worldbuilding The construction of a consistent and coherent imaginary environment in a fantasy text.

Zeugma A figure of speech where a word is applied to two other words, even when it actually only applies to one. An example would be, "She crashed her mother's car and her hopes."

WORKS CITED

INTRODUCTION FOR STUDENTS

Beckett, Sandra L. "Introduction." *Transcending Boundaries: Writing for a Dual Audience of Children and Adults*, edited by Sandra Beckett. Garland, 1999.

Burnett, Frances Hodgson. *The Secret Garden*. 1911, edited by Gretchen Holbrook Gerzina. Norton, 2006.

Butler, Francelia. "The Editor's High Chair: Children's Literature and the Humanities." *Children's Literature* 2, 1973, pp. 8–10.

Griswold, Jerry. *Feeling Like a Kid: Childhood and Children's Literature*. Johns Hopkins UP, 2006.

Kutzer, M. Daphne. *Empire's Children: Empire and Imperialism in Classic British Children's Books*. Routledge, 2000.

Law, Elizabeth. "'Yes, but I'm Eleven': An Editor's Perspective on Condescension in Children's Literature." *The Lion and the Unicorn* 17, 1993, pp. 15–21.

Luke, Allan. *Literacy, Textbooks and Ideology: Postwar Literacy and the Mythology of Dick and Jane*. Falmer, 1988.

Lurie, Alison. *Don't Tell the Grown-Ups: The Subversive Power of Children's Literature*. Back Bay, 1998.

Matthews, Gareth. "Children, Irony and Philosophy." *Theory and Research in Education* 3.1, 2005, pp. 81–95.

Mickenberg, Julia L., and Philip Nel. *Tales for Little Rebels: A Collection of Radical Children's Literature*. New York UP, 2008.

Mielke, Tammy. "Transforming a Stereotype: *Little Black Sambo*'s American Illustrators." *From Colonialism to the Contemporary: Intertextual Transformation in World Children's and Youth Literature*, edited by Lance Weldy. Cambridge Scholars, 2006, pp. 1–15.

Myers, Mitzi. "Impeccable Governesses, Rational Dames, and Moral Mothers: Mary Wollstonecraft and the Female Tradition in Georgian Children's Books." *Children's Literature* 14, 1986, pp. 31–59.

Phillips, Jerry. "The Mem Sahib, the Worthy, the Rajah and His Minions: Some Reflections on the Class Politics of *The Secret Garden*." *The Lion and the Unicorn* 17.2, 1993, pp. 168–94.

Rose, Jacqueline. *The Case of Peter Pan; or, The Impossibility of Children's Fiction*. 1984. U of Pennsylvania P, 1993.

Rowling, J.K. (@jk_rowling). "Canon: brown eyes, frizzy hair and very clever. White skin was never specified. Rowling loves black Hermione." *Twitter*. 21 December 2015, 4:41 a.m., twitter.com/jk_rowling/status/678888094339366914.

Wall, Barbara. *The Narrator's Voice*. Macmillan, 1991.

CHAPTER 1: HISTORICIZING CHILDHOOD

Anderson, Devery S. *Emmett Till: The Murder That Shocked the World and Propelled the Civil Rights Movement*. UP of Mississippi, 2015.

Anglicus, Bartholomaeus. "The Anatomy of Childhood." *Social Life in Britain: From the Conquest to the Reformation*, edited by G.G. Coulton. Cambridge UP, 1919, pp. 45–46.

Ariès, Philippe. *Centuries of Childhood*. Translated by Robert Baldick. Knopf, 1962.

Aristotle. *Generation of Animals: Loeb Classical Library Volume XIII*, edited by A.L. Peck. Harvard UP, 1942.

Ave, Melanie. "'Romeo's' New Status Angers Victim, Mother." *St. Petersburg Times*, 8 August 2007, p. 1B.

Bernstein, Robin. *Racial Innocence: Performing American Childhood from Slavery to Civil Rights*. New York UP, 2011.

Capshaw, Katharine. *Civil Rights Childhood: Picturing Liberation in African American Photobooks*. U of Minnesota P, 2014.

"Declaration by Privy Council of England, 1620." *Childhood in America*, edited by Paula S. Fass and Mary Ann Mason. New York UP, 2000.

DeMause, Lloyd. "The Evolution of Childhood." *The History of Childhood*, edited by Lloyd deMause. Rowan and Littlefield, 2006, pp. 1–74.

Douglass, Frederick. *My Bondage and My Freedom*. 1855. Penguin Books, 2003.

Elgion, John. "Michael Brown Spent Last Weeks Grappling with Problems and Promise." *New York Times*, 24 August 2014.

Freud, Sigmund. "The Sexual Aberrations." *Three Essays on the Theory of Sexuality*. 1905. Translated by James Strachey. Basic, 2000, pp. 1–38.

Goodnough, Abby. "Florida Youth Who Got Life Term for a Killing Is Freed at 16." *New York Times*, 27 January 2004, A12.

Janeway, James. *A Token for Children*. 1671. Deo Gloria, 1994.

Kavesh, Laura. "It Takes a Tough Kid to Be a Poster Child." *Chicago Tribune*, 29 March 1985.

Kidd, Kenneth. *Making American Boys: Boyology and the Feral Tale*. U of Minnesota P, 2004.

Locke, John. *An Essay Concerning Human Understanding*. 1690. Prometheus, 1995.

———. *Some Thoughts Concerning Education*. 1693. Hackett, 1996.

Longmore, Paul. "'Heaven's Special Child': The Making of Poster Children." *The Disability Studies Reader, Fourth Edition*, edited by Lennard J. Davis. Routledge, 2003, pp. 34–41.

Makarechi, Kia. "Besides Michael Brown, Who Else Does the New York Times Call 'No Angel'?" *Vanity Fair*, 25 August 2014.

Marks, Deborah. *Disability: Controversial Debates and Psychosocial Perspectives*. Routledge, 1999.

Mattern, Susan. *Galen and the Rhetoric of Healing*. Johns Hopkins UP, 2008.

Milne, A.A. *The House at Pooh Corner*. 1928. Puffin Classics, 1992.

Mintz, Steven. *Domestic Revolutions: A Social History of American Family Life*. Free, 1989.

The New England Primer. Benjamin Harris, 1687–90.

Riis, Jacob. *How the Other Half Lives*. 1890. Penguin Classics, 1997.

Rousseau, Jean-Jacques. *Emile; or, On Education*. 1762. Translated by Allan Bloom. Basic, 1979.

Schaller, Lyle E. *The Evolution of the American Public High School: From Prep School to Prison to New Partnerships*. Abingdon, 2000.

Singer, P.W. *Children at War*. Pantheon, 2005.

Step by Step; or, Tidy's Way to Freedom. 1862. BiblioBazaar, 2006.

Stowe, Harriet Beecher. *Uncle Tom's Cabin*. 1852. Oxford World's Classics, 2008.

Ward, Geoff K. *The Black Child-Savers: Racial Democracy and Juvenile Justice*. U of Chicago P, 2012.

Wordsworth, William. "Ode." *The Major Works: Including* The Prelude, edited by Stephen Gill. Oxford World's Classics, 2008, pp. 299–302.

Zelizer, Viviana A. *Pricing the Priceless Child: The Changing Social Value of Children*. Princeton UP, 1994.

CHAPTER 2: THE EARLY HISTORY OF CHILDREN'S LITERATURE

Barbauld, Anna Laetitia. *Hymns in Prose for Children*. 1781. 6th ed., Johnson, 1794, *Google Books*.

Bottigheimer, Ruth B. *Fairy Tales: A New History*. State U of New York P, 2009.

Bunyan, John. *A Book for Boys and Girls; or, Country Rhymes for Children*. 1686. Elliot Stock, 1890. Google Books.

Carroll, Lewis. *Alice's Adventures in Wonderland*. 1865, edited by Hugh Haughton. Penguin, 1998.

Carter, Angela. *Little Red Riding Hood, Cinderella, and Other Classic Fairy Tales of Charles Perrault*. Penguin, 2008.

Clark, Beverly Lyon. *Kiddie Lit: The Cultural Construction of Children's Literature in America*. Johns Hopkins UP, 2003.

Commager, Henry Steele. Introduction to the First Edition. *A Critical History of Children's Literature: A Survey of Children's Books in English*, edited by Cornelia Meigs et al. Macmillan, 1969.

Darton, F.J. Harvey. *Children's Books in England: Five Centuries of Social Life*, 3rd ed., revised by Brian Alderson. Cambridge UP, 1982.

Demers, Patricia. *From Instruction to Delight: An Anthology of Children's Literature to 1850*. Oxford UP, 2004.

Eagleton, Terry. *Literary Theory: An Introduction*. 1983. U of Minnesota P, 2008.

Edgeworth, Maria, and Richard Lovell Edgeworth. *Practical Education*. 1798. Harper and Brothers, 1855. Google Books.

Ellis, Alec. *A History of Children's Reading and Literature*. Pergamon, 1968.

Gillespie, Margaret C. *Literature for Children: History and Trends*. W.C. Brown, 1970.

Griswold, Jerry. *The Classic American Children's Story: Novels of the Golden Age*. Penguin, 1996.

Harris, Stephen J. "Ælfric's Colloquy." *Medieval Literature for Children*, edited by Daniel T. Kline. Routledge, 2003.

Hunt, Peter. *An Introduction to Children's Literature*. Oxford UP, 1994.

Kline, Daniel T. *Medieval Literature for Children*. Routledge, 2003.

Marcus, Leonard S. *Minders of Make-Believe: Idealists, Entrepreneurs, and the Shaping of American Children's Literature*. Houghton Mifflin, 2008.

Meigs, Cornelia, editor. *A Critical History of Children's Literature: A Survey of Children's Books in English*. Macmillan, 1969.

Michels, Teresa. *Books for Children, Books for Adults: Age and the Novel from Defoe to James*. Cambridge UP, 2014.

Nodelman, Perry. *The Hidden Adult: Defining Children's Literature*. Johns Hopkins UP, 2008.

Ostry, Elaine. *Social Dreaming: Dickens and the Fairy Tale*. Studies in Major Literary Authors. Routledge, 2002.

Pearson, Lucy. *The Making of Modern Children's Literature in Britain: Publishing and Criticism in the 1960s and 1970s*. Routledge, 2016.

Rusher, J.G. *The Interesting Story of the Children in the Wood: A Historical Ballad*. Rusher, 1840? Google Books.

Townsend, John Rowe. *Written for Children: An Outline of English-Language Children's Literature*. Garnet Miller, 1965.

Trimmer, Mrs. [Sarah]. *An Essay on Christian Education*. F.C. and J. Rivington, 1812. Google Books.

Turner, Elizabeth. *The Daisy; or, Cautionary Stories in Verse*. 1807. Griffith, 1885. Google Books.

Watson, Jeanie. "Introduction." *Children's Literature of the English Renaissance*, by Warren W. Wooden. UP of Kentucky, 1986.

Watts, Isaac. *Divine and Moral Songs, Attempted in Easy Language, for the Use of Children*. 1715. Richardson, 1829. Google Books.

Wooden, Warren W. *Children's Literature of the English Renaissance*. UP of Kentucky, 1986.

Zipes, Jack. *Fairy Tale as Myth / Myth as Fairy Tale*. UP of Kentucky, 1994.

CHAPTER 3: POETRY

Alarcón, Francisco X. *Laughing Tomatoes and Other Spring Poems / Jitomates Risueños y otros poemas de primavera*. Illustrated by Maya Christina Gonzalez. Children's Book Press / Libros para niños, 1997.

Barbauld, Anna Laetitia. *Hymns in Prose for Children*. Printed for J. Johnson, 1781.

Baring-Gould, William S., and Ceil Baring-Gould. *The Annotated Mother Goose: Nursery Rhymes Old and New, Arranged and Explained*. Illustrated by Walter Crane, Randolph Caldecott, Kate Greenaway, Arthur Rackham, Maxfield Parrish, and early historical woodcuts. Bramhall House, 1962.

Barr, John. "Is It Poetry or Is It Verse?" 18 September 2006, *Poetry Foundation*, poetryfoundation.org/articles/68681/is-it-poetry-or-is-it-verse.

Barron, Christina. "Kwame Alexander Wins Newbery Medal." *Washington Post*, 2 February 2015.

Belloc, Hilaire. *Cautionary Tales for Children*. 1907. Rediscovered and illustrated by Edward Gorey. Harcourt, 2002.

Blake, William. "The Chimney Sweeper." *Songs of Innocence*, 1789. In *Blake's Illuminated Books*, edited by David Bindman. William Blake Trust / Tate Gallery, 1991.

Brown, Margaret Wise. *Goodnight Moon*. 1947. Illustrated by Clement Hurd. Scholastic, 1992.

Cadden, Mike. "The Verse Novel and the Question of Genre." *Alan Review*, Fall 2011, pp. 21–27.

Capshaw, Katharine. *Civil Rights Childhood: Picturing Liberation in African American Photobooks*. Minnesota UP, 2015.

Carroll, Lewis. *Through the Looking Glass*. Macmillan, 1872.

Ciardi, John. *The Man Who Sang the Sillies*. Illustrated by Edward Gorey. Lippincott, 1961.

Coats, Karen. "The Meaning of Children's Poetry: A Cognitive Approach." *International Research in Children's Literature* 6.2, 2013, pp. 127–42.

Colley, Ann C. "'Writing Towards Home': The Landscape of 'A Child's Garden of Verses.'" *Victorian Poetry* 35. 3, Fall 1997, pp. 303–18.

Cooper, Mary. *Tommy Thumb's Pretty Song Book*. Vol. II. c. 1744.

Cunningham, Hugh. *The Children of the Poor: Representations of Childhood Since the Seventeenth Century*. Oxford UP, 1991.

Dahl, Roald. *Dirty Beasts*. 1984. Puffin, 2002.

Demers, Patricia, and Gordon Moyles, editors. *From Instruction to Delight: An Anthology of Children's Literature to 1850*. Oxford UP, 1982.

Döhl, Reinhard. "Pattern Poem with an Elusive Intruder." *4 texte (futura 4)*. Edition Hansjörg Mayer, 1965.

Flynn, Richard. "Can Children's Poetry Matter?" *The Lion and the Unicorn* 17.1, 1993, pp. 37–44.

Geisel, Theodor Seuss. *Green Eggs and Ham*. 1960. Penguin Books, 1988.

_____. *Scrambled Eggs Super!* Random House, 1953.

Heyman, Michael, editor. *The Tenth Rasa: An Anthology of Indian Nonsense*. With Sumanyu Satpathy and Anushka Ravishankar. Penguin, 2007.

Howitt, Mary. *Sketches of Natural History*. Effingham Wilson, Royal Exchange, 1834.

Hughes, Langston. *The Dream Keeper and Other Poems*. Illustrated by Brian Pinkney. Knopf, 1994.

Janeczko, Paul B., editor, and Christopher Raschka, illustrator. *A Poke in the I: A Collection of Concrete Poems*. Candlewick, 2005.

Kennedy, X.J. "Strict and Loose Nonsense: Two Worlds of Children's Verse." *School Library Journal*, March 1991, pp. 108–12.

Koch, Kenneth, and the students of P.S. 61 in New York City. *Wishes, Lies, and Dreams: Teaching Children to Write Poetry*. Harper & Row, 1970.

Lear, Edward. "The Owl and the Pussycat." *Nonsense Songs and Stories*. Frederick Warne, 1888.

Lewis, Richard, collector. *Miracles: Poems by Children of the English-Speaking World*. Simon and Schuster, 1966.

Little, Jean. "Today." *Hey World, Here I Am!* 1986. Illustrated by Sue Truesdell. HarperCollins, 1990.

Livingston, Myra Cohn. *The Child as Poet: Myth or Reality?* Horn Book, 1984.

Merriam, Eve. *It Doesn't Always Have to Rhyme*. Atheneum, 1964.

Nel, Philip. *Dr. Seuss: American Icon*. Continuum, 2004.

Newbery, John. *Mother Goose's Melody; or, Sonnets from the Cradle*. Printed for Francis Power and Co., 1791.

Nichols, Grace. *Come on into My Tropical Garden*. Illustrated by Caroline Binch. A. & C. Black, 1988.

Nye, Naomi Shihab. *A Maze Me: Poems for Girls*. Pictures by Terre Maher. Greenwillow, 2005.

Opie, Peter, and Iona Opie. *I Saw Esau*. 1947. Candlewick, 1992.

Paul, Lissa. "Ted Hughes and the 'Old Age of Childhood.'" *Poetry and Childhood*, edited by Morag Styles, Louise Joy, and David Whitley. Trentham, 2010, pp. 33–44.

Prelutsky, Jack. *My Dog May Be a Genius*. Illustrated by James Stevenson. Greenwillow, 2008.

Raybuck, Dorie. "Field Notes: 'This Is Too Much!' Why Verse Novels Work for Reluctant Readers." *The Horn Book*. 30 March 2015, hbook.com/2015/03/featured/field-notes-this-is-too-much-why-verse-novels-work-for-reluctant-readers.

Rosen, Michael. "Robert Louis Stevenson and Children's Play: The Contexts of *A Child's Garden of Verses*." *Children's Literature in Education*, 26.1, 1995, pp. 53–72.

Rossetti, Christina. *Sing-Song: A Nursery Rhyme Book*. 1872. New and enlarged edition. Illustrated by Arthur Hughes. Macmillan, 1893.

Silverstein, Shel. *Where the Sidewalk Ends*. Harper & Row, 1974.

Stevenson, Robert Louis. *A Child's Garden of Verses*. Longmans, 1885.

Styles, Morag. *From the Garden to the Street: Three Hundred Years of Poetry for Children*. Cassell, 1998.

Thomas, Joseph T., Jr. *Poetry's Playground: The Culture of Contemporary American Children's Poetry*. Wayne State UP, 2007.

Thwaite, Ann. *A.A. Milne: His Life*. Faber, 1990.

Van Sickle, Vikki. "Subcategories within the Emerging Genre of the Verse Novel." *The Looking Glass: New Perspectives on Children's Literature* 10.3, 2006, lib.latrobe.edu.au/ojs/index.php/tlg/article/view/74/88.

Watts, Isaac. *Divine and Moral Songs for Children*. 1715. T. Nelson and Sons, 1857. Baldwin Library of Historical Children's Literature, ufdc.ufl.edu/UF00003216/00001/3j.

Webb, Jean. "Conceptualising Childhood: Robert Louis Stevenson's *A Child's Garden of Verses*." *Cambridge Journal of Education* 32.3, November 2002, pp. 359–65.

Weinstein, Amy. *Once Upon a Time: Illustrations from Fairytales, Fables, Primers, Pop-Ups, and Other Children's Books*. Princeton Architectural P, 2005.

Wong, Janet S. *A Suitcase of Seaweed and Other Poems*. Decorations by the author. Margaret K. McElderry, 1996.

CHAPTER 4: FAIRY TALES

Andrews, Travis M. "'Brown skin is not a costume': Disney takes heat for 'Moana' Halloween costume." *Washington Post*, 20 September 2016.

Bacchilega, Cristina. Review of *Fairy Tales: A New History* by Ruth B. Bottigheimer. *Children's Literature Association Quarterly* 35.4, 2010, pp. 468–71.

Baker-Sperry, Lori, and Liz Grauerholz. "The Pervasiveness and Persistence of the Feminine Beauty Ideal in Children's Fairy Tales." *Gender and Society* 17.5, 2003, pp. 711–26.

Betancourt, Manuel. "Elena of Avalor, Disney's New Latina Princess, Is the Right Girl for a Multicultural World." 15 July 2016, mic.com/articles/148769/elena-of-avalor-disney-s-new-latina-princess-is-the-right-girl-for-a-multicultural-world#.hTjDJxoTs.

Bettelheim, Bruno. *The Uses of Enchantment: The Meaning and Importance of Fairy Tales*. Knopf, 1976.

Bottigheimer, Ruth B. "Fairy Tales, Folk Narrative Research and History." *Social History* 14.3, 1989, pp. 323–57.

_____. *Fairy Tales: A New History*. State U of New York P, 2009.

Darnton, Robert. *The Great Cat Massacre and Other Episodes in French Cultural History*. Basic, 1984.

De Haan, Linda, and Stern Nijland. *King and King*. Tricycle, 2002.

Dicker, Ron. "Disney Princesses with Disabilities Redefine 'Standard of Beauty.'" *Huffington Post*, 27 January 2014, huffingtonpost.ca/entry/disabled-disney-princesse_n_4673988.

Duffy, John-Charles. "Gay-Related Themes in the Fairy Tales of Oscar Wilde." *Victorian Literature and Culture* 29.2, 2001, pp. 327–49.

Griswold, Jerry. *The Meanings of "Beauty and the Beast": A Handbook*. Broadview, 2004.

Harries, Elizabeth W. *Twice Upon a Time: Women Writers and the History of the Fairy Tale*. Princeton UP, 2001.

Herman, Doug. "How the Story of 'Moana' and Maui Holds Up Against Cultural Truths." *Smithsonian Magazine*, 2 December 2016, smithsonianmag.com/smithsonian-institution/how-story-moana-and-maui-holds-against-cultural-truths-180961258.

Hornaday, Ann. Review of "The Princess and the Frog." *Washington Post*, 10 December 2009, washingtonpost.com/wp-dyn/content/article/2009/12/10/AR2009121001278.html.

Hurley, Dorothy L. "Seeing White: Children of Color and the Disney Fairy Tale Princess." *The Journal of Negro Education* 74.3, 2005, pp. 221–32.

Hyman, Trina Schart. "'Cut It Down, and You Will Find Something at the Roots.'" In *The Reception of Grimms' Fairy Tales: Responses, Reactions, Revisions*, edited by Donald Haase. Wayne State UP, 1993, pp. 293–300.

———. *Little Red Riding Hood*. Holiday House, 1982.

———. *Self-Portrait: Trina Schart Hyman*. Addison-Wesley, 1981.

Joosen, Vanessa. "Fairy-Tale Retellings Between Art and Pedagogy." *Children's Literature in Education* 36.2, 2005, pp. 129–39.

Kuykendal, Leslee Farish, and Brian W. Sturm. "We Said Feminist Fairy Tales, Not Fractured Fairy Tales! The Construction of the Feminist Fairy Tale: Female Agency over Role Reversal." *Children and Libraries*, 2007, pp. 38–41.

Lewis, Tess. "A Drop of Bitterness: Andersen's Fairy Tales." *Hudson Review* 54.4, 2002, pp. 679–86.

Liberman, Melanie. "Hawaiian Airlines Debuts an Airplane Themed After Disney's Newest Movie." *Travel and Leisure*, 17 October 2016, travelandleisure.com/airlines-airports/hawaiian-airlines-reveals-moana-themed-jets.

Lieberman, Marcia B. "'Some Day My Prince Will Come': Female Acculturation Through the Fairy Tale." *College English* 34.3, 1972, pp. 383–95.

Lozada-Oliva, Melissa. "The Problem with Disney's New Latina Princess; One Size Doesn't Fit All." *Guardian*, 22 July 2016.

McKissack, Patricia. *Flossie and the Fox*. Illustrated by Rachel Isadora. Dial Books for Young Readers, 1986.

Munsch, Robert. *The Paper Bag Princess*. Illustrated by Michael Martchenko. Annick, 1980.

Oates, Joyce Carol. "In Olden Times, When Wishing Was Having: Classic and Contemporary Fairy Tales." *Mirror, Mirror on the Wall: Women Writers Explore Their Favorite Fairy Tales*, edited by Kate Bernheimer. Anchor, 1998, pp. 260–83.

Perrault, Charles. *The Complete Fairy Tales*. Translated by Christopher Betts. Oxford UP, 2009.

Roberts-Gassler, Vicki. "Teaching the Fairy Tale." *Der Unterrichtspraxis / Teaching German* 20.2, 1987, pp. 250–60.

Sale, Roger. *Fairy Tales and After: From Snow White to E.B. White*. Harvard UP, 1978.

Schmiesing, Ann. *Disability, Deformity, and Disease in the Grimms' Fairy Tales*. Wayne State UP, 2014.

Smith, Tyler Scott. "'Snow White in Africa': Afrocentric Ideology in Marilyn Shearer's Tale." *Fairy Tales with a Black Consciousness*, edited by Vivian Yenika-Agbaw, Ruth McKoy Lowery, and Laretta Henderson. McFarland & Company, 2013, pp. 186–201.

Tatar, Maria., editor. *The Annotated Classic Fairy Tales*. Norton, 2002.

———. *The Hard Facts of the Grimms' Fairy Tales*. Princeton UP, 1987.

Von Franz, Marie-Louise. *The Interpretation of Fairy Tales*. Rev. ed. of *An Introduction to the Interpretation of Fairy Tales*, 1970. Shambhala, 1996.

Warner, Marina. *From the Beast to the Blonde: On Fairy Tales and Their Tellers*. Chatto, 1994.

Wilde, Oscar. "The Happy Prince." *Complete Fairy Tales of Oscar Wilde*. Penguin, 1990, pp. 9–22.

Wullschlager, Jackie. *Hans Christian Andersen*. British Library, 2005.

Zipes, Jack. *Breaking the Magic Spell: Radical Theories of Folk and Fairy Tales.* 2nd revised and expanded edition. UP of Kentucky, 2002.

_____. *Happily Ever After: Fairy Tales, Children, and the Culture Industry.* Routledge, 1997.

_____. *The Irresistible Fairy Tale: The Cultural and Social History of a Genre.* Princeton UP, 2012.

_____. Introduction. *The Oxford Companion to Fairy Tales: The Western Fairy Tale Tradition from Medieval to Modern.* Oxford UP, 2000, pp. xv–xxxii.

_____. *The Trials and Tribulations of Little Red Riding Hood.* 2nd ed. Routledge, 1993.

_____. "Why fairy tales are immortal." *Globe and Mail,* 19 November 2010.

_____. *Why Fairy Tales Stick: The Evolution and Relevance of a Genre.* Routledge, 2006.

CHAPTER 5: PICTUREBOOKS, GRAPHIC NOVELS, AND DIGITAL TEXTS

Arnold, Andrew D. "The Graphic Novel Silver Anniversary." *Time,* 14 November 2003.

Bader, Barbara. *American Picturebooks from Noah's Ark to the Beast Within.* Macmillan, 1976.

Bang, Molly. *Picture This: How Pictures Work.* Chronicle Books, 2000.

Bosman, Julie. "Picture Books No Longer a Staple for Children." *New York Times,* 7 October 2010.

Carroll, Lewis. *Alice's Adventures in Wonderland.* 1865. Edited by Donald J. Gray. Norton Critical Edition. Norton, 1992.

Cummins, Julie, editor. *Children's Book Illustration and Design.* PBC International, 1992.

Danielson, Julie. "Just Enjoy the Pictures: Hand-Crafted Versus Digital Art." *The Horn Book,* March/April 2014, pp. 44–47.

De la Peña, Matt. *Last Stop on Market Street.* Illustrated by Christian Robinson. G.P. Putnam's Books for Young Readers, 2016.

De Vicq de Cumptich. Roberto. *Bembo's Zoo: An Animal ABC Book.* Henry Holt & Company, 2000.

"Emily Elizabeth Goes to School." *Clifford the Big Red Dog: Interactive Storybooks.* Scholastic, teacher.scholastic.com/clifford1/flash/story_4.htm.

Geist, J. Nicholas. "The Sailor's Dream Is a Labyrinth, An Instrument, A Place." *Kill Screen,* 2 October 2016, killscreen.com/articles/sailors-dream-labyrinth-instrument-place.

Grieve, Ann. "Postmodernism in Picturebooks." *Papers: Explorations in Children's Literature* 4.3, 1993, pp. 15–25.

Hatfield, Charles, and Craig Svonkin. "Why Comics Are and Are Not Picture Books: Introduction." *Children's Literature Association Quarterly* 37.4, 2012, pp. 429–35.

Hayles, Kathleen N. *Electronic Literature: New Horizons for the Literary.* Notre Dame UP, 2008.

Jones Jr., William B. *Classics Illustrated: A Cultural History, Second Edition.* McFarland & Company, Inc., 2011.

Kümmerling-Meibauer, Bettina. "The Impact of New Digital Media on Children's and Young Adult Literature." *Digital Literature for Children: Texts, Readers and Educational Practices.* Peter Lang, 2015, pp. 57–73.

Lear, Linda. *Beatrix Potter: A Life in Nature.* Penguin, 2007.

Lepore, Jill. *The Secret History of Wonder Woman.* Alfred A. Knopf, 2014.

Marantz, Kenneth. "The Picture Book as Art Object: A Call for Balanced Reviewing." *Wilson Library Bulletin,* 1977, pp. 148–56.

Matulka, Denise I. *A Picture Book Primer: Understanding and Using Picture Books.* Libraries Unlimited, 2008.

McCloud, Scott. *Understanding Comics: The Invisible Art.* HarperPerennial, 1994.

Neuman, Susan B. "The Knowledge Gap: Implications for Early Education." *Handbook of Early Literacy Research*. Vol. 2, edited by David K. Dickinson and Susan B. Neuman. Guilford, 2006, pp. 29–40.

Nikolajeva, Maria, and Carole Scott. *How Picturebooks Work*. Routledge, 2000.

Nodelman, Perry. *Words about Pictures: The Narrative Art of Children's Picture Books*. U of Georgia P, 1988.

Osborne, Harold, editor. *The Oxford Companion to Art*. Oxford UP, 1970.

Prieto, Lucas Ramada. "'Common Places in Children's E-Lit.' A Journey through the Defining Spaces of Electronic Literature." *Digital Literature for Children: Texts, Readers and Educational Practices*. Peter Lang, 2015, pp. 37–57.

Santat, Dan. *Beekle: The Unimaginary Friend*. Little, Brown Books for Young Readers, 2014.

Sendak, Maurice. *Caldecott & Co.: Notes on Books and Pictures*. Farrar, 1988.

Shiga, Jason. *Meanwhile: Pick Any Path. 3,856 Story Possibilities*. Amulet Books, 2010.

Sims, Zach. "Library Board Hears Complaints about Books / Decision Scheduled for Oct. 11 Meeting." *Marshall Democrat-News*, 5 October 2006.

Weiner, Stephen. *Faster than a Speeding Bullet: The Rise of the Graphic Novel*. Nantier Beall Minoustchine, 2004.

Wertham, Frederic. *Seduction of the Innocent*. Rinehart, 1972.

Willems, Mo. *There Is a Bird on Your Head!* Hyperion, 2007.

Yokota, Junko. "The Past, Present and Future of Digital Picturebooks for Children." *Digital Literature for Children: Texts, Readers and Educational Practices*. Peter Lang, 2015, 73–87.

CHAPTER 6: DOMESTICITY AND ADVENTURE

Alcott, Louisa May. *Little Women*. 1868. Signet Classic, 2004.

Armstrong, Nancy. *Desire and Domestic Fiction: A Political History of the Novel*. Oxford UP, 1990.

Ballantyne, R.M. *The Coral Island*. 1857. Oxford UP, 1990.

Baym, Nina. *Woman's Fiction: A Guide to Novels by and about Women in America, 1820–1870*. Cornell UP, 1978.

Burroughs, Edgar Rice. *Tarzan of the Apes*. 1914. Signet Classic, 1990.

Campbell, Joseph. *The Hero with a Thousand Faces*. 1949. New World Library, 2008.

Cawelti, John G. *Adventure, Mystery, and Romance: Formula Stories as Art and Popular Culture*. U of Chicago P, 1976.

Clark, Beverly Lyon. *Kiddie Lit: The Cultural Construction of Children's Literature in America*. Johns Hopkins UP, 2003.

Darton, F.J. Harvey. *Children's Books in England: Five Centuries of Social Life*. 3rd ed., revised by Brian Alderson, Cambridge UP, 1982.

Doyle, Sir Arthur Conan. *The Lost World*. Hodder, 1912. Google Books.

Gammel, Irene. *Looking for Anne of Green Gables: The Story of L.M. Montgomery and Her Literary Classic*. St. Martin's, 2008.

Grant, Julia. "A 'Real Boy' and Not a Sissy: Gender, Childhood, and Masculinity, 1890–1940." *Journal of Social History* 37.4, 2004, pp. 829–51.

Green, Martin. *The Great American Adventure*. Beacon, 1984.

Griswold, Jerry. *The Classic American Children's Story: Novels of the Golden Age*. Penguin, 1992.

Kidd, Kenneth. *Making American Boys: Boyology and the Feral Tale*. U of Minnesota P, 2005.

Kimmel, Michael S. *Manhood in America: A Cultural History*. Free, 1997.

Kutzer, M. Daphne. *Empire's Children: Empire and Imperialism in Classic British Children's Books*. Garland, 2000.

Malarte-Feldman, Claire-Lise, and Jack Yeager. "Babar and the French Connection: Teaching the Politics of Superiority and Exclusion." *Critical Perspectives on Postcolonial African Children's and Young Adult Literature*, edited by Meena Khorana. Greenwood, 1998, pp. 69–78.

Mintz, Steven. *Huck's Raft: A History of American Childhood*. Harvard UP, 2006.

Mitchell, Sally. *The New Girl: Girls' Culture in England, 1880–1915*. Columbia UP, 1995.

Murray, Gail Schmunk. *American Children's Literature and the Construction of Childhood*. Twayne, 1998.

Nodelman, Perry. *The Hidden Adult: Defining Children's Literature*. Johns Hopkins UP, 2008.

Norcia, Megan. "Angel of the Island: L.T. Meade's New Girl as the Heir of a Nation-Making Robinson Crusoe." *The Lion and the Unicorn* 28.3, 2004, pp. 345–62.

Paris, Leslie. *Children's Nature: The Rise of the American Summer Camp*. New York UP, 2010.

Robinson, Joe. "Marooned: 18 Years of Solitude." *Los Angeles Times*, 15 June 2004.

Sachar, Louis. *Holes*. Yearling, 2000.

Said, Edward. *Culture and Imperialism*. Vintage, 1994.

Tompkins, Jane. *Sensational Designs: The Cultural Work of American Fiction, 1790–1860*. Oxford UP, 1985.

Twain, Mark. *Adventures of Huckleberry Finn*, 2nd ed., 1885. Bedford/St. Martin's, 2003.

"What Are the Characteristics of Violent Crimes Against Juveniles?" Trends in Violent Crime Victimization. Juveniles as Victims Related FAQs. OJJDP, 2016. *Statistical Briefing Book*, ojjdp.gov/ojstatbb/victims/qa02502.asp?qaDate=2016.

CHAPTER 7: HISTORICAL FICTION

Atleo, Marlene, et al. "Review of Ann Rinaldi's *My Heart Is on the Ground*." Oyate, 2009. Reposted on americanindiansinchildrensliterature.blogspot.com/2011/03/review-of-ann-rinaldis-my-heart-is-on.html.

Balay, Anne. "Zilpha Keatley Snyder's *The Truth about Stone Hollow* and the Genre of the Time-Slip Fantasy." *Children's Literature Association Quarterly* 35.2, 2010, pp. 131–43.

Barnhouse, Rebecca. *Recasting the Past: The Middle Ages in Young Adult Literature*. Boynton/Cook, 2000.

Brown, David, and Michael Wereschagin. *Gone at 3:17: The Untold Story of the Worst School Disaster in American History*. Potomac Books, 2012.

Collier, Christopher. "Johnny and Sam: Old and New Approaches to the American Revolution." *The Horn Book Magazine* 52, 1976, pp. 132–38.

_____, and James Lincoln Collier. *My Brother Sam Is Dead*. Scholastic, 1974.

Curtis, Christopher Paul. *Bud, Not Buddy*. Dell Yearling, 1999.

_____. *The Watsons Go to Birmingham—1963*. Bantam Doubleday Dell, 1995.

Farrell, Kirby. *Post-Traumatic Culture: Injury and Interpretation in the Nineties*. Johns Hopkins UP, 1998.

Forbes, Esther. "Appendix A: Newbery Acceptance Speech." *Esther Forbes: A Bio-Bibliography of the Author of* Johnny Tremain. By Jack Bales. Scarecrow, 1998, pp. 141–46.

_____. *Johnny Tremain*. 1943. Bantam Doubleday Dell, 1969.

Freud, Sigmund. *Beyond the Pleasure Principle*. 1920. Translated by James Strachey. Norton, 1989.

Ganeshram, Ramin. "My Book on George Washington Was Banned. Here's My Side of the Story." *Guardian*, 18 February 2016.

Hubler, Angela E. "Girl Power and History in the Dear America Series Books." *Children's Literature Association Quarterly* 25.2, 2000, 98–106.

Jennerich, Edward J. "Esther Forbes (28 June 1892–12 August 1967)." *American Writers for Children, 1900–1960*, edited by John Cech. *Dictionary of Literary Biography*. Vol. 22. Gale, 1983.

Lenhart, Chelsea. "Hercules." *George Washington Digital Encyclopedia*, mountvernon.org/library/digitalhistory/digital-encyclopedia/article/hercules.

Lukács, Georg. *The Historical Novel*. 1937. Translated by Hannah and Stanley Mitchell. Merlin, 1962.

MacLeod, Anne Scott. "Writing Backward: Modern Models in Historical Fiction." *The Horn Book Magazine* 74.1, 1998, pp. 26–33.

Manzoni, Alessandro. *On the Historical Novel*. 1850. Translated by Sandra Bermann. U of Nebraska P, 1984.

Murphy, Nora. "Starting Children on the Path to the Past: American Indians in Children's Historical Fiction." *Minnesota History Magazine* 57.6, 2001, pp. 284–95.

"New Statement about the Picture Book 'A Birthday Cake for George Washington.'" *On Our Minds: Scholastic's Blog about Books and the Joy of Reading*, 17 January 2016, oomscholasticblog.com/post/new-statement-about-picture-book-birthday-cake-george-washington.

Nodelman, Perry. "History as Fiction: The Story in Hendrik Willem van Loon's *Story of Mankind*." *The Lion and the Unicorn* 14.1, 1990, pp. 70–86.

——, and Mavis Reimer. *The Pleasures of Children's Literature*. 3rd ed. Allyn and Bacon, 2002.

Novick, Peter. *The Noble Dream: The "Objectivity Question" and the American Historical Profession*. Cambridge UP, 1988.

Rahn, Suzanne. "An Evolving Past: The Story of Historical Fiction and Nonfiction for Children." *The Lion and the Unicorn* 15.1, 1991, pp. 1–26.

Reese, Debbie et al. "Review of Ann Rinaldi's *My Heart Is on the Ground*." Oyate. 2009. Reposted on americanindiansinchildrensliterature.blogspot.com.

Rinaldi, Ann. *The Journal of Jasper Jonathan Pierce: A Pilgrim Boy*. Scholastic, 2002.

Schwebel, Sara L. "Historical Fiction in the Classroom: History and Myth in Elizabeth George Speare's *The Witch of Blackbird Pond*." *Children's Literature in Education* 34.3, 2003, pp. 195–218.

Seale, Doris, and Beverly Slapin. *A Broken Flute: The Native Experience in Books for Children*. AltaMira and Oyate, 2005.

Stack, Liam. "Scholastic Halts Distribution of 'A Birthday Cake for George Washington.'" *New York Times*, 17 January 2016.

Tarr, C. Anita. "'A Man Can Stand Up': *Johnny Tremain* and the Rebel Pose." *The Lion and the Unicorn* 18.2, 1994, pp. 178–89.

Ulanowicz, Anastasia. *Second-Generation Memory and Contemporary Children's Literature: Ghost Images*. Routledge, 2013.

Wehler, Hans-Ulrich. "The Goldhagen Controversy: Agonising Problems, Scholarly Failure, and the Political Dimension." *German History* 15.1, 1997, pp. 80–91.

Wein, Elizabeth. "The Art of the Possible." *The Horn Book Magazine* 85.2, 2009, pp. 163–67.

White, Hayden. *Tropics of Discourse: Essays in Cultural Criticism*. Johns Hopkins UP, 1978.

Wilder, Laura Ingalls. *Little House in the Big Woods*. 1932. HarperCollins, 1987.

——. *Little House on the Prairie*. 1935. HarperCollins, 1963.

Wilson, Kim. "'Are They Telling Us the Truth?' Constructing National Character in the Scholastic Press Historical Journal Series." *Children's Literature Association Quarterly* 32.2, 2007, 129–41.

Yolen, Jane. *The Devil's Arithmetic*. 1988. Puffin Modern Classics, 2004.

Zornado, Joseph. "A Poetics of History: Karen Cushman's Medieval World." *The Lion and the Unicorn* 21.2, 1997, pp. 251–66.

CHAPTER 8: NONFICTION—HISTORY, SCIENCE, LIFE WRITING

Arnold, Caroline. *A Warmer World: From Polar Bears to Butterflies, How Climate Change Affects Wildlife.* Illustrated by Jamie Hogan. Charlesbridge Publishing, 2012.

Balkwill, Frances R. "Writing Science Books for Children." *The American Association of Immunologists,* aai. org/Education/Teaching-Resources/Balkwill-Writing.

Berne, Jennifer. *Manfish: A Story of Jacques Cousteau.* Illustrated by Éric Puybaret. Chronicle, 2008.

Boutet de Monvel, Maurice. *The Story of Joan of Arc.* 1912. Dover, 2010.

Bruner, Jerome. *The Process of Education.* 1960. Harvard UP, 1977.

Buchanan, Andrea J., and Miriam Peskowitz. *The Daring Book for Girls.* HarperCollins, 2007.

Buckley, Arabella Burton. *The Fairy-Land of Science.* Appleton, 1885.

Child, Lydia Maria. *The Girl's Own Book.* Austin, 1833.

Clarke, William. *The Boy's Own Book: A Complete Encyclopedia of All the Diversions, Athletic, Scientific, and Recreative, of Boyhood and Youth.* Vizelly, 1828.

Cole, Joanna, and Bruce Degen. *The Magic School Bus: Lost in the Solar System.* Scholastic, 2010.

Cook, Peter. *You Wouldn't Want to Sail on the Mayflower! A Trip That Took Entirely Too Long.* Illustrated by Kevin Whelan. Scholastic, 2005.

Davetian, Benet. *Civility: A Cultural History.* U of Toronto P, 2009.

Davis, Rocío G. "Asian American Autobiography for Children: Critical Paradigms and Creative Practice." *The Lion and the Unicorn* 30, 2006, pp. 185–201.

DeLuca, Geraldine, and Roni Natov. "Who's Afraid of Science Books? An Interview with Seymour Simon." *The Lion and the Unicorn* 6, 1982, pp. 19–27.

Duke, Nell K., and V. Susan Bennett-Armistead. *Reading and Writing Informational Text in the Primary Grades: Research-Based Practices.* Scholastic, 2003.

Freedman, Russell. *Lincoln: A Photobiography.* Clarion, 1987.

Giaimo, Cara. "Puerto Rico's Parrot Population Is Slowly Recovering." *Atlas Obscura,* 10 April 2018, atlasobscura.com/articles/did-puerto-rico-parrots-survive-hurricane.

Harris, Robie H. *It's Perfectly Normal: Changing Bodies, Growing Up, Sex, and Sexual Health.* Illustrated by Michael Emberley. Rev. ed. Candlewick, 2009.

Holmes, Richard. *The Age of Wonder: How the Romantic Generation Discovered the Beauty and Terror of Science.* Pantheon, 2008.

Horning, Kathleen T. "Newbery and Caldecott Medal Books: Revised, Revamped, and Revitalized." *The Newbery & Caldecott Awards: A Guide to the Medal and Honor Books.* New York: American Library Association, 2009, pp. 11–18.

Kawano, Kenji. *Warriors: Navajo Code Talkers.* Northland Publishing Company, 1990.

Korman, Gordon. *Ungifted.* Balzer + Bray/ HarperCollins, 2012.

_____. "What Makes an Appealing and Readable Science Book?" *The Lion and the Unicorn* 6, 1982, pp. 5–9.

Macaulay, David. *Cathedral: The Story of Its Construction.* Houghton Mifflin, 1973.

Mann, Elizabeth. *Empire State Building: When New York Reached for the Skies.* Mikaya, 2006.

Mickenberg, Julia. "Civil Rights, History, and the Left: Inventing the Juvenile Black Biography." *Melus* 23.2, 2002, pp. 65–93.

Montgomery, Sy. *The Octopus Scientists: Exploring the Mind of a Mollusk.* Photographs by Keith Ellenbogen. Houghton Mifflin, 2015.

Morgan, Emily. *Next Time You See a Spiderweb.* National Science Teacher's Association, 2015.

National Science Teachers Association. *Publications and Products: Outstanding Science Trade Books for Students K–12: 2011 (Books Published in 2010)*, nsta.org/publications/ostb/ostb2010.aspx.

Nelson, Kadir, writer and illustrator. *We Are the Ship: The Story of Negro League Baseball*. Hyperion, 2008.

Norton, Donna. "Moral Stages of Children's Biographical Literature, 1800–1900s." *Vitae Scholasticae* 4.1, 1985, pp. 77–89.

Ostry, Elaine. "Magical Growth and Moral Lessons; or, How the Conduct Book Informed Victorian and Edwardian Children's Fantasy." *The Lion and the Unicorn* 27, 2003, pp. 27–56.

Raschka, Chris. *Arlene Sardine*. New York: Scholastic, 1998.

Raymo, Chet. "Dr. Seuss and Dr. Einstein: Children's Books and Scientific Imagination." *Of Sneetches and Whos and the Good Dr. Seuss: Essays on the Writings and Life of Theodor Geisel*, edited by Thomas Fensch. McFarland, 1997.

Segal, Elizabeth. "In Biography for Young Readers, Nothing Is Impossible." *The Lion and the Unicorn* 4.1, 1980, pp. 4–14.

Sheinkin, Steve. *Bomb: The Race to Build—and Steal—The World's Most Dangerous Weapon*. Roaring Book P, 2012.

Siegel, Siena Cherson. *To Dance: A Ballerina's Graphic Novel*. Artwork by Mark Siegel. Atheneum Books for Young Readers, 2006.

Silver, Donald. *One Small Square: Pond*. Illustrated by Patricia J. Wynne. Learning Triangle, 1994.

Smith, Sidonie, and Julia Watson. *Reading Autobiography: A Guide for Interpreting Life Narratives*. 2nd ed. U of Minnesota P, 2010.

Spinelli, Jerry. *Knots in My Yo-Yo String: The Autobiography of a Kid*. Knopf, 1998.

Stanley, Diane. *Joan of Arc*. HarperCollins, 1998.

Stott, Jon. "Architectural Structures and Social Values in the Nonfiction of David Macaulay." *Children's Literature Association Quarterly* 8.1, 1983, pp. 15–17.

Sutton, Roger. "An Interview with Russell Freedman." *The Horn Book Magazine* 78.6, 2002, pp. 695–704.

Vallone, Lynne. *Disciplines of Virtue: Girls' Culture in the Eighteenth and Nineteenth Centuries*. Yale UP, 1995.

"Welcome to the Robert F. Sibert Informational Book Medal Home Page!" *Association for Library Service to Children*. 2012, ala.org/alsc/awardsgrants/bookmedia/sibertmedal/sibertbout.

CHAPTER 9: FANTASY AND REALISM

Armitt, Lucie. *Fantasy Fiction: An Introduction*. Continuum, 2005.

Cart, Michael. *From Romance to Realism: Fifty Years of Growth and Change in Young Adult Literature*. HarperCollins, 1996.

Cawelti, John G. *The Six-Gun Mystique*, 2nd ed. Bowling Green State U Popular P, 1984.

Culler, Jonathan D. *Structuralist Poetics: Structuralism, Linguistics, and the Study of Literature*. 1975. Routledge Classics, 2002.

Davis, Michael. *Street Gang: The Complete History of Sesame Street*. Vintage, 2008.

Egoff, Sheila A. *Thursday's Child: Trends and Patterns in Contemporary Children's Literature*. American Library Association, 1981.

El-Mohtar, Amal. "'Shadowshaper' Paints a Vibrant Picture." *NPR Books*, 4 July 2015, npr.org/2015/07/04/418597069/shadowshaper-paints-a-vibrant-picture.

Ford, Ashley C. "Daniel José Older Creates Female Black Heroes to Make Fantasy More Real." *Guardian*, 29 June 2015.

Kuznets, Lois R. "'High Fantasy' in America: A Study of Lloyd Alexander, Ursula K. Le Guin, and Susan Cooper." *The Lion and the Unicorn* 9, 1985, pp. 19–35.

Latham, Don. "Empowering Adolescent Readers: Intertextuality in Three Novels by David Almond." *Children's Literature in Education* 39.2, 2008, pp. 213–26.

L'Engle, Madeleine. *A Wrinkle in Time*. 1962. Bantam, 1998.

Marcus, Leonard S. *Margaret Wise Brown: Awakened by the Moon*. Beacon, 1992.

Mendlesohn, Farah. *Rhetorics of Fantasy*. Wesleyan UP, 2008.

Mills, Sophie. "Pig in the Middle." *Children's Literature in Education* 31.2, 2000, pp. 107–24.

Natov, Roni. *The Poetics of Childhood*. Taylor, 2006.

Older, Daniel José. "Day 4: Daniel José Older," *The Brown Bookshelf: United in Story*, 4 February 2016, thebrownbookshelf.com/2016/02/04/day-4-daniel-jose-older.

———. *Shadowshaper*. Arthur A. Levine Books, 2015.

Rabkin, Eric S. *The Fantastic in Literature*. Princeton UP, 1976.

Reese, Debbie. "Daniel Jose Older's Shadowshaper." *American Indians in Children's Literature*. 23 April 2015, americanindiansinchildrensliterature.blogspot.com/2015/04/daniel-jose-olders-shadowshaper.html.

Roberts, Lewis. "Nightmares, Idylls, Mystery, and Hope: *Walk Two Moons* and the Artifice of Realism in Children's Fiction." *Children's Literature in Education*, 2008, pp. 121–34.

Rowell, Rainbow. *Carry On: The Rise and Fall of Simon Snow*. St. Martin's Griffin, 2015.

Sommers, Joseph Michael. "*Are You There, Reader? It's Me, Margaret*: A Reconsideration of Judy Blume's Prose as Sororal Dialogism." *Children's Literature Association Quarterly* 33.3, 2008, pp. 258–79.

Stork, Francisco X. *Marcelo in the Real World*. Scholastic, 2011.

Townsend, John Rowe. *Written for Children: An Outline of English Language Children's Literature*. HarperCollins, 1992.

Watt, Ian. *Rise of the Novel: Studies in Defoe, Richardson, and Fielding*. Penguin, 1957.

Western, Linda. "New Realism—A Second Look." *Wisconsin English Journal* 23.2, 1981, pp. 9–12.

CHAPTER 10: RACE, ETHNICITY, AND CULTURE

Alderson, Brian. *Ezra Jack Keats: Artist and Picture-Book Maker*. Pelican, 1994.

American Indian Library Association. "American Indian Youth Literature Award." *American Indian Library Association*, 14 March 2018, ailanet.org/activities/american-indian-youth-literature-award.

American Library Association. "Coretta Scott King Book Award Governance: Constitution." *American Library Association*. June 1998, ala.org/rt/sites/ala.org.rt/files/content/cskbookawards/docs/CSKBylawsADOPTED062516.pdf.

Aronson, Marc. "Slippery Slopes and Proliferating Prizes." *The Horn Book Magazine* 77.3, 2001, pp. 272–78.

Asian/Pacific Librarians Association. "Literature Awards Guidelines & Nominations." *Asian/Pacific American Librarians Association*, apalaweb.org/awards/literature-awards.

Bader, Barbara. "How the Little House Gave Ground: The Beginnings of Multiculturalism in a New, Black Children's Literature." *The Horn Book Magazine* 78.6, 2002, pp. 657–73.

Banks, Lynne Reid. *The Indian in the Cupboard*. 1980. Yearling, 2010.

Bishop, Rudine Sims. "Reflections on the Development of African American Children's Literature." *Journal of Children's Literature* 38.2, Fall 2012, pp. 5–13.

Capshaw, Katharine. "Ethnic Studies and Children's Literature: A Conversation between Fields." *The Lion and the Unicorn* 38.3, September 2014, pp. 237–57.

_____, and Anna Mae Duane. *Who Writes for Black Children?: African American Children's Literature before 1900.* U of Minnesota P, 2017.

Cart, Michael. *From Romance to Realism: 50 Years of Growth and Change in Young Adult Literature.* Harper-Collins, 1996.

Creech, Sharon. *Walk Two Moons.* Harper Trophy, 1994.

Cummings, Pat. "The Man Who Became Keats." *School Library Journal* 47.5, 2001, pp. 46–49.

Cummins, June. "Leaning Left: Progressive Politics in Sydney Taylor's All-of-a-Kind Family Series." *Children's Literature Association Quarterly* 30.4, 2005, pp. 386–408.

De Manuel, Dolores, and Rocío G. Davis. "Editors' Introduction: Critical Perspectives on Asian American Children's Literature." *The Lion and the Unicorn* 30.2, 2006, pp. v–xv.

Dixon, Bob. *Catching Them Young: Sex, Race, and Class in Children's Fiction.* Pluto, 1977.

Dudek, Debra. "Multiculturalism." *Keywords for Children's Literature,* edited by Philip Nel and Lissa Paul. New York UP, 2011, pp. 155–60.

Hall, Stuart. "New Ethnicities." *Stuart Hall: Critical Dialogues in Cultural Studies,* edited by David Morley and Kuan-Hsing Chen. Routledge, 1996.

Harris, Violet J. "African American Children's Literature: The First One Hundred Years." *The Journal of Negro Education* 59.4, 1990, pp. 540–55.

Holloway, Lynette. "Unswayed by Debate on Children's Book." *New York Times,* 10 December 1998.

Keats, Ezra Jack. "From *Collage: The Memoirs of Ezra Jack Keats.*" *The Lion and the Unicorn* 13.2, 1989, pp. 58–74.

_____. *The Snowy Day.* 1962. Puffin, 1976.

_____. *The Snowy Day.* 50th anniversary ed. Viking, 2011.

Kidd, Kenneth. "Prizing Children's Literature: The Case of Newbery Gold." *Children's Literature* 35, 2007, pp. 166–90.

Kutzer, M. Daphne. *Empire's Children: Empire and Imperialism in Classic British Children's Books.* Routledge, 2000.

Larrick, Nancy. "The All-White World of Children's Books." *Saturday Review of Literature* 48.37, 1965, pp. 63–65, 84–85.

Lester, Julius. "Morality and *Adventures of Huckleberry Finn.*" *Satire or Evasion?: Black Perspectives on* Huckleberry Finn, edited by James S. Leonard, Thomas A. Tenney, and Thadious M. Davis. Duke UP, 1992, pp. 199–207.

_____. *Sam and the Tigers: A New Telling of "Little Black Sambo."* Illustrated by Jerry Pinkney. Dial, 1996.

_____. *The Tales of Uncle Remus: The Adventures of Brer Rabbit.* Dial, 1987.

MacCann, Donnarae. *White Supremacy in Children's Literature: Characterizations of African Americans, 1830–1900.* Routledge, 1998.

Martin, Michelle. *Brown Gold: Milestones of African-American Children's Picture Books, 1845–2002.* Routledge, 2004.

McDermott, Gerald. *Arrow to the Sun: A Pueblo Indian Tale.* Puffin, 1977.

Mikkelsen, Nina. "Insiders, Outsiders, and the Question of Authenticity: Who Shall Write for African American Children?" *Children's and Young-Adult Literature. Special issue of African American Review* 32.1, 1998, pp. 33–49.

"Mission Statement." *We Need Diverse Books,* diversebooks.org/about-wndb.

Moore, Opal. "Othello, Othello, Where Art Thou?" *The Lion and the Unicorn* 25.3, 2001, pp. 375–90.

_____, and Donnarae MacCann. "The Uncle Remus Travesty." *Children's Literature Association Quarterly* 11.2, 1986, pp. 96–99.

Murray, Gail Schmunk. *American Children's Literature and the Construction of Childhood.* Twayne, 1998.

Nieto, Sonia. *Affirming Diversity: The Sociopolitical Context of Multicultural Education.* 3rd ed., Longman, 2000.

Nodelman, Perry, and Mavis Reimer. *The Pleasures of Children's Literature.* 3rd ed., Allyn and Bacon, 2002.

Pinkney, Andrea Davis. "Awards that Stand on Solid Ground." *The Horn Book Magazine* 77.5, 2001, pp. 535–39.

"Publishing Statistics on Children's Books about People of Color and First/Native Nations and by People of Color and First/Native Nations Authors and Illustrators." Cooperative Children's Books Center, ccbc. education.wisc.edu/books/pcstats.asp.

Reese, Debbie. "Rev. of *Arrow to the Sun*, by Gerald McDermott." *A Broken Flute: The Native Experience in Books for Children*, edited by Doris Seale and Beverly Slapin. AltaMira, 2005, pp. 342.

Reese, Liz. "Liz's Story." *A Broken Flute: The Native Experience in Books for Children*, edited by Doris Seale and Beverly Slapin. AltaMira, 2005, pp. 14–15.

Reimer, Mavis. "Making Princesses, Remaking *A Little Princess.*" *Voices of the Other: Children's Literature and the Postcolonial Context*, edited by Roderick McGillis. Garland, 2000, pp. 111–14.

Seale, Doris. "Introduction." *A Broken Flute: The Native Experience in Books for Children*, edited by Doris Seale and Beverly Slapin. AltaMira, 2005, pp. 4–5.

Smith, Henrietta M., editor. *The Coretta Scott King Awards Book: From Vision to Reality.* American Library Association, 1994.

Smith, Katharine Capshaw. *Children's Literature of the Harlem Renaissance.* Indiana UP, 2004.

_____. "Introduction: The Landscape of Ethnic American Children's Literature." *MELUS* 27.2, 2002, pp. 3–8.

Sollors, Werner. "Theory of American Ethnicity, or: '? S Ethnic?/Ti and American/Ti, De or United (W) States S S1 and Theor?'" *American Quarterly* 33.3, 1981, pp. 257–83.

Stott, Jon C. "Joseph Campbell on the Second Mesa: Structure and Meaning in Arrow to the Sun." *Children's Literature Association Quarterly* 11.3, 1986, pp. 132–34.

Taylor, Mildred D. *Roll of Thunder, Hear My Cry.* 1976. Puffin, 1997.

Yolen, Jane. "An Empress of Thieves." *The Horn Book Magazine* 70.6, 1994, pp. 702–05.

CHAPTER 11: GENDERS AND SEXUALITIES

Abate, Michelle. *Tomboys: A Literary and Cultural History.* Temple UP, 2008.

Alcott, Louisa May. *Little Women.* 1868. Signet Classics, 1996.

American Library Association. "Number of Challenges by Year, Reason, Initiator, and Institution (1990–1999)." *American Library Association*, ala.org/advocacy/bbooks/frequentlychallengedbooks/ statistics/1990-99#reasons1990.

American Library Association. "Number of Challenges by Year, Reason, Initiator, and Institution (2000–2009)." *American Library Association*, ala.org/advocacy/bbooks/frequentlychallengedbooks/ statistics/2000-09.

American Library Association. "Top Ten Most Challenged Book Lists." *American Library Association*, 2017, ala.org/advocacy/bbooks/frequentlychallengedbooks/top10.

Balingit, Moriah. "Education Department No Longer Investigating Transgender Bathroom Complaints." *Washington Post*, 12 February 2018.

Bamford, T.W. *Rise of the Public Schools: A Study of Boys' Public Boarding Schools in England and Wales from 1837 to the Present Day*. Nelson, 1967.

Brink, Carol Ryrie. *Baby Island*. 1937. Aladdin, 2003.

Burnett, Frances Hodgson. *Little Lord Fauntleroy*. 1886. Aladdin, 2004.

_____. *A Little Princess*. 1905. HarperTrophy, 1999.

Butler, Judith. *Gender Trouble: Feminism and the Subversion of Identity*. Routledge, 2006.

Carpan, Carolyn. *Sisters, Schoolgirls, and Sleuths: Girls' Series Books in America*. Scarecrow, 2009.

Cart, Michael, and Christine A. Jenkins. *The Heart Has Its Reasons: Young Adult Literature with Gay/Lesbian/Queer Content, 1969–2004*. Scarecrow, 2006.

Coolidge, Susan. *What Katy Did*. 1872. Dover, 2006.

Crisp, Thomas. "It's Not the Book, It's Not the Author, It's the Award: The Lambda Literary Award and the Case for Strategic Essentialism." *Children's Literature in Education* 42.2, 2011, pp. 91–104.

Cummins, June. "Romancing the Plot: The Real Beast of Disney's *Beauty and the Beast*." *Children's Literature Association Quarterly* 20.1, 1995, pp. 23–28.

Daniel, Carolyn. *Voracious Children: Who Eats Whom in Children's Literature*. Routledge, 2006.

Davidoff, Leonore, and Catherine Hall. *Family Fortunes: Men and Women of the English Middle Class, 1780–1850*. U of Chicago P, 1987.

Davis, Julie Hirschfeld, and Matt Apuzzo. "U.S. Directs Public Schools to Allow Transgender Access to Restrooms." *New York Times*, 12 May 2016.

Ellis, Havelock. *Sexual Inversion*. 1897. Vol. 2 of *Studies in the Psychology of Sex*. UP of the Pacific, 2001.

Freud, Sigmund. *Three Essays on the Theory of Sexuality*. 1905. Translated by James Strachey. Basic, 2000.

Gillis, John R. *Youth and History: Tradition and Change in European Age Relations, 1770–Present*. Academic, 1974.

Grahame, Kenneth. *The Wind in the Willows*. 1908. Penguin Classics, 2005.

Hughes, Thomas. *Tom Brown's Schooldays*. 1857. Oxford World Classics, 1999.

Hunt, Peter. *An Introduction to Children's Literature*. Oxford, 1994.

Kidd, Kenneth. "Introduction: Lesbian/Gay Literature for Children and Young Adults." *Children's Literature Association Quarterly* 23.3, 1998, pp. 114–19.

Kincaid, James R. "Producing Erotic Children." *Curiouser: On the Queerness of Children*, edited by Steven Bruhm and Natasha Hurley. U of Minnesota P, 2004.

Lo, Malinda. "2014 LGBT YA by the Numbers." 10 December 2014, malindalo.com/blog/2014/12/2014-lgbt-ya-by-the-numbers.

Mack, Edward C. *Public Schools and British Opinion since 1860*. Columbia UP, 1941.

Maglaty, Jeanne. "When Did Girls Start Wearing Pink?" Smithsonian.com, 8 April 2011.

Mead, Margaret. *Male and Female*. 1949. Harper, 2001.

Mitchell, Sally. *The New Girl: Girls' Culture in England, 1880–1915*. Columbia UP, 1995.

Padilla, Branden. "Target's Decision to Gender Neutralize Causes Controversy." *Los Angeles Times*, 25 September 2015.

Paterson, Katherine. *Bridge to Terabithia*. HarperCollins, 1987.

Patmore, Coventry. *The Angel in the House*. John W. Parker and Son, 1854.

Pattee, Amy. "Commodities in Literature, Literature as Commodity: A Close Look at the 'Gossip Girl' Series." *Children's Literature Association Quarterly* 31.2, 2006, pp. 154–75.

Porter, Eleanor. *Pollyanna*. 1913. Aladdin, 2002.

Quigley, Isabel. *The Heirs of Tom Brown: The English School Story*. Chatto, 1982.

Reed, John. "The Public Schools in Victorian Literature." *Nineteenth-Century Fiction* 29, 1974, pp. 58–76.

Rubin, Gayle. "The Traffic in Women: Notes on the 'Political Economy' of Sex." *The Second Wave: A Reader in Feminist Theory*, edited by Linda Nicholson. Routledge, 1997, pp. 27–62.

Sedgwick, Eve Kosofsky. *Between Men: English Literature and Male Homosocial Desire*. Columbia UP, 1985.

_____. *Epistemology of the Closet*. U of California P, 1990.

Sims, Sue. Introduction. *The Encyclopedia of Girls' School Stories*, edited by Sue Sims, Hilary Clare, Rosemary Auchmuty, and Joy Wotton. Ashgate, 2000, pp. 1–18.

Singh, Rashna B. *Goodly Is Our Heritage: Children's Literature, Empire, and the Certitude of Character*. Scarecrow, 2004.

Stevenson, Robert Louis. "Appendix 1: 'My First Book.'" *Treasure Island*. Oxford World Classics, 2011, pp. 185–92.

Wannamaker, Annette. *Boys in Children's Literature and Popular Culture: Masculinity, Abjection, and the Fictional Child*. Routledge, 2009.

CHAPTER 12: CENSORSHIP AND SELECTION

American Library Association. "Intellectual Freedom and Censorship Q & A." *American Library Association*. 2011, ala.org/advocacy/intfreedom/censorship/faq.

American Library Association Office for Intellectual Freedom, *Intellectual Freedom Manual, Eighth Edition*, American Library Association, 2010.

Asheim, Lester. "Not Censorship But Selection." *Wilson Library Bulletin* 28, 1953, pp. 63–67.

Baker, Vicky. "Battle of the Bans: US author Judy Blume Interviewed about Trigger Warnings, Book Bannings and Children's Literature Today." *Index on Censorship*, September 2015, pp. 44, 64–66.

Behr, Kate. "'Same-as-Difference': Narrative Transformation and Intersecting Cultures in *Harry Potter*." *Journal of Narrative Theory* 35.1, 2005, pp. 112–37.

Blume, Judy. "Is Harry Potter Evil?" *New York Times*, 22 October 1999, nytimes.com/1999/10/22/opinion/is-harry-potter-evil.html.

_____, editor. *Places I Never Meant to Be: Original Stories by Censored Writers*. Simon and Schuster, 1999.

Bosmajian, Hamida. "Children's Literature and Censorship." *ParaDoxa* 2.3–4, 1996, pp. 313–18.

"Canadian Charter of Rights and Freedoms." *Department of Justice, Canada*, 29 March 1982, laws-lois.justice.gc.ca/eng/Const/page-15.html.

Chung, Sandy. "Request to Ban 'Two Boys Kissing' from Virginia High School Library Denied." *School Library Journal*, 29 April 2014.

Cockrell, Amanda. "Harry Potter and the Witch Hunters: A Social Context for the Attacks on *Harry Potter*." *Journal of American Culture* 29.1, 2006, pp. 24–30.

Cortese, Anthony. *Opposing Hate Speech*. Praeger, 2006.

DeMitchell, Todd A., and John J. Carney. "Harry Potter and the Public School Library." *Phi Delta Kappan* 87.2, 2005, pp. 159–65.

Glanzer, Perry L. "Harry Potter's Provocative Moral World: Is There a Place for Good and Evil in Moral Education?" *Phi Delta Kappan* 89.7, 2008, pp. 525–28.

Gribben, Alan. Introduction. *Mark Twain's* Adventures of Tom Sawyer *and* Huckleberry Finn: *The New-South Edition*, by Mark Twain, edited by Alan Gribben. NewSouth, 2011, pp. 7–28.

Gust, Onni. "I use trigger warnings—but I'm not mollycoddling my students." *Guardian*, 14 June 2016.

Heins, Marjorie. *Not in Front of the Children: "Indecency," Censorship, and the Innocence of Youth*. Rutgers UP, 2007.

Hinds, Andy. "Goodnight Moon: The Nauseating Landscape of Childhood Anxiety." *Beta Dad*, 11 April 2011, betadadblog.com/goodnight-moon-book.

Hirsch, Tim. "Banned by Neglect: *Tom Sawyer*, Teaching the Conflicts." *Censored Books II: Critical Viewpoints, 1985–2000*, edited by Nicholas J. Karolides. Scarecrow, 2002, pp. 1–9.

Howard, Douglas L. "Silencing Huck Finn." *Chronicle of Higher Education*, 2 August 2004, chronicle.com/article/Silencing-Huck-Finn/44576.

Jansen, Sue Curry. *Censorship: The Knot that Binds Power and Knowledge*. Oxford UP, 1991.

Jenkins, Christine. "International Harmony: Threat or Menace? U.S. Youth Services Librarians and Cold War Censorship, 1946–1955." *Libraries and Culture* 36.1, 2001, pp. 116–30.

Kearns, Paul. "Public Morality Laws and the Creation and Appreciation of Art: The Postmodern Western Experience." *Legal Convergence in the Enlarged Europe of the New Millennium*, edited by Paul L.C. Torremans. Kluwer, 2001, pp. 143–60.

Kidd, Kenneth. "'Not Censorship but Selection': Censorship and/as Prizing." *Children's Literature in Education* 40, 2009, pp. 197–216.

Kohl, Herbert. *Should We Burn Babar? Essays on Children's Literature and the Power of Stories*. Introduction by Jack Zipes. New, 1995.

Krug, Judith. "Harry Potter and the Censor's Flames." Quoted in Julie Clawson, "Banned Books Week," *One Hand Clapping*, 27 September 2009, julieclawson.com/2007/09/29/banned-books-week.

Kushner, Tony. *The Art of Maurice Sendak: 1980 to the Present*. Abrams, 2003.

Maxwell, Bill. "It's Wrong to Change 'Huck Finn.'" *Times Herald*, 17 January 2011, timesherald.com/article/JR/20110117/OPINION/301179969.

McClure, Amy. "Censorship." *Children's Literature Association Quarterly* 8.1, 1983, pp. 22–25.

Mickenberg, Julia L. *Learning from the Left: Children's Literature, the Cold War, and Radical Politics in the United States*. Oxford UP, 2006.

"Modern Life Leads to More Depression among Children." *Daily Telegraph* (London), 12 September 2006.

Moore, Lorrie. "Send Huck Finn to College." *New York Times*, 15 January 2011.

Pitts, Leonard, Jr. "Don't Change a Word of *Huck Finn*." *Columbus Dispatch*, 9 January 2011.

Postman, Neil. *The Disappearance of Childhood*. Vintage, 1994.

Prose, Francine. "Why Is 'Slave' Less Offensive?" *New York Times*, 24 June 2011.

Ravitch, Diane. "Thin Gruel: How the Language Police Drain the Life and Content from Our Texts." *American Educator* 27.2, 2003, pp. 6–19.

Rowling, J.K. *The Tales of Beedle the Bard: Translated from the Original Runes by Hermione Granger: Commentary by Albus Dumbledore: Introduction, Notes and Illustrations by J.K. Rowling*. Children's High Level Group, 2008.

Watkins, Boyce. "Cutting N-word from Twain Is Not Censorship." *CNN Opinion*, 6 January 2011, cnn.com/2011/OPINION/01/06/watkins.twain.nword/index.html.

West, Mark I. "Teaching Banned Books." *Teaching Children's Literature: Issues, Pedagogy, Resources*, edited by Glenn Edward Sadler. MLA, 1992, pp. 51–58.

——, editor. *Trust Your Children: Voices Against Censorship in Children's Literature*, 2nd ed. Neal-Schuman, 1997.

White, Elon James. "The N-word Belongs in 'Huckleberry Finn.'" *Salon*, 4 January 2011, salon.com/2011/01/04/huck_finn_n_word.

CHAPTER 13: CHILDREN'S LITERATURE AND POPULAR CULTURE

Adams, William Davenport. *A Dictionary of the Drama: A Guide to the Plays, Playwrights, Players, and Playhouses of the United Kingdom and America, from the Earliest Times to the Present.* Chatto & Windus, 1904.

Adorno, Theodor, and Max Horkheimer. *Dialectic of Enlightenment: Philosophical Fragments.* 1947. Edited by Gunzelin Schmid Noerr, translated by Edmund Jephcott. Stanford UP, 2002.

Bailey, Peter A. "Reports on Black Theatre: New York City." *Black World* 25.6, April 1976, pp. 54–61.

Barthes, Roland. *Mythologies.* Translated by Annette Lavers. Farrar, Straus and Giroux, 1972.

Bedard, Roger L. "Sara, Jack, Ellie: Three Generation of Characters." *Children's Literature Association Quarterly* 9.3, Fall 1984, pp. 103–04.

Benjamin, Walter. "Art in the Age of Mechanical Reproduction." *Illuminations: Essays and Reflections.* 1968. Harcourt, Brace, & World, 2007.

Boone, Josh, director. *The Fault in Our Stars.* Fox 2000 Pictures, 2014.

Brecht, Bertolt. *On Theatre: The Development of an Aesthetic.* 1957. Edited and translated by John Willett. Hill and Wang, 1992.

Brittain, Marcus, and Timothy Clark, editors. "Introduction." *Archeology and the Media.* Left Coast P, 2007, pp. 11–66.

Butler, Judith. "Imitation and Gender Insubordination." *The Lesbian and Gay Studies Reader*, edited by Henry Abelove, Michèle Aina Barale, and David M. Halperin. Routledge, 1993, pp. 307–20.

Cassidy, Julie A.S. "Popular." *Keywords for Children's Literature*, edited by Philip Nel and Lissa Paul. Routledge, 2011.

Cawelti, John G. *The Six-Gun Mystique.* 2nd ed. Bowling Green State U Popular P, 1984.

"Culture." *Oxford English Dictionary*, en.oxforddictionaries.com/definition/culture.

During, Simon. "Introduction." *The Cultural Studies Reader*, edited by Simon During. Routledge, 1993, pp. 1–25.

Dunn, Samantha. *Fandom and Fiction: Adolescent Literature and Online Communities.* MA Thesis. Iowa State University, 2016, lib.dr.iastate.edu/etd/15158.

Edgerton, Gary. *The Columbia History of American Television.* Columbia UP, 2007.

"Fidelity." *Oxford English Dictionary*, en.oxforddictionaries.com/definition/fidelity.

Fiske, John. *Understanding Popular Culture, Second Edition.* Routledge, 2010.

Fleming, Victor, director. *The Wizard of Oz.* MGM, 1939.

Frus, Phyllis, and Christy Williams. "Introduction: Making the Case for Transformation." *Beyond Adaptation: Essays on Radical Transformations of Original Works*, edited by Phyllis Frus and Christy Williams. McFarland & Company, 2010.

Gerzina, Gretchen. *Frances Hodgson Burnett: The Unexpected Life of the Author of The Secret Garden.* Rutgers UP, 2004.

Green, John. *The Fault in Our Stars.* Dutton Books, 2012.

Gubar, Marah. *Artful Dodgers: Reconceiving the Golden Age of Children's Literature.* Oxford UP, 2009.

Haviland, Virginia, and Margaret N. Coughlan. *Yankee Doodle's Literary Sampler of Prose, Poetry, and Pictures: Being an Anthology of Diverse Works Published for the Edification and/or Entertainment of Young Readers in American Before 1900.* Thomas Y. Crowell, 1974.

Hood, Robert. "Scribblings: A Playground for Fear: Horror Fiction for Children." *Robert Hood*, 1997, roberthood.net/scribbls/children.htm.

Hutcheon, Linda. *A Theory of Adaptation.* Routledge, 2006.

Jarvis, Shawn. "Drama and Fairy Tales." *The Oxford Companion to Fairy Tales: The Western Fairy Tale Tradition from Medieval to Modern*, edited by Jack Zipes. Oxford UP, 2000, pp. 137–41.

Jenkins, Henry. "*Star Trek* Rerun, Reread, Rewritten: Fan Writings as Textual Poaching." *Critical Studies in Mass Communication* 5.2, June 1988, pp. 85–107.

Kutzer, M. Daphne. "'I Won't Grow Up—Yet': Teen Formula Romance." *Children's Literature Association Quarterly* 11.2, 1986, pp. 90–95.

Lamb, Charles, and Mary Lamb. *Tales from Shakespeare*. 1807. Wordsworth Limited Editions, 1994.

Lefebvre, Benjamin. "Introduction: Reconsidering Textual Transformations in Children's Literature." *Textual Transformations in Children's Literature: Adaptations, Translations, Reconsiderations*, edited by Benjamin Lefebvre. Routledge, 2013.

Lurie, Alison. *Don't Tell the Grown-Ups: The Subversive Power of Children's Literature*. Back Bay Books, 1998.

McClintock, Michael. "High Tech and High Sorcery: Some Discriminations between Science Fiction and Fantasy." *Intersections: Fantasy and Science Fiction*, edited by George Slusser and Eric Rabkin. Southern Illinois UP, 1987, pp. 26–35.

McLane, Maureen N. "Dating Orality, Thinking Balladry: Of Milkmaids and Minstrels in 1771." *The Eighteenth Century* 47.2, Summer 2006, pp. 131–49.

Monaco, James. *How to Read a Film: The Art, Technology, Language, History, and Theory of Film and Media, Revised Edition*. Oxford UP, 1981.

Morrow, Robert M. *Sesame Street and the Reform of Children's Television*. Johns Hopkins UP, 2006.

Mulvey, Laura. "Visual Pleasure and Narrative Cinema." *Film Theory and Criticism: Introductory Readings*, edited by Leo Braudy and Marshall Cohen. Oxford UP, 1999, pp. 833–44.

Penley, Constance. "Brownian Motion: Women, Tactics, and Technology." *Technoculture*, edited by Constance Penley and Andrew Ross. U of Minnesota P, 1991, pp. 135–62.

Ratcliffe, Rebecca. "JK Rowling Tells of Anger at Attacks on Casting of Black Hermione." *Guardian*, 5 June 2016.

Richards, Patricia O., Debra H. Thatcher, Michelle Shreeves, Peggy Timmons, and Sallie Barker. "Don't Let a Good Scare Frighten You: Choosing and Using Quality Chillers to Promote Reading." *The Reading Teacher* 52.8, 1999, pp. 830–40.

Rose, Jacqueline. *The Case of Peter Pan; or, The Impossibility of Children's Fiction*. U of Pennsylvania P, 1993.

Sargent, Lyman Tower. Introduction. *British and American Utopian Literature, 1516–1985: An Annotated, Chronological Bibliography*. New Garland, 1988, pp. xi–xiv.

Schwartz, Alvin. *Scary Stories to Tell in the Dark*. HarperCollins, 2010.

Sleator, William. "What Is It about Science Fiction?" *Only Connect: Readings on Children's Literature*. 3rd ed., edited by Sheila Egoff, Gordon Stubbs, Ralph Ashley, and Wendy Sutton. Oxford UP, 1996, pp. 206–13.

Sobol, Donald J. *Encyclopedia Brown and the Case of the Secret Pitch*. 1965. Puffin, 2007.

Stahl, J.D. "Media Adaptations of Children's Literature: The Brave New Genre." *Children's Literature Association Quarterly* 7.3, 1982, pp. 5–9.

Sterling, Christopher H., and John Michael Kittross. *Stay Tuned: A History of American Broadcasting, Third Edition*. Taylor & Francis, 2009.

Stowe, Harriet Beecher. *Pictures and Stories from Uncle Tom's Cabin*. John P. Jewett & Co., 1853.

Syme, Rachel. "The Fault in Our Stars: Love in a Time of Cancer." *NPR Books*, 17 January 2012, npr.org/2012/01/17/145343351/the-fault-in-our-stars-love-in-a-time-of-cancer.

Talbot, Margaret, "The Teen Whisperer," *New Yorker*, 9 and 16 June 2014, newyorker.com/magazine/2014/06/09/the-teen-whisperer.

Tosenberger, C. "Mature Poets Steal: Children's Literature and the Unpublishability of Fanfiction." *Children's Literature Association Quarterly* 39.1, 2014, pp. 4–27.

Tran, Diep. "The Top 10 Most Produced Plays of the 2016–17 Season." *American Theatre*, 21 September 2016, americantheatre.org/2016/09/21/the-top-10-most-produced-plays-of-the-2016-17-season.

Varty, Ann. *Children and Theatre in Victorian Britain*. Palgrave Macmillan, 2008.

Williams, Raymond. *Keywords: A Vocabulary of Culture and Society, Revised Edition*. Oxford UP, 1985.

Wilson, Jacqueline. "Children's Books: My Inspiration." *Guardian*, 31 July 2015.

Wojcik-Andrews, Ian. *Children's Films: History, Ideology, Pedagogy, Theory*. Garland, 2000.

Wolf, Matt. "The Fault in Our Stars: Slickly Produced Weepie Sells Truth Short." *The Arts Desk*, 18 June 2014, theartsdesk.com/film/fault-our-stars.

CHILDREN'S BOOK AWARDS

As we discuss in Chapter 12, there are many different types of awards presented around the world each year to recognize notable works of children's literature. We do not attempt to present exhaustive lists of those awards or prizewinners here since they are readily available online, but we include lists of the Caldecott Medal and Newbery Award winners from the United States since 1970 to provide our readers with a quick reference. First awarded in 1985, the Phoenix Award is presented by the Children's Literature Association; it recognizes a children's book of high literary merit 20 years after its original publication. The Phoenix Picture Book Award was first presented in 2013. Both lists are provided in full.

THE CALDECOTT MEDAL (SINCE 1970)

The Caldecott Medal is named for Randolph Caldecott, the British illustrator. Presented annually since 1938 by the American Library Association, the award recognizes the most distinguished picturebook published in the United States.

1970 *Sylvester and the Magic Pebble* by William Steig (Windmill Books)

1971 *A Story A Story*, retold and illustrated by Gail E. Haley (Atheneum)

1972 *One Fine Day*, retold and illustrated by Nonny Hogrogian (Macmillan)

1973 *The Funny Little Woman*, illustrated by Blair Lent; retold by Arlene Mosel (Dutton)

1974 *Duffy and the Devil*, illustrated by Margot Zemach; retold by Harve Zemach (Farrar)

1975 *Arrow to the Sun* by Gerald McDermott (Viking)

1976 *Why Mosquitoes Buzz in People's Ears*, illustrated by Leo and Diane Dillon; retold by Verna Aardema (Dial)

1977 *Ashanti to Zulu: African Traditions*, illustrated by Leo and Diane Dillon; text by Margaret Musgrove (Dial)

1978 *Noah's Ark* by Peter Spier (Doubleday)

1979 *The Girl Who Loved Wild Horses* by Paul Goble (Bradbury)

1980 *Ox-Cart Man*, illustrated by Barbara Cooney; text by Donald Hall (Viking)

1981 *Fables* by Arnold Lobel (Harper)

1982 *Jumanji* by Chris Van Allsburg (Houghton Mifflin)

1983 *Shadow*, translated and illustrated by Marcia Brown; original text in French by Blaise Cendrars (Scribner)

1984 *The Glorious Flight: Across the Channel with Louis Bleriot* by Alice and Martin Provensen (Viking)

1985 *Saint George and the Dragon*, illustrated by Trina Schart Hyman; retold by Margaret Hodges (Little, Brown)

1986 *The Polar Express* by Chris Van Allsburg (Houghton Mifflin)

1987 *Hey, Al*, illustrated by Richard Egielski; text by Arthur Yorinks (Farrar)

1988 *Owl Moon*, illustrated by John Schoenherr; text by Jane Yolen (Philomel)

1989 *Song and Dance Man*, illustrated by Stephen Gammell; text by Karen Ackerman (Knopf)

1990 *Lon Po Po: A Red-Riding Hood Story from China* by Ed Young (Philomel)

1991 *Black and White* by David Macaulay (Houghton Mifflin)

1992 *Tuesday* by David Wiesner (Clarion Books)

1993 *Mirette on the High Wire* by Emily Arnold McCully (Putnam)

1994 *Grandfather's Journey* by Allen Say (Houghton Mifflin)

1995 *Smoky Night*, illustrated by David Diaz; text by Eve Bunting (Harcourt)

1996 *Officer Buckle and Gloria* by Peggy Rathmann (Putnam)

1997 *Golem* by David Wisniewski (Clarion)

1998 *Rapunzel* by Paul O. Zelinsky (Dutton)

1999 *Snowflake Bentley*, illustrated by Mary Azarian; text by Jacqueline Briggs Martin (Houghton Mifflin)

2000 *Joseph Had a Little Overcoat* by Simms Taback (Viking)

2001 *So You Want to Be President?*, illustrated by David Small; text by Judith St. George (Philomel)

2002 *The Three Pigs* by David Wiesner (Clarion/Houghton Mifflin)

2003 *My Friend Rabbit* by Eric Rohmann (Roaring Brook Press/Millbrook Press)

2004 *The Man Who Walked Between the Towers* by Mordicai Gerstein (Roaring Brook Press/Millbrook Press)

2005 *Kitten's First Full Moon* by Kevin Henkes (Greenwillow Books/HarperCollins)

2006 *The Hello, Goodbye Window*, illustrated by Chris Raschka; text by Norton Juster (Michael di Capua Books/Hyperion Books for Children)

2007 *Flotsam* by David Wiesner (Clarion)

2008 *The Invention of Hugo Cabret* by Brian Selznick (Scholastic Press, an imprint of Scholastic)

2009 *The House in the Night*, illustrated by Beth Krommes; text by Susan Marie Swanson (Houghton Mifflin)

2010 *The Lion and the Mouse* by Jerry Pinkney (Little, Brown)

2011 *A Sick Day for Amos McGee*, illustrated by Erin E. Stead; text by Philip C. Stead (Roaring Brook Press/Macmillan)

2012 *A Ball for Daisy* by Chris Raschka (Schwartz & Wade Books/Random House, Inc.)

2013 *This Is Not My Hat* by Jon Klassen (Candlewick Press)

2014 *Locomotive* by Brian Floca (Atheneum/Simon & Schuster)

2015 *The Adventures of Beekle: The Unimaginary Friend* by Dan Santat (Little, Brown)

2016 *Finding Winnie: The True Story of the World's Most Famous Bear*, illustrated by Sophie Blackall; text by Lindsay Mattick (Little, Brown)

2017 *Radiant Child: The Story of Young Artist Jean-Michel Basquiat* by Javaka Steptoe (Little, Brown)

2018 *Wolf in the Snow* by Matthew Cordell (Feiwel and Friends/Macmillan)

THE NEWBERY MEDAL (SINCE 1970)

The Newbery Medal is named for British publisher John Newbery. Given annually since 1922, the award is presented by the American Library Association for the most distinguished work of children's literature published in the United States.

1970 *Sounder* by William H. Armstrong (Harper)

1971 *Summer of the Swans* by Betsy Byars (Viking)

1972 *Mrs. Frisby and the Rats of NIMH* by Robert C. O'Brien (Atheneum)

1973 *Julie of the Wolves* by Jean Craighead George (Harper)

1974 *The Slave Dancer* by Paula Fox (Bradbury)

1975 *M.C. Higgins, the Great* by Virginia Hamilton (Macmillan)

1976 *The Grey King* by Susan Cooper (McElderry/Atheneum)

1977 *Roll of Thunder, Hear My Cry* by Mildred D. Taylor (Dial)

1978 *Bridge to Terabithia* by Katherine Paterson (Crowell)

1979 *The Westing Game* by Ellen Raskin (Dutton)

1980 *A Gathering of Days: A New England Girl's Journal, 1830–1832* by Joan W. Blos (Scribner)

1981 *Jacob Have I Loved* by Katherine Paterson (Crowell)

1982 *A Visit to William Blake's Inn: Poems for Innocent and Experienced Travelers* by Nancy Willard (Harcourt)

1983 *Dicey's Song* by Cynthia Voigt (Atheneum)

1984 *Dear Mr. Henshaw* by Beverly Cleary (Morrow)

1985 *The Hero and the Crown* by Robin McKinley (Greenwillow)

1986 *Sarah, Plain and Tall* by Patricia MacLachlan (Harper)

1987 *The Whipping Boy* by Sid Fleischman (Greenwillow)

1988 *Lincoln: A Photobiography* by Russell Freedman (Clarion)

1989 *Joyful Noise: Poems for Two Voices* by Paul Fleischman (Harper)

1990 *Number the Stars* by Lois Lowry (Houghton Mifflin)

1991 *Maniac Magee* by Jerry Spinelli (Little, Brown)

1992 *Shiloh* by Phyllis Reynolds Naylor (Atheneum)

1993 *Missing May* by Cynthia Rylant (Jackson/Orchard)

1994 *The Giver* by Lois Lowry (Houghton Mifflin)

1995 *Walk Two Moons* by Sharon Creech (HarperCollins)

1996 *The Midwife's Apprentice* by Karen Cushman (Clarion)

1997 *The View from Saturday* by E.L. Konigsburg (Jean Karl/Atheneum)

1998 *Out of the Dust* by Karen Hesse (Scholastic)

1999 *Holes* by Louis Sachar (Frances Foster)

2000 *Bud, Not Buddy* by Christopher Paul Curtis (Delacorte)

2001 *A Year Down Yonder* by Richard Peck (Dial)

2002 *A Single Shard* by Linda Sue Park (Clarion Books/Houghton Mifflin)

2003 *Crispin: The Cross of Lead* by Avi (Hyperion Books for Children)

2004 *The Tale of Despereaux: Being the Story of a Mouse, a Princess, Some Soup, and a Spool of Thread* by Kate DiCamillo, illustrated by Timothy Basil Ering (Candlewick Press)

2005 *Kira-Kira* by Cynthia Kadohata (Atheneum Books for Young Readers/Simon & Schuster)

2006 *Criss Cross* by Lynne Rae Perkins (Greenwillow Books/HarperCollins)

2007 *The Higher Power of Lucky* by Susan Patron, illustrated by Matt Phelan (Simon & Schuster/Richard Jackson)

2008 *Good Masters! Sweet Ladies! Voices from a Medieval Village* by Laura Amy Schlitz (Candlewick)

2009 *The Graveyard Book* by Neil Gaiman, illustrated by Dave McKean (HarperCollins)

2010 *When You Reach Me* by Rebecca Stead (Wendy Lamb Books/Random House)

2011 *Moon over Manifest* by Clare Vanderpool (Delacorte Press/Random House)

2012 *Dead End in Norvelt* by Jack Gantos (Farrar, Straus and Giroux)

2013 *The One and Only Ivan* by Katherine Applegate (HarperCollins)

2014 *Flora & Ulysses: The Illuminated Adventures* by Kate DiCamillo (Candlewick Press)

2015 *The Crossover* by Kwame Alexander (Houghton Mifflin Harcourt)

2016 *Last Stop on Market Street* by Matt de la Peña (G.P. Putnam's Sons/Penguin)

2017 *The Girl Who Drank the Moon* by Kelly Barnhill (Algonquin Young Readers/Workman)

2018 *Hello, Universe* by Erin Entrada Kelly (Greenwillow Books/HarperCollins)

PHOENIX AWARD

1985 *The Mark of the Horse Lord* by Rosemary Sutcliff (Oxford)

1986 *Queenie Peavy* by Robert Burch (Viking)

1987 *Smith* by Leon Garfield (Constable)

1988 *The Rider and His Horse* by Erik Christian Haugaard (Houghton Mifflin)

1989 *The Night Watchmen* by Helen Cresswell (Faber)

1990 *Enchantress from the Stars* by Sylvia Louise Engdahl (Atheneum)

1991 *A Long Way from Verona* by Jane Gardam (H. Hamilton)

1992 *A Sound of Chariots* by Mollie Hunter (Mollie Hunter)

1993 *Carrie's War* by Nina Bawden (Gollancz)

1994 *Of Nightingales That Weep* by Katherine Paterson (Crowell)

1995 *Dragonwings* by Laurence Yep (HarperCollins)

1996 *The Stone Book* by Alan Garner (Collins)

1997 *I Am the Cheese* by Robert Cormier (Pantheon)

1998 *A Chance Child* by Jill Paton Walsh (Macmillan)

1999 *Throwing Shadows* by E.L. Konigsburg (Atheneum)

2000 *Keeper of the Isis Light* by Monica Hughes (Atheneum)

2001 *The Seventh Raven* by Peter Dickinson (Gollancz)

2002 *A Formal Feeling* by Zibby Oneal (Viking)

2003 *The Long Night Watch* by Ivan Southall (Methuen)

2004 *White Peak Farm* by Berlie Doherty (Methuen)

2005 *The Catalogue of the Universe* by Margaret Mahy (Dent)

2006 *Howl's Moving Castle* by Diana Wynne Jones (Greenwillow)

2007 *Memory* by Margaret Mahy (Dent)

2008 *Eva* by Peter Dickinson (Delacorte)

2009 *Weetzie Bat* by Francesca Lia Block (HarperCollins)

2010 *The Shining Company* by Rosemary Sutcliff (Farrar, Straus and Giroux)

2011 *The Mozart Season* by Virginia Euwer Wolff (Henry Holt & Company)

2012 *Letters from Rifka* by Karen Hesse (Henry Holt & Company)

2013 *The Frozen Waterfall* by Gaye Hiçyilmaz (Farrar, Straus and Giroux)

2014 *Jesse* by Gary Soto (Scholastic)

2015 *One Bird* by Kyoko Mori (Henry Holt & Company)

2016 *Frindle* by Andrew Clements (Simon & Schuster Books for Young Readers)

2017 *Wish Me Luck* by James Heneghan (Farrar, Straus and Giroux)

2018 *Restless Spirit: The Life and Work of Dorothea Lange* by Elizabeth Partridge (Viking Juvenile)

PHOENIX PICTURE BOOK AWARD

2013 *Owen* by Kevin Henkes (Greenwillow)

2014 *The Bear* by Raymond Briggs (Julia Macrae)

2015 *My Map Book* by Sarah Fanelli (HarperCollins)

2016 *Goose* by Molly Bang (Blue Sky Press)

2017 *Tell Me a Season* by Mary McKenna Siddals and Petra Mathers (Clarion Books)

2018 *Cendrillon: A Caribbean Cinderella* by Robert D. San Souci and Brian Pinkney (Simon & Schuster Books for Young Readers)

ACKNOWLEDGMENTS

We are very appreciative of the support we have received from everyone at Broadview Press. We are especially grateful to publisher and editor Marjorie Mather, who has guided us through the production of the second edition with thoughtfulness and efficiency. It has been a tremendous pleasure to work with her. We thank production editor Tara Trueman for helping us navigate the final stages of producing the book and ensuring that all the parts came together. We are grateful for George Kirkpatrick's wonderful design and the keen eye of copy-editor Juliet Sutcliffe. We thank illustrator and graphic artist Scott McKowen for continuing to collaborate with us for the second edition.

Thank you to all of the readers who have embraced the book and encouraged us to produce a second edition. While working on *Reading Children's Literature*, we have been guided by suggestions from many readers and instructors. For their invaluable suggestions, we would like to thank Rosie Arenas, California State University, Fresno; Russell Barrett, Blinn College; Penny Bryan, Chapman University; Brenda Connel-Ross, The University of Texas at El Paso; Thomas Crisp, Georgia State University; Brenda Dales, Miami University; Laretta Henderson, University of Wisconsin–Milwaukee; Nancy J. Johnson, Western Washington University; Don Latham, Florida State University; Judith Lechner, Auburn University; Patricia A. Leek, The University of Texas at Dallas; Kelly Loughman, editor of *LibrarySparks*; Roni Natov, CUNY–Brooklyn; Megan Norcia, Brockport, SUNY; Elaine Ostry, SUNY Plattsburgh; Peggy Rice, Ball State University; Sara L. Schwebel, University of South Carolina; Lynne Vallone, Rutgers University–Camden; Nancy Walker, University of La Verne; Lance Weldy, Francis Marion University; Lorinda Cohoon, University of Memphis; Meghan Sweeney, UNC Wilmington; Gwen Tarbox, Western Michigan University; Erika Travis, California Baptist University; Scott Zaluda, Westchester Community College, SUNY; Ron Christiansen, Salt Lake Community College; Meghann Meeusen, Western Michigan University; Mary Anna Violi,

Indiana University South Bend; Laura Apol, Michigan State University; Marva Solomon, Angelo State University; Eileen Hinders, University of Memphis; Joseph Michael Sommers, Central Michigan University; Stephanie White, Cameron University; Susan Gentry, Tunxis Community College; Charlsie Prosser, Baker University; Robert Goldberg, Prince George's Community College; and Catherine Posey, Shasta Community College.

At the Graduate Center/CUNY, we would like to thank Meira Levinson, Dale Ireland, Kristi Fleetwood, Hilarie Ashton, Christina Quintana, Elaine Housseas, and Christian Lewis for research assistance at various stages of the project. Jason Tougaw's collegial support is very much appreciated as well, and the many insights of Balaka Basu and Kate Broad. Conversations with Paige Gray, Amy Hicks, and Laura Hakala were also helpful and encouraging. We would like to thank the faculty and staff of McCain Library and the de Grummond Children's Literature Collection at the University of Southern Mississippi, especially curator Ellen Ruffin and assistant curator Danielle Stoulig.

We would like to thank Maura Shea for her creative and meticulous contributions to *Reading Children's Literature* over many years; her work has truly shaped the book. We also appreciate Steve Scipione's early and ongoing support. We are particularly grateful to Glenn Burger, Chair of English at Queens College/CUNY, for his timely advice and insight at a time when we needed it the most.

Carrie Hintz is grateful to her husband Peter Hamilton for his encouragement and kindness during the long process of developing the second edition, Carol and Art Hintz for being such steadfast supporters, and the entire Hamilton clan for cheer and encouragement. Eric L. Tribunella also thanks his spouse, Jerrid S. Boyette, for his continued support and encouragement.

PERMISSIONS ACKNOWLEDGMENTS

TEXT

Alarcón, Francisco. "Chile/El chile" and "Prayer of the Fallen Tree" from *Laughing To-matoes and Other Spring Poems/Jitomates Risueños y otros poemas de primavera*. Copyright © 2005. Reproduced by permission of Children's Book Press, an imprint of Lee & Low Books, Inc., 95 Madison Ave, New York, NY 10016.

Dahl, Roald. "The Pig" from *Dirty Beasts*. © 1983 by Roald Dahl and The Roald Dahl Story Company Limited. Reproduced in the United Kingdom and Commonwealth by permission of David Higham Associates. Reproduced in the United States by permission of Puffin, an imprint of Penguin Young Readers Group, a division of Penguin Random House LLC. All rights reserved.

Hughes, Langston. "Children's Rhymes" from *The Collected Poems of Langston Hughes*, edited by Arnold Rampersad with David Rossel, Associate Editor, copyright © 1994 by the Estate of Langston Hughes. Reproduced in the United Kingdom and Commonwealth by permission of Harold Ober Associates. Reproduced in the rest of the world by permission of Alfred A. Knopf, an imprint of the Knopf Doubleday Publishing Group, a division of Penguin Random House LLC. All rights reserved. Any third party use of this material, outside of this publication, is prohibited. Interested parties must apply directly to Penguin Random House LLC for permission.

Little, Jean. "Today" from *Hey World, Here I Am!* by Jean Little and illustrated by Sue Truesdell. Text Copyright © 1986 by Jean Little. Reproduced in the United States by

591

IMAGES

de Angeli, Marguerite. Cover illustration from *The Door in the Wall* by Marguerite de Angeli, copyright © 1990. Reproduced by permission of the Estate of Marguerite de Angeli.

De Brunhoff, Jean. Illustration from *The Story of Babar* by Jean De Brunhoff. Copyright © 1933; copyright © renewed 1961 by Penguin Random House LLC. Reproduced by permission of Random House Children's Books, a division of Penguin Random House LLC. All rights reserved.

Deenie. Cover illustration from *Deenie* by Judy Blume. Copyright © 1976 by Dell. Reproduced by permission of Random House, Inc.

Degen, Bruce. Illustration from *The Magic School Bus: Lost in the Solar System* by Joanna Cole, illustrated by Bruce Degen. Text copyright © 1990 by Joanna Cole. Illustrations copyright © 1990 by Bruce Degen. Reproduced by permission of Scholastic Inc.

Disney. Still from *The Little Mermaid*, copyright © 1989 Disney. Reproduced by permission of Disney, Inc.

Disney. Still from *Maleficent*, copyright © 2014 Disney. Reproduced by permission of Disney, Inc.

Emberley, Michael. Illustration from *It's Perfectly Normal* by Robie H. Harris; illustrations by Michael Emberley. Text copyright © 1994 by Bee Productions, Inc. Illustrations copyright © 1994 by Bird Productions, Inc. Reproduced by permission of the publisher, Candlewick Press, Somerville, MA.

Feelings, Tom. Illustration from *To Be a Slave* by Julius Lester, illustrations by Tom Feelings, copyright © 1968 by Tom Feelings. Reproduced by permission of Dial Books for Young Readers, an imprint of Penguin Young Readers Group, a division of Penguin Random House LLC. All rights reserved. Any third party use of this material, outside of this publication, is prohibited. Interested parties must apply directly to Penguin Random House LLC for permission.

Fitzhugh, Louise. Illustration from *Harriet the Spy* by Louise Fitzhugh, copyright © 1964 by Louise Fitzhugh, renewed 1992 by Lois Anne Morehead & E. Seward Stevens. Reproduced by permission of Delacorte Press, an imprint of Random House Children's Books, a division of Random House LLC. All rights reserved. Any third party use of this material, outside of this publication, is prohibited. Interested parties must apply directly to Penguin Random House LLC for permission.

Frank, Anne. Anne Frank diary page, © 1942 by Anne Frank Fonds/Getty Images. Reproduced by permission of Getty Images.

Gammell, Stephen. Illustration from *Scary Stories to Tell in the Dark* by Alvin Schwartz, illustrated by Stephen Gammell. Illustrations copyright © 1981 by Stephen Gammell. Reproduced by permission of HarperCollins Publishers.

Holland, Richard. Illustration from *Yeh-hsien (Chinese Cinderella)* retold by Dawn Casey with illustrations by Richard Holland. Copyright © 2006 Mantra Lingua UK, 2006 www.mantralingua.com. Reproduced by permission of Mantra Lingua.

Hollander, John. "Kitty and Bug" from *Types of Shape* by John Hollander, Yale University Press, copyright © 1991.

Hurd, Clement. Illustration from *Goodnight Moon* by Margaret Wise Brown and illustrated by Clement Hurd. Reproduced by permission of HarperCollins Publishers.

Jacobs, Neil. Harry Potter Book Burning. Copyright © 2001 Neil Jacobs/Getty Images. Reproduced by permission of Getty Images.

Keats, Ezra Jack. Illustration from *The Snowy Day* by Ezra Jack Keats, copyright © 1962 by Ezra Jack Keats; copyright renewed © 1990 by Martin Pope, Executor. Reproduced by permission of Viking Children's Books, an imprint of Penguin Young Readers Group, a division of Penguin Random House LLC. All rights reserved. Any third party use of this material, outside of publication, is prohibited. Interested parties must apply directly to Penguin Random House LLC for permission.

Keystone. Nazi Book Burning. Copyright © 1933 Keystone/Getty images. Reproduced by permission of Getty images.

Lawson, Robert. Illustration from *The Story of Ferdinand* by Munro Leaf, © 1936 by Munro Leaf and Robert Lawson, renewed © 1964 by Munro Leaf and John W. Boyd. Reproduced by permission of Viking Children's Books, an imprint of Penguin Young Readers Group, a division of Penguin Random House LLC. All rights reserved.

Lionni, Leo. Illustration from *Swimmy* by Leo Lionni, copyright © 1963, renewed 1991 by NORAELEO LLC. Reproduced by permission of Alfred A. Knopf, an imprint of Random House Children's Books, a division of Penguin Random House LLC. All rights reserved.

Lynch, P.J. Cover illustration from *Sarah, Plain and Tall* by Patricia MacLachlan, copyright © 1985 by Patricia MacLachlan. Cover illustration © 1998 by P.J. Lynch. Reproduced by permission of the publisher, Candlewick Press, Somerville, MA.

Macaulay, David. Illustration from *Cathedral: The Story of Its Construction* by David Macaulay. Copyright © 1973 by David Macaulay. Reproduced by permission of Houghton Mifflin Harcourt Publishing Company. All rights reserved.

Maze, Deborah. Illustration from *Edmund and the White Witch* by C.S. Lewis with illustrations by Deborah Maze. Reproduced by permission of HarperCollins Publishers.

McCarty, Peter. Illustration from *Hondo and Fabian* by Peter McCarty. Copyright © 2002 by Peter McCarty. Reproduced by permission of Henry Holt Books for Young Readers. All Rights Reserved.

McCurdy, Michael. Illustration from *Johnny Tremain* by Esther Forbes, illustrated by Michael McCurdy. Illustrations copyright © 1998 by Michael McCurdy. Reproduced by permission of Houghton Mifflin Harcourt Publishing Company. All rights reserved.

McKowen, Scott. Cover illustration from *Anne of Green Gables* by Lucy Maud Montgomery. Illustration copyright © 2011 by Scott McKowen. Reproduced by permission of Scott McKowen.

McKowen, Scott. Cover illustration from *Adventures of Huckleberry Finn* by Mark Twain. Illustration copyright © 2006 by Scott McKowen. Reproduced by permission of Scott McKowen.

McKowen, Scott. Cover Illustration from *The Wind in the Willows* by Kenneth Grahame. Illustration copyright © 2005 by Scott McKowen. Reproduced by permission of Scott McKowen.

McNicholas, Shelagh. Cover illustration from *I Am Jazz* by Jessica Herthel and Jazz Jennings, illustrations by Shelagh McNicholas. Copyright © 2014. Reproduced by permission of Random House, Inc.

Nappi, Rudy. Cover illustration from *The Clue in the Old Stagecoach* by Carolyn Keene, cover illustration by Rudy Nappi. Reproduced by permission of Random House, Inc.

INDEX

From the Publisher

A name never says it all, but the word "Broadview" expresses a good deal of the philosophy behind our company. We are open to a broad range of academic approaches and political viewpoints. We pay attention to the broad impact book publishing and book printing has in the wider world; for some years now we have used 100% recycled paper for most titles. Our publishing program is internationally oriented and broad-ranging. Our individual titles often appeal to a broad readership too; many are of interest as much to general readers as to academics and students.

Founded in 1985, Broadview remains a fully independent company owned by its shareholders—not an imprint or subsidiary of a larger multinational.

For the most accurate information on our books (including information on pricing, editions, and formats) please visit our website at **www.broadviewpress.com**. Our print books and ebooks are also available for sale on our site.